Environmental Politics

Environmental Politics

Domestic and Global Dimensions

SIXTH EDITION

JACQUELINE VAUGHN
Northern Arizona University

Australia • Brazil • Japan • Korea • Mexico • Singapore • Spain • United Kingdom • United States

WADSWORTH
CENGAGE Learning

Environmental Politics: Domestic and Global Dimensions, Sixth Edition
Jacqueline Vaughn

Acquisitions Editor: Carolyn Merrill

Assistant Editor: Katherine Hayes

Editorial Assistant: Angela Hodge

Marketing Manager: Amy Whitaker

Marketing Assistant: Josh Hendrick

Marketing Communications Manager: Heather Baxley

Content Project Management: PreMediaGlobal

Art Director: Linda Helcher

Print Buyer: Paula Vang

Rights Acquisitions Account Manager, Text: Katie Huha

Rights Acquisitions Account Manager, Image: Amanda Groszko

Production Service: PreMediaGlobal

Cover Designer: Grannan Graphic Design

Cover Image: manfredxy/istockphoto

For product information and technology assistance, contact us at
Cengage Learning Customer & Sales Support, 1-800-354-9706

For permission to use material from this text or product, submit all requests online at **www.cengage.com/permissions**
Further permissions questions can be e-mailed to
permissionrequest@cengage.com

Library of Congress Control Number: 2010923647

ISBN-13: 978-0-495-89897-9

ISBN-10: 0-495-89897-X

Wadsworth
20 Channel Center Street
Boston, MA 02210
USA

Cengage Learning is a leading provider of customized learning solutions with office locations around the globe, including Singapore, the United Kingdom, Australia, Mexico, Brazil, and Japan. Locate your local office at **www.cengage.com/global**

Cengage Learning products are represented in Canada by Nelson Education, Ltd.

To learn more about Wadsworth, visit **www.cengage.com/wadsworth**

Purchase any of our products at your local college store or at our preferred online store **www.cengagebrain.com**

Printed in the United States of America
1 2 3 4 5 6 7 14 13 12 11 10

For my dad

Contents

List of Tables

List of Figures

Preface

On April 22, 1970, people around the world celebrated what has become an annual event, the observance of Earth Day, now in its fourth decade. Senator Gaylord Nelson, a Democrat from Wisconsin and the "father" of Earth Day, wrote that his goal that year "was to show the political leadership of the Nation that there was broad and deep support for the environmental movement. While I was confident that a nationwide peaceful demonstration of concern would be impressive, I was not quite prepared for the overwhelming response that occurred on that day." Individuals at two thousand universities, ten thousand high schools and grade schools, and thousands of communities in the United States participated in the event, as did millions of others globally. In 1980, Nelson commented, "To anyone who has paid attention, it is clear that the environmental movement now is far stronger, far better led, far better informed, and far more influential than it was ten years ago. Its strength grows each year because public knowledge and understanding grow each year." To many, Earth Day has become both a way of showing support for the environment and a way of encouraging groups and individuals to adopt a more sustainable lifestyle while celebrating the planet's resources and biodiversity.

I was an undergraduate student at the University of California, Santa Barbara on the first Earth Day in 1970. I remember sitting on the cool grass on the back of the student union overlooking the lagoon, not knowing that the events of the day would result in a sea change of attitudes about the environment. At the time, Earth Day felt like a somewhat spontaneous spring celebration rather than the beginning of a social movement, or at least nothing on the scale that Gaylord Nelson had envisioned. Decades later, I had the opportunity to speak with the senator, and he waxed poetic about his dreams for that day. This book is, in part, about those dreams.

In fall 2008, the dreams of many individuals were wrapped up in another movement, this time to elect the president of the United States. An opening in the political window meant that there would be a change in the nation's policies toward the environment. The policy rollbacks of the administration of George W. Bush would ostensibly be altered by a new president, and when Barack Obama won the general election in November, pundits and academicians joined members of the public in attempting to second-guess what those changes might look like. In my classes, there seemed to be a certain cautious optimism that President Obama would work harder to protect natural resources, and that global climate change would find its way to the top of the political agenda. Despite the attention paid to the struggling economy, the battles over health care, and the troop surge in Afghanistan, students felt that it was only a matter of time before Congress and the president did—well, did *something*.

This sixth edition of *Environmental Politics* is designed to identify and explain the way government has addressed environmental problems from the colonial period through the first year of the Obama administration. As in previous editions, the process model is used as a paradigm for exploring environmental politics and policy. I have found that in many of my classes, it is a useful model for understanding the interaction among institutions, such as the president and Congress, administrative agencies, courts, and state and local governments. The process model also provides a way to explain the role of nongovernmental organizations both in the United States and abroad as essential stakeholders, as well as the role of the media and public opinion in a world that is increasingly electronically connected. Ultimately, the process model allows us to understand how politics affects policymaking and progress toward solving environmental problems. Thanks to the suggestions of reviewers and students, there is now a greater emphasis on relating the policy process to the outcomes of decision making, and an integration of national and international policies in an increasingly globalized world.

Although the organization of the book remains basically unchanged, many sections have been completely rewritten and updated to reflect upon the most recent political events worldwide. There are expanded sections on the role of state and local governments, particularly in their efforts to deal with climate change. Events that have occurred during the past three years—from the coal ash spill in Tennessee to the Copenhagen Conference of the Parties to the Kyoto Protocol—are covered, as well as changes such as the renaissance in nuclear power and in the definition of wetlands. Although there are only a small handful of legislative victories to report, the Omnibus Public Lands Management Act of 2009 is covered in detail. Each of the "Another View, Another Voice" segments has been revised to provide a personal glimpse of an individual or organization that has made an impact on a particular policy issue. The "Thinking Globally" segments from the previous editions have now been integrated directly into the text to make reading more seamless.

As before, the book does not attempt to provide in-depth coverage of every issue, but it does provide an overview that goes beyond the "headline news" approach. Sections at the end of every chapter that suggest books for further reading represent the newest books that have become available since 2008, so that readers will become aware of the resources that have become available since the fifth edition was published. Similarly, the appendices include an updated list of major U.S. environmental legislation and international environmental agreements.

To place environmental politics in context, the introduction identifies some of the events that have occurred over the last decade that have affected the development of environmental politics, from the listing of the polar bear as an endangered species to the opening of China's Three Gorges Dam. The historical overview of Chapter 1 explores the philosophical and political beginnings of environmental concern, while Chapter 2 identifies the key stakeholders who influence policy. Chapter 3 provides an expanded analysis of the role of political institutions, following the process model. It covers the appointments and initiatives of the Obama administration, and the complicated maze of federal rulemaking. Chapters 4 through 11 are devoted to specific environmental problems, with the addition of issues that have arisen in the past three years. Although many of the problems are overlapping and interrelated, these chapters update the reader on the most critical issues and analyze the progress that has been made. New to Chapter 2 is coverage of the Blue/Green Alliance and the role of social networking, and Chapter 4 revisits the 2001 Roadless Rule and the most recent court action on the controversial regulation. Some issues have reappeared on the political agenda and are covered in more depth in this edition, such as the controversy over nuclear waste storage at Yucca Mountain, Nevada, explained in Chapter 5, along with enduring ones like air-quality regulations in Chapter 8. In Chapter 6, there is an expansion of coverage of oil drilling and offshore wind projects, and in Chapter 7, the issue of wetlands protection is revised. Chapter 9 explores endangered species delisting, and Chapter 10 covers climate-change conferences from Bali to Copenhagen. Population and sustainability issues are covered in Chapter 11, and in the final chapter, six "emerging issues" are identified, from the backlash over bottled water to the new "locavore" movement.

A portion of the royalties from this book, as well as from the third, fourth, and fifth editions, has been donated to the Jack and Ruby Vaughn Graduate Internship Scholarship at Northern Arizona University, named in honor of my parents. The scholarship is awarded to a student pursuing an internship in public service, and although the size of the award is small, the opportunities it can provide are endless. Your support, comments, and suggestions from the past five editions, along with this one, are greatly appreciated and integral to its success.

About the Author

Jacqueline Vaughn is Professor of Politics and International Affairs at Northern Arizona University, where she specializes in public policy. Professor Vaughn holds a Ph.D. in political science from the University of California, Berkeley, where she also attended the Graduate School of Public Policy. She taught previously at the University of Redlands and at Southern Oregon University. Professor Vaughn has a broad spectrum of nonacademic experience in both the public and private sectors. Her environmental background stems from her work with the South Coast Air Quality Management District in southern California, and with Southern California Edison, where she served as a policy analyst. Professor Vaughn's previously published books include *The Play of Power; Green Backlash: The History and Politics of Environmental Opposition in the United States; Disabled Rights: American Disability Policy and the Fight for Equality; Environmental Activism: A Reference Handbook; George W. Bush's Healthy Forests: Reframing the Environmental Debate* (co-authored with Hanna Cortner); *Managerial Discretion in Government Decision Making* (co-authored with Eric Otenyo); and *Waste Management: A Reference Handbook*.

Acknowledgments

The words "thank you" are never sufficient to show my appreciation for the hard work of those who are involved in developing a book manuscript, and the support of the many individuals who make sure that it is completed successfully. For this sixth edition, I remain indebted to Don Reisman, now with Resources for the Future Press, for his initial signing of the book. The cycle continues with the support of Carolyn Merrill at Cengage/Wadsworth, along with Angela Hodge. Three faculty reviewers provided insightful comments on how to approach this edition: Kristian Alexander at the University of Utah; Len Broberg at the University of Montana; and Marjorie Hershey at Indiana University. Two graduate students, Jim Buthman and Jessica Kagele, provided assistance in tracking down obscure statistics, updates, and vital information that made their way into each chapter. But without the comments, positive and otherwise, of the students in POS 359, I would have neither the motivation nor the feedback I need to undertake this effort every few years.

Introduction

While the 1970s have historically been known as the "environmental decade," the first decade of the twenty-first century could arguably have taken its place. The news headlines, agency regulations, legislation, state and local initiatives, interest group actions, court cases, and crises rivaled those that started the original Earth Day. Some events appealed to the media and public for years, while others seemed to disappear and garnered little interest after leaving the political and policy agenda. For instance:

- The polar bear was listed as an endangered species, the first animal to be identified by the U.S. Fish and Wildlife Service out of concern for global warming's impact on its habitat.

- The Avian Flu (H5N1) and Swine Flu (H1N1) raised awareness of the threat of pandemics around the world.

- Reports showed that 80 percent of U.S. electronic waste is sent to Asia, where it threatens worker safety and the environment.

- Over 3,250 kilometers of an Antarctic ice shelf collapsed as regional temperatures warm.

- The BP oil spill off the Louisiana coast became the worst environmental disaster in U.S. history.

- Scientists alleged that officials within the Bush administration censored their global climate-change findings to alter their reports.

- The Three Gorges Dam in China opened, with its reservoir displacing nearly 2 million people.

- Former Vice President Al Gore received the Nobel Peace Prize on behalf of the Intergovernmental Panel on Climate Change.

- The UN reported that more than 15 million hectares of tropical forest are lost each year to logging, agriculture, and other threats.

- China officially overtook the United States as the world's biggest greenhouse-gas emitter.

- A study estimated that 38 million animals are smuggled from Brazil each year for sale on the black market.

Do these events sound familiar to you, or have you forgotten when and why they were important when they happened? Did they appear on your personal "radar," or did you ignore them because you were concerned about other events, problems, or issues? If so, you are not alone. Recent public opinion polls show that although people are concerned about the environment, it does not make the "top ten" list of problems today. Instead, jobs and the economy, the wars in Iraq and Afghanistan, health care, and other issues occupy our interest. A crisis, such as the Tennessee coal ash spill or the Asian tsunami, captures our immediate concern, and then fades away until some other event makes headlines.

To understand how and why this happens, it is first important to develop an overview of the policymaking process and the people who have a stake in policy outcomes. One way of doing so is through Anthony Downs's 1972 theoretical model, called the "issue-attention cycle." According to Downs, the public's interest in an issue, such as the preservation of natural resources, goes through a cycle of ebb and flow—a process that is continuous, but not always predictable. Initially, a condition must be recognized as a problem; subsequent steps to solve that problem make up the policy process.[1] Public policies are those developed by the arms of government, like the Department of Agriculture or the Nuclear Regulatory Commission. Downs's model helps explain why some issues find their way to the policy agenda and others do not.

John W. Kingdon presents a similar concept by starting with the question, "How does an idea's time come? What makes people in and around government attend, at any given time, to some subjects and not to others?"[2] He notes that little is known about the predecisional process when agendas change from one time to another, how a series of alternatives is narrowed down from a large set of choices to a very few, and how subjects drift onto the agenda and then drift off. "The patterns of public policy, after all, are determined not only by such final decisions as votes in legislatures, or initiatives and vetoes by presidents, but also by the fact that some subjects and proposals emerge in the first place and others are never seriously considered."[3]

There are many approaches to policy study, including political systems theory,[4] group theory,[5] elite theory,[6] institutionalism,[7] and rational choice theory.[8] Other political scientists, such as James Anderson, have built upon the ideas of earlier theorists to conceptualize policymaking as a sequential model of stages that represent distinct periods of time, political institutions, and actors inside (official policymakers) and outside (unofficial policymakers) government. Some participants in making policy serve as gatekeepers, acting as checkpoints where a determination is made about what problems the government ought to consider.[9]

All of these models are useful in understanding how environmental policy is influenced by politics. This book relies upon an amalgamation of previous theorists' work as a way of illustrating what many consider to be the processes of solving problems, using stages as a metaphor for what takes place.

1. *Problem identification and agenda setting*: In this stage, policy issues are brought to the attention of government officials in a variety of ways. Conditions become problems when there is sufficient belief that something ought to be done about them; not all conditions become problems, however. Some problems are uncovered by the media; others, like wildfires, become prominent through crisis or another type of focusing event. In some cases, there is a gradual accumulation of knowledge by scientists or issue specialists; once a critical mass of information is collected, reports are issued and press conferences held, as has happened with global warming. There may be a technological breakthrough that leads to a call for change, such as the development of hybrid-fueled cars. Sometimes, organized groups may demonstrate or lobby officials to focus attention on the problem, which is how Greenpeace activists gained support for the protection of marine mammals. Celebrities like Leonardo di Caprio or Ted Danson may use their status to bring a problem to the government's attention. Some problems may exist without being recognized except by a few isolated individuals or groups, who clamor to have their voices heard. Other problems are so immediate or visible that there is an immediate call for resolution. Once identified, problems are said to be part of the policy agenda, a list of subjects or problems to which people inside and outside of government pay serious attention at any given time.

   Agenda setting is also affected by processes such as election results and changes in the partisan balance in the White House or Congress; economic ups and downs in inflation, stock market performance, or consumer confidence; swings in public opinion; and the national mood. The agenda is subjected to forces like the motivations of individuals seeking to bring about change, trade-offs among political actors, and persuasion. But overall, the process is a dynamic one that is in a constant state of change.

2. *Policy formulation*: After a problem is identified as worthy of government attention, policymakers must develop proposed courses of action to solve it. Policy formulation may involve a variety of actors, which will be covered in more detail in Chapter 3. Some policies come directly from the president, such as President Barack Obama's plan to increase the use of renewable energy. Other policies, such as the opening of roadless areas on public lands, are developed by federal agencies or Cabinet-level departments, such as the U.S. Forest Service, a topic that is explored in Chapter 4. Congress and state legislatures are often the source of policy initiatives, including Oregon's landmark "bottle bill," which established cash refunds for recycled products, and California's vanguard air-pollution regulations. Interest groups, the subject of Chapter 2, often place pressure on legislators or provide their expertise on matters that are scientifically or technically complex. The control of greenhouse gases, for example, has been made more difficult due to issues of scientific uncertainty and the application of the precautionary principle, discussed in Chapter 10.

3. *Policy adoption*: The acceptance of a particular policy is a highly politicized stage, often involving legislation or rulemaking, that legitimizes the policy.

This is usually referred to as the "authorization phase" of policymaking, and it often occurs outside the public's direct view. Hearings on competing proposals, meetings among stakeholders, and the publication of new standards of regulation may be conducted with minimal public participation or media attention. The process of making a choice among competing alternatives (such as different air-quality bills in Congress) has been studied extensively by political scientists, who often refer to this area as the "decision sciences."

Although important policy outcomes may be the result of informal, intuitive judgments, three theories of decision making are generally used when trying to explain policy adoptions. The rational-comprehensive theory is used to explain the procedures for maximizing the attainment of specific goals. These goals are intended to solve problems that can be clearly identified and defined. It is the process of problem definition that makes this approach quite difficult.

Incrementalism, in contrast, involves making relatively limited changes—fine tuning—rather than major alterations in policy. Incrementalism is built on the premise that there is no single "right" answer to problem solving, but rather a limited number of potential choices. This type of decision making tends to be conservative and is unlikely to lead to innovative solutions.

Multiple advocacy calls for the use of a "broker" who brings together a wide range of (often conflicting) alternatives and opinions. Leaders listen to the various arguments and ideas as they are presented, ideally with a neutral perspective. Although this format allows for greater participation by numerous actors, not all actors are equal in their resources, powers, or level of information about the nature of a problem.

4. *Policy implementation*: To put an agreed-on policy into effect, this fourth stage involves conflict and struggle as the administrative machinery of government begins to turn. Affected groups must now turn their attention from the legislative arena to the bureaucracy, and in some cases the judicial branch, to get the policy to work. Usually, implementation is conducted through a complex administrative process, which may force agencies to make decisions based on very broad, ambiguous legislative intent, as was the case with the 1990 Clean Air Act. Implementation may become politicized and may force agencies to compete against one another for government resources and attention. The interest groups that were instrumental in getting the policy problem identified and placed on the policy agenda may become enmeshed in the implementation process, making further demands on the bureaucracy. Contending interests, such as those seeking protection for a specific endangered animal, will push their own agendas forward, often at the expense of the initial policy they sought to have adopted.

5. *Policy evaluation*: An ongoing process, this stage involves various determinations as to whether the policy is effective. This appraisal may be based on studies of program operations, systematic evaluation, or personal judgment; but whatever the method, the evaluation may start the policymaking process

all over again. Public policies are usually evaluated by the agencies that administer them, by the Government Accountability Office (GAO),[10] or occasionally at the president's request. Policy evaluation takes a number of forms. Researchers may use cost-benefit analysis to determine whether the amount of money being spent on a project is matched by the value obtained. They may conduct an evaluation midway through the implementation process so that changes can be made or errors corrected. However, policy evaluation also takes many other forms. Elected officials may make a determination about how well a policy is doing based on comments they receive not only from their constituents but also from organized groups attempting to lobby their support or responding on the basis of partisan concerns.

However, the elements of this model of policymaking are not separate, distinct events: Policymaking is an organic, even messy, process of defining and redefining problems; formulating and implementing policies, and then reformulating them; and moving off and back on the policy agenda. Throughout each of the chapters that follow, these policy terms will be used to show how various problems—from waste management and biodiversity to water pollution and energy—go through the various stages of the policy process. Although not every scholar of environmental policy agrees with the precise terminology used here, it is a way of helping explain what happens.

Understanding the policy process allows us to consider the various points where public participation is allowed or encouraged. It helps to explain why some problems seem to be ignored while others have a mercurial rise to prominence. Knowledge of the political aspects of policymaking points toward determining which actors play the most important role, and in which arena. For those seeking changes in environmental policy, this book provides a guide for activists as well as those seeking to understand what has already happened.

1

A Historical Framework for Environmental Protection

"Environmental decisionmaking can and should be made more
data-driven and rigorous. A more fact-based and empirical
approach to policymaking promises systematically better
results."
— EXECUTIVE SUMMARY, 2008 ENVIRONMENTAL PERFORMANCE INDEX[1]

While concern about the environment has been an issue since before the United States was founded, the country now ranks 39th among nearly 150 others in its overall environmental performance, according to one widely respected study released in 2009.

For the last decade, Yale University and Columbia University have measured the environmental performance of nations around the world to determine their effectiveness in meeting specific environmental goals. The Environmental Sustainability Index (ESI), published between 1999 and 2005, was developed to evaluate environmental sustainability, and the Environmental Performance Index (EPI), first published in 2002, was designed to supplement the environmental targets of the United Nations Millennium Development Goals. The most recent EPI ranks 149 countries on six policy categories (environmental burden of disease, water, air pollution, biodiversity and habitat, productive natural resources, and climate change) using twenty-five performance indicators, such as sulfur dioxide emissions, critical habitat protection, fisheries trawling intensity, and pesticide regulation.

The United States does not fare well on the EPI in several categories. On a scale of 100, the U.S. score of 81.0 is the lowest of the Group of 8 industrialized nations. European countries led the list, topped by Switzerland, Sweden,

Norway, and Finland, along with Austria, France, Latvia, Costa Rica, Columbia, and New Zealand.[2] The U.S. ranking is "slipping," according to officials, because of low scores on three different analyses of greenhouse gas emissions and its performance on a new indicator for regional smog, where the country ranks at the bottom of the list.[3] As the study notes, "quantitative performance metrics have reshaped decisionmaking processes in many arenas."[4]

Another study, the Climate Change Performance Index (CCPI), released in Copenhagen in December 2009, also ranked the United States low. Researchers from Germanwatch and the Climate Action Network (CAN) Europe placed the United States fifty-third out of fifty-seven industrialized countries and emerging economies that together account for more than 90 percent of global energy-related carbon dioxide emissions. The study includes emissions figures provided by the International Energy Agency but also weights an assessment of climate policy based on a survey of national climate experts.[5] The groups' overall response to current climate change policies was not optimistic. The author of the study noted, "Because the CCPI represents a relative ranking, countries are ranked against one another as well as against the criteria of keeping temperature rise below the dangerous level of two degrees. Therefore, since no country is thus far adequately on the path toward halting dangerous climate change, the three top spots are empty once again this year."[6] Brazil was the biggest mover on the index, with Canada and Saudi Arabia at the very bottom.

As is the case elsewhere, in the United States, concern about other issues—the economy, national security, or health care—push the environment down on the public policy agenda. It may even languish toward the bottom as other issues are perceived to be more pressing or more important. Such has been the case for much of the twenty-first century. Government efforts to protect the environment are a direct reflection of public opinion as to what issues should be a priority, and how many dollars, personnel, or hours should be devoted to solving various problems. Like items on a crowded meeting's agenda, the environment must compete with other issues seeking the attention of policymakers, and often, time runs out while other problems are considered.

The governmental agenda is also affected by environmental disasters and crises that make headlines. Some, like the 100,000-ton oil spill caused by the sinking of the supertanker *Torrey Canyon* off the coast of England in 1967, have been upstaged by more recent events such as the 2010 BP oil spill that contaminated fragile wetlands along the Gulf Coast. The radiation leak at the Soviet Union's Chernobyl plant in April 1986 has become synonymous with contemporary concerns about nuclear power that are reflected in congressional debates over a nuclear waste site at Yucca Mountain, Nevada. The December 26, 2004, tsunami that devastated Southeast Asia made other environmental problems pale in comparison to the death and destruction experienced by millions of people. These types of "focusing events," as they are called by policy scholars, are crises that "come along and simply bowl over everything standing in the way of prominence on the agenda."[7]

The development of an environmental policy agenda can be viewed in two ways. First, it is a history of ideas, a philosophical framework about our relationship to nature and the world. This history is punctuated with names ranging from Thomas Malthus and Charles Darwin to Karl Marx and Francis Bacon, to modern commentators Barry Commoner, Garrett Hardin, Rod Nash, Paul Ehrlich, and David Suzuki. Second, it is a factual history, made up of events, individuals, and conditions. This chapter focuses on factual history to identify six distinct periods in the development of policies to protect the environment. It also summarizes the ways in which public opinion and attitudes about the environment have framed the environmental debate and resulting policy.

GERMINATION OF AN IDEA: FROM THE COLONIAL PERIOD TO 1900

Even before the American states were united, there was an awareness of the need to limit the use of the new land's natural resources. As early as 1626, members of the Plymouth Colony passed ordinances regulating the cutting and sale of timber on colony lands. Other colonial leaders recognized the importance of preserving the region's resources, prohibiting the intentional setting of forest fires, and placing limits on deer hunting. In 1681, William Penn, proprietor of Pennsylvania, decreed that for every five acres of land cleared, one must be left as virgin forest. In 1691, Massachusetts Bay leaders began to set aside "forest reservations"—large stands of pines valued for their use as ships' masts. Forest preservation became an entrenched principle of colonial land management as early as the seventeenth century.[8]

The 1700s and 1800s are noteworthy because of the shift that took place in how the Western world viewed wilderness. The Old World view of wilderness as repugnant and inhabited by horrible beasts was replaced by a New World perspective of a nation struggling to conquer nature rather than fleeing from it. In the Puritan view, for instance, humans could carve a garden from the wilderness, conquering wild nature, which was to many an obstacle to be overcome. The taming of the frontier became a goal in an age which idealized progress, often in the name of God. Similarly, the Romantic movement's appreciation of wilderness for its aesthetic value flourished in the eighteenth and nineteenth centuries, with cities as the intellectual heart of the new movement. Primitivism and deism took on new importance as writers such as Alexis de Tocqueville and Jean

Jacques Rousseau, and scientists like William Bartram, saw the new country as a living laboratory. A New York writer, Charles Fenno Hoffman, revealed in his letters the pleasures of visiting the Adirondacks, while John C. Fremont's journal of his 1842 trip to Wyoming made wilderness both sublime and appealing. When coupled with the growing spirit of nationalism and the portrayal of wilderness by artists such as Thomas Cole, it was not unexpected that efforts to preserve the lands for their sheer beauty alone would commence.[9]

Another View, Another Voice: George Perkins Marsh

He is nicknamed "The Versatile Vermonter," but he is best known for his book that appeared a century before the environmental movement had a name. George Perkins Marsh (1801–1882), author of *Man and Nature: Physical Geography as Modified by Human Action* (1864), wrote a treatise on humanity's wastefulness, the relationship between animals and plants, deforestation, water consumption, and what we now refer to as the "balance of nature" long before 1960s environmentalists would call for society to serve as stewards of the earth in restoring the land. He is considered by many to be the first American environmentalist.

Marsh was born in rural Woodstock, Vermont, in the foothills of the Green Mountains, a setting that would color his views as much as the homeschooling in Latin and Greek he received as a child. He attended the prestigious Phillips Academy in Andover, Massachusetts, but left to go to Dartmouth College, where, uninspired, he taught himself four languages and graduated at the age of nineteen in 1820. He began his career as a teacher, but left his first position to return to Woodstock to study law. Marsh was admitted to the bar in 1825, and moved to Burlington, Vermont, where he went through a series of mostly unsuccessful business ventures. He then ran for Congress in 1843 as a member of the Whig party, serving until 1849, when he was appointed as the U.S. minister to Turkey by President Zachary Taylor. By this point in his life, he spoke twenty languages and was an accomplished diplomat, traveling extensively and gathering samples for the Smithsonian Institution, which he had helped found while he served in Congress. In 1861, President Abraham Lincoln appointed Marsh as the first U.S. minister to the United Kingdom of Italy, a position he would hold for over 20 years. He became known as the Patriarch of American Diplomacy for his service; he was buried in Rome, where he lived the last two decades of his life. He was married twice; he supported education

for women and feminism before it was considered fashionable to do so.

Man and Nature is a long and formidable compendium of a lifetime's worth of observations by a well-traveled and educated man, based on both his youth in New England and his public service in the Middle East. Upon its publication, it received considerable public acclaim; the U.S. Forest Service's Gifford Pinchot called it "epoch-making," and it was his work that many environmental historians believe led to the development of the U.S. forest system. A century before *ecology* became a household term, Marsh profiled the dangers of disasters like earthquakes and the technological and economic forces that transform nature, sounding a clarion call that action be taken before humans destroyed nature altogether. Some of his ideas, such as importing camels to be used by the military in the Southwest, were implemented but impractical. Others, such as identifying the consequences of technology before decisions are made, played a huge role in the development of the environmental movement generations after *Man and Nature* was published. By describing the interrelatedness of humans and their environment, Marsh added a new perspective to the science of geography, and provided much of the underpinnings of today's environmental awareness, even though he is not as well-known as more contemporary authors like Rachel Carson.

SOURCES:
Paul Brooks. *Speaking for Nature: How Literary Naturalists from Henry Thoreau to Rachel Carson Have Shaped America.* Boston: Houghton Mifflin, 1980.
David Lowenthal. *George Perkins Marsh: Versatile Vermonter.* New York: Columbia University Press, 1958.
"George Perkins Marsh: Renaissance Vermonter." http://www.clarku.edu/departments/marsh/about. Accessed June 11, 2009.
George Perkins Marsh. *Man and Nature: Physical Geography as Modified by Human Action.* Cambridge, MA: Belknap Press of Harvard University, 1965.

During the eighteenth century, the nation was consumed with the building of a new government, but individual states made efforts to preserve the resources within their boundaries. Massachusetts in 1710 began to protect coastal waterfowl and in 1718 banned the hunting of deer for four years. Other states, such as Connecticut (1739) and New York (1772), also passed laws to protect game.[10] Political leaders at the beginning of the nineteenth century expressed interest in studying soil erosion; both Washington and Jefferson wrote of their concerns about the lands at their estates. The opening of the Erie Canal in 1825 brought pine forests within the reach of eastern markets and forced states to confront the issue of timber poaching—one of the first environmental crimes.[11]

In 1866, German scientist and philosopher Ernst Haeckel coined the term *ecology*, and the subject became a thriving research discipline.[12] Still, there was no philosophy of protection that dominated either American or European thought. Studies of the popular literature of the 1870s led some historians to conclude that the environmental movement came alive with the advent of sportsmen's magazines. In October 1871, *The American Sportsman*, a monthly newspaper, marked a turning point in environmental history when it became the first publication to interrelate the subjects of hunting, fishing, natural history, and conservation. Two years later, *Forest and Stream* advocated the protection of watersheds, scientific management of forests, uniform game laws, and abatement of water pollution.[13] Diminishing supplies of fish in the Connecticut River resulted in development of the fish culture industry and the formation in 1870 of the American Fisheries Society, the first biological society to research a diminishing natural resource. A year later, the U.S. Fish Commission was created, the first federal agency responsible for the conservation of a specific natural resource.[14]

Adventure and exploration enhanced the public's interest in the environment throughout the nineteenth century. Lewis and Clark's transcontinental explorations beginning in 1804, and John Wesley Powell's journey down the Colorado River in 1869, increased Americans' awareness of the undiscovered beauty of the frontier.[15]

Tremendous urban population growth between 1870 and the turn of the century led to new environmental problems, including contamination of drinking-water sources and dumping of garbage and sewage. The problems were most evident in the cities of the Northeast and Midwest, where the population increases were the most rapid. Although New York remained the nation's largest city, nearly tripling its population over the thirty-year period, Chicago had the biggest percentage increase—nearly sixfold. Similarly, Philadelphia, St. Louis, and Boston nearly doubled the sizes of their populations. Although industrial development did not reach the West Coast's cities as quickly, San Francisco, which served as the major shipping port, doubled its population between 1870 and 1890. The biggest increase was in Los Angeles, which grew to over twenty times its size from 1870 to 1900. American cities became centers of industry; and industry, with its accompanying population growth, meant pollution. By 1880, New York had 287 foundries and machine shops and 125 steam engines, bone mills, refineries, and tanneries. By the turn of the century,

Pittsburgh had hundreds of iron and steel plants. Chicago's stockyards, railroads, and port traffic filled the city with odors and thick, black smoke.[16]

Pollution problems caused by rapid industrial growth resulted in numerous calls for reform, and women became key leaders in cleaning up the urban environment. Upper-class women with extended periods of leisure time, believing that "the housekeeping of a great city is women's work," formed civic organizations dedicated to monitoring pollution and finding solutions to garbage and sanitation problems. The first of these groups, the Ladies' Health Protective Association, was founded in 1884 with the goal of keeping New York City's streets free of garbage. The Civic Club of Philadelphia, formed in 1894, began by placing trash receptacles at key intersections. Other groups were organized in Boston (the Women's Municipal League) and St. Louis (the Women's Organization for Smoke Abatement).[17]

The nation's environmental awareness was enhanced by the actions of specific individuals. George Catlin first proposed the idea of a national park in 1832.[18] Henry David Thoreau spoke poetically in 1858 of his return to a natural world.[19] George E. Waring built the first separate sewer system in Lenox, Massachusetts, in 1876 and was a pioneer in the study of sanitary engineering. Waring, known as "the apostle of cleanliness," crusaded about the impact of garbage on public health and was responsible for the beginnings of contemporary solid waste science.[20] Later, after the turn of the century, progressive reformers like Dr. A. Wilberforce Williams brought advice on hygiene and sanitation to the urban black community.[21]

The concept of preserving natural areas came from a variety of sources. In 1870, a group of explorers recommended that a portion of the upper Yellowstone River region be set aside to protect its geothermal features, wildlife, forests, and unique scenery. The result, the establishment of Yellowstone National Park in 1872, was the beginning of a pattern of preserving large undisturbed ecosystems. The public endorsed the idea, and Congress responded by creating Sequoia, Kings Canyon, and Yosemite National Parks in 1890, followed by Mount Rainier National Park in 1899. Interest in trees and forests was an important element of preservationism, symbolized by the proclamation of the first Arbor Day on April 10, 1872. The event was the culmination of the work of J. Sterling Morton, editor of Nebraska's first newspaper, and Robert W. Furia, a prominent nursery owner who later became governor. The two men convinced the Nebraska state legislature to commemorate the day with tree plantings to make Nebraska "mentally and morally the best agricultural state in the Union." More than 1 million trees were planted the first year, and Nebraska became known as the "Tree Planter's State" in 1895. With the Forest Reserve Act of 1891, the U.S. Congress set aside forest lands for preservation for the first time. Several years later, President Grover Cleveland ordered lands to be protected because few states were willing to protect their forests from logging.

The founding of the Sierra Club by John Muir in 1892 marked the beginning of interest in a more broad-based environmental organization.[22] Although the early organizations have been called "pitifully weak" in membership and finances, these early groups had a strong sense of determination. Most groups debated the scientific management of resources rather than organizing to protect them. But the idea of preserving land and natural resources was germinating within American society.[23]

PROGRESSIVE REFORMS AND CONSERVATIONISM: 1900–1945

Despite these whispers of ideas and early efforts, most environmental historians place the beginning of an actual "movement" at the turn of the twentieth century, when conservationism became a key element of the Progressive era. The term *conservation* sprang from efforts by pioneers such as Frederick H. Newell, George Maxwell, and Francis G. Newlands to construct reservoirs to conserve spring floodwaters for later use during the dry season. The concept behind conservation was "planned and efficient progress."[24]

In the United States, the infant environmental movement split into two camps: preservationists and conservationists. Under the leadership of Pinchot, the conservationists believed that sustainable exploitation of resources was possible. The preservationists, led by John Muir, sought to preserve wilderness areas from all but recreational and educational use. Generally, the conservationists' position won, at least at the national level.

Before the turn of the century, there had been little federal consideration of conservation. The zenith can be traced to May 13–15, 1908, when 1,000 national leaders met to attend the White House Conference on Resource Management, coordinated by Pinchot. This meeting was one of the first official agenda-setting actions in environmental policymaking.[25] At the end of the conference, the leaders asked the president to create a National Conservation Commission to develop an inventory of all natural resources. Roosevelt did so, appointing Pinchot as its chairman. By mid-1909, forty-one states had created similar organizations.[26] Pinchot organized the Conservation Congresses, which convened to discuss the familiar subjects of forest, soil, and water problems and management, and eventually expanded to include issues such as public control of railroads, regulation of speculation and gambling in foodstuffs, coordination of governmental agencies, and creation of better rural schools.[27] The congresses provided an opportunity for debate among federal, state, and local conservation leaders, but were heavily politicized. Bitterness and internal struggles brought an end to the annual events in 1917. Of prime importance to many conservation leaders was the "public land question." The possibilities of unlimited economic growth in the West caused President Theodore Roosevelt to appoint a Public Lands Commission in 1903. While many hoped the commission would promote orderly growth, there was also concern that the old practice of disposing of nonagricultural lands to private owners would give way to public ownership and management.[28] During the presidencies of Theodore Roosevelt, William Howard Taft, and Woodrow Wilson, Congress created new national forests, passed laws to protect historic sites and migratory birds, and enacted the National Park Service in 1916.

The Progressive era is noted also for the birth of conservation organizations such as the National Audubon Society in 1905, the National Parks Association in 1919, and the Izaak Walton League in 1922. Pinchot organized the National Conservation Association in 1909, with the group's primary interests being limited to water power and mineral leasing, reflecting an extension of Roosevelt's policy. The group disbanded in the 1920s. Progressive era reforms were focused on efficiency, striving to make better use of natural resources. The reformers were not radicals in the traditional political sense, so progressive conservation posed only a modest threat to the existing distribution of power in the United States.[29]

As use of the term *conservation* broadened, it gradually lost its initial meaning. Roosevelt began referring to the "conservation of human health," and the National Conservation Congress devoted its entire 1912 session to "the conservation of human life." While conservationists focused attention on the sustainability of natural resource use, progressives in urban areas began working for new laws and regulations to reduce pollution and protect public health. Cities were the first to regulate air pollution; the first clean-air laws were enacted in the late 1800s. Public health advocates and activists such as Alice Hamilton and Jane Addams provided the impetus for state and local regulatory programs to improve water quality, provide for sanitation and waste removal, and reduce workers' exposure to toxic chemicals.[30]

During the 1930s, the environmental movement again became a battle between conservation and preservation. As a result, environmental leaders redoubled their efforts to preserve scenic areas. In 1935, Aldo Leopold founded the Wilderness Society to protect public lands, and the National Wildlife Federation (1936) served as the first of the conservation education organizations, sponsoring National Wildlife Week in schools beginning in 1938. Conservation organizations were closely allied with the four major engineering societies: the American Society of Civil Engineers, the American Society of Mechanical Engineers, the American Institute of Electrical Engineers, and the American Institute of Mining Engineers, all of which spearheaded the drive for efficiency. The Great Depression brought the federal government into new areas of responsibility, including environmental policy. Federal conservation interest intensified with the growth of agencies with specific resource responsibilities, beginning with the Tennessee Valley Authority in 1933, the Soil Conservation Service in 1935, and the Civilian Conservation Corps, which from 1933 to 1942 gave productive work to 2 million unemployed young men. By the time the United States entered into World War II, conservation and resource management were firmly entrenched as part of the federal government's environmental mission.

RECREATION AND THE AGE OF ECOLOGY: POST–WORLD WAR II TO 1969

After World War II, Americans' interest in the environment shifted to a new direction. Concern about the efficient scientific management of resources was replaced with a desire to use the land for recreational purposes. Over 30 million Americans toured the national parks in 1950. The parks were, in the words of one observer, "in danger of being loved to death," because roads and services were still at prewar levels.[31] National Park Service (NPS) Director Conrad Wirth presented Congress with a "wish list" of park needs that came to be known as "Mission '66"—a 10-year improvement program that would coincide with the fiftieth anniversary of the NPS. That plan served as the blueprint for massive growth in national parks as well as recreational areas during the next twenty years.[32] Habitat protection became the focus of groups like the Defenders of Wildlife, founded in 1947 to preserve, enhance, and protect the diversity of wildlife and its habitats. In 1951, the Nature Conservancy began to acquire, either through purchase, gift, or exchange, ecologically significant tracts of land, many of which are habitats for endangered species.

The 1960s brought a battle between those who supported industrial growth and those who worried about the effects of pollution caused by growth. It was a decade when an author's prose or a single event could rouse the public's indignation. The 1960s marked the beginning of legislative initiatives that would be fine-tuned over the next forty years and of tremendous growth in environmental organizations.

Two authors brought public attention to environmental problems during this decade. Rachel Carson, in her book *Silent Spring*,[33] and Paul Ehrlich, in *The Population Bomb*,[34] warned the world of the dangers of pesticides and the population explosion, respectively. Several authors served up "doom-and-gloom" predictions of the problems facing the planet, and there was a spirit of pessimism regarding the environmental situation. In January and February 1969, two oil spills 5.5 miles off the coast of Santa Barbara, California, hit a public nerve like never before. Only eight days into his administration, President Richard Nixon was faced with an environmental crisis for which he was totally unprepared. The media captured the essence of the spills with images of birds soaked in gooey, black oil and pristine, white beaches soiled with globs of oil that washed up with each tide.[35]

Legislatively, the 1960s heralded a period of intense activity (see Appendix A). In a carryover of issues from the postwar period, parks and wilderness remained high on the public's and legislature's agendas. By 1960, the number of national park visitors had grown to 72 million, and Congress responded by creating the Land and Water Conservation Fund to add new wilderness areas and national parks. Congress also expanded recreational areas with the passage of the National Wilderness Act in 1964 and the Wild and Scenic Rivers and National Trails Acts in 1968. President Lyndon Johnson, as part of his environmental policy, which he called "the new conservation," sought congressional support for urban parks to bring the land closer to the people.[36] Johnson's wife, Lady Bird, spearheaded the drive to improve the nation's roadways through her highway beautification program and sought, and found, congressional support for the 1965 passage of the Highway Beautification Act.[37]

Although there were several legislative precursors during the 1940s and 1950s, many hallmark pieces of pollution legislation were enacted during the

1960s, with the signing of the first Clean Air Act in 1963 (amended as the Air Quality Act in 1967) and the Water Quality Act in 1965. The Endangered Species Preservation Act (1966) marked a return to the federal interest in animal and plant habitat that had begun earlier in the century.

Political leadership on environmental issues during the 1960s focused on several individuals, and environmental organizations began to grow. Senator Edmund Muskie of Maine was among the most visible, but he turned out to be the target of considerable criticism, especially when he became a leading contender for the Democratic presidential nomination. A 1969 report by Ralph Nader's consumer organization gave Muskie credit for his early stewardship in the air pollution battle but accused the senator of subsequently losing interest.[38] Other leaders, such as Senator Henry Jackson of Washington (who chaired the Senate Interior and Insular Affairs Committee and was largely responsible for shepherding the National Environmental Policy Act [NEPA] through Congress) and Representative John Dingell of Michigan, were primarily involved in the legislative arena. Not only did the number of environmental groups expand during the 1960s, but existing ones experienced tremendous growth. New organizations like the African Wildlife Foundation (1961), the World Wildlife Fund (1961), the Environmental Defense Fund (1967), and the Council on Economic Priorities (1969) broadened the spectrum of group concerns. Meanwhile, the Sierra Club's membership grew tenfold from 1952 to 1969, and the Wilderness Society expanded from 12,000 members in 1960 to 54,000 in 1970.[39]

One of the most compelling themes to emerge from the decade of the 1960s was that the federal government must take a more pervasive role in solving what was beginning to be called "the environmental crisis." The limited partnership between the federal government and the states was insufficient to solve what was already being spoken of in global terms.

EARTH DAYS AND DEREGULATION: 1970–1992

In August 1969, Wisconsin Senator Gaylord Nelson was on his way to Berkeley when he read an article in *Ramparts* magazine about the anti–Vietnam War teach-ins that were sweeping the country. Nelson, one of the few members of Congress who had shown an interest in environmental issues, thought a similar approach might work to raise public awareness about the environment. In September, he proposed his idea during a speech in Seattle. Later that fall, he incorporated a nonprofit, nonpartisan organization, Environmental Teach-In, and pledged $15,000 of his own funds to get it started.[40] In December 1969, Nelson asked former Stanford student body president Denis Hayes to serve as national coordinator for what was to become Earth Day on April 22, 1970. Hayes, who postponed plans to enter Harvard Law School, worked with a $190,000 budget, purchasing a full-page ad in the *New York Times* to announce the teach-in. Not everyone was supportive. President Nixon, who had presented a thirty-seven-point environmental message to Congress a few months earlier, refused to issue a proclamation in support of Earth Day. Instead, the White House issued proclamations for National Archery Week and National Boating Week.[41]

Certainly, 1970 marked a watershed year for new environmental organizations, with the founding of the Center for Science in the Public Interest, Citizens for a Better Environment, Environmental Action, Friends of the Earth, the League of Conservation Voters, and the Natural Resources Defense Council. Greenpeace and Public Citizen were formed the following year. This period marks the beginning of a turnaround in leverage, as business and industry mobilized to slow the pace of environmental legislation (see Chapter 2). Environmental organizations were no longer able to monopolize the policy debate to serve their own interests. The range of environmental issues had become so extensive that organized environmental groups were unable to act effectively in all areas. Even more important, many issues had become matters not for public debate and legislative action, but for administrative choice, an area in which politics was dominated by technical issues that placed a premium on the financial resources necessary to command expertise. This gave considerable political advantage to administrators and private corporate institutions, which employed far more technical personnel than did environmental organizations.

The American public's attitude about the environment has never been very stable, and the decade of the 1970s is a perfect example. When George Gallup asked respondents in his national survey to identify the most important problem facing the nation in November 1967, the environment did not even make the list; nor did it appear when the question was asked in three surveys in 1968 or another survey in 1969. The Vietnam War and the economy overshadowed other concerns of Americans during that period. Not until May 1970 (after Earth Day) did the topic appear as an issue, when it ranked second and was mentioned by 53 percent of those responding. By June 1970, the subject had dropped off the list, replaced in the number-one spot by the campus unrest caused by the Vietnam War. Pollution and ecology returned to the list in March 1971 (ranked sixth, with only 7 percent of respondents naming these as the most important problem); by June 1971, these two topics ranked tenth. Environmental issues reemerged as a topic of concern in August and October 1972, and in March 1973, when the subject ranked sixth. But in May 1973, although pollution was ranked as the fifth-most important problem facing the nation, it began to be overshadowed by another problem—the energy crisis, which ranked thirteenth. In January 1974, Gallup found that the public considered the energy crisis to be its most important problem, being selected by 46 percent of the public. By July, that ranking dropped to number four, mentioned by 4 percent of those surveyed—a figure that stayed relatively constant throughout the rest of the decade.

President Nixon, whose position on environmental protection often reflected public opinion, used the signing of NEPA on January 1, 1970, to declare the next 10 years as "the environmental decade," and instructed his staff to rush the issue of new legislative proposals. NEPA became one of the nation's most important environmental statutes by requiring an extensive analysis of the environmental impact of proposed projects and the development of ways to minimize negative impacts. With his creation of the Environmental Protection Agency (EPA) by executive order in 1970, Nixon moved ahead in the race with Congress to take advantage of the public's mood.

In the meantime, Congress too was firmly on the environmental protection bandwagon, enacting more than 20 major pieces of legislation, many of which were refinements of earlier bills. Other laws, such as the Marine Mammal Protection Act (1972), the Federal Environmental Pesticides Control Act (1972), the Resource Conservation and Recovery Act (1976), and the Toxic Substances Control Act (1976), brought the federal government into new areas of environmental protection.

As had been the case in the 1960s, unexpected events periodically refocused attention on the environment.[42] The 1973 Arab oil embargo pushed energy to the top of the policy agenda, although a succession of presidents had sought to make the United States "energy-independent." President Jimmy Carter pushed through most of his energy conservation program while turning down the White House thermostat and wearing a sweater indoors. Nuclear power, which was being touted as a cleaner, more reliable alternative to foreign oil, suffered a major setback in 1979 when cooling water at the Three Mile Island nuclear power plant near Harrisburg, Pennsylvania, dipped below safe levels and triggered a meltdown. Although no radioactive fuel escaped and no one was injured, the accident cast a shadow of doubt over the entire nuclear energy program.

During the summer of 1978, media coverage of incidents near the Love Canal in Niagara Falls, New York, reawakened American concerns over toxic waste. The abandoned canal had been used as a dumping ground for waste during the 1940s by the Hooker Chemicals and Plastics Corporation, which filled in the site and sold it to the Niagara Falls Board of Education for $1. A school was then built near the site, which was located in the midst of a residential area. When local health officials found higher than normal rates of birth defects, miscarriages, and other medical problems among Love Canal residents, President Carter ordered the federal government to purchase the 240 homes nearest the site; the government eventually spent more than $30 million in relocation costs.[43]

Similar incidents occurred in 1979 in West Point, Kentucky, where 17,000 drums of leaking chemicals were discovered, and in 1983 in Times Beach, Missouri, where high levels of dioxin were thought to have contaminated the entire town. The Hudson River was found to be contaminated by more than a million pounds of polychlorinated biphenyls (PCBs), and well water in the West was contaminated with cancer-causing trichloroethylene (TCE). The impact of publicity surrounding Love Canal and similar disclosures can be seen in public opinion polls. In July 1978, Resources for the Future (RFF) surveyed Americans' attitudes at a time when the inflation rate topped 10 percent and an endangered fish, the tiny snail darter, had stopped progress on the Tellico Dam. The RFF survey found that environmental public support continued to hold firm, with the number of people who felt "we are spending too little on environmental protection" increasing despite widespread economic problems.[44]

Just as the 1969 Santa Barbara oil spill had galvanized public opinion, the December 3, 1984, leak of deadly methyl isocyanate gas at a Union Carbide plant in Bhopal, India, reawakened interest in environmental disasters, becoming a focusing event for toxic regulations. The leak, which killed more than 2,000 people and injured 200,000, was brought closer to home when it was revealed that an identical Union Carbide plant was located in Institute, West Virginia. The public and governmental outcry resulted in a shutdown of the plant for several months for inspections and safety checks. These events also caused a shifting of legislative gears as interest changed to toxic and hazardous waste and the health impacts of pollution. With congressional enactment of the Resource Conservation and Recovery Act and the Toxic Substances Control Act in the 1970s, the foundation was laid for the Comprehensive Environmental Response, Compensation, and Liability Act ("Superfund") in 1980 (reauthorized in 1986) and the Hazardous and Solid Waste Amendments in 1984. Concerns about health found their way into the Safe Drinking Water Act Amendments of 1986 (an expansion of the 1974 law) and the Federal Insecticide, Fungicide, and Rodenticide Act Amendments of 1988.

But the 1980s brought an increase in the pessimistic attitudes Americans had toward the efforts that had been made in the previous decade. A Cambridge Reports survey from 1983 to 1989 found that respondents believed that the overall quality of the environment was worse than it had been five years before, with a sharp increase in pessimism beginning in 1987.[45] When the question of "most important problem" was asked again during the 1980s by a Gallup poll, energy often made the list of most important problems, although the environment did not. A separate Gallup survey conducted in September 1989 found that 66 percent of the respondents said they were "extremely concerned" about the pollution of sea life and beaches from the dumping of garbage, medical wastes, and chemicals into the ocean, with the same percentage also expressing extreme concern about the pollution of freshwater rivers, lakes, and other sources of drinking water. Fifty percent of those surveyed said they were extremely concerned about air pollution, and 41 percent expressed concern over the disposal of household garbage and trash.[46]

The 1980s environmental policy agenda was molded most by the administration of President Ronald Reagan, whose main concern was to reduce the amount of governmental regulation (see Chapter 3). Reagan's budget cuts and personnel decisions and a weakening of the previous decade's legislative efforts had a profound effect on policy for the next ten years. Despite those changes, public concern over environmental degradation had risen substantially in this period, commanding support from large majorities. What was less clear at the end of the 1980s was the strength of the public's commitment to environmental protection.[47]

After declaring himself "the environmental president" after his 1988 campaign, George H. W. Bush was faced not only with the Reagan legacy of environmental slash-and-burn but also with a host of newly discovered environmental problems and crises, many of which had a global focus. Two major pieces of legislation enacted during the Bush administration were the Clean Air Act Amendments of 1990 and the 1992 Energy Policy Act, both of which represented a break in the legislative gridlock that had characterized Congress under Republican administrations. Environmental organizations, many of which experienced a decline in membership growth after the initial burst of activity in the early 1970s, received a booster shot with Earth Day 1990. The Gallup organization classified about 20 percent of the American public as hard-core environmentalists—those who call themselves "strong environmentalists" and feel that major disruptions are coming if we do not take drastic environmental actions, even at the cost of economic growth.[48]

Perhaps the most important development of this period was the globalization of environmental protection. The 1992 Earth Summit in Rio de Janeiro refocused the need for environmental issues to be viewed globally, rather than locally. It also provided dramatic evidence of the need for international cooperation to solve the larger issues of global warming, transboundary pollution, and biodiversity, and raised the critical question of whether the industrialized world is willing to pay for environmental protection in developing countries. It also spotlighted the North–South split (the split between nations of the Northern and Southern Hemispheres) between industrialized and developing nations—a controversy that would reemerge over the next two decades. In 1992, the Gallup International Institute's Health of the Planet survey showed that concern about the environment was not limited to wealthy industrialized nations of the Northern Hemisphere. In half of the twenty-two nations surveyed, environmental problems were rated as one of the three most serious problems, and only small percentages of people in any nation dismissed environmental issues as not serious. The survey found that air and water pollution were perceived as the most serious environmental problems affecting nations, with the loss of natural resources mentioned most often by residents of other nations.[49] The Bush administration's global focus was on trade, however, rather than on the environment. The president all but ignored the 1992 Earth Summit, opening the door, some hoped, for a candidate who would bring an end to the Reagan/Bush policies.

GLOBAL AWARENESS AND GRIDLOCK:
1993–2000

The inauguration of President Bill Clinton and Vice President Al Gore in 1993 marked yet another turning point in environmental politics. The vice president was widely known as an aggressive advocate of environmental regulation and author of a best-selling call to environmental arms, titled *Earth in the Balance*.[50] The president gave Gore responsibility for developing the administration's environmental policies, pleasing environmental group leaders who believed Clinton was going to follow through on his campaign pledges. Although the environment never surfaced as a key issue in the 1992 presidential campaign, Clinton administration officials immediately called for peaceful coexistence between environmentalists and business as the administration prepared its legislative agenda. Early in 1993, the Clinton administration proposed sweeping changes in public

lands policies, including raising grazing fees and imposing hard-rock mining royalties and below-cost timber sales in national forests, as part of a budget bill
aimed at reducing the federal deficit. The proposals were immediately attacked
by members of Congress from Western states, many of whom were Democrats
or represented states where Clinton had won in 1992; as a result, the president
quickly retreated and shifted his attention to other policy initiatives.

In October 1993, the administration's initiative to add grazing-fee hikes and
new environmental safeguards for grazing lands to the Interior Department appropriations bill failed when the Senate was unsuccessful in ending a filibuster of
the bill by Republicans and Western Democrats. The proposals were eventually
dropped from the bill, but not until Western Senators blasted the administration
as launching a war on the West. However, while the Senate resisted changes, the
media gave increasingly favorable attention to Secretary Bruce Babbitt's efforts to
get Westerners to pay fair prices for using public lands and to increase environmental protection. Babbitt's agenda of reorienting the Bureau of Reclamation
away from dam building and toward water conservation, amending the Endangered Species Act to increase habitat preservation, and updating mining and logging policies raised tremendous opposition among some in the West while
encouraging many others who believed such changes to be long overdue. Babbitt argued that public lands policy should be guided by the idea of "dominant
public use," requiring the preservation of ecosystems, rather than "multiple use,"
in which logging, mining, and ranching interests dominate. Babbitt argued that
dominant public use requires policymakers to look at the needs for biodiversity,
watershed protection, and landscape, as well as the opportunities for extractive
industries, and to set priorities accordingly.[51] However, by the time Congress
adjourned in 1994, the only conservationist legislation that had been enacted
created two new national parks in California, Death Valley and Joshua Tree,
and a third protected area, the Mojave Desert.

In 1994, Republican candidates in a number of Western states were successful in running against Babbitt and Clinton's Western lands reforms. The Republicans effectively integrated attacks on Democrats for launching a war on the
West with antitax, anti-Washington, and antiregulation rhetoric. The election
in 1994 of a Republican Congress shifted the attention to the economic costs
and regulatory burdens of environmental protection. There was a growing belief
that environmental politics had been guided by popular opinion rather than by
science. Critics pointed to sweeping governmental regulations enacted during
the Reagan and Bush administrations to reduce concentrations of toxic compounds in water, air, and land even when there was little scientific evidence of
risk to humans. Congress, responding to highly publicized concerns about the
dangers of asbestos, radon, and toxic waste dumps, quickly wrote legislation
that has cost the government and business an estimated $140 billion a year.
Even William Reilly, the EPA administrator under Bush, has said that action in
the past was "based on responding to the nightly news. What we have had in the
United States is environmental agenda-setting by episodic panic."[52]

When the American economy was relatively healthy, few bothered to question the cost-benefit ratio for such expenditures. But with resources growing

increasingly scarce and with the federal government placing a new emphasis on domestic problems like crime, drugs, health care, and the urban infrastructure, this questioning of environmental priorities seemed long overdue. The 1994 House "Republican Contract with America," written by Newt Gingrich and other Republican House leaders, outlined a set of national issues for House Republican candidates to run on and, after the Republicans won, played a major role in shaping the policy agenda. Among other things, the contract promised to "roll back government regulations and create jobs."[53] Frank Lutz, the Republican pollster who worked with Gingrich in creating the Contract with America, told his clients that "Americans believe Washington has gone too far in regulating and they want to turn the clock and paperwork back." Party strategist William Kristol suggested that Republicans immediately identify regulatory "excesses," and he organized a meeting entitled, "What to Kill First: Agencies to Dismantle, Programs to Eliminate, and Regulations to Stop." William Niskanen, head of the Cato Institute, called on Congress to "rein in what I call the 'Nanny State.' Stop telling states where to set speed limits.... Stop telling businesses about whether and when employees and customers may smoke."[54] Heritage Foundation analysts published "real life 'horror' stories of individuals who have lost their property or had their business harmed because of overzealous government regulators" and offered the following agenda for reforming regulation: force environmental agencies to base their evaluations of proposed regulations on sound scientific criteria; place a ceiling on the estimated total cost of all regulations promulgated by the agency; force regulators to account for the costs of their proposals, whenever possible; insist that regulators rely on markets rather than red tape; and enact legislation specifying exactly when the federal government must compensate property owners for regulatory takings.[55]

The Contract with America did not mention the environment directly, but it included numerous provisions aimed at reducing regulation and promoting economic development rather than preservation. These provisions included requirements that Congress fund the regulatory mandates imposed on states and that agencies perform cost-benefit analyses before issuing regulations, reduce paperwork requirements, compensate landowners for costs resulting from regulation, and formulate a regulatory budget of compliance costs being imposed on business. Republicans in Congress sought to reduce environmental regulation by cutting EPA and Interior Department budgets, attaching riders to appropriations bills that reduced specific protections, and introducing major rewrites of the leading environmental laws.

However, Republican efforts to reduce environmental regulation were short-lived. To begin with, environmental groups challenged the new Republican agenda in the spring of 1995. The largest environmental organizations proposed an Environmental Bill of Rights, to be signed by Americans throughout the nation and presented to Congress and the White House.[56] President Clinton began vetoing appropriations bills with provisions aimed at reducing environmental protection and saw his popularity climb. That encouraged more vetoes and more challenges to the Republican agenda, and by 1996, the Republicans had abandoned their attacks on environmental laws and programs. Clinton skillfully positioned himself between the Republican radicals and popular environmental programs during the 1996 presidential campaign, and his reelection was, in part, the result of his willingness to challenge the congressional Republicans' deregulatory agenda. Bruce Babbitt had become one of the most popular members of the Clinton administration, and he led the criticism of the Republican Congress, which contributed greatly to the president's political rehabilitation in 1996. He was most effective at drawing attention to the Republican Congress's environmental agenda, particularly when he charged that some Republicans were seeking to sell off the national parks. Babbitt's shift from public lands issues in the West to national environmental issues defused criticism of him from inside the administration and in the environmental community.[57] Congress and the White House came together to pass new pesticide and safe drinking-water laws in the summer of 1996, which were widely heralded as examples of the potential of bipartisan environmentalism. But the demands for more environmental protection and less burdensome regulation are not easily satisfied, a factor that characterized environmental politics in Clinton's second term.

President Clinton began his second term on the heels of a Harris public opinion poll that showed (despite Republican claims to the contrary) that Americans continued to favor strong environmental policies and did not support reducing the powers of the EPA. Researchers found that over half those surveyed believed that the EPA is needed now more than when it was founded.[58] The study confirmed the findings of another Harris Poll conducted just a few months earlier that found 60 percent of the public opposed to the Republicans' efforts at environmental deregulation, which indeed had failed miserably during Clinton's first term. By 1998, the Harris Poll "feel good index," which measures how people feel about their lives, noted substantial increases in the number of respondents who felt good about the quality of the air, water, and environment where they live and work.[59]

Against this backdrop, many assumed that the president would capitalize on rising public support for environmental protection by proposing new initiatives or the reform of older laws like the Endangered Species Act and Superfund. But Clinton's administration became so engrossed in dealing with scandal and impeachment proceedings that the last four years of his term as president are marked by few notable environmental achievements. The business of retaining the presidency in times that were tumultuous both nationally and globally left Clinton neither time nor congressional support for proposals that environmental groups had long hoped would be passed. Despite his 1993 pledge, Clinton and Vice President Al Gore were more often seen at largely symbolic photo opportunities with the press than at bill-signing ceremonies in the White House.

Clinton and Gore observed Earth Day in April 1998 by traveling to Harper's Ferry, West Virginia, to help volunteers maintain America's longest footpath, the 2,157-mile-long Appalachian Trail. The president used the occasion to urge Congress to "end its attacks on the environment and help build on America's conservation legacy."[60] Later that year, they went to the New River in North Carolina to formally designate fourteen American Heritage Rivers.

While the president used the Council on Environmental Quality to trumpet an accelerated cleanup of toxic waste sites and a reduction of paperwork at the EPA,[61] several other initiatives hit a dead end. For example, the administration's efforts at issuing more stringent air-quality standards were struck down by a federal court in 1999. The EPA had tried to issue new regulations for particulate matter and ozone, but the court ruled that the standards had not been based on public health concerns and thus constituted an unconstitutional delegation of power to the agency by Congress.[62] Attempts to strengthen right-to-know laws about toxic chemical releases were overshadowed by research that showed existing laws to be ineffective. In mid-1999, a study by the Environmental Working Group showed that almost four of every ten factories tracked by the EPA over a two-year period were guilty of significant violations of air-quality regulations. The study noted that although major violations were punishable by fines that could have ranged into the millions of dollars, government officials had disregarded guidelines for setting the amounts, and in some cases, offending firms paid no penalty at all. The report blamed the EPA for poor oversight and state regulators for enforcement failures.[63] A 1999 EPA study also found that, rather than meeting the administration's goals of a reduction in toxic chemical releases, the amount of toxic chemicals released into the environment by industrial plants had actually increased. The report attributed the increase to factories sending their metal wastes to landfills instead of to recycling centers, thus ending years of steady decline in toxic chemicals entering the environment.[64] But the president did herald the fact that the administration had established a Brownfields National Partnership, which brought together the resources of more than a dozen federal agencies to help thousands of communities clean up abandoned pieces of land that had been contaminated by previous industrial use. Moreover, in October 1999, Clinton used his weekly radio address to announce that, effective January 1, 2000, new rules would significantly lower the amount of twenty-seven dangerous chemicals, including dioxin, that companies could use before reporting discharges to the public.

Clinton could point to some victories in the area of natural resource protection. For example, the federal government agreed to acquire mining property near Yellowstone National Park and to decontaminate the site from the effects of earlier mining activities. Among the more noteworthy preservation accomplishments was the acquisition of the largest privately owned stand of ancient redwoods in the Headwaters Forest in northern California—a deal negotiated among the landowner, the federal government, and the state. The president also sought funds to continue the restoration of the south Florida ecosystem and to purchase 50,000 additional acres of land on the northern edge of Everglades National Park—issues important to the region's politically powerful leaders.

On a global level, the administration called on a reluctant Congress for more bilateral and multilateral environmental assistance to address issues such as biodiversity and to fund contributions to the United Nations' environmental agencies.

In the area of global climate change, the United States participated in negotiations calling for cuts in greenhouse gas emissions, which became formalized as the Kyoto Protocol in December 1997; but by the end of the decade, there was little sign that the projected reductions would be realized. Although the United States signed the treaty in 1998, Clinton could not persuade Congress to ratify the agreement or to begin implementing the necessary reductions in greenhouse gas emissions.

Clinton's "commonsense environmental reforms," such as helping American business compete more effectively in the global market through environmental technology, were not new, and they lacked the luster of even the Bush administration's environmental efforts. The president had, for the most part, piggy-backed on proposals that preceded his administration, thus disappointing environmental leaders who had supported the Clinton–Gore ticket as a potential for reawakening the nation's environmental conscience. Those hopes became lost in issues that, by the end of 1999, had pushed the environment almost to the bottom of the political agenda: sexual scandals, impeachment, conflict in the Balkans, and violence in the workplace and the schools.

Most observers have commented that, although there was some disappointment that the Clinton–Gore ticket failed to live up to its advance billing as proactive on environmental protection, the administration was able to stop the Republican-controlled Congress from dismantling controversial laws like the Endangered Species Act or cutting agency budgets, as had been feared. Clinton abolished the controversial Council on Competitiveness and was widely praised for his appointees. The Clinton administration was able to build on the groundwork laid by congressional leaders and environmental organizations. His goal, Clinton said, was to block attempts to roll back safeguards for the nation's food, water, and air: "I want an America in the year 2000 where no child should have to live near a toxic waste dump, where no parent should have to worry about the safety of a child's glass of water, and no neighborhood should be put in harm's way by pollution from a nearby factory."[65]

In the 2000 presidential race, neither Al Gore nor George W. Bush paid much attention to the environment as an issue. Gore received endorsements from environmental groups like the Sierra Club and the League of Conservation Voters, but seemed to abandon his once-ambitious environmental agenda. Just months before the election, a Gallup Poll survey found that 29 percent of the respondents considered the candidates' position on the issue of the environment extremely important, ranking it ninth overall behind issues such as education, the economy, health care, and Social Security. According to the poll,

> The environment's mid-range importance in terms of the presidential race this year is similar to the relatively low "seriousness" rating Americans give it in relation to other problems facing the country. Only a slim majority of Americans believed that environmental problems are an extremely or very serious problem—putting it fifth on the list of seven problems tested.[66]

ROLLBACK: 2001–2008

Just prior to leaving office in January 2001, Clinton decided to wield his power as president, using the 1906 American Antiquities Act, to make last-minute designations of national monuments—actions that some believe salvaged his environmental record. While the move pleased environmental leaders, it added more responsibilities to an already financially strapped National Park Service. The actions also infuriated members of Congress, who felt the designations had been made without appropriate consultation with political leaders or the public. They responded by opening the 2001 session with a series of bills designed to repeal the president's actions.

After the bitter presidential race, it was clear that George W. Bush did not assume office with a policy mandate, especially an environmental one. His appointments set the tone for his actions, with critics noting that many of the key positions were given to corporate interests, especially those in the oil industry. His appointee for Secretary of Energy, Spencer Abraham, was a longtime opponent of increasing fuel efficiency standards. Gale Norton, named Secretary of the Interior, was a supporter of opening up oil drilling in the Arctic National Wildlife Refuge, and she had served under controversial Reagan appointee James Watt. Ann Veneman, Secretary of Agriculture, had served on the board of directors for the first company to bring genetically engineered food to consumers.

Bush and Congress may have been trying to gauge public opinion about environmental problems in the new millennium as the president developed his own environmental agenda. If that were the case, they would have found that Americans were anxious, but moderate in their views. In a Gallup Poll survey in March 2001, almost half of those surveyed viewed the current state of environmental conditions in the United States as "good" or "excellent," with 42 percent saying they worry "a great deal" about the quality of the environment. Combining the two ratings, only a quarter of Americans are "highly concerned" about the environment. Yet when asked what steps are necessary to address the Earth's environmental problems, 27 percent report that "immediate and drastic" action is needed.[67]

The nation's economic situation clearly affected other poll results, which showed that 57 percent say protection of the environment should be given priority over economic growth—down from 67 percent in 2000. About a third favored giving priority to economic growth, "even if the environment suffers to some extent," an all-time high for the measure. When asked what they thought was the most important problem facing the country, respondents ranked the environment sixteenth on the list, and only 2 percent of respondents named it as the primary issue.[68]

During his first term, Bush made clear that his environmental agenda would be different from that of his predecessor. On his first day in office, Bush ordered a 60-day moratorium on all Clinton regulations and executive orders that had not yet gone into effect, including the controversial monument designations. He retracted his campaign pledge and support for regulating carbon dioxide emissions at power plants and announced that the United States would not adhere to the limits on emissions that were part of the Kyoto Protocol. Shortly after the announcement, he went a step further by saying that the United States would withdraw from the treaty altogether. The abrupt change angered environmental groups and the rest of the world's leaders, who met in Johannesburg in 2002 in an attempt to finalize global climate change policies. Bush refused to attend, sending secretary of state Colin Powell instead. But the president was on solid ground in terms of public opinion. Surveys showed that most Americans believe the effects of global warming are already occurring or likely to occur in their lifetime. But barely one-third of those questioned predicted that global warming will pose a serious threat to their way of life. When asked about the environmental issue they worry about most, respondents ranked global warming twelfth out of the thirteen issues tested—just barely ahead of acid rain.[69]

The Bush administration has been compared to that of Ronald Reagan, especially in relation to oversight of the regulatory process. The president had called for stricter cost-benefit analyses and more rigorous risk assessment studies prior to the approval of any new environmental regulations. Critics believe this opens up the process to industry interests, which have a greater influence on policymaking than ever before. Vice President Dick Cheney quickly filled the role of the president's surrogate on energy policy (discussed in Chapter 6), which, along with energy-related air-quality issues, were at the forefront of political maneuvering.

Most noticeably, however, Bush made clear his intention to do whatever he could to roll back the Clinton administration's environmental efforts, along with thirty years of legislation to protect natural resources. On May 20, 2002, the Council on Environmental Quality (CEQ) established the NEPA Task Force, charged with reviewing current practices and procedures. While the charge to the group sounded harmless at first, environmental organizations quickly realized that the administration planned to water down if not altogether repeal the law. The director of the task force denied reports the group was out to gut NEPA, saying, "We're out there to try to make it better. In common parlance, we want to cut the fat if there's fat out there and we want to beef up the beef."[70] An April 2002 memorandum from the chair of the CEQ stated that the task force would "focus on modernizing the NEPA process," citing the terrorist attacks of September 11, 2001, as one reason for the analysis of the law.[71] Another target of the administration was the Northwest Forest Plan, which was adopted in 1993 after the Forest Summit in Portland, Oregon, to set aside millions of acres of federal forests to protect endangered wildlife, but still allowed the logging of nearly 1 billion board feet of timber annually. An April 2002 U.S. Forest Service internal memo entitled "Fixes to the Northwest Forest Plan" telegraphed the administration's plans to increase timber production on lands previously off-limits to harvesting. The president has the authority to make changes to the Forest Plan without Congressional approval.[72] The administration followed through on its pledge to streamline NEPA, and by October 2002, the House of Representatives had already held hearings and was in the process of amending proposals to repeal portions of the law.

One of the president's major legislative achievements during his first term was passage of the Healthy Forests Restoration Act, which he signed in December 2003. The law and its accompanying regulatory framework (discussed in Chapter 4) began to serve as a template for similar strategies on issues from grazing to mining. He revived efforts to permit oil exploration and drilling in the Arctic National Wildlife Refuge and continued to support efforts to open a long-term nuclear waste site in Nevada.

Results from public opinion polls during Bush's first term reinforced his choice of positions on key environmental issues. The Gallup/CNN/*USA Today* polls conducted between April 2001 and January 2005 showed that the president's approval ratings for how he was handling the environment went from 46 to 53 percent; the ABC News/*Washington Post* surveys from March 2001 to January 2005 ranged from a low approval rating of 41 percent in June 2001 to a high of 54 percent in January 2002. A more extensive Public Relations Society of America [PSRA]/*Newsweek* poll found that the percentage of those who approved of the president's handling of the environment remained consistently higher than the percentage of those who disapproved of his performance between April 2001 and January 2004.[73]

Any hopes that environmental advocates might have had that the 2004 presidential campaign might put the spotlight on problems like pollution and sustainability were quickly deflected and, for the most part, the environment was a nonissue. Democratic presidential nominee John Kerry received the League of Conservation Voters' endorsement for his "unparalleled record on environmental issues," along with the support of forty-eight Nobel Prize–winning scientists. But the issues of terrorism, the continuing war in Iraq, and accusations over Kerry's Vietnam War record allowed Bush to sidestep any serious consideration of issues his opponent tried to raise. Bush defeated Kerry by more than 3 million popular votes and thirty-four electoral college votes.

At the start of Bush's second term, his environmental approval ratings began to drop. PSRA/*Newsweek* reported that 45 percent of those surveyed in March 2005 said they disapproved of the way in which the president was handling the environment, and 41 percent approved. That dip in rankings corresponds to the March 2005 poll by Harris Interactive, which found an even larger gap, with 36 percent approving and 47 percent disapproving. The numbers did not appear to be tied to any particular environmental issue or problem, but they do correlate to the public's growing disapproval of the Iraq war and backlash against a proposed revision of Social Security regulations.[74]

Overall, the Bush administration solidified its environmental agenda from both a partisan and strategic perspective. Republican members of Congress were tutored in how to stay "on message" and how to neutralize opposition. Those who might potentially flee from the fold were brought back by framing environmental problems as being caused by bureaucratic red tape and unnecessary regulatory hurdles, so that they need not appear to be anti-environmental. One confidential memo advised members to "use the three words Americans are looking for in an environmental policy: 'safer,' 'cleaner,' and 'healthier'" and to "emphasize common sense." Despite numerous environmental report cards from advocacy groups that criticized the Bush administration's approach to environmental policy, the president's focus on foreign policy allowed numerous regulatory actions and legislative initiatives to proceed almost without focused opposition. The administration had found a successful strategy for pushing its environmental agenda without making it seem like it was on the policy agenda at all.

But environmental policy during the Bush administration can also be characterized by what *High Country News* called "an eight-year soap opera" due to scandals and intrigue involving key agencies and officials. J. Steven Griles, who held the number-two spot within the Department of the Interior, resigned in 2004 amidst the brouhaha over lobbyist Jack Abramoff, whose clients included Indian tribes who had been told to donate money to the Bush campaign in exchange for access to administration officials. Secretary of the Interior Gale Norton resigned in 2006; during her tenure, the agency issued drilling permits at a record pace and increased the number of snowmobiles allowed in Yellowstone National Park, but she was only indirectly linked to the Abramoff scandal. Julie MacDonald, a deputy assistant at Interior, resigned in 2007 after allegedly tinkering with the agency's own scientific findings, derailing efforts to implement the Endangered Species Act. And an estimated third of the staff members at the Minerals Management Service (MMS) were accused by federal investigators of accepting gifts and consorting with oil industry representatives between 2002 and 2006. The director of the MMS, Rejane Burton, resigned in 2007 after accusations were made that energy companies failed to pay $1 billion in royalties to the federal government.[75]

Controversies over wolf reintroduction, the government's failure to take action on climate change and greenhouse gases, and the lack of leadership in international controversies over oceans and fisheries made the Bush administration's last two years seem as though his presidency was ending with a whimper, some critics charged. Certainly the administration was successful in keeping the environmental movement at bay. But a presidency that was tied up in long-running courtroom battles, staffing scandals, and bad publicity on environmental issues would not be remembered for many successes, if any.

OVERTURES AND INITIATIVES: 2009–

The slide that marked the last two years of the Bush administration was expected to change once Barack Obama became president. Although the environment was seldom mentioned on the campaign trail, voters had a clear choice between the candidacy of Obama and John McCain. Obama, for instance, called for 25 percent of U.S. electricity to come from renewable sources by 2025, pledging a $150 billion investment over 10 years in research and development of renewables, biofuels, and clean coal technology. McCain, in contrast, supported a greater reliance on nuclear power, pledging to build dozens more facilities if he were elected president.

But public opinion showed that there was still little interest in the environment in comparison to other issues. Just before Obama took office in January 2009, 60 percent of adults nationwide said economy/jobs was the most important problem facing the country in a *CBS News/New York Times* poll. By September 2009, 41 percent of those responding picked the economy and jobs as the most important problem facing the country, followed by health care at 19 percent. The environment did not even make the list of the top seven problems on either the January or September surveys, mired deeply in the "other" category. Similar results were posted in a Bloomberg poll, although climate change eked out 2 percent of the respondents, and energy policy received 2 percent in a late August *CNN*/Opinion Research Corporation Poll. The only area where the numbers appeared slightly higher was in a Diageo/Hotline Poll from July 2009, where registered voters were asked which issue they thought would be the most important in determining how they would vote in the elections for Congress in 2010. While the economic stimulus package garnered half of those responding, energy and climate change initiatives, which were coupled as a single option in the survey, were the choice of 7 percent of those answering.[76]

While the stimulus package and the deployment of troops to Afghanistan in support of a surge there were two of the more visible actions Obama took during his first year in action, supporters enthused that the president kicked off his environmental initiatives by building a strong team of White House advisers, cabinet members, and agency staff (outlined in Chapter 3). The Natural Resources Defense Council (NRDC), for instance, noted that Obama moved quickly to put clean energy and climate protection at the top of an "assertive agenda." Citing the administration's follow-up to a 2007 U.S. Supreme Court ruling, the EPA declared carbon emissions and other greenhouse gases a threat to public health, the first of several steps taken to improve the country's response to global warming. The president's actions, including developing greenhouse-gas and fuel-efficiency standards for cars and light trucks, once implemented, are expected to save 1.8 billion barrels of oil.[77] Other elements of an energy-focused record included making $50 billion available for renewable energy investments and improvements in the energy efficiency of homes, cars, and workplaces. Following up on campaign pledges, $3.4 billion was also made available to modernize the energy grid.

Aside from energy and climate issues, Obama was given high marks for maneuvering legislation through Congress establishing the Omnibus Public Land bill (see Chapter 4), canceling the sale of seventy-seven oil and gas leases in the Red Rock Canyon wilderness in Utah, and blocking what would have been the largest mountaintop removal coal mining operation in Appalachia. New standards were put in place to reduce toxic mercury and soot emissions from power plants, and the administration advanced efforts to secure a global treaty on mercury pollution. The NRDC also gave Obama credit for initiating strategic partnerships with China, India, and Latin American counties to expand international cooperation on clean-energy goals.[78]

FURTHER READING

Kevin C. Armitage. *The Nature Study Movement: The Forgotten Popularizer of America's Conservation Ethic.* Lawrence: University Press of Kansas, 2010.

Douglas Bevington. *The Rebirth of Environmentalism: Grassroots Activism from the Spotted Owl to the Polar Bear.* Covelo, CA: Island Press, 2009.

Karl Boyd Brooks. *Before Earth Day: The Origins of American Environmental Law, 1945-1970.* Lawrence: University Press of Kansas, 2009.

Marcus Hall. *Greening History: The Presence of the Past in Environmental Restoration.* New York: Routledge, 2009.

Ann Campbell Keller. *Science in Environmental Policy: The Politics of Objective Advice.* Cambridge, MA: MIT Press, 2010.

Sandra Mitchell. *Unsimple Truths: Science, Complexity, and Policy.* Chicago: University of Chicago Press, 2009.

Ted Steinberg. *Down to Earth: Nature's Role in American History.* New York: Oxford University Press, 2008.

David B. Woolner and Henry L. Henderson. *FDR and the Environment.* New York: Palgrave Macmillan, 2009.

Tom Wolf. *Arthur Carhart: Wilderness Prophet.* Boulder: University Press of Colorado, 2008.

2

Participants in the Environmental Debate

"I don't regret doing what I felt was right. I don't regret trying
to protect the environment. I had good intentions, and I don't
regret that I dedicated so much of my life to this."
— ECO-SABOTEUR CHELSEA GERLACH[1]

Chelsea Gerlach grew up in Sweet Home, Oregon. Her mother was a pre-
school teacher and her father worked at an electronics company; after they
divorced, Chelsea moved to the Eugene area and lived with her mother, who
received graphic mailings from Greenpeace and Sea Shepherd about whale hunting. At age fifteen, Gerlach worked for the Northwest Youth Corps maintaining
hiking trails, and got her first view of forest clear-cuts. In 1995, while a student
at Evergreen State College, she read the Unabomber Manifesto, which had been
published in the *Washington Post*. She became involved with the local Earth First!
group, participating in blockades of old-growth timber sales, and eventually,
joined an Earth Liberation Front (ELF) underground cell, or small group, of activists. For the next several years, she served as a communiqué sender, alerting
the media after an arson event and relaying messages. On October 19, 1998,
she and another ELF activist, William Rodgers, were involved in arson of buildings at a Vail, Colorado, ski resort that caused $12 million in damage. The ski
resort had planned to expand into an 885-acre wilderness area that was report-
edly home to the last wild lynx that had been spotted in Colorado.[2] No one was
injured or killed.[3]

After the fires, Gerlach continued her activism with ELF, but left Eugene in
2001 and spent six months hiding out in Canada, then moved to San Francisco

and then to Portland, living an underground life with another activist. Their life away from the ELF cell was, as she puts it, "hard. We couldn't talk to any of our new friends about our past. I had a pre-paid cell phone to call my family, and I was very careful about when and where I turned it on."[4]

In November 2005, Gerlach, who had started working as a disk jockey, was arrested outside a coffee shop in northwest Portland. At an FBI office, they showed her photographs of a Bonneville Power Administration tower that the ELF activists had brought down, and told her that other members of the loosely knit group were talking to the authorities. She says she resisted cooperating with officials for two months. "I didn't think it was ethical to put someone else in jail so I could get out of jail." But others did cooperate with the FBI, and they were planning on testifying against her. "I was facing a mandatory minimum of thirty-five years, and it reached a point where I felt my cooperation wouldn't put anyone in jail. So I talked."[5]

More than a half-dozen individuals were arrested, and in January 2006, a federal grand jury indicted eleven persons on sixty-five counts, charging them with a series of seventeen arson attacks and charges of conspiracy from 1996 to 2001 in California, Colorado, Oregon, Washington, and Wyoming. Using improvised incendiary devices, the twenty- and thirty-year-old suspects claimed responsibility as members of either the Earth Liberation Front or the Animal Liberation Front. The defendants called themselves "a family who pledged to protect each other" but denied they were terrorists because they did not seek to harm anyone. Included among the group were college students and a thirty-nine-year-old millionaire. One of those arrested, William Rodgers, who had masterminded the Vail arson attack, committed suicide in jail.[6] Another, Stanislaus Meyerhoff, claimed he had come from a family of bigots, apologizing to those in the courtroom. "A million times over I apologize, to all of you hardworking business owners, employees, researchers, firemen, investigators, attorneys, and all citizens whose property was destroyed, whose holidays were ruined, whose welfare was thwarted, and whose sleep was troubled." He was sentenced to thirteen years in prison.[7]

The proceedings involving the ten members of "The Family" may attest to the observation that "radical environmentalism failed. Whether radical environmentalists admit it or not, they failed," according to James Johnston of Forest Service Employees for Environmental Ethics. After federal, state, and local agencies began making arrests under "Operation Backfire" in 2005, incidents involving radical environmental groups such as ELF decreased dramatically. Although there are still sporadic crimes by environmental and animal-rights activists, some argue that "a violent chapter in the environmental movement ended—with a whimper."[8]

Whether radical environmentalism is really "dead" is open to discussion and debate, and there is little doubt that many of the ideas that led activists like

Chelsea Gerlach to move from civil disobedience to violence are still alive and well. Just prior to the 2005 arrests, John Lewis, Deputy Assistant Director of the FBI, told members of the U.S. Senate Committee on Environment and Public Works,

> One of today's most serious domestic terrorism threats comes from special interest extremist movements such as the Animal Liberation Front (ALF), the Earth Liberation Front (ELF), and Stop Huntingdon Animal Cruelty campaign. Adherents to these movements aim to resolve specific issues by using criminal "direct action" against individuals or companies believed to be abusing or exploiting animals or the environment.[9]

The radical beliefs and tactics of groups like ALF, ELF, and Earth First! are an important part of the environmental debate. Radical organizations shun traditional structure and administrative rules, preferring militant action—termed "monkeywrenching" and "ecotage"—to the traditional political strategies used by mainstream environmental organizations. Study results regarding the motivations of environmental radicals vary. One researcher says that these activists are driven by a combination of spiritual conviction, science, and politics, including a deeply held belief that the Earth is sacred.[10]

Are the tactics of radical environmentalists effective in changing policy? Generally, their actions are shunned by both environmental organizations and groups associated with the environmental opposition. Some actions may, in fact, be counterproductive. Mink ranchers say that when saboteurs release the animals from their cages into the wild, they simply hasten their deaths. At the University of Washington's Center for Urban Horticulture, a fire allegedly set by environmental radicals damaged the work of researchers seeking to save endangered plants and efforts to find trees that could be used instead of logging old-growth stands.[11] But the mainstream groups also use the radicals as a foil, realizing that the posturing and activities of such groups cause their own agendas to be perceived as much more reasonable and acceptable in contrast.

This chapter continues with a discussion of how the concept of group theory[12] can be used to explain how unofficial participants in the policymaking process influence environmental policy, deciphering the actions of the primary actors and stakeholders in the debate over the environment and natural resources. Adherents to this approach believe that political decisions are the result of the struggles among competing interests with access to the political process. Key to understanding group theory is the assumption that some groups will have more political access than others because of superior financial resources, leadership, organization, or public support for their cause.[13] Although this book does not attempt to delve into the theoretical debate over applying the pluralist tradition of

Another View, Another Voice: Tim DeChristopher

Bidder #70 looked different from the men in the suits at the December 19, 2008, Bureau of Land Management auction of sixteen parcels totaling nearly 150,000 acres of federal land in Utah. He entered the room after the bidding had begun, and watched a young woman weeping at the thought that the acreage would be used for oil and gas exploitation, rather than preserved for future generations. The young man grabbed a bidding paddle, posing as a legitimate bidder. Tim DeChristopher, a twenty-seven-year-old University of Utah economics student, had recently attended an event commemorating the twentieth anniversary of the death of Edward Abbey, best known for his stories of the Monkey Wrench Gang, and the themes seemed to have resonated for the young environmentalist.

DeChristopher notes that his participation in letter-writing campaigns and actions like riding his bicycle seemed inconsequential in comparison with the threats posed by global climate change, and that he felt a conflict within himself. At the auction, he repeatedly raised the paddle to bid successfully on 22,500 acres, knowing full well that he did not have the funds to pay for the lands he won. "I tried to resist the Bush administration's attempt to defraud the American people," he says. "Many of us have sat around countless times saying how much we needed someone to do something. If I am not willing to take a stand for my generation, then who will?"

"I thought I could be effective by making bids, driving up prices for others and winning some bids myself," he said. He ended up as the successful bidder on thirteen parcels totaling $1.7 million he does not have. Although he had spoken openly with Bureau of Land Management officials about his motivations and values, that did not stop the federal government from arresting him. He had hoped that the incoming Obama administration would not press charges, but DeChristopher was charged by the U.S. Attorney with two felony counts: making a false statement to the government and violation of the Federal Onshore Oil and Gas Leasing Reform Act, which establishes a competitive process for oil and gas leases on federal land. If he is convicted, the charges could carry a $750,000 fine and ten years in prison.

"I've been hoping that someone would come out and be the leader and someone would put themselves on the line and make the sacrifices necessary to get us on a path to a more livable future. And I guess I just couldn't wait any longer for that someone to come out there and had to accept the fact that someone might be me," he says. DeChristopher had expected that a decision by new Secretary of the Interior Ken Salazar would nullify the auction, and he believes that due process was not followed. Two attorneys agreed to represent him, and an online website was established to help pay for his legal fees. Funds were collected in small increments to help pay for the first payment on the lands he "bought" at the auction. Officials argued that a down payment on the cost was due on the day the lands were purchased, and that DeChristopher had failed to make the required payment.

The legal action against him proceeded, with an indictment by a federal grand jury and trial scheduled for late 2009. In June 2009, the Department of the Interior dropped its $81,000 administrative fine against DeChristopher, saying that the civil action was on hold until criminal charges were resolved.

SOURCES:
Paul Foy. "Feds Back Off Fine for Activist." *Deseret News.* June 13, 2009. http://www.deseretnews.com/article/705310357/Feds-back-off-fine-for-activist.html?linkTrack=rss-30. Accessed June 16, 2009.
Paul Foy. "Tim DeChristopher Throws Utah Oil and Gas Drilling Leases Auction into Chaos." December 19, 2008. http://www.huffingtonpost.com/2008/12/21/tim-dechristopher-throws-_n_152661.html. Accessed June 16, 2009.
"Tim DeChristopher, Environmental Prankster, 'Wins Again.'" January 9, 2009. http://www.huffingtonpost.com/2009/01/09/tim-dechristopher-environ_n_156668.html. Accessed June 16, 2009.
Tim DeChristopher. "Why I Disrupted a Fraudulent Auction." One Utah. December 20, 2008. http://www.oneutah.org/2008/12/20/why-I-disrupted-a-fraudulent-auction/. Accessed June 16, 2009.
"Utah Student Who Prevented Bush Admin Sell-Off of Public Land Charged for Disrupting Auction." Democracy Now. April 3, 2009. http://www.democracynow.org/2009/4/3/utah_student_who_prevented_bush_admin. Accessed June 16, 2009.

American politics to other countries to explain their environmental politics, it does describe the role of international stakeholders in the environmental debate. The chapter begins with an overview of the major mainstream U.S. environmental organizations, followed by a discussion of the environmental justice movement and the development of an environmental opposition. This is followed by an analysis of the role of the media in shaping public opinion and the environmental debate. The chapter then shifts to a discussion of international activism, ranging from nongovernmental organizations to the Green Party movement and to the international governmental organizations that attempt to protect the environment on a global scale. The chapter touches briefly on these participants' strategies, successes, and failures, and summarizes their participation in the policymaking process.

U.S. ENVIRONMENTAL ORGANIZATIONS

In the 100 years since the founding of the first American environmental associations, there has been a gradual evolution of the movement. Seven of the ten most powerful groups (known collectively as the "Group of Ten") were founded before 1960. Most have influential local or regional chapters and have expanded their interests from land and wildlife issues to broader, "second-generation" issues, which are not necessarily site- or species-specific.[14] Membership in environmental organizations has ebbed and flowed over the past four decades, often in response to the government's environmental initiatives or electoral change. With the flurry of environmental legislation enacted in the late 1960s and early 1970s, membership in these organizations grew enormously. When energy replaced the environment as a key issue during the Carter administration, the groups' direct-mail campaigns generally yielded just enough members to replace those who failed to renew. But two of Reagan's appointees, Secretary of the Interior James Watt and Environmental Protection Agency (EPA) Administrator Anne Burford, were perceived as a threat to the movement. This resulted in a surge in membership as environmental organizations warned potential members of what might happen if they did not have the funds to closely monitor Reagan administration policies. But by the early 1990s, even though the environment appeared to be a core value for most Americans, membership decreased again, with many of the groups reducing staffing, closing field offices, and narrowing their program focus to just a few key issues. But for the most part, membership in these groups has grown over the last decade, especially for the groups focused on litigation as a strategy for forcing compliance with environmental protection statutes and regulations, as seen in Table 2.1.

Mainstream organizations have as a common strategy an emphasis on lobbying, although their specific focus often varies. The Sierra Club, the Wilderness Society, and the National Parks Conservation Association, for example, have tended to emphasize the preservation of public lands for future generations. Groups such as the National Wildlife Federation and Izaak Walton League, with a large percentage of sports enthusiasts and hunters within their constituencies, are more involved with habitat preservation for wildlife. Friends of the Earth and other smaller groups are involved in a broad range of issues, from

TABLE 2.1   **Membership of "Group of Ten" Environmental Organizations (1995–2010)**

Group	Year Founded	Membership 1995	Membership 2010
Sierra Club	1892	570,000	1.3 million
National Audubon Society	1905	570,000	500,000
National Parks Conservation Association	1919	450,000	325,000
Wilderness Society	1935	310,000	400,000
National Wildlife Federation	1936	1.8 million	4 million
Nature Conservancy	1951	825,000	1 million
World Wildlife Fund	1961	1.2 million	1.2 million
Environmental Defense	1967	300,000	500,000
Greenpeace*	1969	1.6 million	2.8 million
Natural Resources Defense Council	1970	185,000	1.2 million

*Figures for Greenpeace membership are worldwide.

SOURCE: Individual organization websites, brochures, and staff.

factory farms and energy policy to protection of the Potomac River and public health.

When the Environmental Defense Fund (now called Environmental Defense) was founded in 1967, a new breed of organization joined these mainstream groups. Environmental Defense—and later, the Natural Resources Defense Council (NRDC)—made environmental litigation an art form, moving group strategy from the legislative to the judicial arena. These groups have benefited from the citizen suit provisions in virtually every federal environmental statute since the 1970 Clean Air Act. The provisions allow "any person" to sue private parties for noncompliance with the law; and to sue not only for injunctive relief, but for civil penalties. This allows those who sue to recover the cost of attorneys' fees and "mitigation fees" in lieu of, or in addition to, civil fines. The question about when and whether to enter the court system is a controversial one. During the debate over the Healthy Forests Restoration Act in 2002 and 2003, environmental groups were demonized for filing lawsuits.[15]

Other mainstream groups, although smaller in size and resources, conduct research or grassroots campaigns. Two of the most prominent are the Environmental Working Group (EWG) and the League of Conservation Voters (LCV). One of the newer watchdog organizations, EWG was founded in 1993 and is considered one of the most effective lobbying organizations in Washington. It was the first to raise questions concerning the health risks of a substance used to make Teflon, and it has released reports on how environmentally sensitive areas in Utah were being leased to oil and gas companies. The LCV, founded in 1970, has two goals: to help elect pro-environment candidates and to monitor congressional performance. It is not the group's members that give it clout, but its annual report, the National Environmental Scorecard, which ranks the voting records of each member of Congress on environmental legislation.

Some environmental organizations are characterized by their emphasis on a single issue. These groups rarely shift from their area of concern to another issue, although some overlap is developing. Clean Water Action, founded in 1971, conducts research and lobbies on issues related to drinking-water and groundwater resources. Recognizing the interrelatedness of pollution, Clean Water Action also became involved in the passage of the 1986 Superfund legislation and the 1990 Clean Air Act Amendments. The Clean Air Network is an umbrella organization that brings together national and grassroots groups to promote implementation of the Clean Air Act and oppose efforts by industry to weaken its provisions. The Defenders of Wildlife work, as their group's name implies, to protect wildlife habitats through education and advocacy programs. Founded in 1947, the group is now working to strengthen the Endangered Species Act and develop funding for wildlife refuges.

Among the more recently created environmental organizations are those, often with a purely regional base of operation, seeking to preserve individual species. Many of these groups were organized in the 1980s after the initial burst of momentum in the environmental movement had passed. Although these groups limit their activities to individual species, they often form coalitions to preserve natural habitats and wildlife ranges. Their membership is typically smaller (10,000 to 40,000) and may include researchers dedicated to scientific study of the species. Typical of such groups are Bat Conservation International, founded in 1982, and the Mountain Lion Preservation Foundation, founded in 1986. Both of these organizations emphasize education as well as research and habitat studies. The Mountain Lion Preservation Foundation, for example, has developed an aggressive media campaign in California to educate the public on the habitat needs of this animal, as well as lobbying for a permanent state ban on the hunting of the mountain lion (also known as the cougar, puma, or panther).

Also relatively new on the political scene are evangelical groups and those associated with faith communities. Among the largest is the Evangelic Environmental Network, "grounded in the Bible's teaching on the responsibility of God's people to 'tend the garden.'" The organization provides educational materials to mobilize individuals and churches relating to the spiritual and moral aspects of public policies on energy and the environment. Another group, the Christian Life Commission (CLC), the public policy arm of the Baptist General Convention of Texas, mobilized its members against the state's governor's plan to speed the approval process for eighteen new coal-fired power plants. The CLC urged its 2.3 million members to voice their opposition to the plants to the state legislature, and also affirmed a resolution advocating for sound environmental policies. Other faith groups have supported the Endangered Species Act as part of their beliefs that scripture requires them to be stewards of the Earth.

More recently, evangelical groups have focused on global climate change. Organizations such as the Evangelical Youth Climate Initiative and the Evangelical Call to Action on Climate Change urge their followers to help solve the global warming crisis because they recognize the impact will be hardest on the poor, the vulnerable, and future generations. The Southern Baptist Convention on the Environment and Climate Change calls for a "unified moral voice" to solve problems, stating that humans must care for Creation and take responsibility for humans' contributions to environmental degradation. Other faith-related activities are more like those of traditional green groups, urging their members to reduce energy consumption, monitor water use, and recycle. In 2002, the "What Would Jesus Drive?" campaign called attention to gas-guzzling vehicles through a catchy public relations effort and bumper stickers.

Property-oriented groups, such as Ducks Unlimited and the Nature Conservancy, represent examples of long-standing organizations that focus their efforts on management and preservation. Both groups mentioned here have invested private funds for purchasing lands that are then reserved for wildlife habitats. One of the older environmental groups, Ducks Unlimited, with chapters throughout the United States, was founded in 1937 by hunters seeking to preserve wetland habitats. The Nature Conservancy, founded in 1951, has privately purchased land for habitat protection throughout the United States as well as global ecological preserves that are home to endangered species. The organization is also known for developing creative solutions to land acquisition, such as working with landowners and other groups to create conservation easements where further development is prohibited.

Another subgroup is comprised of organizations that originated or are based in the United States, have members throughout the world, and have broadened their interests to more global concerns. The largest international environmental organization, Greenpeace, was founded in 1969 as the Don't Make a Wave Committee by a small group of Sierra Club members and peace activists. In 1971, a crew of eleven activists leased a fishing vessel, the *Phyllis Cormack,* to bear witness to and protest nuclear weapons testing in the Aleutian Islands, although the boat never reached its destination. But the activity focused worldwide attention on the issue of nuclear testing, and shortly afterward, the group took the name Greenpeace.

Its initial effort was the Save the Whales campaign, which was later expanded to include other sea animals such as dolphins and the Steller sea lion. Since then, Greenpeace has extended its concerns to six major efforts that parallel the expansion of environmental policy: saving ancient forests, stopping global warming, exposing toxic pollutants, protecting the oceans, eliminating the threat of genetic engineering, and ending the nuclear age. Headquartered in Amsterdam, Greenpeace now has offices in forty countries worldwide and maintains consultative status to the United Nations.[16]

Greenpeace activities have often bordered on violence, as was the case in 1989 when a Greenpeace ship protested a Trident missile test and was rammed by a U.S. Navy vessel. The group is known, too, for its ability to use the media to its advantage, as demonstrated when its activists are pictured in small boats placing themselves between whales and whaling ships. Activists enjoyed the media spotlight in July 2009 when a dozen protesters breached a secured area at South Dakota's Mount Rushmore to unfurl a 2,275 foot sign over the edge of the monument next to the granite head of Abraham Lincoln. The organization said the sign, which read "American Honors Leaders, Not Politicians, Stop Global Warming" was part of a global day of action to urge world leaders to take the actions necessary to avert runaway climate change. The timing of the activism was designed to coincide with the "Group of 8" (G8) meeting of the world's industrialized nations in L'Aquila, Italy. Although they acknowledged that the action was illegal, Greenpeace leaders said that they did not believe any damage had been done to the national memorial. Federal officials disagreed, however, indicting eleven people on federal trespassing charges, noting that Greenpeace had even hired a helicopter to film the activists as they unfurled the banner.

Environmental organizations have periodically attempted to put aside their individual interests and have formed coalitions in an attempt to advance their collective interests. Coalitions are especially important to groups engaged in long-term policy struggles, such as public land management, air and water pollution, and global climate change. In 1946, the Natural Resources Council of America was formed to bring together conservation organizations to serve as an information-sharing body and sponsor policy briefings and surveys of public opinion on issues such as energy needs and conservation. Coalitions have also been formed to lobby specific pieces of legislation, such as the National Clean Air Coalition, which came together during debate over the 1977 and 1990 Clean Air Act Amendments.

Coalitions sometimes are made up of strange bedfellows. As one researcher notes, "The historic relationship between labor and environmental activists has been complicated and uneven; policy issues over the past three or four decades have found them alternately as allies and opponents."[17] One group, the Blue Green Alliance, formed in 2006 by the United Steelworkers and the Sierra Club, marks a major departure from the historically adversarial relationship of labor and environmental groups. The coalition, which works on issues ranging from energy and climate change to transportation and workers' rights, recognizes the potential for expanding the number and quality of jobs in the green economy.[18]

Coalitions can be powerful; in January 2007, former Interior Solicitor William Myers withdrew his name from consideration for a seat on the Ninth Circuit Court of Appeals after more than 180 environmental, Native-American, public health, civil rights, labor, and religious groups condemned his nomination. Their activism marked the first time in history that a judicial nominee has been forced to withdraw primarily due to his environmental record, according to the legal defense group Earthjustice.[19]

THE ENVIRONMENTAL JUSTICE MOVEMENT

From the early 1960s through the 1980s, the majority of mainstream environmental organizations focused on issues related to natural resource management and preservation, along with efforts to control air and water pollution. Their leadership (and support) came primarily from middle-class and upper-middle-class whites, and surveys found that members of environmental groups were considerably better educated, more likely to have white-collar jobs, and more likely to have high incomes in comparison to the larger population.

At the same time, the civil rights movement had become a fixture in American politics, with a focus on bringing jobs and social justice to poor communities and improving the economic conditions of minorities and people of color. Often, community leaders made trade-offs between bringing jobs and industry into neighborhoods faced with high unemployment and the cost of exposing workers and their families to industrial pollution and toxic hazards, a condition political scientist Robert Bullard refers to as "job blackmail."[20] Bullard notes that, eventually, there was a convergence of environmentalism and the civil rights movement that called for a balancing of economic development, social justice, and environmental protection. In cities like Los Angeles, African-American and Latino groups formed in the mid-1980s to fight the siting of municipal and hazardous waste incinerators in poor, largely minority neighborhoods. Native-American groups have organized against landfills on their reservations, which are not subject to federal or state environmental laws, and farm workers in California's Central Valley protested the hazardous waste landfill and a proposed incinerator in one tiny community.[21]

These community struggles developed a political focus from two hallmark events. In 1987, the United Church of Christ (UCC) Commission for Racial Justice published a controversial study, *Toxic Wastes and Race in the United States: A National Report on the Racial and Socio-Economic Characteristics of Communities with Hazardous Waste Sites,* which concluded that the poor and members of racial minority groups were being treated inequitably in the siting of such facilities.[22] The report was followed in October 1991 by the First National People of Color Environmental Leadership Summit in Washington, D.C. The meeting produced a set of Principles of Environmental Justice that called upon people of color to secure their economic and social liberation, which had been denied them as a result of the "poisoning of our communities and land and the genocide of our peoples." In calling for environmental justice, the summit's leaders demanded the right to participate as equal partners in environmental decision making, free from any form of discrimination or bias. But it also placed a responsibility on individuals to make personal and consumer choices in their lifestyles that minimized the use of natural resources and produced as little waste as possible.

Subsequently, national civil rights leaders criticized environmental organizations and political decision makers for "environmental racism"—a term used to describe the fact that "whether by conscious design or institutional neglect, communities of color in urban ghettos, in rural 'poverty pockets,' or on economically impoverished Native American reservations face some of the worst environmental devastation in the nation."[23]

Responses to these charges varied. Civil rights organizations like the National Association for the Advancement of Colored People and the American Civil Liberties Union have begun working side by side with mainstream environmental organizations such as the Natural Resources Defense Council. Larger environmental groups, such as the Sierra Club and the Wilderness Society, have attempted to diversify their governing boards and staff, with a corresponding "trickling down" to state governments that, in turn, have begun to enact some form of environmental justice laws.[24]

At the federal level, the EPA responded with the creation of the Environmental Equity Workgroup in 1990 to assess the evidence that minority and low-income communities bear a higher environmental risk burden than does the general population, and how EPA might deal with any disparities. EPA created an internal Office of Environmental Justice in 1992, and a year later, the National Environmental Justice Advisory Council (NEJAC) was established to provide stakeholder input and to serve as a forum for discussion. The council's charter was renewed in 2003. In 1994, President Bill Clinton issued an executive order that instructed federal agencies to integrate environmental justice into their ongoing missions, and EPA administrator Carol Browner announced that she would make environmental equity a part of her agency's decisionmaking processes. After the Clinton administration left office, the issue of environmental justice appeared to have stagnated within the executive branch. Although EPA Administrator Christine Whitman recommitted the agency to "integrating environmental justice into all agency programs,"[25] NEJAC meetings have been infrequent and considered to be more symbolic than substantive.

There is, however, a discordant note among those who believe that the environmental justice movement is facing challenges it cannot overcome. University of Maryland professor and Brookings Institution scholar Christopher H. Foreman Jr. has argued that many goals of the environmental justice movement— such as community empowerment, social justice, and public health—are difficult for federal officials to address using the environment as a policy "hook." He also believes that such advocacy directs community attention away from the problems that pose the greatest risks and "may therefore have the ironic effect of undermining public health in precisely those communities it endeavors to help." He cautions that there are significant political hurdles to be overcome as well, such as a lack of congressional support and the infeasibility of attempting to ban new siting in and near low-income communities and communities of color. Many leaders concur with Foreman's conclusion that what is really at stake, not only in the environmental justice movement but also in the environmental movement itself, is what he calls "an abiding hunger for livable communities."[26]

But there is still a significant amount of evidence that there are disparities in facility locations. The UCC Commission for Racial Justice did a follow up study to its 1987 report as part of the twentieth anniversary of the original study that led to the environmental justice movement. The 2007 report used 2000 census data and distance-based methods to determine the location of hazardous waste facilities to examine disparities by region and state, with a separate analysis of metropolitan areas, where most hazardous waste facilities are located. The application of the new methods showed that racial disparities in the distribution of hazardous waste sites are greater than previously reported. People of color make up the majority of those living in host neighborhoods within 3 kilometers (1.8 miles) of the nation's 413 hazardous waste facilities, according to the new study, with the majority of those persons of Hispanic or Latino origin.[27]

There is also a global element to environmental racism, whether the issue be toxic waste dumping in poorer, usually nonwhite countries (see Chapter 5), exploitation of resources by multinational corporations, or "eco-catastrophes." The term refers to events like toxic gas releases or oil spills that result in severe environmental damage. In the Niger Delta region of Africa, for example, grassroots groups like Environment Rights Action and the Niger Delta Human and

Environmental Rescue Organization have documented incidents where oil lines have burst or punctured, spilling crude oil. The spills, often in remote areas, are sometimes not discovered immediately, and land, water, and fish and wildlife are degraded or die. One researcher notes, "Foreign oil companies doing business in Africa are typically immune from paying for their mistakes. They engage in practices that are not tolerated in their home countries and they get away with atrocities.... This has led some to question whether companies operating abroad should be held to the same standard that their countries of origin demand."[28]

ENVIRONMENTAL OPPOSITION
IN THE UNITED STATES

The Progressive Era ideals of the conservation movement had almost universal support throughout the early twentieth century, although the early groups were still dominated by business organizations, which were much more influential in the political arena. As the goals of the movement began to expand from conservation to environmentalism in the late 1960s and early 1970s, so, too, did the potential impact on business and industry, which had never really felt threatened before. The development of an organized environmental opposition involved three interests—farmers and ranchers, industry, and grassroots activists, composed of wise use, property rights, and county supremacy.

The initial concern of farmers and ranchers was the tremendous influx of city dwellers who sought the tranquility of rural life after World War II. "Recreationists," as they were called, brought tourist dollars to rural economies badly in need of them, but they also brought with them litter, congestion, and noise. Urban visitors seldom paid much attention to property lines, and major battles developed over public access along the California coastline and through inland wetlands. Farmers who were used to controlling predators on their private property were suddenly facing raptor protection programs and angry wildlife enthusiasts who sought preservation of wolves and coyotes. Agricultural land use also came under fire, as environmental groups sought to legislate farm practices relating to pesticide use, soils, and irrigation. As development, including oil pipelines and utility transmission lines, began to intrude onto rural areas, farmers felt even more threatened.[29]

The two issues that have most galvanized farmers have been proposals to restrict the use of agricultural pesticides and herbicides, and agricultural use of water. In the case of pesticide use, rural interests have formed a coalition with chemical companies and their associations, bringing together such disparate groups as the American Farm Bureau Federation and the National Agricultural Chemical Association, along with the National Association of State Departments of Agriculture; the Association of American Plant Food, Pesticide, and Feed Control Officers; the National Association of County Agents; and the Christmas Tree Growers Association. But the land-use issue has become even more controversial because of the Sagebrush Rebellion and the development of the grassroots environmental opposition movements discussed later in this chapter.

Industry Interests

Industry interests have traditionally opposed environmental rules, for two reasons: the cost of complying with regulations threatens a company's ability to make money, and there is little incentive for voluntary compliance. Sometimes, industry opposition results from disagreement over the goals or means used to protect the environment. Yet industry leaders recognize that they (and their employees and their families) breathe the same polluted air and face the same toxic contamination as the rest of America. Industry's role has been described as "marked not by agreement on values but by tactics of containment, by a working philosophy of maximum feasible resistance and minimum feasible retreat."[30]

Businesses were initially slow to recognize the potential impact of the environmental movement on their operations, characterizing the activities of most groups as no more than a fad. But officials within the pulp and paper industry began, in the late 1950s, to understand how desires for more recreation land would likely mean a call for reduction in logging activities and expansion of wilderness area designations. Eventually, other industry leaders became alarmed at the rapid pace of environmental legislation, which accelerated during the late 1960s and into the 1970s. They countered by forming trade associations and nonprofit research groups or "think tanks" to further their aims, pouring millions of dollars into education and public relations. The American Forest Institute, for example, was specifically created to justify the need for increased, rather than reduced, timber production. The oil industry has been especially hard hit as the environmental movement gained more clout. Companies have been ordered by the courts to pay for special cleanups or fines, and have faced lengthy and costly litigation due to compliance suits brought by environmental groups.

Today, industries affected by environmental regulations rely on a fourfold approach in their opposition to environmental groups:

1. There is a continuation of the public relations campaigns that began in the early 1960s to paint industry with an environmentally green brush. Chevron Oil, for example, ran advertisements in national publications promoting its "People Do" projects to protect the habitat of endangered species to counter the public backlash that results after every oil spill.

2. Industry has taken a more proactive role in crafting legislation and seeking allies, rather than simply reacting to initiatives proposed by environmental groups. The chemical industry, which for years was accused of intransigence, decided in the late 1980s to move toward a pollution prevention approach as a way to improve the marketability of its products. They were active in the debate over the 1990 Clean Air Act Amendments, and politicians gave the industry's lobbyists credit for drafting its own legislation rather than just opposing what was on the table. During the administration of George W. Bush, lobbyists for the energy industry were accused of being too aggressive in the policymaking process, virtually handing over their demands to the president (see Chapter 6).

3. Virtually every sector of the economy relies on a stable of federal and state lobbyists to review legislation that could potentially affect its operations.

In 2009, the Center for Responsive Politics identified 10,764 registered lobbyists, down from a high of 15,384 in 2007. Although federal law prohibits them from contributing directly to candidates, corporations can form political action committees (PACs) that funnel campaign contributions directly to legislators as a way of enhancing their access to the political system. Companies and trade associations also employ their own scientists, economists, and policy experts to refute the claims made by environmental groups, and usually have more financial resources to devote to this strategy than do grassroots groups.

4. Once programs reach the implementation stage, most industry interests regroup to press their case through the administrative maze. Because many implementation decisions are made by low-level administrators, or in a less public arena than Congress, industry has been much more successful in molding programs at this phase of the policy process, although recent studies have shown that the influence of business tends to vary based on the nature of the conflict.[31] EPA rule development has frequently been hampered by companies arguing that information about products and processes constitutes trade secrets or is proprietary. Industry lawyers have also launched a flurry of lawsuits aimed at regulations and enforcement actions.

Still, it is important to note that industry interests are not monolithic. There is sufficient competition within the economy to provide competition in certain sectors. The stereotype of "big business" speaking with a single voice is more mythology than reality. While it may be in some companies' interest to share information or form coalitions, there is at least an equal amount of distrust over who will have the most to gain (or lose) from legislators and regulators.[32]

Grassroots Activists

In 1988, a different type of environmental opposition surfaced as an outgrowth of a meeting of 250 groups at the Multiple Use Strategy Conference, sponsored by the Center for Defense of Free Enterprise. One of the group's leaders, Ron Arnold, applied the phrase "wise use" (originally used by conservationist Gifford Pinchot) in describing twenty-five goals to reform the country's environmental policies, including opening up national parks and wilderness areas to mineral exploration, expanding visitor facilities in the parks, and restricting application of the Endangered Species Act. Grassroots opposition is now focused on three issues led by large umbrella organizations: wise use, property rights, and the county supremacy movement. The umbrella groups serve as a clearinghouse for information and share a deep antigovernment sentiment and opposition to efforts by government and environmental groups to regulate further the use of public and private lands, and natural resources. Although some of the opposition efforts are supported by private interests, ranging from the Mountain States Legal Foundation to agricultural groups, and oil, timber, and mining companies, there is a strong grassroots component of individuals who perceive the government to be intruding into their lives by telling them what they can do with their private property or how lands and resources within the public domain ought to be used. It is difficult to estimate the membership of these groups; many individuals are members simply because they belong to another group that has supported one or more of the umbrella groups' tenets. The members of the American Farm Bureau Federation (AFBF), for example, are counted as members of the wise-use movement simply because the AFBF has endorsed some wise-use policies.

The Sagebrush Rebellion began in the 1970s as an effort by wealthy ranchers and others to gain control of public lands in the West. The movement had proponents in government in the 1980s, particularly Secretary of the Interior James Watt. The movement was reinvigorated in the early 1990s as the wise-use and county-supremacy movements garnered attention. Although there are similarities between the wise-use movement and the Sagebrush Rebellion of the late 1970s and early 1980s, one difference between the two is that the current efforts are marked by steps to broaden the base of support beyond purely western issues. Like other political movements, the groups employ a wide variety of strategies and tactics to push their agenda forward. The Blue Ribbon Coalition, which represents motorized recreational interests, tracks legislation and alerts its members to contact their congressional representatives when a bill affects their interests. Some of the more militant opposition groups, like the Sahara Club, boast of vandalizing property or disrupting environmental group activities. In addition to cattle ranchers resisting higher grazing fees, the grassroots efforts tap into gulf shrimpers opposing the use of turtle-excluding devices, Alaskans seeking to expand oil drilling, and private property owners from Eastern states battling the National Park Service over boundary disputes. The three movements are well-organized, tapping into an electronic network that keeps even the most isolated adherents in touch with one another.[33]

From a political standpoint, the grassroots opposition has had moderate success legislatively. During President Clinton's first term, it stalled proposed grazing fee increases and was able to get congressional approval for a brief moratorium on listings under the Endangered Species Act. Organizations like the Mountain States Legal Foundation and the Individual Rights Foundation have led the legal fight against federal lands. Between 1991 and 1995, fifty-nine Western counties passed ordinances that claimed authority to supersede federal environmental and land-use laws and regulations, and thirty-four counties in Nevada, California, Idaho, New Mexico, and Oregon passed ordinances challenging federal control of local lands.[34] The resolutions declared that federal land in the county actually belonged to the state and that the county alone had the authority to manage it. Although the resolutions were not technically law, local officials were enforcing them as though they were. The Justice Department challenged the ordinances as illegal and sought an injunction to ban their enforcement.

The courts have dealt a serious blow to county-supremacy groups by striking down ordinances that would have given counties the right to determine how public lands within their boundaries would be used. Most individuals involved in the property-rights movement are mired in a legal system that takes years to resolve issues, thus reducing their ability to accomplish goals. The grassroots movements have as much success as they do because they have been led by policy entrepreneurs, charismatic individuals who have capitalized on the public's distrust of the government's natural resource policies, as well as mistrust of the federal government in general, and turned that distrust into self-perpetuating organizations. Although they have often been at odds with most environmental organizations, some opposition group leaders appear to be seeking common ground and compromise as a more effective way of influencing environmental policy during an era when the vast majority of Americans still adhere to a protectionist ethic. But the wise-use movement's adherents are highly motivated; moreover, they are well-organized through a network of websites, e-mail, and grassroots chapters, and continue to press their concerns forcefully.

Although they were not an organized group, on May 9, 2009, an estimated two hundred off-road vehicles and motorcycles, encouraged by a local member of the Kane County Board of Supervisors, rode their vehicles up the bed of the Paria River in the Grand Staircase-Escalante National Monument in southern Utah. The riders were protesting the 1996 creation of the monument by President Bill Clinton, and a Bureau of Land Management plan for the area that prohibited general off-road driving, although nearly one thousand miles were left open to vehicles. Within the monument was the Paria River canyon, and a flat, sandy-bottomed "phantom road" that was part of a federal Wilderness Study Area. The Paria River canyon was formally closed to vehicles in 2000.[35] In 2003, county officials began tearing down the BLM's road closure signs, arguing that the dirt tracks were "highways," and put up their own signs in 2005 claiming that the roads were open to off-highway vehicle use. Environmental groups said that the county's action threatened sensitive Wilderness Study Areas, and eventually, the BLM notified Kane County that their illegally posted signs must come down. The battle continued as environmental groups filed a lawsuit seeking to force the Department of the Interior to take further enforcement action, and in late 2005, Kane County and an adjoining county filed their own suit against the BLM, challenging the management plan for the monument. They argued that the Paria riverbed is a road, and that closure to motor vehicle traffic constitutes federal impingement on states' rights. The battle continued for the next several years; in a 2007 document, the BLM urged voluntary compliance, saying that "Visitors choosing not to participate in the voluntary closure should follow 'Leave No Trace' and 'Tread Lightly' guidelines." In early 2009, the 10th Circuit Court of Appeals rejected Kane County's assertion that it owned many of the roads and cow paths, keeping areas off-limits to riders.[36]

The bed of the Paria River is covered by the BLM's transportation plan, and it prohibits motorized recreation in the river. But the May 2009 protesters ignored the agency in an act that they characterized as civil disobedience, despite the fact they knew the riverbed was off-limits to riders. "We're mad as hell and aren't going to [take] it anymore," one official announced through a bullhorn before the riders took off. The demonstration had been highly publicized, so BLM officials were present, writing down license plate numbers and photographing riders to record potential violations.[37] While typical of the types of grassroots activism of the 1980s and 1990s by environmental opposition groups, the Paria River riders represent a new chapter in protests in a region that was at the heart of the Sagebrush Rebellion. This does not mean a new movement is about to emerge, but it does indicate that some of the emotions and arguments of those earlier decades are still there.

THE ROLE OF THE MEDIA

The media play two important roles in bringing environmental problems to the attention of both the public and policymakers. One, they report events and conditions that are considered to be "newsworthy," and two, in doing so, they may help to convert a problem to an item on the policy agenda. For example, most Americans are probably familiar with the 1989 Exxon *Valdez* oil spill in Alaska because of the massive amount of publicity surrounding the event. In the aftermath of the *Valdez* spill, policymakers rushed to create new disaster protocols for marine cleanups, safety regulations were reviewed, groups formed to help save birds and marine mammals, and engineers and oil company officials discussed the design of oil tankers.

But there was little media coverage of the 2005 oil cleanup operations at the site of the *Selendang Ayu* wreck on Unalaska Island, considered the worst Alaska oil spill in the last twenty-five years. The incident, in which a Malaysian freighter broke in two in December 2004, received only minor attention from the press. Nor was there much attention paid to a complaint by the Hawaii State Department of Health against Chevron Hawaii Refinery, Inc. in 2005. The agency assessed a fine of $107,000 against the company for failing to obtain a permit for storage of hazardous waste. Chevron operates a refinery on Oahu that processes crude oil from Alaska that is transported in tankers with the same potential for a massive spill. Why would media coverage of one incident influence policy, while the two events just described would not?

Part of the reason stems from what political scientists Roger Cobb and Charles Elder call the governmental agenda and the systemic agenda.[38] They define the *governmental agenda* as those problems to which political leaders decide to give their more serious attention. Not all problems identified by the media will make their way to the governmental agenda, especially if there is little public knowledge of the issue. This is the situation with the events that took place in Alaska and Hawaii in 2005. The *systemic agenda*, in contrast, includes those issues that are perceived by members of the political community as being worthy of public attention and are part of the jurisdiction of governmental authority. The systemic agenda is primarily made up of discussion items; often, there are few distinct or specific answers to a perceived problem. While the environment is most commonly thought to be a problem dealt with on all levels of government, the media often focus on issues that are more localized or regional.

This represents the second major role of the media's coverage of the environment. If an issue or problem is not yet widely recognized by the public, the media can make it more salient, that is, worthy of attention. The most common way in which the media perform this function is through long-term, comprehensive coverage, including follow-up stories and features. In this sense, the discretion the media have is not so much to tell people or leaders what to think, as what to think about.[39] International media coverage of the *Valdez* has continued for more than two decades, with follow-up stories on the trial of the ship's captain, the costs of cleanup, and the anniversary of the tanker spill.

Sometimes, the media affect the agenda-setting process by choosing which stories to cover and which to ignore, a process that leads to what researchers Peter Bachrach and Morton Baratz have called *non-decision making*.[40] The suppression of discussion may not always be deliberate, but it may also be enough to keep a problem from agenda status. In 1989, for instance, a steam tube ruptured in the McGuire nuclear facility outside Charlotte, North Carolina, and the plant's operators quickly shut down the reactor. Local television crews arrived within minutes, followed by national media and preparations for a community evacuation. Network newscasters reported "a terrifying nuclear 'accident'" even though the event was over in less than an hour and no radiation was released either inside or outside of the plant. The widely publicized incident was the subject of months of public hearings, and local and national environmental organizations demanded that the nuclear facility be closed. In contrast, a petroleum refinery in Pasadena, Texas, exploded that same year. Over three hundred workers were injured, and twenty-three were killed. Although the nightly news carried helicopter footage of the fiery blaze, the story subsequently vanished from the media.[41] The difference is reflective of the media's (and public's) perceptions about energy and fears about anything nuclear.

However, the media have brought a number of environmental problems to the governmental agenda that might never have been considered serious problems without highly visual coverage. Sensitivity toward the plight of endangered species is a result of extensive coverage of whales, dolphins, and other marine mammals, especially when there are highly charged images of overfishing. When the media do not have direct access to these images, they often rely on videos or photographs provided by interest groups, which are more than willing to share graphic illustrations of clear-cut forests, uranium mine tailings, or plumes of smoky pollutants rising from industrial smokestacks. Media coverage thus becomes important in shaping public opinion, which in turn, may shape how decisionmakers choose to respond to perceived problems.

The media cover the environment because it is politically attractive to do so. Without media coverage of environmental problems, for instance, most Americans would undoubtedly continue to believe that pollution and other issues were no longer serious, and thus not worthy of government action. It is also likely that they would fail to connect the environmental problems of one nation with global issues, such as the United States' emission of greenhouse gases and global climate change. But the short life span of any media coverage, from a fifteen-second sound bite to a photo opportunity with the president when legislation is signed, moves any environmental issue on and off the policy agenda. Even the enduring problems like sustainability and resource depletion are given limited coverage when other events, such as the treatment of prisoners in Iraqi prisons or celebrity trials, seem to capture more of the public's attention.

Another type of media presence is found in electronic cyberspace—a phenomenon that has changed the policy process considerably due to three factors:

1. It gives the public access to the identification of global problems and the discussion of issues that previously might have gone unnoticed. In addition, the Internet has made access to news easier and more immediate, regardless of a person's geographic location or income level. Anyone with access to a computer can read major international newspapers, watch simultaneous coverage of events anywhere in the world, or read e-books online.

2. A positive consequence of the growing reliance on the Internet is that it serves as an important resource and research tool for activists and leaders in developing countries. Prior to the late 1990s, many nations were unable to access, let alone store, published collections of journals in paper form. The economic impact of journal subscriptions, as well as storage space, was beyond the reach of most universities and libraries. Even smaller microfiche versions were difficult to work with and required equipment that often was unavailable. Now scholarly information, especially technical journals, is available online.

3. Organizations now rely heavily upon the Internet to instantaneously transmit information and to mobilize their members, solicit contributions, and provide a sense of cohesiveness that would be impossible through traditional group meetings and periodic publications. Groups can influence the policy process by informing members when Congress is about to vote on legislation or when an appointee is going through the process of confirmation. Little-known problems can be made more visible when they are posted on a website, no matter how geographically distant they might be from the person reading them. Links to other organizations and information further expand the reach of a group with limited resources.

Social networking, through Facebook, Twitter, and other sites, has totally changed the way many groups operate, and, some argue, replaced traditional news media as a source of information. One blog asked whether Twitter "is the CNN of the new media generation."[42] Created in 2006, and with message limitations of 140 characters or less, Twitter is constantly being updated, providing up-to-the-moment coverage of breaking events. In Iranian protests in 2009, for instance, activists used cell phones and Twitter to convey photographs and live video of demonstrators, giving other Twitter supporters a view that traditional journalists could not provide because they had been ousted from the country. Twitter is also used by the media who have a feed to readers directing them to their sites, augmenting their coverage. Interest groups also have the ability to circumvent traditional media by releasing information without the usual press conferences or press releases. In a few short sentences, "tweets" can provide the instantaneous details of a meetup, protest, or other last-minute event. While the credibility of tweets remains a serious problem (deaths of very live people have been reported and transmitted globally within a few minutes), and news can easily be manipulated without the need for fact checking, real-time web services may be the future of group mobilization, replacing traditional media outlets.

As the world's communications networks expand, the media and cyberspace become additional tools for participants in the environmental debate. Whether the focus is group mobilization, information transfer, outreach, or the shaping of public opinion, the process is sometimes subtle and difficult to ascertain. But it is also clear that without the media, most environmental problems would never find their way to the policy agenda.[43]

INTERNATIONAL ACTIVISM

Concern about the environment is universal. Although this chapter has thus far focused on development and tactics of the environmental movement and opposition groups in the United States, the environmental debate involves a number of international actors. Some global activism parallels what was taking place in the United States during the nineteenth century, beginning with the founding of the Commons, Open Spaces, and Footpaths Preservation Society in Britain in 1865. There appears to be a trend in industrial nations that ties the development of environmental awareness to business cycles; in Britain, for example, support for environmental protection has been strongest toward the end of periods of sustained economic expansion. With greater economic prosperity, people shift their interest from immediate material needs to the nonmaterial aspects of their lives. As a result, economic advances in the late 1960s and early 1970s led to a tremendous growth spurt in the membership of existing nature groups and the formation of new groups, paralleling activity in the United States during that same period.

Nongovernmental organizations (NGOs) now play a key role in environmental policymaking in both industrialized and developing countries. The term is used to describe all organizations that are neither governmental nor for-profit, and it may include groups ranging from rural people's leagues and tribal unions to private relief associations, irrigation user groups, and local development associations. NGOs can be classified as grassroots organizations (membership-oriented, often in developing nations), service NGOs (supporting the development of grassroots groups), or policy-specific (environment, human rights, family planning). One characteristic many of the groups have in common is that they are often parochial—concerned almost exclusively about environmental issues in their region. A typical example is the group Dasohli Gram Swarajya Mandal, which began a logging public awareness campaign in India in 1964 that led to the Chipko Andalan movement. Chipko, which means "to cling to," literally is composed of India's tree huggers, Himalayan Indians who launched protests over logging. Indian environmentalists developed political clout over the issue of proposed dams and hydroelectric projects, but have often limited their activism to specific projects. These groups not only help shape policy but also play a major role in generating demands within individual countries for governments to comply with and implement the global agreements they have signed.

NGOs are growing in both number and influence, particularly in developing nations. Unlike their counterparts in Northern Hemisphere countries, NGOs in the south perform somewhat different functions. They often fill a vacuum left by ineffective or nonexistent government programs or extend the reach of resource-poor national governments. They may also forge links with NGOs whose issues are decidedly nonenvironmental, such as the networking that is beginning to occur between human rights and economic development NGOs. Last, NGOs in developing countries may serve as an independent voice for public participation, either in opposition to a government program or by placing pressure on government to create new programs (see Table 2.2).

Studies of NGOs indicate that they are evolving in three directions: the southern NGOs are seeking greater autonomy from those in the north; NGOs are forming international networks and coalitions to keep abreast of issues; and they are performing new roles in legal defense and policy research. The first trend appears to be the most critical as Southern Hemisphere NGOs seek to distance themselves from their dependence on their northern partners. Long dependent for financial support on their northern donors, these groups now seek the transfer of the technical expertise they need to gain independence. They hope to set their own environmental protection agendas rather than have the terms of their activities dictated by outside sources that they perceive to be less familiar with local problems. Technological advances such as facsimile machines and computer-linked networks have allowed groups to coordinate their efforts on a global scale, and they have steadily increased their presence in the diplomatic world as well. NGOs held a parallel conference at the 1972, 1992, and 2002 United Nations environmental meetings, and several organizations were accredited by the United Nations to participate in the preparatory meetings leading up to the summits. Although these trends indicate that NGOs are growing in numbers as well as importance, their influence on global environmental protection is still limited by a lack of stable funding sources and political sophistication.

Only a handful of organizations have begun to address the global issues of concern to many of the mainstream organizations in the United States, such as global warming and stratospheric ozone depletion. Friends of the Earth International, for example, has affiliates throughout the world, as does Greenpeace. NGOs are especially important in regions where environmental concern has only recently begun to emerge, as evidenced by the founding of a Russian affiliate of Greenpeace. Without the support of an international organization and its resources, environmental activists in the republics of the former Soviet Union would have little voice for their efforts to draw international attention to decades of environmental degradation.

Of particular concern to some NGOs is the lack of capacity, especially those groups that have become financially dependent on large, international NGOs that are legally registered in developing countries, such as Conservation International and the Nature Conservancy. While registration provides greater accountability to national governments and donors, they also compete for scarce local dollars, which may decrease efforts to strengthen local institutions. Large groups push their own global agenda, while local groups that are essential for long-term conservation efforts struggle for funds.[44]

Cultural differences are the major factor behind the variations in how environmental interests become structured or operate. In democratic nations, the

T A B L E 2.2   Major International Environmental and/or Developmental Nongovernmental Organizations (NGOs)

A Rocha International

Amazon Watch

Amigos de la Tierra

Asian Nature Conservation Foundation

Bureau of International Recycling

Center for International Climate and Environmental Research

Consejo Iberico para la Defense de la Naturaleza

Corporate Watch

Cousteau Society

Earth Action

Earth Charter Initiative

Earth Council

Earthscan

Earth Watch Institute

EUROPARC Federation

Friends of the Earth

Global Witness

Green Cross International

Greenpeace International

International Council of Environmental Law

International Rivers Network

International Wildlife Coalition

Inuit Circumpolar Conference

Islamic Academy of Sciences

Nature Conservancy

Physicians for Social Responsibility

Public Services International

Rainforest Action Network

Rainforest Alliance

Taiga Rescue Network

World Business Council for Sustainable Development

World Commission on Dams

World Conservation Union

World Rainforest Network

World Resources Institute

World Water Council

World Wide Fund for Nature

pluralist system legitimizes interest group membership. But acceptable tactics in one nation may be considered unacceptable or even criminal in others. In non-democratic countries such as the People's Republic of China, the government crackdown on Western influences has made it difficult even for NGOs such as the World Wildlife Fund to have much of an impact, leaving little room for environmental groups, domestic or foreign. International pressure and the government's expanded involvement in international trade and politics have led to substantial advances in China's environmental policies; and small groups, such as Friends of Nature, have been successful at lobbying against clear-cutting of old-growth forests.[45]

The most cohesive and powerful environmental movements are found in western Europe, where public opinion polls have shown that support for the environment is especially strong and continues to grow. Still, the environmental movement in Europe is best characterized as diverse, with each group developing its own structure, strategy, and style. Coalition building is a common strategy, with umbrella groups monitoring proposed legislation and lobbying. Group activism has historically been focused on the issues of nuclear power and nuclear weapons, leading to massive public protests in 1995 when the French government resumed weapons testing in the South Pacific. Great Britain is well known for direct action, a phenomenon that changed environmental activism completely in the 1990s. While some analysts characterize the increasing militancy and radicalism as simply a pendulum swing, others feel it represents a new spirit and ethos.

Not content to try to influence politicians or institutions, protesters have seen direct action as disruption seeking to delay environmentally damaging projects and to escalate their costs. At many sites of direct action, there was an avowed goal of actually stopping particular projects going ahead by getting in the way, damaging equipment, and creating physical obstacles like tunnels, as well as building a groundswell of opinion to make the project politically untenable.[46] Protesters have stopped road-building projects—especially in pastoral or scenic areas, incinerator and waste facilities—and research on genetically modified foods.

GREEN POLITICAL PARTIES

On a global level, Green political parties vary considerably in strength and impact on their respective political systems, in membership, and in the percentage of the electorate they represent. The term *green party* is sometimes used generically, and many groups represent a broader social movement or consist of activists focused on a single issue. In the United States, the first national green party organization formed at a 1984 meeting of sixty-two activists on the campus of Macalester College in Minnesota. Known as the Green Committees of Correspondence after the grassroots efforts of rebels during the Revolutionary War, the group defined "greenness" as interweaving "ecological wisdom, decentralization of economic and political power wherever practical, personal and social responsibility, global security, and community self-determination within the context of respect for diversity of heritage and religion. It advocates nonviolent action, cooperative world order, and self reliance."[47]

The definition that developed from the 1984 meeting was later developed as the "Ten Key Values": ecological wisdom, grassroots democracy, decentralization, community-based economics, feminism, respect for diversity, personal and global responsibility, and future focus/sustainability. The goal was to develop grassroots organizations throughout the United States, but the process was slow and there was dissension among group members, who questioned whether their activities were primarily symbolic or whether a Green political party was realistic.

Throughout the 1990s, most Green Party victories were at the local level, especially on city councils in California. In 1996, the National Association of State Green Parties was created as a more conventional structure for nominating candidates under the Green Party USA. A surge of activism occurred in 2000, when consumer activist Ralph Nader was nominated as the party's presidential candidate, along with running mate Winona LaDuke. Although the Green Party candidates did not win any electoral votes, they were widely publicized by the media and picked up about 2.8 million popular votes nationwide, enraging Democrats, who believed that defections from voters in Florida and New Hampshire cost Al Gore the election. In Florida, Nader collected more than 97,000 votes; George W. Bush narrowly won the state, by 537 votes.

In 2004, Nader ran for president under the banner of the Reform Party USA, but his name ended up on the ballot in only thirty-four states, compared to forty-four in 2000. He had few resources except for student volunteers, and liberals feared he might once again serve as a campaign spoiler. Instead, the Green Party nominated two relative unknowns, David Cobb and Pat LaMarche. Overall, 430 Green candidates ran in 356 races, in 41 states, for 74 types of offices, with 63 victories. By year's end, there were 212 elected Green Party members in 27 states, 75 of them in California.[48]

By 2008, the Green Party's attraction seemed to have faded almost completely at the national level, overshadowed by the two major parties' candidates. Although Nader's name was among those listed at the party's Chicago convention in July, the Greens nominated former Georgia congresswoman Cynthia McKinney as their presidential nominee. Her running mate, commentator and political activist Rosa Clemente, was a political unknown, and together, the two received only 161,603 votes, or 0.12 percent of the national popular vote. The picture was brighter at the local and state levels, however. The party secured a seat in the Arkansas legislature; additional positions on the local level in California; county commissioner seats in California, Colorado, Florida, Maine, Massachusetts, and Oregon; advisory neighborhood positions in the District of Columbia; and a public service district position in South Carolina.[49]

International green parties are often more difficult to track, because they frequently change their names or form new alliances with other groups to bolster their political clout. In Hungary, for example, "greens" were initially called "blues" in reference to the Blue Danube Circle (those opposed to the building of the Nagymaros Dam); and in Poland, the largest environmental organization was not a party per se, but the Polish Ecology Club.

The first green party was the United Tasmania Group, which contested the local elections in the Tasmanian region of Australia in 1972. Although the party was unsuccessful in the ten elections it contested before its dissolution in 1976, it was instrumental in placing the environment at the top of the Australian political agenda. The major wave of green party activity has been in Europe, primarily because the structure of European political systems allows political parties, even small ones, a role in policymaking. During the 1970s, one of the first green parties to form was in Germany, where a loose coalition of groups, the Bund Burgerini-tiativen Umweltschutz (BBU), organized massive demonstrations opposing nuclear energy but exercised little political power. Over the past three decades, the German Greens have formed several electoral alliances, becoming what many believe is the most powerful environmental force in Europe. Their increasing role in national politics has come despite the death of one of their most influential leaders, Petra Kelly, in 1992. For instance, in January 2009, the Greens of the German state of Hesse received 13.7 percent of the vote, the highest percentage ever for Greens in any state.

The achievements of the German Greens have not been matched elsewhere, however. Initially, green parties' successes seemed to be limited to getting their members elected at the local and regional levels. In countries such as Sweden, where legislative seats are allotted based on a threshold level of representation, green parties have struggled to attract the necessary numbers of voters or often have been shut out of the process entirely. Even in those countries with proportional representation, most green parties have had little support, in large part because they modeled their strategy on the atypical German model. The "fading of the greens," as the phenomenon has been called, is not an indication of the public's lack of environmental interest or its saliency as a political issue. One observer has argued that in one sense the national green parties simply outlived their usefulness once the major political parties adopted the greens' issues as their own.[50] In addition, many environmental activists, sensing that structural barriers limited their ability to attain status as a potent political entity, shifted their energies toward affecting legislation and policy through NGOs.

During the 1990s, efforts focused on building coalitions of international green groups, developing a Global Green Network (GGN) and issuing joint statements on French nuclear testing in the South Pacific (1996) and the Kyoto climate change agreement (1997). In 2001, eight hundred representatives from seventy-two countries met in Canberra, Australia, to adopt a Global Green Charter; Green Federations were formed, representing regional attempts at organizing individual countries' parties.[51] In February 2004, the first European-wide political party, the European Green Party, was founded, bringing together thirty-two green parties. The first goal of the new party was to establish common campaign materials with posters, graphics, and slogans that would be used throughout Europe in the June 2004 parliamentary elections. The new party won 34 seats in the 732-seat parliament, and 6.6 percent of the vote overall.

In subsequent elections, international green parties have increased their visibility by standing in national elections. In 2004, the Canadian Greens, using the campaign slogan, "Someday is now," contested all 308 ridings, finishing fifth nationally with 4.3 percent of the vote. In Australia's 2004 election, they fielded candidates in every House of Representative seat and for all State and Territory Senate positions.

INTERNATIONAL GOVERNMENTAL
ORGANIZATIONS

The concept of protecting the global environment through some form of international regime or institution did not occur until well into the twentieth century.[52] The UN Charter of 1945, for instance, included no mention of the environment in its mission. Although forty or more international environmental agreements were signed prior to World War II, most international governance was conducted through regional commissions. In 1909, for example, the United States and Canada formed the International Joint Commission to deal with transboundary issues between their shared 3,000-mile border; the United States and Mexico signed a similar treaty in 1906.

Since then, international governmental organizations (IGOs) have become important participants in the global effort to protect the environment. The United Nations has increasingly served as a diplomatic platform for negotiation of international agreements. In 1949, the UN held its first environmental Conference on the Conservation and Utilization of Resources. Five years later, it sponsored the Conference on Conservation of Living Resources of the Sea, which resulted in the International Convention for the Prevention of Pollution of the Sea by Oil.

The UN entered a second phase of international environmental protection on January 17, 1972, when its General Assembly passed a Resolution on Development and Environment that criticized highly developed nations for improper planning and inadequate coordination of industrial activities that had led to serious environmental problems worldwide. In language highly critical of the United States, the UN General Assembly called upon the industrialized nations to provide additional technological assistance and financing, starting a decades-long debate over who should bear the cost of environmental cleanup in developing nations.

Today, environmental IGOs have begun to bring together the often competing issues of environmental protection and economic development. They can be structurally divided into two types: (1) organizations and programs developed under the auspices of the UN, and (2) IGOs made up of states or national government bodies. The primary UN body charged with natural resource protection is the UN Environment Programme (UNEP), which was conceptualized at the 1972 Stockholm Conference on the Human Environment. UNEP was established in 1973 and is facilitated by a secretariat in Nairobi—a significant siting, as it is the only major global UN agency headquartered in a developing country. It is directed by a fifty-eight-member Governing Council, made up of representatives elected by the UN General Assembly and based on geographic region.

The mission of the agency is set forth in ten-year-long work plans known as the Montevideo Programmes. Each work plan sets out the tasks and goals the UNEP expects to achieve; the 1992–2002 work plan identifies eighteen areas for global environmental action.

UNEP has been widely criticized for becoming too bureaucratic and unwieldy and for problems with its financial management. It is primarily funded through voluntary contributions from member nations, and throughout the 1990s it faced a financial crisis that many observers believed could not be overcome. A subsequent compromise reorganization created a smaller advisory body that is charged with reviewing UNEP's administrative structure and making recommendations for change. Most recently, the organization has focused on outreach efforts to promote global observances related to children and the environment, planting trees, and cleanup efforts.

In the last decade of the twentieth century, the issues of environment and development became even more closely intertwined. The Commission on Sustainable Development (CSD), established in 1993 as a body within the UN Economic and Social Council, has the primary responsibility for implementing the recommendations that were produced from the 1992 United Nations Conference on Environment and Development in Rio de Janeiro. The recommendations, known as Agenda 21,[53] encourage national and subnational governments to integrate environmental and economic concerns, but the CSD has no legal authority and has only the power to make recommendations. Another major IGO, the UN Development Programme (UNDP), is more active on the issues of development and trade.

Most funding for global efforts to protect the environment comes from the Global Environmental Facility (GEF), which was originally established in 1991 as a pilot project under the organizational umbrella of the World Bank. GEF has now become the largest multilateral source of funding for grants to individual countries for environmental projects. It, too, has been criticized because it focuses its funding priorities on only four areas: climate change, the conservation of biological diversity, the protection of international waters, and ozone depletion. Most of GEF's grants have been made to developing countries based on recommendations by its own scientific panel of experts. In contrast, the handful of IGOs that affect natural resource policy are made up of states or national government bodies. The most visible is the European Union Environment Agency, which serves as a regional IGO.

International governmental organizations are critical to global environmental protection for a number of reasons. They allow problems like water or air pollution to be approached from an integrated perspective, rather than unilaterally. By standardizing policies such as acid deposition emissions, they recognize the importance of transboundary issues. They provide a forum for the diplomatic negotiation of issues, such as whaling, and serve as a clearinghouse for information and scientific research. The drawback of IGOs is that they have limited powers and virtually no enforcement capabilities. When a nation fails to abide by an international regime, such as the Convention on International Trade in Endangered Species of Wild Fauna and Flora, there is little an IGO can do except attempt to apply the force of public opinion to the rogue state. However, forums like the UN are critical, because without them, there would be no singular body or mechanism for disputes to be aired or problems to be addressed. Efforts to reform IGOs and make them stronger have failed to date, largely due to a lack of financial support and a fear by some developed nations that they might force industrialized countries to turn over valuable technology to poorer nations. A more likely future for IGOs is the continuing development of regional bodies and agreements, such as those that have been created as a result of the North American Free Trade Agreement and the General Agreement on Tariffs and Trade.

In addition, other major UN-based IGOs, like the Food and Agriculture Organization (FAO), United Nations Children's Fund (UNICEF), and the UN Population Fund (UNFPA), are assuming a more active role in environmental and development issues. Each of these IGOs is now interacting with UNEP and UNDP to coordinate global environmental initiatives (see Table 2.3).

TABLE 2.3   Major International Environmental and/or Developmental Intergovernmental Organizations (IGOs)

Commission for Environmental Cooperation (CEC)

Commission on Sustainable Development (CSD)

European Union Environment Agency (EUEA)

Food and Agriculture Organization (FAO)

Global Environmental Facility (GEF)

Intergovernmental Panel on Climate Change (IPCC)

International Atomic Energy Agency (IAEA)

International Council for the Exploration of the Sea (ICES)

International Fund for Agricultural Development (IFAD)

International Labour Organization (ILO)

International Maritime Organization (IMO)

International Monetary Fund (IMF)

International Oil Pollution Compensation Fund (IOPCF)

United Nations Children's Fund (UNICEF)

United Nations Development Programme (UNDP)

United Nations Education, Scientific, and Cultural Organization (UNESCO)

United Nations Environment Programme (UNEP)

United Nations Industrial Development Organization (UNIDO)

United Nations Population Fund (UNFPA)

World Bank

World Food Programme (WFP)

World Health Organization (WHO)

World Meteorological Organization (WMO)

FURTHER READING

J. Robert Cox, ed. *Environmental Communication and the Public Sphere,* 2nd ed. Thousand Oaks, CA: Sage, 2010.

Magali A. Delmas. *Governance for the Environment: New Perspectives.* Cambridge: Cambridge University Press, 2010.

E. Gene Franklin, ed. *Green Parties in Transition.* Surrey, UK: Ashgate Publishing, 2008.

Anders Hansen. *Environment, Media and Communication.* New York: Routledge, 2010.

Frederick P. Miller, Agnes F. Vandome, and John McBrewster, eds. *Green Politics.* Beau Bassin, Mauritius, 2009.

Norman Miller. *Environmental Politics: Stakeholders, Interests, and Policymaking,* 2nd ed. New York: Routledge, 2009.

Steven Milloy. *Green Hell: How Environmentalists Plan to Ruin Your Life and What You Can Do to Stop Them.* Washington, DC: Regnery Publishing, 2009.

Erik Qualman. *Socialnomics: How Social Media Transforms the Way We Live and Do Business.* New York: Wiley, 2009.

3

The Political Process

"This legislation—just to give you a sense of the scope—this
legislation guarantees that we will not take our forests, rivers,
oceans, national parks, monuments, and wilderness areas for
granted; but rather we will set them aside and guard their
sanctity for everyone to share."
— PRESIDENT BARACK OBAMA[1]

On March 30, 2009, President Barack Obama joined legislative leaders, tribal representatives, officials from a half-dozen federal agencies, and representatives of the disability community in the East Room of the White House in signing the Omnibus Public Land Management Act of 2009, considered by both the administration and by observers as "among the most important in decades to protect, preserve, and pass down our nation's most treasured landscapes to future generations."[2]

What the president's remarks did not cover, however, is the fact that the legislation included nearly 170 different bills that had been hammered out in sometimes tense negotiations to produce a single measure on which a majority of the members of the House and Senate could agree. The "Omni," as it is known, formally establishes the National Landscape Conservation System to protect the most environmentally and historically significant lands controlled by the Bureau of Land Management. The new system covers 26 million acres and 850 sites, including the Canyons of the Ancients National Monument in southwest Colorado, the Agua Fria National Monument in Arizona, and Nevada's Black Rock Desert National Conservation Area, requiring the agency to make conservation a priority when managing these areas.[3] In addition, it will protect nearly 2 million acres of new wilderness land under bills such as the Sequoia and Kings

Canyon National Parks Wilderness Act, more than 1,000 miles of newly designated wild and scenic rivers under bills such as the Lewis and Clark Mt. Hood Wilderness Act of 2007, new conservation areas through bills like the Washington County Growth and Conservation Act, and will withdraw from oil and gas leasing over 1.2 million acres of landscape in western Wyoming's Bridger-Teton National Forest.

The measure is important not only for what it will do to protect environmentally sensitive areas, but also because it represents both the best and the worst of the legislative process. Using the model outlined in the Introduction to this book, the Omni is an example of how the policy window opened with the election of President Obama in November 2008. Bills that had been bottled up for years, such as the Owyhee Public Lands Management Act of 2007, were made part of a huge wilderness protection measure that developed sufficient legislative support less than three months into the new administration. Idaho Republican Senator Mike Crapo had worked for eight years to shepherd the measure through grassroots negotiations that included local governments, ranchers, environmental groups, and representatives of the Shoshone-Paiute tribe.[4] Omnibus bills, which are defined as multiple bills presented to Congress as a single measure, are a response, according to one researcher, to the growing number and complexity of issues. They represent an important and widely supported core proposal, and because these bills are more likely to be enacted, more controversial related bills may be added on to them. Omnibus bills may be subjected to less scrutiny than the individual bills of which they are made up, and this gives ancillary proposals they carry along a better chance of becoming law.[5]

In this case, several provisions were added that probably would not have survived legislative scrutiny on their own. The Izembeck and Alaska Peninsula Refuge and Wilderness Enhancement Act includes the building of a road the Wilderness Society calls "unnecessary and ecologically harmful" through fragile wetlands in a National Wildlife Refuge. "This provision," the group said, "has no place in a lands bill focused on protecting America's natural resources."[6] Another provision was seemingly tacked on for no apparent reason, the Christopher and Dana Reeves Paralysis Act, which coordinates research activities through the National Institutes of Health that will facilitate collaboration of scientific research to find a cure for paralysis, and which will promote enhanced rehabilitation for Americans with paralysis. Bills that are not germane to the main mission of the omnibus bill are called *policy riders*, and while sometimes innocuous, they deflect attention from the major purpose of the legislation.

Omnibus bills represent bipartisan efforts, and in that sense, they can be considered positive representations of the democratic process. But they can also be heavily politicized, as the heads of each party take part in the scramble to determine which bills are included and which are not. "Because the aggregate of bills in the omnibus package have different—and sometimes competing—goals, member accountability is blurred. Constituents cannot readily discern which or which combination of proposals their representatives support."[7] The Energy Policy Act of 2005 is another example of an omnibus measure that encompassed dozens of different bills that appear to have satisfied numerous competing interests.

Congress is only one of the official stakeholders responsible for the development of policy. The institution is often thought of as a check on the power of the president and the courts; it involves a highly complex and historically formal set of stages and procedures that can be mystifying. Chapters 1 and 2 provided an overview of the political context in which environmental policy is made, outlining the historical development of environmental consciousness and awareness and identifying the key stakeholders who participate in the environmental debate. Policy scholars characterize those activities and actors as the first and second stages of the policymaking process: problem identification and agenda setting, followed by policy formulation. This chapter continues with an explanation of the third stage, policy adoption, and then moves to the fourth stage, policy implementation. The discussion begins with an analysis of two government institutions that are often referred to as the "official policymakers": the president and Congress. It includes an overview of the legislative process in which policies are chosen (or not chosen) for further action, and the role of the courts in reviewing legislation and interpreting cases. The last portion of this chapter analyzes the increasing role of state and local governments in environmental policymaking, and some of the reasons why their work is slowly beginning to break up the environmental gridlock that has characterized the last three decades.

PRESIDENTIAL LEADERSHIP

Most scholars consider the president to be one of the key stakeholders in setting the policy agenda and in directing the discussion of potential options in formulating policy. By examining the actions of individual presidents since 1970 (the first Earth Day) it is possible to see how each one has used his powers to appoint officials in the executive branch agencies and to provide guidance on environmental policy direction, to use the federal budget and the regulatory process to implement (or not implement) policy, to use the media to get his environmental message to the public, and to issue executive orders that may circumvent a reluctant Congress.

Historically, the president has had a limited role in environmental politics, with much of the power delegated to the executive branch agencies.[8] Not until

Richard Nixon's tenure began in 1969 did the environment become a presidential priority, and even then, Nixon was reluctant to act. After years of study and staff negotiations, Nixon agreed to a federal reorganization plan calling for an independent pollution control agency that later became the Environmental Protection Agency (EPA), discussed later in this chapter.

Using his power to appoint the head of the agency, Nixon set the tone for the first generation of environmental agency activities. The EPA opened its doors under the stewardship of William Ruckelshaus, a graduate of Harvard Law School and former Indiana assistant attorney general. Although he had virtually no background in environmental issues, Ruckelshaus had the support of Nixon's attorney general, John Mitchell, and was confirmed after only two days of hearings. On the day of his selection as administrator, Ruckelshaus was briefed by Nixon, who gave him the impression that he considered the environmental problem "faddish."[9] Ruckelshaus came to the EPA with three priorities: to create a well-defined enforcement image for the agency, to carry out the provisions of the newly amended Clean Air Act, and to gain control over the costs of regulatory decision making.[10] In setting up the agency, Ruckelshaus decided that each regional organization within the EPA should mirror the full agency's structure, with staff capabilities in every program area and delegation of responsibility to regional offices, creating an organizational structure that gave the agency a rare capability to make decisions, move programs ahead, and motivate people to produce high volumes of work.[11] Inside the EPA, morale was high, in large part due to the accessibility of Ruckelshaus to his staff. Outside, he became a forceful spokesperson for the public interest and was well-respected by both sides in the environmental debate. Early on, Ruckelshaus concentrated on air and water pollution, assigning three-quarters of his staff to that task. As a result, there was an improvement in noncompliance with air-quality standards in most cities, and the agency effected a change from aesthetic concerns about the recreational uses of water to health concerns.[12]

Nixon's efforts to give credibility to the Department of the Interior were not nearly as successful. It appears that the creation of the EPA relegated the Department of the Interior to backseat status as far as environmental issues were concerned. A succession of secretaries came and went (see Table 3.1) while the EPA administrators garnered publicity and notoriety. Despite these efforts, there is some doubt as to how much Nixon really cared about the environment as an issue. Some staff members believed the Nixon reorganization experts were neither proponents nor opponents of environmental reform; their specialty was management and organization. They focused on the environment because that was the area in which political pressures were creating a demand for action.

Typical is the case of Walter Hickel, whom Nixon chose in late 1968 as the new Secretary of the Interior, setting off a storm of protest. Hickel, who had grown up in Kansas and lived on a tenant farm during the Depression, was a Golden Gloves boxer who loved to fight. As governor of Alaska, he was accused of being a pawn of the U.S. Chamber of Commerce and of the oil industry. After four days of defensive hearings, his nomination was confirmed. Hickel's bold style was his undoing; he offended the president in a rambling letter about

T A B L E 3.1   **Department of the Interior and EPA Leadership (1970–2010)**

President	Secretary of the Interior	EPA Administrator
Nixon	Rogers Morton (1971–74)	William Ruckelshaus (1970–73)
Ford	Rogers Morton (1974–75)	Russell Train (1973–77)
	Stanley Hathaway (1975)	
	Thomas Kleppe (1975–77)	
Carter	Cecil Andrus (1977–81)	Douglas Costle (1977–81)
Reagan	James Watt (1981–83)	Anne (Gorsuch) Burford (1981–83)
	William Clark (1983–85)	William Ruckelshaus (1983–85)
	Donald Hodel (1985–89)	Lee Thomas (1985–89)
Bush (G.H.W.)	Manuel Lujan Jr. (1989–92)	William Reilly (1989–92)
Clinton	Bruce Babbitt (1993–2001)	Carol Browner (1993–2001)
Bush (G.W.)	Gale Norton (2001–06)	Christine Whitman (2001–03)
	Dirk Kempthorne (2006–09)	Mike Leavitt (2003–04)
		Steve Johnson (2005–09)
Obama	Ken Salazar (2009–)	Lisa Jackson (2009–)

Nixon's policies (eventually leaked to the press) after the Kent State shootings. The gaffe came at a time when the president's staff was considering the reorganization proposal that would have elevated Hickel to head the new Department of Natural Resources. He was fired Thanksgiving Day, 1970.[13]

In 1971, Nixon chose Earl Butz as his Secretary of Agriculture; Butz was an academician who had taught and served as an administrator at Purdue University and had worked in the U.S. Department of Agriculture (USDA) for three years. But as would become the case with subsequent presidents, leadership of the Forest Service would be less controversial and more stable. Edward Cliff, who had been named chief in 1962, served for ten years before Nixon named his replacement, John McGuire, who would serve Nixon, Ford, and Carter.

To Nixon's credit, it should be noted that it was under his administration that the United States first began to take a more global approach to environmental protection. Ruckelshaus was successful in convincing Nixon of the important role the United States could play at the UN Conference on the Human Environment in June 1972 in Stockholm. Although the United States was not totally in agreement with the priorities of the United Nations Environment Programme, which grew out of the Stockholm conference, Nixon used his persuasive power as chief executive to convince Congress to pay the largest share (36 percent) of the new Secretariat's budget.[14]

When Gerald Ford took over as president upon Nixon's resignation, he made few changes in the way environmental policy was being conducted, preferring to follow the overall policy direction of his predecessor when it came to the environment. Russell Train remained head of the EPA under Ford and served in that position until Ford was defeated by Jimmy Carter in 1976. Carter kept most of Nixon's other environmental appointees, including Secretary of the Interior Rogers Morton and Secretary of Agriculture Robert Berglund. For the most part, the crush of environmental programs that marked the Nixon years slowed considerably under Ford, for three reasons. One, the energy shortage created by the 1973 Arab oil embargo pushed pollution off the legislative agenda for several years (see Chapter 6). A second factor was a growing concern that the cost to industry to comply with EPA standards was slowing the economy at a time when expansion was needed. Last, the environmental momentum of the early 1970s faded by 1976, and Ford did little to refuel it. Congressional initiatives expanded the EPA's authority with the Safe Drinking Water Act of 1974, the Toxic Substances Control Act of 1976, and the Resource Conservation and Recovery Act (RCRA) of 1976 (legislation discussed in Chapter 6 and Chapter 7), but Ford's unsuccessful presidential campaign made him an observer, rather than a participant, in the policymaking process. The environmental slate for Gerald Ford is clean, albeit empty.

In 1976, groups such as the League of Conservation Voters gave presidential candidate Jimmy Carter high grades for his environmental record as governor of Georgia, although his campaign focused more on other issues, such as human rights and the economy. President Carter openly courted environmental groups during his single-term administration, and he counted on their support to carry him through to reelection in 1980, when he lost to Ronald Reagan. He received high marks from environmental groups that believed he would emphasize environmental issues in his administration, but he initially offended one of the environmental movement's heroes, Maine Senator Edmund Muskie. Carter began by choosing Douglas Costle to head the EPA over the objections of Muskie. Costle, a Seattle native, attended Harvard and the University of Chicago Law School and had worked at the Office of Management and Budget under Nixon. His main environmental credential was a stint as Commissioner for Environmental Affairs in Connecticut, but he had a strong financial management background from working at the Congressional Budget Office.

Under Costle, the EPA became the first federal agency to adopt Carter's plan of zero-based budgeting. Costle's main aim in taking over the agency was "to convince the public that EPA was first and foremost a public health agency, not a guardian of birds and bunnies."[15] Taking Costle's lead, Congress responded by passing the Superfund authorization in late 1980, establishing a $1.6 billion emergency fund to clean up toxic contaminants spilled or dumped into the environment. The result was a major shift in the agency's regulatory focus from conventional pollutants to toxics. This allowed the agency room to grow, and justified a 25 percent budget increase at a time when the president was preaching strict austerity.

Carter had a number of environmental achievements during his term, including passage in 1980 of the landmark Alaska National Interest Lands Conservation Act, or Alaska Land Bill, which brought millions of acres of pristine wilderness under federal protection. As part of his attempt to gain group support, Carter convinced Congress to consider a windfall profits tax on oil to fund solar research and pushed stronger energy conservation measures. But the inability of Congress to develop a comprehensive energy policy under his administration has led most observers to conclude that Carter was not an especially effective leader in environmental policy or in protecting the environment.

The eight years of Ronald Reagan's administration mark a stormy chapter in environmental politics. Critics believe that he almost single-handedly destroyed the progress that had been made in the area of pollution control. Supporters point to his legislative achievements and say the picture was not so bleak after all; but critics argue that those successes came as a result of congressional initiative, not from Reagan. During his stints as governor of California and then as president, Reagan was heavily influenced by pro-business interests like Colorado brewer Joseph Coors, who urged him to take a more conservative approach to environmental regulation. Coors and his allies were represented in Reagan's inner circle by Nevada Senator Paul Laxalt, and they focused their attention on the appointment of a conservative Secretary of the Interior who would show prudent respect for development interests, especially in the West.[16]

In an example of how presidential appointments can influence policy, their candidate was James Watt, a Wyoming native who had served as a member of the Nixon transition team in 1968 to help Walter Hickel through his confirmation hearings as Secretary of the Interior, and was then appointed Deputy Secretary for water and power. In 1977, he founded the Mountain States Legal Foundation, a conservative anti-environmental-regulation law firm, and was later connected to the leadership of the Sagebrush Rebellion (see Chapter 2). Although some of Reagan's advisors preferred Clifford P. Hansen, former governor and senator from Wyoming, for the Department of the Interior slot, Watt's rhetorical style and ability to bring in dollars as a conservative fund-raiser for Reagan gave him a decided edge. He was a spokesperson for the New Right, among those who believed Reagan was drifting too close to the political center.[17]

Watt divided people into two categories—liberals and Americans—and called the Audubon Society "a chanting mob."[18] He perceived environmentalists as "dangerous and subversive,"[19] suggesting they sought to weaken America and to undermine freedom. He called them extremists and likened them to Nazis. More telling, however, was the comparison of Watt to his predecessor, Cecil Andrus, who had said, "I am part of the environmental movement and I intend to make the Interior Department responsive to the movement's needs."[20] Watt discovered that he had great independence in molding the agency to conform to his policy interests. Among his first directives, he ordered a moratorium on any further national park acquisitions and announced his intention to open up federal lands to mining and logging. He proposed to permit leasing of 1.3 million acres off the California coast for offshore oil and gas exploration and auctioned off 1.1 billion tons of coal in the Powder River Basin of Montana and Wyoming, actions that infuriated environmentalists. By summer 1981, Watt had made enough enemies that the Sierra Club, National Wildlife Federation, and Audubon Society gathered more than 1 million signatures seeking Watt's ouster. Together, ten organizations urged President Reagan to fire Watt, issuing a stinging indictment that purported to show how he had subverted environmental policy.

His supporters, however, point out that under Watt, the federal government spent more than $1 billion to restore and improve the existing national parks, and 1.8 million acres were added to the nation's wilderness system. Watt's vision was to develop America's energy resources and to remove what many perceived as excessive regulation of business, efforts at which he was successful.[21] But by late 1982, Watt was under heavy criticism for his actions, although he was blunt enough to say out loud what many in the Reagan administration were thinking. Reagan called Watt's record "darn good"[22] but urged him to reconcile with environmental groups, to whom he had stopped speaking just six weeks into his job. They continued to criticize him for refusing to touch more than $1 billion in the Land and Water Conservation Fund, which had been set aside for national park acquisition, and for spending only about half of the amount of funds for land acquisition appropriated by Congress.[23]

Watt's bluntness turned out to haunt him after he banned the musical group The Beach Boys from performing a concert on the Capitol Mall, embarrassing the president and the first lady (a great admirer of the musicians), who rescheduled the event. Then, in a speech before Chamber of Commerce lobbyists, Watt recalled that an Interior Department coal advisory panel comprised "a black, a woman, two Jews, and a cripple," a remark widely criticized in the press. Eventually, this made Watt a major liability to Reagan, who then asked for his resignation. Shortly thereafter, Reagan appointed William Clark, a man whose term was as undistinguished as Watt's had been tumultuous, to head the Department of the Interior. Clark served less than a year and a half and was replaced by Donald Hodel, another moderate.

Reagan's appointment of Anne (Gorsuch) Burford as administrator of the EPA proved to be even more of an embarrassment than Watt. Burford, a former member of the Colorado legislature, became one of the youngest of Reagan's appointees despite her lack of administrative experience. She began her term as administrator by reorganizing the agency, abolishing divisions only to reestablish them later. The EPA's highly politicized staff members demoralized careerists, and the agency was constantly under siege both from environmental groups (who believed Burford's appointment signaled Reagan's support for industry interests) and from members of Congress. More telling, perhaps, was the loss of a fifth of the EPA's personnel and the major cuts in the agency's budget that began in 1980.[24]

Under Burford, the Office of Enforcement was dismantled, and personnel within the agency found their positions downgraded. Environmental professionals were often passed over for promotion by political appointees, and neither of the two original associate administrators served more than 100 days.[25] The Reagan administration became embroiled in further controversy when several top EPA administrators, including the agency's general counsel, were investigated for or accused of conflict of interest, perjury, giving sweetheart deals to polluters who had influential political ties, and other misdeeds. By the end of Reagan's third year in office, more than twenty senior EPA employees had been removed from office and several key agency officials had resigned under pressure.[26]

The biggest fall was Burford's. In fall 1982, John Dingell, chairman of the House Committee on Energy and Commerce, initiated an investigation of alleged abuses in Superfund enforcement and sought EPA documents as part of the case. Dingell subpoenaed Burford to appear in court to provide the committee with the documents, but based on Justice Department advice, she declined to do so, citing the doctrine of executive privilege. In December 1982, the House voted to declare her in contempt of Congress. Eventually a compromise was struck that allowed the committee to examine nearly all the documents they sought, and the contempt citation was dropped.

The contempt charge was coupled with charges of EPA mismanagement of cleanup operations after discovery of the toxic chemical dioxin in roadways at Times Beach, Missouri. The project had been handled by EPA Assistant Administrator for Hazardous Waste, Rita Lavelle, who was eventually fired by Reagan. Lavelle was the only EPA official to face criminal charges, and she was convicted of perjury and obstructing a congressional investigation. She was sentenced to six months in prison and fined $10,000. The incident cast further doubt on Burford's ability to manage the agency, and she resigned March 9, 1983. At a press conference two days later, Reagan said he believed that it was he, not Burford, who was the real target of Congress's action. He said that he never would have asked for her resignation.[27] Congress did not let up even after Burford resigned. At the end of August 1984, a House Energy and Commerce Oversight Committee concluded that from 1981 to 1983, "top level officials of the EPA violated their public trust by disregarding the public health and environment, manipulating the Superfund program for political purposes, engaging in unethical conduct, and participating in other abuses."[28]

To return the EPA to some semblance of credibility, Reagan again used his power to appoint agency leadership. He called upon the EPA's first administrator, William Ruckelshaus, who returned to coordinate salvage operations. Ruckelshaus restored morale to the middle-level EPA staff, reversed the adversarial posture of the EPA toward Congress and the media, and brought in new and experienced administrators to replace political appointees.[29] During his second stint as administrator, Ruckelshaus revised the standards for the lead content in gasoline and declared an emergency ban on ethylene dibromide (EDB), a pesticide widely used in grain and food production. Ruckelshaus served until after Reagan's reelection, when the president appointed his third EPA administrator, Lee Thomas.

Thomas, a South Carolina native, became the first nonlawyer to head the agency. He had previously worked in the Federal Emergency Management Administration (FEMA) and headed the Times Beach Task Force that led to Rita Lavelle's firing. When Lavelle left, Thomas took over her position as coordinator of hazardous waste, Superfund, and RCRA programs. Seen as a career EPA employee, he redefined the agency's mission. On the one hand, he focused attention on localized concerns such as medical waste and the garbage crisis that was threatening urban areas. At the same time, he brought attention to global concerns like the weakening of the ozone layer and chlorofluorocarbons (CFCs).

Thomas made sure that the EPA became an active participant in international forums and returned the environment to the policy agenda.[30] Another major achievement was the full restoration of the EPA's reputation for strong enforcement, especially after the agency reached a 1985 agreement with Westinghouse Corporation to spend $100 million to clean up toxic waste at its Indiana facilities. This was followed in 1986 by an agreement with Aerojet General to clean up a toxic dump near Sacramento (estimated to cost the company $82 million) and in 1988 by a $1 billion cleanup agreement with Shell Oil and the U.S. Army at the Rocky Mountain arsenal near Denver.

Keeping to the tradition of naming farmers to head the Department of Agriculture, Reagan appointed John Block, a West Point graduate, farmer, and former Illinois Secretary of Agriculture. Block was followed by Richard Lyng, owner of a family seed and bean firm who had served under Reagan in California. The Forest Service, unlike the other agencies, had one chief during the Reagan administration—Max Peterson, who served until George H. W. Bush named Dale Robertson as his successor.

Many environmentalists believed George H. W. Bush's campaign promise to be "the environmental president" when he appointed William Reilly to head the EPA in 1989. Reilly, who had previously served as head of the U.S. branch of the World Wildlife Fund, was the first environmental professional to serve as administrator. He had also established a reputation as a moderate while serving with the Washington, D.C.–based Conservation Foundation. The Sierra Club took a wait-and-see attitude, declaring that Reilly was "clearly tagged to be the administration's good guy in a very tough job."[31] Reilly's agenda was different from those of the Reagan appointees. In several early speeches and articles, he reiterated the need for pollution prevention as "a fundamental part of all our activities, all our initiatives, and all our economic growth," making it the theme of EPA's Earth Day celebrations in April 1990.[32] He also pointed to science and risk assessment "to help the Agency put together a much more coherent agenda than has characterized the past twenty years."[33] Reilly and Bush were jointly praised for having broken the legislative gridlock that characterized clean-air legislation since the amendments had last been revised in 1977 (see Chapter 8).

Some observers believe, however, that Reilly's efforts were often derailed by members of the White House staff, especially by Chief of Staff John Sununu, who ridiculed EPA pronouncements on global warming and wetlands preservation, and by budget director Richard Darman, who once called Reilly "a global rock star."[34] Sununu was criticized by environmentalists, who believe he blocked serious international negotiations on global warming. Reilly was caught up in White House politics again in June 1992 when a memo to President Bush on negotiations at the Earth Summit was leaked to the press; some insiders believe that Vice President Dan Quayle's office was responsible.

Bush's other appointees were given mixed reviews, from Michael Deland, head of the Council on Environmental Quality (CEQ) and an ardent environmentalist, to James Watkins, Bush's Secretary of Energy, who won praise for his commitment to alternative energy and energy conservation policy, although critics of the administration felt that his views had not been translated into substantive policy change. The appointment of Manuel Lujan Jr., a former congressional representative from New Mexico, as Secretary of the Interior was criticized by environmental groups that believed he favored the logging and mining interests of the West. Lujan's critics became even more alarmed when he agreed in October 1991 to convene the so-called Endangered Species "God Squad" to review the denial of timber permits on Bureau of Land Management (BLM) property because they threatened the habitat of the northern spotted owl, a species that had been declared threatened the previous year. But the Secretary's supporters argued that he was taking a more reasonable approach to the Endangered Species Act and simply invoking a mechanism provided for under law. Equally controversial was the president's wetlands policy. By redefining what constitutes a wetland, the administration had exempted thousands of acres of land from federal protection—a move that pleased the business community and angered environmentalists, who took the matter to court.

Did Bush live up to his claims as "the environmental president?" In his 1991 message on environmental quality, Bush pointed to adoption of an international agreement on CFCs, enactment of the Oil Pollution Act of 1990, enactment of an environmentally progressive farm bill, and his commitment to environmental stewardship. He noted that in 1990, the EPA's enforcement staff had a record of felony indictments that was 33 percent higher than that for 1989. His America the Beautiful tree-planting initiative sought to add 1 billion new trees annually over the next 10 years.[35] In December 1990, he established the President's Commission on Environmental Quality to build public/private partnerships to achieve concrete results in the area of pollution prevention, conservation, education, and international cooperation. Critics counter that under Vice President Dan Quayle, the Council on Competitiveness thwarted congressional intent by preventing agencies from issuing regulations required by environmental laws. Henry Waxman, chairman of the House Subcommittee on Health and the Environment, accused the council of "helping polluters block the EPA's efforts" through its regulatory review process.[36] Proving that almost everything he did offended someone, Bush was criticized by both environmentalists and conservatives.

Voters had a clear choice on environmental issues in the 1992 presidential election. While Bush proposed giving greater consideration to protecting jobs in enforcing the Endangered Species Act, Bill Clinton ran on an environmentalist's dream platform. His vice presidential running mate, Tennessee senator Al Gore, had solid ties to Congress and was an outspoken advocate for the environment. A key provision of the Clinton campaign was a promise to limit U.S. carbon dioxide emissions to 1990 levels by the year 2000 to halt global warming—an issue that Bush was soundly criticized for failing to support at the Earth Summit. Clinton also pledged to create recycling and energy conservation incentives, to set national water pollution runoff standards, and to support a forty-miles-per-gallon fuel standard. In direct contrast to Bush, Clinton promised to restore to the UN Population Fund monies that had previously been cut off and to oppose drilling in the Arctic National Wildlife Refuge. These viewpoints, along with his appointments to executive branch agencies, gave environmentalists room for hope and a sense of renewed executive branch leadership.

Clinton faced a unique situation during his first term. During his first two years as president, he worked with a Democratic Congress, while the sea-change congressional elections of 1994 made a historic transfer of power of both houses to the Republicans, effectively bottling up the few legislative initiatives the administration tried to make. Even during the first two years, Clinton's environmental successes were minimal. Clinton's White House staff initially set the tone by eliminating the Council on Competitiveness, which both Bush and Reagan had used to sidestep EPA regulations, and by proposing to replace the CEQ with a new White House environmental policy office. The CEQ was a statutory agency of Congress, not subject to presidential fiat, and therefore could not be abolished. But it was merged in 1994 with the new Office of Environmental Policy, headed by Gore protégée Kathleen McGinty. The president also appointed a Council on Sustainable Development—made up of business leaders, representatives from environmental groups, and government officials—that issued a 1996 report calling for a change from conflict to collaboration to maximize environmental protection. Less than a month into his administration, Clinton also endorsed a Senate bill to create the Department of the Environment, elevating the EPA to Cabinet-level status. Similar legislation had been introduced in Congress before but never gained sufficient support, especially when the Republicans took control of Congress. Clinton's Office of Environmental Justice, established in 1994 by executive order, was the first effort by any administration to deal with the issue.

Clinton's initial appointees also gave his supporters hope that the president could bring organizational change to key agencies. Former Mississippi congressman Mike Espy became the first African American to serve as Secretary of Agriculture, having developed a reputation for his strong stance on consumer protection and hunger in his home state. He served only two years and was replaced in 1995 by Daniel Glickman, another former member of Congress from Kansas who had served on the House Agriculture Committee. Unlike previous presidents who relied upon career Forest Service insiders who had served as chiefs of the agency for ten years, Clinton had two chiefs during his administration—Jack Ward Thomas and Mike Dombeck.

Clinton's first term was marked by the signing of only two environmental measures of any significance—the 1994 California Desert Protection Act and bipartisan-supported revisions in safe drinking-water amendments in 1996. In both cases, the groundwork for passage had been laid by Congress, and both measures reflect legislative momentum rather than presidential leadership. The majority of the nation's most important domestic environmental problems—grazing fees on public lands, designations of wetlands, storage of hazardous and nuclear waste, reauthorization of Superfund legislation—remained trapped in the legislative gridlock of a divided government. Environmentalists criticized the administration for switching sides and accepting a logging compromise in 1995 that opened old-growth forests to salvage timber cuts, and for compromising with automakers on implementation of the 1990 Clean Air Act Amendments. Industry groups were just as upset with the White House. There were some small preservationist victories, such as policies to reintroduce wolves into Yellowstone National Park and continuation of protection for the Arctic National Wildlife Refuge and the Tongass National Forest in Alaska. The 1997 Interior Department appropriations bill avoided the controversies that plagued the 1996 bill and actually increased overall spending for the department because of emergency funds for fighting Western fires.[37] However, the first Clinton term was hard on the EPA, resulting in staff cutbacks for research by one-third and a shift toward external rather than in-house research. One report on the agency found that the agency's ability to produce sound environmental studies had been diminished and that the "quality of science produced in the EPA [had] plummeted into a state of crisis."[38]

In the area of global environmental politics, Clinton had promised to accelerate and expand U.S. involvement in international preservation efforts, expecting support from Gore and a new legion of activist Democratic members to implement a wide-ranging but unfocused plan. The president failed to establish a timetable to meet proposals to reduce emissions of greenhouse gases, but Clinton can be credited with his prompt signing of the biodiversity treaty that had been adopted at the Earth Summit in 1992. Clinton followed up by establishing a National Biological Service to survey American species—a program that immediately became the target of Republican budget slashers. Clinton also followed up on a campaign promise to restore support for international family planning programs and the Global Environmental Facility, a fund to help developing countries meet their global environmental obligations under international treaties, but these programs also were slashed by the new Republican majority in Congress. Clinton promised early in his first term that the United States would take the lead in addressing global climate change, and he proposed an energy tax in 1993 as part of his deficit reduction plan, but he abandoned both of those efforts in the face of strong opposition from the Republican-controlled Congress. These policy failures undermined the U.S. leadership in global environmental diplomacy that had seemed so certain when the Clinton–Gore ticket was first elected. By 1996, the administration had given modest support to legally binding limits on greenhouse gases, to be set sometime after the year 2005, but had failed to rally support to ratify the biodiversity convention.[39]

Clinton's administration will be remembered as one in which the president was successful in blocking Republicans who not only sought a major regulatory overhaul for laws covering issues such as wetlands, mining reform, and the Endangered Species Act but also tried to use the budget process to reduce environmental regulations and agency activities.[40] But environmental policy did not become a priority of the administration until blocking congressional environmental protection rollbacks became politically potent. Despite his efforts to reinvent government and make regulation more efficient, Clinton met with resistance virtually every time he sought collaborative agreements on environmental problems.[41] During his second term, he had largely abandoned global environmental concerns, while his promises to protect Social Security, education, and health care from Republicans became core issues. As one political scientist, Martin Nie, has noted, "Clinton found himself to be not 'the candidate of change' in regard to the environment, but the defender of the environmental status quo."[42]

George W. Bush used his powers to set an entirely different environmental agenda than Clinton had created. As outlined in Chapter 1, Bush relied on presidential powers to appoint executive branch officials who shared his views, especially those related to energy policy, forests and logging, and global climate change. Because most of the appointees did not require Senate confirmation, Bush filled his administration with allies who had industry and corporate experience. The new appointees were ready to carry out a three-pronged environmental agenda: reverse or delay Clinton-era programs and initiatives; move forward with new initiatives that would, at a minimum, stall the environmental momentum of the previous eight years; and use the regulatory process to circumvent Congress.

Immediately after Bush took office, Andrew Card, the president's Chief of Staff, announced that the administration would be reviewing the Clinton initiatives by issuing an order calling for a sixty-day implementation moratorium. Some environmental leaders saw the move as a way for the president to begin rolling back the progress made under Clinton. Bush also attacked the Clinton administration's agenda by using the power of the purse and his control over the appropriations process. The first draft budget called for a 4 percent reduction in the EPA's funding, and similar cuts were proposed for other federal agencies with environmental policy responsibilities.[43]

During the 2000 presidential campaign, Bush talked about his support for the reduction of carbon dioxide emissions, and EPA administrator Christine Todd Whitman told a gathering of environmental ministers that the administration would support an internationally coordinated response to climate change (see Chapter 10). Bush then told Republican leaders that his campaign statements on the subject had been a "mistake" and that a Cabinet-level review had found that his prior position was incompatible with domestic energy production goals. He charged that the Kyoto Protocol, which had been supported by Clinton, was "fatally flawed" because it would lead to economic harm to the United States without establishing mandatory carbon-emission targets for developing countries.[44]

One of the Clinton administration's successes was a directive to the EPA to strengthen provisions of the Safe Drinking Water Act by developing a revised standard for arsenic, which occurs naturally in some water but is also a by-product of mining and wood processing. The original threshold standard had been established in 1942, but National Academy of Science (NAS) researchers subsequently found links to lung and bladder cancer in a 2001 study requested by Whitman. In a twist of political fate, the NAS report confirming the danger of arsenic-laced drinking water was released on September 10, 2001—the day before the terrorist attacks on New York's World Trade Center and the Pentagon. What might have been an important EPA policy announcement was eclipsed by coverage of the attacks; Whitman quietly announced a reduction in the arsenic standard a month later.

Bush earned what the Sierra Club called "at least three dozen environmental black marks" in his first year of office. Among the actions cited by the group were Bush's attempt to weaken efficiency standards for central air conditioners, a proposal to cut energy-efficiency research and development by 27 percent, a proposal to increase the BLM budget for oil drilling and exploration by $15 million and decrease its budget for conservation by the same amount, and a move to weaken Clinton's roadless initiative for national forests, discussed in more detail in Chapter 4.[45]

The second prong of the Bush environmental agenda called for the president to introduce his own programs, most of which favored industry interests over natural resource protections. This included proposals to allow oil exploration in the Arctic National Wildlife Refuge and in the Rocky Mountains, a Healthy Forests Initiative and proposed legislation to repeal appeals procedures under the National Environmental Policy Act (NEPA) just as the 2002 wildfire season was ending, and an announcement that the federal government would pay $235 million to buy mineral rights near the Florida Everglades. Bush introduced his unsuccessful Clear Skies Initiative and changes in New Source Review regulations of emissions from diesel-fueled engines (see Chapter 8).

Following the example set by his father, Bush angered environmental organizations and foreign leaders when he decided not to attend the UN Earth Summit in Johannesburg, South Africa, in September 2002. The president stayed at his ranch in Crawford, Texas, further isolating the United States from the global environmental debate and making firm his decision not to capitulate on his controversial global-warming policy.

Even before the November 2004 presidential election, George W. Bush telegraphed that he planned to make substantial changes to his Cabinet and key advisors, including several associated with environmental issues. During his cabinet shuffle, nine of the fifteen members resigned, two more than under Clinton or Reagan, both of whom served two terms.[46] One scholar noted, "He's looking for more responsiveness in his Cabinet. It looks like they want people who will be able to sell his policies on Capitol Hill rather than policy experts."[47] The president's power to appoint, and especially to appoint individuals who agree with his policy positions, is key to understanding the tremendous power of the White House when it comes to the environment.

The Bush administration's second term can be characterized by the comings and goings of his environmental team, several of whom were replaced by appointees who appeared to be more willing to capitulate to the White House staff and to Vice President Dick Cheney. Secretary of Agriculture Ann Veneman, along with several other top political appointees in the department, announced that they would step down from their positions two weeks after the election. Veneman had been criticized for a hands-off role by farmers and fiscal conservatives. In September 2002 she was diagnosed with breast cancer, and even though she recovered fully, the nation's first female Secretary of Agriculture announced her resignation in a one-page letter saying she wanted to try something new. Less than three weeks later, the president announced his nomination of Mike Johanns, two-term governor of Nebraska, to replace Veneman. Johanns, who grew up on a dairy farm in Iowa, acknowledged his interests in rural economic development and his close relationship with the agriculture community. He seemed to have less interest in grazing and other key environmental policies administered by the department.[48]

One of the most controversial of Bush's Interior Department appointments was Mark Rey, Undersecretary of Agriculture for Natural Resources and Environment, whose job it is to oversee the U.S. Forest Service. Prior to working for

Bush, Rey had worked as a timber industry lobbyist for twenty years, and also worked for Republican Senator Larry Craig from Idaho in an effort to rewrite national forest legislation.[49]

Rey had also been instrumental in crafting the contentious 1995 Salvage Rider, which had been attached to an appropriations bill, allowing the Forest Service to bypass environmental laws in designated salvage logging areas.[50]

From 2001 to 2005, Bush made three appointments to the position of EPA administrator, reflecting his attempts to reconcile his policy views with the agency's mission and leadership. His first appointee, Christine Todd Whitman, a former governor of New Jersey, was called an unlikely choice for the position. "From the outset it was clear she knew relatively little about environmental policy and would have preferred a more high profile post," noted one observer, who called her two-year term "relatively unremarkable."[51]

Whitman appeared to have difficulty adhering to the administration's views, especially on global warming, and some criticized her for insensitivity toward the concerns of state and local governments. Others felt that the agency's internal battles reflected fundamental differences over agency direction and Whitman's attempt to distance herself from lobbyists. She resigned in May 2003 and was replaced by another governor, Utah's Mike Leavitt, in November 2003. Leavitt, in contrast, was considered an antiregulatory advocate who won praise from oil, gas, and off-road vehicle interests while being attacked by environmental groups. His low-key, soft-spoken style seemed to fit well with the Bush administration's desire to keep environmental issues out of the news.[52]

Leavitt fit the administration's leadership needs at the EPA for a year before Bush appointed him Secretary of Health and Human Services just after the 2004 election, replacing former Wisconsin governor Tommy Thompson. The vacancy at EPA left the agency in limbo for several months, with some observers speculating that Bush preferred that the EPA be run from the White House. In January 2005, Stephen L. Johnson became acting administrator; he had previously served as acting deputy administrator and worked at the EPA for twenty-four years. President Bush nominated Johnson as administrator in March 2005, becoming the first EPA administrator to rise from the agency's professional ranks.

At the Department of the Interior, Bush had initially appointed former mining industry lobbyist Gale Norton, who had spent four years at the conservative Mountain States Legal Foundation, co-founded by Reagan's controversial Secretary of the Interior James Watt. Lower-level appointees represented the oil, gas, and mining industries. After Norton left in 2006, she was replaced by former Idaho governor Dirk Kempthorne, who appeared to take direction squarely from the White House and from the vice president.

In addition to his appointees, Bush also used the regulatory process and administrative rulemaking to further advance his political agenda. While one set of offices within the White House focused on legislation (and an uncooperative Congress), another worked to institute moratoriums on rules that had been promulgated under the Clinton administration, such as the 2001 Roadless Rule.

When possible, Bush repealed old rules and fought for the development of new ones that matched his political mission. Revisions of rules related to NEPA were coupled, for instance, with an executive order that required every agency to create a regulatory policy office run by a political appointee, whose sole job was to manage the process of regulatory review. This parallel process had the intended effect of making sure that what could not be done in one political arena could be accomplished in another.

But President Bush also used his power as chief executive to do what his predecessor had done, creating the largest single conservation area in the history of the United States. The 1906 Antiquities Act gives the president the power to designate national monuments without consulting Congress, and Bush used that power in June 2006 to sign a proclamation designating the 14,000 square miles of federal waters of the Northwestern Hawaiian Islands a national monument. The monument is more than 100 times larger than Yosemite National Park, larger than forty-six of the fifty states, and home to 1,400 surviving monk seals, the entire population of the critically endangered species. It became the first national monument in Hawaii, and the first to be managed by the Department of Commerce under the National Oceanic and Atmospheric Administration (NOAA).[53] Using the Antiquities Act was important because not only was the president able to designate an island chain in the Pacific as a national monument and the world's largest protected marine area, but the action was perhaps the administration's most enduring environmental legacy.[54]

During the 2008 election, Democratic candidate Barack Obama and his running mate Joe Biden used social networking and their appeal to the media to push an environmental agenda, more than they actually talked about issues on the campaign trail. Since the United States was deeply involved in economic difficulties and the wars in Iraq and Afghanistan, those issues rose to the top of the campaign agenda. When environmental issues did get mentioned, they were usually coupled with the issue of energy; reducing the country's reliance on fossil fuels, using renewable sources such as wind and solar power, increased automobile fuel economy, and taking a lead role in climate change negotiations were all part of the Obama policy agenda. Less often mentioned were programs and positions on wilderness and public lands, water pollution, and endangered species and habitat protection.

As president, Obama followed the trend of other contemporary presidents, using his power to appoint to set the tone for his new administration. Some choices of new officials seemed questionable, such as the appointment of Steven Chu, director of the Lawrence Berkeley Laboratory, as Secretary of the Energy. Although Chu was a Nobel Prize–winning physicist, there was some doubt among conservation groups whether he had the experience necessary to stand up to oil and gas interests who sought to open up coastal and Alaskan oil fields to exploration and drilling. Perhaps to soften the impact of the appointment, he brought back former EPA administrator Carol Browner to serve as the White House coordinator of energy and climate change, positioning a more experienced leader in the key role of energy czar. Among her credentials was the fact that she had been the longest-serving administrator in the EPA's history, and once worked as a legislative aide for Senator Al Gore.

At EPA, the president appointed Lisa Jackson, Commissioner of the New Jersey Department of Environment Protection, as administrator. Jackson, who has a background in chemical engineering, spent twenty years in the environmental field, with experience in both land use management and compliance and enforcement within the state agency. At the Department of Agriculture, Obama's choice of Tom Vilsack, former governor of Iowa, won unanimous support from the U.S. Senate but some criticism from environmental groups, who faulted his support for ethanol and genetically modified organisms as evidence he had already been captured by corporate agriculture interests. He also had been an early candidate for president in 2008, and was a supporter of Hillary Clinton in the primary election. His counterpart at Interior, Colorado senator and lawyer Ken Salazar, satisfied those who wanted a true Westerner within the cabinet. Salazar's long family history in Colorado, endorsements by the Sierra Club and Wilderness Society, and seven-year tenure with the Colorado Department of Natural Resources gave him broad-based experience and even industry support.

Obama reached out to others with conservation and environmental experience in his choices at other federal agencies. Nancy Sutley, the deputy mayor for energy and environment in Los Angeles, was chosen as chairwoman of the Council on Environmental Quality, the group that provides advice to the president on environmental issues. Prior to her stint in Los Angeles, she served as energy advisor to California Governor Gray Davis, and spent ten years as deputy secretary for policy and intergovernmental relations for the California EPA. Perhaps more importantly, she was a special assistant to the new energy coordinator, Carol Browner. As had been the case with President Bush, Obama named a longtime U.S. Forest Service employee as the agency's chief. Tom Tidwell, who spent thirty-two years with the Forest Service in a variety of positions in eight national forests, also worked in the Washington Office of the agency as a legislative affairs specialist. Together, Obama's appointees appeared to lean toward the middle ground on environmental policy, a fact not lost on industry, ranching, oil and gas, and environmental groups.

In addition to his appointees, Obama had a potent tool to use in advancing his environmental agenda—the $787 billion stimulus package passed by Congress in February 2009, the American Recovery and Reinvestment Act. The stimulus package gave the president billions of dollars to direct to specific programs that had been at the mercy of the Bush administration, including additional funding for the EPA, the National Park Service, and the Forest Service. Candidate Obama had promised to look toward those with more scientific expertise than his predecessor, in a stinging rebuke to the Bush administration, which had been accused for years of ignoring or editing scientific data in policy recommendations. But in the first year of his administration, critics charged that President Obama had done little to lead environmental agencies, bogged down in the battle over health care reform and the wars in Iraq and Afghanistan.

CONGRESSIONAL POLICYMAKING

"When Congress passes a statute, it reflects the outcome of an agenda setting process that typically may include many months, if not years, of discussion about an issue." This terse statement sums up one of the key roles of Congress in formulating and adopting environmental policy. Congress must initially identify and frame a problem, a process that Rochefort and Cobb refer to as *ownership*: the way in which a legislator characterizes a problem, identifies the causes and potential solutions, then determines which institutional structures, such as committees and subcommittees, will address the issue.[55] Unless a problem is identified by a person (or institution) with the authority to do something about it, it never reaches the policy agenda. In addition, the problem must be given sufficient attention (such as by a major newspaper, or the issuance of a public report) to push it ahead of the dozens of other problems Congress must consider.

How are problems brought to the attention of legislators, and how do they find their way to the policy formulation phase? One way to think about the process is to imagine a member of Congress standing on the street and trying to hear the myriad voices of a crowd of interest-group members, all of whom are trying to get the member's attention. As the legislator tries to hear what they are shouting about, the din becomes even louder, and more group members join the crowd. At some point, no one can hear one another, and, with a shrug of shoulders, the member of Congress gives up, heading back to the staff members who will try to sort out the various "voices" that have been shouting out their concerns.

Such is the case with the contemporary Congress. Contrary to popular fiction and high-school civics tests, legislators do not toil at their desks all night trying to come up with legislation to solve a perceived problem they have heard about while visiting their district and meeting with local leaders. Today, it is more likely that representatives of interest groups from each part of the political spectrum will make an appointment with draft legislation in hand, citing the appropriate section of the U.S. Code that needs to be changed, in their opinion. They bring in volumes of data and reports to bolster their cause, perhaps with a petition or letters of support from constituents and other interests who agree with them. And in most cases, the group representatives do not meet with the member of Congress at all; a staff member will probably ask for an executive summary of the reports and studies, perhaps in a one- to two-page format that can be further summarized for presentation to the legislator.

In another instance, representatives from agencies and departments will be the ones seeking the appointment and handing over proposed legislation. They are experts at not only the legislative process but also the status of current research on an issue. Staff from the EPA, for instance, are in an excellent position to explain the technicalities of water quality law and convoluted permit processes to someone from the district who has complained about what appears to be an illegal discharge from a local facility. Members of Congress tend to be subject-matter experts, but the expectation of expertise can reach only so far.

It helps, too, if those shouting for attention have gained entrance to a congressperson's office by donating to the legislator's campaign fund. It is a widely held belief that campaign contributions do not buy a member's vote, but they do provide access to the staff and sometimes to the legislator directly. This is particularly true at the national level, where the cost of running for office has skyrocketed over the last two decades. The level of influence can be seen, in part, by looking at federal campaign contributions and lobbying expenditures as reported to the Federal Election Commission and, more recently, by analysis by groups such as OpenSecrets.org. As the latter group points out, billions of dollars are spent each year by companies, labor unions, and nongovernmental interests who try to sway members of Congress with their ideas and their dollars. The actual number of registered lobbyists in Washington, D.C. has remained about

---

Another View, Another Voice: The U.S. Chamber of Commerce

Among the "loudest" voices of those attempting to get Congress's attention is the U.S. Chamber of Commerce, a powerful interest group that represents 3 million businesses; more than 96 percent of its members are small businesses with 100 employees or fewer. The organization's staff includes hundreds of policy analysts, lobbyists, lawyers, and communication experts, with an office near the White House. Its mission is "to advance human progress through an economic, political, and social system based on individual freedom, incentive, initiative, opportunity, and responsibility." But that statement does not really identify the activities of the complex and sometimes controversial business interest group.

The Chamber is noteworthy for the 2,500 forums and meetings it holds annually, and for the eleven major programs it operates, ranging from TradeRoots, which supports free-trade legislation and grassroots efforts to assist companies in expanding into the global marketplace, to the Institute for a Competitive Workforce that focuses on workforce development and education issues. Of particular importance is the fact that the group maintains its own in-house law firm, the National Chamber Litigation Center, which defends business interests and sues government agencies, and the Institute for Legal Reform, which informs voters about state-level races for attorneys general and the judiciary, as well as fighting for legal reform legislation. Between 1998 and 2009, the Chamber was the top lobbying client in the country, spending over $477 million, more than double what was spent by the American Medical Association—a lobbying giant—and the nearly $187 million of big spenders such as General Electric, the $168 million of the American Hospital Association, and the American Association of Retired Persons' expenditures of $159 million.

On the environmental front, the U.S. Chamber of Commerce is active on every level and every conceivable issue that might affect business interests. One of the most prominent issues has been New Source Review (NSR), the policy that establishes emissions standards under the Clean Air Act for new and modified stationary sources of air pollutants, such as power plants and factory operations. The Chamber supports a streamlined permitting process for businesses, backs rules that clarify the effects of routine maintenance and repair, and opposes legislative attempts to block NSR efforts. The group has also lobbied actively on transboundary air pollution, expediting environmental review of projects triggered under NEPA, and energy supplies. Critics of the Chamber point to the group's support of the Yucca Mountain nuclear waste repository (or a suitable alternative site for nuclear waste storage) as an example of its efforts to promote the interests of business over sound science. One other contentious issue deals with public lands, especially support for the multiple use of land, including cattle grazing and timber sales. The Chamber has repeatedly opposed efforts to implement the 2001 Roadless Rule and any efforts to eliminate road construction in national forests.

In many ways, the views of the U.S. Chamber of Commerce are the antithesis of most environmental organizations. But its powerful voice is reinforced by its long history of support for business interests and the resources it brings to the legislative arena.

SOURCES:
OpenSecrets. "Top Spenders." http://www.opensecrets.org/lobby/top .php. Accessed June 11, 2009.
U.S. Chamber of Commerce. "About Us." http://www.uschamber.com/ about. Accessed June 11, 2009.
"U.S. Chamber of Commerce." http://www.sourcewatch.org/index.php. Accessed July 21, 2009.

the same over the last ten years, from 10,684 in 1998 to 10,764 in 2008. What has changed is the amount of money spent on lobbying during that same period; from $1.44 billion in 1998 to $3.27 billion in 2008.[56]

The committee system in Congress becomes the mechanism for the policy adoption phase. Committees and their myriad subcommittees may hold public hearings, issue reports, or consider budget requests on how to deal with the problem. The House and Senate leaders also play primary roles in environmental policy as they set the agenda for their chambers and determine what issues will be given priority, based largely on the way an issue is defined. The use of symbols and rhetoric, congressional committee jurisdictions, the nature of the participants, and many other factors explain how environmental policies are defined, shaped, and implemented.

The most striking thing about environmental policymaking in Congress is its fragmentation. James Anderson refers to this issue in his discussion of majority building in Congress as a part of the policy adoption phase of policymaking.[57] The authorizing committees have primary responsibility for writing environmental laws. In the House, the Natural Resources Committee primarily focuses on bills dealing with public lands, national parks, and natural resources. The Energy and Commerce Committee has broad jurisdiction over energy, the environment, and health. The Transportation and Infrastructure Committee has responsibility for water projects, pipelines, and hazardous materials. Several other committees regularly get involved in environmental issues, such as the Agriculture Committee and the Science and Technology Committee. Then there are committees that have a say in how much money is raised from special environmental taxes (the Ways and Means Committee), how much is spent on environmental programs in general (the Budget Committee), and how funds are distributed to specific agencies and programs (the Appropriations Committee). Each committee is further divided into subcommittees that create additional overlaps. The Senate is almost as fragmented for environmental policy, with a similar set of budget-related committees (the tax committee is Finance rather than Ways and Means). The Energy and Natural Resources and the Environment and Public Works committees are the major players, but the Agriculture, Nutrition, and Forestry Committee is also a regular participant in major environmental initiatives.

House leaders have taken a particular interest in environmental regulation, vowing to reduce its cost and intrusiveness. In the past, the House Government Reform and Oversight and Senate Governmental Affairs, as well as other committees, have given particular scrutiny in oversight hearings and investigations of the U.S. Forest Service and the EPA. The chairs of committees play enormously important roles in deciding what bills are moved through the process and what committee resources are aimed at what issues. Oversight of the actions of the many agencies involved with environmental programs becomes just as important as adopting policy in the evaluation phase of the process. For instance, members of the House have been carefully watching the actions of the Bureau of Land Management's Wild Horses and Burros program. Since Congress passed the Wild Horses and Burros Act in 1971, the agency has been tasked with responsibility for the care of about 37,000 animals (33,100 horses and 3,800 burros currently grazing on public land in the Western states).[58]

In a little-noticed action in 2004, Senator Conrad Burns of Montana, in deference to ranchers wanting to protect federal lands for their cattle, amended the 1971 law to allow for the slaughter of animals older than ten years that had been unsuccessfully placed up for adoption three times.[59] In August 2008, BLM officials announced that they were considering euthanizing 6,000 horses in the BLM's care because of a lack of space at its corrals and pastures, skyrocketing hay and grain prices, and an economic downturn that reduced the number of animal adoptions from 5,700 in 2005 to 3,700 in 2008.[60] The action was legal under the agency's policy of establishing an "appropriate management level" (AML) for wild horses and burros on public rangelands. The AML considers droughts, wildfires, and other factors that reduce forage, while allowing the BLM to gather thousands of animals and put them up for adoption or sale.

Headlines announcing the "slaughter of wild horses" caught the attention of animal protection groups such as the Humane Society of the United States and the American Wild Horse Preservation Campaign. These organizations, along with smaller nonprofits around the West, pounced on members of Congress to do something about the BLM, which they argued was mismanaging the program so badly that they created an emergency on their own. Critics noted that the agency rounded up the animals to put them in holding pens knowing that there were insufficient adoptive homes for them. The chairman of the House Subcommittee on National Parks, Forests, and Public Lands wrote a letter to the BLM asking the agency to wait on conducting euthanasia because of concerns about the BLM's inability "to administer the budget of the Wild Horses and Burros program with any trace of fiscal accountability." Agency officials countered that they were doing their best to balance the wild horses and burros with other public land uses, including cattle grazing, oil and gas development, and recreation, in disagreement with House members who argued that the BLM was mismanaging the program. They believed that the current $37 million budget was inadequate and that $77 million would be needed by 2012 to maintain the program "as is."[61]

But election pressures and other issues intervened in the wild horses example, moving it further down the policy agenda. Members of Congress who had seemed so focused on the issue in the late summer of 2008 did not take decisive action on bills, so the problem of BLM oversight languished through the fall. A year later, a newly elected Congress seemed sufficiently energized by thoughts of thousands of animals being killed to pass a measure by a vote of 239 to 185 in the House. The Restore Our American Mustangs Act (ROAM) would step up fertility control measures, encourage more adoptions, and provide as much as 19 million additional acres on which the horses and burros could roam freely. The issue of shrinking rangeland was one of the key problems cited by supporters of the bill; they complained that the acreage for the animals had been reduced from 54 million acres in 1971 to about 34 million acres in 2007.[62] When the congressional efforts seemed stalled, in October 2009, Secretary of the Interior Ken Salazar proposed the creation of seven new wild horse preserves to accommodate 25,000 nonreproducing horses, including a preserve in the East and one in the Midwest, a measure that would go beyond the ROAM act but that would still require congressional approval.

Congressional turnover can have a dramatic effect on the policy agenda and legislative activities. When the 111th Congress convened in January 2009, for instance, congressional committees and subcommittees reflected the changes brought by the 2008 elections, as seen in Table 3.2. Committee

T A B L E 3.2   Congressional Committees and Subcommittees with Environmental Jurisdiction, 111th Congress (2009–2010)

Senate
Agriculture, Nutrition, and Forestry
    Rural Revitalization, Conservation, Forestry, and Credit
    Energy, Science, and Technology
    Domestic and Foreign Marketing, Inspection, and Plant and Animal Health

Energy and Natural Resources
    Energy, National Parks, Public Lands and Forests, Water, and Power

Environment and Public Works
    Children's Health
    Clean Air and Nuclear Safety
    Green Jobs and the New Economy
    Superfund, Toxics, and Environmental Health
    Transportation and Infrastructure
    Water and Wildlife

House
Agriculture
    Conservation, Credit, Energy, and Research
    Department Operations, Oversight, Nutrition, and Forestry
    Horticulture and Organic Agriculture
    Livestock, Dairy, and Poultry
    Rural Development, Biotechnology, Specialty Crops, and Foreign Agriculture

Energy and Commerce
    Energy and the Environment
    Health

Natural Resources
    Energy and Mineral Resources
    Insular Affairs, Oceans, and Wildlife
    National Parks, Forests, and Public Lands
    Water and Power

Science and Technology
    Technology and Innovation
    Energy and the Environment
    Research and Science Education

Transportation and Infrastructure
    Highways and Transit
    Railroads, Pipelines, and Hazardous Materials
    Water Resources and Environment

House Select Committee on Energy Independence and Global Warming structures, leadership, budgets, and staffs are allocated based on a ratio of Republicans to Democrats that gave the Democrats a majority in both the Senate and in the House of Representatives. Committees may alter their membership and even their names, reflective of the broader policy agenda. For instance, in the Senate, there is a Subcommittee on Green Jobs and the New Economy, a name that would not have existed a decade ago before the topic became more popular in the media. Similarly, in the House, there is a Subcommittee on Horticulture and Organic Agriculture, representing a growing interest in the organic farming movement. Specialized committees can also be created to deal with ad hoc issues and problems, such as the House Select Committee on Energy Independence and Global Warming.

Although Congress has primary responsibility for policy formulation and adoption, the nature of the institution has hampered that role. Congress's inability to develop an overall national environmental policy has been termed "environmental gridlock,"[63] referring to the contrast between the institution's rapid pace and initiative during the 1960s and 1970s in comparison with the body's current inability to move forward with a legislative agenda. There are a number of reasons explaining why Congress may be "stuck" in moving forward:

1. The fragmentation of the committee system decentralizes both power and the decisionmaking process. Environmental issues do not "belong" to any one committee within Congress. Many of the House and Senate's standing committees claim some environmental jurisdiction. Depending on the title of a particular piece of legislation and the subject matter, there is a great deal of latitude in deciding which committee(s) should have jurisdiction over that subject. When environmental issues are "hot," a certain rivalry exists that causes competition among committees as to which one will have the greatest chance of influencing the bill's content.

2. The pressures of an increasing number of "green" groups and industry interests have made it more difficult to build a congressional consensus. The same committee fragmentation that characterizes the modern Congress also gives interest groups more access to the legislative process. If a group feels one committee is less accommodating to its interests, it may seek a more favorable venue before another committee or subcommittee. At any one point in the legislative process, dozens of groups may be vying for members' attention, and environmental groups have lost the power advantage they once enjoyed in the agenda-setting phase of the policy process.

3. Members of Congress often lack the time and expertise needed to produce sophisticated legislation. One criticism of Congress is that it is "an assembly of scientific amateurs enacting programs of great technical complexity to ameliorate scientifically complicated environmental ills most legislators but dimly understand."[64] The result is often legislation that is watered down or intentionally vague.

4. Localized reelection concerns override a "national" view of environmental policymaking. It is difficult for a member of Congress from southern Oregon to convince a colleague from an urban district in New York of the

relative importance of a bill barring timber exports to Japan. As reelection pressures mount (especially in the House, where the fever strikes every two years), bargaining becomes an essential style of policymaking. Members with little personal interest in an issue often could not care less about the legislative outcome, and only by bargaining for something of value to their own district do they have a reason to become involved. Votes on pork-barrel projects such as dams and parklands, for example, are often based on the "you scratch my back, I'll scratch yours" principle, with no thought given to consistency or even to the regional impact of the decision. Local concerns determine which authorizations get funded and which do not; and legislators in positions of seniority, especially members of the powerful budget committees, are particularly adept at bringing projects and facilities "back home."

5. The domination of the Republican Party in Congress (and from 2001 to 2008 in the White House) seriously challenged the existing structure of environmental policymaking. During the Clinton administration, Republican leaders sought to rewrite major laws, reduce the resources of the EPA and other agencies, and reshape the regulatory process so that agencies would be much less likely to intrude on industrial and commercial activities. Although the extreme antiregulatory agenda was blocked by more moderate Republicans, the party often fails to take into account widespread public support for environmental, health, and safety regulation.

As a result, the most recent congressional sessions are noteworthy for their lack of partisan environmental legislation, especially in comparison to prior years. The Republicans can claim some victories, such as the 1995 closure of the Office of Technology Assessment (OTA). Congress had established OTA in 1972 to provide its committees with neutral analyses of scientific and technical issues, but defunded the $22 million program as part of an antiregulatory sweep in the 104th Congress. That same year, Congress voted to close the U.S. Bureau of Mines, which was created in 1910 in response to concerns about health and safety conditions in the nation's mines. Although Congress terminated all of the bureau's programs, many of its functions were simply transferred to the U.S. Geological Survey, the Department of Energy, and the Bureau of Land Management.

THE EXECUTIVE BRANCH AGENCIES

Despite the prolonged public interest in conservation and environmental protection outlined in Chapter 1, the federal government's involvement is actually relatively recent. During the first 100 years after the nation's founding, both the president and Congress were much more deeply involved with foreign affairs, paying little attention to internal domestic problems until the growth of the country literally demanded it. The creation of a federal environmental policy was sporadic and unfocused, with responsibility for the environment scattered among a host of agencies. Today, environmental policy is largely in the hands of unelected but often partisan officials in the Department of the Interior, the Department of Agriculture's Forest Service and Fish and Wildlife Service, and the EPA. These agencies have jurisdiction over the implementation of most of the nation's environmental policies.

Under its first Secretary, Thomas Ewing, the Department of the Interior was given domestic housekeeping responsibilities different from those of today's Cabinet-level department. Initially, the department controlled the General Land Office, Office of Indian Affairs, Pension Office, and Patent Office, as well as supervising the Commissioner of Public Buildings, Board of Inspectors, the Warden of the District of Columbia Penitentiary, the census, mines, and accounts of marshals of the U.S. courts. Gradually, a shift occurred as the agency's responsibilities were transferred to other agencies within the executive branch. Eventually, the need to manage newly discovered public resources, especially land and mineral rights, led to the development of several agencies that later came under the Department of the Interior's umbrella, as seen in Table 3.3. The Secretary of the Interior is nominated by the president and confirmed by the Senate, as are the agency directors.

Another agency within the Department of the Interior, the U.S. Fish and Wildlife Service, has a convoluted past, starting in 1871 with the creation of the U.S. Commission on Fish and Fisheries—charged with studying and recommending solutions to the decline in food fishes—in the Department of Commerce, and in 1885, with the creation of the Division of Economic Ornithology and Mammalogy in the Department of Agriculture. It was renamed the Bureau of Biological Survey and given jurisdiction over the interstate shipment of wildlife and importation of species. In 1903, within the first federal bird reservation established by President Theodore Roosevelt, the Biological Survey took over management of what later became the national wildlife refuge system. Under Chief Jay Norwood "Ding" Darling, the Survey took on a more ambitious agenda, and in 1934, the bureau began acquiring wetlands and wildlife habitat throughout the United

T A B L E 3.3   Agencies of the U.S. Department of the Interior

Agency	Established
Bureau of Indian Affairs	1824
Bureau of Land Management[*]	1946
Bureau of Reclamation[**]	1902
Minerals Management Service	1982
National Park Service	1916
Office of Surface Mining Reclamation and Enforcement	1977
U.S. Geological Survey	1879
U.S. Fish and Wildlife Service[***]	1940

*Originally in War Department; transferred to Interior in 1849
**Combined the responsibilities of the General Land Office, created in 1812, and the Grazing Service, established in 1934
***Combined the responsibilities of the Bureau of Fisheries, established in 1871, and the Bureau of Biological Survey, created in 1885

States. The Bureau of Fisheries and the Biological Survey were moved to the Department of the Interior in 1939, and a year later were combined to create the Fish and Wildlife Service. The agency created two new bureaus in 1956: the Bureau of Commercial Fisheries and the Bureau of Sport Fisheries and Wildlife. In 1970, the Bureau of Commercial Fisheries was transferred to the Department of Commerce and renamed the National Marine Fisheries Service.

In thirty years, the agency had been split between two Cabinet-level agencies (Agriculture and Commerce), expanded its jurisdiction beyond fish and birds to wildlife habitat and wetlands, and created new divisions in response to congressional legislation like the Endangered Species Act and the Federal Aid in Sportfish Restoration Act. Today, the Washington Office of the agency is divided into seven directorates:

1. Wildlife and Sportfish Restoration Programs
2. National Wildlife Refuge System
3. Migratory Birds
4. Fisheries and Habitat Conservation
5. Endangered Species
6. International Affairs
7. Law Enforcement

The U.S. Forest Service, which is now part of the Department of Agriculture, was originally called the Division of Forestry when it was established in 1876 under the leadership of Forestry Agent Franklin Hough. When Gifford Pinchot became chief of the division in 1898, he asked to have his title changed from "Chief" to "Forester," noting that there were many chiefs in Washington, D.C., but only one forester. That title remained in effect when the Division of Forestry was changed to the Bureau of Forestry in 1901 and then to the Forest Service in 1905. The "Forester" title remained in effect until 1935, when the title "Chief" was readopted under Ferdinand Silcox. See Table 3.4 for a list of Department of Agriculture and U.S. Forest Service leadership.

It was not by accident that the Forest Service was placed under the jurisdiction of the Department of Agriculture while most of the land and natural resources agencies were part of the Department of the Interior. At the time, trees were considered a crop—a commodity just like cotton or soybeans. The Forest Service is also charged with providing a sustained yield of other natural resources, such as water, forage, and wildlife, while maintaining its mission, "Caring for the Land and Serving People." The 155 national forests and 20 national grasslands comprise 191 million acres (77.3 hectares) of land—an area equivalent in size to the state of Texas—in 44 states, Puerto Rico, and the Virgin Islands.

The agency's 33,000 employees work in four levels of national forest offices:

Ranger districts. Most of the on-the-ground activities take place in the more than 600 ranger districts, ranging in size from 50,000 acres (20,000 hectares) to more than 1 million acres (400,000 hectares). The staff level at each district office may include from 10 to 100 people, with

TABLE 3.4 **Department of Agriculture and U.S. Forest Service Leadership (1962–2010)**

President	Secretary of Agriculture	Chief, U.S. Forest Service
Nixon	Earl Butz (1971–1974)	Edward Cliff (1962–1972)
		John McGuire (1972–1974)
Ford	Earl Butz (1974–1976)	John McGuire (1974–1976)
Carter	John Knebel (1976–1977)	John McGuire (1976–1979)
	Robert Bergland (1977–1981)	
Reagan	John Block (1981–1986)	R. Max Peterson (1979–1987)
	Richard Lyng (1986–1989)	Dale Robertson (1987–1988)
Bush (G.H.W.)	Clayton Yeutter (1989–1991)	Dale Robertson (1988–1993)
	Edward Madigan (1991–1992)	
Clinton	Michael Espy (1993–1994)	Jack W. Thomas (1993–1996)
	Daniel Glickman (1995–2001)	Mike Dombeck (1997–2001)
Bush (G.W.)	Ann Veneman (2001–2005)	Dale Bosworth (2001–2007)
	Mike Johanns (2005–2009)	Gail Kimbell (2007–2009)
Obama	Tom Vilsack (2009–)	Tom Tidwell (2009–)

responsibilities for trail construction and maintenance, operation of campgrounds, management of vegetation and wildlife habitat, and public outreach and education.

National forests. Each national forest comprises several ranger districts and is managed by a forest supervisor, who coordinates the activities among the districts, allocates the budget, and provides technical support.

Regions. There are nine regions with the Forest Service, numbered 1 through 10 (Region 7 has been eliminated). Regions represent broad geographical areas that usually include several states and are managed by a regional forester. The regional offices coordinate activities within national forests, allocate budgets, and provide guidance in the development of forest planning.

National office. The Washington Office (WO), as it is called, provides broad direction and policy for the agency. The person in charge is the chief, who reports to the undersecretary for natural resources and environment in the Department of Agriculture.[65]

The EPA, in contrast, is an independent agency in the executive branch; it is headed by an administrator, a deputy administrator, and nine assistant administrators, all nominated by the president and confirmed by the Senate. Each administrator has responsibility for a specific set of functions related to the environment, as seen in Table 3.5. The agency also divides the country into ten geographic regions, with field offices that monitor and support environmental policies in their

TABLE 3.5   EPA Administrative Offices (by function)

Administration and Resources Management

Air and Radiation

Enforcement and Compliance Assurance

Environmental Information

International Affairs

Prevention, Pesticides, and Toxic Substances

Research and Development

Solid Waste and Emergency Response

Water

SOURCE: U.S. Environmental Protection Agency. "About EPA." http://www.epa.gov/epahome/organization.htm. Accessed July 17, 2009.

area, as seen in Table 3.6. The EPA has responsibility for administering and implementing a broad spectrum of environmental laws. In one sense, it is a regulatory agency, issuing permits, setting and monitoring standards, and enforcing federal laws, but nearly half of its annual budget goes toward grants to states, nonprofits, educational institutions, and other entities for projects such as building wastewater-treatment facilities or conducting research. The agency manages its own laboratories throughout the country and sponsors partnerships with businesses, nonprofit organizations, and state and local governments. The EPA also conducts public education and publishes information about its activities, including an annual report available electronically.

TABLE 3.6   EPA Regional Office Responsibility by State and Territories

Region 1	Connecticut, Maine, Massachusetts, New Hampshire, Rhode Island, Vermont
Region 2	New Jersey, New York, Puerto Rico, U.S. Virgin Islands
Region 3	Delaware, Maryland, Pennsylvania, Virginia, West Virginia, District of Columbia
Region 4	Alabama, Florida, Georgia, Kentucky, Mississippi, North Carolina, South Carolina, Tennessee
Region 5	Illinois, Indiana, Michigan, Minnesota, Ohio, Wisconsin
Region 6	Arkansas, Louisiana, New Mexico, Oklahoma, Texas
Region 7	Iowa, Kansas, Missouri, Nebraska
Region 8	Colorado, Montana, North Dakota, South Dakota, Utah, Wyoming
Region 9	Arizona, California, Hawaii, Nevada, Guam, American Samoa
Region 10	Alaska, Idaho, Oregon, Washington

SOURCE: U.S. Environmental Protection Agency. "Regions." http://www.epa.gov/epahome/regions.htm. Accessed September 8, 2005.

The president also receives policy advice on environmental matters from the CEQ, created as part of the 1970 NEPA. Members of CEQ recommend policy to the president and to some degree evaluate environmental protection programs within the executive branch and environmental impact statements prepared by federal agencies. The CEQ has no regulatory authority; its recommendations are purely advisory.

Although the EPA, Department of Agriculture, and Department of the Interior are responsible for most policy implementation, they share jurisdiction with several other federal agencies, as seen in Table 3.7.

Sometimes, an agency may have powers and an interest level comparable to that of a Cabinet-level department or the EPA, as is the case with the Nuclear Regulatory Commission, which is currently engaged in relicensing nuclear power plants and supervising their operation. Other agencies, such as the Federal Aviation Administration (FAA), may not have environmental concerns as their primary mission but may be affected by regulations or legislation implemented by other agencies. Thus, the FAA was consulted in 1990 when air-quality officials within the EPA began to consider legislation that would govern the amount of particulates released in aircraft exhaust emissions.

T A B L E 3.7   Other Federal Agencies and Commissions with Environmental Policy Jurisdiction

Department	Agency or Commission
Commerce	National Bureau of Standards
	National Oceanic and Atmospheric Administration
Defense	Army Corps of Engineers
Energy	Federal Energy Regulatory Commission
	Office of Civilian Radioactive Waste Management
	Office of Conservation and Renewable Energy
Health and Human Services	Food and Drug Administration
	National Institute for Occupational Safety and Health
Labor	Mine Safety and Health Administration
Transportation	Federal Aviation Administration
	Federal Highway Administration
	Materials Transportation Bureau
	National Transportation Safety Board
Commissions and/or Regulatory Agencies	Consumer Product Safety Commission
	Federal Maritime Commission
	Federal Trade Commission
	Nuclear Regulatory Commission

RULEMAKING AND NEPA

Administrative agencies are constantly engaged in the process of rulemaking—interpreting congressional intent and translating ideas into specific procedures, or rules. Congress enacted the Administrative Procedure Act of 1946 (APA) to establish standard procedures that agencies would use because they are the source of rules. The APA's definition is: "A 'rule' means the whole or part of a statement of general or particular applicability and future event designed to implement, interpret, or prescribe law or policy"...[66] The compilation of the rules made by the Executive Branch is found in the Code of Federal Regulations, or CFR, which is divided into fifty subject areas, called *titles* and *chapters*. Environmental rules can be found in several of the titles, because some issues overlap distinct topics. Title 10, for instance, deals with rules involving energy; Title 18 covers the conservation of power and water resources. Other titles that involve environmental policies include Mineral Resources (Title 30), Navigation and Navigable Waters (Title 33), Parks, Forests, and Public Property (Title 36), Protection of the Environment (Title 40), Public Lands (Title 43), and Wildlife and Fisheries (Title 50).

When Congress passes a new statute and it is signed by the president, the rulemaking process begins in earnest once authorization to proceed with rulemaking is given. The process of drafting a rule usually involves lawyers working for the affected agency, along with technical staff who are familiar with the intricacies of the subject and its impact on those who will be affected by the new rule. Other stakeholders may include the president, members of Congress, consultants to affected parties, researchers, and groups and individuals supporting or opposing rule development.

Congressional legislation is often vague, indicating a general intention rather than a specific goal or description of how what it seeks to do will be accomplished. Usually, the draft rule undergoes a comprehensive external review; if the subject of the rule overlaps agencies, the process may be done concurrently, or one agency may take the lead in collecting relevant information, consulting with experts, and making sure the rule meets any legal requirements. The notice of proposed rulemaking appears in the *Federal Register*, which is published five days a week, indicating which title of the CFR would be affected, an overview of what the proposed rule would do, and information about how the public can participate in the process. This often involves hearings on the issue and provides the opportunity for groups and individuals to contribute written comments. Meanwhile, an agency may be conducting research studies, performing cost-benefit analyses, and determining the environmental impact if the rule is implemented.

Legislation that states Congress's intention to increase salvage timber that can be harvested after a major wildfire, for instance, must be compared to the existing rules in the CFR, and a proposed draft rule developed. Congress might signal what it wants the U.S. Forest Service to do—make more salvage timber available—without specifying how much salvage timber should be logged in what regions of the country, or how quickly it expects the process to be implemented.

Environmental organizations are likely to be monitoring the *Federal Register* to see what the agency plans to propose, or representatives might be asked to participate informally in the drafting of a rule. The timber industry is doing the same thing, and both sides are preparing comments and various forms of evidence for submission to the agency, which then considers the comments and may issue a revised rule based on public input. An interest with extensive resources, such as the pulp and paper industry, often conducts its own studies and analysis of the impact of a rule. Smaller organizations or individuals may not be able to participate fully in rulemaking if they are unable to provide an agency with similar studies refuting industry claims. Still, groups can mobilize their membership to participate during the written comment period or to appear at public hearings.

Sometimes, an agency will schedule a hearing at a location outside Washington, D.C. so that those most affected by the proposed rule will have an opportunity to participate. A rule on salvage timber harvesting might be heard in a logging community in Oregon, for example. But the agency managing the rule is also subject to political pressures, so hearings may be held at a time and place more convenient to trade associations in Washington. Individuals may not be able to participate because they cannot afford the time and money to travel to the capital, and their voices may thus be muted. This is one reason so many environmental organizations have established a presence in Washington, D.C.—it allows them to monitor and participate in the various stages of rulemaking.

Once a final rule has been approved and published in the *Federal Register*, it must still undergo scrutiny by the Office of Management and Budget and by Congress. If major revisions are needed, the process may start over; in some cases, a rule is abandoned. Rules that survive the process undergo formal congressional scrutiny, and a Notice of Final Rulemaking is published in the *Federal Register*. If a rule makes it through the entire process, it then becomes part of the CFR. There will still be work for agencies to do—interpreting the rule in its final form, making technical corrections once the rule is implemented, and preparing for litigation.[67]

Corollary to the rulemaking process are the procedures required for compliance with NEPA. The statute was designed to improve the quality of decision making, inform the public of the federal government's major programs and potential environmental impacts, and ensure that the public was involved in agency decisions through the process of scoping (soliciting public input through newsletters, legal notices, and hearings, for instance). Once a major activity is proposed, all federal agencies must conduct an evaluation of the potential environmental impact of a project. Agencies initially categorize their actions as (1) projects normally requiring an environmental impact statement (EIS), a full and exhaustive study of the range of issues and effects the project might have; (2) actions requiring a less exhaustive study, called an environmental assessment (EA); or (3) projects for which neither an EA or EIS is required because there is no significant impact on the human environment, called a Finding of No Significant Impact (FONSI). The EIS generally determines whether the project will have a significant impact on the human environment, a definition that often leads to court interpretation of what NEPA really means and requires. There is less public participation in the development of a FONSI or an EA than in an EIS; the latter document generally includes:

- A project summary that states potential issues, controversies, and conclusions
- A statement of the proposed project's underlying purpose
- The identification and comparison of proposed alternative courses of action
- A full description of the affected environment
- A description of the environmental consequences of each alternative

The legal notice of the start of the NEPA process is published in the *Federal Register*, and members of the public are invited to submit letters or other information, such as independently conducted studies, relevant to the proposed project. There may be a time period when the federal government agency in charge of the project accepts comments, usually 30 to 90 days, and then the comment period is closed. The agency may prepare a draft version of the EIS (DEIS) which is then adjusted or expanded in response to comments or studies that were submitted by individuals, academicians, researchers, state and local governments, tribes, interest groups, and other entities with a stake in the outcome of the project. Comments may range from a handful on less contentious issues to hundreds of thousands on large projects or those for which the impact affects a large number of persons. The DEIS is reviewed in light of the comments, and the resulting document, the final EIS (FEIS) is again published. NEPA documents are generally available at public libraries in the communities where projects are being considered, and online through the website of the department proposing the project.

The NEPA process, like rulemaking in general, involves arcane, bureaucratic processes that are subject to litigation at each step. There are twists and turns that require stakeholders to monitor each and every notice, action, and deadline in order to remain an active participant. One need not be a lawyer to participate in rulemaking or NEPA activities, but one does need to know how to track each layer of the process, how to access documents, and how and when public participation is in order. Missing a deadline by a single day can eliminate a party from potential legal recourse in the future, or result in projects moving forward with minimal public input.

COURTS AND ENVIRONMENTAL POLITICS

The courts have two primary functions in the making of environmental policy: to exercise their authority for judicial review and to interpret statutes through cases brought to them. In doing so, they use the Constitution to determine the legality of actions of the executive and legislative branches, and define the meanings of laws that frequently are open to differing interpretations. Often, courts have the authority to determine who has access to the judicial process and may play an activist role in policymaking through their decisions. Courts can choose whether to hear a case, based on the concept of ripeness—whether there are concrete issues to be adjudicated, rather than hypothetical disputes. They may also determine what remedy is most appropriate, such as forcing statutory compliance or ordering the payment of punitive monetary damages to deter future violations.[68]

Before the passage of the major environmental laws of the 1970s, most courts' involvement in environmental issues was limited to the adjudication of disputes between polluting industries and citizens affected by pollution under the common law of nuisance. The result in most cases was a cease-and-desist order and, perhaps, a fine. The new generation of environmental laws opened up a variety of opportunities for private parties, usually environmental groups, to use the courts to compel agencies to take actions mandated by statutes or to sue polluters when government officials failed to enforce the law. Administrative requirements for environmental assessments of projects funded or carried out by federal agencies under NEPA spawned hundreds of administrative appeals and lawsuits challenging agency actions. Studies of NEPA litigation show that the willingness of the courts to review agency decisions, especially in the early 1970s, resulted from various factors including public support for the environment, a tendency toward strict enforcement of statutory procedural requirements, and most important, timing. When NEPA was enacted, the courts were generally tightening their review of agency decision making and increasingly taking a "hard look" at agency actions.[69]

Several important environmental decisions came about during this period of judicial activism. Interpreting congressional intent in the opening words of the 1970 Clean Air Act, the U.S. Supreme Court upheld a district court order that instructed the EPA to prevent the "significant deterioration" of air quality in regions that had already met federal standards. A 1973 decision by the District of Columbia Circuit Court forced the EPA to prepare plans to reduce ozone and carbon monoxide (key components of smog) for cities using transportation control measures. The legal concept of "standing"—the right of an individual or group to bring an issue before a court—was greatly expanded as well. The constitutional basis for standing is found in Article III, which gives courts the authority to decide "cases and controversies," and has historically been interpreted to mean that an individual had the right to bring a suit only when there was a clear showing that the person had been harmed, in terms of either personal injury or loss of property. Thus, most suits against polluting industries could be brought only by citizens actually affected by the pollution. Environmental groups found it difficult to qualify as litigants in most suits because many courts did not consider environmental harm to be personal in nature, so litigation was infrequent. Gradually, however, the courts began allowing members of environmental groups to sue on behalf of the public interest, thereby increasing the number of lawsuits against industries, and later against agencies, that failed to comply with environmental laws and regulations.[70]

It has been argued, however, that U.S. Supreme Court justices may defer to administrative decisions when cases brought before them are exceptionally technical. In analyzing cases involving environmental issues brought before the Court between 1972 and 1991—the heyday of environmental legislation—Robert Percival found that about one-third of the cases were decided unanimously, with another third generating only one or two dissents. As environmental problems and laws become more complex, it appears that the courts have taken a less active role in intervening in established policies.[71]

As the issue of regulatory takings became more controversial, the courts became more important as they addressed the issue on Fifth Amendment grounds. Two U.S. Supreme Court decisions moved the courts closer to a policymaking role in land-use decisions. In a 2001 case, *Palazzolo* v. *Rhode Island*, the Court considered whether a property owner was entitled to challenge an environmental regulation that was in place when the land was acquired.[72] The case involved an owner who sought to fill eleven tidal wetland areas to build a private beach club. The state denied his request for a permit, refusing to give the owner an exemption because the activity did not serve a compelling public interest that benefits the public as a whole. Other courts had ruled that similar regulations form part of the title to the property, precluding the owner from raising a takings challenge against the rule.

In a second case in April 2002, the U.S. Supreme Court upheld the constitutionality of a nearly three-year-long moratorium on development around Lake Tahoe and local governments' regulation of land use. Several hundred owners of land in the area purchased property prior to 1980 changes in a compact established between California and Nevada. Under the compact administered by the Lake Tahoe Regional Planning Agency, development in environmentally sensitive areas was halted. The landowners argued that even though the action did not take away their future right to develop, it was a temporary taking during the moratorium period. They sought compensation for their losses. The justices ruled against the landowners in a 6–3 decision, affirming the right of local governments to use various techniques of land-use control, even if the control affects the value of private property.[73]

There is much evidence to conclude that the courts are the political arenas of choice for resolving all types of environmental disputes, although this is not necessarily a new development. On the one hand, the courts have been used to ensure enforcement of environmental regulations. The Natural Resources Defense Council, for example, successfully filed suit against the Department of Energy in 1984 to compel the agency to comply with environmental laws at its nuclear weapons facilities. In 2001, a coalition of environmental groups took similar action against the U.S. Fish and Wildlife Service, claiming the agency had failed to protect the spotted owl and the Pacific fisher under the provisions of the Endangered Species Act (ESA).

Over the past few years, environmental organizations have monitored the use of the courts carefully, arguing that there has been a systematic violation of laws and that judges have ruled consistently against the president's policies and strategies. The Defenders of Wildlife Accountability Project, undertaken in conjunction with the University of Vermont's Law School, analyzed all reported cases in which the Bush administration presented legal arguments regarding an existing environmental law, regulation, or policy before federal judges or magistrates between January 21, 2001, and October 31, 2003. The project released three reports dealing with NEPA, national forests, and the ESA, noting that since taking office in 2001, the Bush administration worked systematically to undermine environmental law and weaken environmental protection.[74]

In one 2002 case involving the ESA, the judge admonished the executive branch, "What gives the Federal Government the right unilaterally to decide what agreements it will comply with and what it won't comply with? Indeed, this is not an agreement. It's a court order.... The Federal Government is not above the law."[75]

On the other hand, it is usually to industry's advantage to litigate environmental regulations because the process has the net effect of stalling the implementation of new rules, as has frequently been the case with the 1990 Clean Air Act regulations. Industry can demur during the policy formation and adoption stage, thereby avoiding the bad press that comes from intrusive lobbying, in hopes of moving the courts closer to their position. Led by the American Trucking Associations, Inc., the U.S. Chamber of Commerce, the National Association of Manufacturers, and three states (Michigan, Ohio, and West Virginia), industry groups challenged the 1997 EPA standards for ozone and particulate matter. They argued that the setting of the standards was both arbitrary and unconstitutional because that power belonged to Congress, not an executive branch agency. In its February 2001 decision, the U.S. Supreme Court ruled in favor of the EPA; the case was remanded to the U.S. Court of Appeals, which supported the more stringent air-quality health standards in 2002. The importance of the case lies in the fact that it took five years for the legal fight to be decided.[76]

Similarly, federal agencies can rely upon the judicial arena to force compliance. In *Michigan* v. *EPA*, the U.S. Court of Appeals ruled in favor of the agency's attempts to enforce requirements that twenty-two state implementation plans be revised to show efforts to reduce nitrogen dioxide emissions in order to mitigate nonattainment of ozone standards in downwind states, an issue discussed further in Chapter 8. Northeastern states had previously complained to the EPA that they were unable to meet National Ambient Air Quality Standards due to the interstate transport of pollutants.[77]

Judicial challenges to agency actions have come to dominate the process of issuing regulations, and virtually every major agency decision is highly scrutinized. Regulatory officials must anticipate a lawsuit any time they take an action of any consequence. It is difficult to assess the benefits that have come from more careful agency action when contrasted to the disadvantages of a regulatory process that is slow, expensive, and cumbersome. But some researchers believe that rulemaking increases public participation and agency accountability, despite the complexity of the process.

STATE AND LOCAL POLICYMAKING

For most of the past thirty years, the federal government has been given low marks in its efforts to deal with the most serious environmental problems: water and air pollution, the handling of municipal and hazardous wastes, the protection of endangered species and habitats, and the management of public land resources, from wilderness areas to forests, grazing areas, minerals, and energy. The prevailing pattern has been fragmentation, and efforts to integrate federal, state, and local policymakers have been inconsistent and often unsuccessful.

Beginning in the 1950s, states developed resource management agencies, most often to deal with forests or mining activities on state lands. However, the overall state interest in environmental problems like pollution was minimal. The local government contribution came from concerns about public health and air pollution, a function that local health departments gradually conceded to government scientists. In contrast, jurisdiction over water pollution was taken away from health officials and made a separate agency in most cities.[78]

Federal mandates, which began to proliferate in the late 1960s and 1970s, forced states to create environmental agencies on a single-media basis, such as state air-quality boards or water commissions. It was clear, however, that the federal government expected the states to be the implementing agencies, while the federal agencies provided funds for planning, monitoring, management, and technical studies.[79]

Gradually, three patterns of state initiative emerged. Some states, such as New York and Washington, created "superagencies" or "little EPAs" for purposes of administrative efficiency. In some cases, this was done for political acceptability, rather than to integrate an entire program of environmental management.[80] Minnesota, for example, created its Pollution Control Agency (PCA) in 1967 and shifted responsibility for water pollution control from the state health department to the PCA, giving it air and solid waste authority as well. Most of these consolidated programs include a citizen board, which often comes under criticism because of a perception that its members lack sufficient technical expertise. A second pattern was to create a totally new environmental agency focusing on pollution control. Illinois, for example, created a powerful, full-time, five-member Pollution Control Board with a full research staff, the Institute for Environmental Quality. In states like California where environmental issues are highly politicized, the single-media approach still reigns. The California Environmental Protection Agency was created in 1991 by executive order of the governor. Although the Cabinet-level agency is ostensibly charged with coordinating the deployment of state resources, it maintains six boards, departments, and offices for air quality, pesticide regulation, toxic-substances control, waste management, environmental health, and water resources. The heads of each agency are frequently selected not so much for their technical background as for their partisanship, and as a result, leadership changes hands with the election of a new governor and party.

As the technical competence of state government grows, so too has an "environmental presence" that some business and industry interests find unacceptable. They sometimes turn to the federal government for regulatory relief and federal preemption of state authority.[81] The New Federalism, which actually began with the State and Local Fiscal Assistance Act of 1972, is exemplified by the Reagan administration's philosophy of "getting government off the backs of the people."[82] Reagan's belief in a reduction in the scope of federal activity, privatization, and the devolution of policy and fiscal responsibility to the states resulted in an EPA unwilling to serve as policy initiator or congressional advocate. To fill that void, state officials began to band together to lobby collectively.

During the 1980s, states were characterized as somewhat passive in their environmental leadership, with implementation of the 1986 Superfund amendments often cited as an example. One study found very low levels of compliance with the law, with some states in complete ignorance of the requirements of the statute.[83] However, other researchers have concluded that there is an "unevenness" in compliance with environmental regulations for a number of reasons, and that states are now taking a much more active role than they did during the 1980s and early 1990s. Among the reasons used to explain why some states approach environmental protection more comprehensively than others is the "severity argument"—that those states with the most concentrated population growth and urbanization (and therefore the most severe pollution problems) take the most active role in dealing with them. This may also be tied to states where the environmental movement has been strong and has pressured local officials to enact environmental regulations more stringent than those of the federal or state government, as is the case in several Western states.

The "wealth argument" states that there is a direct relationship between the state's resource base and its commitment to environmental protection. States with budget surpluses or other resources may use those funds directly for environmental mandates, as compared to states where monies are extremely limited and where environmental problems compete with issues like education, crime control, and health care. The "partisanship argument" is that states with a Democratic-leaning legislature are more likely to work toward environmental protection than are those that are Republican-controlled.[84]

California, which has been at the forefront of state-level environmental initiatives, has moved forward on policies ranging from integrating its waste-management programs to establishing air-quality standards that go beyond EPA rules. It has been proactive in developing new programs as well. For instance, in August 2004, Governor Arnold Schwarzenegger unveiled a new plan to encourage installation of solar panel systems on 1 million new and existing homes by 2017. "The proposal is about smart, innovative, and environmentally friendly technologies that will help improve the state's ability to meet peak electricity demand while cutting energy costs for homeowners for years to come," the governor said.[85]

Despite efforts at developing cooperative arrangements between what the federal government wants states to do and what states are willing or able to do, there is still a need for strong federal oversight and funding. Without the presence of the federal government, states' willingness to implement environmental programs does vary dramatically. When policy cues involve highly detailed, domain-specific knowledge, vertical or "picket fence" federalism may develop vertical working relationships. Coercive controls, in contrast, appear to be the least effective approach for federal officials attempting to secure compliance.[86]

The other layer of government that has had an impact on environmental policymaking is local government, especially on the issue of global climate change, discussed in more detail in Chapter 10. Mayors have led the way on reductions of greenhouse gas emissions in their communities, committing their cities to a 7 percent reduction below 1990 levels by the year 2012. The lead organization in this effort has been the U.S. Conference of Mayors, whose Climate Protection Agreement was endorsed by the group in June 2005.

Local government participation is characterized by policy entrepreneurs—individuals who recognize the opportunity for bringing an issue to the policy agenda just when the timing is right to do so. Former Seattle mayor Greg Nickels, who launched the Mayors' Climate Protection Agreement, has noted that global warming is also "local" warming. On the same day that the Kyoto Protocol took effect in 141 countries that ratified it, February 16, 2005, he challenged mayors across the country to join Seattle in taking local action to reduce global warming. On March 30, 2005, ten mayors representing more than 3 million Americans agreed to do so.

Former mayor Rocky Anderson of Salt Lake City, Utah, initiated the Salt Lake City Green program to slash the city's own greenhouse gas emissions to 21 percent below 2001 levels by 2012; the city exceeded that goal by reducing emissions to 31 percent below 2001 levels by 2007. The city began with retrofitting lighting in public buildings, replacing incandescent bulbs with compact fluorescent bulbs, saving $33,000 a year in electricity. Those cost savings allowed Salt Lake City to become the state's largest purchaser of wind power, actions that reduced carbon dioxide emissions by more than 1,100 tons. Even more effective in reducing greenhouse gases was the city's decision to capture and utilize methane from its wastewater-treatment plant and its landfill, generating electricity and reducing carbon dioxide through the use of a cogeneration plant. In the transportation sector, the city built a green-certified intermodal hub where all modes of transportation come together at one place in the city. Future buildings owned or managed by the city must be certified to meet environmental standards. Anderson has noted that although these types of efforts are economically beneficial, there is still a belief among some local government leaders that good environmental practices run counter to good business practices.[87]

Other mayors have jumped on the green bandwagon, making it appear that there is a virtual race to see who can be the greenest of them all. While Chicago mayor Richard Daley announced that his city would be the greenest in America by planting trees, fast-tracking green buildings, and creating more rooftop gardens, New York mayor Michael Bloomberg announced that his city would become the greenest by becoming the leader in reducing greenhouse gases. Cities of all sizes have made commitments to set their own targets for reducing carbon dioxide emissions, increasing the use of nonautomobile transportation, installing solar panels on both public and private buildings, and taking steps that outpace anything the federal government has done.

What remains to be determined is what the appropriate balance for responsibility among the federal, state, and local governments ought to be. Clearly, some issues, such as water and air pollution, cross boundaries and are unlikely to be solved by unilateral state actions. Waste-management sites, in contrast, are located in local jurisdictions but are governed by federal Superfund legislation.[88] Other problems, such as global climate change, are believed to be better solved by a national approach, something that has not been accomplished under previous administrations.

Some scholars feel that states are the home of policy innovation because they have greater flexibility than do local governments or the federal bureaucracy. Environmental groups have turned to the states out of frustration with congressional gridlock, and to the courts when all else fails. Under the Clinton administration's National Environmental Performance Partnership Program (NEPPS), efforts were made to substantially reform the federal–state relationship in environmental policy in 1995. Through grants and specific goals, NEPPS was designed to focus on environmental improvement, with states given some flexibility to determine how to meet goals under a results-oriented policy. But the program has been given mixed grades, with analysts concluding that there were few real gains.[89]

Under the Obama administration, it is likely that this devolution of environmental policymaking will continue, perhaps shadowing the efforts of the Clinton administration. If local governments and states can prove their ability to meet specific goals, such as reductions in carbon dioxide emissions or compliance with air-quality standards, the federal government may continue the process of providing grants and technical assistance in further efforts to meet national goals through a different kind of federalism than was in existence during the Bush administration.

FURTHER READING

Elizabeth Berry. *Obama's Motley Crew*. Raleigh, NC: LuLu.com.

Albert Breton, Giorgio Brosio, Silvana Dalmazzone, and Giovanna Garrone, eds. *Governing the Environment: Salient Institutional Issues*. Cheltenham, UK: Edward Elgar Publishing, 2009.

Frans H. J. M. Coenen. *Public Participation and Better Environmental Decisions: The Promise and Limits of Participatory Processes for the Quality of Environmentally Related Decision-Making*. New York: Springer, 2008.

Jeffrey E. Cohen. *Going Local: Presidential Leadership in the Post-Broadcast Age*. Cambridge, UK: Cambridge University Press, 2009.

Scott A. Fritsch and Sean O. Kelly. *Jimmy Carter and the Water Wars: Presidential Influence and the Politics of Pork*. Amherst, NY: Cambria Press, 2008.

Christopher McGrory Klyza and David J. Sousa. *American Environmental Policy 1990–2006*. Cambridge, MA: MIT Press, 2008.

Oran R. Young, Leslie A. King, and Heike Schroeder, eds. *Institutions and Environmental Change*. Cambridge, MA: MIT Press, 2008.

4

The Lands Debate

"Afghanistan will become again the tourist destination for
Central Asia, for Americans, Europeans, for people of the
world. You can hold me to that. In five years. You can grab
me by the tie and hold me to it."
— PRINCE MOSTAPHA ZAHER, DIRECTOR, AFGHANISTAN NATIONAL
ENVIRONMENTAL PROTECTION AGENCY[1]

On June 18, 2009, Ambassador Karl Eikenberry was in Band-e-Amir, Afghanistan, sitting in a swan-shaped paddleboat on one of the area's six mountain lakes, about 140 miles from Kabul. The former three-star U.S. Army general cruised quietly across the still waters as various Afghan leaders joined him in a dedication ceremony that was both symbolic and pragmatic. According to an ancient legend, Imam Ali, son-in-law of the prophet Mohammed, used magic to build the dams connecting the lakes, and prayed in the nearby valley. Until 1996, when the Taliban took control of the area, located in Bamiyan Province, the region was the most popular tourist area in the country. It was best known for two huge statues of Buddha that had been carved into the red cliffs 1,500 years ago, when the region was known as a center of Buddhist pilgrimage in a land that is now under Muslim rule. But under the Taliban, elders had proclaimed that the two statues, which were 180 and 121 feet tall, were idols that were forbidden under Sharia law, and that they must be destroyed. In March 2001, Taliban militants used dynamite to blast the statues into millions of stone fragments, mostly destroying the site that some considered one of the wonders of the world. The United Nations designated the Bamiyan ruins as an endangered World Heritage site in 2003, and in 2009, with almost $1 million in U.S. aid, the lakes and cliffs became Afghanistan's first national park.

Band-e-Amir was supposed to have become a national park in the 1960s, but history and violence intervened. It was not until after the two statues were destroyed that the rest of the world seemed to recognize the need for some sort of protective status for the land. The World Conservation Society helped to identify the park's boundaries, working with Afghanistan's National Environmental Protection Agency (NEPA) to try to protect the remaining wildlife, many of which have already been lost. A recent survey found that the region is home to ibex, wolves, foxes, a type of small sheep called the *urial*, smaller mammals, fish, and bird species such as the Afghan snow finch, the only bird found exclusively in Afghanistan. Many of the fish that used to be found in the six deep lakes have been killed by men blasting the pristine waters with hand grenades.[2] But the head of NEPA sees the potential of the park, which is now a ten-hour drive for those willing to ignore U.S. State Department warnings or occasional sectarian violence to visit the site. As the head of NEPA sees it, gesturing at the red cliffs, "Look at this. It is poetry for the eyes. Poetry for the soul. Poetry for the spirit."[3]

His words might have been spoken in the United States nearly 150 years ago, at the same time American explorers and artists were seeing the beauty of the American West. They, too, experienced a reverence for the land and felt the need to preserve both its scenic beauty and the animals that inhabited it. Expeditions in the Montana territories in 1869 and 1870 marveled at what they termed "curiosities" and "wonders," proposing that instead of being divided up by land speculators, the areas surrounding the geysers and hot springs become a great national park.[4] Their appreciation for the sights they encountered, publicized in a series of articles in *The New York Times* and in *Scribner's Monthly*, led to public support for what Congress would designate as the first U.S. national park, Yellowstone, in 1872.

This chapter examines the public lands, and the controversies that surround them, from several perspectives. First, there is an overview of the scope of the public lands that make up the U.S. public domain, followed by a summary of the issues facing the nation's protected areas and national parks. Second, there is an explanation of U.S. forest policy and the most recent efforts to deal with the mounting cost of fighting wildfires. The section that follows covers wilderness and the battle over the designation of roadless areas, and a summary of the issues related to grazing rights and mining on public lands. The chapter then moves to a discussion of state and local land use regulations, and trends in U.S. land management.

THE PUBLIC LANDS

Today, the total area of the United States is 2.3 billion acres. When the United States was in its infancy, "public lands" referred to the area between the

Appalachian Mountains and the Mississippi River that were held by seven of the original thirteen colonies—the land-claim states. In 1780, New York agreed to surrender its claim to the unsettled territory in order to persuade Maryland to sign the Articles of Confederation, deeding it to the federal government and creating the first land considered part of the "public domain." By 1802, the public domain consisted of over 1.8 billion acres.

The government, however, was not interested in being in the land business. Soldiers who served in the Revolutionary War were given land instead of monetary compensation; other parcels were sold to raise revenue for the new nation. Millions of acres were sold to private owners under the Ordinance of 1785, which allowed the sale of parcels of land to the highest bidder at a minimum price of $1 per acre, with a 640-acre minimum. In 1812, the General Land Office took over the administration of the land disposal process, and Congress aided the effort through passage of the Armed Occupation Law of 1842, which gave 160 acres of land in exchange for fighting the Native Americans in Florida. Couples willing to settle in "Oregon Country" could receive 640 acres. From 1812 until 1946, the General Land Office sold or gave away over 1 billion acres of public land, including 132 million acres granted to railroads.[5]

The federal government slowed its marketing approach to public land, however, when it established Yellowstone National Park. This shift in both attitude and policy—from selling land to preserving it—was mainly the result of the Progressive Era and the pleas of Thoreau and Emerson for government intervention to protect natural areas. Under growing pressure from the conservation movement, Congress began to tighten up the government's somewhat cavalier attitude toward land in the public domain. With passage of the 1891 Forest Reserve Act (repealed in 1907), the federal government began to set aside forest land to protect future timber supplies. The American Antiquities Act of 1906 gave the president authority to withdraw federal lands from settlement and development if they had national or historic interest, and the 1920 Mineral Leasing Act authorized leases, rather than outright sales, of public lands for extraction of oil, gas, coal, and other minerals.

Today, the federal government holds responsibility for managing over 650 million acres of public lands. The Bureau of Land Management (BLM) manages nearly half the public domain (261 million surface acres, a total area nearly as large as Oregon and California combined), of which over 88 million acres are in Alaska. Most of the rest of the BLM lands are in eleven Western states, and the following six states each have more than 100,000 acres: Alabama, Arkansas, Louisiana, Minnesota, South Dakota, and Wisconsin. The U.S. Forest Service (USFS) is responsible for another 192 million acres, 141 million of them in the West. Other public domain lands are the responsibility of the U.S. Fish and Wildlife Service (93 million) and the National Park Service (NPS) (83 million); the remainder is administered by other federal agencies like the Department of Defense.

A parallel system to agency management is the National Landscape Conservation System (NLCS), initially established in 2000 by Secretary of the Interior Bruce Babbitt. However, because he did so without congressional designation, the system's status could be reversed at any time. President Barack Obama

TABLE 4.1   The National Landscape Conservation System (2009)

Category	Number	BLM Acres
Monuments and National Conservation Areas	37	9,364,387
Wilderness Areas and Study Areas	767	21,452,505
Wild and Scenic Rivers	67	1,164,894
National Historic and Scenic Trails	15	

SOURCE: Bureau of Land Management. "NLCS Summary Tables." http://www.blm.gov/wo/st/en/prog/blm_special_areas/NLCS/summary. Accessed August 24, 2009.

formalized the NLCS in 2009 under the Omnibus Public Land Management Act, providing a framework for managing specially designated conservation areas as part of the BLM's multiple-use mission. The new law combined over 1.2 million acres of newly designated conservation area lands, adding to the existing NLCS units of national monuments, wilderness, wild and scenic rivers, historic and scenic trails, as seen in Table 4.1.

The new designations for the NLCS included 26 miles of California's Amargos Wild and Scenic River, 9 miles of the Pacific Northwest National Scenic Trail in Washington, and 209,610 acres of the Dominguez-Escalante National Conservation Area in Colorado. Despite the protective labels, the NCLS lands are threatened and being rapidly degraded, according to a 2009 study by the Sonoran Institute, one of the groups that lobbied for the inclusion of the NCLS in the omnibus legislation. It reported that the "crown jewel" lands of the system are under siege due to growth and development, vandalism, illegal off-highway driving, poor staffing, and a lack of oversight. There is only one BLM ranger assigned for every 200,000 acres of land, with total funding in 2007 for all NCLS units amounting to only $2 per acre. "When you consider that almost 22 million people in the West live within 25 miles of BLM lands today, it underscores how woefully inadequate current staffing and funding plans are to truly protect these amazing landscapes and culturally rich areas."[6]

The formalization of the NCLS was supported by dozens of environmental organizations, including the umbrella group the Conservation System Alliance, a coalition of seventy-four recreational, environmental, religious, and other groups who pushed the measure along with the Bush administration. Opposition to the designation was scant and scattered, with no major efforts to block the law. Even the Blue Ribbon Coalition, which promotes enhanced access to public lands but opposed the NCLS, did not actively fight it since the group hoped passage of the omnibus law would increase federal spending on BLM lands.[7]

One reason why public lands face such daunting challenges is that each agency has its own clientele, some of which overlap, and its own agenda regarding how it implements federal law. The conflicts created by shared jurisdiction are epitomized by the term *multiple use*, which refers to those federal lands that have been designated for a variety of purposes, ranging from grazing to recreation. By its very name, a multiple-use designation means that groups compete for the permitted right to use the land. A second component of the multiple-use policy is sustained yield, which means that no more forage or timber may be harvested than can be produced.

Several legislative efforts demonstrate the government's continued commitment to the multiple-use concept. Congress enacted the Multiple Use Sustained Yield Act (MUSYA) of 1960 and, four years later, the Classification and Multiple Use Act. These two pieces of legislation recognized that land held within the public domain might be used for activities other than logging and grazing, although the laws were minimally successful in changing patterns of use that had existed for decades. When the Federal Land Policy and Management Act was enacted in 1976, it reiterated the government's position on multiple use. The legislation required full public participation in land-management decisions and specified that all public lands under federal management were to continue under federal ownership unless their sale was in the national interest. Critics of multiple use, however, call the policy a charade, arguing that it is a smokescreen used by the federal government to justify the exploitation of public lands and resources by favored commodity interests.[8]

"THE BEST IDEA AMERICA EVER HAD":
THE NATIONAL PARKS

In the policy process, one of the most difficult tasks is finding a way to stimulate government to take action; equally perplexing is the question of why some problems are acted upon while others are not. Policy scholars believe that, oftentimes, government does not take action until the public considers a situation troubling or it causes discontent. If the public thinks that a condition is normal, inevitable, or its own responsibility, then nothing is likely to happen because that condition is not perceived as a problem. Conditions do not become public problems until they are defined as such, articulated by someone, and then brought to the attention of government.

Such is the case for America's national park system. Early naturalists and explorers of the West sought some form of preservation for the scenic wonders they discovered in the latter half of the nineteenth century. Led by John Muir, preservationists believed that only by setting aside areas of wilderness where no commercial or industrial activity was permitted could their value be preserved forever. But historians note that although there is a mythological aura to the telling of the national park story, reality actually has its roots in the efforts of the Northern Pacific Railroad Company to monopolize tourist traffic into the area that is now Yellowstone. Company officials, like other railroad entrepreneurs, wanted to prevent private land claims and limit competition for tourism, while establishing trade corridors for themselves. Tourism emerged in the nineteenth century "as an economic land use attractive to business investment. The success of such investment depended in part on the preservation of scenery through prevention of haphazard tourism development and other invasive commercial uses such as mining and lumbering."[9]

When President Woodrow Wilson signed the National Park Service Act in 1916, he brought thirty-six national parks under a single federal agency, in what was termed by former British ambassador to the United States James Bryce "the best idea America ever had." The concept of a national park has now been copied by more than 120 other nations worldwide. But the popularity of the idea has also led to a tremendous amount of fragmentation. Congress has enacted legislation that creates myriad numbers and types of designations, most of which are under NPS authority but some of which have been managed with other federal agencies. This fragmentation is illustrated in Table 4.2.

Fragmentation in management and administration is complicated by the varying sizes of sites within the NPS system, from the largest area, Wrangell–St. Elias National Park and Preserve in Alaska (13.2 million acres) to the smallest unit, the Thaddeus Kosciuszko National Memorial in Pennsylvania (0.02 acre). The agency is attempting to channel increasingly limited funds to an increasing number of properties, creating a deferred maintenance backlog of between $9 billion and $11 billion. In addition, the NPS faces the threat of climate change, according to a 2009 report from the Natural Resources Defense Council and the Rocky Mountain Climate Organization. The report notes that climate change poses "an immediate threat to America's recreational, historical, and scenic gems," and that some parks may simply disappear in whole or in part (due to sea level rise) if greenhouse gas emissions are not reduced significantly.[10]

Because legislative bodies are asked to deal with thousands of policy problems each year, only a small fraction of them will receive serious consideration. Because of limitations on their time and resources, policymakers will choose to act on only a few problems, which then constitute the policy agenda. When there is substantial disagreement over the best solution to a problem, as is the case with the national parks, policymakers may choose not to put the item on the agenda, deciding instead to deal with other priorities or issues for which the choices are clearer.

Funding decisions may be based on many different factors, such as the political clout of an individual legislator, pressures from affected stakeholders, media coverage of a problem in a particular park unit, or the recommendations of the NPS itself. Nonprofit organizations that lend financial support to the national park may make recommendations on what projects should be prioritized, but park staff may not always agree. In some cases, where public funding is unavailable, private groups may choose to work in conjunction with the NPS to complete a project. In Yosemite National Park, for instance, there was virtual agreement that major improvements were needed at the base of Yosemite Falls. Exhaust from diesel tourist buses, a lack of parking space for cars, degraded landscape, insufficient signage, and accessibility were obvious problems. Over the year, visitors had created their own trails, destroying vital habitat and watershed areas in an effort to get closer to the falls or to take photographs.

The nonprofit Yosemite Fund successfully raised over $13.5 million from 14,500 contributors over an eight-year campaign to create a fifty-two-acre visitor area at Yosemite Falls. The largest public–private partnership in the park's history, the project is one of about 250 funded by the organization since it was created in 1988, contributing over $50 million to research, infrastructure repair,

TABLE 4.2 **Designation of National Park System Units**

NPS Unit	Description	Examples
National park	Large places with a variety of attributes, including historic assets	Bryce Canyon (UT), Grand Canyon (AZ)
National monument	Places on government lands designated by the president with historic or scientific interest	Fort Pulaski (GA), Statue of Liberty (NY)
National preserve	Areas with characteristics of the national parks, but where Congress has permitted hunting, trapping, and oil and/or gas exploration and extraction	Big Cypress (FL), Tallgrass Prairie (KS)
National historic site	A single historical feature associated with its subject	Ford's Theater (D.C.), Vanderbilt Mansion (NY)
National historical park	Historic parks that extend beyond single properties or buildings	Chaco Culture (NM), San Antonio Missions (TX)
National memorial	A site commemorative of a historic person or episode	Lincoln Boyhood (IN), National World War II Memorial (D.C.)
National battlefield	Parklands including sites, parks, and military parks	Manassas (VA)
National recreation area	Sites focused on water-based recreation or near major population areas	Chattahoochee River (GA), Whiskeytown (CA)
National seashore	Sites on the U.S. coast	Cape Cod (MA), Cape Hatteras (NC)
National lakeshore	Lakeshore sites that are all located on the Great Lakes	Sleeping Bear Dunes (MI), Apostle Islands (WI)
National river	Includes major waterways, recreation areas along rivers, and wild and scenic rivers	Mississippi River (MS), Bluestone (WV)
National parkway	Roadways intended for scenic motoring and the parkland paralleling the roadway	Blue Ridge (SC), Natchez Trace
National scenic trail	Lengthy, multistate linear parklands authorized under the National Trails System Act of 1968	Appalachian, Potomac Heritage
Other designations (examples)	The White House Poplar Grove (national cemetery) City of Rocks National Reserve Ebey's Landing (national historic reserve)	

SOURCE: Adapted from National Park Service. http://www.nps.gov/legacy/nomenclature.html. Accessed October 9, 2009.

restoration, and interpretive outreach.[11] Without support groups, most national parks would be struggling even more than they are now.

Although there is little dispute that the country's existing national park units are in trouble and need vast amounts of additional resources, Congress has been pressured by various types of stakeholders to continue adding more and more lands and historical sites as protected areas. For instance, perceiving a "problem," members of Congress responded to interest groups' lobbying by enacting the 1994 California Desert Protection Act, which created more than 7.5 million acres of federally protected land in the California desert. This was the largest land withdrawal since the Alaska National Interest Lands Conservation Act of 1980 (ANILCA) and the largest wilderness law in any of the lower forty-eight states. The act included the creation of three national parks, totaling nearly 4 million acres: Joshua Tree, Death Valley, and East Mojave. The first two parks had been managed as wilderness areas by the NPS for more than a decade.[12]

U.S. FOREST POLICY

About one-third, or approximately 730 million acres, of U.S. land area is forested; two-thirds of that (about 480 million acres) is considered timberland, capable of growing commercial crops of trees. The federal government owns about 20 percent of those lands; 7 percent is owned by state and local governments, 1 percent by Native American nations, 58 percent by private nonindustrial owners, and 14 percent by the forest industry. American timber management is complex and involves concerns about jobs, economic diversity, endangered species and their habitats, and global warming. At opposite ends in the policy debate are timber companies and environmental groups, with federal agencies caught squarely in the middle.

Federal stewardship of the nation's forest resources can be traced back to 1873, when the American Association for the Advancement of Science petitioned Congress to enact legislation to protect and properly manage U.S. forests. Despite the creation of a special bureau in 1876, timber-management practices were rife with scandal and exploitation. In the late 1890s and early 1900s, the Cornell School of Forestry engaged in intensive logging, called *clear-cutting*, in the Adirondacks, where virtually every tree was cut down and removed. The forest-products industry was criticized for its cut-and-run practices of stripping timber, abandoning the land, and quickly moving on to other areas where trees were plentiful. The result was soil degradation, flooding, and the loss of wildlife habitat.

Forest policy was truncated by a division of responsibility between the commodity-oriented Division of Forestry (in the Department of Agriculture) and the General Land Office (in the Department of the Interior). In 1901, the Division of Forestry changed its name, becoming the Bureau of Forestry; four years later, it became the Forest Service. From 1910 to 1928, the agency concerned itself primarily with fire prevention and control, and Congress had little power over forests on private lands.[13]

It was not until the Forest Service gradually began increasing the harvest of national forest land after World War II that the agency became the target of

Another View, Another Voice: George B. Hartzog Jr.

Often called "the man behind the scenery," George Hartzog Jr. served as the seventh director of the NPS from 1964 to 1973. The emphasis, perhaps, should be on "service," since much of his career with the agency was spent on three goals: expanding the system to save important areas before they were lost; making the system relevant to an urban society; and opening positions to people who had not previously had much access to them, especially minorities and women. Under his leadership, the NPS saw the largest expansion of the national parks in its history, adding sixty-nine units.

He was born in 1920 in Smoaks, South Carolina, brought up in poverty, and able to attend only one semester at Wofford College in South Carolina, leaving school to help support his family. He worked in gas stations and hotels until he got a job as a law clerk in Walterboro, South Carolina. Studying on his own, he was admitted to the South Carolina Bar in 1942 without attending a single day of law school. After World War II, he went to Washington, D.C., and served as an attorney for the General Land Office, then transferred to the NPS in 1945. He also returned to college at American University in Washington, D.C., graduating with a Bachelor of Science degree in 1953. He was appointed superintendent for the Jefferson National Expansion Memorial in 1959, and he left the agency briefly in 1962 to become executive director of Downtown St. Louis, Inc. He returned to the NPS as associate director in 1963, becoming director a year later under Secretary of the Interior Stewart L. Udall.

As director, Hartzog's vision for the agency matched that of President Lyndon B. Johnson, under whom he served. Johnson saw a Great Society; more than 2.7 million acres were added to the NPS during Hartzog's tenure, many of them in urban areas, including the Gateway National Recreation Area in New York and the Golden Gate National Recreation Area in San Francisco. He was a proponent of the 1966 Historic Preservation Act, expanding the NPS's mission from wilderness preservation to create the National Register of Historic Places. He created the proposal for, and shepherded through Congress, the Volunteers in Parks Program, and initiated the Bring Parks to People program, the Summer in the Parks program, and the Parks for All Seasons programs. He also expanded the NPS environmental education curricula, and developed partnerships between the parks and public schools and civic organizations. One of his greatest achievements may be an amendment he initiated to the Alaska Native Claims Settlement Act of 1971, reserving a selection of 80 million acres of National Interest land from State and Native Interest lands for possible addition to the national park system. From these and other lands, in 1980, Congress more than doubled the size of the national park system, adding more than 43 million acres.

In 1969, when President Richard Nixon cut the NPS budget, Hartzog made an unprecedented move, closing all of the national parks, including the Grand Canyon and the Washington Monument, for two days a week. "Even my own staff thought I was crazy," he said. Because of the public backlash against the parks' closing, Congress restored the funding for the agency. The action exemplifies the leadership of the man credited with being the greatest director in the National Park Service's history, except for the two founders, Horace Albright and Stephen Mather. He died at age eighty-eight in 2008, one of the unsung heroes of the preservation movement in the United States

SOURCES:
"George B. Hartzog, Jr. – The Man." http://www.hehd.clemson.edu/PRTM/Hartzog. Accessed June 11, 2009.
Matt Schudel. "Obituary, George B. Hartzog, Jr., 88." *The Washington Post.* July 6, 2009. http://www.washingtonpost.com/wp-dyn/content/article/2008/07/05/AR2008070501577.html. Accessed June 11, 2009.
National Park Service. "George B. Hartzog, Jr." http://www.nps.gov/history/history/online_books/director/hartzog.pdf. Accessed June 11, 2009.

environmental interests. The need for timber that resulted from postwar economic growth conflicted with public demand for recreational use of the nation's forests. Congress perceived the Forest Service as a commodity and income-producing agency, and timber harvests increased from 3.5 to 8.3 billion board feet during the decade of the 1950s.[14] In addition to competing public pressures, the development of a comprehensive federal forest policy was thwarted by the lack of congressional direction other than broad mandates. As a result, the Forest Service operated under the dual traditions of planning—utilitarian and protective—that were the legacy of its first chief, Gifford Pinchot, who believed that wise use and preservation of forest resources were compatible goals. The resulting policy—multiple use—meant that the national forests were to serve competing interests: ranchers seeking land for grazing their livestock, recreational visitors seeking to spend their leisure time outdoors, and miners hoping to make their fortunes on as-yet-undiscovered lodes.

Policy was also affected by the postwar increase in leisure time, when Americans began driving to national forests in an increasing number of automobiles over newly improved highways. Over a seventy-year period from 1924 to 1994, with an exception during the 1980s, recreational visits to national forests exceeded those of the national parks. The concept of multiple use began pitting recreationists and those desiring a wilderness experience against other users, such as livestock owners, timber companies, and mining interests. The passage of MUSYA in 1960 gave the Forest Service discretion over how best to manage the national forests by balancing the interests of competing stakeholders. Congress followed with another major statute, the Wilderness Act, in 1964, designating more than 9 million acres of public land the National Wilderness Preservation System, which has grown to over 100 million acres as a result of the Alaska National Interest Lands Conservation Act.

The transformation of forest policy in the 1970s has been said to have five fundamental components: the emergence of the organized environmental movement, the enactment of new laws like the Forest and Rangeland Renewable Resources Planning Act (RPA) of 1974 and the National Forest Management Act (NFMA) of 1976, the expansion of congressional control over policy through specific statutory provisions, increased judicial scrutiny of administrative actions, and increased public participation through formal procedural avenues—creating what one scholar has called a "pluralist forest regime." Critics argued that the Forest Service was out of step with the emerging ethic of environmentalism, and the agency became perceived as an enemy of the people. Congressional leaders began to recognize the growing criticism over the federal government's lack of long-term planning, and the increasing polarization of forestry issues between the timber industry and environmental groups. Both the RPA and its amendments (the NFMA) provided the Forest Service with some direction, requiring inventories of forest resources and an assessment of the costs and benefits of meeting the nation's forest resource needs.[15]

Although the legislation satisfied some critics, forest policy was far from complete, and the agency came under fire from its own employees, who alleged the Forest Service had been captured by timber interests and was inconsistent in its implementation of the law. In 1988, former staffer Jeff DeBonis founded a group called the Association of Forest Service Employees for Environmental Ethics (AFSEEE) as a way of encouraging its members to speak out against agency policies and abuses. The organization began as an in-house protest against the Forest Service policy of clear-cutting—the logging of all trees within a given stand.

The practice, in addition to being aesthetically unpleasing, often leads to erosion, and has been widely criticized by environmental groups. DeBonis's organization marked one of the first times government employees had rallied against a particular cause, although some observers felt his actions were not constructive, given the Forest Service's history of institutional loyalty.[16] But DeBonis and his group believed the agency had forgotten its mission of serving the public and had become totally politicized.[17]

Current forest policy evolved from battles between environmental groups and timber companies during the 1980s, when the Reagan and Bush administrations supported massive logging in the Pacific Northwest. At one point, more than 5 million board feet of timber were being cut per year in Washington and Oregon.[18] The most heavily logged areas were also home to several endangered or threatened species, including the northern spotted owl. In 1991, a federal judge ordered a ban on logging until a species recovery plan for the bird was adopted. The controversy continued for two more years until 1993, when the Clinton administration brought the parties together in an attempt to work out a compromise. The result was the Northwest Forest Plan, an ecosystem management proposal that covered 24 million acres of forest in three states. Under the proposal, up to 1.1 million board feet of timber could be harvested, allowing some mills to continue operation. The program has now entered into the policy implementation stage. The Forest Ecosystem Management Assessment Team, a group of more than 100 scientists, has been given responsibility for coordinating the plan. Their efforts are complicated because over the last century, logging has been conducted in a haphazard manner that has created a patchwork of heavily logged and reforested areas throughout the region. Full implementation means tying these patches of land together while balancing timber harvests and ecosystem protection.[19]

Many environmental organization leaders believe the plan has been a failure, charging that old-growth forests far from urban political constituencies have been heavily logged. There is also criticism that, at least initially, the program did not adequately protect key watersheds, approximately 8 million acres of which are within the boundaries covered by the plan. Supporters, however, argue that the new timber regulations immediately reduced logging 80 to 85 percent below levels of the 1980s—a change few ever imagined would be possible.

FORESTS AND FIRES

The history of U.S. forests has been punctuated by fires, caused both by humans and naturally, as seen in Table 4.3. In 1910, fires burned a forested area about the size of Connecticut, including about 8 million board feet of timber. The fires were economically devastating; eighty-six lives and entire towns were lost, mostly in the West. The newly created Forest Service took on the added responsibility of becoming a firefighting agency, with an objective of spotting and extinguishing every fire before 10 A.M. the next day. Through its Smokey the Bear public-relations campaign, children were taught that "Only YOU can prevent forest fires."[20]

But the unintended consequence of fire-suppression policy was the creation of millions of acres of forests choked with vegetation and small trees with little

T A B L E   4.3   **Historically Significant U.S. Wildland Fires (1825–2010)**

Date	Name	Location	Significance
1825	Miramichi and Maine Fire	New Brunswick/ Maine	3 million acres burned
1871	Peshtigo	Wisconsin/Michigan	3.78 million acres burned; 1,500 deaths
1881	Michigan	Michigan	1 million acres burned; 169 deaths
1902	Yacoult	Washington/Oregon	1 million acres burned; 38 deaths
1910	Great Idaho	Idaho/Montana	3 million acres burned; 85 deaths
1933	Tillamook	Oregon	311,000 acres burned
1987	Siege of '87	California	640,000 acres burned
1988	Yellowstone	Montana/Idaho	1.5 million acres burned
1991	Oakland Hills	California	1,500 acres burned; 25 deaths; 2,900 structures destroyed
1997	Inowak	Alaska	610,000 acres burned
1999	Dunn Glen Complex	Nevada	288,000 acres burned
2000	Cerro Grande	New Mexico	48,000 acres burned; 235 structures destroyed
2002	Rodeo/Chedeski	Arizona	500,000 acres burned
2002	Biscuit	Oregon	500,000 acres burned
2003	Cedar	California	2,400 structures destroyed; 15 lives lost
2004	Taylor Complex	Alaska	1.3 million acres burned
2005	Cave Creek Complex	Arizona	11 structures destroyed; 248,000 acres burned
2006	East Amarillo Complex	Texas	80 structures destroyed; 12 lives lost
2007	Big Turnaround Complex	Georgia	388,000 acres burned
2007	Murphy Complex	Idaho	652,000 acres burned
2007	Witch Creek	California	198,000 acres burned; 1,454 structures destroyed; 2 lives lost
2007	Harris	California	90,440 acres burned; 458 structures destroyed; 10 lives lost
2007	Zaca	California	240,207 acres burned
2008	Montecito Tea	California	1,940 acres burned; 210 structures destroyed
2008	Sayre	California	11,262 acres burned; 630 structures destroyed
2009	Station	California	160,557 acres burned; 209 structures destroyed; 2 lives lost

SOURCES: Adapted from National Interagency Fire Center data. http://www.nifc.gov/fire_info/historical_stats.htm. Accessed October 9, 2009.; and individual wildfire reports.

commercial value. Fires, which had previously been a natural force in thinning forests, were no longer fulfilling that role in the ecosystem; as a result, the dry timber was more fire-prone than ever. Some researchers began warning of the need for ecological restoration, including the use of prescribed burns and some logging, as a way of bringing the forests back to a natural state before suppression was introduced.

Prescribed fire—the deliberate application of fire to wildlands to achieve specific resource-management objectives such as reducing fuel hazards and increasing specific responses from fire-dependent plant species—is just one tool in ecological restoration. William Jordan refers to the concept as the old "notion of helping land recover from the effects of human use" that dates back to biblical times. Jordan, who founded the Society for Ecological Restoration, believes that creating ecosystems for aesthetic purposes is grounded in traditions of landscape design, the pioneering work of Edith Roberts of Vassar College in the 1920s, and landmark work at the University of Wisconsin–Madison Arboretum. He sees restoration as "perhaps one way to resolve the contradiction between community and wilderness—not by keeping them apart but by revealing the wildness at the heart of both."[21]

In 1968, the National Park Service changed its attitude toward fires by adopting a policy to allow "prescribed natural fires"—lightning-caused fires would not be suppressed under certain conditions when officials could control the burning. By the mid-1970s, "fire management" replaced "fire control," due in part to concerns over increasing costs of firefighting. But in 1985, the United States experienced the most severe wildland fire losses of the century up to that point; more than 83,000 fires burned about 3 million acres, destroying or damaging more than 1,400 structures and killing forty-four people.

The use of prescribed burns and the government's evolving fire policies began to change in summer 1988, when people around the world watched in horror as Yellowstone National Park went up in flames. Yellowstone's beauty and resources symbolized what natural parks were all about: tall trees, big mammals, scenic vistas, and open spaces. The fire consumed nearly 1.6 million acres in Montana, Wyoming, and Idaho, as Americans wondered why the federal government did not aggressively pursue the flames in the national park. What began as wonder turned into a public outcry that "indicated public intolerance for widespread use of burning as a tool in areas of high economic and scenic value."[22]

The federal government responded with the Federal Wildland Fire Management Policy and Program Review—an attempt to ensure that policies are uniform and programs are cooperative and cohesive. The policy created an "umbrella" that joined together the Departments of the Interior and Agriculture, together with tribal governments, states, and other jurisdictions with responsibility for the protection and management of natural resources on lands they administer. However, federal officials admit that these efforts must include education efforts to expose the public to accurate information on the environmental, social, and economic benefits that result when prescribed fire is used.[23]

Whatever those benefits might be, the public was unconvinced about the role of prescribed burns in May 2000 when a National Park Service fire got out of control near the town of Los Alamos, New Mexico. The fire started in the Bandelier National Monument and quickly spread to the wildland–urban interface (WUI), a term used to describe the area between natural areas like forests and human development. Other fires later that year burned in interface areas, putting pressure on Congress and the president to take immediate action. The resulting National Fire Plan gave priority to reducing the hazardous fuels that had built up in the WUI, placing an emphasis on community-based approaches and land stewardship contracts. In 2002, the issue gained the attention of the Western Governors' Association (WGA), whose members took the lead in developing a 10-Year Implementation Plan to commit local, state, federal, and nongovernmental organizations to address wildland forest fire and forest health issues.

In 2002—the nation's second-worst fire season—7.1 million acres burned and twenty-one firefighters were killed. Three states—Arizona, Colorado, and Oregon—had their largest-ever wildfires, including the devastating Rodeo/Chedeski Fire in Arizona and the Biscuit Fire in Oregon, each of which burned over 500,000 acres. The 2000 and 2002 fire seasons raised public awareness about the magnitude of the fire problem, deteriorating forests, and the need for fuels reduction to restore forests and protect communities, and opened the policy window for the Bush administration to reshape forest policy.

President Bush stood in the ashes of a fire on Squire Peak in southern Oregon in August 2002, challenging critics of his new Healthy Forests Initiative to "come and stand where I stand. We need to understand if you let kindling build up and there's a lightning strike, you're going to get yourself a big fire."[24] The Healthy Forests Initiative was a blueprint to step up efforts to prevent the damage caused by catastrophic wildfires by expediting procedures for forest thinning and restoration projects. The president charged that current forest policy "is misguided policy. It doesn't work."[25]

Within hours of the announcement, environmental groups were already criticizing the proposal. The Natural Resources Defense Council called it "a smokescreen that misses the target" and "exploits the fear of fires in order to gut environmental protections and boost commercial logging."[26] The Wilderness Society's initial analysis registered concern over the portion of the proposal that would curtail or eliminate administrative appeals and lawsuits challenging fuels treatments and restoration projects.[27] When the president flew to Portland later in the day for a Republican fund-raising event, he was met by several hundred protestors who were angry about the administration's forest policies.

Not surprisingly, timber companies and forestry officials praised the president's announcement. A spokesperson for the American Forest and Paper Association acknowledged that reducing fire danger will cost money and not always produce timber for mills. "This isn't about economics, it's about forest health. You have to value it against what would be lost if you do nothing."[28] The National Association of State Foresters said the initiative was consistent with the goals and objectives of the National Fire Plan, noting, "There is an urgent need for broad-based fuels reduction efforts to prevent another fire season as severe as the one we are experiencing now."[29]

Political supporters of the initiative, such as Idaho governor Dirk Kempthorne, said the president's plan "is just the remedy Idaho and other western states need to reduce the threat of wildfire and protect communities."[30] Governor Bill Owens of Colorado praised the proposals, as did Montana governor Judy Martz, who called for change in the process by which Forest Service projects were developed.[31]

Using both the legislative and regulatory arenas as access points for policy change, the administration delivered a four-part legislative proposal to Congress to "streamline unnecessary red tape that prevents timely and effective implementation of wildfire prevention and forest health projects on public lands." Two of the four proposals called for expediting the reduction of hazardous fuels; a third would repeal the congressional mandate for appeals of Forest Service projects, and the fourth would "establish commonsense rules for courts when deciding on challenges to fuels reduction projects."[32]

Members of Congress responded immediately, with bills designed to implement the Healthy Forests Initiative introduced into both houses. But the pressures of the 2002 elections and the inability to gain consensus for a bipartisan law killed the measures, which were introduced again in the 108th Congress. This time, with the Senate under Republican control and a series of agency reports backing up the need for forest and fire reform, a compromise measure looked promising. Once again, a focusing event made the difference between policy success and failure. A series of wildfires throughout southern California burned hundreds of thousands of acres just as the Senate was deliberating on the Healthy Forests Restoration Act (HFRA); in less than two months, President Bush signed the bill just as Congress went into its holiday recess. Supplementary regulations to implement the legislative provisions continued into 2004 and 2005.[33]

Passage of the HFRA has had a number of spillover effects—a chain of events establishing a principle that guides future policy decisions—that have also changed forest and fire policy. On December 22, 2004, the U.S. Forest Service announced a final rule that drastically altered the implementation of the NFMA. The 1976 law was enacted to control what some considered as out-of-control clear-cut logging on the national forests, and since 1982, Reagan administration regulations have guided the development of forest planning. Although there has been significant criticism of the NFMA, groups like Forest Service Employees for Environmental Ethics have called the rules "moderately effective," noting that annual logging levels on national forests have dropped from 12 billion board feet to about 3 billion board feet.[34]

The new regulations, first proposed in 2002 and effective in January 2005, made broad changes to forest planning procedures, deleting requirements of previous rules to maintain viable populations of plant and animal species and removing detailed procedural requirements concerning species protection. The focus, according to the Forest Service, would make planning more timely, cost-effective, and adaptive.[35] Critics argued that the new Bush administration rules eliminated the environmental "muscle" of predecessor regulations; they not only eliminated limits on clear-cutting and protections for water quality, recreation, or scenery, but also ended public disclosure of the effects a forest plan would have on the environment under NEPA.[36]

Moreover, the strategies used by the Bush administration in gaining support for the Healthy Forests Initiative began to be used in shaping other legislation and rules, from grazing regulations to energy and mining. While most environmental organizations were focused on their opposition to the president's forest initiatives, numerous other rules and regulations were being considered, making it difficult for both supporters and critics to keep up with the barrage of *Federal Register* notices, public hearings, and comment periods.

Several environmental organizations complained that as soon as they finished submitting comments on one rule or environmental impact statement (EIS), they were already behind on several others due at almost the same time. The administration, on the other hand, had the advantage of relying upon different members of Congress and agency officials to shepherd legislation through dozens of hearings that were often held simultaneously or in different regions of the country.[37]

Thus, the perceived rollback in forest policy during the Bush administration was accompanied by a secondary impact—the successful development of political strategies that could also be used in other policy debates.

What is apparent, though, is that the combination of the National Fire Plan and the Healthy Forests Restoration Act have had little impact on hazardous-fuel treatments in the areas that are of particular interest to many policymakers, those within the WUI. These areas, where there has been a dramatic increase in the number of housing units that abut or intermix with wildland vegetation, have also seen a dramatic increase in area burned by wildfire. Over half of the WUI area in the western United States is in forests characterized by high-severity fires that are difficult to control, with the expansion of the WUI resulting in increased wildfire risk to private property. But a 2009 study of the degree to which forest treatments have been located in or adjacent to the WUI found that only 3 percent of the 44,000 total areas treated across the eleven Western states between 2004 and 2008 were within the WUI.[38]

The study's findings are important for policymaking for several reasons. Most of the fuels reduction has taken place in forest ecosystems, but increasingly, human communities in rapidly growing desert exurbs may also be threatened by high-severity wildfire because of the spread of highly combustible invasive plants. Treatments in these areas may also play a key role in fire-mitigation planning. In addition, almost three-quarters of the land within the WUI is privately owned, making it difficult for federal agencies to implement fire-risk reduction treatments in and near communities. As the study's authors note, "Fire mitigation treatments located far from the WUI may play an important role in protecting timber resources and rare or threatened species or ecosystems from high-severity fire, but their effectiveness in direct community protection requires more systematic evaluation. There is strong evidence that the potential for a home to burn is relatively independent of distant wildland-fire behavior. Thus, fire proofing houses and their immediate surroundings should provide the most direct and effective wildfire protection of homes and communities in the WUI."[39] This has implications for not only the over $1 billion spent on fire suppression each year, but also the $2.7 billion spent on fuel treatments between 2001 and 2006. Nine out of ten areas logged for fuel reduction were too far away from human habitation to have much, if any, effect on the wildfire threat to communities.[40] Government may be directing funding at the wrong targets, in the wrong places, without adequate study of where the need and risk are greatest.

WILDERNESS AND ROADLESS AREAS

The development of U.S. wilderness policy is often reduced to the somewhat simplistic battle between the perspectives of Gifford Pinchot and John Muir. In his biography of Pinchot, Char Miller argues that too much has been made of the role of John Muir in protecting American wilderness, as the de facto leader of the preservationist movement, and too little credit given to Pinchot. As the main publicist for what historians call "utilitarian conservationism," Pinchot is sometimes condemned for his failure to embrace the aesthetic conservationists who advocated the maintenance of wilderness as wilderness. Miller believes that Pinchot had an "ability to maintain what might seem to be contradictory impulses—the desire to live simultaneously within and on nature, to exult in its splendors while exploiting its resources."[41]

The preservation of wilderness outlined in Chapter 1 is found in a number of statutory provisions, beginning with the designation of wilderness areas in 1924 under the leadership of Forest Service officials Aldo Leopold and Bob Marshall. The agency began conducting roadless area reviews in 1929 to determine which landscapes should be preserved for back-country recreation and to protect entire ecosystems. After World War II, however, concerns were raised as to how many acres were coming under the protection of wilderness designation, reducing the amount of land available for timber. The forest industry requires an extensive road network in order to both cut and transport logs, with much of the cost subsidized by the Forest Service.

In 1971, the Forest Service conducted a Roadless Area Review and Evaluation (RARE) to determine which wilderness areas within the National Forests might have the potential for road building. Environmental organizations feared that the agency's actions were a preliminary step toward reducing the acreage designated as wilderness, and successfully sued to force the Forest Service to conduct an EIS to identify the impact of any form of development. A second evaluation, RARE II, recommended that 36 million acres of National Forests be opened for logging, grazing, and other resource extraction; but another lawsuit halted any new development within the inventoried roadless areas.

In 1999, the Clinton administration sought to have 58 million acres of roadless National Forests designated as off-limits to future development, raising questions about whether the agency could afford to build more roads in wilderness areas when it already had an estimated $8 billion maintenance backlog for the 380,000-mile road system it manages. Although thirty-eight states and Puerto Rico have inventoried roadless areas within the National Forest system, 97 percent are contained within twelve Western states.

As part of the rulemaking process, the Forest Service held twenty-three public hearings and received over 1.1 million public comments on what would become the 2001 Roadless Area Conservation Rule. It established blanket, nationwide prohibitions limiting timber harvest and road construction or reconstruction within inventoried roadless areas on national forests and grasslands. But the rule's effective date was extended by the incoming Bush administration, and when finally implemented in May 2001, the Secretary of Agriculture announced that amendments to the roadless rule were likely. Later that year, the Forest Service published an Advance Notice of Proposed Rulemaking, requesting public comment on the long-term protection and management of roadless areas.

Meanwhile, a series of lawsuits were filed in federal courts beginning in May 2001, and in April 2003, a court of appeals ruling actually made the rule effective for the first time. The U.S. Department of Agriculture (USDA) announced it would implement the roadless rule, but would propose an amendment to identify how governors might seek relief from the prohibitions of the rule for limited exceptional circumstances in their state. A lawsuit with the state of Alaska was settled in June 2003 to temporarily exempt the Tongass National Forest from the road prohibitions. Then, in July 2003, the U.S. District Court issued a permanent injunction setting aside the roadless rule, finding that it violated the Wilderness Act and NEPA.[42]

In July 2004, while the district court's actions were being appealed, the USDA published a new proposed rule to replace the 2001 version, allowing governors eighteen months to petition for adjustments to management requirements for roadless areas. Public reaction was so extensive that the comment period was extended twice, for a total of 122 days. Finally, on May 5, 2005, the final rule was announced, along with plans for a national advisory committee to assist the USDA in its implementation. Six states submitted petitions before the deadline; five of the six states (California, New Mexico, North Carolina, South Carolina, and Virginia) asked the Secretary of Agriculture to follow the roadless rule in their states. Idaho's petition was for less than one-third of the state's 9.3 million acres. In August 2005, California, Oregon, and New Mexico (later joined by Washington) sued over the state petitions rule, and in September 2006, a federal district court in California enjoined the federal rule, reinstating the 2001 Roadless Rule.[43] The federal government appealed, and in August 2009, the U.S. Court of Appeals for the Ninth Circuit reaffirmed the decision to strike down the Bush administration's efforts to repeal the roadless rule. The justices called the Bush plan "unreasonable" and said that "It was likewise unreasonable for the Forest Service to assert that the environment, [protected] species and their critical habitat would be unaffected" by the move. Earthjustice, one of the groups that had argued the case, said "The court of appeals today affirmed and reinstated throughout the lower forty-eight states the most popular environmental rule of all time. Finally, the Bush administration's attacks on the 2001 Roadless Rule are over, and this administration is now free to pursue President Obama's pledge to 'support and defend' the 2001 rule nationwide."[44] However, the action is anything but final. While the Ninth Court of Appeals was rendering its decision, a parallel 2008 court action by a federal district court judge in

Wyoming invalidated the Clinton roadless rule, and environmental groups appealed that decision to the Tenth Circuit, which has yet to release a decision. In the meantime, Idaho has developed its own rule for roads on forest lands and Colorado is working on a rule, indicating that a clash of circuit courts and state actions is likely to occur.[45]

GRAZING RIGHTS

Cattle became a fixture in the American West long before there were regulations over grazing and public lands. In 1519, Hernando Cortez took the offspring of cattle originally brought to the New World by Columbus to ranches in Mexico. Sometimes roaming wild, the cattle crossed the borders of what would later become Florida, Texas, and California; others were shipped from Europe to New England. By the late nineteenth century, the cattle industry had begun to develop as farms and homesteads were carved out and railroad lines enabled ranchers to get their livestock to market.

Range rules were nonexistent in the emerging nation. Livestock owners strung barbed wire across lands, disregarding public and private land boundaries, and grazing wars broke out between cattlemen and sheepherders over scarce water supplies. By the 1870s, federal rangelands were greatly overgrazed; in 1887, a severe winter, coupled with malnutrition, killed millions of stressed livestock, bankrupting cattle companies that were involved in speculative grazing practices that damaged the lands. Concerns began to grow that grazing interests, along with timber and mining, had monopolized the frontier.[46]

In 1934, Congressional passage of the Taylor Grazing Act established a federal Division of Grazing to work with the General Land Office to establish grazing districts, set fees, and grant permits for use. The two agencies later merged to become the BLM.

Grazing is permitted within national forests, on many national wildlife refuges, and within some national parks. The BLM and the Forest Service administer permits and leases, with fees calculated on the basis of an animal unit month (AUM)—the amount of forage required to feed a cow and her calf, a horse, or five goats or sheep for a month. Access to federal lands is fixed to base property ownership, so that those who own the greatest amount of property get priority for federal grazing privileges. The livestock industry leases an estimated 160 million acres of public lands, mostly in twelve Western states.

The issue of grazing on public lands is complex and polarized, fraught with symbolism, cultural traditions, economics, and environmental concerns. The livestock industry's perspective is best explained through the Colorado-based National Cattlemen's Beef Association (NCBA), which is among the most powerful stakeholders in the debate over public lands grazing. Originally formed as the National Cattlemen's Association, the group focused on deflated grain prices, agricultural legislation like the 1985 Farm Bill, the meatpacking industry, and the declining market share for beef. Gradually, industry leaders realized that by forming a coalition representing the various sectors of the beef market, they would have considerably more political clout. Several groups merged in the mid-1990s—including the Beef Industry Council of the National Livestock and Meat Board, the Beef Promotion and Research Board, the American National CattleWomen, and the U.S. Meat Export Federation—becoming the NCBA.

Ranchers rely on grazing subsidies as a way of providing their industry with a stable source of forage for their livestock. They also believe that public subsidies keep the cost of meat at a reasonable level for consumers and help to sustain the economic base for the rural West. The NCBA notes that more than 90 percent of the land used for grazing throughout the United States is too high, too rough, too wet, or too dry to be used for crops. Using lands for grazing, especially those within the public domain, becomes an important element of local and regional economic vitality. In addition, the NCBA argues, removing the right to graze on public lands would force many livestock producers to reduce their herd numbers, selling their ranch land for conversion to residential development. Livestock ranching becomes, in one sense, a way of maintaining open space and preserving the landscape.[47]

Environmental groups have focused on three primary issues in their attempts to limit or ban livestock grazing on public lands: the subsidizing of the ranching industry, environmental degradation, and the domination of the livestock industry over BLM policy. When the Taylor Act went into effect in 1936, the fee was five cents per AUM, although the Forest Service and the BLM have often differed in the rates they charged. Congress enacted the 1978 Public Rangelands Improvement Act to require a uniform grazing fee, which reached a high of $2.36 per AUM in 1980. The AUM formula continued under a presidential executive order issued in 1986, which stipulates that the grazing fee cannot fall below $1.35 per AUM. The annually adjusted fee is computed by using a 1966 base value of $1.23 for livestock grazing on public lands in sixteen Western states. The figure is then adjusted according to current lease rates for grazing livestock on private lands, beef cattle prices, and the cost of livestock production.

Environmental organizations want the federal government to bring the charges more in line with what it costs to graze animals in the private market, rather than subsidizing ranchers. The direct and indirect cost to taxpayers has been estimated at $130 to $500 million annually, exceeding the estimated revenue from grazing fees (less than $15 million annually).[48] In 2009, the federal grazing fee was $1.35 per AUM for public lands administered by the Bureau of Land Management and $1.35 per head month, a similar calculation for fee purposes. There are an estimated 18,000 grazing permits and leases administered by the BLM and more than 8,000 permits administered by the Forest Service.[49]

In addition to the financial subsidies provided by the federal grazing program, critics point to the ecological damage caused by livestock. Overgrazing is claimed to have led to erosion and stream sedimentation in riparian habitats and to have devastated populations of game birds, songbirds, and fish. In one study, the General Accounting Office (GAO) found that more U.S. plant species are wiped out or endangered by livestock grazing than by any other single factor. Livestock are also major consumers of one of the West's most precious resources—water, which is needed to irrigate hay and other crops. Some groups note that grazing is a major source of nonpoint water pollution. Grazing also forces out populations of wildlife that cannot compete for forage and water.[50]

Environmental advocacy groups have repeatedly criticized the BLM for allowing the cattle industry to dominate the grazing policy debate; one GAO report found that "the BLM is not managing the permittees, rather, permittees are managing the BLM." Occasionally, environmental groups have been successful in forcing the federal government to analyze the impact of grazing, as was the case in 1974 when the Natural Resources Defense Council won a landmark suit that forced the BLM to develop 144 EISs on grazing. But in response, ranchers fought back in a Rocky Mountain West movement during the late 1970s; environmentalists called it "The Great Terrain Robbery," but it is better known as "The Sagebrush Rebellion."

During the late 1970s, several Western groups were formed by conservatives and ranchers dissatisfied with BLM policies. The movement had three objectives: to convince state legislators to pass resolutions demanding that BLM and Forest Service lands be transferred from the federal government to individual states, to create a financial war chest for legal challenges in the federal courts, and to develop a broad public education campaign to get western voters to support the movement. The rebellion was portrayed as a "states' rights" issue, although it became obvious that what the organizers really wanted was to eliminate the federal government from having any say in how ranchers used the land. The Sagebrush Rebellion was the first organized and politically viable challenge to the environmental movement since the early 1950s. One observer, however, believes that although there was a rebellion for a time, only one side showed up to fight.[51]

Contemporary grazing policies have been shaped by Presidents Clinton and Bush, especially under the stewardship of Clinton's Secretary of the Interior Bruce Babbitt. The former Arizona governor found himself in a position to reform grazing policy, and in 1990, 1991, and 1992, the House passed grazing fee increases (as high as $8.70 per AUM). But despite successes in the House, the bills died in the Senate or were stripped from the bills in the conference committees.[52] The Clinton administration then entered the grazing-reform debate through the budget process, proposing to raise the grazing fee from $1.92 to $5.00 per AUM as part of its fiscal stimulation package. Western senators quickly opposed the administration's initiative, and the president just as quickly retreated, dropping his demands for public-land reform and reduction of subsidies.

The failure of congressional reform prompted a series of twenty meetings throughout the West, convened by Secretary Babbitt and others. The meetings culminated in a March 1994 Department of the Interior proposal to raise the grazing fee, broaden public participation in rangeland management, and require environmental improvements on rangelands. The proposal, called Rangeland Reform '94, went into effect in August 1995. Rangeland Reform '94 created Resource Advisory Councils (RACs)—comprised of ranchers, conservationists, and other stakeholders to help create grazing policy—authorized permit holders to not use land for up to ten years for conservation purposes and to graze fewer animals than permitted without losing leases, allowed federal officials to consider a permittee's past performance when determining future permits, required grazing land improvements to be owned by the federal government, raised fees to approximately $3.68 per AUM and subsequent fees to be negotiated, and required changes in grazing practices to ensure recovery and protection of endangered species and protect rangelands. Efforts by opponents in Congress to enact legislation to overturn Rangeland Reform '94 were unsuccessful.

Wise-use advocates had achieved few of their policy goals during Clinton's second term. However, they had successfully placed their concerns on the policy agenda, and federal agencies, environmentalists, and members of Congress were all scrambling to anticipate their attacks on public-lands policy and their defense of the traditional West. But when George W. Bush assumed office, grazing issues appeared to have been pushed further down the agenda, failing to capture the interests of ranchers or environmental groups, who moved on to other issues. A few Bush appointees raised eyebrows and voices, such as William G. Meyers, solicitor for the Department of the Interior, who had formerly worked as a lobbyist for the National Cattlemen's Beef Association and sued unsuccessfully to overturn the Clinton grazing-reform regulations. Grazing interests simmered while many environmental organizations moved on to other initiatives introduced by the Bush administration.

In December 2003, the BLM proposed new grazing regulations the administration said would improve the agency's working relationships with public-land ranchers, conserve rangeland resources, and address legal issues while enhancing administrative efficiency. Six public hearings were held in early 2004; 18,000 public comments were received, and the final rule was announced in June 2005. The new rule gives shared title to future permanent range improvements, such as fences, wells, or pipelines, if they are constructed under a Cooperative Range Improvement Agreement, a provision stemming from the Rangeland Reform '94 regulations. The rule also requires the phasing in of grazing-use decreases or increases of more than 10 percent over a five-year period to allow sufficient time for ranchers to make gradual adjustments in their operations. Existing restrictions that limit temporary nonuse of a grazing permit to three years would be removed, and the BLM would have up to twenty-four months (rather than the start of the next grazing season) for the agency to analyze and formulate an appropriate course of action in cases where grazing practices are at issue and need to be corrected. BLM would no longer be able to issue conservation use permits (purchased primarily by conservation groups to rest the land rather than using it for grazing.)[53]

Environmental advocacy groups made clear their opposition to the new rules, which went into effect in July 2005. "We are disgusted but not surprised by this administration's consistent concern for private economic interests at the expense of public awareness and involvement," said a spokesperson for the Center for Biological Diversity. "These new regulations allow the fox to guard the henhouse, and interested parties are left without recourse as soils, water, vegetation, and imperiled species suffer from the economic exploitation of our public lands."[54]

Critics also assailed provisions in the new rule that would redefine the phrase "interested public" in a way that they believe limits the participation of new residents in an area and removes public involvement from biological assessments and evaluations for wildlife. "The Bush administration is making it clear that they want to take the 'public' out of public lands," the Forest Guardians noted. Others said, "The new regs are an unethical political scam from Interior Department appointees in Washington, D.C. BLM is trying to reverse years of progress on rangeland restoration to serve a handful of cowmen at great cost to the public interest."[55]

The grazing rule came under fire just days after it was announced when two former BLM employees revealed that the EIS they prepared had been altered by the Bush administration. A biologist and hydrologist who had contributed to the EIS said their conclusions that the proposed rules might adversely affect water quality and wildlife, including endangered species, were excised and replaced with language justifying less stringent regulations. The original draft of the EIS warned that the new rules would have a significant adverse impact on wildlife, but that phrase was removed, and the revised version concluded that the grazing regulations would be beneficial to animals. "This is a whitewash, they took all of our science and reversed it 180 degrees," said the biologist, who retired before the rule was finalized. The agency's hydrologist, who also retired before the rule was published, said, "Everything in the report that was purported to be negative was watered down. Instead of saying, in the long-term, this will create problems, it now says, in the long-term, grazing is the best thing since sliced bread."[56]

The BLM's manager for rangeland resources said the report was written by a number of specialists from different offices within the BLM. When it was finished in November 2003, the agency believed it "needed a lot of work. We disagreed with the impact analysis that was originally put forward. There were definitely changes made in the area of impact analysis. We adjusted it."[57]

There is little doubt that, like other Bush administration initiatives, the new grazing rules will affect public-lands ranching, although BLM officials denied that the new provisions were a rollback of the Rangeland Reform '94 provisions that established the twenty-four citizen-based RACs across the West. "The rule will continue to require the Bureau to consult with the interested public in all key matters. Clearly, there is no 'locking out' of the interested public from the BLM's grazing decision making process."[58]

MINING LAW AND PUBLIC LANDS

Decades before land-use issues were on the public's environmental agenda, the discovery of gold in California in 1849 and the subsequent gold rush became the foundation for the nation's mining policies. When California was admitted as a state a year later, the area, which was under control of the military, still had no federal regulation of land use, although miners were officially considered trespassers on public lands. The overriding theme was one of economic liberalism. From 1848 to 1866, the military appears to have ignored mining activities, even though the miners themselves realized that some regulations were necessary to fill the legal vacuum.[59]

Responding to miners' efforts to strengthen property-rights claims yet cause minimal disruption to mining activities, Congress enacted one general mining law in 1866, followed by amendments in 1870 that allowed a person or group to patent up to 160 acres and to purchase the claims for $2.50 an acre. Congress recodified the provisions of the 1866 and 1870 laws with the 1872 Mining Law, later signed by President Ulysses S. Grant. The purpose of the law was simple—to encourage the expansion and settlement of the West. At the time, miners, who were confident of the fortunes that they could make in the largely unexplored Western lands, used pickaxes, shovels, and pans to look for mineral treasures. There was little consideration for the environmental impacts of mining—a problem that developed in the twentieth century as the industry used more highly mechanized equipment and dumped mining waste into rivers and streams.

The 1872 law allows an individual who finds a valuable mineral resource on public lands to obtain a mining claim for the deposit. The individual acquires a possessory interest in the claim, making it a form of transferable property, and thus granting the right to extract, process, and market whatever minerals are found. The holder of the claim may also obtain title to the land on which the claim is located at a nominal cost. The result is that the federal government has only minimal authority to control mining. Subsequent laws have fine-tuned the 1872 act, but the government has generally taken a hands-off attitude when it comes to the mining industry, as seen by the paucity of legislation that has been enacted (see Table 4.4).

In August 1996, the issue resurfaced on the political agenda when Crowne Butte Mines, a subsidiary of a Canadian company, applied to purchase twenty-seven acres of public land near Yellowstone National Park. On the lands was a closed mine that had been used sporadically since the late 1800s. The company would have purchased the land, and the minerals beneath it, for only $135 under the terms of the 1872 law. The property is now estimated to contain

TABLE 4.4   Major U.S. Mining Laws

Year	Law	Provisions
1872	Mining Act	Authorizes and governs prospecting and mining for hard-rock minerals on public lands
1920	Mineral Leasing Act	Authorizes and governs leasing of public lands for development of deposits of coal, oil, gas, sulfur, phosphate, potassium, and sodium
1947	Materials Act	Regulates mineral material disposal
1947	Mineral Leasing Act	Authorizes and governs mineral leasing on acquired lands
1955	Common Varieties Act	Regulates minimal material disposal
1973	Mineral Leasing Act	Amends 1947 law to govern oil and gas leasing on federal lands
1977	Surface Mining Control	Regulates coal mining to prevent contaminants from entering groundwater

$650 million in gold, silver, and copper reserves—revenues on which the company would have paid no royalties whatsoever. Environmental organizations like the National Resources Defense Council (NRDC) were also concerned that the cyanide-based chemical extraction process and use of heavy machinery would cause irreparable damage to the Yellowstone ecosystem.

Instead, the Clinton administration negotiated an agreement to purchase the site in exchange for the surrender of Crowne Butte's mining rights, payment of a cleanup fee of over $22 million, and a land swap giving the company federal land worth $65 million. Despite the publicity surrounding the agreement, Congress still refuses to enact legislation that would provide fair compensation to the taxpayer for the value of minerals extracted from public lands, establish long-term monitoring of all mine sites, and set standards for regulating water quality, with special provisions for environmentally sensitive areas.[60]

In January 2001, the Department of the Interior finalized a regulation that gave the BLM the power to veto proposed mining operations that would do "significant irreparable harm" to public lands. Environmental groups tasted victory, but two months later, Bush administration Secretary of the Interior Gale Norton suspended the rule; and in October 2001, she officially rescinded the BLM's authority. The administration also reversed prior policies that protected tribal lands from mining and approved permits for mining in wilderness areas, ending the string of environmental group success stories and returning power to the mining industry.[61]

Just months later, Norton said she supported making mining companies pay royalties for mining on federal land as part of revisions to the 1872 law. Members of Congress, like Representative Christopher Shays of Connecticut, called the statute a "taxpayer ripoff" that provides insufficient environmental protection. More than 557,000 mines have been deserted since the 1800s, costing taxpayers more than $30 billion in cleanup costs, according to one estimate. Companies like Phelps Dodge, the world's second-largest copper producer, have moved operations to Latin America because of federal regulations; officials for Newmont, the world's largest gold producer, have said they would consider the controversial royalty issue.

These examples illustrate how difficult it can sometimes be to get a problem placed on the policy agenda. Although there is almost total agreement on the need for the General Mining Law to be amended and for appropriate environmental safeguards to be placed on public lands, efforts to do so have been unsuccessful for over a century. Mining policy has not captured the interest of the general public, and a strong lobbying effort by extractive resource industries has put pressure on Congress to leave the law alone. Environmental organizations have focused on other issues while powerful Western lobbyists have kept the law intact.[62]

STATE AND LOCAL LAND USE REGULATION

Historically, land-use designations have been the responsibility of local governments, with zoning ordinances and building codes used to restrict and manage growth and unwanted land use. Although federal statutes do impact land use, such as the Surface Mining Control and Reclamation Act and the Coastal Zone Management Act, local governments, and to a lesser extent, states, have attempted to manage land use since the early twentieth century. Regulation of zoning is largely a response to the increase in population and urbanness, and has been ruled constitutional by the U.S. Supreme Court. In 1916, New York City adopted the first comprehensive municipal zoning ordinance, and in 1926, the court approved a zoning ordinance in Euclid, Ohio, that met the test of being reasonable and clearly related to the public health, safety, morals, and general welfare.[63]

States have been successful in their attempts to manage the development of and protect sensitive areas. California adopted Proposition 20, the Coastal Conservation Initiative, in 1972, creating a state-level coastal commission, which would become the basis for the 1976 California Coastal Act, one of the nation's strictest protection programs. It limits development along the state's coastline, requiring developers to obtain permits that must conform to local coastal protection plans. Maryland adopted a similar program in 1984 to protect Chesapeake Bay, creating a Critical Area Commission to control development in a 1,000-foot buffer zone around the bay. Growth management is also the focus of Oregon's 1973 Comprehensive Growth Management Program, which adopted fourteen statewide planning goals and five additional goals applicable to the Oregon coast and the Willamette River. All cities and counties must adopt comprehensive land-use plans to implement the state plan, and the state's Land Conservation and Development Commission has the authority to require revisions in local plans to make sure they are consistent with statewide goals.

But in November 2004, Oregon's voters revised their position on growth management under controversial Measure 37. It states that a private property owner is entitled to receive just compensation when a land-use regulation restricts the use of the property and reduces its fair market value, known as a *taking*. In lieu of compensation, the measure also provides that the government responsible for the regulation may choose to "remove, modify, or not apply" the regulation. While some advocates argued that Measure 37 was simply a way for individual land owners to build the home of their dreams, others noted that it would bankrupt the state as developers rushed to file claims on land marked for multiple homes, subdivisions, and commercial uses. The law gave state and local government only 180 days to rule on Measure 37 claims, and the state's governor noted that municipalities had neither the staff nor financial resources to pay claimants. More than 7,000 claims, worth more than $1 billion in damages, had been filed within the first two years; governments opted to waive regulations because they were unable to pay the claims against them.[64] Similar statewide propositions heated up the ballot box in California and Washington in 2007, and Oregon voters later approved Measure 49, tightening up the standards for receiving compensation under Measure 37 while further restricting development on agricultural, forest, and rural lands.

Regulatory takings have galvanized private property owners through the United States. These people feel the government has unfairly appropriated their land without paying them for its value. The bases for their position are the Fifth

Amendment to the Constitution, which states that private property may not be taken for public use without just compensation, and a 1922 U.S. Supreme Court case that affirmed the concept of a regulatory "taking."[65] For years, the courts have attempted to interpret the meaning of the amendment, especially in cases where privately owned land was needed for public use, such as the construction of a new freeway. Local governments routinely have condemned houses in the freeway path and paid the owners damages, usually the fair-market value of the homes.

In 1985, University of Chicago law professor Richard Epstein published a controversial book that placed the concept of takings in a regulatory context.[66] Epstein argued that all forms of government regulations are subject to scrutiny under the takings clause, leading advocates of private property rights to demand that the government pay those affected for the loss of the right to use their land, regardless of the reason. These people were joined in their efforts by conservative organizations like the Cato Institute and the Federalist Society, who used the takings and property-rights issue to bolster their attempts to reduce government intervention. Since Epstein's book was published, the concept of takings has been applied to a broad range of environmental legislation, from wilderness and wetlands designations to the protection of endangered species.

Under the Endangered Species Act, for example, the federal government has the power to prevent landowners from altering their property in any way that threatens a species or its habitat. From a legal perspective, the reasoning is that the protection of a species (the common good or public interest) must be weighed against the interest of an individual property owner. Proponents of property rights counter that view by arguing that the government should be prevented from imposing on individual landowners the cost of providing public goods. They cite regulations, such as those restricting development that would adversely affect wetlands, as examples in which individuals are unfairly being asked to give up the use of their land without being compensated for their loss. Other cases have involved the expansion of national park boundaries and wilderness designations or instances where a private property owner's land is appropriated for a wildlife refuge or recreational area. To press their demands upon the political system, individuals with property grievances have joined grassroots organizations like the American Land Rights Association, Defenders of Property Rights, and Stewards of the Range. The groups have attempted to gain media attention for their cause and have sought remedies in both the judicial and legislative arenas.[67]

The Supreme Court has not provided clear guidelines for determining when a taking has occurred and when compensation is due. There is little question that, when the government actually takes possession of land, fair compensation must be awarded the previous owner; the problem comes when government regulation places some limit on how property owners can use their land. The Court's decisions send mixed signals concerning the difference between a compensable taking and a regulation with which property owners must comply. In some cases, if the government requires a physical intrusion, the Court has required compensation. The Court assesses the economic impact of a regulation in determining whether it crosses the line to become a taking. But the justices have been unable to decide on enduring principles. They have devised some criteria for assessing government actions, but the weight given each factor varies from case to case. Many decisions appear to be the result of a judgment about whether the Court concludes that a regulation serves an important public purpose and is valid or whether it is unjustifiably meddling in the affairs of landowners and is a taking.[68] Property-rights activists have also pursued their cause in the U.S. Court of Federal Claims, which hears claims against the U.S. Treasury involving $10,000 or more.

TRENDS IN LAND USE AND MANAGEMENT

Given these examples of current land-use controversies, what does this tell us about trends in how America's land-use policies have developed? First, attitudes about the management of public lands have evolved slowly in the United States, from a policy of divestiture and conservation to one of preservation. Those attitudes reflect the changing public consciousness about the environment, which has had its peaks and valleys throughout U.S. history. When citizens are concerned about land use, they demand to be involved and participate fully. When they are apathetic, decisions get made without them.

Second, land-use policies are tempered by politics. Frustrated by their attempts to influence presidential policymaking, environmental groups have often turned to Congress or the president in hopes of exploiting regional and partisan rivalries. Many of the legislative mandates given to the agencies responsible for land management are vague and often contradictory, and Congress has seldom seemed eager to be more explicit in its direction. This is due partly to congressional sidestepping of many of the more controversial conflicts in resource use. Should deserts be opened up to all-terrain vehicles or left in a pristine condition where no one can enjoy them? Should the national parks be made more accessible so that they can accommodate more visitors, or should traffic be limited to prevent destroying the parks' scenic beauty through overuse? Should governmental regulatory agencies tell private property owners how their land can be used? The answers to those questions depend largely on which member of Congress, in what region of the country, is answering them.

Third, the future of public lands appears to have a price tag attached. Although there is a general sense that Americans want to preserve wilderness areas, scenic wonders, and some historic sites, they become less willing to do so when the decisions directly affect their pocketbooks. They may be willing to pay slightly higher fees to use state or national parks, but they rebel when the choice is between preservation of a single species and putting food on their family's table. As a result, land-use policies are more likely to take into account the economic rather than scientific impact of decisions.

Fourth, decisions about land-use policies are often made in the cloistered setting of administrative hearing rooms, and the hearings are poorly attended by those affected by the decision making process and only marginally publicized. The language of resource management is esoteric, and the science often unsubstantiated. Thus, the debate over the future of public lands has historically been dominated by resource users, such as timber and mining companies. More recently, however, environmental groups have "learned the language" of land and forest management, often hiring former industry experts. Still, most Americans know little about what is happening to the millions of acres still under federal control, and only well-organized groups that closely monitor regulatory actions (most of them based in the West) are in a position to speak for the public interest.

Last, it appears that stakeholders are realizing that no progress can be made as long as they stick to highly adversarial positions. Strategies of coordination and collaboration are becoming the rule rather than the exception, whether they are being used to develop community fire plans or private land trusts.[69] Although these initiatives and mechanisms cannot resolve all land-use conflicts, they represent a change in direction from refusing to come to the table at all to at least taking a look at what is on the menu.

FURTHER READING

Bruce L. Benson, ed. *Property Rights: Eminent Domain and Regulatory Takings Re-examined.* New York: Palgrave McMillan, 2010.

Ellen M. Donaghue and Victoria E. Sturtevant, eds. *Forest Connections: Implications for Research, Management, and Governance.* Washington, DC: Resources for the Future Press, 2008.

Derick Fay and Deborah James, eds. *The Rights and Wrongs of Land Restitution: "Restoring What Was Ours."* New York: Routledge Cavendish, 2008.

Sara E. Jensen and Guy R. McPherson. *Living with Fire: Fire Ecology and Policy for the Twenty-First Century.* Berkeley: University of California Press, 2008.

William R. Lowery. *Repairing Paradise: The Restoration of Nature in America's National Parks.* Washington, DC: Brookings Institution Press, 2009.

P. Michael Saint, Robert J. Flavell, and Patrick F. Fox. *NIMBY Wars: The Politics of Land Use.* Hingham, MA: Saint University Press, 2009.

James R. Skillen. *The Nation's Largest Landlord: The Bureau of Land Management in the American West.* Lawrence: University Press of Kansas, 2009.

Stephen Trimble. *Bargaining for Eden: The Fight for the Last Open Spaces in America.* Berkeley: University of California Press, 2008.

Tom Turner. *Roadless Rules: The Struggle for the Last Wild Forests.* Covelo, CA: Island Press, 2009.

Courtney White. *Revolution on the Range: The Rise of a New Ranch in the American West.* Covelo, CA: Island Press, 2008.

5

Waste and Toxics

"It seems like TVA is just throwing darts at the problem, and they don't have a clue how to really fix it."
— DONALD SMITH, RESIDENT NEAR THE KINGSTON FOSSIL PLANT
IN HARRIMAN, TENNESSEE[1]

On December 22, 2009, an earthen dike, or surface impoundment, containing 5.4 million cubic yards of wet coal ash sludge failed in Roane County, Tennessee. The dike at the Kingston Fossil Plant, adjacent to the Emory River and near a residential area, destroyed three houses and flooded more than 300 acres of land. A study by the Tennessee Valley Authority (TVA), which operates the electrical generating plant, found that river water near the spill area contained elevated levels of lead and thallium, substances known to cause birth defects and nervous and reproductive system disorders. Several miles downstream, the river study showed that iron and manganese content exceeded the secondary drinking water standards of the Environmental Protection Agency (EPA). The Tennessee Department of Environment and Conservation released a statement saying that there was no risk unless the coal ash was ingested.[2]

Further tests by the EPA showed that drinking water from the Kingston Water Treatment Plant, downstream of the coal ash spill, did meet drinking water standards, as did 100 private wells that were tested. The TVA also measured windblown ash, finding that more than 25,000 air samples measured below federal levels for particle matter.[3] Residents, however, were not convinced, questioning whether there would be a health hazard once the mud dried out. "There are huge health concerns," noted one resident who was worried about the future of the coal ash spill. "It's going to get in our house. We're going to breathe it. It would be like walking through a dust bowl, and we don't know what is in the dust."[4]

Meanwhile, citizens in rural Perry County, Alabama, began to question the safety of the 8,500 tons of coal ash brought each day by train from Tennessee to the Arrowhead Landfill near where they live. Eventually, 3 million cubic yards of the ash will be brought to the landfill, adding more than $3 million to the county's current $4.5 million budget. The county, whose residents are very poor and 70 percent black, has an unemployment rate of 17 percent, and a third of all households are below the federal poverty line. The work at the landfill has brought in thirty new jobs for local residents. The Arrowhead site was chosen, officials say, because the ash could be brought in by train instead of trucks, because the facility underbid competitors, and because it was large enough to accept all of the ash.[5]

Supporters argue that the money from handling the coal ash will allow Perry County to fund its schools, build roads, and do things it could not have done without the influx of fees from the operation. But critics charge that the residents are being taken advantage of and that there is no plan if something goes wrong. A local newspaper columnist summed up his feelings about concerns over public health and safety: "I won't feel comfortable until I see a delegation from EPA and TVA standing on the courthouse square, each member stirring a heaping spoonful of this coal ash into a glass of Tennessee river water this stuff has already fallen into, and gargling with it."[6]

The job of cleaning up humanity's mess, whether it be household garbage or coal ash from utility power plants, has become a more visible and acute problem on the environmental policy agenda. In years past, the issue has literally and figuratively been buried at the bottom of the pile of environmental problems facing policymakers. Historically, we have simply covered up the refuse of life with dirt or dumped it where it was out of sight (and out of mind). Now, old habits are coming back to haunt us as we produce more waste than ever before and run out of places to put it.

This chapter explores the management of waste and the strategies that are being developed to try to deal with this ongoing, highly politicized, and increasingly global problem. The discussion begins by identifying the various types of waste produced and the attempts that have been made to deal with it, including municipal solid waste. The main focus of the chapter is an analysis of the regulatory framework of waste management and the role of different levels of government that are grappling with a growing problem that has fewer resources for its solution. Two key statutes are analyzed: the Resource Conservation and Recovery Act (RCRA) and the Comprehensive Environmental Response, Compensation, and Liability Act (CERCLA), along with the Brownfields Prevention Initiative under RCRA. Separate sections deal with the policy issue of nuclear waste resulting from civilian use and from the military's attempt to dispose of nuclear weapons. The chapter concludes with an overview of the global waste mess, shipbreaking, and a discussion about the creation of international regimes to control hazardous-waste trade.

THE NATURE OF WASTE: FROM GENERATION TO DISPOSAL

Historians who have studied human development note that there has not always been a refuse problem, at least not of the magnitude seen in modern times. Garbage is primarily an urban issue, exacerbated by limited space and dense populations. It must also be perceived as having a negative effect on human life, or else it is viewed as an annoyance rather than as a health or environmental problem. Such a transition of perception occurred in the United States between 1880 and 1920, when the "garbage nuisance" was first recognized. City dwellers could no longer ignore the piles of garbage and the manure from horse-drawn streetcars that covered sidewalks and streets and polluted local waterways. A sense of community responsibility evolved as citizens developed an awareness of doing something about the problem. Garbage was seen not only as a health issue but also as an aesthetic one, because it detracted from the overall attractiveness of city living. Gradually, municipal governments developed street-cleaning and disposal programs (controlled by health officials and representatives of civic organizations) to begin dealing with the massive wastes generated by a growing industrial society.[7]

Just before the turn of the century, the United States imported one of the most common European methods of waste disposal—the "destructor," or garbage furnace. The British, with insufficient cheap land or water as dumping areas, had turned to incineration, which was hailed as a waste panacea. Cities throughout the United States quickly installed incinerators, while researchers continued to experiment with other European technologies such as extracting oil and other by-products through the compression of city garbage. During the first quarter of the twentieth century, the emphasis was on waste elimination, with little thought given to controlling the generation of waste. After the 1970s, however, the growth of the American economy changed the refuse situation with a dramatic increase in the manufacture of packaging materials—plastics, paper, and synthetics—that became a part of the waste stream. This not only increased the amount of waste but posed new collection and disposal problems for local governments. One researcher estimates that solid waste increased about five times as rapidly as population increased after World War I. The most dramatic change in the composition of waste was the massive increase in the proportion of paper, which by 1975 accounted for nearly half of all municipal refuse. This increase is attributed to rampant consumerism during the 1970s, which fostered a boom in the packaging industry.[8] An even more pervasive waste problem emerged after World Wars I and II with the tremendous increase in chemical products, which were being discharged into the air, water, and land.

THE UNIVERSE OF WASTES

Waste is a generic term used to describe material that has no obvious or significant economic or other benefit to humans. Waste includes five major categories of materials that differ in their physical properties and origins.

The largest component of the waste stream is industrial waste, which is non-hazardous and is generated by activities such as manufacturing, mining, coal combustion, and oil and gas production. It makes up nearly 94 percent of the waste universe. The second-largest segment—about 5 percent—is hazardous waste, which is primarily generated by industry and meets a specific legal definition. It comes under federal regulations because it poses a serious threat to human health or the environment if not handled properly. Sometimes the terms *toxic waste* and *hazardous waste* are used interchangeably, but this is not technically correct. *Toxicity* refers to a substance's ability to cause harm, and thus all waste could conceivably come under that definition. Because some wastes present only a minimal amount of harm if stored or disposed of properly, they are not considered hazardous. To be considered *hazardous*, waste must meet four criteria: the potential to ignite or cause a fire; the potential to corrode; the potential to explode or generate poisonous gases; and the capacity to be sufficiently toxic to health. Federal regulations also classify as "hazardous" any other wastes mixed with hazardous waste, as well as by-products of the treatment of hazardous waste.

The problem of handling hazardous waste has become acute because waste-generating industries in the past were often unaware of or unconcerned about the potential toxic effects of hazardous waste. Dangerous chemicals may percolate from holding ponds into underlying groundwater or wash over the ground into surface water and wetlands. Some hazardous waste evaporates into the air or explodes; other types soak into the soil and contaminate the ground, and some forms bioaccumulate in plants and animals that might be consumed later by humans. Typical hazardous wastes include dioxin, petroleum, lead, and asbestos.

The third category of waste, composing about 1 percent, is municipal solid waste (MSW), the garbage and trash generated by households, offices, and similar facilities. Americans deserve their reputation for being a "throwaway society"; the amount of trash produced per person per day in the United States has jumped from 2.68 pounds in 1960 to 4.62 pounds in 2007, the most recent year for which figures are available. [9] By weight, most MSW consists of containers and packaging (33 percent), followed by yard trimmings and food scraps (25 percent); plastics (12 percent); metals (8 percent); rubber, leather, and textiles (almost 8 percent); wood (6 percent); and glass (5 percent), with other miscellaneous wastes making up about 3 percent of the MSW generated in 2008, as seen in Figure 5.1. Overall, MSW generation grew from 88.1 million tons in 1960 to 121.1 million tons in 1970, 151.6 million tons in 1980, 205.2 million tons in

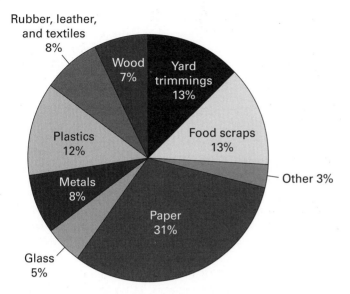

FIGURE 5.1 Municipal Solid Waste Generation (2008)

SOURCE: U.S. Environmental Protection Agency. "Executive Summary: Municipal Solid Waste Generation, Recycling, and Disposal in the United States: Facts and Figures for 2008." http://www.epa.gov/osw/nonhaz/municipal/pubs/msw2008rpt. pdf. Accessed January 5, 2010.

1990, 234 million tons in 2000, and 254 million tons in 2007.[10] The EPA had previously predicted that 216 million tons would be generated by 2000, and 250 million tons by 2010—figures that clearly underestimated Americans' ability to produce trash.

The last two components of the waste stream are medical and radioactive wastes, each of which makes up less than one-tenth of 1 percent of the waste stream. Hospitals and other medical and dental facilities generate more than a half-million tons per year of waste that must be specially managed.[11] This type of waste gained attention in the late 1980s, when miles of beaches in New Jersey and New York had to be closed because improperly handled syringes and vials of blood began washing ashore, raising fears about the spread of acquired immuno-deficiency syndrome (AIDS).

Radioactive waste includes fuel used in nuclear reactors, spent fuel from weapons production, and mill tailings from the processing of uranium ore. This category also includes substances that have become contaminated by radiation, either directly or accidentally.

DISPOSING OF THE PROBLEM

Primitive cultures had an easy answer to disposal—they simply left what needed to be disposed where they had created it. Leftover or spoiled food and excre-ment were allowed to rot on the ground, where they naturally decomposed and returned to the earth as fertilizing compost, completing the naturally occurring ecological cycle. Aside from odors and foraging wildlife, waste did not pose much of a problem until it got in the way of other human activities. As the population grew, people began to burn their waste or bury it in the ground—practices that have remained unchanged throughout most of our history. The method of disposal now used depends largely on what type of waste is being managed, as the following overview indicates.

Burial and Landfills

Dumping and burial have been among the most common ways of disposing of municipal waste, although communities have developed sanitary landfills as a way of avoiding the environmental problems caused by burial. The number of landfills declined as the federal government began regulating waste disposal in the 1960s; the number dropped further in 1979, when the EPA issued minimum criteria for landfill management. One of the biggest concerns about landfill operations has been pollution; because most landfills accept whatever household garbage is collected by waste haulers, there is often little screening of what gets dumped. As a result, landfills may contain a variety of substances, including paints, solvents, and toxic chemicals, that residents routinely put into their curbside trash. In older landfills, leachate (formed when water from rain or the waste itself percolates through the landfill) sometimes seeps into the ground, polluting the surrounding groundwater. Today's sanitary landfills, in contrast, are located on land where the risk of seepage is minimal, and most facilities are lined with layers of clay and plastic. A complex series of pipes and pumping equipment collects and distills the leachate and vents flammable methane gas, which is formed by the decomposition of waste. Many landfills now recover the gas and distribute it to customers or use it to generate electricity.

Historically, the key criterion for landfill operation was accessibility; but that gradually changed to a goal of minimizing health risks. In the 1930s, the United States switched from open dumping to using sanitary landfills, where waste is compacted and buried. Most cities established their landfills in the most inexpensive and accessible land available—typically a gravel pit or wetland—paying little attention to environmental considerations. With the advent of the environmental movement in the 1960s and 1970s, planners began to consider whether a proposed site was near a residential area, was susceptible to natural phenomena such as earthquakes or flooding, or was a potential threat to water quality; they also considered the hauling distance from where the refuse was collected.

In the 1980s, considerable attention was focused on the problem of landfill capacity. Projections warned that only 20 percent of the landfills in operation in 1986 would be open in the year 2008, despite increasing amounts of waste. Due to this shortage of landfill space, the cost of disposal rose astronomically. The shortage occurred because the criteria for what becomes an acceptable disposal site changed, making it difficult to increase both the number and capacity of burial facilities. Disposal costs today increase by as much as a dollar per ton for every mile the garbage is transported. Today's landfill operations are tightly regulated by federal restrictions that govern the location, design, operating and

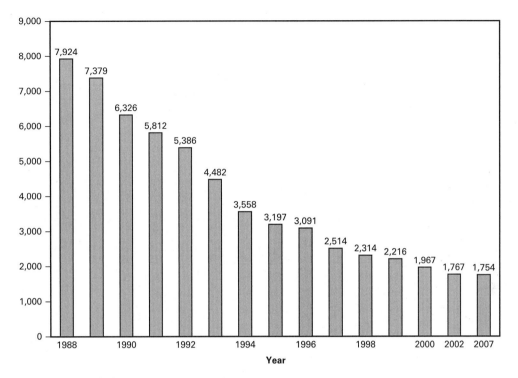

FIGURE 5.2 U.S. Landfills (1988–2007)

SOURCE: U.S. Environmental Protection Agency. "Municipal Solid Waste in the United States, 2007 Facts and Figures." http://www.epa.gov/waste/nonhaz/municipal/pubs/msw07-rpt.pdf. Accessed December 22, 2009.

closure requirements, and cleanup standards for existing contamination. It is important to note that many of those restrictions were added only because of political pressure from environmental organizations. The number of MSW landfills has decreased substantially, from almost 8,000 in 1988 to 1,754 in 2007, as seen in Figure 5.2. About 54 percent of MSW was disposed of in landfills in 2007, and the percentage of MSW going to landfills continues to decrease as other disposal methods increase.

Incineration

Many European nations have been successful at instituting waste-incineration programs to deal with municipal waste. Their modern facilities produce minimal levels of visible emissions and have the added advantage of generating energy while reducing the amount of waste by up to 90 percent in volume and 75 percent in weight.

In contrast, since the first garbage furnace was installed in 1885 on Governor's Island, New York, the United States has been unsuccessful in convincing both policymakers and citizens of the acceptability of incineration as a disposal method. Since the 1980s, most facilities incorporate recovery of an energy product (waste-to-energy, or WTE) such as steam or electricity; as of 2000, there were 102 facilities, but the number had decreased to 87 by 2007, mostly in the northeast United States.[12]

Incineration was initially used as a disposal method because it was considered the most sanitary and economical method available. Modifications of the European technology proved ineffective, however, for U.S. needs. Sanitation engineers became critical of incineration facilities, which often produced gas and smoke emissions because the waste was not completely burned when furnace temperatures were lowered to save on fuel consumption. Beyond their design and operational problems, many incinerators were built by unscrupulous or inexperienced companies; by 1909, 102 of the 180 furnaces erected between 1885 and 1908 had been abandoned or dismantled. Later adaptations of English technology produced a second generation of incinerators, and the facilities flourished until the 1960s. At that point, concerns about air pollution surfaced, and cities such as Los Angeles began to legislate against incinerators, setting standards so high that they virtually outlawed the plants. Although the technology was available to increase efficiency and reduce polluting emissions, the cost of upgrading equipment was high in comparison to disposal in sanitary landfills.

There is still some support for incineration as a concept, especially among those who note the advantage of reducing the volume of waste or of using the incinerator's capacity as an energy generator. Critics argue that even with improved technology, many facilities have suffered from mechanical breakdowns and costly repairs. Attempts to transfer European incineration technology to the United States have often been unsuccessful because American trash contains considerably more plastic that, when burned, produces toxic gases and leads to corrosion of equipment. Even plants that run efficiently are being closely scrutinized for adverse health effects. Environmental groups have raised questions about the toxicity of both the gases and the ash produced by the combustion process.

Despite these objections and problems, officials are taking a second look at waste-to-energy plants for MSW. Most of the plants are called "mass burn" facilities because they use unsegregated waste as a fuel, producing electricity that can then be sold to customers. Refuse-derived fuel plants remove materials that can be recycled from the waste stream, such as plastics and glass, and shred the remaining components, which are then burned in boilers. They have several advantages over other municipal disposal options because they require no change in waste collection patterns, their management can be turned over to a private owner if desired, low-cost financing mechanisms are available, and the market for the electricity they produce is guaranteed under the 1978 Public Utilities Regulatory Policies Act.

Public opposition to incineration has proved to be the most formidable barrier to siting any new facilities, thus ending projects throughout the United States—from the Los Angeles City Energy Recovery (LANCER) facility in Los Angeles to the Brooklyn Navy Yard, where opponents promised to block a proposed incinerator with their bodies. New Jersey residents even rejected a referendum on the state's ballot over an incinerator that had been planned and approved for a decade. Political leaders have found the topic so volatile that it has created an acronym of its own—NIMTOO—for "not in my term of office." The phrase refers to the virtual paralysis over waste-management decision making that keeps municipal officials from approving incineration projects in favor of more expensive disposal solutions. The situation is different from that in Europe, where incineration has been more widely accepted. The difference lies perhaps in the contrast of political systems. Nations like Denmark and Germany have a strong history of centralized decision making, which precludes the kinds of public participation and access to the legal system that allows citizens in the United States to have such an impact on decisions, including the siting of hazardous-waste facilities.

Ocean Dumping

The dumping of wastes into the ocean is one of the few disposal methods that has received almost universal condemnation. Initial objections to the practice were not necessarily environmental—too much of the garbage dumped off the New York coast in the early 1900s floated back to shore. The practice was also considered too costly, because barges had to tow the garbage to deep water to keep it from floating back to the surface and washing up on local beaches. As downstream cities filed lawsuits against upstream cities, the legal ramifications of dumping municipal waste into waterways limited the practice as well. Burial of waste seemed much more attractive and inexpensive to early sanitation engineers by the 1920s. In 1933, New Jersey coastal cities went to court to force New York City to halt ocean dumping. The U.S. Supreme Court affirmed a ruling in 1934, when the practice of ocean dumping of MSW ceased as a major means of disposal.

The Supreme Court ruling applied only to municipal waste, and the ocean dumping of industrial and commercial waste continued unabated. Over the course of the 1960s, an estimated 50 million tons of waste were dumped into the ocean, most of it off the East Coast, where the rate doubled between 1959 and 1968. In the mid-1970s, nearly 120 ocean sites for waste disposal were supervised by the U.S. Coast Guard. Of particular concern has been the use of ocean dumping for toxic wastes. Not until passage of the Marine Protection, Research, and Sanctuaries Act in 1972 was there a federal effort to stop the practice. In 1988, the Ocean Dumping Ban Act restricted offshore dumping of sewage sludge and other wastes.

The ocean depths have also been considered as sites for the burial of radioactive waste; for more than a dozen years, the United States was part of an eight-nation, $100 million research effort that had considerable scientific support. But the issue was so politically sensitive that the research program was cut off as Congress turned its focus to geological storage.

Recycling

The terms *recycling* and *recovery* refer to the reuse of materials. A majority of waste-management analysts believe recycling represents one of the most underused yet promising strategies for waste disposal. There are two aspects of recycling: primary recycling, in which the original material is made back into the same material and is also recyclable (such as newspapers back into newspapers); and secondary recycling, in which products are made into other products that may or may not be recyclable (such as cereal boxes made out of wastepaper). Recycling gained acceptance in the early 1970s as the public became more aware of the garbage crisis, the need to conserve natural resources, and the shortage of landfill space. About 7 percent of the MSW was recovered in the 1960s and 1970s; the amount then increased to nearly 10 percent in 1980, and 14 percent by 1990. In 2007, recycling and composting increased to over 33 percent, diverting more than 85 million tons from disposal.[13]

Recycling can involve both curbside recyclables collection and materials recovery facilities (MRFs). There were an estimated 8,650 curbside programs in operation in the U.S. in 2007,[14] with the most extensive programs in the Northeast, as shown in Table 5.1.

Composting has grown as a method of disposing of certain segments of the MSW stream, such as food scraps, yard trimmings, and other organic materials, from residential, commercial, and institutional sources. In 2007, over 3,500 community composting programs were operating, in addition to individual citizens doing backyard composting. Between 1960 and 1990, the amount of MSW recovered for composting was negligible; by 2007, nearly 21 million tons were being composted.[15]

Recycling is actually less an environmental issue than it is an extremely volatile economic supply-and-demand issue. A shortage of markets for recycled goods represents the biggest obstacle to this waste-management approach. During the early 1970s, recycling gained acceptance not only in the public's mind but economically as well. Rising costs of land disposal and incineration made recycling a booming business. Junked autos, worthless a few years before, were bringing up to $50 each, and prices for copper scrap rose 100 percent. Lead batteries became profitable recycling targets when the price of battery lead rose fourfold. Under President Richard Nixon, the federal government considered providing tax credits and direct cash subsidies to encourage the sale of recycled materials; but a 1974 EPA report recommended that such incentives were

TABLE 5.1   Curbside Recyclables Collection Programs (2007)

Region	Number of Programs	Percent of Population Served
Northeast	3,299	84%
South	797	30%
Midwest	3,749	61%
West	814	76%
Total	8,659	59%

SOURCE: U.S. Environmental Protection Agency. "Municipal Solid Waste Generation, Recycling, and Disposal in the United States: Facts and Figures for 2007." http://www.epa.gov/waste/nonhaz/municipal/pubs/msw07-fs.pdf. Accessed October 26, 2009.

unnecessary, because demand for recycling was high and prices were rising. Some states sought their own forms of monetary incentives—for example, Oregon, which pioneered a bottle-deposit law in 1972. The federal subsidy and incentive concepts never gained acceptance in Congress, however, and were not revived by President Gerald Ford when he assumed office after Nixon's resignation.

Unfortunately for the future of recycling, prices collapsed in 1974 as quickly as they had risen, with wastepaper prices dropping from $60 per ton in March 1974 to $5 by mid-1975. In the late 1980s and early 1990s, supplies of newspapers, cans, plastic, and glass began to pile up when communities and individuals believed they might be able to squeeze cash from trash, even when there were few markets for recycled goods. As demand for recycled goods increased, "recycling bandits" in some communities were taking newspapers out of curbside containers in the middle of the night or yanking them out of landfills.

The EPA's most recent recycling report found that the highest rate of recovery was in the category of containers and packaging (42.7 percent), followed by nondurable goods such as plastics, rubber, leather, and textiles (35 percent), and durable goods such as steel, glass, and wood at 17.6 percent. Among the most recovered products in 2007 were lead-acid batteries (99 percent), major appliances (67.1 percent), corrugated boxes (73.6 percent), newspapers (77.8 percent), steel packaging (64.6 percent), and aluminum cans (48.6 percent).[16]

Recycling can be made more attractive to both consumers and recyclers in several ways. The most obvious is to boost the demand to create an appetite for the swollen supply of materials, or apply sanctions against those who use virgin material. In 1992, for example, the federal government took the incentive route by directing its agencies to purchase environmentally sound supplies, including those made of recycled materials, and several states have enacted similar legislation. Other approaches have included providing tax incentives for new recycling operations, mandating commercial recycling, and recycling organic waste. Nearly every state requires newspaper publishers to use some recycled fiber in their paper. Others have invested money into facilities that turn old newspapers into usable pulp in a process called *de-inking*, so publishers have pushed their suppliers to increase demand.

Is recycling a viable waste disposal alternative in the United States? Recycling programs here have not been nearly as successful as programs in other parts of the world. Even though they do not produce nearly the amounts of waste that the United States does, other countries much more commonly use recycling. Deposits on beverage containers are almost universally used, and more reverse vending machines (where returned containers are accepted) are common in Europe. In Ireland, consumers are charged a small fee (equivalent to about five cents U.S.) for each grocery bag the store must provide, and recycling bins are commonly placed at tourist attractions. Source separation programs are in place throughout Western Europe and Japan, and even in developing nations like Egypt and Thailand, institutionalized scavenging and recycling programs are fully operational.

In Cairo, for instance, the Zabbaleen Environment and Development Program, initiated in 1981, combined the city's municipal sanitation department with a traditional, private-sector program that transports thousands of tons of solid waste to the city's fringe, where it is sorted and recycled. Two historically poor groups, the Waahis and the Zabbaleen, now work with nongovernmental organizations to improve living conditions for the trash pickers and foragers, who are growing in number as desert dwellers move to the city. An estimated 60,000 people in Cairo are supported through waste collection, recycling about 80 to 85 percent of the waste that they collect and diverting it from landfills. Similar programs, although less well-organized, are in place in Brazil, India, and Nepal, although they border on exploitation and face foreign takeovers.[17]

Source Reduction

The EPA first identified source reduction (or waste prevention) as its first preference in the integrated waste-management hierarchy in 1989. This includes the reuse of products and on-site, or backyard, composting of yard trimmings as a way of keeping material out of the waste stream. Source reduction's benefits are threefold. It decreases the amount of waste that must be managed, preserves natural resources, and reduces pollution generated during the manufacturing and packaging process. The Pollution Prevention Act of 1990 required the EPA to develop and implement a strategy to promote source reduction. Source reduction relies largely on behavioral changes, and some corporations have begun to reduce the amount of waste they generate as models for residential consumers.[18] The EPA measures compliance on the basis of practices such as the use of greener materials, such as cleaners and coatings; process changes, such as fume suppressants; work practices; and controls with lighter environmental footprints

Paper versus Plastics

What started in Ireland in 2002 spread to China with the January 10, 2008, announcement that the government has ordered a ban on the production, sale, and use of plastic bags beginning June 1, 2008. The Chinese government's decision comes on the heels of an Earth Day 2007 effort by the Beijing-based Plastic Bags Reduction Network that urged consumers to reduce their plastic bag use by half. Although exact figures are unavailable, Chinese consumers use an estimated 2 to 3 billion of the free plastic shopping bags each year, with about one-fifth of those bags handed out in Beijing. Introduced in China about ten years ago, plastic bags were initially considered a convenience for shoppers, but now they will be sold instead, with some government officials considering fining retailers who give plastic bags away for free.[19]

Worldwatch Institute calls plastic bags "among the most ubiquitous consumer items on Earth." Although no one knows for sure, there are an estimated 4 to 5 trillion nondegradable plastic bags used worldwide each year, with many of them produced in Asia. Most of them are made from petrochemical derivatives that are heated, shaped, flattened into rolls, and then punched out or printed on.

In the United States, where plastic bags were first introduced in 1977, an estimated 100 billion plastic bags are thrown away each year. In 2007,

San Francisco became the first city to outlaw bags at large supermarkets and pharmacies by requiring that the stores provide only recyclable paper bags, compostable plastic bags, or reusable bags, either at no cost or by selling them directly to customers. Another ten cities have adopted bans, but not every municipality has been successful at using negative sanctions like charging a fee for using a noncompostable bag. Seattle initially passed an ordinance to charge consumers twenty cents for each paper or plastic bag used at a supermarket, drug store, or convenience store. But an aggressive effort by the U.S. plastics industry and the American Chemistry Council convinced voters to reject the measure in an all-mail vote in August 2009, despite the fact that supporters said it would encourage the use of more reusable bags and reduce greenhouse-gas emissions. Retailers, including the popular IKEA chain, have tried to encourage shoppers to bring their own bags or else face a five-cent charge on top of their purchase for each one. IKEA, which dropped the price of its reusable Big Blue Bag from ninety-nine cents to fifty-nine cents, said it would donate the first year's proceeds from the sale of its reusable bags in the United States to the conservation group American Forests.

Many of the efforts to reduce plastic-bag use and encourage the use of cloth or other reusable bags have taken place in countries where environmental awareness is already established. Australia's Environment Minister, for instance, said that he hoped to phase out plastic bag use by the end of 2008, and in 2004, New Zealand's government worked with retailers and environmental groups to sign an accord to reduce their use by supermarkets as part of the Make a Difference campaign. The issue has also reached developing countries. Botswana, Rwanda, and Eritrea have imposed bans, and Tanzania has imposed a ban on both the manufacture and import of plastic bags. Before the latest round of political violence there, Kenya was considering a ban, and South Africa, where they are known as the "national flower," banned the thinnest types of bags in January 2002. Other nations, including Papua New Guinea, Bhutan, Zanzibar, Taiwan, and several Indian states now have bans or are considering them. Others, such as Bangladesh, not only impose a ban but have imposed a levy on plastic bags similar to what Ireland has done.

RCRA AND SUPERFUND

Unlike some environmental-protection issues for which the federal government has assumed primary responsibility, waste-management regulations are usually locally enacted and implemented. The issue is complicated because neither policymakers nor the public initially considered waste—especially hazardous waste—to be a serious problem, making it difficult to push the issue onto the policy agenda. Some observers believe that the problem is not garbage per se, but improper management of hazardous waste, litter, and uncontrolled dumping.

Three major pieces of federal legislation underscore the government's hands-off policy toward waste; these laws have placed the problem in the hands of local government. Initially, the focus of regulation was on what was considered the most visible problem—solid waste. In 1965, Congress passed the Solid Waste Disposal Act (SWDA), designed to offer financial and technical assistance to local governments rather than for regulatory purposes. The federal Bureau of Solid Waste Management, housed in the Department of Health, Education, and Welfare, had jurisdiction over solid waste but shared responsibility with the Bureau of Mines in the Department of the Interior. The agencies were underfunded and suffered from heavy personnel turnover; the Bureau of Solid Waste Management moved its headquarters three times in five years. Creation of the Environmental Protection Agency in 1970 led to a consolidation of agency responsibilities, coinciding with the passage of amendments to the SWDA—the Resource Recovery Act of 1970. The legislation authorized a fourteenfold increase in funding, from $17 million to $239 million, for demonstration grants for recycling systems and for studies of methods to encourage resource recovery. The 1970 legislation also provided the foundation for the development of state waste-management programs; by 1975, forty-eight states had developed some form of program, with budgets ranging from zero to $1.2 million. Most of the state waste-management programs were minimal, structuring themselves around the federal support programs rather than using federal assistance to help them develop a more comprehensive effort, and the statute remained essentially nonregulatory.[20]

With the passage of the RCRA in 1976, Congress intruded into what had been essentially local and state jurisdiction.[21] The act required states to develop solid waste–management plans and mandated the closing of all open dumps. The only disposal methods allowed under the legislation were sanitary landfills or recycling, with little attention paid to other potentially effective options such as bottle-deposit or waste-recovery facilities. Another portion of the RCRA dealt with hazardous-waste management, but gave the EPA the responsibility of determining what waste was solid and what waste was hazardous—a task that is not as easy as it might have seemed to Congress at the time the legislation was enacted.

One of the problems faced by some local officials is that there simply is not enough landfill space available in their area to dispose of wastes properly, and despite the RCRA legislation, many states were slow to develop alternatives. Other states have a surplus of landfill capacity. As a result, communities turned to exporting their waste to other states. In a 1978 case involving Philadelphia and New Jersey, the U.S. Supreme Court ruled that attempts by the states to restrict interstate transfers of waste violated the Commerce Clause of the Constitution.[22]

The Supreme Court reiterated that position in two cases in 1992 and two more in 1994; as a result, there was little that states with plenty of landfill space—such as Indiana and New Mexico—could do to stop other states' dumping. Under the Court's ruling, state and local governments cannot ban, impose restrictions on, or place surcharges on solid waste simply on the basis of its origin. Publicly owned facilities, however, can restrict the solid waste that they accept to waste generated within the state.[23]

In the 1980s, Congress seemed to have difficulty developing hazardous-waste legislation that was acceptable to both the industries that produced the waste and the environmental-group supporters who believed the issue was not receiving appropriate attention from federal and state regulators. The 1980 amendments to the RCRA allowed for broad exemptions to what was considered hazardous waste, and another set of amendments in 1984 still failed to remedy earlier deficiencies in the law. The RCRA expired in 1988, with several states still unable to complete the solid waste–management plans required by the 1976 law. Congress chose to rely upon the EPA to "regulate solutions" to hazardous waste, while Congress itself seemed more interested in dealing with MSW problems.[24]

Congressional attempts to pass a sweeping reauthorization of RCRA have been unsuccessful, as the continuing legislative gridlock over solid waste demonstrates. Congress has repeatedly rejected a national bottle-deposit system, avoided the issue of industrial wastes from manufacturing and mining, and rolled back industry-wide recycling rates for paper and plastic. Both business and environmental groups have opposed most reauthorization efforts thus far because proposed legislation neither promotes enough recycling nor creates markets for recycled materials.

Policymaking is often triggered when specific events capture the attention of both the media and the public, and this is especially true of hazardous waste. As discussed in Chapter 1, disclosure of massive contamination at Love Canal in New York, and at a site near Louisville, Kentucky, was the catalyst for a change in the regulatory focus. Citizens began contacting their representatives in Congress, demanding that some form of action be taken, and Congress turned to the EPA for guidance on types of legislative remedies that might be available. Both Congress and the EPA did an environmental policy about-face by shifting their attention from solid to hazardous and toxic waste. Facing political pressures from citizens' groups and public concerns for immediate action shortly after the passage of RCRA in 1976, the EPA's Office of Solid Waste abruptly changed focus. With the election of Ronald Reagan, the federal solid-waste effort was completely eclipsed by hazardous-waste concerns. The EPA's solid-waste budget was reduced from $29 million in 1979, to $16 million in 1981, to $320,000 in 1982; meanwhile, staff was reduced from 128 to 74 in 1981, and 73 of those 74 positions were eliminated in 1982. The RCRA's hazardous-waste provisions require permits for companies storing, treating, or disposing of hazardous waste, and give EPA the authority to levy fines or hold individuals criminally liable for improperly disposed waste. This created a cradle-to-grave program by which EPA regulates hazardous wastes from the time they are generated to the time of disposal.

Abandoned waste sites became an extremely visible problem that forced Congress to revamp the regulatory provisions of the RCRA with the enactment in 1980 of the Comprehensive Environmental Response, Compensation, and Liability Act, more commonly known as "Superfund." The CERCLA legislation initially included a $1.6 billion trust fund authorized over five years to clean up abandoned toxic- and hazardous-waste sites throughout the United States. But further research indicated that the number and magnitude of site cleanups was much larger than originally estimated.[25] Realizing the long-term nature of waste cleanup, Congress reauthorized the program for another five years under the

1986 Superfund Amendments and Reauthorization Act (SARA). Legislators were dissatisfied with the slow pace of cleanup (only six sites had been cleaned up since 1980), so SARA added $8.5 billion to the fund; in 1990, Congress voted to extend CERCLA to September 30, 1994, with another $5.1 billion authorization. Oil and chemical companies were also taxed to augment the congressional appropriation, but that provision of the law was allowed to expire at the end of 1995, further reducing the program's operating budget. Members of Congress were unable to decide the thorny issue of how to finance the program, with debate over how much of a site's cleanup costs should be paid for by government and how much should be paid for by private companies.

Under Superfund, the EPA established a National Priorities List (NPL) of targeted sites in September 1983. The NPL is a relatively small subset of a larger inventory of tens of thousands of potential hazardous-waste sites. Cleanup projects vary considerably from site to site, ranging from an abandoned steel mill to small parcels of land where toxic waste was once stored and leaked into the ground. Most of the sites are landfills, industrial lagoons, and manufacturing sites. In its 2008 Accomplishments Report, the EPA noted that nearly $600 million had been obligated for construction and postconstruction activities and emergency response actions, including more than $55 million for sixteen new projects at fifteen NPL sites.[26]

The agency also notes that it is committed to the concept of "polluter pays," the principle that private parties that engaged in activities that contaminated sites be responsible for their cleanup. In 2008, the EPA secured nearly $1.9 billion to fund cleanup work, with potentially responsible parties (PRPs) agreeing to conduct $1.6 billion in future response work and to reimburse EPA for $232 million in past costs of remediation at Superfund sites. Still, not all new projects ready for construction were funded; nearly 57 percent of Superfund monies went to just seventeen sites.[27]

Most of the nation's hazardous waste is treated or disposed of on-site; only a small percentage is transported off-site for treatment, storage, or disposal. This avoids the problems associated with transporting waste and trying to find a place to take it once it has been removed. Congress also dealt with the cleanup problem under the corrective-action program of the RCRA amendments. The legislation also requires companies that are permitted to operate a hazardous-waste treatment, storage, or disposal facility to be responsible for the cleanup of that facility. Unlike Superfund, where the federal government must find the responsible party, RCRA permittees must themselves submit a cleanup plan.

Underground storage tanks (USTs) present an additional hazardous-waste problem because they may leak and contaminate drinking-water supplies. The United States is estimated to have over 2 million underground tanks that store petroleum and other chemicals, and the EPA estimates that 20 percent of the regulated tanks are leaking or have the potential to leak. Many of the tanks were installed during the 1950s, and their average lifetime use is only fifteen to twenty years. The EPA began regulating the tanks in 1984 under RCRA amendments, requiring owners and operators to meet strict requirements for design, construction, and installation, including repair or closure of systems that do not meet federal guidelines. When the deadline for repairs and replacement of USTs arrived in December 1998, some owners hurriedly tried to replace aging tanks. Thousands of gas stations and other facilities across the United States were forced to close down.

The nation's multiple hazardous-waste programs have come under tremendous criticism from a variety of stakeholders, giving Congress ample reason to avoid or delay reauthorization and providing justification for not increasing the program's budget. In a December 2004 report, EPA projected that as many as 350,000 contaminated sites will require cleanup over the next thirty years under existing regulations, because nearly 10,000 new sites are discovered each year. About 43 percent of the sites involve USTs, and hazardous-waste properties account for another 50 percent; but between the two, they account for only 22 percent of the costs. The remaining 7 percent of sites, including those on the NPL, tend to be larger, more complex, and more costly to remediate, according to the EPA.[28]

Less than 1 percent of the projected average number of sites that would need to be decontaminated by 2033 are part of Superfund, but these would require about 15 percent of the funding. Federal agencies other than the Department of Defense (DOD) and Department of Energy (DOE) have been spending about $200 million annually for site cleanups, but an estimated $21 billion more in cleanup work needs to be done over the next thirty years. The total cost for that period would be $180 to $280 billion.[29]

Another criticism relates to who ought to be responsible for paying for the cleanup. Congress has been divided on the issue of whether to revise the "polluter pays" concept, which involves extensive research and often costly litigation to determine who originally created the waste. Industry has balked at one of the key components of the legislation, known as *joint and several retroactive liability*, which makes polluting companies responsible for the entire cost of cleaning up sites where wastes were dumped decades ago—even if they were responsible for only a portion of the contamination or before dumping was made illegal.

Compensation for individuals seeking to recover damage claims has also been very contentious. Congress continues to be heavily lobbied—a lobbying effort led by the Chemical Manufacturers' Association (CMA)—to make it difficult for an individual to bring legal action against a company believed to be responsible for the improper storage or handling of hazardous waste. Proving that a site caused health problems leads to a complex legal maze from which few plaintiffs successfully emerge. Several obstacles face those victims seeking compensation because of toxic-waste problems, including that many chemical-caused illnesses have a long latency period (perhaps twenty to thirty years) that makes assessment of the effects of exposure difficult. Some state laws mandate that the statute of limitations begins with the first date of exposure, limiting claims by those exposed over a long period of time. In addition, hazardous-waste injuries require potential claimants to submit to (and pay for) sophisticated and expensive medical and toxicological testing, and to pay legal fees that may extend for years. Class-action suits are difficult to pursue because even if a group of workers were exposed to a chemical hazard, the effects on one worker, a forty-year-old male, are likely to be considerably different from the effects on a twenty-something female of childbearing age. Not surprisingly, potential industrial defendants have opposed attempts to legislate ways of easing the compensation process.

One of the most visible legal actions has been pursued against W. R. Grace Company for its actions at a vermiculite mine in Libby, Montana. In February 2005, federal prosecutors charged the company and seven high-ranking employees with releasing cancer-causing asbestos into the air and trying to hide the danger to workers and local residents. The indictment also accused the company and officials of trying to obstruct EPA efforts to investigate the extent of asbestos contamination in Libby, along with wire fraud and violations of the federal Clean Air Act.[30]

W. R. Grace purchased the mine in 1963 from the Zonolite Company for $9 million. Zonolite had operated the facility for decades, mining vermiculite—a mineral frequently used in insulating materials, for fireproofing, and for potting soil. Many homes built in Libby were insulated with Zonolite products, and Grace was considered by many longtime workers to provide "the Cadillac of jobs at the time" in the town.[31] The company is alleged to have covered up reports and health studies dating back to 1976 that showed a link between tremolite asbestos, contained in the ore processed at the mine, and lung diseases, including cancer. The death rate from asbestos in Libby and surrounding areas is forty to eighty times higher than elsewhere in the state, and asbestos exposure has afflicted many people who never even worked in the mine. Dust from the operations settled all over the town, near the railroad tracks where material was carted away, adjacent to a Little League baseball field, and at a high school where mining scraps were used to pave a running track.[32]

The problem gained national attention in 1999 following a report about worker health that ran in a Seattle newspaper. EPA officials began their investigation, which the Montana U.S. Attorney has called a "human environmental tragedy" for which Grace and top officials must be held accountable.[33] In May 2000, the EPA began removing contaminated soil and materials from the town, and in March 2001, the government filed suit to recover its costs under CERCLA. Grace filed for bankruptcy protection in April 2001, after dozens of asbestos-related injury lawsuits had been filed against them for the Libby plant and others where vermiculite was used. The Libby area has been declared a Superfund site, and in 2003, the federal district court in Montana awarded the EPA $54 million for cleanup costs incurred by the agency through the end of 2001.

In 2008, W.R. Grace agreed to pay $250 million, the highest sum in the history of the program, to reimburse the federal government for the costs of investigation and cleanup, including future cleanup costs. The company has faced about 250,000 lawsuits that have been settled or dismissed; an estimated 120,000 actions are still remaining. The case against W.R. Grace continued well into the decade, however, as families of those diagnosed with mesothelioma, asbestosis, and lung cancer continued their battle against the firm. Lawyers for the injured claimed the pollution has killed about 225 people and sickened another 2,000.[34]

BROWNFIELDS AND PORTFIELDS

The term *brownfield* refers to a slightly different type of waste site, defined by the EPA as abandoned, idled, or underused industrial and commercial facilities where expansion or redevelopment is complicated by real or perceived environmental contamination. As part of a partnership between the federal government and local communities, EPA manages these sites under the Brownfields Economic Redevelopment Initiative and the RCRA Brownfields Prevention Initiative, launched in 1998. President George W. Bush signed the Business Liability Relief and Brownfields Revitalization Act (the "Brownfields Law") in January 2002, amending CERCLA by providing funds to assess and clean up brownfields. Funding is used to assess and test for contamination at a site and to arrange for voluntary cleanup with a goal of reuse and redevelopment. There are also tax incentives available as part of the Taxpayer Relief Act to spur cleanup and redevelopment in distressed urban and rural areas.

Benefits of the program include preventing further contamination and associated potential health threats; revitalizing communities around abandoned sites; preserving valuable agricultural land and green space; and providing environmental job training for residents affected by brownfields. The EPA estimates that an estimated 25,000 jobs have been created thus far, with about $6.5 billion in leveraged funding from the private and public sectors. Overall, there are an estimated 450,000 brownfields in the United States.[35]

Equally important is the development of the environmental expertise needed to attempt to reclaim these sites, some of which are on tribal lands or closed military bases. Carnegie Mellon University has established training programs in conjunction with the University of Pittsburgh, and sponsored numerous conferences in conjunction with the EPA. Such efforts also have an international component, with several European universities developing technology and training on-site.

The concept of developing a similar type of program for the nation's busy ports comes from the Portfields Initiative of 2003. Three communities that had been recipients of EPA Brownfields Assessment Pilot grants— New Bedford, Massachusetts; Tampa, Florida; and the Port of Bellingham, Washington—were selected as Portfields Pilot Ports because they already had shown success in partnering with federal agencies. The program is designed to revitalize port communities through waterfront revitalization, facility planning, and habitat restoration. The initiative is led by the EPA and the National Oceanic and Atmospheric Administration (NOAA), each of which has provided modest financial assistance, with technical assistance and administrative support from the Economic Development Administration, the U.S. Department of Labor's Employment and Training Administration, the U.S. Army Corps of Engineers, and the Maritime Administration. The program has been expanded through a peer-to-peer program with representatives of six southern Louisiana ports.[36]

At the Bellingham site, the community is working on a Central Waterfront Redevelopment Project, cleaning up a fifty-acre site where properties had been identified as contaminated, including a former landfill. With the Portfields Project, there are additional properties that can be redeveloped, along with restoration of habitat for endangered salmon species, expansion of the local Coast Guard station, design and construction of transportation infrastructure to accommodate the waterfront redevelopment project, and other elements that expand the initial brownfields project. The portfields concept is built on the expectation that maritime trade will double by the year 2020, and that businesses are looking for additional sites for manufacturing, shipping, and tourism.[37] By partnering with the federal government, local communities can leverage the limited funds that are available during the economic downturn, and bring jobs to depressed areas.

NUCLEAR WASTE

Among the more politicized waste-management problems to find their way onto the policy agenda are those involving the back end of the nuclear fuel cycle and the disposal of nuclear waste from military bases and nuclear weapons facilities. *Back-end waste* refers to solids, liquids, gases, and sludge that must be treated to remove contaminants or diluted to reduce their toxicity and then stored. Radioactive waste decays at varying rates, so different types of disposal are needed for different types of waste. Although low-level radioactive waste can safely be stored in containers that are buried in shallow trenches, researchers have had to look at alternatives for disposing of high-level radioactive waste. Under the provisions of the 1982 Nuclear Waste Policy Act, the DOE was required to assume ownership of these wastes in 1998 and to store them. The initial plan was to store the waste in a temporary aboveground site, to be used only until a permanent site was ready.

After years of bitter congressional debate over where the repository would be located, in 1987, Congress directed that DOE focus on one site—Yucca Mountain, Nevada, located about ninety miles northeast of Las Vegas. State officials and the Nevada congressional delegation have protested the siting ever since, joined by environmental organizations and some scientists who believe the location is unsafe. In 1998, the Senate Energy and Natural Resources Committee refused to consider a bill that would have created an interim high-level nuclear-waste facility next to the Yucca Mountain site. The Clinton administration and Nevada senators opposed the legislation, which was supported by the utility industry. Their lobbyists argued that almost 40,000 tons of nuclear wastes—consisting primarily of used reactor fuel rods—are piling up at power plants in thirty-four states while the government fails to provide the centralized storage promised under the 1982 law.

The issue also reached the bureaucratic agenda of the Nuclear Regulatory Commission (NRC) through the Nuclear Waste Technical Review Board, which was established by Congress to review the DOE's work. The Yucca Mountain site came to exemplify what happens when scientists disagree and inconsistency occurs among studies. One 1997 DOE study found that rainwater, which could dissolve nuclear waste, has seeped from the top of the mountain, running down nearly 800 feet at a rate much faster than scientists had expected. This finding led Nevada officials to claim that the site should be disqualified as a suitable location. Hydrologists and officials of the Nuclear Energy Institute (a trade association for nuclear utilities) disagreed, however, noting that the water was not flowing like a household faucet running at forty-five gallons per minute; instead, only minuscule amounts were dripping through the cracks in the rock strata.[38]

The EPA had originally been seeking a site that would be stable for 10,000 years. However, a 1998 study by the California Institute of Technology and the Harvard-Smithsonian Center for Astrophysics in Cambridge, Massachusetts, warned that the ground around the site could be considered stable only over the next 1,000 years. Using DOD satellites, researchers found that the Yucca Mountain region was seismically active and therefore the geological foundation could stretch more than three feet in the 1,000-year period. The movement could crush any canisters of nuclear waste buried there, potentially exposing a wide area of the Southwest to radiation.

The DOE turned in late 1998 to another study, which found reasonable assurance that Yucca Mountain would meet long-term safety standards for many thousands of years. After years of research on the site's hydrology and geology, scientists reported that the performance of a geological repository over such long periods cannot be proven beyond all doubt; they added that uncertainties can be reduced but never completely eliminated. The 80,000 tons of used reactor fuel, which would be placed 1,000 feet below the surface, will remain deadly for an estimated 300,000 years.

While scientists argued over the reliability of various studies, politicians and interest groups continued the lengthy battle in Washington, D.C. Secretary of Energy Spencer Abraham noted that a permanent underground depository was far preferable to storing waste in temporary, aboveground facilities at 131 sites near cities and waterways. He also raised the issue of national security, which became especially salient after the terrorist attacks on the World Trade Center in 2001. "Scientists have studied the safety and suitability of Yucca Mountain for the past 24 years at a cost of more than $4 billion," he notes. "The science is sound, and the national interests served by a permanent repository are compelling."[39] Members of Nevada's congressional delegation introduced legislation to fund more studies of long-term solutions for storage, with one representative stating that "Yucca Mountain is a politician's solution to a problem that requires real science and will have consequences lasting hundreds of thousands of years. A problem of this magnitude deserves solutions founded on the recommendations of scientists, and not subject to the clumsy intrigues and estimations of shortsighted politicians."[40]

At the same time Yucca Mountain's fate was being debated, the federal government approved a plan to store 5 million cubic feet of transuranic waste (tools, rags, clothing, and other materials contaminated with uranium or plutonium isotopes during nuclear weapons production). The Waste Isolation Pilot Project (WIPP) complex near Carlsbad, New Mexico, took nearly twenty years to plan, develop, and build, at a cost of nearly $2 billion. The mile-square maze of tunnels in a geological salt formation a half-mile underground was further delayed by legal challenges until 1998, when it was formally certified by the EPA. Environmental groups opposed the project because of concerns about the health risks of shipping nuclear waste by truck to the site and fears that the location was geologically unstable.

Nonetheless, on March 26, 1999, the first shipment, consisting of 600 pounds of nuclear debris from the Los Alamos National Laboratory, was trucked to the site, with only a handful of protestors as witnesses. Secretary of Energy Bill Richardson claimed that the WIPP's opening was part of the cleanup of the legacy of the Cold War and its waste. "The opening of this facility is a step to meeting this obligation," he said.[41]

President George W. Bush attempted to end the stalemate over Yucca Mountain on February 15, 2002, by approving the site. Under the 1982 statute, Nevada responded by vetoing the president's action. In his statement of reasons for disapproving the project, Nevada governor Kenny Guinn told Congress:

> Nevada will not allow it to happen. Not simply because it is the wrong thing to do, at the wrong time, from the standpoint of environmental equity. Even when carrying the load of others, Nevadans will never tire of serving their country for a worthy cause. We will not permit Yucca Mountain to happen—and it will not happen—because the project is manifestly not a worthy cause.... I assure you, the only thing inevitable about Yucca Mountain is that it will plot the course of so many other doomed DOE mega-projects.[42]

Not unexpectedly, the U.S. House of Representatives voted to override the Nevada veto in May 2002; and two months later, the U.S. Senate followed. On July 23, 2002, President George W. Bush signed legislation that officially designated Yucca Mountain as the nation's nuclear-waste dump, paving the way for DOE to seek a license for the project. Nevada senator Harry Reid blamed the outcome on nuclear lobbyists and their "unending source of money" that perpetuated what he called "the big lie" that the facility was urgently needed. Nevada's other senator, John Ensign, raised the NIMBY—"not in my backyard"—issue, saying no one wanted to reopen the debate. Their arguments were countered by Alaska's Frank Murkowski, who said nuclear power itself would be threatened, the government could face lawsuits, and lawmakers would have to start looking all over again for a waste site.[43]

Murkowski was right on one point—a variety of lawsuits have been filed by the State of Nevada—and Reid moved to cut $153 million from the $489 million Bush had requested for Yucca Mountain in the following year's budget, citing more pressing priorities. Nevada also filed a petition with the NRC seeking a change in rules that would require the DOE to prove the site will be safe. Governor Guinn and other state officials continued to oppose Yucca Mountain despite the president's action, stating that they believed their best chance to defeat the project was in the federal courts, "where impartial judges will hear the factual and scientific arguments as to why Yucca Mountain is not a safe place to store this nation's high-level nuclear waste."[44] Environmental groups, still dissatisfied with the government's solution, renewed their focus on the handling and transport of the waste, calling the proposed shipments a "mobile Chernobyl." The debate over the project's safety, funding, and transportation of waste simmered, with the Nevada Commission on Nuclear Projects calling the repository project a "dead man walking."[45]

During the 2008 presidential campaign, candidate Barack Obama showed his support for shutting down the Yucca Mountain operation completely, telling a Las Vegas newspaper, "I believe all spending on Yucca Mountain should be redirected to other uses, such as improving the safety and security of spent fuel at plant sites around the country and exploring other long-term disposal options."[46] Obama was accused of playing politics, rather than using good science, by one newspaper that wrote in an editorial that the move was designed to please Senate Majority Leader Harry Reid and bring Nevada into the Democrats' win column.[47]

Whether the action was politically inspired or not, Obama fulfilled his campaign promise with his first set of budget announcements, saying the program at Yucca Mountain "will be scaled back to those costs necessary to answer inquiries from the Nuclear Regulatory Commission while the administration devises a new strategy toward nuclear waste disposal," a policy roughly translated, one source noted, as "Yucca Mountain is dead."[48] The project has thus far cost $7.7 billion, and the president's proposal of $197 million for fiscal year 2010 would be only enough to allow the licensing project to continue before the NRC. Senate leaders, pushed by Reid, have also slashed the NRC's budget by 13 percent, limiting its ability to process the Yucca Mountain license—a secondary tactic that could seriously damage any forward movement on the facility, or licensing for new nuclear reactors.[49] The expectation is that key staff members in the Obama administration will revisit the issue over the next year, and in the meantime, dry-cask storage of waste, the current method of storing material, will remain a safe, short-term solution.

But some lawmakers in Washington have refused to let the project die, adding legislative language to an energy and water appropriations bill in 2009 that would establish and fund a Blue Ribbon Commission that would look at alternatives to Yucca Mountain, including a review of the Nevada project itself. At this point, there is no "plan B" for handling and disposing of high-level radioactive waste, a problem that grows more important as the United States considers reviving its nuclear energy program, as discussed more in Chapter 6.

CLEANING UP MILITARY WASTE

Also unresolved as a policy issue are the prospects for long-term environmental cleanup of military bases. For decades, the DOD held itself exempt from environmental legislation under the guise of national security. Environmental groups accused the agency of disposing of solvents, dead batteries, dirty oil, and unexploded shells and bombs by dumping them on-site, thereby contaminating the underlying water or soil. In the 1980s, the DOD was estimated to be generating 500,000 tons of toxic waste per year—more than the amount being generated by the top five U.S. chemical companies combined. One agency report identified nearly 20,000 sites at 1,800 military installations that showed varying levels of contamination, nearly a hundred of which warranted placement on the NPL.[50]

In 1984, the courts directed the DOE to accept responsibility for the cleanup resulting from decades of military weapons production at over 100 sites in thirty states around the country. Since 1989, DOE has spent over $20 billion on cleanup tasks, with the end nowhere in sight. Many researchers believe it will take decades before cleanups at all weapons sites are completed, at a total cost of almost $150 billion, while others believe the sites may be too contaminated ever to be cleaned up.[51]

To facilitate public oversight and monitoring, in 1998, a coalition of thirty-nine environmental groups reached agreement over a 1989 lawsuit that requires the DOE to provide greater access to information about the cleanup process. Now the agency must create a publicly accessible database on contaminated facilities and provide $6.25 million to help citizen's groups and Indian tribes conduct technical and scientific reviews of cleanup activities.[52]

Two of the nation's most controversial military sites are the Atlantic Fleet Weapons Training Area and the Naval Ammunitions Facility on Vieques Island, Puerto Rico. The U.S. Navy purchased about two-thirds of the land area in 1942, primarily from large sugar-plantation owners, for live ordnance delivery and amphibious assault landings by the Marine Corps during World War II. Tons of live and spent munitions, including depleted uranium, have been found on Vieques, along with dozens of sites on the Navy's Camp Garcia, where there is visible evidence that hazardous materials were released. The landfill at the fifty-five-acre camp is filled with over 3,000 tons of construction debris, scrap metal, and general waste; there are industrial or manufacturing areas where gasoline, diesel, and waste oil were stored and soil may be contaminated; and four lagoons used to treat domestic wastewater and two storage areas for waste batteries must also be cleaned up.[53]

In 1978, the governor of Puerto Rico filed suit to stop the Navy from using the portions of the land it owns, and adjacent waters, for training operations, but a request for injunction was denied. The problem reached the policy agenda in the late 1990s after a series of highly publicized demonstrations where protesters, including celebrities and political figures, sought an end to the use of an island as a bombing range. Over 9,000 people live on the island, and the Committee for the Rescue and Development of Vieques, an advocacy organization, claims that over 1,000 acres of the island still contain live ammunition. In February 2000, President Bill Clinton announced that a compromise had been reached that would allow the Navy to resume inert bombing in exchange for $40 million in housing and infrastructure aid for Puerto Rico.

Vieques exemplifies the difficulties that arise when a military site is involved—jurisdictional disputes, which are fairly common in environmental politics. The EPA does not control or manage contaminated facilities; its role is regulation and enforcement. The intent of Congress was to make the agency independent so that compliance could be assured. At the same time, the DOD operates under its own political agenda and direction; thus, environmental remediation is not always its highest priority. While staffers talk of a partnership arrangement between the two agencies, in reality there has been more study and discussion than actual cleanup, and there are often overlapping statutory provisions and goals. Under RCRA, the EPA signed a Consent Order with the Navy to conduct an investigation of any environmental damage. This statute was applicable because, at the time, the Navy was still conducting bombing on Vieques; Superfund applies only to sites that are no longer in use. The Navy had already conducted its own investigation, as had the Puerto Rican Environmental Quality Board.

As part of the Defense Authorization Bill for fiscal year 2001, the Navy turned over 8,148 acres of land to the Municipality of Vieques, the U.S. Department of the Interior, and the Puerto Rico Conservation Trust. About half of the land was to be used to promote economic development and employment opportunities for the island's residents. Then, in 2003, the Navy announced that it would discontinue using Vieques as a bombing range. About 3,100 acres were to be transferred to the U.S. Fish and Wildlife Service as a wildlife refuge, and all temporary facilities and structures would be demolished. The Navy pledged a cleanup as the Principal Responsible Party, this time under Superfund standards, because the site was no longer active.[54]

The twist in the dispute is that the new designation—the Vieques and Culebra National Wildlife Refuges—while ostensibly designed to protect endangered plant and animal species, restricts public access to contaminated sites. Any Superfund designation that adds Vieques to the NPL may use different cleanup standards and prioritization of remediation because the goal is to protect wildlife, not human lives.

In 2005, the Navy began detonating unexploded bombs on the island, and groups protested what EPA called "open detonation" because military toxins were being dispersed on the island's residents as part of the cleanup process. In addition, by fencing off wilderness zones, protesters argue, the Navy says that there are no threats to humans due to contamination in the areas and therefore no cleanup is necessary.[55] To satisfy residents' complaints about the pace of the cleanup, Democratic Representative Jose E. Serrano of Puerto Rico secured $1 million in the 2004 omnibus spending bill for assistance. Still another federal agency, the NOAA, is now involved in providing assistance to the DOD, EPA, and Department of the Interior.[56] Vieques was eventually added to the NPL under CERCLA in April 2005.

The Vieques example illustrates how complex the issue of cleaning up waste at military facilities has become. A site cleanup can be politicized when political leaders sense a threat to their constituency and use contamination as a way of showing how they are working for those living in their area.

There can be turf battles among competing agencies or competition for limited federal dollars. Human health appears to have become almost secondary, as has science, in determining where problems are placed on the waste-policy agenda.

AMERICAN POLICY STALLED: TOO LITTLE, TOO LATE

Various agencies and analysts are exploring a number of waste-management strategies, ranging from technological solutions such as soil washing, chemical dechlorination, underground vacuum extraction, and bioremediation (the use of microbes to break down organic contaminants) to the use of price incentives and cost-based disposal fees. Despite these proposals, the waste-management issue has been called an "environmental policy paradox." Even though officials have been aware of the shortage of landfill space for decades and could have anticipated the need for alternatives, they have been unable to develop a viable long-term policy to deal with the problem. Observers point to the lack of a publicly perceived crisis; the incentives that have caused policymakers to choose short-term, low-cost options; and the incremental nature of the policy process. Regarding hazardous waste, officials at the federal level have failed to follow through on policy development with an appropriate level of resources to clean up the thousands of identified sites in the United States. In addition, the involvement of organized crime in the disposal industry has been connected to illegal disposal, or "midnight dumping," of hazardous wastes—a problem not yet solved by government officials at any level.

It is equally accurate to characterize America's waste-management practices as the policy of deferral. The inability of policymakers to plan now for future disposal needs (whether the waste be solid, hazardous, or radioactive) simply means that they are putting off until tomorrow an inevitable, and growing, environmental-protection problem. Future generations will be forced to deal with the mounting heaps of trash, barrels of toxic waste, and radioactive refuse that are already piling up in our cities, at chemical companies, and at utilities all around the country. Other analysts note that there is a lack of information about the full costs of various disposal alternatives. Without sufficient research into the "true" costs of waste-management strategies, it is impossible for the most efficient systems to be developed.

Meanwhile, it appears as if the future of American waste management will involve a combination and integration of disposal methods, rather than any single strategy. Technological strategies and price incentives are of little value, however, until the legislative gridlock is broken and policymakers get serious about finding a solution, rather than just passing stopgap measures for short-term fixes. We know the problem is there, but no one seems willing to get down and dirty to tackle it.

INTERNATIONAL WASTE TRADING

Until recently, most nations dealt with their waste problems independently of one another. Due to various developments in the way waste is managed, the issue has now become globalized, especially when developed countries attempt to ship their waste abroad. The issue gained international prominence in 1988 when 3,000 tons of a flaky black material was dumped on a Haitian beach. A barge carrying the substance had entered the port with a permit to unload "fertilizer," which later turned out to be ash laced with toxic residue from a Philadelphia municipal incinerator.

The hazardous-waste trade is now one of the most important global environmental-policy issues, for several reasons. There is a great amount of variation in what each nation defines as "hazardous" when it comes to waste. In industrialized countries, most substances that pose a potential risk (usually from manufacturing) are given hazardous status. In developing nations, the lack of technical expertise and testing facilities might mean that the list of substances considered hazardous is closer to guesswork than to science. The most common definition used internationally refers to wastes that, if improperly managed or disposed, could harm humans and/or the environment because they are toxic, corrosive, explosive, or combustible.[57] The complexity of waste types also requires specialized disposal techniques in order to reduce risk potential. Dumping large quantities of sometimes unknown substances in landfills is not the most desirable option, but it is comparatively inexpensive. One study found a tremendous disparity in hazardous-waste disposal costs between developed and developing nations, ranging from $2,000 per ton in one European country to $40 per ton in an African nation. With fewer regulatory controls and enforcement mechanisms, the economic incentive for waste trade is understandable.

A study of waste trading among rich nations found that the major waste-disposal firms often operate far outside their own country of origin, and mergers of large companies are a common phenomenon. One of the largest European disposal companies, Generale des Eaux of France, has operations in Chile, Australia, and New Zealand. Sometimes, the management of these firms may have an inadequate communication infrastructure with its partners and local authorities.[58]

Waste management has also gained a more global focus as the nations of the former Soviet Union have appealed to the industrialized world for assistance in dealing with the phenomenal amount of toxic waste and radioactive materials produced from decades of military activity and inattention to environmental contamination. For decades, billions of gallons of liquid radioactive waste were secretly pumped underground near major rivers in Russia, and scientists have little information about the potential risk the practice now poses. It is estimated that cleaning up nuclear power plants like Chernobyl will take as long as 100 years and will cost billions of dollars more in financial assistance. Although the area of the former Soviet Union continues to suffer from massive pollution of its water and air from manufacturing and other industrial processes, radioactive contamination is by far its most pressing, and most expensive, challenge. Existing international institutions are simply not prepared to deal with either the cost or the coordination of this legacy of the communist regime.[59]

The United States is now attempting to lend its expertise to dealing with spent nuclear fuel from decommissioned Russian submarines. The U.S.-funded Nunn-Lugar Program opened a facility in the Arctic port of Severodvinsk in 2002 that is expected to unload spent nuclear fuel from six submarines each year as part of U.S. efforts to help Russia secure and eliminate weapons of mass destruction. Still unanswered, however, is what to do with the nuclear waste from the submarine reactors, although Russian officials have previously said they would build a dump site on a remote Arctic archipelago.

It is the perceived inequity of how hazardous waste is handled that has also made it an increasingly global issue. Organizations like Greenpeace call efforts to ship waste abroad "toxic terrorism," and the group's members have helped publicize the lack of monitoring and regulations over what materials are being transported, often under the guise of recycling. Many poor countries are willing to accept hazardous wastes, even though they may lack the necessary facilities or processes to deal with them. But in a study of hazardous waste trading, Dr. Kate O'Neill notes, too, that many less developed countries—especially Africa—that are supported by international environmental organizations are now refusing to accept the waste from industrialized nations. Waste trade among the United States, Canada, and Mexico is lawful under the North American Free Trade Agreement (NAFTA), as are shipments within the United States to Native American tribal lands. There are also bilateral and regional agreements, such as one between France and Germany, the Waigani Convention of 1995 addressing the South Pacific, and the 1996 Barcelona Convention governing waste trade in the Mediterranean region.[60]

Hazardous-waste trade remains high on the policy agenda despite more than thirty years of attempts to develop an acceptable international regime. At the 1972 UN Conference on the Human Environment, delegates made a commitment to regulate waste trading, although it was not until 1984 to 1985 that a UN Environment Programme committee developed the Cairo Guidelines to implement that pledge. The guidelines included notification procedures, prior consent by receiving nations, and verification that the receiving nation has requirements for disposal at least as stringent as those of the exporter. Despite those restrictions, a coalition of African nations argued that the agreement was tantamount to exploitation or "waste colonialism." In 1987, the United Nations attempted to devise an agreement that would satisfy the African nations (who sought an outright ban on exports) and exporters (still seeking inexpensive ways of disposing of their wastes). In 1989, two attempts were made to restrict further the international trade in wastes. A group of sixty-eight less industrialized nations from Africa, the Caribbean, and the Pacific, collectively known as the "ACP countries," joined with European Community (EC) officials in signing the Lome Convention, which banned all radioactive- and hazardous-waste shipments from the EC and ACP countries. A second agreement—the Basel Convention on the Control of Transboundary Movements of Hazardous Wastes and Their Disposal, which took effect in 1992—did not ban waste trade but allowed hazardous wastes to be exported as long as there is "informed consent" or full notification and acceptance of any shipments. Even though members of the EC and other nations had pledged not to export their hazardous wastes regardless of the Basel Convention, twelve African states subsequently signed the Bamako Convention in 1991, banning the import of hazardous wastes from any country—a move that further emphasized their determination not to become a dumping ground for other countries.

Led by Greenpeace, many environmental groups pointed out the deficiencies in the Basel Convention—especially the lack of a clear definition of "hazardous waste." The prior notification procedures were attacked as being ineffective, the convention did not cover radioactive waste, and there were no incentives for source reduction and waste minimization. Exporters circumvented the various international agreements simply by relabeling waste as being destined for recycling rather than disposal.[61]

After a series of meetings among the parties to the convention, and despite opposition from hazardous-waste producers—the United States, Canada, Australia, and Japan—the Basel Ban Amendment was adopted in September 1995. The amendment banned exports of hazardous waste destined for disposal, as well as waste designated for recycling purposes. Attempts were made to convince member nations that they should not ratify the amendment, focusing on Technical Working Group meetings that were less visible to press their arguments. A new nongovernmental organization, the Basel Action Network (BAN) formed to lobby governments and gain grassroots support. Jennifer Clapp points out that what made the Basel Convention and the subsequent Basel Ban Amendment so noteworthy was the increased activism and lobbying of the global recycling industry. In the late 1990s, the industry employed some 1.5 million workers and was worth about $160 billion per year. Despite the industry's clout, however, countries began to ratify the Ban Amendment, in large part due to the continuing pressure of environmental organizations.[62]

Despite agreements among various countries to implement source-reduction strategies, the total amount of hazardous waste generated among Organization for Economic Cooperation and Development (OECD) countries has increased substantially since 1989. What is most important, however, is that countries differ substantially when it comes to imports and exports, generation of wastes, and disposal. Middle Eastern countries produce over 1 million tons of hazardous waste per year, but only Saudi Arabia has even a minimal level of disposal facilities. In English-speaking Africa, 2.23 million tons are produced annually, and over half of that total comes from South Africa. But only South Africa, Namibia, and Mauritius have commercial waste facilities. Although the countries of the former Soviet Union have reported a gradual reduction in the amount of hazardous waste that is being produced, they face a disposal crisis, due largely to the stockpiles left over from the Cold War.[63]

It appears that waste-trade regulation will consist of two types of strategies: voluntary, regionally based agreements like NAFTA, and unilateral actions taken by individual countries that attempt both waste minimization and the use of more advanced technologies to deal with their own waste. On the global level, there is a call for a commonly accepted definition and classification of hazardous waste, the creation of an international clearinghouse for data on management and toxicity, and increased monitoring.

There has been some success, however, in reaching international agreement on persistent organic pollutants, or POPs. In 1998, over 100 governments met in Montreal, Canada, for talks on an international agreement to minimize emissions and releases of twelve POPs (or the "dirty dozen"), such as dichloro-diphenyltrichloroethane (DDT) and polychlorinated biphenyls (PCBs), into the environment. The issue was returned to the UN Environment Programme agenda because of growing scientific evidence that exposure to even very low doses of certain pollutants can lead to a number of diseases like cancer, immune and reproductive system disorders, and interference with infant and child development. Over 170 types of POPs have been found in human tissue, and more types have been found in animals.

The globalized nature of the problem stems from two factors: (1) decaying and leaching chemicals from dump sites; and (2) toxic drums, first used from 1950 to 1980, that circulate through a process called the "grasshopper effect." Pollutants released in one part of the world can—through a repeated, and often seasonal, process of evaporation and deposit—be transported through the atmosphere to regions far away from the original source. Through bioaccumulation, the pollutants are also absorbed in the fatty tissue of living organisms, where concentrations can become magnified by up to 70,000 times background levels. The result is that POPs can be found in humans and other animals in regions thousands of miles away, such as the Arctic. Researchers believe that some POPs may last more than 100 years in the natural environment, creating a long-term policy problem.

As a follow-up to the 1979 Geneva Convention on Long-Range Trans-boundary Air Pollution, the meeting resulted in the Protocol on Persistent Organic Pollutants, which focuses specifically on eleven pesticides, two industrial chemicals, and three by-products/contaminants. The agreement's objective is the elimination of any discharges or emissions of POPs; a ban on the production and use of some products, such as toxaphene and endrin; the scheduled elimination of other products like DDT and PCBs in the future; and a requirement that parties reduce emissions of other substances, such as dioxins, below 1990 levels.

This is an area of international environmental policy where issues overlap—waste management and transboundary pollution—and the need for collaboration and cooperation are essential. Depending upon how the POPs issue is framed, countries may view the problem as one that is largely the concern of individual states, or one that is profoundly global.

SHIPBREAKING

In August 2007, the television news program *60 Minutes* aired an episode focusing on a problem most people have heard little about—the shipbreaking industry of Bangladesh. It focused on the city of Chittagong on the Bay of Bengal, where men rip apart huge ships that have outlived their usefulness, often earning $1 for a day's worth of backbreaking, dangerous work. The industry began in Bangladesh in 1965 when a violent storm left a giant cargo ship on the beach, and local residents began dissecting it for the parts and metal components. Soon after, the Bay of Bengal became a port of sorts for vessels that are sold to scrap recyclers by the ton of steel; scrapping a ship can yield a profit of $2 million. But the Bay of Bengal also became a toxic-waste dump that operates twenty-four hours a day, with outdated ships ending up on the shores of Bangladesh and other developing countries where wages are low and occupational safety laws virtually nonexistent. The shipbreaking yards are home to child labor, appalling work conditions, and toxic waste, often in violation of international agreements.[64]

A December 2008 report by Greenpeace and the International Federation for Human Rights says that, on average, at least one worker is injured each day and one dies each week in the scrapping operations. An estimated 700 ships are scrapped each year, mainly in five countries: China, Bangladesh, India, Pakistan, and Vietnam, with some in Turkey. While Bangladesh has imposed a ban on the shipbreaking activities without government clearance, newspapers have reported that the country is failing to meet its obligations under the Basel Convention.[65]

This issue is becoming more critical as a whole generation of ships reaches obsolescence. Previously, shipbreaking was done in the docks of Europe, Greenpeace notes, but as these countries became more conscious of environmental problems like toxic waste, operations moved to developing countries where environmental laws are nonexistent or unenforced. The global fleet grew from 15,000 ships in the 1960s to 62,000 in 2000, with most ships having a working lifespan of about thirty years. That means that the number of vessels reaching the age of decommissioning, from cargo ships to cruise liners, will be growing in the future. The result is that beaches throughout Asia are littered with machinery, leaking barrels, rags, and piles of metal, with the air poisoned by open fires and the land and surrounding watersheds contaminated by toxic metals, dioxins, asbestos, and other POPs. "You can see workers with bare hands using acetylene torch cutters to dismantle huge sea carriers into small pieces. They don't have gloves, they're unprotected from toxic substances, explosions, and falling steel," Greenpeace says. The organization reports that in 2000, an explosion in a gas tanker killed twenty to forty workers in Bangladesh, which does not enforce mandatory regulations that ensure that the ships are free of gas residues before they are dismantled, as India does. So ships are now moved out of Indian yards and sent to Bangladesh.[66]

Another View, Another Voice: Syeda Rizwana Hasan

Rizwana Hasan won an important victory in March 2009. The Bangladesh High Court directed the government to close operation of all shipbreaking yards that operate without clearance from the Department of Environment. The order followed a writ filed by the Bangladesh Environmental Lawyer's Association (BELA), five years of negotiations and lobbying by the group, and successful petitions in 2006 to stop an ocean liner and an oil tanker from entering Bangladeshi waters, where they were scheduled for dismantling. From 2005 to 2007, more than 250 ships, with a total weight in excess of 2.5 million tons, were broken on the shores of Bangladesh. About 95 percent of each ship was comprised of steel coated with paint made of hazardous chemicals such as lead, cadmium, arsenic, zinc, and chromium, along with components such as asbestos, oil, and grease.

Rizwana Hasan grew up in a politically active family, and received a master's degree in law before joining BELA at age twenty-four and becoming one of the nation's leading voices for environmental protection. She manages six offices with nearly sixty staff members, and in 2009, she was named one of the winners of the Goldman Prize for her work in spearheading increased governmental regulation and heightened public awareness of shipbreaking.

In 2003, she filed a petition with the Bangladesh Supreme Court to prohibit aging ships from entering the country unless they were certified to be free of toxic substances, a requirement of the Basel Convention on hazardous-waste trading, and to prohibit shipbreaking unless the government enacted and enforced legislation protecting both workers and the environment. Using a list of ships listed as hazardous by the organization Greenpeace, she filed petitions against the two ships, and later a third vessel, which was allowed to enter the country. However, she was successful in obtaining an injunction against the breaking of the ship, which had already begun, and persisted in her legal battle until the court ordered compensatory fees be paid by the company. Even though the dismantling had already begun, it became the first time in the history of Bangladesh that a polluter had been fined.

Hasan continues her work to encourage the government to regulate more actively Bangladesh's thirty-six shipbreaking yards, and to make sure the 2009 order of the High Court is enforced. Using the Greenpeace list, she is seeking to have all ships designated as posing a contamination risk precleaned before entering the country's waters. She is also expanding her work to other countries where shipbreaking activities continue, such as India, Pakistan, and Turkey. The Goldman Prize also cited her efforts to advocate on other environmental issues, such as wetlands preservation, regulation of commercial shrimp farming, traditional forest rights preservation, and vehicular and industrial pollution.

SOURCES:
Environmental Law Alliance Worldwide. "Bangladesh: Ship-Breaking Victory." Spring 2009. http://www.elaw.org/news/advocate/2009-spring. Accessed August 30, 2009.
"Save Shipbreaking Sector, Cry Jobless Workers." *Toxic Trade News*. March 22, 2009. http://www.ban.org/ban_news/2009/090322_save_shipbreaking_sector.html. Accessed August 30, 2009.
"Siyeda Rizwana Hasan." http://www.goldmanprize.org/2009/asia. Accessed June 11, 2009.

FURTHER READING

Elizabeth Blum. *Love Canal Revisited: Race, Class, and Gender in Environmental Activism.* Lawrence: University Press of Kansas, 2008.

Sarah Cellard and Diane Millis. *The Eco-Living Handbook: A Complete Green Guide for Your Home and Life.* London: Carlton Books, 2010.

James J. J. Clark and Paul F. Rosenfeld. *The Risks of Hazardous Wastes.* Norwich, NY: William Andrew Publishing, 2010.

Jacob D. Hamblin. *Poison in the Well: Radioactive Waste in the Oceans at the Dawn of the Nuclear Age.* Piscataway, NJ: Rutgers University Press, 2008.

Gavin Harper. *A Nuclear Waste: Nuclear Power, Climate Change and the Energy Crisis.* London: Zed Books, 2010.

Anne Maczulak. *Cleaning Up the Environment: Hazardous Waste Technology*. New York: Facts on File, 2009.

Christopher Rootes and Liam Leonard, eds. *Environmental Movements and Waste Infrastructure*. New York: Routledge, 2010.

J. Samuel Walker. *The Road to Yucca Mountain: The Development of Radioactive Waste Policy in the United States*. Berkeley: University of California Press, 2009.

6

The Politics of Energy

"I don't like to call it a disaster, because there has been
no loss of human life. I am amazed at the publicity
for the loss of a few birds."
— FRED L. HARTLEY, PRESIDENT OF UNION OIL COMPANY, 1969[1]

On January 28, 1969, the fog that regularly drifts over the beaches of Santa
Barbara, California, lifted slightly, encouraging early-morning joggers, students at the nearby campus of the University of California, and winter visitors
staying in ritzy Montecito to stroll along the coast's beautiful beaches. The area
is known as an area of pristine, soft sand, minimal piles of kelp, and gorgeous
sunrises. But that morning, the tide brought in gobs of gooey, oily tar that stuck
to feet like molasses that would just not rub off. The oil washed up along with
the tide, depositing the goo in wavy lines and bringing with it an odor of
petroleum.

Five miles out to sea at Platform Alpha, an offshore drilling rig operated by
Union Oil, a pipe was being extracted from a 3,500-foot well. Pressure built up
as drilling mud was pumped back down the well, straining the casing, despite an
emergency attempt to cap it. A burst of natural gas blew out the mud, causing a
blowout and cracks to form in the seafloor surrounding the well. Oil and natural
gas rose to the surface for eleven days while 3 million gallons of oil escaped into
the ocean waves. Eight hundred miles of ocean were impacted, and thirty-five
miles of coastline were covered in up to six inches of oil. In addition to the
gooey mess being deposited onto the shoreline, rescuers counted 3,600 dead
ocean-feeding seabirds, dead seals and dolphins washed ashore, and unknown
fish and other invertebrates were killed. Secretary of the Interior Walter J. Hickel
and President Richard M. Nixon both viewed the damage.[2]

While the oil spill is credited by many as being the crisis that led to the founding of the grassroots environmental movement, one of the long-term impacts of that morning was the call for a moratorium on all offshore drilling. A newly formed group, Get Oil Out (GOO) gathered more than 100,000 signatures on a petition for a ban, and Union Oil gas credit-card holders were urged to cut up their plastic cards in protest against the company. The State Lands Commission (SLC), which regulates drilling along the California coast, banned offshore drilling for forty years, and federal and state oil-drilling regulations were strengthened. The experience of the Santa Barbara oil spill seemed to generate sufficient opposition to coastal drilling to slow, if not completely stop, any new efforts to drill along the Outer Continental Shelf (OCS).

But a number of factors intervened between the blowout and 2009, when the SLC considered whether to grant an oil lease sought by the Plains Exploration and Production Company. In 1994, new drilling in state waters was banned with the California Coastal Sanctuary Act. The Arab oil embargo, rising fuel prices, concerns about the country's reliance on fossil fuels, and military operations in the oil-rich Middle East, along with the fact that there are still gobs of oil on Santa Barbara's beaches, were vivid reminders of controversy and political debate over offshore drilling. In 2008, when the county's board of supervisors voted to support an expansion of oil drilling off the Santa Barbara coast, Republican presidential convention delegates were shouting "Drill, baby, drill." Senator John McCain and then-President Bush supported a lifting of the ban. The oil company agreed to pay the state $100 million after legislation authorizing the lease is signed into law, a boost to California's struggling state budget.

The SLC was being pressured to approve the lease despite opposition by California governor Arnold Schwarzenegger. Secretary of the Interior Ken Salazar announced that the Obama administration favored offshore drilling as part of a larger U.S. energy plan, although he criticized what he called the "midnight timetable" of the Bush administration. To complicate matters further, in April 2009, the county board, with a new Democratic-leaning majority, voted 3–2 to reverse its earlier decision to allow offshore drilling. The county is one of several entities that must approve the lease bid; the state legislature failed to gain sufficient support to supplant a ruling by the SLC.[3]

The Santa Barbara controversy is only one of many taking place as the nation's policymakers weigh the option of expanding offshore oil and natural-gas production. In the last few days of the Bush administration in January 2009, officials released a draft of a proposed program that would have allowed thirty-one energy-exploration lease sales (four areas off Alaska, three areas off the Atlantic coast, two areas off the Pacific coast, and three areas in the Gulf of Mexico) between 2010 and 2015. The rationale for the program was that energy prices may increase as global economies recover, and the nation needs access to more dependable sources of energy. After an initial 60 days of public comment, the Obama administration extended the public comment period for another 180 days, holding four hearings to gather public input. By the time the public-comment period ended in September 2009, the federal government had received more than 450,000 comments, which are under review by the Minerals Management Service.[4]

Although there is agreement about the potential economic crisis that would transpire if the nation's energy supplies were disrupted, "there are emerging concerns that deserve equal attention, namely the resilience of the domestic energy infrastructure—oil and gas terminals and pipelines, nuclear power plants, and the electricity grid—to terrorist attacks."[5]

This change in focus, which is part of the process of problem definition and the framing of energy policy, has pushed energy issues higher on the environmental agenda. A July 2008 public-opinion survey found that Americans are about evenly split on whether energy exploration and building new power plants is more important than conservation,[6] and analysts note, "Like it or not, Americans must confront the reality that oil prices are set by worldwide markets that respond to many economic and political factors beyond the U.S. government's control."[7]

Energy has been called a "transparent" sector of society because no one buys or uses it as an end in itself. All demand for energy is indirect and derived only from the benefits it provides. People do not buy gasoline because they want gasoline, but because they need it for their cars to take them where they want to go. Similarly, a manufacturing plant needs electricity only to run the machines that make the products the company sells.

Our growing electricity needs make the debate both timely and controversial. Two-thirds of American oil consumption is from the transportation sector—highways, air routes, and long-distance railroads—with no other fuel potentially viable for these uses.[8] Large developing countries such as China and India are also fueling the energy debate as the demand for automobiles and other consumer goods increases and the countries rely on fossil fuels.

This chapter examines the changing politics of energy, reviewing the various energy sources and looking at the political environment and regulatory aspects of energy policy, from the nuclear-power debate to increasing consumer interest in fuel-efficiency ratings. The chapter concludes with an overview of global energy trends and projections for changes in energy use and carbon dioxide emissions.

THE ENERGY PIE

Energy is needed to produce goods and services in four basic economic sectors: residential (heat for rooms and hot water, lighting, appliances), commercial (including air conditioners in commercial buildings), industrial (especially steel, paper, and chemicals), and transportation (of both people and goods). Historically, the crux of the energy-policy debate has been to find efficient, environmentally safe, economical, and stable sources of supply to meet those needs. The United States has periodically experienced global energy transitions that mark changes in energy supplies and needs. In 1850, the United States derived nearly 90 percent of its energy needs from wood, which remained the dominant fuel into the late nineteenth century. In 1910, coal replaced wood as the dominant fuel, capturing 70 percent of all energy produced and consumed. Along with the transition from wood to coal came the migration from rural areas to the cities, the development of an industrial base, and the railroad era. In 1970, oil and gas reached the 70 percent level and became dominant fuels, and it was not until 1990 that geothermal, solar, and wind power sources became a statistically significant source of energy in the United States.

Edward Teller, the "father of the atomic bomb," once commented:

> No single prescription exists for a solution to the energy problem. Energy conservation is not enough. Petroleum is not enough. Nuclear energy is not enough. Solar energy and geothermal energy are not enough. New ideas and developments will not be enough. Only the proper combination of all these will suffice.[9]

Teller suggests that the answer to our global energy needs is like a recipe for an "energy pie," which is essentially the situation in the United States today; it must be found in a blend of energy sources and strategies, rather than in a single fuel. This concept would seem relatively reasonable were the costs and benefits of various forms of energy equal, but that is far from the case. Some forms of energy are relatively inexpensive to produce but are not in abundant supply. Other sources are expensive but less polluting. Still others are considered unsafe but could be made available to consumers around the world for pennies a day, improving the standard of living for millions of people in developing nations. Figure 6.1 illustrates the 2010 energy pie, with a comparison of fuel production projected for 2030. The figure shows that there are only minor changes expected over the next twenty years, with a slight increase in U.S. biofuels capacity.

Fossil Fuels

For thousands of years, humanity's primary sources of power were draft animals, water, and wind. Industrialization and the introduction of fossil fuels for power followed the invention of machines that could harness natural power sources. Oil, coal, and natural gas became the elements of what has been called the "fossil fuel revolution"—the expansion of power sources and, subsequently, the rise of

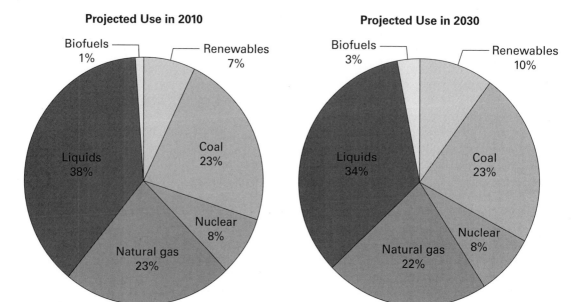

FIGURE 6.1 Primary Energy Use by Fuel (Quadrillion BTUs)

SOURCE: U.S. Department of Energy. Energy Information Administration. Annual Energy Outlook 2009 with projections to 2030, at at www.eia.doe/gov/oiaf/aeo/demand, accessed October 13, 2009.

the United States as a superpower in the global economy. Although developing nations are still largely dependent upon biomass energy (primarily fuelwood), industrialized countries have expanded their fuel mix through petroleum exports and an increasing reliance upon nuclear power.

Initially, the United States depended on "Old King Coal" as its primary fuel source. Demand came from the transportation industry, as railroads moved westward, and from metal industries (iron and steel) that forged the new tracks. Coal, found in thirty-eight states, was a relatively inexpensive and reliable energy source, and by the end of World War I, it accounted for about 75 percent of total U.S. energy use. Between then and World War II, automobiles began to be mass-produced; moreover, trucks and diesel locomotives requiring petroleum reduced the country's dependence on coal, while natural gas replaced coal in household furnaces and heaters. After World War II, new household appliances appeared—electric dishwashers, clothes dryers, and washing machines—that further expanded the demand for electricity.[10] Whereas coal still accounts for about one-quarter of the energy pie, the average age of coal-burning plants is twenty-five years; consequently, facilities are quickly becoming outdated and closing down, partially in response to the air-quality concerns outlined in Chapter 8.[11]

The United States has huge reserves of natural gas, which makes up another quarter of the energy pie; the country is estimated to have the sixth-largest proven reserves of natural gas in the world. Initially heralded as a clean, virtually pollution-free source of energy, the expansion of natural-gas production has been heavily criticized by environmental organizations. A proposal for a pipeline from Wyoming to California was derailed when researchers found that the planned route passed through habitats of the endangered desert tortoise.

About 20 percent of the U.S. energy pie is made up of crude oil, most of it imported from the Persian Gulf. In October 1973, nations of the Organization of the Petroleum Exporting Countries (OPEC) sharply increased the price of a barrel of oil from an average cost of $4 a barrel to nearly $12, leading to a fuel crisis that, at least momentarily, focused the political agenda on energy. In late 1975, Congress passed the Energy Policy and Conservation Act, which called for a phased deregulation of oil. But as quickly as they had surfaced, concerns about the country's energy policies faded; even a second energy crisis from 1979 to 1981 that raised crude oil prices from $14 to $37 a barrel failed to ignite public interest. Americans assumed that there was an unlimited supply of fuel available—it was simply a matter of turning on the spigot. Upon assuming office in 1981, President Ronald Reagan accelerated the process for price decontrols, making energy policy more market-oriented and reducing the federal government's role. The high cost of imported crude oil led to a reduction in U.S. petroleum consumption between 1978 and 1982; there was more fuel substitution, more efficient consumption of oil, a diversification of supply sources, and price-induced conservation. By the mid-1980s, OPEC nations sharply lowered the price for crude oil; from 1985 to 1986, the cost for imported oil fell from $27 a barrel to $14 a barrel.[12]

In August 1990, Iraq's leader, Saddam Hussein, ordered his troops into Kuwait, once again threatening the world's oil supplies. Few Americans showed much evidence of concern about whether their local gasoline pumps would go dry. The price of oil, which averaged $16 a barrel at the end of July 1990, exceeded $28 by late August and reached $36 a barrel in September. Realizing that the long-term demand for crude oil would be jeopardized by prolonged periods of high oil prices, OPEC nations boosted their oil production to make up for the supply lost during the Iraqi invasion. Prices quickly began to fall, and more importance was placed on energy conservation.

When President George H. W. Bush signed the Energy Policy Act of 1992—the first major legislative attempt to curb U.S. oil dependence in more than a decade—his action failed to generate more than a single day's media headlines. Even repeated bombings of Iraq by the United States and its allies in 1998, intense political unrest in the Middle East, a rise in oil prices that began in late spring 1999, and the terrorist attacks of September 11, 2001, did not seem to resonate with the American public as having a potential impact on petroleum supplies.

By 2005, when gasoline prices topped $3 per gallon in some parts of the country, consumers began paying more attention, as they did in 2008 when prices approached $5 per gallon and some pundits said prices could top $20 per gallon. Sales of hybrid vehicles such as the Toyota Prius and Honda Insight, and the natural-gas-powered Honda Civic GX, grew at an annual growth rate of 89 percent. These cars still made up a small fraction of the new vehicle market, and consumers added their names to waiting lists and paid more than the suggested manufacturer prices just to get better mileage. President Bush's Hydrogen Initiative, which called for spending $1.2 billion over five years to develop vehicles with hydrogen fuel cells and infrastructure technologies, faced many obstacles. The high cost and technological barriers associated with the fuel's distribution, storage, and use are likely to place this option several decades away—not fifteen years, as the president predicted.[13]

Congress, sensing an opening in the policy window, came back to the issue of drilling in the Arctic National Wildlife Refuge (ANWR) in April 2005. The House handed the president a victory by agreeing to provisions that would open up the coastal plain to oil drilling. The administration argued that environmentally responsible exploration and development could provide up to 1 million barrels of oil per day using less than 2,000 acres of the refuge's total land area. Then, in 2007, the president called on the nation to invest in new technology to reduce the country's dependence on foreign oil. At the heart of Bush's plan was a proposal to increase the amount of alternative fuels in the nation's vehicle fuel supply to 35 billion gallons by 2017, up from 5 billion gallons in 2006. The president's proposal, which seemed designed to assist the nation's farmers, would focus on corn-based ethanol, a move criticized by economists, who said it would drive up corn prices. Bush also called for stricter gas-mileage standards, with a 4 percent increase in fuel efficiency beginning in 2010 for cars. But the two prongs of the president's energy proposals seemed contradictory; since ethanol gets poorer gas mileage than gasoline, a mandate for greater use of alternative fuels could undermine efforts to achieve increased fuel economy.[14]

Ethanol and alternative fuels lost traction as a policy issue as the price of gasoline declined, and with the election of President Obama in November 2008, fossil-fuel policy took a number of different twists. In March 2009, after Congress lifted a moratorium on drilling in September 2008, the administration announced that it would auction off leases in the Gulf of Mexico that included 4.2 million acres that had been off-limits since 1988. The Department of the Interior (DOI) estimates that undiscovered oil reserves total 86 billion barrels, four times the nation's official proven reserves.[15] Then, in May 2009, the president summoned key Democratic lawmakers to Washington to try to build consensus around his energy policy. They agreed to support a "Cash for Clunkers" program that would give $3,500 or $4,500 to car buyers who agreed to replace their low-efficiency gasoline-powered vehicles with new, more fuel-efficient ones. Congress appropriated $3 billion to the program, which at least temporarily gave car dealers a positive bounce in sales. In October 2009, the president announced a $3.4 billion package to improve the country's energy grid, but the message was overshadowed by the World Series, health care and climate change proposals that were before Congress, and the deaths of more Americans in Afghanistan. Despite campaign promises to change the nation's energy mix to include more renewable fuels, the Obama administration faced major barriers from other issues on the policy agenda that captured the attention of both Congress and the public.

THE RETURN OF RENEWABLES

Renewable energy sources could conceivably serve as an alternative to our existing reliance on fossil fuels. These sources have been used extensively in other countries but, with the exception of hydropower, not in the United States.

Supporters of renewable energy sources point out that they produce no waste to be disposed of and no greenhouse gases. They generally are safe for workers, and facilities can be constructed more quickly than can plants using fossil fuels or nuclear power. Their biggest drawbacks are unreliability as a fuel source and the higher cost of producing and distributing the electricity they generate. But the subject of renewable energy returns to the policy agenda from time to time due to focusing events like the massive electric power blackouts over most of the northeastern United States in 1965, the Arab oil embargo in 1973, and historic highs in the cost of crude oil in 2005 and early 2008.

The political process has greatly affected U.S. attention to alternative fuel sources, and the federal government's support for renewable-energy research can be tied to both electoral cycles and the cost of oil. The passage of the 1978 Public Utilities Regulatory Policies Act (PURPA), for example, requires utilities to purchase power from nonutilities at an "avoided cost" rate (the rate of expense the utility would have incurred had it generated the energy itself). PURPA became an incentive for alternative sources like cogenerators (large, industrial power users produce steam and electricity for their own needs and sell the excess to local utilities) and small hydroelectric plants that were guaranteed a market for the electricity they generated. Although hydroelectric power is among the cheapest sources of energy available, its use is becoming more limited, as environmental groups have lobbied against the siting of new dams along waterways. Other forms of renewable energy—solar, wind, and geothermal power—were hailed as promising energy sources during the 1970s, when the newly created Energy Research and Development Administration funded proposals for "soft" energy. But by the mid-1980s, political support had faded and research dollars disappeared.

Despite limited federal support for alternative energy in the 1980s and 1990s, state governments moved forward with their own policies. Regulatory bodies can require utilities to develop a portfolio of energy sources, called *renewable portfolio standards* (RPS), including power generated by renewable energy providers, to make the cost of environmentally friendly energy more acceptable to consumers. The quantity of renewable energy or capacity is measured either in absolute units (such as Iowa, which requires its two utility companies to get 105 megawatts (MW) of power from renewable sources) or as a percentage share of retail sales, as seen in Table 6.1. RPS purchase obligations generally increase over time (based on legislative requirements), and retail suppliers, such as a utility company, must demonstrate compliance on an annual basis and face penalties for noncompliance.[16]

The direction of renewable energy appeared to be changing in 2004. President Bush announced a new Solar Energy Development Policy, establishing a framework for land managers to use in processing right-of-way applications for commercial solar energy projects on public lands managed by the Bureau of Land Management (BLM). The scale is significant because the DOI manages one in every five acres of land in the United States, and the BLM has jurisdiction over 261 million acres of the DOI land. In 2004, the solar-energy program was a key part of the president's energy proposals, with a focus on public land in the Southwest, where solar-energy

T A B L E 6.1   States with Renewable Energy Standards (2009)

State	Year Adopted	% Renewable Energy	By Year
Arizona	2006	15	2025
California	2006	20	2010
Colorado	2010	30	2020
Connecticut	2007	27	2020
Delaware	2007	20	2019
District of Columbia	2008	20	2020
Hawaii	2004	20	2020
Illinois	2007	25	2025
Iowa	1983	105 megawatts	
Maine	2007	10	2017
Maryland	2008	20	2022
Massachusetts	2008	15	2020
Michigan	2008	10	2015
Minnesota	2007	30	2020
Missouri	2008	15	2021
Montana	2005	15	2015
Nevada	2005	20	2015
New Hampshire	2007	23.8	2025
New Jersey	2006	22.5	2021
New Mexico	2007	20	2020
New York	2004	24	2013
North Carolina	2007	12.5	2021
Ohio	2009	12.5	2025
Oregon	2007	25	2025
Pennsylvania	2004	8	2021
Rhode Island	2004	16	2020
Texas	2005	5,880 megawatts	2015
Washington	2006	15	2020
Wisconsin	2006	10	2015

production is thought to have the highest potential. Generators producing about 370 MW of solar power are already installed in the West, mostly in southern California. 370 MW would supply energy for 370,000 homes. A typical large electricity-generating plant produces 1,000 MW. But by 2005, when the president made another attempt to gain congressional support for his energy policies, solar energy was mentioned in the context of tax incentives and research and development, rather than new initiatives or funding for specific projects. Instead, solar power appeared to have lost out to hydrogen, ethanol, and biomass for transportation fuels, and to nuclear power for electricity.

Under the Obama administration, solar power has been touted as one of the most reliable forms of alternative energy, with additional support from California governor Arnold Schwarzenegger. Dozens of companies, hoping to capitalize on federal stimulus dollars, have sought approval for applications to place solar mirrors on more than a million acres of public lands. In order to qualify for 2009 stimulus funds, the firms needed to break ground by the end of 2010. But projects have been stymied by two factors: the economic recession slowed down the bureaucratic maze for permits, and concerns over endangered species could stop projects altogether. In June 2009, the U.S. Ninth Circuit Court of Appeals ordered the U.S. Fish and Wildlife Service to reconsider its decision not to list the flat-tailed horned lizard as an endangered species, and a coalition of environmental groups sued the agency in October 2009 for slashing critical habitat designations for Peninsular bighorn sheep, both of which have been found on the site of a proposed solar array in southern California. Another solar-energy project in the state's Ivanpah Valley is the home of threatened desert tortoises and endangered cactuses. Company officials are looking at various forms of mitigation, from buying conservation land elsewhere to moving the tortoises.[17]

At least at the state and local levels, another promising renewable energy source now gaining governmental support is wind power, which dates back to around 50 A.D. in China, Afghanistan, and Persia. A Danish inventor, Poul La Cor, built a practical four-blade windmill in 1891; the first utility-scale wind generator was built on the shores of the Caspian Sea in 1931.[18] An estimated 6 million small windmills operated in the United States between 1850 and 1970. They were owned primarily by farmers to provide electricity for their family's use and for tending to the farm animals. Wind-power companies were supported by the U.S. Federal Wind Energy Program after the energy crisis of the 1970s, with an estimated 17,000 machines installed between 1981 and 1990. Suppliers received a 15 percent federal energy tax credit, and in California, where large-scale wind farms were built, a 50 percent credit encouraged additional wind-power development.[19]

Several new projects have gone from the wishful-thinking stage to probable as the technology progressed and citizens became more accustomed to seeing wind turbines on the landscape. The American Wind Energy Institute (AWEI) reports that by the end of 2008, Texas had surpassed both Iowa and California in terms of installed wind-power capacity, as seen in Table 6.2. Wind is classified into power classes based on wind speed. Class 1 is the lowest at about 13 miles per hour (mph), and Class 7 (27 mph) is the highest; large utility-scale turbines usually require Class 4 (17 mph) winds or higher. In addition to wind speed, companies considering land as potential wind farms must survey sites for their potential environmental sensitivity and distance from urban areas. Land-use conflicts may eliminate some areas, such as forests, farmlands, or

TABLE 6.2   Top Ten States, Total Wind-Power Capacity (2009) (in megawatts)

State	Existing	Under Construction	Rank (existing)
Texas	8,361	1,096	1
Iowa	3,043	409	2
California	2,787	20	3
Minnesota	1,805	40	4
Washington	1,575	405	5
Oregon	1,408	426	6
New York	1,264	21	7
Colorado	1,068	174	8
Kansas	1,014	0	9
Illinois	915	703	10

SOURCE: American Wind Energy Association. "U.S. Wind Energy Projects." http://www.awea.org/projects. Accessed September 9, 2009.

rangeland. Although most policymakers support efforts to diversify energy sources, the projects can also be politically controversial. Alameda County, California, placed a moratorium on new wind farms because turbines had killed hundreds of birds of prey; and in Tucker County, West Virginia, hundreds of bats that had flown into the turbines were killed. In Cape Cod, Massachusetts, residents opposed a project that they felt would spoil their view. Environmental groups have raised questions about the potential impact of wind farms on fish populations and migratory birds.[20]

There is an important change that characterizes U.S. wind policy as we enter the next decade: an increasing competition among projects for wind development dollars. Although over $15 billion in federal stimulus funds were initially made available for renewable energy, including wind power—money that previously went to California, Texas, and states in the Midwest—that money is now being split between onshore and offshore projects.

States in the East have been fiercely competitive over funding for offshore projects, with the region being called the "Saudi Arabia of Wind." States in the mid-Atlantic and Northeast regions have fought for years over which one would be the first one to be actually brought online, with the Cape Wind project off the coast of Massachusetts closest to fruition. The proposed 130-turbine project, which is estimated to create 150 permanent jobs, received final approval from the state in 2009. The turbines will be spaced six to nine football fields apart, allowing room for small draft boats to maneuver.[21] Meanwhile, offshore projects are still in the planning or approval stage in Delaware, New Jersey, Rhode Island, Maryland, New York, and North Carolina.

Another View, Another Voice: S. David Freeman

If you live in California—or, for that matter, Tennessee—you might recognize S. David Freeman's name. If you're a conservationist, have an interest in renewable energy, or believe there's a future in hydrogen cars, you probably have read his book, *Winning Our Energy Independence: An Energy Insider Shows How.* In April 2009, he was appointed by Los Angeles Mayor Antonio Villaraigosa as the deputy mayor assigned to carry out his environmental agenda. He is a political mover and shaker who has a career in public utilities, and whose voice might be influencing the Obama administration's energy policies.

Simon David Freeman was born in Chattanooga, Tennessee, in 1926; his father was an umbrella repairman and his mother helped out with his store. He served as a U.S. Merchant Marine in World War II, transporting gasoline across the North Atlantic, then received a B.S. in civil engineering from Georgia Tech, and an L.L.B. from the University of Tennessee. He held positions as energy advisor in both the Johnson and Nixon White Houses, but he is best known as chairman of the Tennessee Valley Authority (TVA) from 1977 to 1981. Freeman was appointed to that position by President Jimmy Carter, where he turned the agency's focus from growth to conservation. He launched a $1 billion air pollution–mitigation program and an energy-efficiency effort that reached more than 1 million homes. He subsequently headed public power utilities in Texas, New York, and Sacramento.

His shining hour may have been his work with the Los Angeles Department of Water and Power, where in 1997 he laid off thousands of workers and cut the $8 billion of debt the facility owed in half. His popularity has ebbed and flowed along with his career path, with even friends noting, "He can be just terribly difficult to get along with. But you forgive all the momentary stuff for the strength of his character and the depth of his experience and the fact that he will be plain."

"It's time the words 'public power' are pronounced again in public," he says. "It was public power that turned the lights on in rural America." He left the agency in 2001.

In September 2005, he was appointed to the Los Angeles Board of Harbor Commissioners by Mayor Villaraigosa, a slightly different post for Freeman. The Commission oversees the management and operations of the Port of Los Angeles, one of the busiest, most successful seaports in the United States. In 2006, he helped negotiate an agreement with the Port of Long Beach to reduce lethal, cancer-causing diesel emissions from oceangoing ships, railroads, trucks, and cargo-handling equipment. The reductions included the use of cleaner diesel fuel, more efficient engines, catalytic converters, and switching to liquefied natural gas or even hydrogen in the future. Freeman said there was also the possibility of switching to a maglev train to haul shipping containers away from the port to huge freight yards.

He has won awards from the Los Angeles Coalition for Clean Air, National Wildlife Association, and Global Green for his devotion to clean air, clean water, and renewable energy. While in Sacramento, when voters decided to mothball the troubled Rancho Seco nuclear generating facility, he replaced the lost 913 MW by buying up old and inefficient refrigerators, offering rebates for solar-panel and wind-energy projects, and planting thousands of trees to serve as a natural air-conditioning system.

As for the use of renewable energy, Freeman says he is "cautiously optimistic. Let's outlaw new coal-fired plants and new nuclear plants and let's order Detroit to make plug-in hybrids and treat this as a life-or-death issue, which is what it is." He notes that "It will take twenty-five, thirty years to phase out the existing coal-fired plants and have an all-renewable world. But I'm not a member of the Sierra Club. I'm a utility executive that ran major utilities, and I can tell you there is no reason why the electric power industry can't be all renewable."

SOURCES:

David Gilson. "Power Q & A: S. David Freeman." *Mother Jones.* April 21, 2008. http://www.motherjones.com/politics/2008/04/power-qa-s-david-freeman. Accessed August 11, 2009.

S. David Freeman. *Winning Our Energy Independence: An Insider Shows How.* Salt Lake City: Gibbs Smith, 2007.

Port of Los Angeles. "Commissioners." http://www.portoflosangeles.org/commission_Commissioners. Accessed August 11, 2009.

Todd Purdum. "California's Leader in Singing the Praises of Public Power." *New York Times.* January 27, 2001. http://www.nytimes.com/2001/01/27/us/public-lives-california-s-leader-in-singing-the-praises-of-public-power.html?pagewanted=1. Accessed February 18, 2007.

James Sterngold. "Port Pollution Revolution Coming." *San Francisco Chronicle.* June 28, 2006. http://articles.sfgate.com/2006-06-28/news/17299551_1_ports-diesel-emissions-cleaner-diesel-fuel. Accessed February 18, 2007.

David Zahniser. "Villaraigosa Picks S. David Freeman as Environment Deputy." *Los Angeles Times.* April 17, 2009. http://articles.latimes.com/2009/apr/17/local/me-freeman17. Accessed August 11, 2009.

Michael Zielenziger. "Green Rules." *California Magazine.* January-February 2007. p. 22.

THE NUCLEAR POWER DEBATE

Support for nuclear power as an energy source began in the United States in 1960, when the utility company Southern California Edison announced plans to build a huge facility at San Onofre, California. Pacific Gas and Electric made a similar announcement of plans to build a privately funded plant at Bodega Bay, California, although the latter project was never built. The companies were encouraged by the Atomic Energy Commission (AEC), the federal agency charged with regulating the new facilities. The AEC announced its objective of making nuclear power economically competitive by 1968 in those parts of the country that were dependent upon high-cost fossil fuels. In 1962, as an incentive for utility companies to build large-capacity nuclear plants, the AEC offered to pay part of the design costs. The rush to build began; orders for new plants grew steadily between 1966 and 1974, and then dropped off sharply between 1975 and 1978. No orders for nuclear generating units have been placed by a utility or government agency since 1978, and no new facility has been issued a full-power operating license since 1996. About 8 percent of the nation's energy comes from the 104 nuclear power plants currently operating in the United States.

What happened to undermine the promising beginnings of nuclear power? Many factors were at work:

1. The growth of the environmental movement in the early 1970s, combined with zealous antiwar sentiment, led to a strong sense of public opposition to anything associated with nuclear weapons, including nuclear power as an energy source.

2. That same public pressure led to increased government sensitivity about the impacts of new projects, as seen in the history of legislation outlined in Chapter 1. In 1971, the U.S. Court of Appeals ruled that the AEC had failed to follow the provisions of the National Environmental Policy Act in licensing the Calvert Cliffs facility near Baltimore, Maryland; the court made a similar ruling on the Quad Cities nuclear power station on the Mississippi River in Illinois. Both decisions focused attention on the environmental impacts of nuclear facilities and led to increased scrutiny of license applications.

3. Media coverage of a malfunctioning cooling system at Three Mile Island in 1979 and the explosion of a nuclear reactor at Chernobyl in 1986 made utilities still considering nuclear power think twice about the effects of widespread public opposition to such projects. These attitudes are still prevalent today and have accounted for the general reluctance of policymakers even to consider this power source as an option.

4. Economics played a key role in scuttling the building of new facilities. Government estimates on the growth in demand for electricity in the 1970s turned out to be overly optimistic. As the demand for energy decreased, the cost of building new plants rose, making them cost-ineffective. In 1971, the estimated cost of building a typical facility was $345 million, but by 1980,

the figure had climbed to $3.2 billion. The federal government had spent nearly $18 billion in subsidizing the commercial development of nuclear power by 1980, and smaller utilities could not afford to build on their own.

5. In addition, construction and licensing of new plants were taking as long as ten years, delaying the point at which utilities could begin passing the costs on to consumers and recouping their investments. Financial horror stories began to proliferate. Of the five nuclear reactors started in the 1970s by the Washington Public Power Supply System, only one has been completed, and the utility ultimately defaulted on $2.25 billion in bonds in 1983. When the Long Island Lighting Company began building its Shoreham plant in April 1973, the cost was estimated at $300 million. The project was delayed by protests from nearby residents and by federally mandated design changes, and the cost escalated to $5.5 billion by the time the plant was completed in December 1984.[22] Suddenly, plans for all types of power plants—not just nuclear—were being shelved as too costly.

However, utility companies are now rethinking their options. The initial forty-year operating licenses of about 10 percent of current nuclear reactors in the United States are scheduled to expire by the end of 2010. The Electric Power Research Institute notes, however, that because the facilities have been well-maintained and the Nuclear Regulatory Commission (NRC) has carefully scrutinized the safety and environmental records, the inherent operational limitations have been extended. In 2000, the NRC extended the license renewals for two nuclear plants for an additional twenty years; the industry expects to be revitalized, supplying some of the most competitive power generators available.[23]

The industry itself continued moving forward, in large part due to the support of the Bush administration. Nuclear Power 2010, a program initiated to address issues affecting the expansion of nuclear generation, is a cost-shared government-industry effort to pave the way for new light-water nuclear plants. According to the program's goals, to maintain nuclear power's contribution to the U.S. energy portfolio would require the building of new nuclear plants at a rate of three to four per year, starting in 2010. To keep this pace on track, the Bush administration favored an Early Site Licensing Permit that would approve sites for new nuclear plants prior to a power company's commitment to build. This, along with other regulatory changes and legislation under the Energy Policy Act of 2005, would accelerate nuclear power development, the administration believed.[24]

By the end of 2009, the Energy Information Administration referred to a "nuclear renaissance" as the NRC began considering new applications for commercial nuclear reactors. The first application in over three decades was filed in July 2007, and by the end of 2008, twenty projects were on file. While this does not mean that projects will be built or even started, the agency notes, the significant number of applications, along with the expense of gathering the required data for the NRC, may indicate "future commitments by the industry to increase capacity."[25]

As of 2009, facilities were proposed in fifty states. Notably, there was only one state—Idaho—in the West where a company had applied for an application for a commercial nuclear reactor. The TVA's Watts Bar 2 plant had originally been issued a construction permit in January 1973; the last newly built commercial reactor to go online was Watts Bar 1 in 1996. In the 1980s, the utility decided there was insufficient demand to merit completion of the second reactor, which is about 80 percent complete. TVA estimates it will take about five more years to finish the work, at a cost of about $2.5 billion. But if completed, Watts Bar 2 would likely become the first new U.S. reactor completed in the twenty-first century.[26]

Will nuclear power ever be reconsidered as a major source of energy? The answer to that question has little to do with science or technology, and much to do with politics and the economy. Some industry officials believe that such a change can take place only if Congress streamlines the regulatory framework for licensing facilities. Other analysts feel that utilities would be more likely to gain public acceptance for new nuclear facilities if they were sited or expanded near existing plants rather than in new areas. Public opposition to nuclear facilities, although still strong, appears to have leveled off. Attempts to close down facilities or ban nuclear power altogether have not been successful in some states, suggesting that Americans may not be so disenchanted with nuclear power as to close down the industry completely. But most observers believe that, unless Congress moves forward with a plan to store nuclear waste (see Chapter 5), the nuclear energy debate will remain at a standstill.

CAFE STANDARDS AND ALTERNATIVE FUELS

Environmental groups have long sought to address the nation's energy problems through revisions to new car corporate average fuel economy (CAFE) standards. The standards, designed to increase the fuel economy of cars and light trucks, were initiated in 1975 by the Energy Policy and Conservation Act, and are implemented by the National Highway Traffic Safety Administration (NHTSA), which sets the standards for vehicles sold in the United States. The Environmental Protection Agency (EPA) calculates the average fuel economy for each manufacturer; cars and light trucks are considered separately. The NHTSA standards, beginning with model year (MY) 1978, required cars to meet a fleet average of 27.5 miles per gallon (mpg) by 1985. The NHTSA required light-duty trucks (pickup trucks, minivans, and sports utility vehicles) to achieve a fleet average of at least 20.7 mpg. This was a substantial increase for cars, which averaged 16 mpg in 1977, and for new trucks, which averaged about 13 mpg.[27] Between 1978 and 1985, there were significant reductions in oil consumption, although studies were inconclusive regarding whether the change was due to reduced gasoline prices or to implementation of the new CAFE standards. Automakers had changed as well, producing smaller, more lightweight cars that were more fuel-efficient. But the unintended consequence of the new policy was an increase in traffic fatalities that were attributed to the size and weight of the smaller cars. This raised the issue of whether safety was being sacrificed for fuel economy.

From MY 1990 to 2010, the CAFE standard remained at 27.5 for cars, staying at about 20 mpg for light trucks from MY 1984 to 2004. Policy changed on December 19, 2007, when President George W. Bush signed the Energy Independence and Security Act (EISA), setting a goal of 35 mpg by 2020, a measure that would increase the fuel economy standards by 40 percent. In April 2008, the U.S. Department of Transportation proposed a 4.5 percent per year increase over the five-year period ending in 2015, a 25 percent total improvement, exceeding the 3.3 percent baseline proposed by Congress in 2007. For passenger cars, the proposal would increase fuel economy from 27.5 mpg to 35.7 mpg by 2015. For light trucks, the standard would rise from 23.5 mpg in 2010 to 28.6 mpg in 2015. The change in CAFE standards was estimated to save nearly 55 billion gallons of fuel and a reduction of 521 metric tons of carbon dioxide emissions, along with a $100 billion savings in fuel costs by consumers over the lifetime of the vehicles covered by the proposal. NHTSA and the EPA subsequently prepared a rulemaking to cover vehicles for MY 2012 through 2016.[28]

One of the more controversial elements of the proposal was that it would allow auto manufacturers to earn credit for exceeding the CAFE standards, which were designed to serve as an incentive for companies to exceed the goals. Under the EISA, the NHTSA was directed by Congress to establish a credit trading and transferring system that allows manufacturers to transfer credits among appliance categories, as well as selling them to other manufacturers. Credits, once earned, could be "banked" for five years, but could not be used to meet the minimum CAFE standard.

Organizations like Resources for the Future support higher gasoline prices instead of increases in CAFE standards. This would motivate new-car buyers to demand better fuel economy from the manufacturers, and once that demand was established, automakers would be less reluctant to produce more fuel-efficient vehicles. Higher gas prices have the added benefit of forcing the public to drive less, to maintain their cars better, or to carpool—strategies that reduce the emissions of carbon dioxide.[29] Public response to having to pay more to drive bigger vehicles that are fuel-inefficient is not likely to be supportive.

Under the Obama administration, in January 2009, the Department of Transportation was told to review the Bush administration's proposal, and to finalize the MY 2011 standard by the end of March 2009. The department subsequently issued a new standard that is about 1 mpg lower than the CAFE standard recommended under Bush, saving an estimated 887 million gallons of fuel and reducing carbon dioxide emissions by 8.3 million metric tons. But the Obama rulemaking was challenged in court by the Center for Biological Diversity, leading to manufacturer uncertainty as to which standard will be in place for future model years of vehicles. A few months later, Obama proposed a fuel-economy program that went beyond the Bush years by adopting uniform federal standards that would regulate both fuel economy and greenhouse-gas emissions. This standard would cover MY 2012 to 2016, when a standard of 39 mpg for cars and 30 mpg for trucks would go into effect. This proposal gained the support of manufacturers because it provided some measure of certainty, at least for the next several model years.

THE HISTORY OF POLICY PARALYSIS

Historically, U.S. energy policy has been separated by type of fuel, with different institutional associations and interests for each type, and few attempts at coalition building. Coal interests from the Northeast have dealt with the Bureau of Mines, while states with uranium were more likely to converse with the Atomic Energy Committees in Congress and the NRC. Seldom did jurisdictional boundaries cross over from one fuel to another; as a result, terms like *disarray*, *turmoil*, and *inertia* are often used to describe U.S. energy policy. Those terms are in part applicable due to the maze of legislative and regulatory obstacles that have developed, along with a profusion of competing interests. The result is an energy policy that is highly segmented and neither comprehensive nor effective. Although many analysts have attempted to explain why U.S. energy policy has been so ineffective, the consensus appears to be that the government has intervened unnecessarily rather than allowing market forces to allocate scarce energy resources. How did such a policy develop?

Before 1900, the U.S. government had an ad hoc approach to what was perceived to be an unlimited supply of energy resources. A sense of abundance and virtual giveaways of public lands resulted in many valuable resources coming under private ownership. Although there were early rumblings of competition among interests representing the various fuels, it was not until after the turn of the century that the government began to intervene. To assure a stable and competitive oil market, the government relied upon the Sherman Anti-Trust Act in 1911 to break up the Standard Oil monopoly, and during World War I, President Woodrow Wilson established the Petroleum Advisory Committee to allocate American supplies. After the 1921 Teapot Dome scandal, in which officials were convicted of leasing federal lands to oil companies in exchange for bribes, the Federal Oil Conservation Board was created to oversee the oil industry. By the 1930s, the federal government's role had changed to one of consumer protection, expanding its jurisdiction with the Natural Gas Act of 1938 and the creation of the TVA. An attempt was never made to coordinate policy across fuel and use areas. Each area of energy supply—coal, gas, hydropower, oil, and nuclear power—was handled separately, as was each consumption sector—utilities, transportation, industrial, and residential. During the 1950s, as Congress approved a massive interstate highway system and transportation network, the Supreme Court ratified the Federal Power Commission's power to regulate natural gas prices, which held prices artificially low as gas consumption skyrocketed.[30]

As the environmental movement developed in the late 1960s and early 1970s, the process of developing energy policy became increasingly complex as more interests demanded to be included in the decision making process. At the same time, the importance of energy as a political issue brought in congressional leaders who sought to respond to their constituents' demands that something be done about the long lines at the gas pumps and rising prices for fuels. Between 1969 and 1973, a confluence of negative factors and events changed the history of American energy policy forever. First, predictions by a few officials about a dependence on foreign oil came true. Although the United States first began importing oil as early as 1947, oil from Arab sources reached over a million barrels a day by 1973, more than double the amount imported eighteen months earlier and 30 percent of total U.S. demand. Second, domestic oil production decreased because of price disparities with foreign oil and increasing costs for exploration and recovery. Third, new environmental legislation discouraged production of coal and nuclear power and brought a delay in completion of the trans-Alaska pipeline at the same time that Americans were driving more miles than ever. Finally, the highly publicized Santa Barbara oil spill in 1969 led to a moratorium on offshore drilling, further restricting American oil production. The result was a nation made vulnerable to the vagaries of Middle Eastern politics.

The Nixon administration's approach to energy policy in the 1970s was marked by a series of failed attempts to do something about the impending crisis. Initially, the government imposed an Economic Stabilization Program, which not only froze prices on crude oil and petroleum products for 90 days but also froze wages and prices nationwide. In early 1973, Nixon restructured the country's mandatory oil-import quota plan, which had limited foreign oil imports and allowed an unlimited purchase of home heating oil and diesel fuel for a four-month period. This action was followed by the creation of a handpicked Special Committee on Energy comprised of key Nixon advisers, who recommended that steps be taken to cope with price increases and fuel shortages. The strategy was to increase energy supplies, with little concern for modifying demand or conserving energy. By midyear, the administration's mandatory fuel-allocation program had led to the closure of hundreds of independent gasoline stations. Then the administration shifted its policies once again by proposing that $100 million be spent on research and development for new energy technology and creation of a Federal Energy Administration to coordinate policy.

In October 1973, OPEC members, resentful of U.S. aid to Israel, voted to cut their oil production and to end all petroleum exports to the United States, resulting in a sharp increase in world oil prices and forcing the Nixon administration to drastically revise its approach. Nixon responded with Project Independence to eliminate foreign oil imports by 1980, and Congress enacted the Emergency Petroleum Allocation Act to distribute fuel supplies evenly.

Analyses of the politics of energy during this period point out several lessons learned from the 1973 crisis. For example, a "cry-wolf syndrome" arose when the first warnings appeared about dependence on foreign oil. One survey had even found that most Americans were unaware that the United States imported any oil and were unable to understand how the most technically advanced nation in the world was simply unable to produce enough oil to meet demand. As a result, the concerns were often ignored or disbelieved. Decisions were often based on misleading or poor-quality information, and confused and often contradictory policies resulted. A turnover in leadership (four different people held the position of White House energy policy coordinator in 1973) exacerbated the problem. From 1971 to 1973, the role of "energy czar" passed through the hands of seven men, each of whom had a different concept of what U.S. energy policy should be. Some, such as Secretary of Agriculture Earl Butz, were given new titles and responsibilities; others, such as George Lincoln, were made heads of agencies that were then abruptly abolished (Office of Emergency Planning).[31] Last, by treating each fuel source separately and allowing the disparate interest groups to be so deeply involved in the decision making process, the government never really took control of the crisis.

Public opinion about energy policy has changed over time in response to fuel supplies and the state of the economy. Support for more oil and coal production peaked at the height of the second energy crisis in 1980, according to one study. When gasoline prices soared, support for offshore drilling and strip-mined coal became popular. As the economy improves, however, the public takes a more pro-environmental stance. After the Three Mile Island incident, support for nuclear power dropped dramatically, although, ironically, the same trend did not hold true for the 1986 accident at the Chernobyl nuclear facility.[32] Although Greenpeace has chronicled a substantive list of nuclear accidents and events at facilities around the world since World War II, only a handful have been widely publicized. As a result, most consumers in the United States believe that with minor exceptions, nuclear power production has been safe.

As a result of the 1973 oil crisis, a host of agencies took turns formulating energy policy. The Federal Energy Administration was created in May 1974, but the agency lacked both direction and a clear sense of mission. It was designed to bring together smaller agencies that had historically been in conflict with one another and was caught between the competing objectives of regulating prices and expediting domestic resource development. After Nixon's resignation, Congress attempted to pick up the pieces by enacting the Energy Policy and Conservation Act of 1975, which levied a windfall-profits tax on oil to control imports and gave the president the power to ration gas in an emergency. Other provisions included appliance standards, improved fuel-efficiency standards, and authorized petroleum stockpiling.

The politics of energy took a different turn during President Jimmy Carter's administration. The creation of a separate, Cabinet-level Department of Energy in 1977 underscored the nation's crisis mentality and reflected Carter's campaign promise to reorganize government. The agency was charged with regulating fuel consumption, providing incentives for energy conservation, and conducting research and development into alternative energy sources. In 1977, an acute natural-gas shortage led Carter to propose his National Energy Plan (NEP), and he characterized the energy situation as "the moral equivalent of war." The NEP differed from the Nixon administration's strategies because it called for greater fuel efficiency and conservation rather than increased production. In 1977, Congress also replaced the Federal Power Commission, which had been created in 1920, with the Federal Energy Regulatory Commission (FERC), giving the agency responsibility for oversight of the electric power and natural gas industries.

By the time Congress passed the National Energy Act in October 1978, Carter's NEP had been gutted. In retrospect, it has been argued that the Carter proposal was doomed from the beginning. Members of Congress found that their constituents were unwilling to make sacrifices (like reducing the number of miles they drove yearly) because they did not think there really was an energy shortage. Voters made it clear that they believed the entire energy crisis was concocted by the big oil companies to force prices upward and generate bigger profits. In addition, the Carter administration was guilty of taking its case directly to the people, rather than developing a program in consultation with Congress.

The Reagan administration, in contrast, marks an eight-year period of amicable cooperation between the petroleum and coal industries and the administration, and a dramatic shift in energy research and development.[33] Reagan's strategy, outlined in his 1981 National Energy Plan, was to limit governmental intervention as much as possible—especially with regard to regulatory agencies—while supporting nuclear power and cutting research funds for alternative energy sources. Renouncing the Carter administration's goal of meeting 20 percent of the nation's energy needs through solar power by the year 2000, Reagan even had his staff remove the solar panels Carter had installed at the White House. Reagan was unsuccessful in dissolving the Department of Energy, which he viewed as indicative of Carter's "big government" approach. Federal subsidies for alternative energy sources like wind power were eliminated by the mid-1980s, further reducing industry incentives. The Reagan presidency was marked by a return to the strategies of the 1960s—including reliance on the free market to control prices, dependence on fossil fuels, tax benefits for oil producers, and little support for conservation.

George H. W. Bush continued the policies initiated by his predecessor. His 1991 national energy strategy sought to achieve roughly equal measures of new energy production and conservation. A cornerstone of that policy was to open up 1.5 million acres of the 19-million-acre ANWR in northeast Alaska for oil and gas exploration. After the Persian Gulf War in 1991, Congress seemed more inclined to move forward on energy policy, finally enacting the comprehensive Energy Policy Act of 1992 just prior to the November election. The new law allowed restructuring of the electric-utility industry to promote more competition, provide tax relief to independent oil and gas drillers, encourage energy conservation and efficiency, promote renewable energy and cars that run on alternative fuels, make it easier to build nuclear power plants, authorize billions of dollars for energy-related research and development, and create a climate protection office within the Department of Energy. Critics point out that the bill did not address the issue of automobile fuel efficiency (one of the planks in Bill Clinton's environmental platform) and did not significantly reduce U.S. dependence on foreign oil, but rather capped existing levels of use. Still, it marked the first time in a decade that Congress was able to compromise on the most contentious provisions—those dealing with alternative fuels and energy-related tax provisions.[34]

Early in his presidency, Bill Clinton proposed a broad tax on all forms of energy in order to raise federal revenue to reduce the budget deficit. The proposed tax—called a "BTU tax" because it was based on the heating ability of different fuels as measured in British thermal units (BTUs)—would have raised the prices of gasoline, electricity, and other energy sources. Environmental groups supported the measure as a way to promote conservation and to begin moving away from fossil fuel consumption. The tax would have raised approximately $22 billion per year, only a tiny fraction of the $6 trillion U.S. economy, but opposition from Democratic and Republican senators representing energy-producing states killed the idea.[35] The administration was successful in raising gasoline taxes by 4.3 cents per gallon in 1993, however, as part of its deficit-reduction plan. During the summer of the 1996 campaign, when gas prices jumped 17 percent, Republican candidate Bob Dole called for a repeal of the gas tax, and President Clinton called for an investigation of the oil companies and ordered the release of 12 million barrels of oil from the nation's Strategic Oil Reserve to soften the price increase.[36] Increasing energy taxes sufficiently for significant conservation or revenue purposes requires more political skill than recent presidents and their congressional allies have been able to muster. Clinton's record on energy policy did improve in 1998 when he announced a twelve-year extension of the federal ban on new oil and gas drilling off the East and West Coasts. The drilling moratorium had been imposed by President Bush in 1990 and was scheduled to expire in 2000. Although environmental organizations had hoped the president would make the federal ban permanent, the extension until 2012 was considered a reasonable compromise between environmental protection and the interests of oil and gas firms, which had argued that improved technology is making drilling safer.

The president extended the drilling moratorium (which is permanent in marine sanctuaries) by executive order in June 1998. Two months later, California senator Barbara Boxer urged Secretary of the Interior Bruce Babbitt to ban drilling on forty existing, yet undeveloped, leases off the coast of California.[37] The leases, owned by several different oil companies, were not made a part of Clinton's drilling moratorium and include portions of the Santa Maria Basin, termed "the Saudi Arabia of California." The area is a vast reservoir of more than 500 million barrels of petroleum and a still-undetermined volume (billions of cubic feet) of natural gas. To lease owners, the oil and gas resources could mean a reduction of the nation's dependence on imported oil. Any interference in their legal right to develop the leases would constitute an illegal taking, although some observers believe that some kind of plan could be arranged to compensate the oil companies for the billions of dollars already spent on buying up leases. To environmental groups like the League for Coastal Protection and the Environmental Defense Center in San Luis Obispo, California, a potential leak not only poses environmental hazards, it also threatens the region's economy, which is largely dependent on tourism. But as one representative of the Western States Petroleum Association (the region's main oil industry trade group) put it, "There are a lot of [oil] resources off this coast. When it comes down to it, it's hard for me to believe that the Congress and the Secretary of the Interior are willing to walk away from them."[38]

Those factors were of key importance to incoming President George W. Bush, who issued his plan for a national energy policy in May 2001, appointing Spencer Abraham as his Secretary of Energy. As part of his proposal, Bush sought to increase supplies of oil and gas by opening up drilling in the ANWR. Bush made reducing the United States' dependence upon foreign oil his top domestic priority, even though attempts to open up exploration within the refuge had been tried unsuccessfully for decades. Geologists believe the refuge has the largest untapped reserve of oil in the country. Environmental groups criticized the plan, and even as war with Iraq threatened oil supplies and prices at the pump rose significantly, Congress refused to approve the president's drilling proposal.

The Bush administration also looked to other domestic sources of fossil fuel—five basins along the Rocky Mountains, which the industry refers to as the "Persian Gulf of natural gas."[39] The U.S. Geological Survey estimated that 137 trillion cubic feet of natural gas and several billion barrels of oil could lie within the region, centered around Colorado, Montana, New Mexico, Utah, and Wyoming. Although the federal government owns some of the area and drilling rights beneath some private lands, the patchwork system of ownership and conflicting laws over land use have led to confusion and fragmentation, making a comprehensive drilling plan difficult. The administration established a task force in May 2001 to speed decisions on drilling permits because industry officials complained that red tape and rigid legal interpretations were strangling domestic energy production. "We're hoping," said the chair of the Independent Petroleum Association of America, "that the seemingly endless reviews come to a conclusion."[40]

Attempts to move the administration's energy proposals forward were thwarted in part to allegations surrounding Vice President Dick Cheney and the National Energy Policy Development Group. Cheney convened the group, also called the "energy task force," to develop an assessment of the nation's energy needs and to make recommendations to the president. The members, government officials with extensive experience within the energy industry, met for three months in closed-door sessions before releasing their report in May 2001. As one critic noted, "The report was an orgy of industry plunder, recommending the transfer of billions of dollars of public wealth to the oil, coal, and nuclear industries. Paying lip service to conservation and environmental concerns, the report focused almost exclusively on deregulation, giant subsidies, and tax breaks for every major corporate polluter in the energy field."[41]

The issue became supercharged when the task force refused to make its records public. The General Accounting Office unsuccessfully filed suit in federal district court; the U.S. Supreme Court ruled against the Sierra Club and the organization Judicial Watch in 2004. In a May 2005 unanimous decision, the U.S. Court of Appeals for the District of Columbia ruled against the two groups again, supporting the Bush administration's contention that Cheney was free to meet with energy-industry lobbyists in 2001 when the national energy policy task force was meeting. The justices noted that the Open Meetings Act was not applicable to the case because two White House officials had testified that industry members offered opinions only at advisory meetings and did not have a vote during the internal deliberations of the task force. The court noted that the smaller stakeholder meetings were forums to collect individual views, rather than to bring a collective judgment to bear. Another suit, filed under the Freedom of Information Act by the Natural Resources Defense Council, resulted in the organization's eventually gaining access to about 20,000 documents, but no logs from the vice president's meetings were included.

Environmental organizations charged that the task-force proposals were a form of payback for corporate leaders who had contributed to the president's reelection campaign. Others referred to "corporate cronyism" because the task-force members had conflicts of interest with the decisions being made about companies they had represented or worked for. Senate Democrats were able to block the task force's 105 proposals in legislative form, but the administration countered by moving them to the regulatory arena, where they did not require congressional approval. Several Clinton-era regulations were eliminated, and Clean Air Act provisions were substantially weakened. Although the incident may have been a minor public-relations nightmare for the president, the end result was that most of the task-force recommendations were implemented. The court rulings appear to have brought an end to litigation regarding Cheney's group.

President Bush's proposals in 2005 differed substantially from how the public viewed the energy debate. Polls showed that Americans preferred energy conservation to increased production of domestic energy supplies, with 56 percent opposing the president's plans to open up exploration and drilling for oil in the ANWR. Despite their opposition to specific policies, however, three out of five Americans said they expected Bush to do a good job in improving the nation's energy policies.[42]

In March 2005, President Bush traveled to Columbus, Ohio, where he called upon Congress to pass an energy bill that would meet four major objectives: promote conservation and efficiency, increase domestic production, diversify the nation's energy supply, and modernize the energy infrastructure while upholding the responsibility to be good stewards of the environment.[43] The proposal was not new, but rather a reiteration of the president's call for a comprehensive energy bill that had been announced when he first came into office. Bush may have perceived that the policy window was opening during his second term in a way that it had not been in 2001. With larger partisan majorities in the House and the Senate resulting from the 2004 elections, uncertainty over oil supplies in the Middle East, and historic highs in the cost of crude oil, the political environment certainly was more promising than in previous years.

Some researchers believe that each episode of short supply and higher energy prices contributes to the perception that the nation lacks an energy policy, and that we have failed to learn from past lessons. One study notes, however, that in the three decades since the 1973 Arab oil embargo, the period has been one of general price and supply stability that is generally broken with shorter episodes when price became more volatile and supplies of fuel less certain. It is not that energy policy has failed to be responsive to crises; rather, it is hard in the face of lengthy periods of stability and declining prices for conventional fuels to sustain certain policy courses that shield the nation from the occasional episodes of instability.

GLOBAL ENERGY USE AND SUPPLIES

While most of this chapter has focused on domestic energy use and production, there is a different image altogether when one looks at the global picture. Energy policy transcends the traditional boundaries of the nation-state and cannot be resolved by a single country. It is an issue that possesses a present imperative that forces nations to press for resolution. For example, oil is a finite commodity; thus, it is crucial that alternative energy sources be found. The resolution of energy scarcity requires policy action—it will not resolve itself. Finally, energy is a global issue because of its persistence on the policy agenda—there is no consensus on how to solve the problems of supply and demand that have been identified.

Energy consumption is closely tied to economic development. Throughout the 1990s, forecasters believed that as we entered the next century, in addition to increasing demand, there would be a changing profile of fuel use. But many factors determine the world's demand for energy, and expectations for economic growth and energy market performance in many areas of the world are changing dramatically.

One way to look at the development of energy policy on a global scale is to examine projections for energy consumption. According to the U.S. Department of Energy's Energy Information Administration, world marketed energy consumption is projected to increase by 44 percent from 2006 to 2030. What is particularly noteworthy is the fact that energy demand in developing countries (defined as those outside the Organization for Economic Cooperation and Development, or OECD) increases by 73 percent, compared with an increase of 15 percent in developed countries. Although energy demand has been reduced because of the economic downturn of 2008 to 2010, there is an expectation that as economies recover, demand for energy in the long term will rise.[44]

Fossil fuels continue to be the dominant element of the world's "energy pie" in most projections; however, their share falls from 36 percent in 2006 to 32 percent in 2030 due to increasing oil prices that will lead many energy users to switch to other sources of fuel whenever possible, especially natural gas. The cost of a barrel of oil on the world market, which reached $147 in mid-July 2008, has fallen dramatically since then, but is expected to rise from $61 per barrel in 2009 to $110 per barrel in 2015 and $130 per barrel in 2030. Some countries, including the United States, will begin to rely more on unconventional fuels, such as oil sands, biofuels, coal-to-liquids, and gas-to-liquids, accounting for 13 percent of the world liquid supply in 2030.[45]

Renewable energy sources will continue to flourish, with an emphasis on hydropower, wind power, and biomass. World renewable energy use for electricity generation is expected to grow by nearly 3 percent per year, with the renewable share of world electricity generation growing from 19 percent in 2006 to 21 percent in 2030. Eight developed countries, for instance, already have wind turbines installed offshore: Denmark, Belgium, Sweden, Finland, Germany, the United Kingdom, the Netherlands, and Ireland. Five others—France, Italy, Norway, Poland, and Spain, plan projects by 2015. Although only twenty-five countries were producing geothermal power in 2005, an additional twenty-two new countries were expected to add to that total by 2010, according to the U.S. Geothermal Energy Association and the International Geothermal Association. The organizations noted that the success of geothermal development in a country is linked to government policies and initiatives, with the extent of future geothermal project development appearing to depend more on adequate funding and sustained policy support than geological factors.[46]

Another energy issue that continues on the policy agenda is nuclear power. As of September 2008, there were 439 operating nuclear reactors worldwide, with a total installed capacity of 372 gigawatts in thirty-one countries. In 2008, the International Atomic Energy Agency (IAEA) announced that while it had increased its projections for nuclear generation in 2030, nuclear's share of global electricity generation had decreased by 2 percent in 2007, with a 6 percent drop in the European Union. One reason for the drop in nuclear's share of the energy pie was the fact that seven units of the complex at Kashiwazaki, Japan (the world's largest nuclear power plant in power output capacity) remained offline following a severe earthquake in the region in July 2007; German reactors that have been taken off the grid for major repairs; and problems in French facilities because of generic problems found in their steam generators. The "Big Six" nuclear powers—the United States, France, Japan, Germany, Russia, and South Korea—saw their global share of nuclear-generated electricity drop from about 75 percent in previous years to 68 percent in 2007.[47]

Nuclear power remains an important segment of the energy pie in the countries of the former Soviet Union, with Lithuania depending upon nuclear power plants for over 80 percent of its electricity supply. Older nuclear plants in the former Soviet republics pose unique energy-production problems. With the collapse of the Soviet regime and the accessibility of formerly classified information, researchers are learning about flaws and previously unreported incidents at several nuclear facilities. Observers point to the lack of replacement parts for reactors, an aging infrastructure, insufficient security, and limited employee training as evidence that some states cannot operate existing facilities effectively.[48]

The primary challenge for the world's nuclear power supply appears to be the fact that there has been no significant new building of facilities for years, and the average age of current plants has been increasing steadily to about twenty-four years. While some utilities envision nuclear plants with lifetimes of forty to sixty years (unlikely, since the average age of plants that have been shut down is twenty-two years), the pace at which new plants would have to be built is almost impossible to meet. To maintain the same number of operating facilities around the world, 70 reactors would have to be planned, completed, and started up by 2015—one every 1.5 months—and an additional 192 units would have to be online over the subsequent decade—or one every 18 days, a target that cannot be met. The reality is that there will be less reliance on nuclear power over the years to come unless lifetime extensions beyond forty years become standard, which would raise safety and maintenance questions.[49]

International nuclear-power advocates also face the challenge of security issues, ranging from concerns about plant safety and radioactive-waste disposal to fears that weapons-grade uranium may be produced from facilities installed to enrich uranium for civilian nuclear-power programs.[50] This has been the case between the United States and Iran as policymakers grappled with the problem of inspection of Iran's facilities and leaders' claims that the country was not intending to use uranium for weapons.

Although developing countries appear to recognize the inevitable demand for more energy capacity as their economies and population grow (especially electricity for residential use), the source of new power remains controversial. Global opposition is growing for new energy production from hydropower, due to the impact of megaprojects like the huge dams being built in China and India. There are an estimated 45,000 large dams in the world, and most of them were constructed during the 1970s. Half of the world's dams are in China and India, many of them previously financed by the World Bank. Facing opposition from environmental groups and concerns about costs and benefits, the Bank did not provide funding for China's controversial $25 billion Three Gorges Dam, the largest hydroelectric project in history. The dam spans 1.3 miles of the Yangtze River, creating a 400-mile-long reservoir, and generating about 10 percent of the country's energy. But in the process, the dam has also inundated 19 cities and 326 villages, forcing the relocation of nearly 2 million people.[51]

One final global strategy to meet the world's energy needs is the so-called "conservation alternative"—a dramatic change in consumption patterns world-wide. Proponents believe that we must all go on an "energy diet," and that rather than looking for new sources of power, we should be conserving what is available and getting more out of it. Thus far, however, whereas there has been support for conservation as a key element of future energy planning, international rhetoric has failed to result in any substantial changes—evidence of the kind of institutional immobilization characterizing the stage in the policy process when governments fail to see a "problem" that requires them to take action. In the case of energy, most Americans do not have a sense that anything is "wrong." As population growth in the industrialized world has slowed, the demand for energy is also slowly decreasing, due in part to technological advances. Still, industrialized countries account for one-half of all energy consumption in the industrial sector worldwide, with the United States using one-half that amount.

World concern about carbon-dioxide (CO_2) emissions is an important element of global energy policy, especially since the Kyoto Protocol went into force (see Chapter 10). Projections indicate CO_2 emissions are likely to grow from 29.0 billion metric tons in 2006 to 33.1 billion metric tons in 2015 and 40.4 billion metric tons in 2030. What is especially important about those figures is that most of the increase in CO_2 emissions is expected to be in non-OECD countries. In 2006, non-OECD emissions exceeded OECD emissions by 14 percent, but by 2030 that figure is expected to soar to 77 percent, due to strong economic growth and reliance on fossil fuels.[52]

This is where the Kyoto Protocol and the Copenhagen conference become especially important. While developing nations demand that the United States and other OECD countries reduce their CO_2 emissions, China, India, and other countries say they will continue to maintain policies of only voluntary emissions reductions. Policy analysts note that this is the kind of situation in which policy-makers seldom are willing to move forward. The conditions associated with energy use have not produced sufficient anxiety, discontent, or dissatisfaction that would cause the public to seek a remedy. In order for this to happen, people would have to have some criterion or standard by which the troubling condition is judged to be not only unreasonable or unacceptable but also appropriate for government to handle. The world's primary consumers of energy simply do not sense that a problem exists; they continue to purchase fuel-guzzling vehicles and increase their residential use of power at a rate that signals complacency and inattentiveness rather than awareness of a global environmental problem.

FURTHER READING

Michael Ball and Martin Wietschel, eds. *The Hydrogen Economy: Opportunities and Challenges*. Cambridge: Cambridge University Press, 2009.

Paul Ekins, ed. *Hydrogen Energy: Economic and Social Challenges*. London: Earthscan, 2010.

Robert Foster et al., eds. *Biomass Energy: Renewable Energy and the Environment*. Boca Raton, FL: CRC Press, 2010.

Steven Gorelick. *Oil Panic and the Global Crisis: Predictions and Myths*. Wiley-Blackwell, 2009.

Jay Inslee and Backen Hendricks. *Apollo's Fire: Igniting America's Clean Energy Economy*. Covelo, CA: Island Press, 2009.

Jerry McBeath et al. *The Political Economy of Oil in Alaska: Multinationals vs. the State*. Boulder, CO: Lynne Rienner, 2008.

Phil O'Keefe, Geoff O'Brien, and Nicola Pearsall. *The Future of Energy Use*. London: Earthscan, 2010.

Jim Pipe. *Biofuels: A Threat to Food*. New York: Franklin Watts, 2010.

John Randolph and Gilbert M. Masters. *Energy for Sustainability: Technology, Planning, Policy*. Covelo, CA: Island Press, 2008.

7

The Politics of Water

"There are more and more dams that people cannot afford to
repair and maintain. It's a growing infrastructure crisis."
— HELEN SARAKINOS, RIVER ALLIANCE OF WISCONSIN[1]

When Wisconsin was settled by Europeans in the nineteenth century, the
new settlers quickly made plans to put the over 40,000 miles of creeks,
streams, rivers, lakes, and water passages to work. The state now has about 3,800
dams. The state is typical of the United States as a whole; former Secretary of the
Interior Bruce Babbitt once observed that the country has been building, on average, one dam a day since the signing of the Declaration of Independence.[2]
Dams pose numerous issues for water managers. Those built in the country's
early history are indicative of the infrastructure problems faced by states such as
Wisconsin. Some, such as the Ward Paper Mill Dam in central Wisconsin, that
were built for sawmills and paper mills, are no longer needed for that purpose.
Removal of the dam is the most cost-effective method of dealing with a costly
repair problem. Although there is no official tally of how many dams have been
removed, the group American Rivers reports that about 500 dams have been
removed in the United States since 1912—over half of them in the last twenty
years. After Wisconsin, the most dams have been removed in Pennsylvania,
California, and Ohio.[3] Other states, such as Washington, are back in the dam-
building business, having just created a $200 million fund to build new dams and
other water projects to control water for agriculture along the Columbia River.[4]

The "public good" concept, similar to the metaphor of a commons as
discussed in Chapter 10, is an excellent starting point for understanding how
water policy flows from both local and global problems. Management of water
resources involves two major issues: the availability of water and its quality.

Water scarcity and water pollution are global issues that have become increasingly politicized worldwide. The basic issue is that while the world's population tripled in the twentieth century, demand for water increased sixfold. About 0.025 percent of the world's water supply is easily and economically available for human use—the rest is "locked up" in oceans, polar ice caps, and surface collectors such as lakes and rivers, in clouds, or under the Earth's surface yet too deep to be drilled in wells.

Even when water is available, it is often contaminated and unfit for human use. The debate over how best to improve water quality focuses on two issues: first, the pollution of surface waters (rivers, streams, lakes, wetlands, and even drainage ditches), largely from discharges directly into waterways; and second, the pollution of groundwater, which flows beneath the Earth's surface and serves as a primary source of drinking water.

This chapter examines water-resource supply and management, both in the United States and internationally. The first half of the chapter briefly reviews water-use trends; the second half focuses on water pollution and an analysis of how politics have affected water quality, especially in preserving wetlands. The chapter concludes with a review of the political factors that have led to a water-policy stalemate in both developing and industrialized nations.

TRENDS IN WATER USE

How much water do we need, and how much do we have? That question is at the heart of the water-management debate, which is complicated by inexact science and reporting methodologies that are inconsistent over time. The U.S. Geological Survey (USGS) has been compiling water-use data since 1950 to analyze the source, use, and disposition of water resources at the local, state, and national levels. In the agency's reports, water use is divided into eight categories: public supply, domestic, irrigation, livestock, aquaculture (fish farms and hatcheries), industrial, mining, and thermoelectric power. All of these categories are subject to factors such as population growth and shifts, economic trends, legal decisions, and periodic droughts. In 2005, for instance, the most recent year for which statistics are available, water use was affected by climatic extremes. Much of the West experienced severe drought, and weather in the Midwest and Northeast was characterized by prolonged periods of conditions that were cooler and wetter than normal.[5]

Estimates show that total water usage in the United States increased steadily from 1950 to 1980, declined more than 9 percent from 1980 to 1985, and has varied less than 3 percent across the five-year intervals since 1985. Water use peaked in 1980 because of large industrial, irrigation, and thermoelectric power withdrawals; but the implementation of federal legislation has affected industrial use because of requirements that encourage conservation, greater efficiency, and technologies that decrease water use. About 410,000 million gallons of water were withdrawn per day for use in the United States during 2005, with about 80 percent of the total withdrawal from surface water.[6]

Agricultural water use is also behind water-policy decisions. Irrigation is the answer to growing crops in areas that receive insufficient natural rainfall. Piping systems and wells transfer water from natural sources (lakes, streams, or aquifers) to fields, basically altering the natural hydrological cycle. In California, for instance, more than half of the state's withdrawals were for irrigation.[7] There are also differences in the way agricultural water is used. It takes 500 to 1,500 tons of water to irrigate a ton of potatoes, 3,500 to 5,700 tons of water to produce a ton of chicken, and 15,000 to 70,000 tons of water to produce a ton of beef. Can future water needs be predicted without knowing if people will eat 2,300 calories per day (the minimum level of health set by the Food and Agriculture Organization) or 3,300 calories per day, as people in the wealthier nations do? What portion of those calories will come from meat? It is estimated that all the grain fed to U.S. livestock is equivalent to the amount needed to feed 400 million people.[8]

Statistics like these represent policy trade-offs. Should water be prioritized to produce power and increase industrial capacity? Should the emphasis be placed on conserving water for personal use and for drinking, or for agriculture to feed hungry people? Should resources be directed toward developing more efficient practices and technology, or toward expansion of the water-supply infrastructure? The answers to these policy choices vary considerably from one region to another, as the following discussion illustrates.

WATER RESOURCE MANAGEMENT
IN THE UNITED STATES

American water policy is among the most politicized in the world. As this overview indicates, it is colored by political appointments and powerful industry lobbies. U.S. water policy has recently changed as political clout has shifted from the farm and agricultural lobby, which controlled policy at the turn of the century, to the urban interests now dominating Congress. Water management in the United States has primarily been the responsibility of two federal agencies, although that responsibility is shared with many public and private entities ranging from local sewage companies and irrigation districts to state water boards. The Army Corps of Engineers (ACE), originally created in 1802 under the Department of the Army, became the main construction arm of the federal government. In 1824, Congress gave the Corps authority over navigational operations, and the agency gained additional jurisdiction through the Flood Control Act of 1936. Just four years after Franklin Roosevelt began his New Deal, the Corps embarked on a reservoir construction program that erected ten large dams a year, on average, for fifty years. The authority was expanded further in 1972 with passage of the Clean Water Act, which broadened its jurisdiction to include wetlands permits.

The Reclamation Service (later renamed the Bureau of Reclamation) was authorized by Congress in 1902 with responsibility for aiding Western settlement in a seventeen-state area.[9] The Bureau was popular among Western farmers because its charter included a limitation to serve only those landowners who held title to 160 acres or less; thus, the agency rapidly came to be influenced by local interests. During its early years, the Bureau constructed massive water-development projects, canals, and public-works programs, such as Washington's Grand Coulee Dam (the largest single-purpose peacetime appropriation in U.S. history) and California's Central Valley Project. Between them, the two federal agencies quickly established a reputation as the home of the pork barrel—congressionally approved water projects that benefited a single district. Projects such as dams and flood-control channels brought a visible product (and jobs) to the home base of a member of Congress, paid for by liberal cost-sharing formulas and substantial federal financing. In 1920, the Federal Water Power Act created the Federal Power Commission, which was replaced in 1977 by the Federal Energy Regulatory Commission (FERC). The commission was initially responsible for regulating the nation's water resources, but its charter was eventually redirected to oversee the electric-power and natural-gas industries.

A close-knit relationship has always existed between the congressional oversight committees, the two agencies, and local water-interest lobbies. Decisions on which projects to fund, and at what level, were frequently made by those leaders with the most political clout—or because of pressure from campaign contributors—rather than on the merits of good water management. Around 1900, for example, the National Rivers Congress, comprised of powerful business figures, contractors, and members of Congress (who were honorary members of the group), began monitoring ACE projects. This group of lobbyists was extremely successful at convincing Congress to continue authorizing funds for projects that had long since been completed. The water lobby became so powerful that in its heyday in the early 1960s, the chair of the House Appropriations Committee would boast that "practically every Congressional district" was included in the omnibus public-works bills, and that "there is something here for everybody."[10]

For the most part, America's growth spurt continued unabated after World War II, and few questioned the advisability of massive undertakings by the Corps and the Bureau of Reclamation. New water technology, modern farming and cropping techniques, and widespread pesticide use made agricultural expansion a key element of the postwar boom, with cheap, government-subsidized water the key. Land irrigated with government-financed water grew from 2.7 million acres in 1930 to more than 4 million acres after the war and to nearly 7 million acres by 1960. But during the late 1950s and mid-1960s, water-resource planning changed from an emphasis on economic development to municipal, industrial, and recreational purposes. The water lobby was forced to make some concessions to environmental groups, which were outraged when projects began to infringe upon scenic or preserved areas—such as a proposal to build Echo Park Dam in Dinosaur National Monument.[11] The Sierra Club mobilized its members upon learning about a plan to build a hydroelectric plant in the Grand Canyon—and in so doing, the group lost its federal tax-exempt status.

By the mid-1970s, environmental groups had turned their attention to water issues and were becoming a potent force in policymaking. Groups such as the Sierra Club, the American Rivers Conservation Council, the National Wildlife Federation, and the Natural Resources Defense Council (NRDC) pressured Congress to follow the requirements of the National Environmental Policy Act (NEPA) and used litigation as a tool for forcing compliance with new legislative initiatives. Bolstered by environmental support during his campaign, President Jimmy Carter began his administration in 1977 by developing a "hit list" of nineteen water projects that were to be deleted from the federal budget, including the Central Arizona Project. Carter underestimated the powerful water-industry lobby, however, which was able to convince Congress to restore all nineteen appropriations.

Water industry officials cheered the 1980 election of Ronald Reagan, believing his appointment of Robert Broadbent, a Nevada legislator, as head of the Bureau of Reclamation was a positive omen. It turned out to be a conflicting sign, however, as Reagan continued Carter's cost-sharing requirements on water projects (the portion of a water project to be borne by the federal government). As state and local governments began to realize that they might have to pay a larger share of the cost for many of the projects, they became less attractive, and in some cases, financially burdensome. Part of the shift in policy can be traced to the growing clout of urban political interests over those of agriculture, as city politicians began to question why farmers were getting all the cheap water.[12]

Equally important was the discovery of dead waterfowl at the Kesterson National Wildlife Refuge in California's San Joaquin Valley. Ducks and geese were dying of a mysterious sickness that not only killed them but resulted in birth deformities in their chicks. The eventual cause was found to be selenium, a trace element that can be toxic in high concentrations. The selenium was carried by the San Luis Drain from the politically powerful Westlands Water District in Fresno and Tulare Counties. In 1985, Secretary of the Interior Donald Hodel called for a halt in the drainage by June 30, 1986; but by then, the public had lost its patience with the Bureau of Reclamation's projects and its negligence.[13] By 1987, the policy change became clear when James Zigler, the Department of the Interior's Assistant Secretary for Water and Science, announced that the bureau was changing its mission from an agency based on federally supported construction to one based on resource management. The empire-building days of the Corps and the Bureau were over, replaced by an administration that was paying more attention to urban needs for a stable water supply than to agricultural interests seeking cheap water for their fields.

Like other natural resources, water is often assumed to be in endless supply, and many Americans just pay their monthly water bill (usually from a local or municipal water district) without complaint. Similar in structure to other types of public utilities, water costs may be limited and users are seldom penalized for overconsumption, even in arid regions of the West. However, pricing inequities continue to be at the heart of the battle over water management in the United States. The "real" cost of providing and distributing water is often impossible to determine, and historically, municipalities have been reluctant to try to pass those costs on to developers and commercial interests. City leaders often avoided charging a new business the true cost of water delivery for fear it would discourage economic growth. As a result, the rate structure has often allowed large users to benefit because of a system that charges the user less for using more water. Favored customers often receive preferential pricing, and some cities served by the same water district often unknowingly subsidize the water costs of other cities in their area through complex pricing arrangements. Residential users tend to subsidize industrial users throughout most of the United States today.

Another new wrinkle has been the development of "water markets"—transactions ranging from transfers of water rights to the sale and lease of either those rights or the land above the water source. Market transfers are dependent upon the concept of reallocating water supplies, rather than coming up with new sources of water. Part of the affection for the market concept was purely economic—new capital projects were becoming increasingly expensive and politically unpopular in much of the West. One group even began purchasing water rights in Colorado as an investment, with the expectation that as supplies diminished the rights could be sold for a tidy profit. Cities such as Phoenix and Scottsdale also have been active in the water market, buying thousands of acres of farmland outside their city limits to have a water source as their population increases and water within city boundaries runs short. Reallocation is gradually being looked upon as an alternative to finding a new allocation as the primary mode of water development.[14]

Water management is also highly dependent upon weather patterns, which may vary in both the short and long term. Much of the attention on water supply is focused on the West because of extensive drought. For decades, the Midwest and Northeastern United States have been characterized by periods of conditions that are cooler and wetter than normal, with above-average precipitation. As a result, water-management issues are lower on these regions' environmental-policy agendas than they are in the Southwest.

A single season's change in weather patterns, especially amounts of precipitation, can lead to accelerated government policymaking. The winter storms of 2004 and 2005, for instance, filled lakes and reservoirs throughout much of the Southwest and reduced overall water demand in many areas. In June 2005, Arizona officials projected that the state would not need to draw upon its full allocation from the Colorado River, and agreed to store some of the extra water in its underground "water banks" to benefit Nevada, which has dealt with years of drought and urban expansion. The deal requires Nevada to pay Arizona $330 million to store its water, and when the state needs to draw water supplies, it will take it directly from the Colorado River drainage into Lake Mead. Arizona, in return, will take less water from the Colorado and will instead pump its allocation from the water banks using wells. The agreement provides additional revenue for Arizona while Nevada maintains a reliable source of water in Arizona's "bank."[15]

The American water wars have also touched our southern border with Mexico, where the Colorado River flows on its way to the Gulf of California. In 1922, Congress approved the Colorado River Compact, which divided up the river's resources, giving the three lower basin states (California, Arizona, and Nevada) and the four upper basin states (Wyoming, Colorado, New Mexico, and Utah) 7.5 million acre-feet for each region. (An acre-foot is the volume of water that covers one acre to a depth of one foot, or 325,851 gallons. This is about enough water to serve one or two households for one year.) It should be noted, however, that the actual flow of the river is closer to 14 rather than 15 million acre-feet. Congress also authorized the building of the Hoover Dam in 1928, giving the United States total control over the Colorado River—a situation that understandably made our Mexican neighbors nervous. Seeking to keep Mexico as a wartime ally, the United States signed a treaty in 1944 that assigned 1.5 million acre-feet to Mexico and created the International Boundary Water Commission to administer the treaty. In the early 1960s, a combination of population growth, the drilling of wells on the U.S. side, saline runoff from drainage projects, and construction of the Glen Canyon Dam in Utah began affecting both the quantity and quality of Mexico's water allocation. It took nearly ten years for the two sides to reach an agreement that, in 1973, guaranteed Mexico a fair share of the Colorado River in usable form. The responsibility for implementing the numerous treaties between the two countries that relate to water and resolving any differences belongs to the renamed International Boundary and Water Commission.

Today, the issue of maintaining an adequate supply for Mexico remains unresolved. Stakeholders have identified several problems that require U.S. and Mexican collaboration and cooperation. Among them are the need for an international collaborative plan for surface water and groundwater, the quantity of water flowing through the Rio Grande, competition between El Paso and Ciudad Juarez for the same water sources, and development of a sustainable water supply.[16]

The growing pressure to tap more and more of the Earth's water resources is having some negative impacts. More urban communities are tapping into underground aquifers, drying them up as residential and agricultural demand increases. In cities such as Beijing, Mexico City, Houston, New Orleans, and Phoenix, water levels are dropping as a result of heavy pumping, leading to subsidence—literally, the sinking of the city. In addition to a reduction in the availability of a valuable commodity, it is unlikely that the water in the aquifers will ever be fully replaced. Water is being withdrawn from aquifers much faster than it can be recharged—replenished by rain and runoff.

The water scarcity and management problem has two basic solutions: conservation and technology. The first is relatively straightforward—convince users to use less. The second involves a wide range of options, from ancient to modern technological solutions. Water conservation is being implemented in many regions, ranging from urban communities to rural irrigation improvements, in an attempt to reduce residents' dependency upon existing sources. Some of the easiest conservation efforts have been accomplished by metropolitan water districts that have enacted consumption ordinances or made water-saving showerheads and low-flow toilets available. These efforts are not temporary responses to drought; studies indicate that by 2010, southern California will have enough water to fulfill only 70 percent of its needs, making demand-management practices a more likely strategy for reducing consumption.[17]

WETLANDS PROTECTION

Although the water-resource debate in the United States has focused primarily on the issue of supply, water quality is an equally enduring problem for policymakers. Historically, legislative efforts to reduce pollution at the source have been ineffective, as will be seen later in this chapter. Scientists are also looking at wetlands restoration as another strategy for improving water quality. Wetlands are sensitive ecological areas that serve as breeding grounds for migratory birds and as plant habitats. They also serve as natural flood- and storm-control systems, and some communities are experimenting with using wetlands as a way of treating wastewater. For the most part, wetlands protection was not really considered a policy problem to be dealt with until the 1970s, primarily because the public did not value wetlands as a resource. But during the 1980s, suburban sprawl, development, and increased use of land used for agriculture led to a decline in wetlands acreage, and calls by groups like Ducks Unlimited for the government to take action.

One difficulty encountered by policymakers is determining the scope of the problem of wetlands protection. In order to formulate policy, scientists and researchers within the government must be able to define what the term *wetlands* means and then inventory how many acres of land fall under that definition. The Clean Water Act of 1972 included provisions requiring anyone seeking to build or otherwise conduct business that would alter the landscape of wetlands to first obtain a permit from the ACE. Of particular interest in the act is Section 404, which makes it unlawful to put dredged or fill material into navigable waters—the term *wetlands* was never mentioned in the legislation. The ACE's interpretation of this section was that navigable waters were only those subject to the ebb and flow of the tide that are or might be used for interstate or foreign commerce, or for transportation.

Four agencies—the Department of Agriculture, the Environmental Protection Agency (EPA), the Department of the Interior, and the ACE—have developed regulations to implement the law and to designate which areas are defined as wetlands, among them an estimated 77 million acres of wetlands that are privately owned. State departments responsible for wetlands also have developed their own definitions, further complicating policymaking. Because each agency has its own interpretation of the wetlands designation, the importance of wetlands preservation has collided with private property rights and become one of the most contentious water-management issues in the United States.

The U.S. Fish and Wildlife Service (FWS) has adopted this definition from a 1979 report; it is also used by the U.S. Department of Agriculture's Natural Resources Conservation Service (NRCS):

> Wetlands are lands transitional between terrestrial and aquatic systems where the water table usually at or near the surface of the land is covered by shallow water. For purposes of this classification wetlands must have one or more of the following three attributes: (1) at least periodically, the land supports predominantly hydrophytes; (2) the substrate is predominantly undrained hydric soil; and (3) the substrate is nonsoil and is saturated with water or covered by shallow water at some time during the growing season of the year.[18]

In contrast, the ACE and the EPA use the following definition, developed in 1977:

> Wetlands are those areas that are inundated or saturated by surface or groundwater at a frequency and duration sufficient to support, and that under normal circumstances do support, a prevalence of vegetation typically adapted for life in saturated soil condition. Wetlands generally include swamps, marshes, bogs, and similar areas.[19]

While there is agreement that wetlands are transition areas between aquatic ecosystems and uplands, that is where the agreement ends and the policy debates (and court action) begins. How do you tell whether a piece of land is a wetland? Depending on the agency, they have three characteristics:

1. Hydrology (the presence of water) on land that is subject to periodic inundation or saturated soil conditions (based on records such as flood maps or debris lines)
2. Hydrophytes (an estimated 7,000 plants able to grow in saturated conditions in the United States, of which about a quarter grow only in wetlands)
3. Hydric soils (that reflect periodic inundation by showing evidence of large amounts of organic matter because saturation prevents oxidation of plant materials)

These criteria are then applied through aerial-photo interpretation and other sources of information to prepare wetland maps, along with on-site field investigation to determine precise wetland boundaries, a process called *delineation*.[20] The disagreement comes over how wet, and for how long a period of time, a system must be to qualify as a wetland. The contentious areas are those where there is infrequent flooding or saturation, such as flats, playa, riparian zones, and some depressions that lack wetland vegetation some of the time, or those that lack characteristic soils. In the definitions above that are used by the four agencies, the FWS and NRCS require only one of the three parameters, while the ACE/EPA definition requires both hydrology and vegetation.

With regard to how many acres are considered wetlands, the Emergency Wetland Resources Act of 1986 directs the FWS to inventory the nation's wetlands and provide reports to Congress. The FWS National Wetland Classification System has been used to prepare the National Wetland Inventory maps, and for the NRCS Natural Resources Inventory. The agency publishes a Status and Trends Report that documents trends in the acreage of the nation's wetlands. Data from the most recent inventory, covering the period from 1998 to 2004, shows 107.7 million acres of wetlands in the conterminous United States. During the study period, there was a net gain of 191,750 acres, for an average annual net gain of 32,000 acres.[21] The EPA is in the process of preparing its own study, the National Wetland Condition Assessment, a statistical survey of the quality of U.S. wetlands. In conjunction with state and tribal partners, the survey is designed to determine the regional and national ecological integrity of wetlands, with both a baseline and statistically valid set of wetland data, and promote collaboration across jurisdictional boundaries. That report is due in 2013.[22]

Despite the lack of vital information and agreement on a definition of what constitutes a wetland, and how many acres meet the definition, policy has become highly politicized, largely because of federal court decisions in the 1970s and 1980s. In *U.S.* v. *Holland* in 1974, a Florida court ruled that wetlands adjacent to navigable waterways, such as mangrove swamps, were navigable waters, and therefore within the jurisdiction of the Clean Water Act, requiring an ACE permit. Another federal court case in 1977 further expanded the definition of *navigable* when a home developer was told a permit was required for a sixty-acre building site because it was a wetland, even though it was inundated only 17 percent of the time. And President Jimmy Carter added to the debate with Executive Order 11990 in 1977, requiring all federal agencies to consider wetlands protection in their actions. To respond to the court and the president, in 1977, the ACE redefined *wetlands* as "waters of the United States to include isolated wetlands and lakes, intermittent streams, prairie potholes, and other waters that are not part of a tributary system to interstate waters or to navigable waters of the United States, the degradation or destruction of which would affect interstate commerce."

Perhaps the most notable attempt at making wetlands policy came at the height of the 1988 presidential campaign when George H. W. Bush announced on the shores of Boston Harbor that there would be "no net loss" of the nation's remaining wetlands—a concept that was the brainchild of then-president of the Conservation Foundation William K. Reilly (later Bush's nominee to become administrator of the EPA). During the 1992 presidential campaign, the phrase came back to haunt Bush as one of the major failures of his administration, eliciting criticism from both environmental groups and property owners.[23]

In contrast to the president's policy, a December 1991 report by the National Research Council recommended that the United States embark upon a policy of wetlands restoration, with a goal of a net gain of 10 million acres of wetlands by 2010—a program that went far beyond the Bush administration's policy of "no net loss." Failure to implement such a policy, the report warned, would lead to permanent ecological damage that would reduce the quality of American life.[24] Restoration has subsequently become a key element of wetlands policy. While conservation ecologists argue over what the term means, the generally accepted definition of *restoration* is the return of an ecosystem to a close approximation of its condition prior to disturbance; the basic goal is to renew native ecosystems to sites where they once existed. When applied to wetlands, this generally involves a series of restoration-related activities, ranging from the creation of wetlands in an area that was not a wetland in the recent past (100 to 200 years) and that is not adjacent to existing wetlands, to enhancement (the modification of specific structural features of an existing wetland to accentuate one or more values of a site), to reallocation or replacement (converting an existing wetland to a different type), to mitigation. The latter term is perhaps the most important, since it is the basis for most legal action. Under Section 404 of the Clean Water Act, wetlands may legally be destroyed, but their loss must be compensated for by the restoration, creation, or enhancement of other wetlands.[25]

In order to determine how the no-net-loss policy should be interpreted and implemented, in 1987, each of the four agencies developed its own technical manual to guide field staff, with another unified version published in 1989, and a new manual proposed by the ACE in 1991. That same year, President Bush announced his Coastal America Initiative, coordinated by the Council on Environmental Quality (CEQ), to establish a partnership among federal agencies responsible for the management, regulation, and stewardship of coastal living resources. Wetlands protection came under the proposal, focusing on regional activities that provide direct local and watershed action as well as national projects.[26]

Although the Coastal America Initiative continued to operate when President Clinton took office in 1993, the new administration reexamined federal wetlands policies almost immediately, in large part due to court rulings that questioned whether the government had the authority to place sanctions on those who failed to meet wetlands permit criteria.

In 1995, the debate resumed as the Republican-controlled Congress sought to rewrite a Clean Water Act that would have established another new classification scheme for wetlands. Under the proposal, the least valuable lands would no longer be protected by the federal government, and less protection would be given to the remaining wetlands. The measure also would have required government agencies to compensate landowners for any loss in property values of 20 percent or more resulting from wetlands regulations, but the proposals failed to obtain sufficient bipartisan support. In 1999, the ACE expanded its jurisdiction again, taking on navigable waterways plus "waters such as intrastate lakes, rivers, streams (including intermittent streams), mudflats, sandflats, wetlands, sloughs, playa lakes, or natural ponds, the use, degradation, or destruction of which would affect interstate or foreign commerce."[27] Clinton was unable to make significant progress with a new wetlands policy due to congressional leaders working at cross-purposes, stalling any major programs. In addition, just as Clinton was leaving office in January 2001, the U.S. Supreme Court issued a decision concerning what the court termed "isolated" waters used as habitat for migratory birds, further confusing the definition of *wetlands*.

President Bush moved forward in his water-policy changes, announcing a new wetlands initiative on Earth Day 2004 that called for restoring at least

1 million acres of additional wetlands, improving the condition of at least 1 million acres of existing degraded wetlands, and extending protection to at least 1 million acres of imperiled wetlands by 2009. Overall, the Bush policy would move beyond his father's "no net loss" of wetlands through expanded incentive and partnership measures, such as the Department of Agriculture's Wetland Reserve Program, and through grants under the Department of the Interior's North American Wetlands Conservation Act, also signed by George H. W. Bush.[28]

A year later, the CEQ released a report noting that on the first anniversary of the president's wetlands initiative, 328,000 acres had been restored or created, 154,000 acres had been improved, and 350,000 acres had been protected. CEQ chairman James Connaughton emphasized once again the administration's preference for incentives to encourage private stewardship and conservation partnerships rather than government enforcement: "Working collaboratively with private landowners and local officials has proven remarkably effective in improving and sustaining America's wetlands."[29]

What does not appear to have happened over the last ten years, though, is agreement among the agencies on both policies to protect wetlands and the definition of the term. ACE districts differ, studies show, on their interpretation of the jurisdiction of the agency, and what actions trigger the need for a federal permit when a wetland is involved. Despite efforts to coordinate their actions, the federal agencies still appear to overlap one another when it comes to surveying and inventorying lands that might be deserving of federal protection. Overall, wetlands seem to lack the urgency that they did in the 1970s and 1980s. As long as the standard of "no net loss" appears to have been met, stakeholders have moved on to other types of habitat loss, and few attempts at policy change have actually occurred.

Although President Barack Obama has been steadfast in his desire to restore the wetlands decimated by Hurricane Katrina, there has been less activity on the definition of *wetlands*. It has been reported that top administration officials have sent the Senate Environment and Public Works Committee a list of principles to guide legislation clarifying the term "waters of the United States," urging the panel to make the definition of covered water "predictable and manageable."[30]

EVERGLADES RESTORATION

The Florida Everglades encompasses an ecosystem that once stretched from the Kissimmee chain of lakes to Florida Bay. The Everglades, a subtropical wetlands in the southern region of the state, provides habitat for diverse plant and animal species and a landscape of cypress swamps, coastal lagoons, sawgrass sloughs, and coral reefs. In 1947, Marjory Stoneman Douglas referred to the Everglades as a "river of grass—a unique region of the earth, remote, never wholly known."[31] In its natural state, the area also serves as a complex freshwater filtration and distribution system. However, that system has been altered by human decisions and policies. In the late 1800s, inhabitants began building primitive canals to drain the region, and by the end of the twentieth century, an estimated 1,700 miles of canals and levees had been built; in 1948, Congress directed the ACE to drain much of the marsh area to prevent flooding. More than half of the area was lost to development; the Central & Southern Florida Project (CSFP), designed to provide flood protection and water management, led to unintended adverse effects on the ecosystem.[32]

It was not until 1992 and the Water Resources Development Act (amended in 1996) that the ACE, responsible for much of the building of the canals and levees, was directed to reevaluate the performance and impacts of the CSFP. The agency's mission changed from stemming the flow of freshwater to capturing, storing, and redistributing water, and regulating the quality, quantity, timing, and distribution of water flows.[33] The Everglades Restoration Act of 2000 authorized $1.4 billion in federal spending to begin work on a handful of projects; there are about sixty elements that will take twenty to thirty years to construct, at an estimated cost of between $7.5 and $8.7 billion, split evenly between the federal government and the state of Florida, making it the world's largest ecosystem-restoration project. The Comprehensive Everglades Restoration Plan (CERP) is a framework and guide that covers sixteen counties over an 18,000-acre area of central and southern Florida, including surface-water storage reservoirs, management of Lake Okeechobee, underground water storage, reuse of wastewater, improved water conservation, treatment of wetlands and improved water delivery to estuaries, removal of barriers, and storage of water in existing quarries.[34]

In March 2003, the Corps and the South Florida Water Management District, partners in the implementation of CERP, developed a vision statement and a set of guiding principles to accomplish the project's goals. The vision is to restore, preserve, and protect the South Florida ecosystem while providing for other water-related needs of the region, including water supply and flood protection. The statement notes:

> Although the future Everglades ecosystem will be a "new" Everglades because it will be smaller than the pre-drainage system, restoration will have been successful if the new system responds to the recovery of these defining characteristics by functionally behaving as a wild Everglades system rather than as a set of managed, disconnected wetlands.[35]

Not unexpectedly, implementation of a policy of this magnitude has not been without pitfalls, both political and practical. Some of the CERP funding comes from property taxes levied on owners in the sixteen-county region covered by the project. It is the only taxing district in the region whose leaders are appointed by the governor, rather than elected by voters, thus increasing the politicization of the process.[36] A 2009 report found that project-specific planning and design are under way, with some components actually under construction. State rulemaking for the first water reservations had been initiated to ensure that water intended for natural systems is safeguarded from other uses. But two National Academy of Sciences reviews of CERP found that funding and progress are lagging behind schedule, although the scientific program is comprehensive and of high quality.[37]

THE NATURE AND CAUSES OF WATER POLLUTION

In 1965, when he signed the Water Quality Act, President Lyndon B. Johnson (LBJ) predicted that Washington's Potomac River would be reopened for swimming by 1975.[38] Yet the Potomac's tidal basin, with its Japanese cherry trees, has been called "the best-decorated sewer in the world," making LBJ's prediction premature and unrealistic, as is the case with most of the legislative attempts to improve the quality of America's water supply. Several factors have contributed to make the nation's waterways and drinking water as polluted now as they were in the 1960s. The debate over how best to improve water quality focuses on two issues: first, pollution of surface waters (rivers, streams, lakes, wetlands, and even drainage ditches), largely from discharges directly into waterways; and second, the pollution of groundwater, which flows beneath the Earth's surface and is the source of nearly half of the nation's drinking water. Sources of groundwater contamination include landfills, biocide applications on farmland and urban lawns, underground storage tanks, leakage of hazardous waste, and waste-disposal wells.

The current level of water pollution is due largely to massive industrialization and inadequate waste-disposal strategies that took place in the United States during the mid- to late-nineteenth century. At that time, local officials were generally reluctant to antagonize industry by trying to stop the widespread practice of simply dumping industrial wastes into the closest waterway. Most of the early government concerns dealt with navigational hazards rather than health. In 1886, Congress prohibited the dumping of waste into New York Harbor; this was followed by the 1899 Refuse Act, which prohibited the dumping of solid waste into commercial waterways. Not until the U.S. Public Health Service was formed in 1912 was serious consideration given to monitoring pollution levels. Today, much of what is known about trends in surface-water quality comes from the USGS, which monitors waterways through its National Ambient Stream Quality Accounting Network (NASQUAN), which began collecting information in 1974. Groundwater quality, in contrast, must be monitored either from wells or at the tap.

Basically, water contaminants can be divided into the following categories:

1. *Organisms:* Biological contaminants, including bacteria, parasites, and viruses, are included in this category. These occur in most water sources, although there are usually fewer in groundwater than in surface water. Human and animal wastes carry fecal coliform and fecal streptococcus bacteria, which may enter the water source from improper sewage treatment, cattle feedlots, or through failing, leaching septic tanks.

2. *Suspended and totally dissolved solids:* Soil particles, inorganic salts, and other substances may make water brown or turbid (cloudy) and may carry bacteria and other harmful substances that pollute water. The problem is particularly acute in areas with significant erosion, including logged watersheds, construction sites, and abused rangelands. Agricultural practices are thought to be the largest single source of unregulated water pollution.

3. *Nutrients:* Some contaminants, such as phosphorus, iron, and boron, can be harmful when ingested in excess quantities. Nitrates, which are not harmful in limited concentrations, occur naturally in some vegetables, such as beets and cabbage, and are used in the meat-curing process.

4. *Metals and toxics:* A wide spectrum of heavy metals is commonly found in drinking water; among the most dangerous of these metals is lead. In 1991, the EPA issued new regulations requiring municipal water suppliers to monitor lead levels, focusing on households at high risk (those with lead service pipes), and at the location where lead content is likely to be the highest—at the consumer's faucet. In areas where water-quality standards are not met, suppliers must add bicarbonate and lime to lower the water's acidity chemically. Other contaminants include radioactive minerals and gases. Toxic concentrations usually come from sources such as pesticides and chemical solvents used in a variety of manufacturing processes.

5. *Municipal wastewater discharges:* Domestic sewage accounts for a large percentage of the materials handled by municipal wastewater-treatment plants, but other substances also routinely enter the wastewater stream, including hazardous chemicals dumped down drains and sewers by individuals, industries, and businesses.

Americans have reason to be concerned about water quality. An EPA report based on the 2000 National Water Quality Inventory (required under the Clean Water Act) found that about 40 percent of the nation's streams, 45 percent of lakes, and 50 percent of estuaries that were assessed were not clean enough to support uses such as fishing and swimming. States, tribes, territories, and interstate commissions assessed approximately 700,000 miles of rivers and 17.34 million acres of lakes in the 2000 survey, or about one-third of the U.S. waters. The water-quality standards used in the assessment consist of three elements: the designated uses assigned to waters (such as drinking, swimming, or fishing); criteria to protect those uses (such as chemical-specific thresholds that should not be exceeded); and policies intended to keep waters that do meet standards from deteriorating from their current condition.

THE POLITICS OF WATER QUALITY

Like many environmental issues, the politics of water quality is not linked to a single act of legislation. One factor that makes water policy somewhat difficult to understand is that Congress has given regulatory responsibility for water quality to the EPA and other agencies under several legislative mandates, as seen in Table 7.1.

Some of the authority comes not from water-pollution legislation, but from related laws. The Resource Conservation and Recovery Act (RCRA), for example, gives the EPA the authority to regulate the treatment, transport, and storage of both hazardous and nonhazardous waste. The Comprehensive Environmental

T A B L E 7.1   Major U.S. Water-Quality Laws

Year	Law	Provisions
1948	Federal Water Pollution Control Act	Authorized Surgeon General of the Public Health Service to prepare comprehensive programs for eliminating or reducing the pollution of interstate waters; gave the Federal Works administrator responsibility to assist state and local governments in constructing sewage-treatment plants
1961	Amendments of 1961	Stipulated that federal agencies consider water quality as part of the planning process for reservoirs; gave authority to the Secretary of Health, Education, and Welfare to assess water quality in the Great Lakes region
1966	Clean Water Restoration Act	Authorized the Secretary of the Interior to conduct a comprehensive study of the effects of water pollution in U.S. estuaries; prohibited discharge of oil into navigable waters
1970	Reorganization Plan #3	Abolished the Federal Water Quality Administration from the Department of the Interior, and transferred all functions to the EPA
1970	Water Quality Improvement Act	Amended prohibitions on discharges of oil; authorized a National Contingency Plan to minimize damage from oil discharges; authorized demonstration projects to control mine water pollution and water pollution within the Great Lakes watersheds; provided direction for water-quality agencies on compliance with applicable standards
1972	Federal Water Pollution Control Act Amendments	Stipulated broad national objectives to restore the nation's waters; expanded provisions related to pollutant discharges; defined liability for discharges of oil and hazardous substances; established National Pollutant Discharge Elimination System (NPDES) authorizing EPA to issue permits for discharges; authorized the ACE to issue permits for discharges of dredged or fill material into navigable waters
1977	Clean Water Act	Developed "best management practices"; authorized funds to complete the National Wetlands Inventory; authorized the ACE to issue permits for activities that cause only minimal environmental effects; transferred some regulatory responsibilities to states
1987	Water Quality Act	Established Chesapeake Bay Program, Great Lakes Program; required states to develop strategies for toxic cleanups in waters; increased penalties for violations of permits; enhanced state reporting of harmful effects of acidity on lakes; funded state nonpoint-source-management programs under EPA authority; required the EPA to study and monitor water-quality effects attributable to dams; authorized program for nomination of estuaries of national significance

Response, Compensation, and Liability Act (CERCLA), more commonly known as "Superfund," gives the EPA responsibility when groundwater is contaminated by inactive waste sites or accidental chemical releases. The Toxic Substances Control Act (TSCA) gives the EPA regulatory authority over the manufacture, use, and disposal of toxic chemicals, and the Federal Insecticide, Fungicide, and Rodenticide Act (FIFRA) regulates certain pesticides, which can also enter groundwater. Despite the overlap of these regulatory mandates, Congress has also enacted legislation specifically targeting surface and groundwater pollution.

Surface Water

The process of placing surface water on the political agenda has been a long one. Before World War II, only a few environmental organizations seemed interested in the deteriorating condition of America's lakes, rivers, and streams. The Izaak Walton League was among the first to draw attention to the contamination problem, noting in a report published in the late 1920s that 85 percent of the nation's waterways were polluted and that only 30 percent of all municipalities treated their wastes, many of them inadequately. Industrial interests like the American Petroleum Institute, the American Iron and Steel Institute, and the Manufacturing Chemists Association insisted that "streams were nature's sewers," and convinced key legislators that industrial dumping posed no environmental threat.[39]

The initial attempts to regulate surface-water pollution were weak and ineffective. In 1948, Congress passed the first Water Pollution Control Act, which established the federal government's limited role in regulating interstate water pollution. The law also provided for studies, research, and limited funding for sewage treatment. It also authorized the Surgeon General to prepare or adopt programs for eliminating or reducing pollution in cooperation with other agencies and the industries involved. The emphasis on a cooperative approach, coupled with provisions that were both cumbersome and often unworkable, gave the law little impact. In 1952, a report to Congress indicated that not a single enforcement action had been taken, and Congress began to hold hearings on a revision to the legislation. The 1956 amendments to the act eliminated many of the difficulties of the 1948 law, but they still limited Congress's role to interstate waters and allowed Congress to delegate much of its authority to implement the law to the states. The amendments did, however, condition federal funding of sewage-treatment facilities on the submission of adequate water-pollution plans by the states. This provided an incentive for states to write water-quality standards to meet state goals for surface-water pollution. Still, only one enforcement action was filed under this authority over the next fifteen years.

During the 1960s, Congress, led by Senator Edmund Muskie of Maine, became restless over the slow pace of water-pollution control, because it was obvious that states were doing an inadequate job. In 1965, passage of the Water Quality Act established a June 1967 deadline for a water-quality standard for interstate waters and streamlined federal enforcement efforts. A year later, the

Clean Water Restoration Act provided $3.5 billion in federal grants for the construction of sewage-treatment plants and for research on advanced waste treatment. These early attempts at water-quality legislation were weak and ineffective. They allowed the states to classify waterways within their jurisdictions, so a state could decide that a particular stream was best used for industrial use rather than for swimming. The use designation of the Cuyahoga River in Ohio, for example, was waste disposal—a fact that did not seem to bother most residents until the river caught fire in 1969. From an enforcement standpoint, the initial pollution laws were meaningless. In the two decades before 1972, only one case of alleged violation of federal water-pollution-control law reached the courts; and in that case, over four years elapsed between the initial enforcement conference and the final consent decree.

President Richard Nixon's February 1970 message to Congress on the environment called for a new water-pollution bill, which eventually became the 1972 Federal Water Pollution Control Act. The main emphasis of the legislation was on technological capability. In addition to establishing a regulatory framework for water quality, the bill gave the EPA six specific deadlines by which it was to grant permits to water-pollution sources, issue effluent (wastewater) guidelines, require sources to install water-pollution-control technology, and eliminate discharges into the nation's waterways to make them safe for fishing and swimming. A key component of the legislation was the establishment of the NPDES, which made it illegal to discharge anything at all unless the source had a federal permit to do so. The NPDES had a historical basis in the 1899 Refuse Act, which had previously been thought to apply only to discharges that obstructed navigation. But the U.S. Supreme Court broadened the interpretation of the act in two cases that made it applicable to any industrial waste.[40]

Water quality continued to capture media interest when consumer advocate Ralph Nader publicized contamination along a 150-mile stretch of the Mississippi River, between Baton Rouge and New Orleans, known as the "petrochemical corridor." Public outcry after a February 1977 spill of carbon tetrachloride (a potential carcinogen) into the Ohio River, which contaminated Cincinnati's water supply, further fueled the legislative fires, although Congress took no action to strengthen the 1972 law. The act was amended in 1977, but it was not until the mid-1980s that policymakers and environmental groups generally agreed that the 1972 legislation had been overly optimistic in setting target dates for the standards to be met. Little progress had been made in improving the overall quality of the nation's waterways, although given the pace of the country's population growth and economic expansion, the argument could be made that at least the situation did not get much worse, or deteriorate as rapidly as it could have. In 1987, Congress enacted a new legislative mandate—the Water Quality Act—over two vetoes by President Ronald Reagan. The new legislation expanded congressional authority to regulate water pollution from point sources—a confined conveyance, such as a pipe, tunnel, well, or floating vessel (such as a ship) that discharges pollutants—as well as from nonpoint sources, which is basically anything else. The Water Quality Act also required every state and territory to establish safe levels of toxic pollutants in freshwater by 1990.

Groundwater and Drinking Water

The main groundwater source of drinking water is aquifers—layers of rock and earth that contain water, or could contain water. For most of the twentieth century, groundwater was thought to be a virtually unlimited natural resource, constantly filtered and replenished and available for human use and consumption. Currently, about half of all drinking water is supplied through groundwater.

As a policy issue, water quality has often suffered from differences of opinion over where the regulatory responsibility ought to lie, with regulatory authority divided between drinking water and groundwater. Federal authority to establish primary drinking-water standards (those applying to materials that are human health standards) originated with the Interstate Quarantine Act of 1893, which allowed the Surgeon General to make regulations covering only bacteriological contamination. But the first U.S. primary drinking-water standard was not set until 1914 by the U.S. Public Health Service, whose main concern was the prevention of waterborne diseases. The federal standards were applicable only to systems that provided water to an interstate common carrier. From 1914 to 1974, the standards were revised four times—in 1925, 1942, 1946, and 1962—and were gradually extended to cover all U.S. water supplies.

Groundwater regulatory authority was treated somewhat differently from the way drinking-water regulatory authority was treated. There were those who felt that the federal government should not be responsible for regulating and cleaning up groundwater. President Dwight Eisenhower, for example, believed water pollution was a "uniquely local blight" and felt that the primary obligation for providing a safe drinking-water supply ought to rest with state and local officials, not with the federal government.[41] But with the creation of the EPA in 1970, the federal government reaffirmed its policymaking authority for water quality. With passage of the 1974 Safe Drinking Water Act, the EPA was authorized to identify which substances were contaminating the nation's water supply and set maximum contaminant levels, promulgated as the National Primary Drinking Water Regulations. The act was amended in 1986 to accelerate the EPA's regulation of toxic contaminants, and included a ban on lead pipe and lead solder in public water systems. It mandated greater protection of groundwater sources and set a three-year timetable for regulation of eighty-three specific chemical contaminants that may have an adverse health effect known or anticipated to occur in public water systems.

During the summer of 1996, Congress and the Clinton administration, anxious to provide some evidence to voters that they were able to address pressing national issues, enacted amendments to the Safe Drinking Water Act. The amendments gave more discretion to states and local governments to determine what contaminants pose a threat to human health. The new law emphasized controlling the greatest risks for the most benefit at the least cost. It required local water agencies to issue annual reports disclosing the chemicals and bacteria in tap water. The reports must be written in simple, accessible language and sent to residents enclosed with their utility bills. Agencies must notify the public when water contaminants pose a serious threat. The law also authorized a $7.6 billion revolving fund to loan money to local water agencies for construction of new facilities. Small water systems can get waivers from compliance with the federal regulations. The measure was criticized by some Democrats for including water-related projects in states where Republicans were in tight reelection campaigns, and by environmental groups for weakening national water-quality standards.[42]

Public policies designed to address the risks associated with drinking-water contamination are not always founded on science and frequently are the result of political maneuvering. For example, just three days before he left office in 2001, President Bill Clinton proposed new regulations that would limit the amount of arsenic in drinking water from 50 parts per billion—a standard that had been in place since 1942—to 10 parts per billion. The administration was responding to studies showing that even minute amounts of arsenic could be linked to an increased incidence of lung and bladder cancer. Environmental groups had sought an even lower standard—3 parts per billion. Shortly after taking office, however, President George W. Bush suspended implementation of the new standard, arguing that there was insufficient proof that it was needed. Officials in many rural communities, which depended upon wells as a drinking-water source, had complained to the new administration that they could not afford to comply with the federal regulation.

EPA administrator Christine Whitman solicited new studies, including one from the National Academy of Sciences and others dealing with benefits and cost-effectiveness. Meanwhile, environmental groups attacked the president's action, running controversial advertisements that, some felt, suggested that Bush's decision would actually increase arsenic levels. Conservatives argued whether the government should be in the business of setting contaminant standards at all, noting that there will be substantial costs and minimal benefits for some communities. "Rather than wade into a debate over how much arsenic is acceptable in drinking water, the Bush administration should have reframed the issue as a debate over who is to make decisions for local communities: local citizens or the Feds," one columnist commented.[43]

Whether succumbing to public pressure, convinced by studies it had commissioned, or influenced by a combination of factors, the EPA changed direction on October 31, 2002, by announcing that the Clinton administration's standard would be implemented. A critic wrote:

> With its decision on arsenic, the EPA has reverted to the "Washington-knows best" mindset that has dominated environmental policy for far too long. Whitman can claim she's protecting Americans from arsenic in their water, but users of small water systems will be left holding the bill.[44]

TOXIC CONTAMINATION

Until the early 1960s and the publication of Rachel Carson's *Silent Spring*, Americans paid little attention to the millions of gallons of toxic chemicals that were routinely being poured into waterways, dumped onto remote sites, or even stored on private property. The dangers posed by the storage and handling of toxic chemicals were either unknown or ignored. Unless there is a focusing event, there is little incentive to move toxic contamination onto the political agenda as a water-quality issue.

Groundwater can be contaminated from a variety of human sources—from dumping to runoff from agriculture use. Homeowners, for example, may unknowingly pour products down their kitchen drains or toilets that contaminate the sewage stream. Some toxic contamination has been deliberate; in other cases, the groundwater was accidentally polluted long before researchers and officials even knew contamination was possible, or the extent to which it could be cleaned up.

A complication in the problem of toxic water contamination is that policies related to water quality have often conflicted with other environmental rules and regulations—what policy analysts refer to as *spillover*. The 1990 Clean Air Act Amendments, for instance, required some cities and states with the worst air quality to sell gasoline that was reformulated with oxygenates to improve combustion and reduce air pollutants. Manufacturers responded to the federal mandate to produce reformulated gasoline by adding methyl tertiary-butyl ether, or MTBE, in 1992. Some concerns were initially raised that MTBE exhaust created adverse health effects, but a more serious problem developed when the chemical, classified as a possible human carcinogen, began showing up in drinking-water tests in the early and mid-1990s in California.[45] In 1999, California governor Gray Davis issued an executive order calling for the prohibition of MTBE in gasoline on grounds that it polluted underground drinking water when gasoline leaked from underground storage tanks. MTBE producers subsequently sued, arguing before the U.S. Court of Appeals that the state's action conflicted with the federal Clean Air Act, but the court upheld the ban in a June 2003 decision. By 2005, California's Department of Health Services had detected nearly 13,000 sources of MTBE in water in more than half the state's counties—the majority in Los Angeles County. The assistant city attorney for Santa Monica, California, estimated it could take decades to clean up the contamination.[46]

While California quickly moved forward with its ban and monitoring program, federal policy became mired in election-year politics. Under the Clinton administration, the Clean Air Act Advisory Committee created the MTBE Blue Ribbon Panel, which held meetings and published a September 1999 report. The final recommendations included a substantial nationwide reduction in the use of MTBE, accelerating research on MTBE and its substitutes, and over twenty specific actions to improve the nation's water-protection programs.[47]

In March 2000, EPA Administrator Carol Browner announced the beginning of regulatory action under the Toxic Substances Control Act to reduce or eliminate use of MTBE in gasoline. A draft regulation that said that "[t]he use of MTBE as an additive in gasoline presents an unreasonable risk to the environment" was sent by the EPA to the White House in January 2001, just as Clinton was leaving office.[48]

Under the Bush administration, the EPA did not move forward with the proposal, despite dozens of studies and background papers on the environmental impacts of the additive's use. Instead, the new Congress considered proposals that would shield industry from lawsuits related to the additive. Environmental groups accused the president of favoring companies that contributed over $1 million to Republican candidates. "This is a classic case of the Bush administration helping its campaign contributor friends at the expense of public health," said the director of the Clean Air Trust.[49] Nearly twenty states have now banned MTBE on their own.

Some forms of toxic contamination are legal and permitted by officials. The nation's pulp and paper mills have been targeted by environmental groups as among the biggest polluters of U.S. waterways, with bleaching plants the source of millions of pounds of chlorinated compounds annually. Among the compounds identified in bleach effluent are dioxins (a generic term applied to a group of suspected carcinogens that are the by-products of other substances or processes), which have been shown to cause reproductive disorders in animals, and immune system suppression and impaired liver function in humans.

The pace at which toxic contamination has been regulated and enforced, both at the federal and state levels, has been uneven and decidedly sluggish. The Clean Water Act of 1972 required the EPA to impose the best available pollution-control technology standards on industries that discharge toxic waste into rivers, lakes, and estuaries, as well as sewage-treatment facilities. The agency did not take action to implement the law until 1976, when a lawsuit forced it to agree to regulate twenty-four of more than fifty industrial categories, including organic chemicals, pharmaceuticals, and pulp and paper. In 1987, Congress amended the legislation and ordered the EPA to update the old standards and to begin regulating additional categories by February 1991. When the congressional deadline passed, the NRDC filed suit in U.S. District Court to force the agency to comply with the 1987 law. In its suit, the NRDC noted that the EPA had not developed rules for four of five industrial plants that dump toxic substances directly into surface waters. In 1992, the EPA agreed to settle the lawsuit and extend federal standards to sixteen additional industry categories between 1996 and 2002, including industrial laundries, pesticide manufacturers, and hazardous-waste facilities and incinerators.

Similarly, the states have failed to comply with the 1987 Water Quality Act provisions, which required them to impose limits on toxic pollution in their waters by 1990. In 1991, the EPA announced that it would impose federal rules on the twenty-two states and territories that had not set their own standards to reduce levels of toxic compounds, including pesticides, solvents, and heavy metals.

Why has water pollution taken so long to gain policymakers' attention, and why has the EPA been so reluctant to move forward on the legislative mandates? There are several possible explanations for the current status of water-pollution control:

1. EPA officials cite staff and budgetary constraints that virtually crippled the agency during the 1980s, especially under President Reagan, that put many water-quality initiatives on hold.

2. The federal government had delegated much of its responsibility to the states, which are required to issue permits to industries that discharge

pollution into surface water. The permit limits vary from state to state and have generally been much more lenient than federal controls.

3. Water-quality issues have tended to take a backseat to air-quality issues when it comes to the political arena. Congressional committees have focused on the more politically visible issues of smog and auto emissions rather than water quality. Although the 1972 law eliminated the gross pollution that causes rivers and lakes to look or smell bad, the more invisible but nevertheless hazardous toxic pollutants have been largely ignored until recently.

4. The overlapping of jurisdictions and responsibilities between the federal and state governments has led to a competition among agencies.

5. Both environmental groups and public officials reluctantly admit that the compliance deadlines of the 1972 legislation were extremely unrealistic, forcing the EPA to scramble to come up with new rules that even the agency leadership knew were not attainable.

6. Despite attempts at innovative conservation strategies and protection of existing sources, one of the compelling factors in water-quality policy today is cost. Many of the new federal requirements place a severe burden on small communities that cannot afford expensive water-treatment plants on budgets that are already stretched thin. Small communities may not be able to take advantage of some treatment technologies, for example, and may not have access to alternative water supplies. Thus many of the proposed solutions may benefit large urban areas, leaving smaller, rural communities with few alternatives.

But the problem of drinking-water quality may be tied primarily to a lack of regulatory enforcement. A December 2009 study by the *New York Times* found that more than 20 percent of the nation's water-treatment systems have violated key provisions of the Safe Drinking Water Act over the last five years. Since 2004, 49 million people have had water delivered to them that contained illegal concentrations of chemicals like arsenic, radioactive chemicals like uranium, or dangerous bacteria. Records accessed by the newspaper found that fewer than 6 percent of the water systems that broke the law were ever fined or punished by state or federal officials. The problem of enforcement affects parts of every state, indicative of "significant reluctance within the EPA and Justice Department to bring actions against municipalities, because there's a view that they are often cash-strapped, and fines would often be paid by local taxpayers."[50]

INTERNATIONAL WATER SCARCITY AND QUALITY

As one of the world's most industrialized countries, the United States has the advantage of technology and monetary resources to support attempts to preserve water resources and to ensure a safe supply of drinking water. To most Americans, water quality is as much a matter of aesthetics as of health—a view shared among developed countries. But from a global perspective, the concerns and attention paid to the issue of managing water resources are quite different.

What differences are there between water management in the United States as compared to other nations? First, in most developing countries, water policy has been almost totally health-based; little attention is paid to the recreational or scenic value of waterways—values considered luxuries in economies struggling to fund any type of environmental program at all. Although all nations respond to the problem of water scarcity through the strategies outlined earlier in this chapter, what minimal environmental resources developing countries have must be spread thinly between air and water pollution, with groundwater contamination receiving the bulk of funds. Many countries have only marginal enforcement operations to handle water pollution, and legislation to control and punish polluters is weak where it exists at all. There is a shortage of lawyers with expertise in environmental law and even fewer judges who are informed or sympathetic.

Second, water-management policies in many developing countries have led to soil erosion and desertification, which threaten nearly a third of the Earth's surface. Desertification refers to the process by which the land gradually becomes less capable of supporting life, and nonproductive. Desertification has four primary causes: overgrazing on rangelands, overcultivation of croplands, waterlogging and salting of irrigated lands, and deforestation. An additional 100 million acres, mostly in India and Pakistan, are estimated by the UN Environment Programme to suffer from salinization, which occurs in dry regions when evaporation near the soil surface leaves behind a thin salt residue. Salinity also affects water quality in Peru and Mexico, where the annual loss of output as a result of salinization is estimated at 1 million tons of food grains, or enough to provide basic rations to 5 million people.

Third, an enduring drought has led to not only a water shortage but also declining water quality. In China, for instance, more than half of the nation's 700 cities suffer chronic water shortages, causing $15 billion in lost industrial output every year. An estimated 23 million people are short of drinking water, and more than 73 million acres of farmland have been damaged. The problem stems from the fact that China has about as much water as Canada but 40 times more people. As the cities grow, the demand increases, wetlands dry up as water is diverted, and species of fish are disappearing.[51]

Fourth, most countries responding to water problems do so on a place-specific basis, using scientific, engineering, and institutional knowledge that has limited transferability, according to the organization Resources for the Future. Some simply cannot afford the technologies and strategies that have been internationally accepted to face individual environmental challenges, whether on a municipal or corporate level. Foreign investors come into an area using pollution-control measures that correspond to their own capabilities and profit-making agendas, with little regard for local culture and values. As a result, "it is difficult to develop commonly understood and generally applicable management policies, practices, and interventions at regional or global scale."[52]

Fifth, the potential for conflict over transboundary water pollution and shared watercourses is much greater on other continents than it is in North America. Almost 40 percent of the world's population lives in international river basins; nearly fifty countries on four continents have more than three-quarters of their total land in the 214 multinational river basins, including fifty-seven in

Another View, Another Voice: Ma Jun

Although he is not well-known outside the United States, Ma Jun's book, *China's Water Crisis*, has been compared to Rachel Carson's *Silent Spring*. In 2006, *Time* magazine named him one of the 100 most influential people in the world, even though he was not yet forty years old. He is the founder of the Institute of Public and Environmental Affairs in Beijing, and the online China Water Pollution Map, a searchable database of information about the country's polluted lakes and rivers.

Ma did not start out as an environmental advocate. He obtained a degree in journalism from Beijing International Studies University, and from 1993 to 1999, he was a researcher in the Beijing bureau of Hong Kong's *South China Morning Post*. As a journalist, he traveled with his colleagues throughout the country. Then, in 1999, he published his first book, which explains how all seven of China's drainage basins throughout the country have been polluted by human activities, primarily the constant struggle for more and more hydropower and flood prevention. He focuses on the country's two major rivers, the Yellow and the Yangtze. He also looks at China's large-scale reservoirs, the diminishing water table, and the abuse of aquifers. The book was translated into English in 2004, and Ma was selected to attend the prestigious Yale World Fellows Program. During his studies, he researched a comparison between Chinese and Western water systems, concluding that public pressure not to pollute was a major difference in outcomes.

To further influence Chinese water policies, he formed the research institute in June 2006 in Beijing, although perhaps "institute" is too strong a term to describe the four employees who work out of a small apartment. The team developed a database of about 2,500 companies that have been officially cited for exceeding pollution-discharge standards between 2004 and 2006; the database is now expanded to more than 8,000 companies with the help of knowledgeable volunteers. The database, which is available to the public, is designed to embarrass companies, since the maximum fine for polluting watersheds is just over $25,000 in U.S. dollars, which he considers to be much too low. "The pre-condition for any meaningful participation should be to allow those who are affected to have access to the information," he says. Executives from companies have tried to get their names erased from the database, something that happens only when Ma is convinced that an independent environmental audit warrants doing so. It is Ma's hope that companies considering doing business with Chinese firms will consult his database as a way of placing additional pressure on them.

One of his latest projects is the Green Choice Initiative, another program developed in conjunction with twenty other nongovernmental organizations to inform the public about sustainable consumption. The program has publicized the names of twenty-five major consumer-goods companies that have been cited for violating Chinese environmental standards, about half of which are foreign.

Ma does not consider himself to be one of the world's most influential people, despite the accolade from *Time*. "If that were the case," he says, "I would be far more effective."

SOURCES:
Ma Jun. "Ecological Civilization Is the Way Forward." October 31, 2009. http://www.chinadialogue.net/article/show/single/en/1440. Accessed December 18, 2009.
Nancy Yang Liu and Lawrence R. Sullivan. "China's Water Crisis: Ma Jun." http://www.eastbridgebooks.org/ChinasWaterCrisisMoreInfo.html. Accessed December 17, 2009.
Ed Norton. "Ma Jun." *Time*. April 30, 2006. http://www.time.com/time/magazine/article/0,9171,1187271,00.html. Accessed December 17, 2009.
Jean-Francois Tremblay. "Ma Jun." *Chemical and Engineering News*, 85, no. 40 (October 1, 2007). http://www.pubs.acs.org/cen/business/85/8540bus2. Accessed December 17, 2009.
Ke Zhang. "Group Monitors China's Water Polluters." *WorldWatch Institute*. September 26, 2006. http://www.worldwatch.org/node/4622. accessed December 17, 2009.

Africa and forty-eight in Europe. Thirteen of the river basins are shared by five or more countries; in Europe, four river basins are shared by four or more countries and regulated by more than 175 treaties. In developing countries, in contrast, there are significantly fewer agreements on shared water resources. Africa has a complex system of river basins, but fewer than forty treaties regulate their use. In Asia, only thirty treaties have been drawn up to regulate the five basins shared by four or more countries.[53]

International cooperation on water issues can be traced back to the sixteenth century, when water was viewed as an economic commodity; control over water focused on navigation of watercourses and the shared use of water for agriculture, fishing, and, later, industry. Over time, pollution of watercourses among neighboring nations, along with concerns about downstream users, led to hundreds of regional agreements over water use. The 1997 United Nations Convention on the Law of the Non-Navigational Uses of International Watercourses sought to codify what historically was customary law. The lack of support for the agreement is due in part to new definitions of watercourses, which originally were considered parts of rivers or lakes that straddled or crossed borders. Now, that perspective is seen as too narrow as countries address problems like riparian areas, the relationship between surface water and groundwater, and the role of state sovereignty.[54]

Finally, environmental organizations in the United States have a longer history and have been much more successful than have their counterparts in other countries in raising the public's awareness about water quality. For instance, Clean Water Action, known initially as the Fisherman's Clean Water Action Group, was formed in 1971 and subsequently focused on implementation of the Clean Water Act of 1972. Over time, it has become a clearinghouse for a national coalition of state and local advocacy organizations that focus on clean and affordable drinking water.[55] In many developing nations, polluted waters have always been a way of life, and there is little knowledge regarding the care and advantages of clean water. As a result, there have been fewer grassroots efforts to demand stronger enforcement and less media attention to gross violations and health risks.

Although efforts are being made to transfer American technology to both developed and developing nations to improve water quality, most observers believe the best that can be done for now is to buy time. Early efforts at providing assistance in the former Soviet Union were often poorly thought out or were abandoned before fulfillment, leading some governments to rethink their aid plans. As one researcher notes:

> What the West needs at this point is not a detailed blueprint for future action, but a new intellectual framework for approaching the problem: patience is necessary. More importantly, policymakers must think in terms of multiyear time frames, collective action, mechanisms for developing joint strategies, and coordination.[56]

FURTHER READING

Robin Kundis Craig. *The Clean Water Act and the Constitution*, 2nd ed. Covelo, CA: Island Press, 2009.

Holly Doremus and A. Dan Tarlock. *Water War in the Klamath Basin: Macho Law, Combat Biology, and Dirty Politics*. Covelo, CA: Island Press, 2008.

Robert Glennon. *Unquenchable: America's Water Crisis and What to Do About It*. Covelo, CA: Island Press, 2009.

Norris Hundley Jr. *Water and the West: The Colorado River Compact and the Politics of Water in the American West*, 2nd ed. Berkeley: University of California Press, 2009.

Wolfram Mauser. *Water Resources: Sustainable and Equitable*. London: Haus Publishing, 2009.

Megan Mullin. *Governing the Tap: Special District Governance and the New Local Politics of Water*. Cambridge, MA: MIT Press, 2009.

Alex Prud'homme. *Clean, Clear, and Cold: The Fate of Fresh Water in the Twenty-First Century*. New York: Scribner, 2010.

Edella Schlager and William Blomquist. *Embracing Watershed Politics*. Boulder: University Press of Colorado, 2008.

Terie Twedt and Teri Oestigaard. *A History of Water*. London: I.B. Tauris, 2009.

8

Air Quality: Pollution and Solutions

"It was unlike anything I've ever seen—you could look
directly at the sun and not have a problem, due to the
thickness of the haze."
— DR. STACI SIMONICH ON AIR POLLUTION AT THE 2008 BEIJING OLYMPICS[1]

When Beijing, China, was awarded the Summer Games of the XXIX Olympiad in 2001, critics pointed to a number of issues, ranging from the country's record on human rights to the lack of sufficient infrastructure to handle the crowds expected for the August 2008 games. But one of the most difficult problems the city and surrounding venues faced was air quality, affecting both spectators and athletes. Air pollution in Beijing, a city of nearly 12 million, has been historically among the worst in the world, and the International Olympic Committee's medical commission recognized that there might be some risk to athletes. One of the prime causes and contributors to air pollution is automobiles, with an estimated 3.3 million cars estimated to use the city's streets. Although China saw significant improvements in air quality during the late 1990s and early 2000s, emissions of nitrogen oxide, carbon monoxide, and volatile organic compounds cover the city with clouds of contamination resulting from reinvigorated economic growth and continued expansion of the transportation system. Concentrations of fine particulate matter and ozone often exceed healthful levels, especially in summer, and past gains in air quality have been lost in recent years.[2]

The Beijing Organizing Committee of the Olympic Games (BOCOG) developed specific proposals, implemented in more than a dozen phases, to improve air quality in time for the Games to begin. The number of subway lines was doubled, factories were required to retrofit facilities with pollution-control equipment, urban parks were built, and more than half of the city's automobiles were pulled off the road. Just before the Games, production was stopped at several chemical and oil-fueling units, with plans to close down forty facilities within six months after the Olympics were over. Despite these efforts, a joint American–Chinese study conducted before, during, and after the events found that although $20 billion was spent on "greening" the city, the level of particulate pollution in Beijing was 3.5 times as bad as at the games in Sydney in 2000, three times as bad as at the 1996 Games in Atlanta, and twice as bad as in Athens in 2004. The 2009 study found, more importantly, that weather conditions, such as rainfall and strong winds, played a much larger role than the efforts made by the city of Beijing to reduce particulate matter. Researchers did not discount Beijing's efforts, nor was there evidence of any health effects of short-term exposure, but they did note that it demonstrates the difficulty of trying to control pollution at the local level, since air masses tend to move regionally.[3]

The government's optimism about what can be done to control air pollution is not new. On August 14, 1943, Los Angeles mayor Fletcher E. Bowron announced at a press conference that the city's smog would be entirely eliminated within four months.[4] The city's air quality at the time was perceived as a product of the region's burgeoning industry—a relatively recent urban development. But air pollution was a problem long before the mayor of Los Angeles made his prediction. There are references to the fumes produced at the asphalt mining town of Hit, about 100 miles west of Babylon, in the writings of King Tukulti in around 900 B.C., and in 61 B.C., the philosopher Seneca reported on the "heavy air of Rome" and its "pestilential vapors and soot." Marco Polo refused to use coal as a fuel because of its smoky odors. Foreigners traveling to Elizabethan England were astonished and revolted at the filthy smoke produced by domestic fires and workshops.[5]

The history of cleaning up urban air pollution is marked by small successes on what has proven to be a much longer road than most early municipal officials ever anticipated. Three characteristics can be used to describe global attempts to improve air quality: (1) In the United States, local government historically has been given most of the responsibility for pollution control; (2) policy efforts have been split between those who desire improvement because of impaired visibility and for aesthetic reasons, and those who recognize the health effects of pollution, especially particulate matter and ozone; and (3) in most other parts of the world, national governments, rather than municipalities, have taken the initiative for improving air quality, with varying degrees of success. This chapter reviews these characteristics and the challenge of developing policies to control air pollution both in the United States and in other countries. It also explores the ways in which the problem has been expanded to other concerns such as toxic air pollution, visibility, and transboundary air pollution.

THE COMPONENTS OF AIR POLLUTION

Until well into the twentieth century, the components of pollution were thought to be primarily smoke and soot (suspended particulate matter) and sulfur dioxide—waste products from home heating, industrial facilities, and utility power plants. With industrialization and the advent of the automobile, that list has expanded to include a broad range of emissions, including some considered toxic. These pollutants are found in the atmosphere; although most are human-made, some, like particulate matter, include the fine particles of dust and vegetation that are natural in origin and small enough to penetrate the most sensitive regions of the respiratory tract.

As Table 8.1 indicates, the term *air pollution* is usually applied internationally to the six conventional (or criteria) pollutants identified and measured by the Environmental Protection Agency (EPA): carbon monoxide, lead, nitrous oxides, ozone, particulate matter, and sulfur oxides.[6] The EPA's Office of Air Quality Planning and Standards reviews the status of the six pollutants, which are measured in parts per million (ppm) by volume, milligrams per cubic meter of air, and micrograms per cubic meter of air. The EPA periodically makes changes in the national standards for air quality, usually lowering the levels of pollutants that are considered to exceed allowable exposure. Based on federal legislation, the EPA sets target dates by which regions throughout the United States are required to meet the standards; if they are not met, various sanctions are imposed. These range from fines for noncompliance to actually shutting down polluting facilities.

There are three primary categories of sources for conventional pollutants: stationary or point sources, such as factories and power plants; mobile sources,

TABLE 8.1   Components and Health Effects of Air Pollution

Criteria Pollutant	Sources	Health Effects
Carbon monoxide (CO)	Motor vehicles	Interferes with ability of the blood to absorb oxygen
Lead (Pb)	Motor vehicles, lead smelters	Affects kidneys, reproductive, and nervous systems; accumulates in bones; may cause hyperactivity in children
Nitrous oxides (NO_x)	Electric utility boilers, motor vehicles	Causes increased susceptibility to viral infections, lung irritation
Ozone	Formed by a chemical reaction of NO_2 and hydrocarbons	Irritates respiratory system; impairs lung function; aggravates asthma
Particulate matter (PM)	Combustion from industry; forest fires; windblown dust; vehicles	Organic carcinogenic (PH_{10}) compounds can migrate into lungs, increasing respiratory distress
Sulfur oxides (SO_2)	Utility plant boilers, oil and chemical refineries	Aggravates symptoms of heart and lung disease; increases respiratory illnesses and colds

including cars, trucks, and aircraft; and domestic sources, such as home heating or consumer products.

Current air-quality law establishes two types of standards for conventional pollutants. Primary standards set limits to protect public health, including the health of "sensitive" populations such as asthmatics, children, and the elderly. Secondary standards set limits to protect public welfare, including protection against decreased visibility and against damage to animals, crops, vegetation, and buildings.

AIR QUALITY AND HEALTH

The most serious air-quality impact that concerns policymakers now is health. It is difficult to pinpoint exactly when concerns about health effects of air pollution made their way to the policy agenda. One factor that made it difficult for policymakers to reach consensus on what to do about air pollution was the lack of a consensus about its sources. Smoky chimneys and smokestacks were considered part of the price urban dwellers paid for living in an industrialized society, and most people were probably unaware of any damage to their health.

The emphasis on the health effects of pollution was due largely to the role of the U.S. Public Health Service, which was given responsibility for air-pollution legislation from 1959 until the passage of the Clean Air Act in 1963. Although little policy initiation occurred before 1963, the Surgeon General did convene the First National Conference on Air Pollution in 1958, and Oregon established the first state air regulatory agency in 1952.

Hundreds of published studies have identified the health effects of urban ozone pollution. People breathing ozone, even at concentrations below the current national standards, appear to be susceptible to increased respiratory hospital admissions, frequent and severe asthma attacks, inflammation of the upper airways, coughing and breathing pains, reaction to irritants, sensitivity to allergens, and decreased lung function much like what smokers experience. Epidemiological studies show a strong correlation between increased mortality and ozone pollution.

Dozens of studies have focused on the impact of pollution on children, who are most at risk. One report, the Children's Health Study conducted by the University of Southern California over an eight-year period, found that children aged ten to eighteen suffered clinically significant reductions in lung function as they reached adulthood. Fine particulate matter, rather than ozone, appeared to have the greatest effect on lung capacity, which was particularly important because researchers monitored older children and over a longer period than previous researchers had done.[7]

Reports by environmental and consumer groups have given the public more information than ever before on the status of the air quality not only in their own state, but throughout the nation. The reports have received considerable attention from the media, and they have served as a way of keeping air quality on the political agenda. Usually published in nontechnical formats, the reports have become a way of keeping score on how much progress the EPA and its

TABLE 8.2   Top Twenty Metropolitan Areas with the Worst Ozone Air Pollution, (2000–2009)

2000 Rank	2009 Rank	Metropolitan Area*
1	1	Los Angeles–Long Beach–Riverside, CA
2	2	Bakersfield, CA
4	3	Visalia–Porterville, CA
3	4	Fresno–Madera, CA
5	5	Houston–Baytown–Huntsville, TX
11	6	Sacramento–Arden–Arcade–Truckee, CA–NV
14	7	Dallas–Ft. Worth, TX
8	8	Charlotte–Gastonia–Salisbury, NC–SC
12	9	Phoenix–Mesa–Scottsdale, AZ
**	10	El Centro, CA
**	11	Hanford–Corcoran, CA
**	12	Las Vegas–Paradise–Pahrump, NV
6	13	San Diego–Carlsbad–San Marcos, CA
7	14	Washington–Baltimore–Northern Virginia, DC–MD–VA– WVA
**	15	Cincinnati–Middletown–Wilmington, OH–KY–IN
13	16	Philadelphia–Camden–Vineland, PA–NJ–DE–MD
16	17	New York–Newark–Bridgeport, NY–NJ–CT–PA
**	17	St. Louis–St. Charles–Farmington, MO–IL
12	19	Knoxville–Sevierville–La Follette, TN
**	20	Birmingham–Hoover–Cullman, AL

*The U.S. Census Bureau revised definitions for metropolitan statistical areas in 2003, making some comparisons with previous reports difficult.
**These metropolitan areas were not listed among the top 20 in the 2000 report.
SOURCE: American Lung Association. "State of the Air 2009." http://www.lungusa2.org/sota/2009/SOTA-2009-Full-Print.pdf. Accessed July 14, 2009.

state counterparts have made per year. In addition, more information is available than ever before on the health impacts of air pollution—much of it distributed on the Internet.

The American Lung Association (ALA) issues an annual public report assessing U.S. air quality on a national basis. Metropolitan areas and counties are ranked according to short-term and year-round particle pollution and for ozone pollution, a major component of smog. Over time, the rankings of various areas have changed somewhat, although California's South Coast Air Basin (which includes Los Angeles, Orange, Riverside, and San Bernardino Counties) is perennially identified with the nation's worst air quality, as seen in Table 8.2. The list of U.S. cities most polluted by year-round particle pollution (Table 8.3) provides a slightly different, although equally disturbing, view of metropolitan air quality.

At the opposite end of the pollution spectrum are the nation's cleanest cities for ozone air pollution (see Table 8.4). What makes the information intriguing is

TABLE 8.3 Top Twenty Metropolitan Areas Most Polluted by Year-Round Particle Pollution (2009)

Rank 2009	Metropolitan Area
1	Bakersfield, CA
2	Pittsburgh–New Castle, PA
3	Los Angeles–Long Beach–Riverside, CA
4	Visalia–Porterville, CA
5	Birmingham–Hoover–Cullman, AL
6	Hanford–Corcoran, CA
7	Fresno–Madera, CA
8	Cincinnati–Middletown–Wilmington, OH–KY–IN
9	Detroit–Warren–Flint, MI
10	Cleveland–Akron–Elyria, OH
11	Charleston, WV
11	Louisville–Jefferson County–Elizabethtown–Scottsburg, KY–IN
11	Huntington–Ashland, WV–KY–OH
14	Macon–Warner Robins–Fort Valley, GA
14	St. Louis–St. Charles–Farmington, MO–IL
16	Weirton–Steubenville, WV–OH
17	Atlanta–Sandy Springs–Gainesville. GA–AL
18	Indianapolis–Anderson–Columbus, IN
18	Rome, GA
20	York–Hanover–Gettysburg, PA

SOURCE: American Lung Association. "State of the Air 2009." http://www.lungusa2.org/sota/2009/SOTA-2009-Full-Print.pdf. Accessed July 14, 2009.

TABLE 8.4 Cleanest Cities for Ozone Air Pollution, 2009 (Alphabetically, by Metropolitan Statistical Area)

Billings, MT

Carson City, NV

Coeur d'Alene, ID

Fargo, ND–Wahpeton, MN

Honolulu, HI

Laredo, TX

Lincoln, NE

Port St. Lucie–Sebastian–Vero Beach, FL

Sioux Falls, SD

SOURCE: American Lung Association. "State of the Air 2009." http://www.lungusa2.org/sota/2009/SOTA-2009-Full-Print.pdf. Accessed July 14, 2009.

that many of these areas, such as Colorado Springs, Colorado, and Spokane, Washington, have a population of about a half-million persons, and Honolulu, Hawaii, is nearing 1 million. This shows that even in urban areas, pollution is influenced by factors other than population, such as weather and topography.

PUBLIC POLICY RESPONSES

For most of the twentieth century, air pollution was considered a local problem in the United States. As a result, most of the efforts to do something about it have been accomplished by municipal governments. By 1912, industrial smoke, the hallmark of urban growth after the turn of the century, was regulated in twenty-eight U.S. cities with populations of 200,000 or more. Smoke was the prime target of most ordinances because it was visible, but little attention was paid to controlling the problem.[8]

Until the passage of the Clean Air Act in 1963, the federal government took only minimal interest in the problem. In 1912, the Bureau of Mines conducted research on smoke control, which at the time was considered to be the only form of pollution. In 1925, the Public Health Service began to study carbon monoxide in automotive exhaust, but for the most part, the federal role was minor. In 1948, a six-day smog siege in Donora, Pennsylvania, killed twenty people and sickened 6,000 residents, focusing national attention on a problem that until then had been considered unique to Los Angeles. The Donora incident was followed in December 1952 by a similar sulfurous smog episode in London, and in 1953 by another incident in New York, resulting in 200 deaths.[9] All three events lent some urgency to the problem. As city officials began to realize the irrelevance of political boundaries to pollution control, they began to coordinate their regulatory efforts.

The discovery in 1949 that automobiles were a prime source of pollution forestalled statewide controls on industrial sources, and local government stepped in to fill the void left by federal inaction. In 1955, Los Angeles officials began to coordinate their efforts with the nation's top automakers, and Congress appropriated $5 million for research into motor-vehicle emissions—the beginning of federal intervention in urban air-pollution regulation. Research in the early 1960s debunked the idea that pollution was a problem only in the area immediately adjacent to the source or in urban areas. Studies began to show that pollution was being transported over long distances, causing environmental damage in regions far removed from the actual source. Long-range transport of sulfur and nitrogen compounds across international boundaries—a phenomenon known as "acid rain"—made air pollution a global problem. These findings made air quality much more than a simple local question and focused problem solving on Congress.

During the 1960s, four members of Congress did attempt to bring the federal government back into the air-pollution policy debate: Edmund Muskie, senator from Maine; Abraham Rubicoff, former Secretary of the Department of Health, Education, and Welfare (HEW); Kennedy Roberts, member of

Congress from Alabama; and Paul Schenck, member of Congress from Ohio. Their efforts were largely responsible for passage of the pioneering 1963 Clean Air Act, which expanded research and technical assistance programs, gave the federal government investigative and abatement authority, and encouraged the automobile and petroleum industries to develop exhaust-control devices. In November 1967, President Lyndon Johnson signed a second air-quality bill, which left the primary responsibility for air-pollution control with the state and local governments, suggesting that the federal agencies study, but not establish, national automobile-emission standards.

Meanwhile, environmental groups were pressuring Muskie to produce a new federal bill. The senator, an early contender for the 1972 Democratic presidential nomination, felt the sting of their criticism. A 1970 report by consumer activist Ralph Nader referred to "the collapse of the federal air pollution effort" and laid the blame squarely on Muskie's shoulders.[10] Muskie and the members of his Public Works Committee staff, relying on estimates provided by the National Air Pollution Control Administration (a part of HEW), proposed tough new federal standards for air quality and a timetable by which the standards had to be met through the filing of state implementation plans (SIPs). States have the option of deciding how to meet federal standards by controlling polluters within their jurisdiction, and the SIP is submitted to the EPA, which determines its adequacy. The EPA then prepares a federal implementation plan (FIP) that ensures the federal standards will be met.

The 1970 Clean Air Act required the newly created EPA to (1) develop federal air-quality standards, the National Ambient Air Quality Standards, or NAAQS; (2) establish emission standards for motor vehicles, effective in 1975; and (3) develop emission standards and hazardous emission levels for new stationary sources. The legislation went further than ever before by giving the EPA responsibility for regulating fuels and fuel additives, and for certifying and subsidizing on-the-road inspections and assembly-line testing of auto emission control systems.[11] The act was the first technology-forcing directive to be placed in legislation, requiring automakers to reduce emissions per vehicle by 90 percent. States faced a formidable task when the 1970 act gave them responsibility for preparing emission-reduction plans that would achieve the new federal standards within three years. If the states did not comply, the legislation authorized the EPA to step in and promulgate a federal plan. In addition to facing tight deadlines for plan preparation, neither the states nor the newly created EPA knew very much about translating federal standards into emission limits on sources. Therefore, relatively crude rules—like requiring all sources to diminish emissions by some specified percentage—were often employed.[12]

Critics charge that the 1970 law had several major faults. First, there was some ambiguity over the intent of the act with regard to the setting of auto-emission levels. The legislation gave automakers a one-year extension if they made a good-faith effort to comply but found that technology was not available to meet the new standards. Second, Congress appropriated only minimal amounts for research into the development of control devices that were in some cases required but did not yet exist. Third, stationary sources such as steel mills and utility power plants faced serious problems because control devices were either prohibitively expensive or technologically unfeasible.[13]

Five major automakers (Chrysler, Ford, General Motors, International Harvester, and Volvo) responded in early 1972 by filing for an extension of the requirement that they meet emission standards by 1975, arguing that they needed additional time to comply with the law. EPA administrator William Ruckelshaus denied their request for an extension, so the automakers appealed to the federal court, which ordered Ruckelshaus to review his original denial.[14] The automobile manufacturers argued that the necessary catalyst technology would not be available in time to meet the federal deadline, and Chrysler and American Motors testified that, even if the vehicles could be mass-produced in time, they would break down.[15] Ruckelshaus again denied the request for an extension, then reconsidered and granted the automakers what they were seeking, setting interim standards that the automobile companies did not appeal.

Implementation of the 1970 law was further hampered by what one observer has called "the enduring reluctance of the public to make significant sacrifices for the sake of healthy air."[16] The nation was locked into a pattern of rapid inflation and high unemployment, which was coupled with the imposition of an oil embargo by the Organization of the Petroleum Exporting Countries (OPEC) in October 1973. With rising concern over energy supplies, in March 1974, President Nixon proposed a package of thirteen amendments to the 1970 Clean Air Act, thereby freezing the interim 1975 auto-emission standards for two more years. In 1975, the automakers applied for another one-year extension, which was granted by new EPA administrator Russell Train, largely as a result of claims that the catalysts produced a sulfuric acid mist.[17]

By 1975, the deadline for states to attain the pollution standards expired, and many areas were still not in compliance. The NAAQS for ozone, which had been set at 0.08 ppm, was routinely being violated. Industry pressure to relax the emission standards on automobiles resulted in the passage of new Clean Air Act amendments in 1977. The legislation suspended the deadlines for automakers and extended to 1982 the deadlines by which states were to have attained federal standards. If a state's implementation plan made all reasonable attempts to meet the standards but was unable to do so, the state had to submit a second plan that would bring the area into compliance no later than December 1987. This issue primarily affected California. A key element of the 1977 law was a provision, shepherded through Congress by the Sierra Club, that states be required to show that any new sources of pollution would not worsen existing pollution conditions. This complex concept, known as *prevention of significant deterioration* (PSD), required businesses to install the best available control technology (BACT) to ensure that any potential pollution was minimized.

The concept had first been outlined in a 1972 Sierra Club suit against EPA administrator William Ruckelshaus[18] in which the organization argued that EPA guidelines under the 1970 Clean Air Act would permit significant deterioration of the nation's clean air, violating congressional intent. The federal district court agreed, ruling that the EPA could not approve state implementation plans that degraded existing air quality even if the region still met national air-quality standards. The EPA appealed, but the U.S. Supreme Court's 4–4 ruling in 1973 upheld the district court's decision. The EPA proposed new regulations to implement the Court's ruling in 1974.

The 1977 amendments required more aggressive antipollution programs and gave the EPA authority to designate those regions that did not meet federal standards as "nonattainment" areas. The amendments included a new provision requiring the EPA to reevaluate the NAAQS and to revise them as necessary, at least once every five years. Researchers from Johns Hopkins University recommended, for example, that the ozone standard be lowered from 0.08 to 0.06 ppm to protect public health. Despite concerns about the health risks of ozone, the EPA actually weakened the NAAQS in 1979 when it raised the one-hour standard to 0.12 ppm. Even with the revised ozone levels, by 1982, numerous areas were still out of compliance. Even though the 1977 amendments required the EPA to review the NAAQS every five years, the agency missed the 1985 deadline, giving itself a two-year extension. In 1990, the EPA missed another five-year deadline.

The EPA showed more flexibility toward industry with the introduction in 1979 of a "bubble" policy, which allowed businesses to find the least expensive method of reducing pollution from an entire plant or series of plants rather than from an individual source (as if the entire facility were under a regulatory bubble). The policy allowed companies to choose how to reduce emissions and to use more innovative strategies than were previously required. The Clean Air Act was scheduled for reauthorization in 1981, but a change in policy direction came with the Reagan administration. As a result, the 1970 legislation remained virtually unchanged until 1990.[19] Chief among the congressional barriers to a new law were Representative John Dingell, a Democrat from Michigan (and chairman of the House Energy and Commerce Committee), who stalled efforts to enact legislation that would impose new standards on automakers; and Senate Majority Leader Robert Byrd, a Democrat from West Virginia, who protected the interests and jobs of the coal miners in his region affected by acid rain proposals.

Clean-air legislation regained its place on the policy agenda in the late 1980s, partly because of changes taking place in Congress. Restless Democrats in the House were openly expressing their hostility to Dingell and Henry Waxman of California, members of the House Energy and Commerce Committee, whose personal battles were perceived as holding up the reauthorization. The result was the formation of the Group of Nine—moderate Democrats hoping to break the legislative logjam over urban smog. In the Senate, Byrd was replaced as majority leader by George Mitchell of Maine, who promised an end to the deadlock. Both houses had the opportunity to end the deadlock when the Bush administration unveiled its own clean-air proposal, forcing the key players to resolve their differences.[20]

The resulting legislation, signed by President Bush in 1990, contained several proposals that went far beyond those in the 1970 and 1977 acts. The bill established five categories of nonattainment (*marginal, moderate, serious, severe,* and *extreme*) and set new deadlines by which areas in those categories must meet federal ozone standards. Only one area, the Los Angeles/South Coast Air Basin, was classified as extreme by the EPA and was given twenty years to meet federal standards. In contrast, severe nonattainment areas were given fifteen years from November 1990 (the enactment date of the amendments) to comply; serious areas, nine years; moderate areas, six years; and marginal areas, three years. Plants emitting any of 188 toxic air pollutants were required to cut emissions, and they would be forced to shut down by 2003 if these emissions subjected nearby residents to a cancer risk of more than 1 in 10,000. Chemicals that harm the Earth's protective ozone layer were to be phased out more rapidly than required under the Montreal Protocol, to which the United States is a signatory (see Chapter 10). One of the bill's most contentious portions dealt with acid rain, requiring an annual reduction of sulfur dioxide emissions by 10 million tons by the year 2000, and annual nitrogen dioxide emission reductions of 2.7 million tons by that same date. The cost of the legislation, ranging from $25 to $35 billion dollars, was hotly debated.[21]

President Bush called passage of the 1990 Clean Air Act "the cornerstone of our environmental agenda." But the battle was far from over. Implementation of the 1990 act has been just as controversial as its development. Congressman Waxman charged, "We'll never see clean air in large parts of the country."[22] Several factors hindered implementation of the 1990 air-quality amendment. Among the hurdles faced by the EPA was the regulatory time frame of the 700-page legislation. The implementing regulations are among the most complex the agency has ever issued. Although the issue of nitrous oxide emissions (one of the two chemicals that cause acid rain) took only two pages of the 1990 act, the regulations crafted by the EPA took hundreds of pages. Due to the large volume and complexity of the rules, the EPA has been forced to rely upon outside consultants for many of its rulemakings and on its advisory committees for assistance in deciding which rules to tackle first. Many of those advisory groups, such as the Acid Rain Advisory Committee, with forty-four members, were packed with industry members and few representatives of environmental groups.[23] The most complex provisions of the law are those dealing with air toxics, an area in which EPA staff members are notoriously short on expertise.

Within a year after the 1990 law was passed, Congress began stepping back from the thrust of the 1990 amendments. One portion of the legislation, for example, was designed to require state and local planners to adhere to air-quality goals when formulating transportation projects. Theoretically, the intent was to force municipalities to look for alternatives to increased use of single-occupancy vehicles. But in 1991, President George H. W. Bush proposed, and Congress accepted, plans for a 185,000-mile national highway system that would increase auto use—at odds with the intent of the air-quality act—by giving the most funds under the program to those states with the highest gasoline use.[24]

President Bush's 1992 State of the Union message stalled the implementation process when the president announced a 90-day freeze on all federal regulations and then extended it another 120 days after that. The freeze affected several clean-air regulations, including the Pollution Prevention Act, which required polluters to report on the amount of toxic chemicals they generate in order to be authorized to release them. Later that year, the president overruled an EPA regulation requiring industries to obtain permits that include limits on the pollution emitted by each plant. Industry had originally sought the right to exceed the limits after making minor changes in plant operations, without going through the costly and time-consuming process of obtaining a new permit. Citizen groups considered the permit process an important opportunity for public participation; and the EPA, which drafted the regulation, agreed. Bush then overturned the regulation as a part of his emphasis on deregulation.

In November 1993, the Senate Environment and Public Works Committee issued a "report card" on implementation of the Pollution Prevention Act. The EPA received A's for its acid-rain and stratospheric-ozone programs, a B for its small-business-assistance program, a C for its management of the state implementation plan process, and D's for development of air toxics standards and for the implementation of the California Low Emission Vehicle Program.[25] The Senate study trumpeted the success of the acid-rain program in devising a market-based approach to environmental regulation and emphasized the importance of environmental quality–based performance standards that create incentives for the development of new technologies.

Since the mid-1990s, most of the revisions in air-quality policy have been regulatory, rather than legislative. Congress has attempted no major changes to the 1990 statute, relying instead upon the regulatory agencies to fine-tune the implementation of the law. President George W. Bush's Clear Skies Initiative, announced on February 14, 2002, set mandatory emissions caps for three harmful air pollutants: sulfur dioxide, nitrogen oxides, and mercury. American power plants would be required to reduce air pollutants by an average of 70 percent, which the EPA predicted would allow most areas of the country to meet federal air-quality standards. The cost was staggering, however—an estimated $6.5 billion annually by 2020, which officials said would be offset by benefits to human health and visibility.[26]

One element of the Bush administration's air-quality policy dealt with new-source review regulations, originally established in 1977 and revised under the Clinton administration, that require power plants, factories, and oil refineries to upgrade their pollution-control equipment when a facility built before 1977 is expanded or improved. The Clinton-era rules were expected to reduce emissions from the nation's dirtiest plants by up to 95 percent.

The president announced his proposal to relax the Clinton regulations, which industry officials had called "overly burdensome," in June 2002. The Clear Skies legislation considered by Congress in 2002 and 2003 would have established a national "cap-and-trade" program that would set a ceiling on polluting emissions. Companies that reduced more than their share of emissions under the cap would be able to trade and sell emissions credits to companies that exceeded their emission permits. The changes were said to save companies billions of dollars that would have been spent on repairing aging facilities, an expense that executives said would ruin the industry.[27]

One bright spot on the administration's air-pollution agenda came in December 2003, when the EPA's Clean Air Mercury rule went into effect.

The rule permanently caps mercury emissions from coal-fired power plants using two mechanisms: by requiring facilities to install new control technology, and through a market-based cap-and-trade rule that would give companies flexibility in cutting emissions in two phases. Mercury was considered an important element of the Bush plan because it is a toxic, persistent pollutant that accumulates in the food chain and is usually absorbed by humans when eating fish. The rest of the Clear Skies measures failed to get sufficient support in Congress.

Because the legislative route to change appeared to have ended, the Bush administration again relied upon the regulatory process for change. On March 10, 2005, the day following the end of the Clear Skies Initiative in a Senate vote, the EPA issued the Clean Air Interstate Rule (CAIR), which acting EPA Administrator Steve Johnson said "will result in the largest pollution reductions and health benefits of any air rule in more than a decade."[28] The final rule permanently caps emissions of sulfur dioxide and nitrogen oxides in twenty-eight states in the eastern United States and the District of Columbia. The agency estimated the rule would result in $85 to $100 billion in health benefits and $2 billion in visibility benefits per year by 2015, annually preventing 17,000 premature deaths and reducing the number of lakes and streams considered acidic.[29]

Not surprisingly, the reaction to CAIR and to the defeat of Clear Skies was mixed. The president of the industry group Americans for Balanced Energy Choices said that coal-based electricity generators would have to invest about $52 billion in new technology to comply with the new rule, preferring the legislative approach rather than regulation.[30] But Environmental Defense, an organization often at odds with the EPA on environmental protection, called the new rule a "big win for clean air." The group's comments echoed the language in the EPA's news releases on CAIR, while saying that the Clear Skies proposals would clear the way for polluters to pollute more and were full of loopholes.[31]

As had been the case with the Healthy Forests Initiative described in Chapter 4, the Bush administration used a two-pronged approach, shepherding its proposals through the legislative and regulatory arenas simultaneously. Although the impact on air-quality policy of CAIR and the mercury rules will not be as significant as that of the parallel timber/wildfire efforts on national forests, the strategy is proving to be a successful one for making policy change.

Ozone

Ozone, a photochemical oxidant that is a major component of smog and a major health and environmental concern, has been the most controversial of the criteria pollutants in the implementation of the 1990 Clean Air Act.

The ALA took the EPA to court in 1991 to force the EPA to revise the 1979 ozone standard of 0.12 ppm, which was supposed to have been reviewed in 1985 and in 1990. The agency missed both review deadlines, and the ALA contended that the EPA disregarded new scientific studies on the health effects of ozone. In 1994, responding to another ALA challenge, the EPA agreed to conduct a review of the studies.

Throughout the budget process in 1995, Congress included additional riders to appropriations and balanced budget bills that would have restricted the EPA's

---

Another View, Another Voice: Vickie Patton

Litigation, one of interest groups' key strategies in affecting policy, is considered technical and sometimes as impersonal as the agencies that regulate pollution and natural resource issues. Cases typically involve teams of attorneys, each a specialist in a segment of environmental law, and often they have degrees in related scientific fields and practical expertise that gives them an edge over their competitors. But there are real people and real faces behind the courtrooms and appellate briefs, and Vickie Patton, senior attorney with the group Environmental Defense, is one of them. She is considered a top expert and litigator in the field, handling national and regional clean-air programs and representing the nonprofit, nonpartisan organization's 400,000 members at the highest court level, the U.S. Supreme Court.

She grew up in Tucson, Arizona, where she saw the tremendous growth that typifies the desert Southwest, and learned about the region's water issues firsthand. She received her undergraduate degree in hydrology from the University of Arizona, and then a law degree from New York University School of Law in 1990. She initially worked in the Office of General Counsel for the EPA at its Washington, D.C. office, specializing in air-quality issues. As an EPA employee, she received the agency's highest award, the Gold Medal for Exceptional Service, gaining invaluable knowledge about the EPA's inner workings.

Patton joined Environmental Defense in 1998, moving to its Boulder, Colorado, office. There, she worked on two important and successful 2007 U.S. Supreme Court cases, one involving pollution controls on factories and another dealing with the government's obligation to regulate greenhouse-gas emissions. She has also been involved in cases related to mercury emissions from coal-fired power plants, visibility in

national parks and wilderness areas, interstate air pollution, and other air-quality initiatives. A scholar as well as a litigator, she has published numerous articles in law reviews and environmental journals, and has been an adjunct professor at the University of Colorado, Boulder School of Law.

One co-worker has said that she "has the tenacity of a bulldog and the genius of an Einstein"; she and her family have installed solar panels on their house, ride bicycles whenever possible, and drive a hybrid car. Saying "There's no time to lose" in getting Congress to adopt and agencies to implement greenhouse-gas emission laws, Vickie Patton couples her legal work with membership on the EPA's national Clean Air Act Advisory Committee and the Initiatives Oversight Committee of the Western Regional Air Partnership.

Recently, she represented a coalition of organizations, including the American Lung Association, documenting the public health effects from marine vessels, including tankers and cruise ships, on the 87 million Americans who live in port areas. "The dangerous air pollution from these floating smokestacks is a serious health threat to tens of millions of Americans who live and work in port cities. Cleaning up these big ships will chart a course for cleaner air and healthier communities," she says.

SOURCES:
Environmental Defense Fund. "Meet Superstar Attorney Vickie Patton." News release. July 24, 2007. http://www.environmentaldefense. org/article.cfm?contentID=6659. Accessed August 9, 2007.
American Lung Association, Environmental Defense Fund, National Association of Clean Air Agencies, and Puget Sound Clean Air Agency. "Protecting American Health from Global Shipping Pollution." March 30, 2009. http://www.edf.org/pressrelease.cfm?contentID=9469. Accessed June 12, 2009.
Environmental Defense Fund. "Vickie Patton." http://www.edf.org/page. cfm?tagID=956. Accessed March 8, 2010.

---

implementation of the Clean Air and other acts, but President Clinton's vetoes blocked those measures, and Congress abandoned them in 1996. That same year, the EPA issued a three-volume document analyzing hundreds of new scientific studies that found evidence of adverse health effects from ozone levels allowed by the 1979 NAAQS.[32]

In July 1997, after public hearings and a formal comment period, the EPA issued a new eight-hour ozone standard of 0.08 ppm; in 1998, Congress set a July 2000 deadline for the next round of attainment designations. These actions prompted lawsuits from three states and several industry interests that believed there was no possibility of complying with the stricter ozone standard.

Proponents of the new standard, such as Earthjustice, praised the EPA for taking "a major step forward in public health protection from ozone."[33] The various challenges to the 1997 standard were heard by the U.S. Court of Appeals; in a 1999 decision, the court ruled that the EPA had violated a little-known constitutional theory—the nondelegation doctrine. But the court reaffirmed that the EPA was to make the designations using the NAAQS.[34] When the statutory deadline for the agency to make new designations expired, the EPA still had not complied with the congressional mandate.

In 2001 and 2002, the courts reversed the earlier rulings, rejecting industry arguments and upholding the EPA's authority to set the ozone standard at 0.08 ppm. Even after the court rulings, the EPA failed to make the attainment designation deadline. Environmental groups accused the EPA of "dragging its feet" in implementing tougher air-quality standards; and in May 2002, Earthjustice, a public-interest law group representing several other organizations, filed notice to take EPA to court once again.[35] In November 2002, the EPA entered into a consent decree with the environmental groups and agreed to set new ozone designations, using the 0.08 ppm standard, no later than April 2004. The agency complied; the 2004 ozone designations classified 126 areas, representing 474 counties and 31 states, as nonattainment areas. The South Coast Air Basin in southern California was the only area rated "severe" for ozone; three other California areas were ranked as "serious." Most of the designations placed areas in the categories of *moderate* or *marginal*.[36]

The implementation process for the new ozone rules was contained in a 279-page document that immediately came under fire by groups that turned to the administrative rulemaking process to air their grievances. A coalition of environmental organizations filed petitions to seek reconsideration of new Bush administration rules on new-source review, future designations of nonattainment areas, and clean fuel blends. Two industry coalitions filed petitions asking the EPA to extend deadlines for compliance with the ozone standard for large metropolitan areas because existing and potentially new pollution programs would not enable them to comply in time. Other legal actions were being pursued by the South Coast Air Quality Management District and six Northeastern and mid-Atlantic states. Complicating the issue was the fact that rural areas may be penalized in the classification system because their air is polluted by upwind pollution sources transported from other areas.[37]

Then, in 2004, the EPA adopted rules that environmental groups argued weakened the ozone standard, and a group of public health and environmental organizations, led by Earthjustice, successfully sued the agency in federal court in December 2006. The EPA appealed the court's ruling, but lost on appeal in a June 2007 ruling when the same court ruled the EPA violated the Clean Air Act, urging the EPA to "act promptly in promulgating a revised rule that effectuates the statutory mandate by implementing an eight hour [ozone] standard, which was deemed necessary to protect public health a decade ago." A spokesperson for the American Lung Association said bluntly, "Today's court decision puts us closer to having air that does not make people sick."[38]

In March 2008, the EPA abided by the court's ruling, concluding that the 1997 ozone standards were not adequate to protect public health and public welfare with an adequate margin of safety. The agency strengthened the ozone standard from 0.08 ppm, the 1997 standard, to a new standard of 0.075 ppm. The Clean Air Act requires states to recommend to the EPA which areas are and which areas are not meeting the revised standards no later than March 2009, and for the EPA to issue final designations no later than March 2010. However, the EPA can take up to an additional year if insufficient data is available for designation. The new ozone standard does not mean that the battle over smog is over; no doubt there will be battles over the final designations once they are made.

Particulate Matter

The reduction of fine particulate matter (PM) has been approached through the regulatory arena rather than through legislation. As with ozone, research published in the 1990s focused attention on the health effects of particulate pollution, and many scientists became convinced that fine particles were the most serious public health threat from air pollution. The health effects of particulate matter at levels below the national air-quality standards (as well as when air quality exceeds the standards) include increased respiratory hospital admissions, increased frequency and severity of asthma attacks, increased school absences, increased respiratory symptoms such as wheezing and coughing, increased hospitalization for cardiovascular problems, and increased mortality. In two major studies of particulate pollution, the risk of early death was estimated to be from 17 to 26 percent higher in areas with high levels of particulate matter 10 micrometers in diameter or smaller (PM10). A study by the Natural Resources Defense Council (NRDC) estimated that 64,000 people may die prematurely from cardiopulmonary causes linked to particulate air pollution. The research focused on the health effects of fine particles, released during combustion, that were not easily expelled by the respiratory system's normal safeguards when breathed by humans.[39]

The goal of air-quality standards, as Congress provided in the Clean Air Act, was to "protect the public health" with an "adequate margin of safety." In the face of compelling research in peer-reviewed scientific publications concerning the health effects of particulates in November 1996, the EPA proposed a new standard for particulate matter 2.5 micrometers in diameter or smaller (PM2.5) to regulate fine particles. The agency noted that the new particulate standards would result in 60,000 fewer bronchitis cases, 9,000 fewer hospitalizations for respiratory problems, fewer visits to doctors, less use of medication, less suffering by those with respiratory disease, improved visibility in national parks and wilderness areas, and prevention of as many as 20,000 premature deaths a year. The EPA also argued that every dollar spent on emissions reductions from 1970 to 1990 resulted in $15 to $20 worth of reduced health-care costs. Critics like the U.S. Conference of Mayors and the Air Quality Standards Coalition, comprised of industry executives, testified in congressional hearings that the proposed standards were too expensive and urged the EPA to do more research before finalizing the regulations.

It was not until 2004 that the EPA issued the country's first rules and designations for particulate matter—eight years after they were first proposed. The agency set standards for small particles, which aggravate those with lung and heart diseases, at $PM_{2.5}$—approximately one-thirtieth the size of an average human hair. In announcing the Clean Air Fine Particle Rules, the EPA reported that certain areas in twenty states as well as all or part of 224 counties nationwide (and the District of Columbia) had not attained national standards. These states have three years to submit plans to the EPA (similar to those for ozone pollution) that show how they will meet the $PM_{2.5}$ standards. The plans must show how standards will be attained by 2010, with a five-year extension possible for those with severe PM problems.[40]

Diesel Emissions

In past years, the EPA has regulated emissions from cars, sports utility vehicles, trucks, and nonroad vehicles, but one piece of the "clean diesel puzzle" has been missing—diesel locomotive and marine engines. In March 2007, the EPA issued new regulations, which cover 40,000 marine vessels and nearly 21,000 diesel locomotives, to cut annual emissions of nitrogen oxide by 80 percent and fine particulate matter by 90 percent. The agency estimates that by 2030, the new rule's health benefits will outweigh the costs by 20 to 1, preventing 1,500 premature deaths and 1,100 hospitalizations a year.[41]

The rules are an important part of the policy process for several reasons. First, the regulations will affect major metropolitan areas where air-pollution levels, especially nitrous oxide (NO_x), which is a component of smog, are already high. Diesel locomotives are the largest remaining uncontrolled source of air pollution in many cities. The emissions benefits are expected to be the equivalent of taking three-quarters of a million diesel trucks off the road each year, according to the executive director of the National Association of Clean Air Agencies. An attorney for the NRDC said the new rules, which also cover ferries, tugboats, and yachts, limit pollution equivalent to 150 coal-fired power plants.[42] Second, the rules phase in the dates on which manufacturers must meet the stricter standards, allowing some flexibility in compliance. Existing engines must be overhauled; newly built train and ship engines must be modified by 2009, and by 2014, marine-engine manufacturers must treat their exhaust through technological improvements, with makers of train engines given an additional year to do so. Third, the action helps spread the burden of compliance among a larger number of pollution sources, rather than forcing additional measures among polluters who argue they have already done everything possible to reduce harmful emissions.

The federal rules did not initially, however, cover cargo ships, cruise lines, and other major vessels, so—as is often the case in environmental policy—California took its own action to control emissions from these sources. In December 2005, California's Air Resources Board approved regulations to restrict emissions of particulates and gases from the 1,900 vessels that make 10,000 stops each year at ports in Los Angeles, Long Beach, Oakland, and Stockton. Once vessels come within twenty-four miles of the California coast, ships must switch from large diesel engines to smaller auxiliary ones that use cleaner-burning fuel. About 90 percent of the ships covered by the rules are foreign, and opponents charged that the state did not have the right to regulate ships outside its own waters. In addition to controlling the emissions from what one environmental advocate called the "SUVs of the seas," the regulations include operators of cranes, forklifts, tractors, and trucks that move cargo at state ports. Like the locomotive and marine-vessel rules promulgated by the EPA, California's regulation would reduce premature deaths, thousands of asthma attacks, lost workdays, and school absences.[43]

The EPA did not follow suit with its own proposal until March 2009, when the agency's new administrator announced at a press conference at Port Newark, New Jersey, that the United States would seek a 230-mile buffer, called an *emissions control area*, around the country's coastline that would impose some of the toughest emissions standards in the world on large vessels coming into American ports. The proposal was submitted to the International Maritime Organization (IMO), and would go into effect by 2015 at an estimated cost to industry of about $3.2 billion. EPA Administrator Lisa Jackson said it would improve air quality as far inland as Kansas by 2020. If approved in 2010, the program would cut sulfur in fuel by 98 percent, PM emissions by 85 percent, and NO_x emissions by 80 percent from current global requirements.[44]

While many environmental organizations appeared to support the landmark action, one of the first of the Obama administration, there was dissatisfaction that the proposal did not go far enough. Earthjustice, on behalf of a coalition of environmental and indigenous groups, asked the EPA to go a step further by amending the application to the IMO to include the waters off the coast of Alaska. The failure to do so, the organization contended, left "a gaping hole in the nation's environmental and human health protections."[45]

TOXIC AIR CONTAMINATION

Little is known about the health risk posed by the tens of thousands of synthetic chemicals available today. Although research is ongoing, many of the effects of toxic contamination, such as cancer, are not apparent until decades after exposure. Many of these substances are produced by factories and industrial processes, such as pulp and paper processors; but smaller sites, such as municipal waste dumps, dry cleaners, and print shops are also responsible for toxic emission releases. Pesticides and herbicides used in agricultural application also are released into the atmosphere.

Five metals found in air—beryllium, cadmium, lead, mercury, and nickel—are known to pose various hazards to human health. Except for lead, most of these substances pose a risk primarily to those living adjacent to the source, such as a waste dump or factory. Lead, however, is much more widely dispersed as a component of vehicle fuels and paints. Lead poisoning is characterized by anemia and may lead to brain dysfunction and neurological damage, especially in children. Elimination of lead from automobile fuels in the United States, Japan, and Canada has reduced emissions significantly, but few developing countries have attempted to phase out lead in gasoline. The problem is compounded by a lack of emission controls on lead smelters, battery-manufacturing plants, and paint-production facilities.

As is often the case in policy development, government regulation of toxics has typically come on the heels of crisis. In this case, the events occurred outside the United States. In July 1976, an explosion at an herbicide-manufacturing facility in Sevesco, Italy, released a toxic cloud of dioxin and other chemicals that spread downwind. *Dioxin* is a generic term applied to a group of suspected cancer-causing substances that are known to cause severe reproductive disorders as well as immune-system problems and impaired liver function. Although no deaths were directly attributed to the incident, within two weeks, plants and animals were dying, and residents with skin lesions were being admitted to local hospitals. More than 700 people living near the plant were evacuated, and 5,000 others in the surrounding areas were told not to garden or let their children play outside. It took two weeks for local authorities to discover that a toxic chemical had been involved and to implement effective safeguards. The incident resulted in the Sevesco Directive in 1984—an agreement by members of the European Community that plants using hazardous chemicals must inform residents of the nature and quantity of the toxics they use and the risks they pose. Later that year, the accidental release of forty tons of isocyanate at a Union Carbide facility in Bhopal, India, refocused attention on the need to require safeguards in developing nations as well. The incident resulted in death or injury to hundreds of thousands of residents near the plant.

Two landmark pieces of U.S. legislation—the Federal Insecticide, Fungicide, and Rodenticide Act (FIFRA) of 1972 and the 1976 Toxic Substances Control Act (TSCA), which regulates how toxic chemicals are to be used—were a result of such incidents. The laws allow the EPA to regulate chemicals that pose an unacceptable health risk—for example, polychlorinated biphenyls (PCBs), which were first regulated in 1978. In addition, the Emergency Planning and Community Right-to-Know Act of 1986 now gives communities access to information about toxic chemicals in their region. The law calls for extensive data collection and for the creation of state emergency response commissions to plan for chemical-release emergencies. The federal government also coordinates the Toxics Release Inventory (TRI), an annual inventory of toxics releases and transfers of over 650 toxic chemicals from facilities nationwide. As information about the health effects of each substance is gathered, chemicals of little or no toxic concern are removed from the list while others are added. Before a new pesticide may be marketed or used in the United States, it must first be registered with the EPA after a series of health, economic, and cost-benefit studies. If the studies indicate that the risks outweigh the benefits, the EPA can refuse to register the product or regulate the frequency or level of application.

The EPA and state, local, and tribal air programs share the responsibility for controlling air toxics. The federal agency sets the standards for emissions, which state and local programs are responsible for implementing. Some state and local programs have also set their own rules for toxic emissions. EPA uses computer models to estimate ambient air toxics concentrations and population exposures nationwide, a process that introduces significant uncertainties, the agency admits.[46]

Yet some observers believe that U.S. progress toward controlling toxic air pollutants has been glacially slow. Before passage of the 1990 Clean Air Act, the EPA had completed regulations for only seven toxic chemicals, and no information was available on the toxic effects of nearly 80 percent of the chemicals used in commerce. In addition to publishing a list of source categories that emit certain levels of these pollutants, the EPA developed standards for pollution-control equipment to reduce the risk from the pollutants.

In 2002, the EPA took another step in the campaign to understand the health effects of air pollution with publication of the National-Scale Air Toxics Assessment (NATA). The study, which used 1996 emissions data, analyzed thirty-two air toxics and diesel particulate matter (as a surrogate for diesel exhaust) to prioritize pollutants of particular concern, determine their sources, identify the need for additional data collection and research, and establish a baseline for future tracking efforts. The pollutants were selected from 187 toxic air pollutants for which EPA must develop emissions standards.

By developing an inventory of air toxics, the government hoped to characterize potential public health risks in the largest number of urban areas. The study did not identify specific geographic areas with significantly higher risks, nor did it identify the risks associated with each pollutant. The data used were from 1996 because they were the most complete and up-to-date available, although more recent information is still being gathered. These limitations, coupled with the fact that the EPA lacks the scientific information necessary to perform a full assessment of the other 156 air toxics, reduce the potential impact of the study for further regulatory efforts.

However, information on the scope and impact of toxic air contamination has been used in recent studies done by non-EPA researchers. One of the most widely publicized is a 2008 report done by *USA Today* that used an EPA computer model to predict the path of toxic chemicals released by over 20,000 companies across the country. The *USA Today* researchers used emissions reports filed by companies in 2005, rather than the older 1996 reports used by the EPA. The eight-month-long study ranked 127,802 public, private, and parochial schools based on the concentrations and health hazards of chemicals likely to be found in the air outside, with some surprising results. Although the industrial centers of Illinois, Ohio, and Pennsylvania had the highest numbers of affected schools, the 437 schools that ranked worst represented 170 cities across thirty-four states.[47]

The report is noteworthy since children are especially susceptible to air contaminants because of the proportion of air they breathe in relation to their weight, and because their bodies are still developing. Children spend much of their time in schools, so the proximity of the facility to a factory or other pollution source is important. Exposure to certain toxic metals, such as manganese, can also cause mental and emotional problems in addition to physical symptoms.

But what makes the study important from an environmental-policy perspective is that the media picked up the newspaper's report (part of a series), and it was reprinted in thousands of other publications and covered in radio and television reports. Smaller newspapers identified schools in their areas that made the list of toxic "hot spots," so the story took on a local focus throughout the country. The story, while based on scientifically sound methodologies and publicly available information, did not come from an obscure academic publication, but from a mainstream American newspaper that circulates widely and can be picked up on newsstands and in hotel lobbies. It raised questions among millions of readers, viewers, and listeners, increasing the salience of toxic air contamination among those with children and grandchildren, as well as industry leaders and environmental organizations, just a few weeks before the Bush administration left office.

The connection could not have been clearer as President Obama assumed office. Less than three months after the *USA Today* articles appeared, the EPA announced a $2.25 million program that would be the first to specifically target toxic exposure among schoolchildren. The agency said it would fund state and local governments to monitor air pollution around 50 to 100 schools. "Questions have been raised about air quality around some U.S. schools, and those questions merit investigation," said the EPA Administrator.[48] The incident underscores the importance of the media as a conduit for translating hard-to-understand scientific information into ideas and issues that are clear to the public at large. While no research has yet shown what happened in the Obama transition period to bring this issue to the political agenda, or the amount of public pressure placed on members of Congress by the constituents who read the newspaper's coverage, it seems more than coincidental that the issue appeared on the new administration's radar so quickly.

VISIBILITY

Although contemporary air-quality concerns have focused primarily on the health effects of pollutants, it is important to remember that one reason public officials in Los Angeles first considered air pollution a problem was in the context of visibility. Complaints from the public about the haze over the city and the inability to see the mountains that ring the South Coast Air Basin drew attention to the problem long before health issues were studied and their impacts exposed. Visibility began decreasing in the 1940s as the West became more populated. But public interest did not coalesce until 1975, when the National Parks Conservation Association alerted its members to the growing clouds of sulfur dioxide, nitrous oxide, and fine particulates that had begun to build up in the atmosphere, often obscuring the vistas in the Grand Canyon and in Utah's Bryce Canyon. Primary sources of the brownish haze were believed to be fossil-fuel-fired power plants, copper smelters, industrial boilers, chemicals production, and mobile sources like cars and trucks. The pollutants, which can originate hundreds of miles away in urban areas, are transported to other areas on the desert winds.

By 1977, the problem was widespread enough to warrant a special section in the Clean Air Act Amendments; visibility regulations were promulgated in 1980. It is at this point that the National Park Service (NPS) took on the role of leader in visibility research. One controversial 1985 study found that visible plumes from stationary sources were not the most important source of visibility impairment. Rather, regional haze, including soil-related materials, seemed to be the cause. Through the remainder of the decade, disputes focused on whether human sources were responsible for the visibility problems, with the 1987 Winter Haze Intensive Tracer Experiment (WHITEX) tests and other studies determining that emissions from the coal-fired Navajo Generating Plant at Page, Arizona, were the largest contributor. Secretary of the Interior Manuel Lujan Jr. promptly called for a new study, no doubt influenced by the fact that the federal government owned a quarter of the Navajo plant.

From a political standpoint, the NPS studies filled a void left by the EPA. The EPA had moved on to other air-quality issues and focused its regulatory efforts on ozone. The NPS, however, was faced with the daily barrage of questions from park visitors, who wondered why such a national treasure in this part of the largely uninhabited West could become despoiled by urban centers and consumer needs for electric power.

In 1996, the congressionally created Visibility Transport Commission, made up of eight governors, four tribal leaders, and other advisors, made sweeping and unprecedented recommendations designed to gradually improve visibility in sixteen national parks and wilderness areas in the Colorado Plateau. This time, the blame for the veil of haze was shared by fires and dust, along with the everyday actions of residents driving cars and of industries operating refineries. Chimney emissions in eleven states and northwest Mexico were also factors. The commission's recommendations, including a slow, voluntary reduction in emissions that would reduce pollution by 70 percent by 2040, were widely criticized because they failed to address the visibility problem in a timely manner and did not comprehensively identify what some felt was a single source.

TRANSBOUNDARY AIR POLLUTION

Air pollutants do not recognize international boundaries or political jurisdictions. Pollution can be carried on air currents across nations, continents, and oceans. When the sources are so distant that the individual contributors to emissions cannot be determined, the problem is referred to as *transboundary air pollution*. In the 1970s, researchers began to develop a new understanding of the forces that lead to long-range transboundary air pollution and acid deposition; at the same time, environmental crises focused attention on transnational water pollution, as discussed in the previous chapter. These issues are of interest to most Americans when they involve the nations along the U.S. borders—Canada and Mexico. All three countries have a common interest in combining their technological resources to solve problems that literally "drift" into their boundaries. Although the problems are global in scope and importance, they are also somewhat regionalized.

For the United States and Canada, the major border issue is acid rain—or *acid deposition*, as it is also known. For many years, it had gone undetected because in its early stages there was little evidence of its impact. Today, no country on Earth receives as high a proportion of acidic deposition from another nation as Canada receives from the United States. Approximately one-half the total amount of acid deposition that falls on Canada comes from the United States, in comparison to the 20 percent Canadian sources deposit on the United States.[49]

There are three primary components of acid rain: sulfur dioxide, nitrous oxides, and volatile organic compounds (VOCs). The most common of the pollutants, sulfur dioxide, comes primarily from the combustion of coal, which reacts with oxygen in the air. The sulfur content of coal varies considerably with the geographic region in which it is mined, so not all areas experience acid deposition to the same degree. Coal from the western portion of the United States, for example, typically has a sulfur content of about 0.5 percent, which is considered to be very low. In contrast, coal mined in the northern region of Appalachia and some Midwestern states has a sulfur concentration of 2 to 3 percent. Scientists measure acid deposition as wet (rain, snow, fog) and dry (particles and gases). Acidity is measured on a pH scale from 1 to 14, with lemon juice measured at 1, vinegar at 3, and distilled water at 7. Although there is no single threshold value below which precipitation is considered to be "acid rain," readings below 4.5 are generally considered highly acidic. The most widely accepted standard for unpolluted precipitation is 5.6, which is twenty-five times the acidity of pure water.

Acid rain causes several types of environmental damage, and because its effects are not merely localized, it can cause increased acidity levels in bodies of water that are fed by rainfall. The impact can damage entire ecosystems and may show up along the entire food chain. Researchers have found reduced yields of crops attributable to acid rain, and studies show it also contributes to health problems. Soil nutrients are declining in Canada, and the long-term impact also includes damage to our cultural heritage: There is evidence that acid rain has damaged some of the world's most beautiful historical artifacts.

Canada and the United States have a long history of disputes as well as cooperative agreements related to transboundary pollution, the most famous of which is the Trail Smelter Arbitration of 1941. The case involved sulfur emissions from a smelter built in Canada in 1896 just a few miles north of the U.S. border. Originally, the claims against the smelter dealt with plumes of sulfur that traveled across the border and damaged the property of apple growers in Washington State, but the case later formed the basis for questions of jurisdiction in international environmental law that would be reflected in subsequent treaties.[50]

Negotiations on transboundary air-pollution issues between the United States and Canada were driven by Title IV of the 1990 Clean Air Act Amendments and subsequently enacted in the 1991 U.S.–Canada Bilateral Air Quality Agreement. The United States agreed to reduce its sulfur dioxide (SO_2) emissions by 10 million tons below 1980 levels by the year 2000; achieve a permanent national emissions cap of 8.95 million tons of SO_2 per year for electric utilities by 2010; and develop additional standards if it is determined that annual emissions will be exceeded. Canada agreed to reduce its SO_2 emissions; reduce its NO_x emissions by 100,000 tons annually by 2000; and to meet technology-based standards for reducing NO_x from mobile sources. The reductions were expected to come from a tightening of restrictions placed on fossil-fuel-fired power plants, along with the promotion of pollution prevention and energy-efficient strategies and technologies. The International Joint Commission (IJC), a permanent bilateral commission of three members from each country that originally dealt with water-quality issues stemming from the 1909 Boundary Waters Treaty, provides the institutional structure for dealing with transboundary air-pollution issues.

Since the treaty went into force, significant progress has been made; Canada surpassed both of its commitments to reduce emissions of SO_2. The EPA's Acid Rain Program and controls on motor vehicles reduced emissions of SO_2 well below the 1999 limits, with projections that the pattern would continue through 2010. The two countries have now agreed to address the issues of ground-level ozone and PM emissions.

Some U.S. officials consider the U.S.–Canadian response to acid rain as a model for tackling emerging environmental issues. The agreements made by these countries have incorporated input from stakeholders such as utilities, coal and gas companies, emissions-control equipment vendors, labor leaders, academicians, and state and provincial pollution-control agencies, along with environmental organizations. The use of continuous monitoring and reporting systems, excessive emissions penalties, and market-based incentives are said to create a program that will achieve cost-effective emission reductions.

In contrast, the transboundary air-pollution issues between the United States and Mexico are perceived as being more complex and more difficult to solve than are those with Canada. The severity of environmental problems is increasing dramatically, due largely to the growth of industry and population along the Mexican side of the border. In cities like San Antonio, Texas, transboundary water pollution has been more of an issue than air quality due to the area's history of flooding from the San Antonio River.

The United States and Mexico have signed several bilateral air-quality agreements as part of the Agreement on Cooperation for the Protection and Improvement of the Environment in the Border Area. One agreement deals with transboundary air pollution from major stationary sources like factories and studies of potential control measures; another relates to emission limits on copper smelters. Negotiations with Mexico are complicated by state laws that both authorize and limit the scope of authority of local governments, agencies, and authorities, as well as of the state government itself. Texas, for example, established a Texas–Mexico authority "to study all Texas-Mexico issues and problems, including health and environment." It allows the state to "explore, develop, and negotiate interstate compacts relating to trade, infrastructure, and other matters with the appropriate officials of the united Mexican states or any of its political subdivisions or any other foreign trading partners."[51]

Recent studies have shown, however, that transboundary air pollution moves even farther beyond national borders than once was believed. A 2008 report commissioned by the UN Environment Programme found that atmospheric brown clouds, caused mainly by the burning of fossil fuels and firewood, are now covering vast areas of Asia, the Middle East, southern Africa, and the Amazon Basin. They have become one of the newest threats to the global environment, composed of particulate matter, ozone, and other chemicals, causing damage to crop yields and water resources. The study also linked the brown clouds to cardiovascular and respiratory disease, and premature deaths, in China and India. The levels of soot have risen alarmingly in thirteen of the world's megacities, from Bangkok and Beijing to Mumbai and New Delhi.[52] Another study found that pollution from Asia is helping to generate stronger storms over the North Pacific. The researchers found that intensified storms over the Pacific are affecting the Pacific storm track, which can impact the global general circulation by generating more intense thunderstorms.[53]

One way countries have responded to transboundary air pollution is through the multilateral Geneva Convention on Long-Range Transboundary Pollution, which entered into force in 1983. Most European countries, as well as the United States and Canada, are party to the convention, which was originally designed as a response to the problem of acid deposition. The convention calls for scientific cooperation and the sharing of information, and a monitoring program that evaluates European pollutants. Parties agree to exchange data on emissions, and in the protocols agreed upon subsequent to the convention, will share technological and market-based alternatives to reduce certain pollutants to targeted levels.[54] Subsequent protocols have been developed on heavy metals, persistent organic pollutants, and ground-level ozone.

Nations cooperate in addressing problems of transboundary air pollution for several reasons. It may be in their own self-interest to support cooperative pollution-reduction agreements in order to protect the quality of life within their own boundaries. It is to their advantage to help establish dispute-resolution mechanisms so they can pressure their neighbors to comply with environmental accords. Nations may recognize that collective benefits such as a stable climate and healthy oceans are in everyone's interest and compel some sacrifice of the freedom to engage in polluting activities. International organizations, norms, and laws play an important role in reflecting that self-interest. Cooperative efforts are bolstered through scientific research that clearly and compellingly identifies collective threats and offers feasible solutions. As scientific consensus develops over an environmental problem, nations are encouraged to participate in solutions. Some countries seek to be leaders in the global community, while others simply wish to avoid the criticisms of others. Domestic politics plays a critical role, and environmental activists demand that their own governments comply with their global commitments and contribute to collective solutions. Political leaders may see global environmental leadership as central to their own political prospects or part of their personal policy agenda. Industries that must comply with domestic environmental regulations have a strong incentive to urge their governments to pressure other countries to enforce similar standards on their industries. In some cases, economic powerhouses like the United States can compel compliance by other nations that want to continue trade with them or otherwise benefit through cooperative relations.

From an international perspective, there is mixed success in controlling transboundary air pollution. Industrialized nations in Western Europe come close to matching the U.S. record in curbing pollutants, whereas the problems facing Eastern Europe are still being identified. In developing nations, attempts to control emissions that travel from one region to another are often thwarted by policies that encourage economic growth at the expense of the environment. As with many other environmental protection policies, there is no "one-size-fits-all" solution for this problem, and there are only very limited resources to use for policy implementation.

FURTHER READING

Julie Kerr Casper. *Fossil Fuels and Pollution: The Future of Air Quality*. New York: Facts on File, 2010.

Joseph Disano, ed. *National Air Quality: Status and Trends*. Hauppauge, NY: Nova Science Publishing, 2010.

Bhola R. Gurjar, Luisa T. Molina, and C. S. P. Ojha, eds. *Air Pollution: Health and Environmental Impacts*. Boca Raton, FL: CRC Press, 2010.

Ronald E. Hester, ed. *Air Quality in Urban Environments*. London: Royal Society of Chemistry, 2010.

Allan H. Legge, ed. *Air Quality and Ecological Impacts*. Maryland Heights, MO: Elsevier Science.

Tunda Salthammer and Erik Uhde, eds. *Organic Indoor Air Pollutants*. Hoboken, NJ: Wiley-VCH, 2009.

Joel E. Schwartz. *Air Quality in America: A Dose of Reality on Air Pollution Levels, Trends, and Health Risks*. Washington, DC: AEI Press, 2008.

Bruno Sportisse. *Fundamentals in Air Pollution: From Processes to Modeling*. New York: Springer, 2010.

Hans Tammemagi. *Air: Our Planet's Ailing Atmosphere*. Oxford, UK: Oxford University Press, 2009.

John Watt et al., eds. *The Effects of Air Pollution on Cultural Heritage*. New York: Springer, 2010.

9

Endangered Species
and Biodiversity

"When governments take action to reduce biodiversity loss
there are some conservation successes, but we are still a long
way from reversing the trend."
— JEAN-CHRISTOPHE VIE, DEPUTY HEAD OF THE INTERNATIONAL UNION FOR
THE CONSERVATION OF NATURE SPECIES PROGRAMME[1]

There is news on the biodiversity front, and it is not good. The International Union for the Conservation of Nature (IUCN) publishes an analysis of efforts to reduce biodiversity loss, and its 2009 report is not only alarming—it is pessimistic.

In *Wildlife in a Changing World,* the IUCN analyzed 44,836 species on what is known as the Red List, identifying whether progress has been made in various categories, such as geographical region, groups of species, and habitats. The Red List is considered to be the world's most comprehensive information source on the global conservation status of plant and animal species. Only about 2.7 percent of the 1.8 million described species have been analyzed, so figures included in the report are grossly underestimated. Species are added to the list based on a peer-review process involving thousands of scientists around the world. The register divides each species into one of nine categories:

- Extinct
- Extinct in the Wild
- Critically Endangered
- Endangered

- Vulnerable
- Near Threatened
- Least Concern
- Data Deficient
- Not Evaluated

But rather than being simply a listing of species and categories, the Red List is a compendium of information on the threats to species, their ecological requirements, where they live, and information on conservation actions that can be used to reduce or prevent extinctions. The Red List is a snapshot of what is going on in the larger picture of species biodiversity.[2]

The 2009 study found that 869 species are known to be Extinct or Extinct in the Wild, with 290 more Critically Endangered species identified as Possibly Extinct. At least 16,928 species are threatened with extinction. They vary considerably among species types; 27 percent of the 845 species of reef-building coral and six of the seven marine turtle species are threatened with extinction. One-third of amphibians, more than one in eight birds, and nearly a quarter of mammals are threatened with extinction, and the situation with plants is even more dire. Twenty-eight percent of conifers and 52 percent of cycads are threatened, largely because of habitat destruction. Marine birds are more threatened than terrestrial ones.[3] In its November 2009 update, the IUCN noted that more than a hundred plants on the Red List are now extinct, with others in special circumstances that make their existence problematic. The Queen of the Andes, for example, is found in the Andes of Peru and Bolivia, and produces seeds only once in eighty years before dying. Its ability to reproduce may be affected by climate change, and by the cattle who roam freely and trample or eat young plants.[4]

A United Nations interim report released for the 2009 Conference of the Parties to the Convention on Biological Diversity in Bonn, Germany, also painted a bleak picture of the cost of biodiversity loss. *The Economics of Ecosystems and Biodiversity* shows that the loss of forests is costing the world $43 billion every year; compounded over time, the actual value of the loss could be closer to $4.7 trillion. A World Wildlife Fund report on the value of ocean ecosystem services was placed at $21 trillion, but that figure would be substantially reduced if half of commercial fish stocks are depleted by mid-century, as has been predicted.[5]

Similar studies released each year tell the same story: Biodiversity is decreasing due to habitat destruction, hunting, pesticide use, pollution, and other human-made causes, which has led to the extinction of an untold number of species. This chapter links the issues of endangered species and biodiversity, explaining how U.S. and international policy efforts have sometimes been parallel and, at other times, at cross-purposes with each other. The chapter also examines how organized interests have framed biodiversity as a problem and explores the successes and failures of those efforts on both the national and global levels.

ENDANGERED SPECIES

Initially, discussions about endangered species tended to focus on megafauna like elephants and whales, but as knowledge of factors influencing biodiversity has grown, so too has the debate over issues that are just now beginning to emerge in the global environmental arena.

We have only begun to understand the diversity and numbers of life-forms on this planet. As many as 30 million species, primarily insects and marine invertebrates, may currently exist; only about 5 percent of them have been named and identified, or "described." That number is thought to be only a tiny percentage of the species that have inhabited Earth during its millions of years of history—perhaps less than 1 percent of as many as 4 billion. In 2007, the Integrated Taxonomic Information System Species Catalog of Life topped the 1 million species milestone. This worldwide effort catalogs all known living organisms, from plants and animals to fungi and microorganisms, providing access to data maintained by a variety of scientific groups. They hope to complete the listing by 2011, reaching an expected total of about 1.75 million species.[6]

Some species have disappeared because of cataclysmic events, such as changes in sea levels or massive ice movements; the disappearance of others can be attributed to the appearance (and often the intervention) of humans. In rare cases, a species believed to have gone extinct is spotted and biologists rush to confirm the sighting. The ivory-billed woodpecker, the third-largest in the world, was last seen in northeastern Louisiana in 1944. The bird's primary habitat is large trees, and scientists believed it had been pushed into extinction by massive logging in the Southeast. Although there had been some reports of sightings over the past sixty years, none were verified. In February 2004, an amateur bird-watcher kayaking along the Cache River in southeastern Arkansas saw what he thought was an adult male ivory-billed woodpecker, and he reported his find to a local newsletter, which found its way to the Internet. Other birders followed; the birds have been spotted within a two-mile radius of the original sighting. Additional confirmation has come through the recordings of the bird's calls. But experts call the sightings "highly controversial" and note that no unequivocal evidence of the species has emerged.[7]

Species extinction is the most concrete example of biodiversity loss; extinction is defined as when the last member of a species dies. When only a few individuals of the species are left, it becomes functionally extinct, and it becomes extinct in the wild when the only living individuals belonging to that species are maintained in unnatural environments, such as zoos.

Estimates of the current rate of species extinction vary considerably and largely depend upon the period of time covered. From 1600 to 1980, for

TABLE 9.1   Recently Declared Extinct and Critically Endangered Species (2009)

Species	Habitat	Status
Baiji Dolphin	China	Functionally Extinct
Black-Eared Mantella	Madagascar	Critically Endangered
Cuban Crocodile	Cuba	Critically Endangered
European Eel	Sargasso Sea	Critically Endangered
Golden Toad	Costa Rica	Extinct
Hawaiian Crow	Hawaii	Extinct in Wild
Holdridge's Toad	Costa Rica	Extinct
Iberian Lynx	Spain/Portugal	Critically Endangered
Kama'o (Thrush)	Hawaii	Extinct
Peacock Parachute Tarantula	India	Critically Endangered
Po'o'uli (Black-Faced Honeycreeper)	Hawaii	Functionally Extinct
Radiated Tortoise	Madagascar	Critically Endangered
Slender-Billed Vulture	Myanmar	Critically Endangered
Spix's Macaw	Brazil	Extinct
West African Black Rhino	Cameroon	Extinct

SOURCES: "Animals Extinct This Century." http://www.dodosgone.blogspot.com. Accessed July 29, 2009.
International Union for the Conservation of Nature. *The Red List.* http://www.iucnredlist.org. Accessed July 30, 2009.

example, nearly 200 vertebrate extinctions were documented, over half of them birds. Table 9.1 provides an overview of some of the species that have been recently declared Extinct or Critically Endangered by the IUCN.

In the United States, approximately 0.2 to 0.4 percent of all described U.S. species have gone extinct, with the rates higher in some taxonomic groups, such as vertebrates. The Hawaiian Islands are considered an extinction hot spot; although they comprise less than 0.2 percent of the total land area of the United States, they account for about 30 percent of extinctions and 50 percent of possible extinctions.[8]

PROTECTIVE LEGISLATION

The development of laws protecting wildlife can be traced back to earliest legal history, but those laws have often differed as to what has been protected and why. Under Roman law, wild animals, or *ferae naturae*, were given the same status as the oceans and air—they belonged to no one. As Anglo-Saxon law developed, however, an exception was made: Private landowners had the right to wildlife on their property. As land was parceled out to the nobility as "royal forests" around 450 C.E., hunting restrictions began to be imposed, and only the king was given sole right to pursue fish or game anywhere he claimed as his realm. As the English political system developed, very few changes were made to the earlier system, perpetuating a situation in which only the wealthy or nobles were qualified to take game. Those same restrictions found their way to American shores and flourished until the mid-nineteenth century, when a major policy shift occurred as the U.S. Supreme Court established the basis for state ownership of wildlife. The federal government's role in defining the legal status of wildlife was limited to an 1868 statute prohibiting the hunting of fur-bearing animals in Alaska and an 1894 prohibition on hunting in Yellowstone National Park. The states began to regulate fishing within their waters just after the Civil War, and the Court upheld that policy, citing the commerce clause of Article 1, Section 8, of the Constitution. What is important about the decisions of this period, however, is that the states' regulatory authority was based on a fundamental nineteenth-century conception of the purpose of wildlife law—the preservation of a food supply.[9]

Contemporary U.S. biodiversity legislation can be divided into five categories: migratory and game birds, wild horses and burros, marine mammals, endangered species, and invasive species. What is unique about U.S. legislative provisions is that, in addition to offering protection for reasons of aesthetics or biological diversity, Congress has also sought to regulate commerce and trade in these species. As public opinion shifts and the political environment responds, protective legislation for species also changes, although incrementally in comparison to the rate of extinction. New problems, such as the increase in invasive species, have been added to the list of legislative mandates that federal agencies and states must implement.

As an indicator of how recently American concern for endangered species has reached the political agenda, three separate legislative efforts have been enacted—all within the last forty years. The first, the Endangered Species Preservation Act of 1966, mandated the Secretary of the Interior to develop a program to conserve, protect, restore, and propagate selected species of native fish and wildlife. Its provisions were primarily designed, however, to protect habitats through land acquisition—and little else. The species protected under the law were those "threatened with extinction" based on a finding by the Secretary in consultation with interested persons, but the procedures for doing that went no further. It did not limit the taking of these species, or commerce in them, but it was an important first step in the development of the law.

The Endangered Species Conservation Act of 1969 attempted to remedy those limitations by further defining the types of protected wildlife and, more important, by including wildlife threatened with worldwide extinction and prohibiting their importation into the United States—an international aspect not included in the earlier legislation. Instead of using the broad term *fish and wildlife* (which was interpreted as only vertebrates), the 1969 law included any wild mammal, fish, wild bird, amphibian, reptile, mollusk, or crustacean. The list of species was to be developed using the best scientific and commercial data available, with procedures for designation pursuant to the rulemaking in the Administrative Procedure Act. This formalized a process that had been haphazard and highly discretionary under the 1966 act.

President Richard Nixon warned that the two laws did not provide sufficient management tools needed to act early enough to save a vanishing species.

He urged Congress to enact a more comprehensive law, which became the Endangered Species Act (ESA) of 1973. The law has several notable features that distinguish it from previous efforts:

1. It required all federal agencies, not just the two departments identified in the 1966 and 1969 acts, to seek to conserve endangered species, broadening the base of protective efforts.

2. It expanded conservation measures that could be undertaken under the act to include all methods and procedures necessary to protect the species, rather than emphasizing habitat protection only.

3. It broadened the definition of *wildlife* to include any member of the animal kingdom.

4. It created two classes of species: those "endangered" (in danger of extinction throughout all or a significant portion of its range) and those "threatened" (any species likely to become an endangered species within the foreseeable future).

Table 9.2 identifies the number of species in the United States listed as threatened or endangered as of November 2009. It is notable that there are

T A B L E 9.2   Summary of Federally Listed Species Populations in the U.S. (November 2009)

Group	Endangered	Threatened	Active Recovery Plans
Mammals	70	15	59
Corals	0	2	0
Reptiles	13	24	38
Amphibians	14	11	17
Fishes	74	65	102
Clams	62	8	70
Snails	24	11	30
Insects	47	10	40
Arachnids	12	0	12
Crustaceans	19	3	18
Birds	75	15	85
Conifers/Cycads	2	1	3
Ferns and Allies	24	2	26
Lichens	2	0	2
Flowering Plants	573	143	633
Totals	1,011	310	1,135

*Twelve U.S. animal species are counted more than once in the table, primarily because these animals have distinct population segments, each with its own individual listing status.

SOURCE: U.S. Fish and Wildlife Service. "Species Reports." November 2, 2009. http://ecos.fws.gov/tess_public/TESSBox-score. Accessed November 2, 2009.

considerably more plants listed than animals, a fact on which Congress may not have counted when the ESA was enacted.

From an administrative standpoint, the 1973 law was considerably more complex than were previous legislative efforts. It included a circuitous route by which a species was to be listed by the Secretary of the Interior, delisted when the species' population stabilized, and changed from "threatened" to "endangered," and vice versa. The Secretaries of Commerce and the Interior have virtually unlimited discretion in deciding when to consider the status of a species, because the law established no priorities or time limitations. Generally, a species is considered for listing upon petition of an interested group that has developed scientific evidence regarding the species' population. Species that are believed to meet the definition of threatened or endangered are referred to as "candidates" for listing, and the agency then seeks biological information that will complete the status review. The U.S. Fish and Wildlife Service (FWS) notes that because of the number of candidates and the time required to list a species, there is a priority system designed to direct its efforts toward the plants and animals in the greatest need. The highest criterion for listing is the degree or magnitude of threat, followed by the immediacy of threat and the taxonomic distinctiveness of the species.[10]

Listing, however, is but the first phase in a very lengthy process. Once a species is added to the list (which is made official by publishing a notice in the *Federal Register*), the federal government must decide how much of its habitat needs to be protected. The 1973 law is somewhat vague in indicating how "critical" habitat is to be determined and when that determination must be made. The law then requires the government to develop a recovery plan for the species. The law defines *recovery* as the process by which the decline of an endangered or threatened species is arrested or reversed, and threats to its survival are neutralized, to ensure its long-term survival in the wild. The plan delineates, justifies, and schedules the research and management actions necessary to support the recovery of a species, including those that, if successful, will permit reclassification or delisting. Typical recovery plans involve extensive public participation and include the cost of each strategy.

One of the most controversial aspects of the planning process is the assignment of individual species recovery priorities, which signifies the imminence of extinction and the designation of those species to which a known threat or conflict exists (usually from development projects). About one-quarter of the listed species are in conflict with other activities and receive the designation. The law was amended in 1988 to make more specific the requirement that the Secretaries of the Interior and Commerce develop and implement recovery plans, and to require a status report every two years on the efforts to develop recovery plans for all listed species and on the status of all species for which recovery plans have been developed.

The ESA also protects plants; in 1977, it listed the first four plant species (all found on San Clemente Island, off the California coast). Before the 1988 amendments were instituted, it was illegal only to "remove and reduce to possession" listed plants—and then only those on lands under federal jurisdiction. Under the amended provisions, there is a prohibition against maliciously damaging or destroying plants on federal lands; it is now illegal to remove, destroy, or damage any listed plant on state or private land in knowing violation of state law. In 1994, the Secretary of the Interior expanded the law's reach even further by prohibiting "significant habitat modification or degradation where it actually kills or injures wildlife." The regulation would set the stage for a series of legal challenges over the Secretary's authority under the ESA.[11]

By December 2008, when the ESA commemorated its thirty-fifth anniversary, there were a number of accomplishments for the agencies that implement the statute. More than 1,300 species were on the national lists of threatened and endangered wildlife and plants, and 21 species had been downlisted, or reclassified from endangered to the less critical category of threatened, mostly aquatic and plant species. The list of downlisted species includes the American crocodile, the Gila trout, and the Missouri bladderpod. Thirteen species have been downlisted due to recovery, from the West Virginia northern flying squirrel to the Yellowstone population of the grizzly bear. There are 545 final recovery plans and 48 draft plans that cover 1,129 U.S. species, and an additional 124 species have recovery plans under development.[12]

INVASIVE SPECIES

One of the less visible aspects of biodiversity protection involves invasive, or nonnative, species. These species are defined under Executive Order 13112 of 1999 as "an alien species whose introduction does or is likely to cause economic or environmental harm or harm to economic health." The executive order also defines native species as those that, "with respect to a particular ecosystem, other than as a result of an introduction, historically occurred or currently occurs in that ecosystem.

The development of invasive-species policy can be traced back to several early laws, especially the 1900 Lacey Act, which prohibited the import of species on a designated list, and other vertebrates, mollusks, and crustaceans that are "injurious to human beings, to the interests of agriculture, horticulture, forestry, or wildlife, or the wildlife resources of the United States." This important statute allowed for the importation of species for scientific, medical, education, exhibition, or propagation purposes, all under the jurisdiction of the U.S. Department of the Interior. The Lacey Act was amended as part of the 2008 Farm Bill (the Food, Conservation, and Energy Act of 2008) to cover a broad range of plants and plant products, including timber deriving from illegally harvested plants. It represents the increasing concern of policymakers about invasive species and their impact on the nation's agriculture, wildlife, and habitats.

Other laws, such as the Plant Quarantine Act of 1912, gave the U.S. Department of Agriculture (DOA) the authority to regulate the importation and interstate movement of nursery stock and other plants that may carry harmful pests and diseases. The Animal Damage Control Act of 1931, also implemented by the DOA's Animal and Plant Health Inspection Service (APHIS), was focused on damaging species, such as nutria, blackbirds, European starlings, and monk parakeets, to protect against unintentional introductions to field and horticultural crops, forests, aquaculture ponds, public buildings, aircraft, livestock feedlots, and public and private ranges. Some statutes have protected against the introduction of specific species, such as the sea lamprey in the Great Lakes fisheries, noxious weeds, plant pests, and aquatic nuisance species in ballast water, foreign birds, and laws to protect Hawaii's tropical forests. Among the statutes are the Plant Protection Act of 2000, which consolidated and modernized all major statutes pertaining to plant protection and quarantine; the Nutria Eradication and Control Act of 2003, which provides financial assistance to Maryland and Louisiana to eradicate nutria and restore marshland damaged by this species; and the Brown Tree Snake Control and Eradication Act of 2004 (on the island of Guam).[13]

There are a series of regulatory efforts to protect native species in the United States, with a lengthy list of stakeholder agencies. The FWS conducts the listing of organisms as "injurious wildlife" under the Lacey Act, and manages invasive species under the Nonindigenous Aquatic Nuisance Prevention and Control Act of 1990 (amended in 2000); the Alien Species Prevention and Enforcement Act of 1992 makes it illegal to ship plants or animals that are covered under the Lacey Act or the Plant Protection Act through the U.S. mail. Executive Order 13112 also created the National Invasive Species Council, including thirteen departmental representatives, and the Invasive Species Advisory Committee. These bodies developed the 2001 National Invasive Species Management Plan to provide an overall blueprint for federal action.

The FWS also administers a broad range of programs to manage aquatic nuisance species, listings of injurious wildlife, invasive species at the FWS's 545 wildlife refuges, habitat restoration of degraded wildlife habitats impacted by invasive species, integrated pest management, and law enforcement inspectors at thirty-two major U.S. airports, ocean ports, and border crossings to prevent the introduction of injurious wildlife though the agency's wildlife-inspection program.

One of the examples of a destructive species that is at the top of the agency officials' list is the quagga mussel, and its cousin, the zebra mussel, which are native to Eastern Europe and have spread across the oceans to U.S. waterways. The fingernail-size shellfish are voracious breeders, with a female mussel producing a million eggs a year. They often cling to boats, and are believed to have arrived in the United States in the ballast water of transoceanic ships. They have no known predators, and no treatment exists that can destroy them without also killing other wildlife. In time, they can permanently alter a lake's ecosystem. The species was found in Lake Erie in 1989, according to the U.S. Geological Survey, and until 2007, they had never been seen west of the Rocky Mountains. Federal and state officials believe quagga mussels hitched a ride on a boat that was moved by trailer to another water body; they were found in the Lake Mead reservoir, one of the waterways with tributaries along the Colorado River. Divers also found mussels on the mouth of the Colorado River aqueduct and at a pumping station on the western shore of Lake Havasu. The concern is that they will spread to the smaller lakes around Arizona and into southern California, and that they could quickly multiply and inflict serious damage by disrupting the food chain by starving off fish at the top of the web.[14] The problem of invasive species is also being addressed at the global level, with the International Plant Protection Convention of 1951, the Convention on International Trade in Endangered Species of 1973 (discussed later in this chapter), the 1979 Convention on Migratory Species of Wild Animals, and the 1992 Convention on Biological Diversity, which deals with modified organisms and alien invasive species that threaten ecosystems, habitats, or species.

THE MAKING OF WILDLIFE POLICY

Federal authority for the regulation and protection of wildlife is a case study in the growth of the American bureaucracy. It is characterized not only by name changes and power struggles within the agencies, but by external political pressure. Power is shared by several agencies, most of which have their counterparts at the state level. Until 1939, the Bureau of Biological Survey in the Department of Agriculture held regulatory authority for all wildlife—with the exception of marine fisheries, which were under the jurisdiction of the Bureau of Fisheries in the Department of Commerce. Both agencies were absorbed by the Department of the Interior and then consolidated into the U.S. Fish and Wildlife Service in 1940; but in 1956, the Fish and Wildlife Act divided authority into a Bureau of Sports Fisheries and Wildlife and a Bureau of Commercial Fisheries, leaving the organization much the same as it had been prior to 1939. President Richard Nixon's federal reorganization of 1970 transferred the Bureau of Commercial Fisheries to the National Oceanic and Atmospheric Administration, and the agency became the National Marine Fisheries Service, once again under the Department of Commerce. The Bureau of Sports Fisheries and Wildlife went back to its previous designation as the Fish and Wildlife Service in 1974, remaining in the Department of the Interior.

The structure of congressional committees also contributes to the fragmentation of policymaking, because various committees and subcommittees have jurisdiction over different types of animals and their habitats. Political change can add to the confusion over which committee handles which species, as was the case in 1995 when the members of the 104th Congress entirely eliminated the Merchant Marine and Fisheries Committee, which had been in existence for 107 years. Its duties and staff were then parceled out to other committees, making the protection of the oceans and sea life more complex.

Congress, in the 1988 amendments to the ESA, directed federal agencies to monitor more closely those species facing substantial declines of their populations, and to carry out emergency listing when necessary. Generally speaking, the longer a species has been listed, the better the chances for its population to stabilize or improve. For the most part, those species listed for less than three years do not yet have final approved recovery plans, although they may have plans in some stage of development. Recovery outlines are developed within sixty days of publication of the final rule listing a species. The outlines are submitted to the director of the Fish and Wildlife Service to be used as a guide for activities until recovery plans are developed and approved.

In response to criticism from various interests about how the ESA was being implemented, President Clinton established the National Biological Service within the Department of the Interior as a way of improving the existing bank of information on species and their habitat. The agency was given responsibility for developing an inventory of plant and animal populations, but some members of Congress viewed it as a base for advocates seeking to expand the scope of the ESA. Clinton's advisors believed that the new bureau was absolutely essential if the federal government hoped to speed up the process of listing and recovery, which had fallen far behind in the review process.

But the 1995 change from a Democrat-controlled Congress, which supported the ESA in principle, to a Republican one, which sought major reforms, marked a major turnaround for the nation's wildlife policies. The Endangered Species Act officially expired on October 1, 1992, but Congress still appropriates funds and can continue do so unless the act is totally repealed. As one of its initial actions, the Republican leadership declared a moratorium on the listing of any new species under the ESA, using the argument that there was uncertainty about how best to implement its provisions. The moratorium lasted until May 1996, creating an additional backlog of casework for agencies already besieged by budget cuts and an overall lack of resources. Republicans also targeted the National Biological Service, whose budget was included under the Department of the Interior. In a conference agreement, legislators agreed to eliminate the agency and shift most of its functions to the U.S. Geological Survey, whose budget was slashed along with its ability to implement much of its chartered responsibilities. President Clinton vetoed the interior appropriations bill, objecting to provisions that included a 10 percent spending reduction for the department, along with a laundry list of issues relating to grazing on federal lands, offshore oil drilling, and mining patents.[15]

Amending the ESA was a top priority of congressional Republicans in the 104th and 105th Congresses, aiming at a major ESA reform proposal. Several bills sought to eliminate species recovery as the primary goal of the act; they also provided more opportunities for states and landowners to be more involved in decisions related to endangered species, created biodiversity reserves, gave more leeway to landowners, and would reimburse private property owners for loss in land value resulting from endangered-species regulation. Conservatives and property-rights activists kept the pressure on the leadership to pass reform legislation, but failed.

Both the Clinton administration and Congress agreed that the ESA was flawed, but a major disagreement between the two branches was whether the law ought to be repealed so that policymakers could begin with a clean slate, or whether piecemeal, incremental changes could be made that would satisfy all the parties involved. Some reforms were made through the regulatory process, circumventing the legislature and therefore not requiring actual amendments to the law. President Clinton's efforts to defeat Republican plans to gut the ESA were successful, and by the 106th Congress, it appeared that most representatives were prepared to move on to other issues. On Earth Day 1998, President Clinton and Vice President Al Gore called on Congress to support, not thwart, their efforts.[16] Meanwhile, federal agencies and nongovernmental organizations were pressuring the administration to deal with the backlog of listings resulting from the 1995–1996 moratorium.

In 1998, the FWS adopted a new policy called "Listing Priority Guidelines," which was designed to delist and reclassify twenty-nine birds, mammals, fish, and plants that have achieved, or are moving toward, recovery. The two-year project amounted to the most extensive delisting and reclassification since adoption of the ESA in 1973, because sixteen species had been restored in more than twenty-five years. By removing recovered species from the list, the agency could redirect its resources to species with greater needs. Still, the overall numbers were small. By June 2005, forty species, some of which had been listed as early as 1967, had been delisted. Sixteen of the thirty-three were classified as "recovered," nine had become extinct, and the remaining species either had gone through a taxonomic revision or had been delisted erroneously based on new or inaccurate data.[17]

Political struggles and partisanship characterize the progress that is being made in the listing process. In 1980, for example, 281 species (primarily birds and plants) were added to the list; ten years later, 596 (mostly plants) were added. Prior to the 1996 moratorium on listings, 1,053 species were added; a year later, only 79 more were included. Federal officials added an average of 9.5 species a year under the administration of George W. Bush, compared with 65 a year under the Clinton administration and 59 a year under President George H. W. Bush.[18]

Species-recovery plans are a second controversial element of species protection. Prior to the 1990s, the FWS relied upon this strategy to save endangered species, a process that often took years and resulted in limited success. In 1985, for example, the FWS decided to remove the last six California condors from the wild as a way of protecting the species. After a monumental tracking and trapping effort, and amid considerable public opposition and an injunction by the National Audubon Society, staff from the San Diego Wild Animal Park captured the last of the known wild birds in 1987. The government allowed several non-profit groups to begin captive breeding programs, and eventually they began to release young condors back into their natural habitat in southern California and northern Arizona, and to track their activities. Critics believed the reintroduction efforts, which began in 1992, were counterproductive; many of the released birds later died. Supporters of the program grew even more pessimistic when researchers discovered that the first three chicks born in the wild in eighteen years had died within three weeks of one another in 2002. One of the chicks died from ingesting shards of plastic and glass, along with a dozen bottle caps.[19] By 2009, about 125 of the condors lived in the wild, and although they are protected, mortality rates are still high from accidental death.[20]

Another species-management tool, the designation of critical habitat, is designed to provide protection for specific areas deemed essential to the survival of a species once it is listed. The "critical habitat" designation can be extremely controversial, as is the case with the Preble's meadow jumping mouse, which has been listed by the government as a threatened species since 1998. Nearly 31,000 acres were designated for the recovery of the nine-inch-long mouse, which is found in Colorado and Wyoming. In 2005, Secretary of the Interior Gale Norton proposed delisting the mouse after a study found that there was no genetic difference between the Preble's species and a more common Bear Lodge meadow jumping mouse, reducing the need for federal protection. However, developers sought to build within the mouse's habitat, and there were questions from independent scientists whether the study showing the similarity in species was valid. In July 2008, the FWS removed protection for the species in Wyoming but kept the Colorado population of the mouse on the Endangered Species List. The Center for Biological Diversity (CBD) subsequently filed suit against the agency in June 2009, arguing that a patchwork approach to habitat protection "is akin to planned extinction by neglect." The group Defenders of Wildlife argued in the suit that it makes no sense for the protection of an imperiled animal to depend on which side of the state line it lives.[21]

Another policy shift involves transferring responsibility for wildlife management from the federal government to the states. Critics of this concept believe it only passes the responsibility for wildlife control on to the states—it is an unfunded mandate that requires additional staff but no money. Environmental groups, which have traditionally opposed blanket national wildlife-management plans, have sometimes given their approval to localized efforts to deal with specific problem colonies. Officials from the FWS believe the proposal gives states a voice in plans affecting species within its borders. But what does "management" mean, and how should each state respond?

Nowhere is the issue more contentious than in Yellowstone National Park, where preservation of the park's American buffalo herd exemplifies the political considerations state officials are currently facing. Prior to European settlement, an estimated 30 to 75 million buffalo (also known as "bison") roamed the West; by 1890, the animals had almost been wiped out because of target shooting and hunting, including organized hunts conducted from train cars. Reintroduction and intensive wildlife management throughout the Greater Yellowstone Ecosystem has led to the protection of about 3,000 to 3,500 free-roaming animals today.[22]

A major policy shift occurred in 1969, when park managers decided to turn from intensive management to natural regulation, allowing buffalo to extend their range and to migrate beyond the national park boundaries. Researchers have determined that the herds carry the *Brucella* bacteria, which causes cows to abort, although there have been no reported cases of transmission of the organism to domestic cattle that graze on the public lands intersecting the buffalo range and migration routes. The pivotal issue is how buffalo should be "managed" when they cross an administrative park boundary; in the past, animals have been herded with snowmobiles, yelled at and hazed by activists trying to force them back across park borders, and trapped. In winter 1988, near the park's northern boundary, 569 animals were shot; and in 1990, game wardens escorted hunters to a designated shooting area after animal-rights protesters confronted the hunters. The hunt, which one activist compared to "shooting a car," brought negative publicity to the state and numerous protests, and sport hunting was discontinued. Nearly 1,100 buffalo were slaughtered by the agency as a preventative measure to keep the area "brucellosis-free" in 1996. The most controversial action was a March 2003 decision to capture about 110 buffalo, many of which were still within the park when they were herded up. Environmental organizations like the Bear Creek Council and Fund for Animals protested the capture and killing of the buffalo and accused the National Park Service of abusing its discretion. One activist commented, "Sending Yellowstone buffalo to slaughter, the Department of Interior's Park Service has sacrificed treasured wildlife and its own integrity for politics, pure and simple."[23]

Another option, organized sport hunting, was revived in a vote by the state legislature in 2003 and in December 2004 when the Montana Fish, Wildlife, and Parks Commission approved a limited one-month hunting season in an area where buffalo are known to migrate in winter. Montana Department of Livestock officials had recommended the issuance of five licenses; commissioners sought twenty-five, and eventually settled on ten permits. The licenses, issued through a public lottery, would allow a more conventional hunt rather than the escorted, prearranged excursions into the park. A three-month hunt scheduled for November 2005 was also approved by the commission.[24]

The commission's decision led to a strong public outcry against the hunt. Members of one activist group, the Buffalo Field Campaign, announced that they would apply for permits and said they would buy licenses but not participate in the hunt if their names were selected. The clothing company Patagonia announced that it would reimburse the cost of the permits ($75 for residents and $750 for nonresidents) for anyone who decided not to take part. More than 8,300 people paid $3 each to apply for the hunting permits. An Idaho newspaper noted, "If it's the thrill of the hunt that people seek, surely they won't find it here. And if it's the meat that they want, let them go to the supermarket."[25]

But on January 6, 2005, on a 4–1 vote, the quasi-judicial commission agreed to reconsider its position. The reason? Just a few hours before the meeting, three new commission members had been appointed by the state's new governor, Brian Schweitzer, who said he was not opposed to bison hunting but was concerned about the circumstances. "There will be a significant hunt. There's going to be a hunt next year. I just don't want a black-eye hunt. I don't think we should have the equivalent of shooting refrigerators."[26]

On January 10, just five days before the hunt was scheduled to begin, the commission voted to postpone the hunting season for bison in southwestern Montana. But the vote did not end the controversy for long. The following day, the commission voted 3–2 to enter the names of those who had already applied for hunting permits into a lottery for ten bison licenses that could be used for a three-month hunting season beginning in November 2005 over a larger area. The commissioners released an announcement confirming their support for the hunt, which was not expected to be used as a way to regulate the bison populations. Instead, the legislature's intent, they said, was "to allow Montana hunters to harvest wild, free-roaming bison under fair chase conditions and to reduce damage to private property by altering bison behavior and distribution."

The news releases also noted that public bison hunts are already established in several western states, including Alaska, Arizona, South Dakota, Utah, and Wyoming.[27] In September 2005, the commission agreed to establish a ninety-day hunt of twenty-five bison between November 15, 2005, and January 15, 2006. Another twenty-five licenses were authorized for use between January 16, 2006, and February 15, 2006. The licenses allowed hunting over more than 460,000 acres of wildlife habitat in southwestern Montana. Sixteen of the licenses were allotted to Montana's Native American tribes, in accordance with a new state law, and ten more were awarded to hunters who had their licenses drawn in 2004 before the 2005 hunt was postponed.

The Montana commission's action, although controversial and highly visible, is restricted to state efforts to manage wildlife; its impact is therefore somewhat limited. A much more controversial element of species-recovery policy is the habitat conservation plan (HCP). The process of developing these plans stems from two sections in the ESA that provide the means for federal agencies to authorize, fund, or carry out development projects while ensuring that such projects do not jeopardize the existence of the species. However, because private and nonfederal developers were not covered by the statute, problems would be created should a project result in the killing, harming, or harassment of a threatened or endangered species. In 1982, Congress amended the ESA by allowing the creation of HCPs, which allow development to continue even if there is a threat to a species, as long as some form of conservation mitigation takes place. A landowner can be issued a permit to proceed legally with an activity that would otherwise be illegal and harmful to a species by enhancing or restoring a degraded or former habitat, creating new habitats, or establishing a buffer area around existing habitats. The compromise concept was designed to allow developers, environmental groups, and government agencies to come up with "creative partnerships" without halting development altogether or placing a burden on private property owners. Realizing that plans alone were insufficient, the FWS developed Habitat Acquisition Projects to provide up to 75 percent of the cost for purchasing land deemed essential to the development of a comprehensive conservation plan.

The ESA is more likely to be the subject of debate in the judicial arena rather than in Congress, where amendments and repeal attempts have made little progress. Many of the disputes involve private property owners who have sued for compensation for economic losses, to which they believe they are entitled under the Constitution when the government "takes" their land by declaring it part of an endangered or threatened species' habitat. In 1975, the FWS expanded its definition of "harm to a species" by including any action that caused the destruction of critical habitat, even if the species itself was not harmed. In a 6–3 decision in 1995, the U.S. Supreme Court upheld the federal government's definition of what constitutes "harm" under a policy that allowed logging in areas that had been declared critical habitat for the threatened northern spotted owl. In *Babbitt* v. *Sweet Home Chapter of Communities for a Greater Oregon,*[28] the latter a timber-industry-sponsored group, the Court ruled that the common meaning of the term *harm* is broad and in the context of the ESA would encompass habitat modification that injures or kills members of an endangered species. The decision upheld the Secretary of the Interior's 1994 regulation, as the majority of the Court also noted that the statute had been reasonably interpreted. Dissenters on the Court argued that the definition was so broad that it had the effect of penalizing actions regardless of whether they were intended or foreseeable.[29]

Environmental organizations hailed the *Sweet Home* decision as precedent for protecting entire ecosystems rather than individual species. These groups believe that the decision gives government agencies such as the FWS more discretion in implementing the law. But groups within the environmental opposition called upon Congress to take action to alter the ESA. One critic called the Court's ruling "one more step down the road to agency control" and said it gave administrative agencies much more power than the Constitution intended.[30]

Groups like Defenders of Wildlife accused the Bush administration of working "systematically to undermine the Endangered Species Act, employing a wide variety of tactics to circumvent the clear language of the law and to skew its function in favor of corporate special interests."[31] In a study of 120 federal court decisions resolving ESA issues between January 21, 2001, and October 31, 2003, in which Bush administration officials exerted influence over legal strategy and outcome, the administration presented arguments hostile to the ESA in 63 percent of cases, defined as contradicting established legal interpretations of the act. In 89 percent of the "ESA-hostile" cases, courts found that the administration had acted illegally and ruled against them.[32] The study identified several legalistic strategies and tactics that the Bush administration was "using in its systematic effort to sabotage the ESA, including ignoring court orders, slanting science, creating an artificial budget crisis, and helping friends in industry."[33]

There is a growing wave of opinion that the debate over the future of endangered species (and biodiversity in general) is becoming more political and less scientific in nature. Some observers of the process believe that the most important decisions about species survival are being made by political appointees who make policy only in response to the groups who provide financial support for their benefactors. This produces, the observers argue, a system in which there is a natural tension between politicians and scientists; and as the issue of conserving biodiversity becomes more important, it inevitably becomes more political. For political leaders, species-recovery efforts often become media events, as was the case in 1998 when Secretary of the Interior Bruce Babbitt announced that the Peregrine Falcon's numbers had increased sufficiently to be removed from the federal list of endangered species. In 1970, when the bird was initially listed, pesticide poisoning had reduced the bird's numbers to only thirty-nine pairs in the continental United States. By the time of Babbitt's announcement, an estimated 1,600 breeding pairs were thought to exist in North America. Babbitt used the occasion in Stone Mountain, Georgia, to release a small falcon from its cage, commenting, "The Endangered Species Act is working. It's a part of our American spirit and heritage."[34] Although the Peregrine's delisting was highly publicized and applauded, it also could be seen as a policy that favors high-profile species over those that are less attractive or well-known. Thousands of species face similar extinction struggles, and only a few animals, such as the prairie dog and desert bighorn sheep, are the beneficiaries of public support and media attention.

One species that has recently been subject to widespread media coverage is the North American bald eagle. In 1967, there were only 417 breeding pairs of bald eagles in the continental United States, due in large part to the eggshell-thinning chemical pesticide DDT, indicted in Rachel Carson's *Silent Spring*. The species was protected in 1940 by federal legislation, and in 1967, it was added to the Endangered Species List. In 1995, enough breeding pairs were surveyed to downlist the eagle's status to "threatened," and in 2007, it was removed from the list altogether. Forty years after being initially listed, there were an estimated 11,000 pairs. They remain under federal law that prohibits killing or wounding them, or disturbing their nests, and they will continue to be monitored by states until 2012. The attention provided to the bald eagle is more than just because of numbers, many believe. It is an iconic species, highly symbolic, and found in every state except Hawaii. Would it have gotten similar protection had it been a plant species, or, as in the case of the Preble's meadow jumping mouse discussed earlier, a rodent with a limited range?

Environmental-group leaders note three factors that make it difficult to keep biodiversity on the public agenda: a lack of an easily identifiable opponent, a lack of any immediate impact on human lifestyles, and a lack of cohesiveness by large groups around the widespread preservation of species. It is difficult, they say, to generate support or motivate groups to mobilize to action even though species are becoming extinct; one reason is that people's daily lives do not appear to be affected. The most difficult task seems to be convincing people, despite their concerns for endangered species, that there is a relationship between their own activities and the causes of endangerment. Consequently, public attention begins to dissipate as policymakers realize the full costs of implementing protection measures.

A paradox faced by the ESA is that a species is not protected until its population becomes so low that it is likely to become extinct. When that happens, recovery becomes both inefficient and costly. Recovery then begins to compromise the activities of other agencies (international, federal, state, and local), which must change their policies to accommodate the situation, thus increasing the probability of conflict. What this tells us about the future of endangered species and their habitats is that their protection requires the building of a much broader political constituency than the one currently in existence. The actions of isolated organizations dedicated to the preservation of an individual species are unlikely to convince policymakers that there is a need for change. Instead, public policy is more likely to be politicized by groups whose economic prospects are influenced by what happens to their future.

THE ROLE OF ORGANIZED INTERESTS

Government agencies are responsible for implementing the legislative aspects of wildlife protection, but environmental organizations, industry trade associations, and grassroots opposition groups have clashed over how the laws ought to be interpreted. Wildlife protection groups began to flourish in the late nineteenth century, and many of them survived to become the mainstays of the contemporary environmental movement, such as the National Audubon Society, founded in 1905. Others, such as the Wilderness Society (1935) and the National Wildlife Federation (1936), were products of the surge of interest instigated by President Theodore Roosevelt. The vast majority of wildlife organizations, however, have a more recent origin, partly due to a spate of legislative activity just after Earth Day 1970. The National Wildlife Federation, which monitors environmental organizations, reported that of the 108 national wildlife and humane organizations identified in its study, 14 percent had been founded before 1940 and 68 percent since 1966. The decade surrounding the first Earth Day (1965 to 1975) accounted for the founding of 38 percent of all groups with a species orientation.[35]

The tactics used by groups to influence the implementation of wildlife policy range from the traditional to the radical. Some organizations see their role within the context of legislation, such as the Wilderness Society's efforts at lobbying Congress to increase appropriations for habitat protection. Other groups focus on advocating for species by lobbying the implementing agency directly. Among the most contentious groups is the CBD, which initiated one of the largest substantive legal actions in the history of the ESA in 2007. The organization filed a formal notice of intent to sue the Department of the Interior for political interference with fifty-five endangered species in twenty-eight states. At the heart of the suit is the illegal removal of one animal from the Endangered Species List, the refusal to put three animals on the list, proposals to remove or downgrade protection for seven animals, and the stripping of protection from 8.7 million acres of critical habitat for other species. The group maintains that key decisions on the species' fates were made by the former Deputy Assistant Secretary of the Interior Julie MacDonald, rather than by scientists who had studied the species' statuses in depth. In one news release, the CBD called the situation within the agency a "scandal," noting that "the corruption goes much deeper than one disgraced bureaucrat. It reaches into the White House itself through the Office of Management and Budget. By attacking the problem systematically through this national lawsuit, we will expose just how thoroughly the disdain for science and for wildlife pervades the Bush administration's endangered species program."[36]

The lawsuit was prompted by the efforts of MacDonald, who oversaw the FWS as a part of her duties. In March 2007, she was rebuked by the Department of the Interior's Inspector General for pressuring scientists to alter their findings about endangered species and leaking information about them to industry officials, which led to her resignation from the agency in May 2007. In July of that year, the head of the FWS ordered a review of eight of the endangered-species decisions in which MacDonald was involved, based on the recommendations of his regional directors, whom he had asked to study MacDonald's decisions.[37] In December 2008, the Inspector General issued a report that found that MacDonald and other officials had altered scientific evidence regarding the protection of endangered species in more than a dozen cases.[38] Documents found as a result of the investigation showed that rank-and-file scientists had recommended that species be listed, but that pervasive bureaucratic obstacles limited the number of species that might have been listed. Officials estimated that more than 280 species should have been on the list but were "precluded" because of more pressing priorities.[39] The controversy epitomizes how interest groups sometimes need to resort to the judicial arena to seek redress, and how the battle over science and politics spilled over to become a major controversy during the Bush administration.

Several organizations have taken independent steps to preserve species, by-passing the federal bureaucracy. The Nature Conservancy (founded in 1951), for instance, buys up endangered habitats to save the species living on them from extinction. The organization has purchased or negotiated donations of more than 5 million acres worldwide, making the group the custodian of the largest private nature sanctuary in the world. Another notable accomplishment of the group is its Biological and Conservation Data System, a biogeographic database of more than 400,000 entries that can be used to assess species diversity on a region-by-region basis. The system allows the group to establish protection priorities and is also used by public agencies and resource planners in preparing environmental-impact studies.

Conflicts over goals—and species—also bring organizations into the policy process. In New Mexico, the mountain lion is a protected species. It preys on the endangered desert bighorn sheep, which has been declining in population for decades. According to the New Mexico Department of Game and Fish, only about 130 bighorn remain in the state; mountain lions caused thirty of the last forty recorded deaths of these sheep. To relieve predation pressures on the endangered animals, the state decided to allow hunters to kill more mountain lions in designated bighorn habitats.

The policy is opposed by several organizations, including the group called Animal Protection of New Mexico. The organization is concerned that the increase in hunting quotas will reduce the mountain lion population by as much as a third, instead of the 10 percent estimated by the state agency. Some researchers also oppose the plan, believing that it represents an antiquated view of predator species and that there is insufficient evidence to support the expanded hunt. Because mountain lions are extremely elusive, no one really knows how many there are in New Mexico; and the state's kill allowance is based on mathematical models. The two species are on a collision course that pits wildlife managers, hunters, and species' organizations against one another.[40]

Other organizations have taken a collaborative approach to species protection. In August 2002, the FWS removed the Robbins' cinquefoil, a rare member of the rose family, from the Federal List of Endangered and Threatened Plants. The plant is found only in the alpine zone of the White Mountain National Forest in New Hampshire, and it was on the brink of extinction due to disturbances by hikers on the Appalachian Trail and by plant collectors. The 93,000-member Appalachian Mountain Club rerouted the trail away from the primary habitat and worked with national forest officials to erect an enclosure around the primary population of the plant. The New England Wild Flower Society became involved by propagating the endangered plant over several decades, establishing two new populations of the species and reducing the threat of extinction.[41]

fanciful and fearful, focusing attention on the animal's power and beauty. Researchers are in agreement about two things: (1) The mammals are intelligent and have a complex communication system, and (2) hunting has diminished their numbers to the point where most species are now endangered.

Throughout most of the eighteenth and nineteenth centuries, whales were hunted without any type of regulatory regime under the freedom-of-the-seas doctrine of international law. Five species of large whales were hunted without government intervention, four of them to the brink of extinction, until the creation of the International Council for the Exploration of the Sea in 1902. The organization collected statistics on the number of whales in order to begin negotiations for the scientific management of whaling, and attempted to establish some uniformity in the application of national laws. But since most whaling took place on the high seas, outside of national jurisdictions, there was little real regulation of the industry. In 1931, the League of Nations, precursor to the United Nations, adopted an important change, the Geneva Convention for the Regulation of Whaling, and in 1946, the ICRW, which remains the primary international law governing the species.[44]

The ICRW applies to all waters where whales are found, including their migration routes. The purpose of the convention, however, seems contradictory; it calls for both the conservation of whale stocks and the orderly development of the whale industry. The eighty-five-member International Whaling Commission (IWC), which serves as a data-gathering body and monitors whaling activities, has no enforcement capabilities and no provisions for the settling of disputes; any infractions must be taken to the country under which the vessel's flag is being flown. As a result, many vessels register with governments displaying lax enforcement or disinterest in the ICRW, recognizing that they are unlikely to face any type of sanction.

The commission's Scientific Committee provides data on the status of large whale populations, with a focus on what is termed "pre-exploitation" size of the stocks. At its 2009 meeting, for instance, the committee reported that Eastern African humpback whale populations have recovered to over 65 percent of their pre-exploitation size, with increases in abundance for several other stocks of humpback, blue, and right whales in the Southern Hemisphere, although several were reported to have reduced levels compared to their pre-whaling numbers and information remains lacking for other stocks. The commission also discussed the status of the endangered Western North Pacific gray whale, which feeds in an area where oil and gas operations are occurring near Sakhalin Island in the Russian Federation. There are only 130 animals remaining, and efforts to conserve the species are being ramped up as a result of the group's meeting.[45]

In the 1970s and 1980s, activists sought a complete ban on whaling, focusing on a pirate whaling fleet that ignored the IWC and international law. Despite attempts by the United Nations to enact a moratorium on all whaling, the IWC was unwilling to adopt a ban. It was not until more anti-whaling nations joined the international group that there was sufficient support for a moratorium, which was passed by the IWC in 1982 and went into force in 1986. Japan, however, objected to the moratorium, and although the country discontinued commercial whaling, it continued to do so under the label of "scientific" whaling. There is a scientific-permit exception to the IWC, and any government may grant a permit authorizing the killing of whales by its citizens, subject to whatever restrictions the government feels are necessary. Japan conducts its whaling through the Institute of Cetacean Research, a private organization that has focused on minke whales and the Antarctic ecosystem.

In 1992, Norway, Iceland, Greenland, and the Faeroe Islands created their own institution, the North Atlantic Marine Mammal Commission (NAMMC), challenging the IWC and arguing that minke whales had sufficiently rebounded to a population of nearly 1 million animals. Iceland, Norway, and Japan believe that a small number of minke can be harvested without endangering the current population of whales. Another dispute has developed in the United States as the Makah tribe of Washington State has alleged that treaty rights allow it to kill up to five gray whales per year for cultural reasons.

Anti-whaling groups have tried to put pressure on the U.S. government to invoke economic sanctions against countries that continue to hunt whales, regardless of the reason. Some, like the Sea Shepherd Conservation Society, have engaged in radical protests and have attempted to intervene on the high seas, targeting Japanese whalers. Greenpeace has criticized the IWC for failing to obtain accurate information on whale populations, and researchers from New Zealand and Australia have documented the fact that whale meat continues to show up in Japanese fish markets.

These disputes point to a number of critical policy issues. First, the IWC has no enforcement capability, relying only on public and political pressure on nations to obtain compliance with the whaling ban. State sovereignty allows nations to ignore the regime, since all directives are purely voluntary. Second, the creation of a parallel organization (the NAMMC) creates opportunities for nations to opt out of the IWC or to refuse to abide by certain obligations under the moratorium. The existence of the organization poses a challenge to the legitimacy of the IWC in international debate. Third, there is a conflict within the IWC. Its own scientific committee has noted that minke whales can be harvested without threatening the overall population of the species. Other parties have argued that the IWC's data are sufficient to allow for artisanal whaling—local, small-scale whaling—that is not profit-driven and which would meet the needs of aboriginal groups. But the IWC membership has not agreed to these changes, and the debate, both in conference rooms and on the high seas, remains decidedly divisive.

At the 1972 Stockholm Conference on the Human Environment, delegates called for a ten-year moratorium on commercial whaling, but the policy did not go into force until 1986. At that time, the IWC approved a cessation of all commercial whaling while a survey of whale stocks and potential catch limits was conducted. Norway, Japan, the Soviet Union, and Peru lodged formal objections to the moratorium (Peru later withdrew). Iceland officially withdrew as a party to the IWC in 1992, and Japan and Norway threatened to withdraw as well. Although Norway had participated in meetings to resolve whaling controversies as early as 1988, its leaders subsequently announced that it would resume commercial whaling in 1993 because Norway had formally objected to the moratorium from the beginning. Once it resumed the hunt for minke whales, Norway began to increase its catch every year in violation of the moratorium.

Nongovernmental organizations like Greenpeace, EarthTrust, and the Sea Shepherd Society have been at the forefront of efforts to focus attention on whaling practices and the potential for extinction, but their efforts to ban whaling altogether are thwarted by sections of the agreement that contain exceptions to the moratorium. For instance, there is an aboriginal exception to allow whale hunting by certain coastal communities that depend upon subsistence whaling. The IWC has never defined what constitutes an aboriginal group, but Japan has argued that the exception should apply to its coastal villages where whale meat is used for local consumption. The United States has faced a somewhat different circumstance because the federal government signed agreements with tribal groups to allow whaling for cultural or subsistence reasons. Tribes in Alaska and in Washington State have defied the IWC moratorium in controversial hunts that have been an embarrassment to the United States, which has been supportive of anti-whaling policies. In 2002, the IWC's Scientific Committee agreed to create new categories of whale stocks that are subject to aboriginal subsistence whaling, from 2003 to 2006–2007, including Eastern North Pacific gray whales (traditional subsistence needs), West Greenland fin whales (Greenlanders), West Greenland minke whales (Greenlanders), East Greenland minke whales (Greenlanders), and humpback whales. These whales would be used exclusively for local consumption and monitored by the governments of St. Vincent and The Grenadines.[46]

Article VIII allows nations to obtain a permit "to kill, take, and treat whales for purposes of scientific research," thus exempting those parties from the convention. During the 1990s, the Japanese government interpreted the scientific-research clause very liberally, allowing vessels to harvest minke whales, remove tissue and organ samples, and then freeze and later sell the whale meat to consumers. The convention calls for the processing of the carcasses "so far as practicable," with the proceeds dealt with by the government. Japan considered its practice of selling the remaining whale parts as part of its compliance with the convention's instructions.

Several nations have attempted to broker agreements that would bring the parties back into the IWC to find ways of addressing their opposition. In 1994, France proposed a Southern Ocean Whaling Sanctuary; Ireland and Australia proposed a global whale sanctuary in 1997; and a 1998 plan would have allowed countries to hunt whales in their own coastal waters up to 200 miles offshore. At the 2002 IWC meeting in Japan, several proposals for sanctuaries in the South Pacific were defeated. Similarly, the threat of any form of penalty has been ineffective. The United States has the authority to impose trade sanctions on any country that violates the ICRW. Other legislation, such as the Marine Mammal Protection Act and the Fishermen's Protective Act's Pelly Amendment, provides species protection.

Strong and organized opposition to Japan's whale hunts erupted again in June 2005 at the IWC meeting in South Korea. The Japanese delegation submitted plans to the scientific committee of the IWC that would expand the hunting of whales for scientific purposes in the Southern Ocean. Specifically, Japan sought to increase its annual intake of minke whales from 440 to 935 and expand its hunt to include ten fin whales a year in 2005–2006 and 2006–2007, with an increase to forty in 2007–2008. The most publicly contentious proposal was to include fifty humpback whales in 2007–2008; the public has embraced this species since the contemporary whale wars began. Japan also announced that it would leave the IWC if the organization failed to approve a contentious set of rules that would allow limited commercial whaling.[47]

Australia's delegation took the lead in opposing Japan, using its diplomatic missions around the world to put pressure on the country's leaders and to line up the necessary votes to defeat the Japanese proposals. Joined by Britain, France, and Germany, along with Ireland, Italy, Sweden, Mexico, Brazil, Argentina, New Zealand, Austria, Finland, The Netherlands, and Portugal, Australia's foreign minister told Parliament that the nation remains steadfast against any forms of commercial or scientific whaling. The Australian prime minister also warned his Japanese counterpart that the country would face a worldwide backlash over its expansion plans.[48]

The level of public outrage is best illustrated by "a modest proposal" from the Australian press:

> Knowledge-hungry Australian scientists would be able to hunt and kill several hundred Japanese whale scientists per year to obtain important information such as how old they are, where they live and how their loins taste when marinated, barbecued and served with a feisty shiraz. It will be a controversial move, but killing Japanese pro-whalers and dissecting them into tasty bite-sized pieces is the only way to help solve enduring mysteries about this enigmatic species.[49]

Convention on Biological Diversity

A third major international species-protection agreement is the Convention on Biological Diversity, which was negotiated both before and during the Earth Summit in Rio de Janeiro in June 1992. The United States was extensively involved in the six-year drafting and negotiation phases of the agreement, which was opened for signature at the Earth Summit event. Unlike the dissension that marked the initial reservations to CITES, the biodiversity convention gained the support of virtually every member of the United Nations except the United States, with 150 nations and the European Union signing the Convention in Rio de Janeiro. President George H. W. Bush, who had threatened to boycott the conference, refused to sign the biodiversity treaty in an action that embarrassed the U.S. delegation in a highly publicized dispute. Under the terms of the agreement, the parties agree that a state has sovereignty over the genetic resources within its borders, including any valuable drugs and medicines that may be developed from endangered animals and plants. The convention is an important extension of CITES because it commits countries to draw up national strategies to conserve not only the plants and animals within their borders but also the habitats in which they live. Other provisions require countries to pass laws to protect endangered species, expand protected areas, restore damaged ones, and promote public awareness of the need for conservation and sustainable use of biological resources. President Clinton signed the treaty in June 1993, and it was transmitted to the U.S. Senate for ratification. The Senate Foreign Relations Committee supported ratification in a 16–3 bipartisan vote in 1994, but the measure was never sent to the Senate floor for a vote. Since that time, the United States has been allowed only an observer role in Convention on Biological Diversity negotiations and decision making. Currently, under President Barack Obama, the convention remains unratified.[50]

Before the Earth Summit, habitat protection found international support largely through organizations such as the IUCN and by regimes such as the International Convention Concerning the Protection of World Cultural and Natural Heritage, which entered into force in 1972. The World Heritage List is established by an international committee of the United Nations to designate sites of "outstanding universal value." At its June 2002 session in Budapest, Hungary, 9 new sites were added, bringing the total to 730 sites in 125 countries. Whereas some sites are primarily historically or archaeologically valuable, such as the Mahabodhi Temple Complex at Bodh Gaya, India, others, like the marine zone around Cocos Island National Park in Costa Rica, are themselves important ecosystems.[51]

A challenge facing global efforts to preserve wildlife habitats is basically one of economics: In times of declining budgets, many governments are finding it difficult to support parks and reserves over human needs. Countries such as New Zealand, for example, are reorganizing their parks to earn more revenue from them, and several African nations are using tourism as a way of financing wildlife refuges. But there are less obvious problems as well. Most national parks are outlined by some type of physical barrier, such as a fence or moat, but animals within do not always respect those limitations. Large mammals and birds of prey, for example, demand a large ecosystem for their habitat, which may cross national borders. This makes it unlikely that, even when strictly protected, national parks by themselves will be able to conserve all, or even most, species.

The 192 states that are parties to the convention took another step in April 2002, committing themselves to achieve by 2010 a significant reduction of the current rate of biodiversity loss at the global, regional, and national level as a contribution to poverty alleviation and to the benefit of all life on Earth. This target was later endorsed by the World Summit on Sustainable Development and the United Nations General Assembly and then incorporated as a new target under the Millennium Development Goals.[52]

Another View, Another Voice: Ahmed Djoghlaf

Born in 1953 in Algiers, Ahmed Djoghlaf's distinguished career in the diplomatic service and with the United Nations Environment Programme (UNEP) led him to the post of Executive Secretary of the Convention on Biological Diversity in January 2006. In that position, he shares the formidable task of managing not only the existing projects being undertaken through the convention, but those that result from the Conference of the Parties to the CBD scheduled for Nagoya, Japan, in October 2010 and the 2010 International Year of Biodiversity.

His impressive academic credentials include a law degree from the University of Algiers, masters' degrees from Universite Lille Nord de France and St. John's University, and a Ph.D. in political science from the University of Nancy, France. In the 1980s, he worked with the Algerian Ministry of Foreign Affairs, and served as advisor on environmental issues to both the Prime Minister of Algeria (1994) and the Ministers of Foreign Affairs (1992–1993). He has held posts associated with the United Nations since 1986 as part of Algeria's Permanent Mission, in charge of economic and environmental issues, including the UNEP.

In 1994, he was appointed Special Adviser to the Executive Secretary of the CBD in charge of the preparation of the second meeting of the Intergovernmental Committee of the CBD and preparations for the first COP, held in Nassau in December 1994. In this position, he had the opportunity to participate in the CBD's development from the very beginning, including future COP meetings. In 1996, he was named Executive Coordinator of the UNEP/Global Environment Facility, a position where he served until 2003 when he became Assistant Executive Director of UNEP and Director of the Division of the GEF Coordination.

Dr. Djoghlaf links biodiversity, sustainable management of freshwater resources, and global climate change, challenging world leaders to meet the target of significantly reducing the rate of biodiversity loss by 2010. Although some work programs are in place for the convention, he notes that much is still to be done to actually implement the international agreement. At the end of 2010, he says, "all people on the planet will be aware of the challenge, committed, and a partner to change. This is a tremendous revolution."

SOURCES:
Ahmed Djoghlaf. "Message on the Occasion of World Water Day, March 22, 2009." http://www.cbd.int/doc/speech/2009/sp-2009-03-20-water-en.pdf. Accessed July 29, 2009.
United Nations Environment Programme. "Ahmed Djoghlaf." http://www.unep.org/Documents.Multilingual/Default.asp?DocumentID=409&ArticleID=4624&l=en. Accessed July 29, 2009.
Miren Gutierrez. "Q & A: The Threatened Have Some Friends." IPSNews. http://www.ispnews.net/news.asp?idnews=47698. Accessed July 29, 2009.

PROTECTING THE WORLD'S FORESTS

The protection of endangered species has been the center of the biodiversity controversy during the last three decades, but an even longer-running debate has continued over the world's forests, which cover almost one-third of the Earth's surface land. The issue is complicated because the planet is home to a variety of forest ecosystems, from the ancient forests of the United States, to the boreal forests of northern Canada and Russia, to the tropical forests circling the equator between the Tropic of Cancer and the Tropic of Capricorn. Forest resources are spread throughout the planet; they comprise 0.1 percent of the landmass of Egypt and Qatar, in comparison to nearly 96 percent of the Cook Islands.

The management of forest resources has become an interest of global concern because in many instances, the conflicts that have erupted represent a duel between the "haves" and the "have-nots." The issue has pitted environmental activists from urban areas against rural landowners, and representatives of industrialized nations against developing nations that have accused developed countries of "economic imperialism" in their attempts to control the fate of other countries' natural resources. The physical and biological diversity of forests, the large number of forest owners with often conflicting objectives, and increasing demands for wood for fuel, paper, shelter, and artistic uses have made forest management especially challenging for policymakers.

Deforestation is an extremely volatile global environmental issue. The boreal forests of the far north comprise nearly one-third of the world's timberland, serving as a major carbon sink as well as home to plants and animals, and to a million indigenous people who have lived in the forests for centuries. Russia, for example, contains about one-fifth of the world's forests; an estimated 19 percent are currently under threat from logging and mining, according to the World Resources Institute.[53] Massive logging in Canada has disrupted ecosystems, displaced native peoples, polluted rivers with toxic chemicals used in the bleaching of pulp, and subsidized major multinational corporations.[54] An estimated 90 percent of boreal logging is clear-cutting, and 25 percent of these areas do not regenerate, as topsoil erodes during and after logging, which also destroys permafrost, the layer below the topsoil that acts as a heat reservoir in the winter. As the permafrost retreats, risks to the forests from fires, pests, and species composition grows; the downward spiral contributes to the threat of global climate change as the carbon sink is lost, and carbon from dead trees is increasingly released into the atmosphere.[55]

Logging of similar forests in Russia is occurring even more rapidly in an effort to generate much-needed foreign currency. Clear-cutting, combined with emissions from smelters and radioactive pollution, poses a serious threat to forests throughout the former Soviet Union. Scandinavian forests, largely in private hands, are facing similar problems. Private landowners log old-growth forests next to lands where trees are protected. Although reforestation is standard practice, and a few companies have switched to chlorine-free production of paper, biodiversity has suffered. There are major challenges to boreal forests throughout the world: below-cost timber subsidies that waste resources, minimal environmental review of proposed logging efforts, disposal of timberlands that are home to indigenous peoples, and large-scale clear-cutting that threatens the sustainability of forest production.[56]

Because almost all boreal forest policy is governed by sovereign nations rather than by international accord, individual countries have approached timber management in their own way. British Columbia, for example, has developed an ambitious program to replant forest lands that were heavily harvested in the nineteenth and early twentieth centuries. Little value had been assigned to forests, which were continuously cut so the land could be used for agriculture. By the 1940s, officials realized that the provincial forests were not limitless, and timber companies began replanting areas that had been clear-cut. The Forest Act of 1947 recognized the forests as economic resources and established the goal of ensuring a perpetual supply of timber under the principle of sustained-yield forestry. By the early 1970s, provincial officials began to realize that logging rates were not sustainable, as timber cuts continued to climb as the promise of immediate jobs and profits overwhelmed a projected loss of sustainability.

Modernization of logging technology resulted in job losses as timber harvests leveled off and increasing international competition impinged on profits. Preservationists lobbied successfully for the creation of parks that also reduced the potential supply of timber.[57] In 1993, the provincial government, prompted by projections that forest harvests were likely to decline by 15 to 30 percent over the next fifty years, established a Forest Sector Strategy Committee to find ways to balance the competing values of forests and review policies that protect watersheds, wildlife, and the rights and concerns of indigenous peoples.[58]

British Columbia is an important case study in forest management because of its biological, cultural, and geographical diversity. Nearly two-thirds of the Canadian province is forested, providing over 60 percent of the province's export revenues (estimated at over $17 billion a year). Unlike the United States, where the federal government retains control of lands with public domain forests, in British Columbia, 94 percent of the land is publicly owned but managed by the provincial government. The provincial leaders make decisions as to whether the lands are best used for recreation, mining, or logging, or set aside as preserves and parks.

Timber policy in the province has been shaped by rapid population growth and accompanying development, along with the increasing clout of environmental organizations like the Forest Alliance of British Columbia and the Western Canada Wilderness Committee. Along with the Sierra Club and Greenpeace, these groups focused attention on the large temperate rain forest on the west coast of Vancouver Island near the Clayoquot Sound. The area is nearly pristine, with huge tracts of ecologically sensitive habitat and one of the largest protected old-growth forests in North America. As environmental groups sought to ban logging and to establish the area as a protected park, timber interests sought to log the area, supported by the indigenous Nuu-chah-nulth people, whose interests in the forest were primarily economic.

Although the Clayoquot controversy is far from over, the provincial government has established an extremely elaborate forest-management program to protect the area in its present natural state. What makes this forest policy particularly noteworthy is that it was framed by environmental and timber groups based on scientific studies rather than simply rhetoric. Both sides brought in their own foresters and biologists, attempting to convince policymakers of the scientific validity of their claims. The result, as one observer notes, has been a debate imbued with scientific uncertainty crafted by knowledge brokers who continue to attempt to frame forest-management policy in their own terms.[59]

Similar problems plague the world's tropical rain forests, four-fifths of which are concentrated in nine countries: Bolivia, Brazil (with one-third of the worldwide total), Columbia, Gabon, Indonesia (with another third), Malaysia, Peru, Venezuela, and the Democratic Republic of Congo. Two major issues are currently being addressed by global policymakers:

1. Although there is a lack of precise information about the rate of loss, there is consensus among scientists that tropical forests are disappearing at an alarming and ever-increasing rate.

2. There is also agreement that failure to manage tropical forests effectively can result in some negative impacts, including the loss of wood products for fuel and other uses, soil erosion, global warming, shrinking populations of plants in the wild, destruction of fish-breeding areas, and loss of biological diversity and wildlife habitat.

Deforestation in tropical areas occurs primarily on lands not held by private citizens, especially in developing areas, where over four-fifths of closed forest areas is public land. In some countries, nearly 100 percent of all natural forest is government-owned, so that officials have total authority over the use and preservation of the land. Thus, the rates of deforestation vary considerably from one region of the world to another.

The logging of tropical forests and their products has been occurring for nearly 500 years, beginning with the collection of rare and valuable spices such as pepper and cinnamon by Southeast Asian traders. However, early merchants tended to collect only what they wanted and did not destroy the forests in their search for spices. During most of the nineteenth century, Europeans sought African hardwood for furniture but left the rest of the forest intact. Latin American forests, in contrast, were often burned to the ground as Spanish settlers established colonial outposts and set up plantation agriculture. The export of agricultural commodities quickly proved to be a lucrative enterprise for several nations. The United States entered the picture in the 1880s when U.S. investors edged out their Spanish competitors and built huge sugar-processing facilities dependent upon crops in Cuba and in the Pacific islands of Hawaii and the Philippines. The sugar barons' quest for increased profits led to more and more forest acreage being cleared; sugar cane became the primary vegetation in many areas, pushing out tropical woods. The logging of native forests for sugar cane was followed by devoting massive acreage to growing tropical fruits, such as bananas in Costa Rica and Nicaragua.

In the 1920s and 1930s, international journals of forestry documented the rapid destruction of tropical forests. However, little political attention was paid to the problem at that time, as was the case between World War II and the advent of the international environmental movement in the early 1970s. The more highly publicized issues of pollution crowded the top of the environmental-protection agenda, especially in industrialized nations. It was not until the early 1980s that international organizations—such as the UN's Food and Agriculture Organization (FAO), the UN Development Programme, and the World Bank—began to review systematically scientific literature on deforestation.[60]

Some forest-protection issues are of relatively recent origin. In southern Chile, for example, widespread logging did not begin until the 1980s, when native trees were cut and ground into small chips that were shipped to Japan to be processed into paper. Although 30 million acres of Chilean forest are protected in reserves, the 19 million acres estimated to be in private hands are often destructively cut by landowners seeking quick profits. The forestry industry has grown into one of Chile's main export earners. Attempts by groups such as the California-based Ancient Forests International and Chile's National Committee for the Defense of the Flora and Fauna have been largely unsuccessful in convincing the Chilean government to enforce existing regulations that limit cutting and provide for restoration. Few violators are prosecuted and even fewer are convicted by Chilean courts.[61]

Now, as tropical-forest resources are being depleted in some countries, international attention is focusing on regions where commercial logging was previously limited or inaccessible. Because the demand for tropical woods has not slowed, logging cartels are looking at areas of New Guinea, China, and New Caledonia; all are considered hot-spot regions of destruction. This means that more nations, by necessity, will become stakeholders and involved in the debate over forest diversity. China, for example, has come under international criticism due to its huge imports of timber from countries where illegal logging is rampant. After it discovered a smuggling route (controlled by crime syndicates) that sends twenty shiploads a month of exotic hardwood logs from Indonesia to China, a British group, the Environmental Investigation Agency, called China "the largest buyer of stolen timber in the world." Chinese officials respond that it is the responsibility of timber-exporting countries to monitor shipments, not their own customs officials—who they insist check all incoming timber to make certain it is legal.[62]

Efforts to protect tropical forests are much better funded and organized than attempts to preserve the Earth's ancient and boreal forest regions. Environmental organizations throughout the world have rallied against tropical deforestation, agreeing for the most part on the urgency of the problem. But the groups differ significantly in their approaches to what should be done.

Globally, there is a division between the more radical groups seeking to ban trade in timber from virgin rain forests (such as the World Rainforest Movement), and more traditional groups, primarily in the United States, that believe the solution is to "green" the development process. Mainstream organizations such as the World Resources Institute and Friends of the Earth have supported the World Bank's efforts to improve economic conditions in developing countries. Other groups, such as Greenpeace, have established tropical forest units within their organization and lobbied government officials to add more land to existing forest reserves, such as Costa Rica's Monteverde Cloud Forest. Indigenous peoples' groups, such as India's Chipko Andalan movement, have attempted to resist state encroachment upon their homelands. The groups are seeking to control not only forest practices but also mining, the siting of dams, and other projects affecting natural resources and land management.

To slow the world demand for exotic woods, the more radical groups have proposed a ban on the sale of tropical timber. They want the International Tropical Timber Organization (ITTO) to restrict severely timber harvests and trade. Developing nations have been critical of the United States and environmental groups for failing to recognize their people's desire to overcome widespread poverty in areas dependent upon forest products and their allied jobs, including shipping and processing industries. ITTO administers the 1984 and 1994 International Tropical Timber Agreements, but critics argue that the group has the somewhat contradictory roles of both protecting forests and regulating the timber trade upon which many of its member nations depend. Some attempts have been made to reduce trade in tropical wood under CITES, which covers both fauna and flora.

The 1994 agreement contains thirteen specific objectives, but no overarching directives—an issue that has become problematic for the group.

In February 2005, at the United Nations Conference for the Negotiation of a Successor Agreement to the International Tropical Timber Agreement (held in Geneva, Switzerland), efforts to focus future efforts were unsuccessful. Representatives of over 180 governments and organizations agreed to continue policies such as encouraging members to recognize the role of forest-dependent indigenous peoples and to improve the marketing and distribution of tropical timber exports from sustainably managed and legally harvested sources. But administrative problems (the distribution of votes and voluntary funding for projects) remained unresolved, as did the obligation of members to submit timber statistics. ITTO reported that many delegates preferred to play a waiting game on the core issues of finance, scope, and organizational matters, although some "imaginative and radical proposals" were made. "Considerable time was spent on 'ventilating' these proposals but the overall response was cautious, exploratory, and noncommittal."[63]

Because it has been very difficult to reach multilateral regimes using ITTO as a platform, many countries are now making individual agreements with member states. In 1997, the United States worked out a compromise with Brazil to allow the United Nations to monitor trade in mahogany, although environmental groups had sought to have mahogany products included on a list that would have allowed only controlled trade. The United States imported an estimated $37.5 million worth of Brazilian mahogany in 2001, primarily for use in furniture and caskets. Concerned about rampant logging, the Brazilian government outlawed the mahogany trade in October 2001. But in May 2002, U.S. Department of Agriculture officials and Customs agents stopped fifteen shipments of the rare wood during inspections at U.S. ports. Initially, it appeared that the mahogany, worth about $10 million, had been harvested legally, based on documents accompanying the shipments. But at the urging of Greenpeace, which has been documenting mahogany logging in Brazil for several years, the documents were inspected further, and Brazil questioned the validity of the export permits accompanying the shipments.[64]

Other than an outright ban on timber, solutions to tropical deforestation vary in their practicality and level of international support. The World Wildlife Fund and Friends of the Earth, for example, believe that the equipment and the types of forest management being used in these regions need to be modernized. Current harvesting practices, they argue, are inefficient and waste much of the forest's resources. They have called for an end to existing logging practices and feel that technological advances could bring about extraction that is more compatible with sustainable management. Other observers believe that a complete restructuring of timber taxing and sales practices is needed, because governments in these areas receive only a fraction of the rents from logging. Virtually all tropical countries also provide generous tax incentives for timber processing and logging, with the benefits accruing to the wealthiest strata of the population. The most commonly voiced solution is the creation of forest reserves, which many researchers argue is the only way to save tropical forests at this point. They believe that destruction is proceeding too rapidly for restoration to be effective, because a damaged tropical forest does not regenerate quickly. The idea is costly, even when coupled with the concept of debt-for-nature swaps that allow developing countries to repay outstanding loans to industrialized nations and lending institutions by establishing forest reserves as a way of paying off their foreign debt. But even the most optimistic estimates show that tropical deforestation is outpacing any current attempts to slow the rate of loss.

FURTHER READING

Harold B. Carleton Jr. *Endangered Species Act: Primer, Evaluation, and Prospects.* Hauppauge, NY: Nova Science Publishers, 2009.

Mark Cioc. *The Game of Conservation: International Treaties to Protect the World's Migratory Animals.* Athens: Ohio University Press, 2009.

Eric T. Freyfogle and Dale D. Goble. *Wildlife Law: A Primer.* Covelo, CA: Island Press, 2009.

Jane Goodall. *Hope for Animals and Their World: How Endangered Species Are Being Rescued from the Brink.* London: Icon Books, 2010.

Anne Maczulak. *Biodiversity: Conserving Endangered Species.* New York: Facts on File, 2009.

Michael J. Manfredo et al., eds. *Wildlife and Society.* Covelo, CA: Island Press, 2008.

Michael L. Morrison. *Restoring Wildlife: Ecological Concepts and Practical Applications.* Covelo, CA: Island Press, 2009.

Craig Pittman. *Manatee Insanity: Inside the War over Florida's Most Famous Endangered Species.* Gainesville: University Press of Florida, 2010.

John Frederick Walker. *Ivory's Ghosts: The White Gold of History and the Fate of Elephants.* New York: Grove Press, 2010.

10

The Global Commons

"If we do not find the means to develop and enhance
the capabilities to govern and manage common-pool
situations effectively, the absence of such institutions in
the twenty-first century will lead to fundamental social
and economic problems."
— DR. ELINOR OSTROM, 2009 NOBEL LAUREATE[1]

On October 12, 2009, a quiet scholar with a Ph.D. in political science from the University of California, Los Angeles became the first woman ever awarded the Sveriges Riksbank Prize in Economic Sciences in memory of Alfred Nobel. Elinor Ostrom, who considers herself a political economist, was honored for her work challenging the conventional wisdom that common property is poorly managed and should be regulated by central authorities or privatized. In fact, she notes, there are many examples around the world where commons users "create and enforce rules that mitigate overexploitation," such as the grasslands in the interior of Asia, that have been shared for centuries in traditional group-based governance.[2]

The terms *commons* and *common-pool resources* were popularized by American biologist Garrett Hardin in his 1968 essay "The Tragedy of the Commons."[3] Using as an analogy the medieval practice of grazing cattle on an open pasture, Hardin theorized that each livestock herder would graze as many cattle on the pasture (the commons) as possible if acting purely from economic self-interest. The result, of course, would be overgrazing of the commons to the point where all the herds would starve.

Implicit in Hardin's metaphor is the idea of common-property resources, which share two characteristics. The first is that the physical nature of the resource is such that controlled access by potential users is costly, and in some cases virtually impossible. The second characteristic is that each user is capable of subtracting from the welfare of other users.[4] This concept is especially applicable to the two topics covered in this chapter: the atmosphere and the oceans. It also exemplifies how environmental politics has been globalized and transnationalized. A global approach requires policymakers to consider how human activities affect the entire planet, rather than looking only at what is happening in their own backyards.

Issues related to common-pool resources are not new; they have been debated since scientists first began recognizing the impact of human behavior on the environment. But along with Ostrom's Nobel Prize, the expansion of technology, new findings on health effects of pollutants, concerns about national security, and dwindling resources have brought these issues back to the diplomatic table. This chapter explores the new developments in problem identification as well as in policy adoption with an explanation of both U.S. and international perspectives.

THE ATMOSPHERE

Since the 1860s, when British scientist John Tyndall first described a phenomenon we now call the *greenhouse effect*, society has learned how human activities affect the atmosphere and climate. For decades, researchers were unable to agree on whether our future was tied to an impending ice age that would result in continental glaciation or to a warming trend that would melt the glaciers and send coastal cities into the sea. The debate flourished around the turn of the century when Nobel Prize–winning Swedish scientist Svante Arrhenius calculated that a doubling of the carbon dioxide in the atmosphere would raise the Earth's average surface temperature. His calculations were confirmed by American geologists Thomas Chamberlain and C. F. Tolman, who studied the role that the oceans play as a major reservoir of carbon dioxide. In the 1930s, after three decades of warming temperatures and the development of a massive dust bowl in the central United States, other scientists warned of the dangers of rising temperatures, which had already been tied to increasing levels of carbon dioxide in the atmosphere. But between the 1940s and 1970s, global temperatures fell, and many reputable scientists prophesied a new ice age rather than a warming trend.[5] The global-warming forecast was resurrected again in June 1988 when Dr. James Hansen, director of the National Aeronautics and Space Administration (NASA) Institute for Space Studies told a Senate committee, "The greenhouse effect is here."

Humans' ability to cause changes in the atmosphere is a relatively recent phenomenon; primitive peoples did not have the technology to alter the environment as we do today. With the Industrial Revolution came technological devices—the steam engine, electric generator, and internal combustion engine—that have

Another View, Another Voice: Bill McKibben

As a preeminent scholar of the early environmental movement, Garrett Hardin bought attention to the tragedy of the commons and the need to view the Earth's resources from a common-pool approach. Bill McKibben widens that view in a series of books written from the perspective of an environmentalist who warns about global warming, carbon emissions and energy use, and human genetic engineering. In his book, *Deep Economy*, he calls for a reduction in consumerism and explains how he spent a year eating exclusively from the valley around Lake Champlain in Vermont to prove that it could be done without suffering too great a deprivation. "Somewhere there's a sweet spot," he writes, "that produces enough without tipping over into the hyper-individualism that drives our careening, unsatisfying economy."

McKibben was born in Palo Alto, California, in 1960 and grew up in Lexington, Massachusetts. He attended Harvard University, and after graduation, worked for *The New Yorker*. He left the magazine in 1987, moved to the Adirondack Mountains in upstate New York, and became a freelance writer. In 1989, he published his first book, *The End of Nature*, written for a general audience, on the impact of global climate change. It was followed in 1992 by *The Age of Missing Information*, in which he reported on an experiment in which he taped everything on the 100 channels of cable television in the Fairfax, Virginia, system for a single day. He spent a year watching 2,400 hours of videotape, and then compared it to a day spent on the mountaintop near his home. Among his other books are *Hope, Human and Wild*, a comparison of life in Curitiba, Brazil, and Kerala, India; *The Comforting Whirlwind: God, Job, and the Scale of Creation*, which examines the scriptural story of Job and the environment; and *Enough*, which deals with genetic engineering.

McKibben's philosophy goes beyond just writing about global warming. He and a group of Middlebury College students organized a one-day event on Earth Day 2007 called "Step It Up," with a goal of staging more than 1,000 global warming–related events in the United States. "We've got to have more people working on this issue," he says. "We've heard the science, the economics, and even the policy proposals. The only part of the movement we haven't had is the movement itself. We've wasted twenty years." Step It Up is a coordinated campaign that calls for legislation to cut carbon emissions by 80 percent by 2050, a goal that goes far beyond current global agreements such as the Kyoto Protocol and the Copenhagen Accord. Activists are also attempting to green their campuses by persuading administrators to purchase renewable energy and green construction.

He says that he is hopeful, rather than pessimistic, about the opportunities for major cultural and social changes. "My great hope is that when St. Peter finishes his accounting I will have ended up two or three gallons to the good—that I will have persuaded just enough people to change their habits a little bit that it will make up for what I've burned."

SOURCES:
Ira Boudway. "Bill McKibben Says We're Stuffed." http://www.salon.com/books/int/2007/03/23/mckibben. Accessed April 14, 2007.
John Donnelly. "Early Critic of Warming Steps Up Activist Role." *Boston Globe*. March 19, 2007. http://www.boston.com/news/nation/articles/2007/03/19/early_critic_of_warming_steps_up_activist_role/ Accessed April 14, 2007.
"Bill McKibben." http://www.billmckibben.com/bio.html. Accessed April 14, 2007.
"Bill McKibben." http://library.thinkquest.org/26026/People/bill_mckibben.html. Accessed August 7, 2009.
"The Greening of America's Campuses." http://www.businessweek.com/magazine/content/07_15/b4029071.htm?chan=top+news_top+news+index_top+story. Accessed April 14, 2007.

forever altered the planet, the water we drink, and the air we breathe. That ability to alter the environment is threatening to some, but others consider it a natural part of the evolutionary process. Some believe that Earth exists as a living organism in which internal control mechanisms maintain the stability of life—a theory called the *Gaia hypothesis*.[6] According to this theory, environmental problems such as ozone depletion will be brought under control naturally by the environment itself, which will make the necessary adjustments to sustain life. Critics of the theory, however, refer to policies built on such optimism as "environmental brinksmanship" and warn that we cannot rely upon untried regulatory mechanisms to protect the planet from large-scale human interference.

One factor that distinguishes the atmosphere from other environmental issues is that it is not a distinct category in international law. Although scientists recognize "airsheds" from a spatial dimension based on fluctuating masses of air, the idea that the atmosphere is common property that ignores political jurisdictions is still not universally accepted. Developing nations point to industrialized states as the source of the problem, and hold them responsible for coming up with solutions that do not penalize nations seeking to become more developed.

This section of the chapter looks at two issues with obvious global dimensions: climate change and stratospheric ozone depletion. It provides an overview of the scientific controversies and identifies the ways in which the two issues differ politically, with an update on recent policy changes.

GLOBAL CLIMATE CHANGE

Although global climate change is ostensibly a subject for scientific debate, it reached the political agenda at full force between 1997 and 1999. *Global warming* refers to the process by which solar radiation passes through the Earth's atmosphere and is absorbed by the surface or reradiated back into the atmosphere. The phenomenon is also called the *greenhouse effect* because some heat is trapped in the atmosphere, warming the Earth like the panels of a greenhouse, but keeping some of the heat from going back out.

About twenty so-called *greenhouse gases* (GHG) make up the Earth's atmosphere; the five major sources are identified in Table 10.1. Changes in the volume of these gases affect the rate at which energy is absorbed, which then affects the Earth's temperature. Greenhouse gases are emitted or absorbed by virtually every form of human activity (anthropogenic sources), as well as by

T A B L E 10.1   Major Greenhouse Gases

Gas	Where It Comes From
Carbon dioxide	Fossil-fuel sources including utility power plants, refineries, automobiles
Chlorofluorocarbons	Solvents, foam insulation, fire extinguishers, air conditioners
Halons	Compounds used in fire extinguishers
Methane	Natural sources such as decaying vegetation, cattle, rice paddies, landfills, oil-field operations
Nitrous oxides	Fertilizers, bacteria

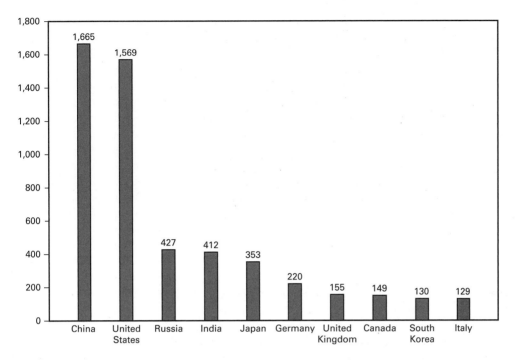

FIGURE 10.1 Total Fossil-Fuel Emissions of Carbon (2006) (in million metric tons)

SOURCE: Carbon Dioxide Information Analysis Center. "Top 20 Emitting Countries by Total Fossil-Fuel CO_2 Emissions for 2006." http://cdiac.ornl.gov/trends/emis/tre_tp20.html. Accessed January 5, 2010.

oceans, terrestrial plants, and animals, all of which contribute to the carbon-dioxide cycle. Scientists are primarily concerned about increases in levels of carbon dioxide because it is difficult to quantify the exact causes and effects of other greenhouse gases. The more carbon dioxide builds up, the more heat is trapped near the Earth.

There are major differences in the amount of carbon emissions generated by each country, with the general rule being that poorer countries emit less carbon than developed ones. The biggest development in fossil-fuel carbon-dioxide emissions stems from the tremendous increase in production and use in China, where figures have increased tenfold since the early 1960s. Since 2000, Chinese fossil-fuel carbon-dioxide emissions have grown nearly 80 percent, surpassing the United States as the world's largest emitter of carbon dioxide emissions, as seen in Figure 10.1.

Although researchers began studying the effect of carbon dioxide on climate in the early part of the twentieth century, the implications of such changes were not seriously considered until the early 1970s. A World Climate Conference in Geneva in 1979, convened by the World Meteorological Organization (WMO), was one of the first efforts at organizing international research, followed by a series of studies and conferences over the next ten years. One of the most respected reports was published in 1987 by the World Commission on Environment and

Development, which recommended a global approach to a broad spectrum of environmental problems, including greenhouse warming.[7]

There is little controversy over the scientific evidence that suggests the levels of carbon dioxide have increased by about 50 percent since the late 1700s, have increased by 25 percent over the past century, and are now increasing at the rate of 0.5 percent each year. Most of the studies agree that continued emissions of greenhouse gases will lead to a warming of the Earth's temperature between 1.5 and 4.5 degrees Celsius (or 2.7 to 8.1 degrees Fahrenheit). So far this century, global average temperatures have risen between 0.5 and 1 degree Fahrenheit.

Why should we be concerned about what seem like relatively small changes in temperature? Several possible scenarios are attributed to global climate change. One of the most respected scientists to have studied the issue, Dr. Stephen H. Schneider of the National Center for Atmospheric Research, believes that the temperature increases will lead to a rise in sea levels through the heating of the oceans, and possibly through the melting of polar ice. Drought and prolonged heat would be expected to lead to more severe air pollution and air stagnation, and to increased energy use, leading to a need for more power production. Some of the changes forecast might not be as negative. Climate change might lengthen the growing season for grain in Siberia, allowing some nations to increase their food production. The flip side of the equation, however, would be a loss to U.S. farmers, who are currently the world's leading grain exporters, along with an accompanying impact on our economy.

Recently, researchers have challenged traditional views about forest-management practices, theorizing that there is also a linkage between global warming and what appears to be an unnatural and unprecedented increase in wildfires. The severity of fires in the United States, Indonesia, and Australia has historically been blamed on forest policies that have suppressed natural fire regimes, promoting dense, overcrowded forests. Some studies using soil deposits as old as 8,000 years now suggest that climate change has resulted in thousands of years of large, intense fires dating back to a cooler, wetter period known as the Little Ice Age. Researchers interpret this information to mean that there is a longer record of climate change that has been continuously in flux.[8]

Are the models and predictions correct? Despite human advances and technological breakthroughs, the atmosphere remains an element of the environment that is imperfectly understood and uncontrolled by humankind. The uncertainty over global climate change comes from three sources: predicting future climate, predicting future impacts, and assessing costs and benefits of policy responses.[9] Polarization among the members of the scientific community has spilled over to the political arena, where policymakers are trying to decide which view is the most reliable. The debate is joined by industry representatives (primarily electric utilities) who argue that it is foolhardy to make costly changes in technology or lifestyle changes until all the evidence is available. They seek support and funding for further study and analysis until a general scientific consensus can be reached.

Nonetheless, a growing body of scientific evidence indicates that, given the various scenarios, it is imperative that steps be taken immediately to avoid the devastating effects of climatic change being forecast. Using the precautionary principle as a basis for decision making, there is general agreement of a need for a major reduction in carbon-dioxide emissions. Such a strategy would require substantive (and costly) changes in the way we live, and not only in the United States. Although the burden of cost is likely to fall disproportionally on the industrialized nations of the Northern Hemisphere, developing countries in the Southern Hemisphere will be asked to make drastic changes in their current patterns of energy use. This raises a host of policy questions. Will industrialized nations share their technology and expertise with the less developed countries? If so, will they also give their financial support to those nations to help them reduce their dependence upon fossil fuels? Could developing countries, already facing massive foreign debt, afford to switch to alternative fuels without aid from the Northern Hemisphere? Is the United States willing to set an example with its policies and rely more on energy conservation and non-fossil-fuel sources?

Despite these uncertainties, one compelling argument is for an "insurance policy" approach. Such a strategy calls for reductions in energy consumption and enhanced conservation—policies that would benefit the United States by reducing the nation's dependence upon foreign oil. The energy savings would have spillover effects as well, such as reducing the need to drill for oil in environmentally sensitive areas and reducing the emissions that contribute to acid rain. Such policies would not solve global climate change, advocates say, but would buy more time for additional research and the opportunity to find better solutions. Even though most scientists admit that additional research is needed to predict the timing and magnitude of potential effects, there is a growing consensus that some initial steps such as those to reduce carbon-dioxide emissions can be taken now without a major economic disruption.

Dealing with atmospheric change became an even more complex issue toward the end of the twentieth century, when scientific debate and political pressures escalated. New studies made scientific consensus more difficult as research funds decreased, especially in the United States. To complicate matters, in 1998, the Environmental Protection Agency (EPA) reported that the catalytic converter, developed by automakers to reduce nitrous-oxide emissions that are a component of smog, is actually contributing to global warming. The EPA found that nitrous-oxide emissions are increasing rapidly, due to more vehicles on the road and an increase in the number of miles traveled by cars that have catalytic converters. Still another study reported that some satellite data that showed a cooling of the Earth's atmosphere were flawed because of "quirkiness" in the satellite orbits. The finding, reported in 1998, seemed to reinforce data showing a gradual global warming, although other scientists downplayed the study.[10]

Other groups began to mobilize to force the issue back onto the political agenda. In 1999, the American Geophysical Union issued a statement claiming that while there has been a "substantial increase" in atmospheric concentrations of carbon dioxide and other greenhouse gases, and that current levels were expected to increase, there was still considerable uncertainty about the effects on the Earth. The group also noted that potential changes might be rapid and geographically unevenly distributed, causing more disruption. Still, the AGU recommended that "the present level of scientific uncertainty does not justify inaction in the mitigation of human-induced climate change and/or the adaptation to it."[11] The Global Coral Reef Alliance and the World Conservation Union also blamed the killing of the world's marine life and coral reefs on global warming and the subsequent increase in sea-surface temperatures. A similar debate erupted on the economic front, focusing on the costs of global warming. A 1998 study by the President's Council of Economic Advisers predicted that American households would pay only $70 to $110 a year more for energy. The study, which relied on an optimistic model that required only small emission reductions from U.S. companies, was heavily criticized by environmental organizations.[12]

While researchers argued among themselves, U.S. policymakers appeared hesitant to make decisions on how to proceed, perhaps due to lukewarm and sometimes conflicting responses by their constituents. A 1997 Gallup Poll found that most Americans believed automobile exhaust was a major cause of global warming but did not want policymakers to take steps that would incur high economic costs, such as great increases in energy costs or unemployment. The study also found that most respondents were opposed to any global treaty that would hold the United States to stricter energy standards than those for other large nations.[13] Another 1997 poll, by the Survey Research Unit at Ohio State University, noted that a substantial proportion of Americans said that they believed in the existence of global warming, and 61 percent believed the results would be bad. Over three-quarters of the respondents said they would be willing to pay higher utility bills in order to reduce the amount of air pollution resulting from some electricity generation. They also advocated significant effort by the government and businesses to combat global warming, while voicing pessimism about how much was actually being done.[14]

Progress toward achieving political consensus (among both scientists and policymakers) was slow until the late 1980s and mid-1990s.[15] The creation of the Intergovernmental Panel on Climate Change (IPCC) in 1988 marked the beginning of contemporary efforts to bring science and policy together, followed by a series of conferences including governments that had previously been working independently on the issue. In 1990, the Second World Climate Conference recommended the development of a Framework Convention on Climate Change (FCCC). Prior to the 1992 Earth Summit in Rio de Janeiro, delegates to the International Negotiating Committee agreed to develop the framework convention; 154 governments signed the document, after which they attended a series of Conferences of the Parties (COPs). In March 1995, the first COP adopted the Berlin Mandate, putting all FCCC parties on a schedule to negotiate and develop a legal instrument at the next COP. A second COP, held in Berlin in July 1996, placed an emphasis on emission reductions from industrialized countries. The first two COPs formulated the protocol and worked toward ratification of the agreement—a difficult task because the agreement requires that it be ratified by 55 percent of the signatories, contributing 55 percent of developed countries' greenhouse-gas emissions, before it can go into effect. Because the United States produces 36 percent of those emissions, its participation became essential for the protocol to succeed.

The parties meeting in Kyoto for COP 3 in December 1997 had an ominous task: to gain the political support of the United States, which historically had refused to agree with the goal of reducing emissions to 1990 levels by the year 2000. The Clinton administration entered the debate in 1993, and policy changed abruptly when the president announced his support for the FCCC but said that the United States wanted the emissions deadline extended to between 2008 and 2012. His position was heavily criticized by members of Congress, who were unconvinced that the purported threat of climate change was serious enough to force Americans to pay more for energy. When Vice President Al Gore addressed the Kyoto COP, he stressed that the U.S. position was that some developing countries should also be willing to reduce their emissions levels, as the industrialized countries had agreed to do. He then chided Congress, saying, "Congress's approach to climate change is: know nothing, do nothing, say nothing."[16] His criticisms were not unfounded. Members agreed to cut $200 million from appropriations for energy efficiency and research into renewable resources; further, they attempted to eliminate funding for any program that even talked about climate change, whether in public forums or administration planning sessions. The result, some officials believed, would be to bar EPA and White House advisors from doing anything, even simply talking about it, to advance the climate-change debate.[17]

The resulting agreement, the Kyoto Protocol to the 1992 Climate Change Treaty, was designed to reduce emissions from six greenhouse gases. The United States, which signed the protocol, agreed to a goal of reducing its carbon-dioxide emissions by 7 percent below 1990 levels by the period between 2008 and 2012. Canada, Japan, and Poland agreed to 6 percent, and the European Union had an 8 percent reduction. An additional 38 countries had average reductions of 5.2 percent, and developing countries such as China only had to set voluntary limits. Databases were to be set to determine carbon stocks at 1990 levels, and annual reports were required. The agreement, however, marked only the beginning of what became a long process of negotiations and conferences, as evidenced by the numerous COPs that subsequently were convened.[18]

At the November 1998 COP 4 in Buenos Aires, participants developed financial mechanisms to assist the developing world in responding to the challenges related to climate change, producing the Buenos Aires Plan of Action. At COP 5 in Bonn, Germany, work continued on strengthening implementation plans for the FCCC. A year later, at COP 6 (held in November 2000 in The Hague), The Netherlands, Russia, Japan, Germany, Canada, and Australia became key signatories; but the deadline for implementation decisions was not met, and the conference was suspended. Although President Bill Clinton signed the protocol, he did not submit it to the U.S. Senate for ratification, where it was unlikely he could gather the necessary votes for passage.

The 2000 presidential election results brought an abrupt turnaround in U.S. policies with the election of George W. Bush. In February 2001, the president announced that the United States would not honor its previous commitment to support the Kyoto Protocol. As negotiations continued at the second session of the Bonn COP in July 2001, the parties outlined basic principles, but enforcement was still an issue. Three months later, delegates from 165 countries meeting in Marrakesh, Morocco, for COP 7 adopted complex legal text requiring industrialized nations to cut or limit greenhouse gases by an average of 5.2 percent from 1990 levels by 2012. The requirements could be offset by managing forest and agricultural areas, known as *carbon sinks*; by providing assistance to developing countries; or through emissions trading that allows countries to buy and sell the right to pollute.[19] At the November 2002 COP in New Delhi, India, environment ministers from 169 nations approved the Delhi Ministerial Declaration just as the talks were poised to collapse. The declaration did not include demands from industrialized countries that developing countries initiate dialogue to make further commitments after the enforcement of the Kyoto agreement, which had been ratified by 96 countries as the conference concluded.

The United States faced a barrage of international criticism for the Bush administration's position on the Kyoto agreement; Greenpeace claimed that the United States was "isolated in the world in its rejection of the protocol." At an April 2001 meeting in New York, Japan's Environment Minister said, "[The Japanese] believe the participation of the United States is crucial. All countries expressed concern and urged the United States to make an open, Cabinet-level review." The head of international negotiations, Dutch Environment Minister Jan Pronk, said that despite the United States' rejection of the protocol, it was alive, and although "not completely healthy, it is recovering."[20] Bush countered with proposals of his own in February and June 2001, announcing that the United States would conduct additional research to address scientific uncertainties and encourage technological innovation, and calling the Kyoto agreement "unrealistic." Critics argued that the administration was doing the bidding of energy-industry lobbyists and auto manufacturers seeking to change the protocol's cuts in greenhouse gases.[21]

The Bush proposal was followed by a slight policy shift two months later, when the administration issued its third formal national communication under the FCCC. The report outlined the president's commitment to reduce greenhouse-gas intensity in the United States by 18 percent over the next decade through voluntary, incentive-based, and existing mandatory measures. It also called for a global partnership, stating that "the United States intends to continue to be a constructive and active Party to the Framework Convention."[22]

The move was heavily criticized for both scientific and political reasons. "The U.S. stands out in the cold," said Princeton University professor Michael Oppenheimer. "This is one of the biggest problems the world is going to face, and the U.S. doesn't have a policy." Other experts warned that European nations required to pay for pollution controls to reduce emissions might try to punish American companies, which do not have to comply, by placing tariffs on U.S. goods.[23]

After languishing at the diplomatic table for years, the Kyoto Protocol was ratified on November 5, 2004, as President Vladimir V. Putin's signature made Russia the 126th country to agree to the global-warming agreement. With the refusal of the United States and Australia to sign the treaty, Russia was left as the only country producing sufficient emissions to reach the 55 percent threshold.

The Russian Federation's decision to join the treaty came after prolonged internal—and surprisingly public—debate. Opponents argued that the treaty would do grave economic harm to the country and would limit industrial growth at a time when the government had promised to double Russia's gross domestic product. The decision to ratify was based less on global environmental concerns than on Putin's ability to bargain with European political leaders to endorse Russia's bid to become a member of the World Trade Organization. In addition, Putin had little to lose because Russia's industrial output had collapsed since 1990—the benchmark year for emissions calculation—so no additional regulations, taxes, or pollution controls would be needed for the country to comply. Ninety days after Russia presented its ratification documents to the United Nations, the treaty's provisions became binding.[24]

POST-KYOTO POLICIES

The structure of future implementation of the agreement changed to incorporate new stakeholders and principles. Canada served as host of the first Meeting of the Parties to the Kyoto Protocol in Montreal, in December 2005. Although the meeting was held in conjunction with the eleventh session of the COP to the Climate Change Convention, it was the initial session involving all the nations that had become signatories to Kyoto.

The Bush administration repeatedly attempted to show its commitment to reducing greenhouse gases through interagency meetings, proposing energy tax incentives that promote greenhouse-gas emission reductions to spur the use of cleaner, renewable energy and more energy-efficient technologies, and continuing support for the Climate Change Technology Program to accelerate the development and deployment of key technologies that can achieve substantial greenhouse-gas emissions reductions, including a Hydrogen Fuel Initiative, the "FutureGen" coal-fired, zero-emissions, electricity-generating power plant, and an internationally supported fusion-energy project. Despite these efforts, however, it was clear to most that the United States was still unwilling to take the most important step—signing on to the Kyoto agreement.

By 2007, when the parties met in Bali, there was an enhanced sense of urgency to getting the United States to participate, since the Kyoto Protocol emissions targets expire in 2012. The "Bali Roadmap" that emerged from the conference focused less on the science of climate change and, finally, more on whether countries had the political will to move forward with negotiations. European nations became the leaders in Bali, partially because they committed to reducing their own emissions and also because they led the call for others to follow. The United States, in comparison, became a laggard nation, basically alone in resisting an agreement. While it could be argued that there was a sense the nation was waiting until a new administration was elected, the conference placed additional pressure on the U.S. Congress to act.

One of the major impediments to change on the part of the United States is illustrated in a public-opinion poll conducted by the Pew Research Center for

People and the Press in late 2009. The survey showed that there has been a steady decline in the percentage of people who think that the average temperature on Earth has been getting warmer over the past few decades. In April 2008, 71 percent of those questioned said there was solid evidence of rising global temperatures, but by October 2009, that number was only 57 percent. At the same time, the number of individuals who said that global temperatures are rising as a result of human activity, such as burning fossil fuels, dropped from 47 percent to 36 percent. The lack of public awareness about cap-and-trade programs—a key element of most climate-change policy initiatives—is also evident in the Pew study. Only 14 percent responded that they have heard a lot about setting carbon-dioxide emission limits, while a majority (55 percent) said they had heard nothing at all.[25]

The lack of understanding about global warming and the potential policies to deal with it are underscored by public opinion that this is not a very serious problem for policymakers to deal with. The Pew Research Center found that only 35 percent of those questioned viewed global warming as a very serious problem, or a somewhat serious problem (30 percent). But these figures are lower than the study undertaken in April 2008, where 44 percent thought global warming was very serious. Previously, from 2006 to 2008, the figures had remained quite stable.[26]

The politics of climate-change negotiations are best characterized by the various divisions among countries, some of which are more likely to experience projected negative impacts than others. As has been the case with many global environmental issues, the split between the industrialized countries of the Northern Hemisphere and the developing countries of the Southern Hemisphere continued in Copenhagen. Though developed countries have been dealing with the issues for over a decade and are aware of the ramifications of the problem, developing nations are less likely to perceive global warming as a potential risk. They are less represented on various international study boards and have devoted fewer resources to research on the potential impact of global climate change. As a result, some are understandably less concerned and less anxious about finding a solution.

One cluster of nations that has had a pronounced impact on post-Kyoto negotiations has been the Group of 77, actually an organization of 130 developing countries that continues to seek deep cuts in carbon-dioxide emissions from industrialized nations. The countries argue that they should not have to make reductions in carbon-dioxide emissions at the expense of their own development. Historically, they have also sought the creation of a fund that would aid in technology transfer and alternatives to fossil fuels.

The thirty-nine nations that make up the Alliance of Small Island States (AOSIS) are likely to be the most affected by climate change and are thus extremely active in negotiations. Projected sea-level increases and storm surges pose a severe risk for low-lying countries as well as nations with coastal ecosystems. Islands like the Maldives and the Cook Islands could be submerged, and there could be widespread damage to coral reefs, saltwater intrusion into freshwater systems, and disruption of tourism. Members of AOSIS have proposed a

20 percent decrease in greenhouse-gas emissions from 1990 levels for all industrialized countries by 2005, a goal that clearly has not been met.

At the Group of Eight (G-8) conference in L'Aquila, Italy, in July 2009, the differences between nations with emerging economies and developed nations looked more like a chasm than a divide. The G-8 countries agreed to a statement setting the goal of holding global warming to an increase of 3.6 degrees Fahrenheit (2 degrees Celsius) by 2020, with a long-range target of cutting emissions among industrialized nations by 80 percent and worldwide by 50 percent by 2050. President Obama admitted that the United States "has sometimes fallen short of meeting our responsibilities. So, let me be clear: Those days are over."[27] China and India, two of the world's biggest polluters, wanted the G-8 countries to commit to reducing carbon emissions to 40 percent over the next decade before they proceed with any reductions of their own. The refusal of developing countries to act until the industrialized world takes action is a key barrier to moving forward in global efforts.

Along with these political divisions, two factors have been identified that make the establishment of an effective climate change agreement problematic. Historically, powerful interests within the United States have been opposed—at least in principle—to any measure to mitigate climate change; and many still do not recognize the scientific legitimacy of the problem. The decision of the United States not to ratify the Kyoto Protocol allows developing countries like China to delay consideration of prevention strategies. The second factor lies within the protocol itself. Many provisions are still vague and unsettled, including agreement on compliance and control procedures. Questions related to the high level of uncertainty in the current protocol must be answered, they argue, "because otherwise ratification by the United States and some other crucial players is unthinkable."[28]

Should public opinion guide policymakers, and how high does the issue rate on the policy agenda? Those questions were at the heart of the debate on the U.S. stance on global warming as officials attended the Conference on the Parties to the Kyoto Protocol in Copenhagen in December 2009. More than two years of negotiations and agreements had been debated prior to the regularly scheduled conference, with many side discussions taking place in the run-up to the meeting. China and India, for instance, the two largest carbon-dioxide emitters in the developing world, agreed in October 2009 to sign a five-year pact to work together to increase energy efficiency and the use of renewable resources, and to develop clean-coal technologies. By signing the agreement, the two countries became a formidable force against industrialized nations that sought specific targets for reductions in carbon-dioxide emissions.

The conference, organized by the United Nations, was supposed to result in a new global framework agreement on climate change. The meeting, attended by world leaders from 193 nations as well as climate scientists and representatives of nongovernmental organizations, was preceded by months of negotiations leading up to the summit itself. President Obama changed his plans to attend the conference several times, finally deciding to attend on the scheduled last day in order to try to broker an agreement among key nations seeking the resolution of three primary issues:

1. Targets for the reduction of greenhouse gases, with expectations that rich countries would cut their greenhouse gas emissions by at least 80 percent by 2050.

2. Disputes over the amount of money rich nations will pay to poor ones to adapt to climate change, with a target figure of $30 billion in the next three years, ramping up to $100 billion a year by 2020.

3. Provisions for the international scientific review and monitoring of greenhouse-gas data, aimed primarily at China's carbon emissions.

The issue of transparency was an important one that focused almost entirely on China. Chinese officials tended to speak in generalities about their intentions, with one noting that the country would "enhance and improve our national communication to the U.N." Beijing would, he said, take part in "dialogue and cooperation that is not intrusive and doesn't infringe on China's sovereignty."[29]

Numerous problems plagued the conference, from street protests and procedural wrangling to a partial boycott by African countries. On one Sunday during the talks, church bells were chimed 350 times throughout Denmark to symbolize 350 parts per million of carbon dioxide in the atmosphere, the highest concentration that some scientists believe the world can handle without major dangerous climate effects. When scientists starting measuring carbon dioxide in 1958 levels were at 315; in 2009, levels reached 390.

The political meetings between the United States and China on the last day of the conference were key, many believed, to its success or failure. President Barack Obama met twice with China's Premier Wen Jiabao in what observers called "a diplomatic frenzy" aimed at bridging the gap between rich and poor nations. Brazilian president Luiz Inacia Lila da Silva said a "miracle" was needed, adding that frustration and discouragement outweighed hope.[30]

By the end of the two-week conference, the miracle did not occur. Despite diplomatic efforts that continued late into the early morning hours of the last day, the result was a three-page nonbinding agreement, referred to as the Copenhagen Accord, which is a beginning step for another one expected to be written and agreed upon in 2011 at the next conference of the parties in Mexico City. The emissions targets of the Kyoto Protocol, involving thirty-seven nations, are scheduled to expire in 2012. The conferees agreed to various emission reductions, from a 20 percent cut by 2020 by the European Union to a 25 percent cut by Japan. China agreed to reduce its "carbon intensity" (the use of fossil fuels per unit of economic output), by 40 to 45 percent, while India, Brazil, and South Africa also agreed to voluntary emissions reductions. Developing nations agreed to report every two years on their actions, which would be voluntary but subject to international consultations and analysis. The latter provision was a compromise between the United States and China, which had argued that such a requirement would be an intrusion on its sovereignty. The industrialized nations also agreed to a $10-billion-per-year, three-year program to fund projects in developing nations that address drought and other impacts of climate change, and to develop clean energy. There was also agreement on a goal of mobilizing $100 billion a year by 2020 for adaptation and mitigation of climate change.[31]

Was this nonbinding international agreement a bold step in climate-change policy, or, as many critics complained, the outcome of a frustrating process that underscored the lack of trust between rich and poor nations? "It's weak. There's nothing ambitious in this text," said one Sudanese delegate. The Chinese were accused of blocking efforts at substantive emissions reductions, and the United States was criticized for coming to the table too late with its plan for a long-range climate aid program. Although China eventually offered to open up its emissions records for inspections by international reviewers, that step came only after the United States negotiated the $100-billion-a-year mitigation fund. That small bit of success was countered by a lack of real cuts in carbon-dioxide emissions, and few new commitments to reduce the greenhouse-gas emissions that cause global warming.[32]

STATE AND LOCAL INITIATIVES

While the United States was attempting to negotiate agreements on the international level, states began taking action on their own, eschewing the federal government's wait-and-see policy that had been in effect for decades. By 2009, twenty-one states had legally binding greenhouse-gas reduction agreements, representing more than 50 percent of the U.S. population, more than 50 percent of the U.S. economic output, and about 37 percent of U.S. emissions. Led by California, the state house became the primary venue for climate-change policy, capping carbon-dioxide emissions of power plants and promoting energy efficiency and renewable energy. Florida and Hawaii set targets of reducing emission levels to 1990 levels by 2025; six Midwestern states agreed to cut emissions within their borders up to 80 percent by 2050. The Northeastern states, which release 10.7 percent of U.S. emissions, agreed to a regional initiative that would reduce emissions by 10 percent below 1990 levels by 2020. The Western Climate Initiative, which includes not only Western states but also Canadian provinces, also took a regional approach to global warming, upping the ante while Washington leaders were unable to come up with a plan on the national level. The result was a patchwork of state laws that made it difficult for businesses to comply with different regulations in different states.

Long a leader in environmental protection, California assumed this role again in 2002 when the state legislature enacted a measure directing the California Air Resources Board (CARB) to develop regulations to reduce greenhouse gases from motor vehicles no later than January 1, 2005. The legislation addressed four greenhouse gases: carbon dioxide, methane, nitrous oxide, and hydrofluorocarbons. In order for the law to be implemented, however, the state needed a waiver from the EPA, under the Clean Air Act, to adopt standards more stringent than those of the federal law, a policy called *preemption*. California had previously been granted more than fifty waivers; the CARB applied for a waiver in December 2005. The EPA denied the request for a waiver in March 2008, and in early 2009, CARB asked for a reconsideration of the waiver denial.

In the meantime, the U.S. Supreme Court was deciding a similar issue in a case brought by twelve states, three cities, and four other petitioners who had filed a petition with the EPA asserting that the agency had sufficient cause to regulate greenhouse gases from new motor vehicles. In *Massachusetts* v. *EPA,* the government argued that Congress did not intend the EPA to regulate carbon dioxide as an air pollutant. The government also argued that even if the EPA had the authority to regulate greenhouse gases, there was no causal link between greenhouse gases and an increase in global surface air temperatures. Lastly, the argument was made that this incremental, piecemeal approach to regulating motor-vehicle emissions conflicted with the president's comprehensive approach to the problem, and that it might hamper the administration's ability to persuade developing countries to reduce greenhouse-gas emissions.[33]

In its ruling against the EPA, a divided Supreme Court noted that the EPA has the authority to regulate *any* [emphasis in original] air pollutant under the Clean Air Act, and regulation is but one strategy that can be used in addition to collaboration and research. The justices pointed out that the EPA did not successfully argue why it believed there was too much scientific uncertainty surrounding climate change, and therefore it would be better not to regulate greenhouse gases at this time. The court also decided that the EPA must render an endangerment determination on whether carbon dioxide was an air pollutant that could reasonably be anticipated to endanger public health or welfare.

The 5–4 decision in the case was important for numerous reasons. It focused attention on the question of whether the Clean Air Act and the National Ambient Air Quality Standards (NAAQS) (discussed in Chapter 8) were the best mechanism for regulating greenhouse gases, since the law takes a state-by-state approach while climate change is global in nature. The ruling also raised the issue of whether carbon-dioxide emissions endangered human health or welfare, a finding that would almost automatically trigger action by the EPA. The role of politics in any potential action was critical; upon taking office, President Obama issued a Presidential Memorandum directing the EPA to assess whether denial of the waiver requested by California was appropriate in light of the Clean Air Act and the decision in the Supreme Court case. This action was in direct opposition to the position of the Bush administration, which was rebuked by the court's decision.

The Obama administration also said that it would be preferable for Congress to adopt new legislation to control greenhouse-gas emissions, rather than relying upon the Clean Air Act. In March 2009, the EPA's new administrator, Lisa Jackson, proposed a rule to require large sources of greenhouse gases to report their emissions to the agency. Although the proposed rule would not require sources to reduce their emissions, this was an important first step in the potential implementation of future controls. Then, in April, 2009, the EPA did issue a ruling that greenhouse gases do endanger public health and welfare within the meaning of the Clean Air Act, an action that set the stage for the agency to regulate greenhouse gases if Congress fails to act decisively on its own.

On June 30, 2009, the EPA granted a waiver to California of Clean Air Act preemption for its greenhouse-gas emissions standards for motor vehicles beginning with the 2009 model year.[34] The notice of decision by the EPA opened the door for not only California's greenhouse-gas regulations, but for other states to follow with regulations of their own. But the agency was widely criticized in October 2009 for a controversial proposed rule that limits greenhouse-gas emissions only from the nation's largest industrial sources. The EPA says the rule will cover nearly 70 percent of greenhouse-gas emission sources—such as power plants, refineries, and cement-production facilities—by requiring those that release more than 25,000 tons of greenhouse gases to demonstrate that they have used the best available pollution controls.[35]

Meanwhile, local governments have enacted their own global-emissions targets and signed on to the U.S. Mayors Climate Protection Agreement, which was presented to the U.S. Conference of Mayors in March 2005. Drafted by Seattle mayor Greg Nickels, the document was designed to "show the world there was intelligent life in the United States after all" by getting cities to commit to the targets in the Kyoto Protocol, even if the federal government failed to act. The agreement calls for matching the Kyoto Protocol's goal to reach a 7 percent reduction below 1990 levels by 2020. The ranks of cities that have signed the agreement range from cities with traditional records of environmental activism, such as Seattle, San Francisco, and Portland, to Arlington, Texas, and Milwaukee, Wisconsin.[36] Local actions, according to a 2007 survey conducted by the U.S. Conference of Mayors, range from the obvious to the innovative. The group found that in 72 percent of the cities responding, vehicles in city fleets run on alternative fuels and/or use hybrid-electric technology. All but 4 of the 134 cities in the survey are using more energy-efficient lighting technologies in public buildings, and two-thirds of the cities have an individual in city government who is responsible on a full- or part-time basis for the city's climate-protection activities. And from a philosophical perspective, 92 percent of the cities consider efforts to reduce greenhouse-gas emissions part of their broader efforts to address public health concerns, such as improving air quality or encouraging active living.[37]

Absent action by Congress, the state and local initiatives will probably make little impact on what is inarguably a global problem. But the actions have kept the issue of climate change on the policy agenda, and have kept pressure on both the Obama administration and Congress to move forward more expeditiously to regulate greenhouse gases.

STRATOSPHERIC OZONE DEPLETION

Ozone is an element of the Earth's atmosphere caused by a photochemical reaction of hydrocarbons (produced mainly from the burning of fossil fuels) and sunlight. Ozone can be both "bad" and "good." At the Earth's surface, ozone is a major component of smog; but higher up in the stratosphere (6 to 30 miles above

Earth's surface), the ozone layer provides a filtering layer of protection against the harmful effects of ultraviolet (UV) radiation. Without such protection against UV radiation, medical experts believe there would be a substantial increase in skin cancers, and genetic changes in some types of plants and animals.

In the early 1970s, scientists warned that the exhaust gases from high-flying supersonic transport planes could damage the ozone layer. In studying components of the high-altitude atmosphere, the researchers discovered that chlorofluorocarbons (CFCs), which are synthetic, reacted with UV light when released into the atmosphere, forming chlorine. Chlorine is known to attack ozone molecules, and the researchers warned that unless steps were taken to reduce CFC production, from 7 to 13 percent of the Earth's protective ozone layer would be destroyed. CFCs are found in thousands of synthetic products and are used primarily in air conditioning and refrigeration, foam packaging, and insulation. They are also used in cleaning the sides of the space shuttles, in sterilizing whole blood, and as a solvent in cleaning computers.

Congress responded in 1977 by including provisions in the Clean Air Act Amendments which authorized the EPA administrator to regulate substances affecting the stratosphere. In 1978, the EPA banned the use of CFCs in most aerosols. At the time, scientists were unable to measure the damage to the ozone layer, but on the strength of theoretical evidence alone, Congress responded.[38]

With the election of Ronald Reagan in 1980, research into CFCs came to a standstill and the search for substitute compounds subsided. Even though the United States had banned CFCs in aerosols, the nonaerosol use of CFCs grew to record levels—and the United States was producing about one-third of the world total.

The issue gained new prominence in 1985, when a group of British scientists (who had been monitoring ozone levels for thirty years) found a "hole" in the ozone layer above Antarctica. The hole, approximately the size of North America, lasted for nearly three months each year.[39] Later that year, the National Science Foundation sent its own team of researchers to Antarctica; although they could not agree on an exact cause, they concluded that chlorine chemistry was somehow involved, and that the hole was getting larger. In 1992, one study by the European Ozone Secretariat and another by NASA concluded that the ozone shield had also thinned markedly over the Northern Hemisphere. Although researchers were unable to discover an ozone hole over North America similar to the one over the Antarctic, they warned that the increased levels of ozone-destroying chemicals were cause for alarm. As the scientific evidence of stratospheric ozone depletion mounted, the environmental protection wheels began to turn in the political arena.

Even though the evidence that CFCs are responsible for ozone depletion is not irrefutable, the government and industry response to CFCs differed from the response to global climate change in four major ways.

Issue Complexity

The issue of stratospheric ozone depletion was perceived as a more "manageable" problem than that of global climate change, which is a much more complex and multifaceted problem than is developing substitutes for CFCs. Whereas industry officials called for more research into greenhouse gases before they were willing to accede to costly changes in production and technology, CFC manufacturers almost immediately agreed that CFC production should be reduced, even without proof that CFCs were damaging the ozone layer.

In 1988, the DuPont Company, inventor and world's largest user of CFCs, announced that it was phasing out production of two types of CFCs altogether. Other manufacturers and users of CFCs followed suit, and competition began to find replacement products and processes. The significance of the CFC strategy, from a political standpoint at least, is that the United States and its industry leaders were willing to take action even before all of the scientific evidence was in. This "preventive action on a global scale" was a unique approach to environmental protection. Rather than bucking the trend and refusing to cooperate, companies such as DuPont immediately began researching alternatives and substitutes for CFCs. And rather than stalling for time, the U.S. government took a leadership role and sought the strongest action possible—a complete ban on CFCs. The cost of finding replacements for the estimated 3,500 applications in which CFCs are used could reach $36 billion between now and 2075, according to the EPA.[40]

As a result, what might initially be seen as an unreasonable cost of compliance is now being viewed as a new marketplace by many in the chemical industry. Forced to find substitutes for products and processes, some companies anticipate higher profits; others fear that substitute substances will have their own complications. For example, hydrochlorofluorocarbons (HCFCs) were originally considered as a replacement for CFCs and halons because they are less harmful to the ozone layer. Hydrofluorocarbons (HFCs), another potential replacement for CFCs, were also considered because researchers were certain that HFCs do not damage the ozone layer. However, because HFCs are a type of greenhouse gas, this choice only complicated the debate by substituting one hazard for another.

Acceptability

The U.S. government accepted the premise that a unilateral phase-out of CFCs was not acceptable for solving such a global problem. The United States initiated an international agreement to phase out CFC production within ten years, a move that led to the signing in September 1987 of the Montreal Protocol on Substances that Deplete the Ozone Layer. The document set a strict timetable of step-by-step reductions in CFCs and other ozone-depleting substances, leading to a complete production ban by 2000. Developing nations were given a ten-year grace period before full compliance is required, but many refused to sign the treaty because of the expense involved in switching to new technology.

After scientists warned that the 50 percent reduction was not adequate to reduce the destruction of the ozone layer, the United States enacted even more stringent domestic legislation via Title VI of the Clean Air Act Amendments of 1990. The legislation required an accelerated phase-out of the compounds that pose the greatest threat to the ozone layer: CFCs, halons, carbon tetrachloride, and methyl chloroform. The act also contained a requirement for the elimination of these compounds as soon as possible, and no later than 2002. Under the terms of the amendments, the EPA now requires the mandatory nationwide recycling of CFCs in motor-vehicle air conditioners, the biggest user of CFCs in the United States. The American efforts were not designed to replace a stronger version of the Montreal Protocol, but instead were expected to serve as a model for future international agreements. Subsequent COPs in London in 1990, in Copenhagen in 1992, Vienna in 1994, and in Montreal in 1997 led to an acceleration of the CFC phase-out, leading to a complete ban by 2010. The conferences also established a global phase-out of methyl bromide (used to fumigate soils and crops), which may be responsible for 10 percent of the ozone lost so far, as a "controlled substance," meaning that emissions would be frozen at 1991 levels. The 1997 amendments set deadlines for the phase-out at 2005 in developed countries and 2015 in developing countries. Several nations did not concede to the methyl-bromide agreement; China opened a new facility and expanded the country's production capacity of the substance to a point that now exceeds the output of methyl bromide by all other developing countries. The 1999 Beijing Amendments set new trade rules for HCFCs and expanded the number of controlled compounds. However, no phase-out schedules have been agreed upon for HFCs or perfluorocarbon (PFC), another potential substitute that is also a greenhouse gas.

Ozone-depleting substances (ODS) are largely a problem emanating from the Northern Hemisphere, but the efforts to raise living standards in the Southern Hemisphere could have a tremendous impact on emissions levels. Participation by developing countries is critical, because increased use of CFCs in China and India could largely negate reductions in emissions throughout the rest of the world. The Montreal Protocol gave developing countries an additional ten years to comply with the production bans and included promises from the Northern Hemisphere to help fund the transition in the Southern Hemisphere to ODS alternatives. A crucial element of the ozone protection agreements was the creation of a multilateral fund to help developing countries finance their implementation of the international commitments. The budget during the fund's three-year pilot phase (from 1991 to 1994) was $1.3 billion. Twenty-five countries contributed $860 million to the core fund, and $420 million came from individual countries for parallel funding or co-funding of specific projects. Thirty-four countries contributed to the replenishment of the fund in 1994, including thirteen recipient countries. In exchange for the new round of financial support, the eighty countries participating in the fund agreed on a restructuring of the governing process. Actions by the thirty-two-member governing council now require support from 60 percent of the members; these members must also have contributed at least 60 percent of the funds.

Only a few countries have implemented laws and regulations to ensure reduction in the manufacturing or use of CFCs. Despite the consensus concerning the threat of ozone depletion, the relatively small number of CFC producers, and other factors that should have led to rapid effective international action, the protocol was still slow in coming (the agreement was signed thirteen years after publication of the first article that suggested the ozone layer was threatened) and slow in being implemented.

Media Coverage

Media coverage of the ozone-depletion issue kept attention focused on U.S. efforts to develop an international agreement and prevented the administration negotiators from weakening the proposed CFC controls. For example, on May 29, 1987, the media published reports that Secretary of the Interior Donald Hodel was attempting to revoke the authority of the U.S. delegation to negotiate significant reductions in ozone-destroying compounds. After newspaper headlines reading, "Advice on Ozone May Be: 'Wear Hats and Stand in Shade'" and "Administration Ozone Policy May Favor Sunglasses, Hats; Support for Chemical Cutbacks Reconsidered," the public outcry over the apparent change in the U.S. position created a backlash that virtually guaranteed the imposition of stringent controls.[41]

Over 200 media correspondents covered the Montreal meeting, and consumers became more aware of the potential impact of continued CFC use. Media coverage of global climate change, in contrast, has been colored by the lack of scientific consensus on the rate of onset and the potential magnitude of the problem. The attention given to greenhouse gases has not been as focused, if only because the potential impacts are more uncertain, less tangible, and less immediate than are those of ozone depletion. Global climate change has lacked an equivalent to the ozone hole upon which the media and public could focus their attention.[42]

But in 2006, one individual, former vice president Al Gore, did manage to change climate change from a scholarly debate to one that infiltrated popular culture, at least for awhile. His book and documentary film, *An Inconvenient Truth*, captured audience attention and over $50 million in box-office receipts. The somewhat bland slide show, which Gore developed in conjunction with science experts, coupled segments on Gore's own experiences and travels with scientific opinion on the effects of global warming. The film won an Academy Award for Best Documentary and made its way through Main Street theater houses, along with campus showings and panel discussions on the message of climate change. In 2009, Gore followed up with another book, *Our Choice: A Plan to Solve the Climate Crisis*. A subsequent media tour did not garner the same kind of attention as *An Inconvenient Truth* had done, but it did spur more public debate on the scientific bases for climate change.[43]

Political Support

The climate-change issue lacks the support of major actors in the political arena, especially the United States. For an international agreement to be effective, it must also be supported by the developing countries, which are becoming dependent upon fossil fuels. This was not the case with CFCs and the Montreal

Protocol. In that instance, sufficient concessions could be made outside the fishbowl of media publicity to allow room for negotiation and compromise. Climate change does not have a similarly low profile; therefore, the process of reconciling differences among developing and industrialized nations to produce a binding agreement will be much more politicized and thus much more difficult.

Still, Richard E. Benedick, who served as one of the U.S. negotiators on the Montreal agreement, believes the impact of the protocol goes beyond science alone:

> In the realm of international relations, there will always be resistance to change, and there will always be uncertainties—political, economic, scientific, psychological. The ozone protocol's greatest significance, in fact, may be as much in the domain of ethics as environment: its success may help to change attitudes among critical segments of society in the face of uncertain but potentially grave threats that require coordinated action by sovereign states. The treaty showed that even in the real world of ambiguity and imperfect knowledge, the international community is capable of undertaking difficult cooperative actions for the benefit of future generations.[44]

U.S. OCEANS POLICY

Nothing exemplifies the concept of a global commons more than the Earth's oceans and seas. They are the source of all living things, a factor in our weather and climate, a source of food, a transportation network, and the home of valuable marine resources. Yet for most of human history, the oceans have also been a dumping ground, assimilating (to some degree) our wastes and receiving little attention from policymakers until the last forty years. Most of the focus has been on international agreements, and the United States has only recently reentered the policy debate on the use of marine resources.

Initially, the U.S. response to dealing with oceans as a part of the total geophysical environment was driven by technology. From the first workable scuba experiments in 1825, to the commercial recovery of bromine from seawater in 1933, to the first offshore oil well built beyond sight of land in 1948, government efforts have been driven by "new and expanded ocean industries [that] offer some of the Nation's most inviting opportunities for economic growth."[45]

The first legislation to define a national oceans policy was the Marine Resources and Engineering Development Act of 1966. The act created the fifteen-member Commission on Marine Science, Engineering, and Resources, commonly referred to as the Stratton Commission after its chair, Dr. Julius Stratton. The commission was charged with examining the development, utilization, and preservation of the marine environment. Its report, "Our Nation and the Sea," recognized the importance of oceans for security, the increasing demands for food and raw materials, the position and influence of the United States in the world community, the importance of oceans for recreational use, and the quality of the environment.

The report also noted the sea's potential as a source of food, drugs, and minerals, as well as depicting the sea as "the last frontier" to be conquered by man. Consideration of humans' impact on the ocean, although mentioned, was secondary to recommendations related to "the full realization of the potential of the sea."[46]

A major recommendation of the commission in 1970 was to create an independent National Oceanic and Atmospheric Administration (NOAA) to ensure "the full and wise use of the marine environment"—language remarkably similar to the terms used by Gifford Pinchot in references to other natural resources. At the time, the Nixon administration was examining a broad executive-branch reorganization plan, with one proposal that would replace the Department of the Interior with a new Department of Natural Resources. The new department would include NOAA and some elements of the Environmental Science Services Administration (ESSA) of the Department of Commerce. Due to political tensions between the White House and the Secretary of the Interior, turf battles led to the inclusion of NOAA within Commerce under Reorganization Plan #4 of 1970.[47]

The reorganization did not include all of the Stratton Commission's recommendations (including one that would have included the Coast Guard under NOAA), but it did extend the Department of Commerce's jurisdiction in programs ranging from the Marine Minerals Technology Center (from the Department of the Interior) and the National Data Buoy Project (from the Department of Transportation) to the National Oceanographic Data Center, previously managed by the U.S. Navy. Nixon's executive order to create NOAA resulted in a merger of some of the nation's oldest agencies, including the United States Coast and Geodetic Survey, created in 1807, the Weather Bureau (formed in 1870), and the Bureau of Commercial Fisheries (1871).[48]

Following the 1970 reorganization, the primary policy instrument was the Oceans Act of 2000,[49] which directs the president to consult with state and local governments and other nonfederal interests on the most pressing issues facing the nation regarding the use and stewardship of ocean and coastal resources. Implementation of the act took place under the jurisdiction of the little-publicized U.S. Commission on Ocean Policy, a sixteen-member group appointed by the president, which first met in September 2001. The commission's work product was fleeting; its charter expired December 19, 2004, as provided for under the terms of the act.

While the commission was developing its initial suite of recommendations, including the establishment of a National Ocean Council in the Executive Office of the President, and a doubling of the U.S. investment in ocean research, a private eighteen-member commission was established by the Pew Charitable Trust. The group's purpose was to focus on "improving ocean stewardship through recommendations to sustain marine life." For more than two years, the Pew Oceans Commission conducted a national dialogue on ocean issues, with fifteen regional meetings, public hearings, and workshops, along with twelve focus groups with fishers. The May 2003 report noted that America's oceans are in crisis, and the government is not making the best use of information already at hand. "The root of this crisis is a failure of both perspective and governance," the report notes. "We have failed to conceive of the oceans as our largest public domain, to be managed holistically for the greater public good in perpetuity."[50]

The Pew group's report focused attention on the dimensions of coastal development and associated sprawl, degradation of coastal rivers and bays, and invasive species that have established themselves in coastal waters. Both commissions recognized overfishing and destructive fishing practices. But the Pew report traced the problem to the Stratton Commission and its reflection of the values of an earlier effort characterizing U.S. ocean governance as being in disarray. "We have continued to approach our oceans with a frontier mentality. The result is a hodge-podge of ocean laws and programs that do not provide unified, clearly stated goals and measurable objectives. Authority over marine resources is fragmented geographically and institutionally."[51]

The Pew report called for a more substantial investment in understanding and managing oceans resulting from changes in perspectives on ocean resources over the last thirty years. "National ocean policy and governance must be realigned to reflect and apply principles of ecosystem health and integrity, sustainability, and precaution. Decisions should be founded upon the best available science and flow from processes that are equitable, transparent, and collaborative."[52]

Stakeholder reaction to the two panels' reports was supportive, but not widely publicized. Acknowledging the unexpected attention to ocean and marine policy after a gap of three decades, some organizations were cautiously optimistic, noting that the recommendations would require a test of political willpower.[53] But as was the case with the Oceans Commission, the Pew Group ceased its work in 2003, indicating that marine policy was slipping down the environmental-policy agenda.

Some groups, noting the impact of the December 2004 tsunami disaster in southeast Asia, tracked legislative responses that authorized additional funding for ocean research and education, along with improved coastal observation data systems. But the tsunami came more than eighteen months after the Pew study was released, and eight months after the U.S. Commission on Ocean Policy's preliminary report was released. A more likely policy driver is national security and, as the U.S. Department of State notes, "the ability to freely navigate and overfly the oceans as essential preconditions for projecting military power."[54]

Statements like this one are important because they indicate that current U.S. ocean policy, while giving lip service to ecological and scientific issues, is at its core an effort to balance interests among competing objectives. "The alternative is increased competition, and conflict over control of the oceans and marine resources to the potential detriment of the United States' interests and the marine environment generally."[55]

Another issue that has plagued U.S. oceans has been coastal pollution, which comes under the jurisdiction of the EPA, which sets standards for water pollution. Responsibility for monitoring beaches is left to the states, whose primary task is controlling sources of beachwater contamination such as runoff from roads and agricultural areas, sewage discharges, boating waste, and stormwater. According to the 2009 report of the Natural Resources Defense Council (NRDC), "Testing the Waters," pollution caused the number of beach closings and advisories to hit their fourth-highest level in the history of the report in 2008. The number of closing and advisory days at ocean, bay, and Great Lakes beaches topped 20,000 for the fourth consecutive year, confirmation, the group said, that the nation's beaches continue to suffer from serious water pollution that puts swimmers at risk.[56]

The problem lies with state and local governments that have failed to implement the federal Beaches Environmental Assessment and Coastal Health (BEACH) Act of 2000, which represents amendments to the Federal Water Pollution Control Act by adding several new sections related to water quality criteria, monitoring, and notification. What the legislation and subsequent rules do not do, however, are enforce controls on pollution sources that lead to conditions such as skin rashes, respiratory infections, meningitis, and hepatitis.

Of particular concern are outdated standards and testing methods. The EPA established recommended health standards for pathogens in 1986, but several environmental groups challenged the agency to update its beachwater-quality standards by 2012 as part of a legal settlement. The EPA will now be required to conduct new health studies and swimmer surveys, approve a water-testing method that will produce same-day results, and protect beach visitors from a broader range of waterborne illnesses.[57]

Typical of many environmental issues, polluted beaches and coastal areas are ignored until there is a focusing event, such as when medical waste washed up on eastern U.S. shores where children were playing. With minimal funding from Congress under the Bush administration, and minimal concern by the public, the issue has languished on the policy agenda for more than two decades. While groups like the NRDC hope that their reports will garner media attention during the summer when they are released annually, the publicity (and public interest) tends to evaporate as children head back to school in the fall and as policymakers move on to less seasonally important issues.

The United States also faces the issue of overfishing of some of its key stocks, but unlike most of the country's maritime policies, the problems are being dealt with at a different governmental level. In the United States, state regulators have taken a key role in protecting local fisheries. In California, for instance, the state Fish and Game Commission voted in 2009 to restrict fishing off more than 20 percent of the state's coastline, moving to enact a historic measure that implements the second of five complexes of reserves and conservation areas. The complexes would create a network along California's 1,100-mile coast to allow dwindling stocks, including rockfish, abalone, and Dungeness crab to rebound.[58]

GLOBAL OCEANS POLICY

U.S. ocean policy focuses on the reconciliation of science and socioeconomic issues that are often based on political will. In contrast, on the global level, the two major ocean-related environmental-policy issues are (1) protection of the world's marine resources and (2) control of marine pollution. Both issues are multifaceted, and few international regimes have successfully dealt with oceanic policy.

One reason for the lack of effective agreements is that we know very little about the oceans; as a result, policymakers are perceived as hesitant and less inclined to sign treaties that might negatively affect their nation in the future. In addition, the oceans affect virtually every country—even landlocked ones—and a rogue state or major international stakeholder can thwart policymaking simply by refusing to adhere to or sign a regime. These problems frame the issue of ocean politics, beginning with the protection of marine resources.

Overfishing

Overfishing is perhaps one of the most critical issues. Fish are an important renewable resource, serving as both a food source and as income for much of the developing world. Once thought of as an inexhaustible bounty of food, marine resources are quickly being depleted because of technological advances and the world's increasing appetite for fish. Awareness of the problem began in 1936 after the publication of John Steinbeck's novel *Cannery Row*, which chronicled the Pacific sardine fishery and the abundance of the sea. Less than thirty years later, the fishery collapsed, and small sardine-fishing enterprises are only now beginning to open. A similar event occurred in Peru from the 1950s to the 1970s, when anchovy fishing made up about one-fifth of the world's entire fish take. In what has been called "the most spectacular collapse in the history of fisheries exploitation," annual landings plunged from 10 million metric tons to less than 1 million metric tons within the next ten years.[59] The UN Food and Agriculture Organization (FAO) estimates that 52 percent of the world's marine fishery resources are fully exploited, and another 24 percent are overexploited. In some areas, catches of commercially valuable fish species may be three times greater than permitted levels due to illegal, unreported, and unregulated (IUU) fishing activities. Production levels in twelve of the FAO's sixteen world fishing regions have fallen to historically low levels.[60]

Global fisheries governance is a patchwork of programs and regimes that reveal a lack of international consensus on global overfishing. The United Nations serves as a forum for many current agreements, such as the 1995 United Nations Agreement on Straddling and Highly Migratory Fish Stocks, also known as the UN Fish Agreement, or UNFA. The UNFA is a framework convention for the management of fish stocks in high seas. Regional fisheries management organizations (RFMOs) exist to deal with issues specific to particular areas (such as the Northwest Atlantic Fisheries Organization), with groups that focus on specific species (Save the Stripers, Menhaden Matter), with legal advocates (the NRDC, the Conservation Law Foundation), or with industrial fisheries. Other stakeholders include processing companies, fishing-boat owners, fisher associations, and indigenous culture organizations.

Driftnets

Among the more controversial overfishing issues is the use of driftnets. These nets hang vertically like curtains in the open ocean and stretch for twenty to forty miles, sweeping over an area of the ocean the size of Ohio. The nearly invisible nets, invented in Japan, are suspended by floats at the ocean's surface and catch fish by their gills as they attempt to swim through. In addition to being extremely efficient at catching fish, the driftnets capture marine mammals, birds, and nontarget fish (called *bycatch*). The Sierra Club estimated that 7 million dolphins were killed between the 1960s and 1980s, when driftnets were commonly used. Driftnets were also blamed for a 1988 crash in the Alaska pink-salmon industry, when Alaskan trawlers took only 12 million fish, rather than an expected 40 million.[61] The use of driftnets virtually ended in 1990 when American environmental organizations urged a boycott of any tuna that was caught in drift nets because of the damage done to the dolphin population. The action led to the labeling of cans as "dolphin-safe" when several companies began to comply. In 1995, the United States and ten other fishing nations agreed that there would be a move towards dolphin-safe fishing practices so that their catch would be allowed into the U.S. market.

A year later, the Clinton administration proposed reversing the ban that allowed only dolphin-safe tuna into the U.S. market and allowed the use of the nets. In an unusual division among environmental organizations, groups such as Greenpeace, the World Wildlife Federation, the National Wildlife Federation, and the Environmental Defense Fund agreed with Vice President Al Gore's proposal to reinstate driftnet use. Their position was that the fishing industry had improved the methods by which tuna are caught. But the proposal was strongly opposed by the Sierra Club and the Earth Island Institute, which called Gore's plan "the dolphin death act."[62]

Driftnet policy stems from the Wellington Convention, also known as the Convention for the Prohibition of Fishing with Long Driftnets in the South Pacific, which entered into force in 1992, but the convention applies only to fishing vessels engaged in driftnet fishing within the convention area. The European Union (EU) also began prohibiting most driftnet use in 1992, and it adopted a more comprehensive ban in 2002. Driftnets continue to be used in the Mediterranean, especially by non-EU countries fishing for bluefin tuna and swordfish.

Marine Pollution

Land-based marine pollution (LBMP) contributes over 70 percent of the oceans' toxic contaminants, creating an overload of nutrients, dredged materials, and synthetic organic compounds that pose a threat when they are taken up through the food chain. They become a human health hazard when they accumulate in food fish, affecting coastal residents who depend upon fish as a primary food source. Floating debris—like bottles and other nonbiodegradable items—and pollution from oil tankers keep this problem in the arena of public interest. Small discharges from ships are more commonplace and sometimes more harmful than tanker spills. The chemical composition of oil varies, as does its environmental impact. Spills in the open ocean, for example, can be more easily dispersed by wind and wave action than can pollution resulting from a spill in a smaller setting.

Marine pollution poses some serious environmental-policy issues that are complicated by the nature of the oceans themselves. First, there is much uncertainty about the short- and long-term effects of ocean pollution. Scientists are still not sure of the potential impact on human health or of the ability of the oceans to adapt to change. Evidence suggests that the marine food chain is easily disrupted and that any major changes could affect the chemical balance between marine organisms and seawater.

Second, marine pollution includes not only what is dumped into the oceans but also its effect on coastal zones and beaches and the world's thirty-five major seas, some coastal and some enclosed by land. Demographic changes are also leading to an increase in land-based marine pollution. Over half the world's population lives within a 120-mile coastal strip representing only 10 percent of the Earth's entire land surface. The residue of coastal life runs into the ocean, where it contaminates ecosystems and can lead to atmospheric deposition. Millions of dollars of tourist business are estimated to be lost every time beaches are closed because of pollution when debris washes ashore. Six of these great bodies of water—the Baltic, Mediterranean, Black, Caspian, Yellow, and South China Seas—are suffering from ecosystem disasters to the point where they are on the verge of collapse.

The political system has approached the protection of the oceans and its resources in several ways, beginning in 1926 with an agreement by seven nations to control oil pollution. In 1954, for example, in response to the growing transport industry, thirty-two nations met to draft the International Convention for the Prevention of Pollution of the Sea by Oil (OILPOL). Representing 95 percent of the world's shipping tonnage, the parties prohibited discharges of oil within fifty miles of the coast, with fines extended to ports that were unable to accommodate waste oil. The act was amended and strengthened in 1962 and 1969, when provisions were attached regulating any type of ship discharges.[63]

Recognizing the limitations of existing oil-pollution regulations, several more agreements were signed over the next ten years: the London Dumping Convention (1972), which limited the disposal of many pollutants at sea, including high-level radioactive waste, and the MARPOL Convention (1973), also known as the Convention of the Prevention of Pollution by Ships. In 1974, the UN Environment Programme prioritized oceans through the creation of the Regional Seas Programme. The program, which covers ten regions and involves more than 120 coastal states, is one of the few regional approaches to solving common-pool problems. The International Convention on Oil Pollution Preparedness, Response, and Cooperation, adopted in 1990, requires parties to establish measures for dealing with pollution incidents, either nationally or in cooperation with other countries. Ships are required to develop and carry an oil pollution emergency plan, and to report incidents to coastal authorities. Parties to the convention, which entered into force in 1995, are required to assist others in the event of a pollution emergency, and provision is made for the reimbursement of any assistance provided.[64]

UN CONVENTION ON THE LAW OF THE SEA

Since the seventeenth century, the oceans have been subject to the "freedom of the seas" doctrine—a principle that essentially limits national rights and jurisdiction over the oceans to a narrow belt of sea surrounding a nation's coastline. The remainder of the seas was proclaimed to be free and belonging to no one—a part of the global commons shared by all. But by the mid-twentieth century, a combination of technology, competing claims to offshore resources, the threat of pollution, and overfishing led to international conflict and instability.

The United States was at the forefront of the challenges to the doctrine; in 1945, President Harry S. Truman unilaterally extended U.S. jurisdiction over all natural resources on the nation's continental shelf; this move was followed with similar actions by Argentina (1946), Chile and Peru (1947), and, in 1950, Ecuador, which asserted its rights over a 200-mile zone. After World War II, Egypt, Ethiopia, Saudi Arabia, Libya, Venezuela, and some Eastern European countries claimed a twelve-mile territorial sea, and several southeast Asian countries claimed rights over the waters separating their island nations.[65]

Although calls for an international regime for the oceans had been made in the late 1950s and 1960s, the Third United Nations Convention on the Law of the Sea (UNCLOS) was not convened until 1973, ending nine years later with the 1982 adoption of the UN Convention on the Law of the Sea, considered by some to be one of the twentieth century's most notable achievements in international diplomacy. The convention was adopted as a package deal, to be accepted as a whole in all its parts without reservation on any aspect. What makes this agreement so important is its comprehensiveness; it establishes more equitable relationships among the member states and distinct zones of sovereignty and jurisdiction for coastal nations. Its 320 articles and nine annexes include rules for the high seas and the rights and duties of members with respect to navigation, protection of the marine environment, and research. It lays down rules for drawing sea boundaries, transit passage for international navigation, and the establishment of a 200-nautical-mile exclusive economic zone (EEZ) over which coastal states have sovereign rights with respect to natural resources and economic activities.

The UNCLOS agreement provides the legal framework to govern the oceans and their resources, recognizing for the first time that the resources of the deep seabed are part of the world's common heritage. The convention did not enter into force until 1994, a year after it obtained the necessary sixty ratifications. A key feature of the convention is an elaborate system of dispute-settlement mechanisms, including compulsory procedures entailing binding decisions by the International Tribunal for the Law of the Sea and the Commission on the Limits of the Continental Shelf. Landlocked and geographically disadvantaged nations have the opportunity, under the agreement, to participate in exploiting part of the zones' fisheries on an equitable basis, with special protection given to highly migratory species of fish and mammals.[66]

The United States initially refused to ratify the convention, and in 1994, Secretary of State Warren Christopher announced that the United States would accept changes that made the agreement more acceptable to business interests. One of the more controversial issues dealt with the mining rights to the seabed floor, a proposal that President Ronald Reagan had rejected in 1982, saying it clashed with free-enterprise principles by requiring mining companies to pay substantial royalties and to share sophisticated technology with developing countries.[67] American negotiators eventually developed an acceptable provision that allows the United States and other industrial countries to have an effective veto over the convention's administrative body, the International Seabed Authority. Despite a 2004 recommendation from the U.S. Commission on Ocean Policy that the United States accede to the convention, the U.S. Senate still refuses to ratify the agreement.

The treaty is typical of the kinds of disputes that are becoming increasingly common between rich and poor countries in dealing with common-pool resources. Wealthy nations such as the United States resent being asked (or forced) to share their more advanced technology with newly developing or poorer countries. There is additional antagonism when poorer countries demand some form of redistribution of wealth in the belief that the oceans and their resources should be more equitably shared. Although the Law of the Sea is now in force, there will undoubtedly be continuing ethical and economic disputes as the convention is fully implemented.

Various theoretical explanations have been put forth as to why some countries seem to have taken a more aggressive approach than others have to resolving common-pool resource problems like those regarding the oceans. Leaders commonly possess a more advanced domestic environmental-policy apparatus, and often are subject to more intense domestic political pressure than other countries. Leaders are most often motivated by being the first to suffer environmental damage; being the first often means being most severely affected as well.[68]

Laggard states, in contrast, may have only a minimal interest in environmental protection or may lack the resources to do so. At times, laggard states may oppose a policy because of economic interests that outweigh environmental ones, or they may be pressured by domestic interests to take a more conservative approach.

This model appears applicable to virtually all of the issues and agreements outlined in this chapter. What the model does not do, however, is provide a sense of how environmental concerns might be made more salient to nations that face daunting economic challenges, or to those leaders who prioritize short-term economic visions over long-term environmental concerns that affect the entire planet.

FURTHER READING

Anthony D. Barnosky. *Heatstroke: Nature in an Age of Global Warming.* Covelo, CA: Island Press, 2009.

Nelson E. Burney, ed. *Carbon Tax and Cap-and-Trade Tools: Market-Based Approaches for Controlling Greenhouse Gases.* Nova Science Publishing, 2010.

Graciela Chichilnisky. *Saving Kyoto: An Insider's Guide to the Kyoto Protocol.* London: Holland Publishers, 2009.

Gary Kroll. *America's Ocean Wilderness: A Cultural History of Twentieth Century Exploration.* Lawrence: University Press of Kansas, 2008.

Justin Lewis and Tammy Boyce, eds. *Climate Change and the Media*. Bern, Switzerland: Peter Lang Publishing, 2010.

Karen McLeod and Heather Leslie. *Ecosystem-Based Management for the Oceans*. Covelo, CA: Island Press, 2009.

David Orr. *Down to the Wire: Controlling Climate Collapse*. Oxford, UK: Oxford University Press, 2009.

Stephen Peake and Joe Smith. *Climate Change: From Science to Sustainability*. Oxford, UK: Oxford University Press, 2010.

Callum Roberts. *The Unnatural History of the Sea*. Washington, DC: Shearwater, 2009.

11

Population and Sustainability

"When my body started burning, I went to my mother and
said, 'Give me water quickly, my skin is scorching.'"
—HASINA AKTER, BANGLADESH ACID-ATTACK VICTIM[1]

Hasina Akter's attack did not make headlines. Every two days, on average,
someone in Bangladesh is injured by an acid attack; 70 percent of the
victims are women. Acid is inexpensive in the country, where it is used for the
dying of textiles and crafting of jewelry. Five years ago, Hasina was attacked by a
man who was an employee of her father after she scolded him for wasting water.
He retaliated by throwing a jar of acid through an open window onto her face.
Her family poured water on the burns and a friend drove her to a hospital as the
acid melted her skin. After undergoing months of surgery and skin grafts, Hasina
was transferred to the Acid Survivors Foundation, run by Monira Rahman,
started in 1999. The organization says that acid disputes are becoming increasingly common for men in South or Southeast Asia to destroy the beauty of
women who have spurned them. "They think, 'If I take [her] beauty away, no
one will marry her."[2] The organization has been honored by the United Nations
Population Fund (UNFPA) for helping to counter gender-based violence. The
attack on Hasina Akter is exemplary of the types of impacts of a burgeoning
world population, pressures on women trying to climb over barriers imposed
by a lack of education and poverty, and constraints on resources that have
brought population and sustainability back to the political agenda.

On October 12, 2009, the United Nations General Assembly officially
commemorated the fifteenth anniversary of the International Conference on
Population and Development (ICPD). In 1994, 179 countries met in Cairo, with

a goal of developing a global Programme of Action for the next twenty years that would link the alleviation of poverty to women's rights and universal access to reproductive health. The "Cairo Consensus" gave priority to investing in people and broadening opportunities, rather than reducing population growth. According to the United Nations Population Fund, the program was firmly grounded in the affirmation of the human rights of all people and centrality of reproductive health, which it defined as "complete physical, mental, and social well being" in all areas related to the reproductive system and processes.[3] Fifteen years later, inadequate resources, gender bias, and gaps in serving the poor and adolescents are undermining further progress while challenges mount, as outlined in Table 11.1.

Population growth and the increased consumption and pollution accompanying it pose a profound challenge to the idea of ecological sustainability. This chapter explores the struggle to manage human population growth from an environmental perspective and the challenges of sustainability. It begins by presenting a summary of the U.S. role in the family-planning debate, the scale of the global population boom, and the factors that have caused the problems to be more acute in some areas than in others, identifying trends and projections. It reviews the evidence for the assumption that not enough natural resources are available, even with enhanced technology, to provide for the growing number of individuals born each year if present demographic trends continue into the new millennium. The chapter then outlines the nature of the policy shifts that now go beyond reproductive health to an emphasis on a global effort to end poverty and work toward sustainability.

THE ROLE OF THE UNITED STATES

Domestically, population-management efforts within the United States are authorized under Title X of the Public Health Service Act, created in 1970. The only federal program devoted exclusively to family planning and reproductive health, it is administered through the Office of Population Affairs under the budget of the Health Resources and Services Administration, a part of the Cabinet-level Department of Health and Human Services. Title X funding ($307.5 million for fiscal year 2009) supports a nationwide network of about 4,600 community-based clinics serving 5 million persons per year. Clinics provide family planning services to low-income and uninsured individuals regardless of their ability to pay.[4]

The U.S. Department of State's Bureau of Population, Refugees, and Migration (PRM) holds primary responsibility for developing and implementing the administration's policies on population, refugees, and migration; it also administers refugee assistance and admissions programs. Along with the U.S. Agency for International Development (AID), which administers U.S. international population programs, PRM coordinates U.S. international population policy through bilateral and multilateral agreements.[5]

TABLE 11.1   World Population Trends, by the Numbers

- The world's population is expected to increase from 6.8 billion in 2005 to 8.9 billion by 2050.
- The 50 poorest countries will triple in size, to 1.7 billion people.
- Overall population growth has declined from 2 percent in 1970 to 1.3 percent in 2005.
- In 2000, young adults aged 15 to 29 comprised more than 40 percent of all adults in 100 nations.
- In most African countries, over half the population is under the age of 15.
- There are 1.2 billion people between the ages of 10 and 19 on Earth as of 2005.
- 61% of married couples are using modern contraception in developing world countries today, compared with 10% to 15% in 1960.
- About 350 million women still lack access to a full range of contraceptive methods.
- Between 2000 and 2015, the number of reproductive-aged couples is expected to grow by 23%.
- The number of children born each day is roughly 225,000.
- The number of women in Africa who will have an unsafe abortion each day is 10,000.
- The lifetime risk of a woman dying in pregnancy or childbirth in West Africa is 1 in 12; in developed regions, the comparable risk is 1 in 4,000.
- The average number of children born per woman in the 1960s, worldwide, was 6.
- The average number of children born per woman today is just under 3.
- Half of the human population lives on or near the world's coasts.
- The number of urban dwellers will rise from 3 billion (48% of the total population) in 2003 to 5 billion (60%) by 2030.
- Today there are 20 cities of more than 10 million people, and 15 of those cities are in developing countries. By 2015, there will be 22 megacities, 16 of them in developing countries.
- Half a billion people live in countries defined as water-stressed or water-scarce; by 2025, that figure is expected to be between 2.4 billion and 3.4 billion people.
- Some 2.8 billion people still struggle to survive on less than $2 a day.
- 5 million new HIV infections occurred during 2003.
- Young people aged 15 to 24 account for half of all new HIV infections—one every 14 seconds.
- 1 in every 35 persons is an international migrant.

SOURCE: Compiled from: United Nations Population Fund. "State of the World Population 2004." http://www.unfpa.org/swp/2004/pdf/en_swp04.pdf. Accessed June 6, 2005.

The U.S. role in global family-planning efforts has been contradictory over time. It is a role that has resulted from changes in political leadership rather than from scientific investigation or research. The policy cycle began with the Foreign Assistance Act of 1961, which prohibited nongovernmental organizations

(NGOs) that receive federal funds from using those funds to pay for abortions as a method of family planning. AID began promoting large-scale national family-planning programs funded through international aid in the early 1960s, providing health-care workers in many developing countries. Congress first earmarked foreign assistance appropriations in 1968, with nearly $4 billion in assistance allocated through AID over the next two decades. Initially, the United States also supported UN programs for education and family planning. But during the administration of President Ronald Reagan, the United States made an abrupt change in policy direction in August 1984 and adopted what came to be known as the Mexico City Policy. The United States cut off its support of the UNFPA and the International Planned Parenthood Federation, the largest multilateral agency and the largest private voluntary organization providing family-planning services in developing countries.

The sudden policy about-face became tied to the issue of abortion, even though U.S. law (the Foreign Assistance Act of 1961 and the 1973 Helms Amendment to the Foreign Assistance Act) explicitly prohibits government funding for abortion programs overseas, and even though legal abortions are permitted in only a few countries. In 1985, the Kemp-Kasten Amendment to the Foreign Assistance Act banned any U.S. contribution to "any organization or program that supports or participates in the management of a program of coercive abortion or involuntary sterilization." The passage of the legislation effectively cut off U.S. support to China's family-planning program, which was alleged to force women to have abortions, despite denials by the Chinese government. Congressional attempts to restore the UN funding by stipulating that the money not be spent in China were vetoed by President George H. W. Bush in November 1989.[6] The Bush administration's position puzzled those who pointed out that by cutting back its aid to the UN program, the United States was actually encouraging the demand for abortion in those nations where there are no other alternatives.

The United States stood virtually alone in its refusal to contribute to the UN program, having previously been the primary donor. But after the U.S. policy change, Germany, Canada, the United Kingdom, Japan, and the Scandinavian countries increased their donations, with Japan becoming the major donor and exceeding what the United States had previously contributed.[7] After years of congressional debate, the result was that from 1986 to 1992 the United States eliminated all contributions to the UN program, with only a few bilateral assistance programs remaining intact.

In 1993, the Clinton administration reversed prior policies and began restoring U.S. aid to the UN program, with $430 million earmarked for international population assistance—the most ever contributed in the history of the program. In 1996, Congress agreed to appropriate $385 million for international family-planning assistance and defeated a proposal by House Republicans to limit assistance to any international program that spent its own funds on any kind of abortion-related services (everyone agreed that U.S. funds could not be used to provide these services). The law required another vote by Congress before the funds could be released, and one of the few pieces of legislation enacted during the first few months of the new Congress in 1997 released the funds.[8]

However, as the UNFPA marked its thirtieth anniversary in 1999, it was clear that the reduced participation of the United States had taken its toll on the organization's efforts to build integrative reproductive-health programs. A four-year decline in donor contributions resulted in a $72 million shortfall in 1999; available resources covered only two-thirds of the fund's commitments to country programs. The result, UN officials said, would be an additional 1.4 million unwanted pregnancies, 570,000 induced abortions, and over 670,000 unwanted births.

Responding to an urgent appeal for funds, the government of The Netherlands pledged an additional 10 million Dutch guilders (about $4.7 million) to the fund for 1999, and another $4 million was awarded by the United Nations Foundation, created by media mogul Ted Turner. His group's contribution allocated $2.3 million to improve adolescent reproductive health in the Pacific region; about $1.1 million to promote Jordanian adolescent girls' health and well-being; and $707,726 to enhance the reproductive health of adolescents in the Russian Federation.

In July 1999, the U.S. Congress voted to restore funding to the UNFPA in fiscal year 2000, due to increasing criticism of the U.S. role. The action was tied to another brokered agreement under which the United States would pay about $1 billion in back dues to the United Nations to retain its voting rights, with a restriction that the funds not be used for any international family-planning groups that support abortion. Women's groups and organizations like Planned Parenthood described the action as a compromise that made the women of the world the bargaining chip.

A new president—George W. Bush—brought a new agenda and another shift in policy. The president had sent a three-member fact-finding committee to China in 2002 to determine whether allegations of forced abortions were true. The committee returned to the United States and wrote in a State Department report that the United Nations program did not knowingly support coercive abortions. In fact, the report concluded that UN programs improved women's lives by helping them prevent unwanted pregnancies through education and birth control, reducing the need for abortions.

The president ignored the report, signing into law the Foreign Operations, Export Financing, and Related Programs Appropriations Act of 2002. In signing the legislation, aimed primarily at the country's war on terrorism, the president included a statement that said the bill does not interfere with U.S. policies regarding bilateral international family planning assistance, ensuring "that U.S. funds are not made available to organizations supporting or participating in the management of a program of coercive abortion or involuntary sterilization." The act also gave the president additional discretion to determine the appropriate level of funding for UNFPA; he subsequently directed that the appropriated funds be transferred to the Child Survival and Health Programs Fund administered by the U.S. Agency for International Development.[9]

Although Congress had agreed to appropriate the funds for UNFPA ($40 million in the 2009 budget year), legislation also gave President Bush the authority to decline to spend the money. The fund's executive director, as well as other family-planning groups, said they were disheartened by the president's action, since one goal of the UNFPA is to encourage women to use voluntary family planning to avoid abortion.

But in January 2009, the political pendulum that has become known as the "Mexico City Policy" (after the city where the U.S. delegation first announced it at the UN Conference on Population) swung back again, as newly elected president Barack Obama quietly issued an executive order striking down the Bush-era ban. The reversal of the Bush administration policy had been a fixture of the presidential campaign for both Obama and candidate Hillary Clinton, but the president's announcement was made with little fanfare.[10] The administration followed up the policy change with a $50 million check to the UNFPA in March 2009, the first time in eight years that the United States had made a voluntary contribution to the organization. But the contribution, made toward paying U.S. dues to the UNFPA, made only a slight dent in what the country actually owed; the United States was $230 million behind in its dues. In 2008, the entire budget of the population organization was $430 million.

The president's actions led to the usual outcry from pro-life and pro-choice organizations. The legislative director of the National Right to Life Committee criticized the president's actions, noting, "President Obama not long ago told the American people that he would support policies to reduce abortions, but today he is effectively guaranteeing more abortions by funding groups that promote abortion as a method of population control." In contrast, the advocacy group Population Action International said that the Bush policy had "severely impacted" women's health and that the Obama announcement "will help reduce the number of unintended pregnancies, abortions, and women dying from high-risk pregnancies because they don't have access to family planning."[11]

SUSTAINABLE DEVELOPMENT

In 1968, when Paul Ehrlich's book *The Population Bomb* first appeared, most Americans were shocked. Ehrlich predicted a population explosion accompanied by massive famine and starvation—a prophecy that did not come to pass. The reason? In the mid-1970s, there was a slight decline in the global population growth rate, and it looked as though the population might stabilize at about 10.2 billion toward the end of the next century. Many demographers called Ehrlich an alarmist, while others argued that population growth was actually a positive force because it accelerated progress and development, forcing humanity to use more ingenuity and resourcefulness. Regardless of the timeliness of the prediction, Ehrlich was correct in pointing out that the Earth is a closed system, with limited resources. How can policymakers deal with population growth, no matter what the actual rate of increase might be, and insufficient resources for that population?

A key phrase often used to answer that question, and one that has appeared often in this book, is *sustainable development*. The term is used to describe policies that balance the needs of people today against the resources that will be needed in the future. It takes into consideration policies related to agriculture production, energy efficiency, health, reduction of poverty, and reduction in consumption. Individuals practice this concept when they recycle cans, bottles, newspapers, and plastics; carpool to work or bicycle instead of commuting alone in automobiles; turn their thermostats down to use less electricity; or install solar heating systems in their home. Each of these actions is recognition that the Earth's resources are not unlimited and that we must restrict our consumption of those resources.

The possibility of sustainable development is built on the idea of carrying capacity. The carrying capacity of an ecosystem is the limit of resource consumption and pollution production that it can maintain without undergoing a significant transformation. If the carrying capacity is exceeded, life cannot continue unless it adapts to a new level of consumption or receives external resources. Carrying capacity is affected by three main factors: the size of the human population, the per-capita consumption of resources, and the pollution and environmental degradation resulting from consumption of each unit of resources. The task of the residents of any ecosystem is to determine the level of resource consumption and pollution production that is sustainable. That level may not be obvious until it is too late, but there are some intermediate indicators, such as the buildup of pollution and an increase in the resultant harms or a decline in a resource as it is depleted more rapidly than it is replenished. According to the WorldWatch Institute, some question exists whether the Earth can even carry today's population at a "moderately comfortable" standard for the long term, let alone with 3 billion more people.[12]

Population growth and consumption in the wealthy countries are the primary sources of global environmental threats. Although population growth rates have stabilized in these nations, consumption of resources and generation of pollution and wastes continue to grow. But population growth in the developing world increases the pressure on the biosphere. The problems of environmental degradation and poverty are intricately intertwined. Many of the most pressing environmental problems are the by-products of modern, industrialized life. As one writer put it, "poverty can drive ecological deterioration when desperate people overexploit their resource base, sacrificing the future to salvage the present." Environmental decline "perpetuates poverty, as degraded ecosystems offer diminishing yields to their poor inhabitants. A self-feeding downward spiral of economic deprivation and ecological degradation takes hold."[13] People in the developing world depend immediately and directly on natural resources for their survival. In their struggle for survival, the poor of the world are likely to harm their environment and make their survival even more tenuous. Further, as resources are stretched for survival, poorer countries will be even less able to mediate the effects of climate change and other problems—unlike residents of the developed world, who will have the resources to protect themselves against at least some environmental threats.

The idea of sustainable development as used by the World Bank, United Nations, industry groups, and others is a very optimistic concept assuming that economic growth will produce the wealth to pay for technological innovations that reduce environmental impacts. Free trade, neoliberal restructuring of national economies and policies, and economic growth and consumption are all compatible with environmental sustainability. But this view of sustainability clashes with the ideas of carrying capacity and scarcity.[14] Studies by ecologists point to an inevitable crisis as exponential growth clashes with the finite resources of Earth. Developed by the Club of Rome, the Limits to Growth computer model—one of the earliest projections of the future of natural resources, technology, and pollution—concluded that by the year 2100, most nonrenewable resources would be exhausted, food supplies would dwindle, and massive famine and pollution would cause widespread deaths.[15] Many have criticized that study, but few challenge the idea of limits; disagreements focus on when they will occur and how the variables interact.

Some optimists believe that pollution in the Western world "will end within our lifetime." They argue that the "most feared environmental catastrophes, such as runaway global warming," are unlikely. Environmentalism, "which binds nations to a common concern, will be the best thing that's ever happened to international relations."[16] Nearly all technical trends are toward new devices and modes of production that are more efficient, use fewer resources, produce less waste, and cause less ecological disruption than technology of the past. Others find that "just about every important measure of human welfare shows improvement over the decades and centuries"—life expectancy, price of raw materials, price of food, cleanliness of the environment, population growth, extinction of species, and the quality of farmland.[17] Some economists argue that we will never deplete resources—Earth's air, water, and crust will serve Earth-dwellers for millions of years to come. The problem is not the existence of these resources, "but whether we are willing to pay the price to extract and use those resources."[18]

The optimists may be right in claiming that human ingenuity can respond to these problems and reverse these troubling trends. But the inexorable pressure from exponential growth threatens to overwhelm even the most optimistic projections. "We may be smart enough to devise environmentally friendly solutions to scarcity," one scholar has written, but we must emphasize "early detection and prevention of scarcity, not adaptation to it." But if we are not as smart and as proactive as optimists claim we are, "we will have burned our bridges: the soils, waters, and forests will be irreversibly damaged, and our societies, especially the poorest ones, will be so riven with discord that even heroic efforts at social renovation will fail."[19]

Another View, Another Voice: Ernest Callenbach

In Ernest Callenbach's world, Ecotopia, sustainable living was such an important concept that Oregon, Washington, and northern California seceded from the rest of the United States to form their own new country. *Ecotopia*, which Callenbach self-published in 1975, tells of a society in which recycling is the norm, bicycles are freely available for people to use, and maglev trains have replaced the internal combustion engine. In Ecotopia, people eat locally and work off their aggression in war games, rather than participating in wars against others.

Callenbach could not find a publisher for his book in 1974, and was told that it was neither a novel or a tract. "Somebody said the ecology trend was over," he says. "I was on the point of burning it." But he persevered, collecting small checks from friends to pay for 2,500 copies to be printed. It has now sold more than a million copies, becoming one of the cult classics of the environmental movement and influencing the development of the Green Party throughout the world.

The author, who has been referred to as a visionary of sustainability, was born in 1929 in Williamsport, Pennsylvania. He attended the University of Chicago, and earned a master's degree in English and communications, specializing in film as an art form. He moved to California and from 1955 to 1991 was on the staff of the University of California Press in Berkeley, where he edited *Film Quarterly* and occasionally taught film courses. He also edited the Natural History Guides at the University of California Press, and became associated with social essayists and thinkers throughout the West Coast who shared his views on technology and human value systems.

Ecotopia is one of several books Callenbach has written, many of them espousing a nontraditional view of society that has been influenced by Edward Abbey and Henry Thoreau. In *Living Poor with Style* (1972), his first book, he writes of ways people can live in a more

sustainable world, followed in 1993 and 2000 with revisions called *Living Cheaply with Style: Live Better and Spend Less.* Those practical ideas eventually are interwoven into *Ecotopia* and a book that becomes the prequel to it, *Ecotopia Emerging*, published in 1981. He is also known for *Ecology: A Pocket Guide* (1998 and 2008) and *Bring Back the Buffalo! A Sustainable Future for America's Great Plains*, which was published in 2000. More recently, he has studied the Yamagishi movement of Japan, a group of several dozen sustainable communities that he believes are modeled after Ecotopia. They are founded on principles similar to those Callenbach used in the novel: living in harmony with the world, sustainable agriculture, democracy, localism, and mutual support. His nonreligious "Earth's Ten Commandments" unexpectedly ended up on a poster popular among environmentalists and ecologists.

Today, Callenbach lectures, tends to his garden, and watches as a new generation of readers learns about *Ecotopia*, which he calls "a lucky little book." It has become required reading at many colleges and universities, especially in courses dealing with literature and the environment. The book was reissued in 2008; Callenbach calls it "very Berkeley" and says that now when he speaks to students, "it apparently doesn't seem that weird to them at all."

SOURCES:
Ernest Callenbach. *Ecotopia*. New York: Bantam Books, 2008.
"Ernest Callenbach." http://www.permaculture.com/node/242. Accessed December 17, 2009.
"Ernest Callenbach Interview." http://www.openexchange.org/archives/Classics/callenbach.html. Accessed December 17, 2009.
Geov Parrish. "The Man Who Invented Ecotopia." *Seattle Weekly*. March 23, 2005. http://www.seattleweekly.com/2005-03-23/news/the-man-who-invented-ecotopia/. Accessed December 17, 2009.
Scott Timberg. "The Novel That Predicted Portland." *New York Times*. December 14, 2008. http://www.nytimes.com/2008/12/15/health/15iht-14ecotopia.18693526.html. Accessed December 17, 2009.

TRENDS IN POPULATION AND PROJECTIONS

In 1798, Thomas Robert Malthus published "An Essay on the Principle of Population," in which he first argued that the "power of population" is indefinitely greater than the power of the Earth to produce subsistence for humanity.[20] One idea that has subsequently dominated the study of demography—the

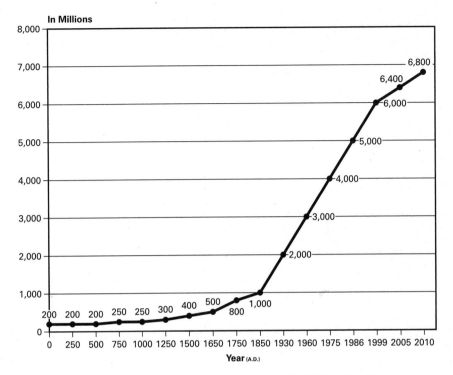

FIGURE 11.1 World Population Growth through (2010) (in millions)

SOURCE: U.S. Census Bureau. "World Population Information." http://www.census.gov/ipc/www/idb/worldpopinfo.php. Accessed January 31, 2010.

science of population—is demographic transition theory, a term used to describe a three-phase ecologic transition that leads to global overpopulation. In the first phase, human demands remain within limits that can be sustained by the environment, so there is enough food, water, and other resources for the needs of the population. In the second phase, human demands begin to exceed a sustainable limit and continue to grow. In the third phase, the ecosystem is unable to sustain the population, because there is little control over birth and death rates, and the system collapses.[21]

Although the demographic transition theory has been criticized,[22] many demographers believe that the Earth has already reached that third stage. The numbers of people already on the planet are staggering, and the projections for the future are considered even more alarming by some observers. The magnitude of growth in world population is disturbing, especially if we look closely at the last 150 years. Figure 11.1 provides a look at the milestone dates in world population growth from the year 1 A.D. through 2010.

As the growth curve in this figure indicates, it took 200 years (from 1650 to 1850) for the global population to double from 500 million to 1 billion, but it took only 45 years (from 1930 to 1975) for it to double from 2 billion to 4 billion, and the trend continues. The UN projections through the year 2025 show an

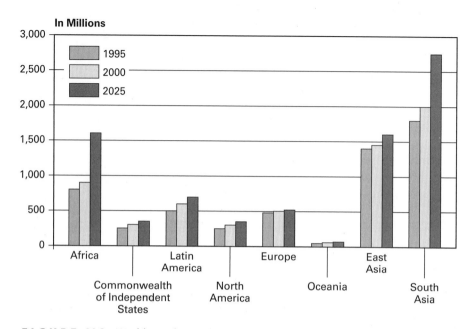

FIGURE 11.2 World Population Growth (1995–2025)

SOURCE: United Nations Population Fund. http://www.unfpa.org. Accessed June 25, 2005.

even greater increase, as seen in Figure 11.2. The world's total population is expected to grow to a projected 8.2 billion by 2025 and to 8.9 billion by 2050.

Demographers have identified several factors to which population increases in some regions can be attributed. Some of those changes began to occur long ago, and others are more recent in origin. First, there have been dramatic changes in our way of life and ability to survive. Humans' transition from hunting and gathering to the agricultural revolution about 8,000 years ago removed much of the risk of dying from starvation, raising the world's overall standard of living, and high death rates kept the number of people in the world from growing rapidly until the mid-eighteenth century. Second, in the category of more contemporary change, the rapid acceleration in growth after 1750 was almost entirely due to the declines in death rates that occurred with the Industrial Revolution. Rapid advances in science lowered the death rate by finding cures for common diseases that had previously wiped out large segments of the population. Introduction of the pesticide dichlorodiphenyltrichloroethane (DDT), for example, dramatically reduced deaths from malaria, which is transmitted by mosquitoes, and similar victories reduced deaths resulting from yellow fever, smallpox, cholera, and other infectious disease. Similarly, acknowledgment of the theory that germs were responsible for disease caused a gradual acceptance of basic sanitary practices such as washing hands and bathing, which further reduced the spread of disease. The impact of DDT and other health and technological advances can be seen clearly in Figure 11.1, where the growth curve begins its steep incline. Advances in medicine have also reduced infant mortality rates to the point where the birth rate continues to exceed the death rate—the bottom line in population growth. The result is that many fewer people die than are born each year.

A primary difficulty in making decisions about population policy is that, in the past, demographic data were often insufficient or contradictory, especially in developing nations. Since the 1970s, however, nearly every nation in the world has conducted some type of census or national population register. Studies of world population by various agencies and organizations have identified several critical trends that go far beyond previous concerns about the growth in population numbers:

1. There are differences in the ages of populations in the industrialized and developing worlds. At the beginning of the twenty-first century, four out of ten adults living in developing countries were aged fifteen to twenty-nine—what the WorldWatch Institute calls a "youth bulge." According to their report, "These youth-laden places were roughly two and a half times as likely to experience outbreaks of civil conflict in the 1990s as other nations. To avoid violence and unrest, governments need to address poverty and the lack of economic opportunity in the short term and high fertility rates in the long term."[23]

2. The population is becoming more urbanized, and due to rural-to-urban migration, the number of persons living in cities is growing twice as rapidly as total population growth. Most of the world's people were predicted to be living in cities by 2007, requiring more social services and resources.

3. Two out of five people struggle to survive on less than $2 per day. "Poverty perpetuates and is exacerbated by poor health, gender inequality, and rapid population growth," the UNFPA reports. "Policymakers have been slow to address the inequitable distribution of health information and services that helps keep people poor. Poor women give birth at earlier ages and have more children throughout their lives than wealthier women."[24]

4. In the past twenty years, the AIDS pandemic has killed more than 20 million people and infected nearly twice that number. In some areas of Sub-Saharan Africa, 25 percent of the workforce is HIV-positive. Studies show, the UN reports, that if 15 percent of a country's population is HIV-positive, its gross domestic product will decline by 1 percent a year, contributing to the cycle of poverty.

5. There were an estimated 175 million international migrants in the world in 2000, an increase from 79 million in 1960. The policy ramifications of migration are widespread, ranging from the tightening of borders to denying financial and social assistance to those entering a country illegally. World Bank economist Herman Daly observes that if globalization leads to uncontrolled migration of cheap labor all over the world, "the strains—on local communities and national economies, both sending and receiving—could be catastrophic." Daly notes, "Immigration is a policy, not a person."[25]

6. As economic reforms have opened up the economies of some nations, food production has increased. But much of the arable land in the less-developed countries is dedicated to the production of cash crops that are used to

generate foreign capital to service debt or finance economic development. Consequently, food production for domestic use suffers. Commodity prices are unstable; when they are high, exporting nations benefit, as revenues exceed those that would result from growing food. However, as world commodity prices have fallen, less revenue is available for debt service and development, and countries have to import food to make up for the shortfall in food grown for local people. Trade agreements prohibit exporting countries from processing food, thereby increasing their profits; shippers, brokers, processors, and wholesalers all live in developed countries and capture the bulk of the profits from food sales. Foreign debt, assistance programs that promote cash-crop production, pressures to generate foreign capital to pay for industrialization, inexorable pressure from population growth, and the increasing use of marginal lands for food production have combined to produce the food crisis in Africa and parts of Asia and Latin America. The problem is not one of scarcity as much as it is of the economic system by which food is distributed. Foreign aid is also a problem: Sending large shipments of food for distribution to poor nations sometimes disrupts domestic food production, drives down prices, and harms local farmers.

GLOBAL POPULATION AND SUSTAINABILITY EFFORTS

The UN has now become the primary agent of worldwide family-planning programs and has made a number of efforts to address the population-sustainability issue. The UN Fund for Population Activities was established as a trust fund in 1967, financed by voluntary contributions from members. During its first fifteen years, the fund allocated over $1 billion in family-planning assistance to member states. Following the 1968 UN Conference on Human Rights, the Tehran Proclamation identified the ability to control one's fertility and therefore access to birth control as a basic human right. The UN organization, renamed the UN Population Fund, has held five world conferences: in Rome (1954), Belgrade (1965), Bucharest (1974), Mexico City (1984), and Cairo (1994). At the Bucharest conference, the UN's World Population Programme of Action was established, led by the United States and other industrialized nations that urged developing countries to set targets for lowering their fertility rates. Many developing nations and Eastern Bloc nations rebelled, accusing the UN of supporting efforts by former colonial masters to suppress emerging nations and limit the strength of their armies. Ten years later, at the Mexico City conference, those misconceptions vanished as leaders from 150 nations committed themselves to voluntary reductions in population growth and strong national family-planning programs. Although there was continuing concern about the continuation of high population growth rates in developing nations, fertility rates had declined modestly since the Bucharest meeting.

In the years intervening between the population conferences, the UN's Conference on Environment and Development, held in 1992 in Rio de Janeiro, indicated how hesitant delegates were to tackle the population issue head-on. For example, the phrase "appropriate demographic policies" was substituted in conference documents for the more traditional phrase "family planning," and many representatives of NGOs were critical of industrialized countries, which they perceived as failing to take responsibility for their own overconsumption of resources. But the meeting did produce, as part of its Agenda 21, a chapter on demographic dynamics and sustainability. Delegates agreed that women's role should be strengthened and their rights fully recognized. They also noted that governments should ensure that women and men have the same right to decide freely and responsibly on the number and spacing of their children. But representatives of the Vatican and the Philippines were successful in weakening the exact language on family planning and in removing any remarks on contraceptives.[26]

At the 1994 Cairo conference, the issue of abortion overshadowed nearly every other agenda item. Delegates reached an uneasy compromise after (as one observer phrased it) "a Vatican-led handful of countries held the meeting hostage."[27]

The final document provided that abortions "should be safe" where they are legal and that they should "in no case … be promoted as a method of family planning."[28] Vatican officials argued that economic reform should be the major focus of global leaders: "Demographic growth is the child of poverty…. Rather than reduce the numbers at the world's table, you need to increase the courses and distribute them better."[29] Other religious groups and foundations launched campaigns aimed at drawing attention to overconsumption in the United States and other wealthy nations, paralleling arguments of economists that the United States needs to save and invest more and consume less.

The "Program of Action," a 113-page document approved in April 1994 by the UN committee responsible for the Cairo meeting, provides the basic outline for a twenty-year plan to promote women's rights and reduce population growth to 7.27 billion by 2015. A central theme embraced by nearly every one of the 150 delegates was the empowerment of women. Although few participants were completely happy with the results of the report, as one observer put it, "conferences and documents like these never get out ahead of where the people who agree to them are comfortable. What these conferences do is take an aerial snapshot of where we're at."[30]

One of the most promising products of the conference was the creation of "Partners in Population and Development: A South–South Initiative," announced by ten developing countries that came together to share their successes in reducing population growth. These successful strategies include offering a wide range of choices for family planning and careful integration with local cultural and political conditions. The Women's Environment and Development Organization, formed in 1989, played a major role in shaping the agenda of the Cairo meeting, and promised to maintain the pressure on governments and international bodies to include gender equality and empowerment of women in family-planning and reproductive-health efforts.

Many challenges remain, however, in determining how to finance and deliver family planning and related services in ways that are consistent with local religious, cultural, social, and economic conditions. In many less-developed countries, family-planning services are still widely seen as a First World idea. Much of the focus will have to be on those countries that have the greatest population growth rates and the fewest resources to help empower women.

Most nations have not adopted explicit policies to manage their population, but there is implicit agreement that the key to balancing resources to people is reducing fertility, especially in those countries where resources are scarce. Family-planning efforts vary considerably in various parts of the world, and thus some countries have made more progress in reducing birth rates than have others. Information about birth control and access to contraception are known to be major causes of declining fertility. According to the 2004 UNFPA study, gaps in reproductive and sexual health care account for one-fifth of the worldwide burden of illness and premature death, and one-third of the illness and death among women of reproductive age.[31] In 2004, the 57th World Assembly recognized the Cairo consensus and adopted the World Health Organization's first reproductive-health strategy to accelerate progress toward the UN's Millennium Goals. Still, complications of pregnancy and childbirth remain a leading cause of death and illness among women—they result in 529,000 deaths each year, mostly from preventable causes.[32]

Globally, most of the countries that initially adopted family-planning programs were Asian and included both large and small nations. India became the first country to adopt an official policy in 1951 to slow population growth, but no other nations followed suit until nearly a decade later, when Pakistan, the Republic of Korea, China, and Fiji adopted similar policies. In the early 1960s, when oral contraceptives and intrauterine devices were first becoming available, about 60 million women, or 18 percent of the women of childbearing age in the developing world, were practicing family planning. By the mid-1990s, about 55 percent of couples in developing countries were using contraception to control their fertility, with about 75 percent in the industrialized nations of the world. In 2009, more than 100 million women lacked access to family planning, and many times that number did not receive other essential reproductive health services.

There are a number of economic, social, and religious reasons for which countries have shunned family planning as a way of bringing the birth rate down, especially in centrally planned countries such as China and Cuba. In many of these cultures, families simply want more children, even though more babies means more mouths to feed. Having more children may also mean more hands at work in the field or more help in caring for aging parents. Population limitation is in direct opposition to the teachings of the Catholic Church, which has encouraged procreation and discouraged birth control and abortion, as is the case in most Islamic nations. When Pope John Paul II assumed office in 1978, the Vatican took a more active role than previously in opposing abortion and contraception. In 1984, the Pope sent a statement to the head of the UNFPA in which he noted that contraception "increased sexual permissiveness and promoted irresponsible conduct," a view that continues to represent the Vatican's perspective with the naming of Pope Benedict. Many couples refuse to use birth-control devices because of rumors and myths about their effectiveness.

In India, women refused to use a loop-shaped intrauterine device when word spread that it would swim through the bloodstream and reach the brain or give the man a shock during intercourse. Vasectomy has been only marginally successful because of fears by men that it would reduce their virility. As a result, the use of contraception varies considerably from one nation to another.

Contraception use is generally highest in the nations of Europe and lowest in Africa—a trend mirrored in population growth rates. Some countries that have recognized the problem have taken steps to make contraception more available and acceptable, while others have made only nominal efforts. Government-sponsored family-planning programs have been the primary mechanism for population control in most developing countries. About a dozen nations have established a Cabinet-level ministry for population, generally in developing countries where the issue is considered serious enough to require an official program. The commitment is often not very firm, however, in countries with an Islamic or Roman Catholic religious tradition. The more successful efforts have been in countries where indigenous NGOs have been the most active. Working at the grassroots level, NGOs appear to develop a greater sense of trust with people than do programs offered by the government or foreign donors. They are also more adaptable to local circumstance and have more flexibility in their operations than do more structured programs.[33]

Generally speaking, economic inequality is the best predictor of fertility rates. Residents of poorer nations want more babies because they are a source of labor, while those in midrange economies choose goods over babies. Citizens of rich nations (such as the United States) can usually afford to have both—babies and goods. For many people in wealthy countries, even though wealth is not evenly distributed, family planning is less of a priority and there is little incentive to limit family size.

In response to a national population crisis in the 1950s and 1960s, China implemented its "later, longer, fewer" program in 1971 to reduce the number of individuals having children at an early age, imposing a limit of two children per family. The policy had little impact on the overall population, and in 1979, the government tightened the policy by mandating that families could have no more than one child. The policy met with internal resistance and external criticism, based primarily on allegations of coerced abortions. China has gradually begun to loosen its one-child policy, although it is too early to estimate the impact on the nation's population. In 2002, China's parliament, the National People's Congress, enacted a national provision that allows provinces to make their own laws to fit special circumstances. Shortly thereafter, the Provincial People's Congress in the rural province of Anhui passed a local birth-control law tailored to its local needs. The law identifies thirteen categories of couples that permit the family to have a second child, such as divorcees where both partners have only one child from previous marriages, farm couples whose first child is a girl, and coal miners—a risky occupation in China.[34]

Concerns about population and sustainability are rarely reflected in legal instruments. Nations retain sovereignty over family-planning policies, and international law is considered "soft" because it typically takes the form of a nonbinding resolution or statement. The 1948 Universal Declaration of Human Rights, for instance, states that men and women have the right to marry and found a family. "The family is the natural and fundamental group unit of society and is entitled to protection by society and the State."[35]

Although the declaration is considered to be customary law, resolutions like the Final Act of the UN International Conference on Human Rights (1988) and the Declaration on Social Progress and Development (1970), which recognize the right to determine the number and spacing of children, are not generally recognized.

IMPLICATIONS FOR POLICYMAKERS

Population management and sustainability are inextricably linked to other types of public policy; social, cultural, and religious beliefs; economics; and political forces that are constantly changing. Population and sustainability have thus become the most critical, yet unresolved, issues facing policymakers today. The consequences of population growth, regardless of the exact magnitude and timing, have considerable repercussions for the resources of both developed and developing nations. The problem is exacerbated by substantial disagreement among scientists as to the seriousness of the problem, making it difficult for policymakers to decide what kind of action, if any, to take. There are also opposing views on whether the population issue ought to be addressed by individual nations, allowing them to develop policies to control their own fertility rates and resource use, or whether the problem should be dealt with on a global scale by organizations such as the United Nations.

For a number of reasons, population management has slipped from the top of the political agenda, both in the United States and globally. Biologist and "population buff" Garrett Hardin, who was at the forefront of the ethical debate over population management, argued that among other factors, a change in public attitude is to blame. He noted that population is a chronic problem rather than a critical one, with the media preferring the latter to the former. As a result, the media is much more interested in covering "crises" such as the continuing conflict in the Middle East than in reporting that a quarter of a million people were born on the day that Iraq invaded Kuwait. Hardin also pointed out that many people fail to make the connection between population size and problems like air pollution from too many automobiles. Finally, he held that population questions raise issues that might be perceived as being selfish, bigoted, provincial, or even racist—criticisms that he himself had to bear.[36]

In the United States, members of Congress have not made population a high priority, because they have little political incentive to do so. Few interest groups support a particular policy, and the nation lacks a strong constituency for policy change in a system where institutional fragmentation is the norm. Most environmental organizations have only tangentially addressed population growth management, preferring instead to focus on more specific resource issues.

But the most important policy implication relates to whether there will be sufficient natural resources to sustain the growth in population, wherever it may occur. A key indicator is the adequacy of the food supply, which has thus far kept pace with population growth in all regions of the world except Africa. But most studies of world population projections note that world food-production potential is dependent upon increasing the amount of land under cultivation and increasing inputs of capital and fertilizers. Developing countries seeking to modernize their agricultural practices risk causing additional harm to the environment, whether by cutting timber in order to grow crops or by adding more chemicals to the soil and water supply. Another important consideration is whether there will be sufficient energy resources for the growing population. Developing countries seeking to modernize and grow will place additional demands on natural resources to produce the power needed for everything from household appliances to factories.

Last, the developing nations still suspect that countries such as the United States are more interested in curbing population growth in poorer countries as a way of protecting the environment rather than concentrating on reducing excess consumption in wealthier nations. This view has been expressed at numerous international conferences and exemplifies the continuing divisiveness between the industrialized nations of the world that already have the benefits of development and those countries that are still seeking to attain them. Some in the South also contend that the real population growth problem is in the North, because the environmental and natural-resource impact of each person in the wealthy world is many times that of residents of the developing world. The UNFPA notes that a child born today in an industrialized country will add more to consumption and pollution over his or her lifetime than will thirty to fifty children born in developing countries. "The ecological 'footprint' of the more affluent is far deeper than that of the poor, and in many cases, exceeds the regenerative capacity of the Earth."[37] If population growth is to be curtailed in the South to reduce pollution and resource use, it must be combined with restraint on the consumptive patterns of the North.

"If Obama wants to go down in history as a great president, he should help bring people to an awareness of this population problem," says the head of World Population Balance, an advocacy group based in Minneapolis. "Population growth is the number-one issue of our time on the planet."[38]

FURTHER READING

Pooran Desai. *One Planet Communities: A Real-Life Guide to Sustainable Communities.* Hoboken, NJ: Wiley, 2010.

Tim Dyson. *Population and Development.* London: Zed Books, 2010.

Robert Engelman. *More: Population, Nature, and What Women Want.* Covelo, CA: Island Press, 2008.

George Friedman. *The Next 100 Years: A Forecast for the 21st Century.* New York: Doubleday, 2009.

Laurie Ann Mazur. *A Pivotal Moment: Population, Justice, and the Environmental Challenge.* Covelo, CA: Island Press, 2010.

Raoner Munz and Albert Reiterer. *Overcrowded World: Global Population and International Migration.* London: Haus Publishing, 2010.

M. Paloma Pavel, ed. *Breakthrough Communities: Sustainability and Justice in the Next American Metropolis.* Cambridge, MA: MIT Press, 2009.

Michael Harrison Smith et al., eds. *Cents and Sustainability: Making Sense of How to Grow Economies, Build Communities and Revive the Environment in Our Lifetime.* London: Earthscan, 2010.

12

Emerging Issues
in Environmental Politics

Each edition of this book attempts to highlight some of the problems and issues that have begun to make their way to the environmental policy agenda. The ideas for this chapter come in part from my reading of current newspapers, journals, and blogs, but also from the students in my courses, who are asked to identify policies that they see as emerging trends. In 2009 and 2010, this is what we see happening in our environmental world.

BOTTLED-WATER BACKLASH

With slogans like "No Way Perrier" and "Evian is naive spelled backwards," cities are increasingly confronting activists demanding an end to single-serve bottled water. On January 1, 2008, Chicago became the first U.S. city to levy a five-cent surcharge on every bottle of water purchased by consumers as a way of encouraging residents to drink tap water. More than three dozen U.S. cities, counties, and schools have endorsed or adopted some form of back-to-the-tap initiative to reduce or ban bottled-water use. Corporate leaders have followed suit, no longer purchasing bottled water for meetings or eliminating plastic bottled-water containers from vending machines and company cafeterias.

Although California cities and counties have been the vanguard of the bottled-water restrictions (Los Angeles mayor Tom Bradley issued the first order restricting the use of city funds for purchasing bottled water in 1987), activists have turned their sights on city governments in Louisville, Ann Arbor, St. Louis, Salt Lake City, and Vancouver. At its 2008 annual meeting, the U.S. Conference of Mayors endorsed a resolution encouraging cities to phase out, where feasible, government use of bottled water and promote the importance of municipal water.[1]

The increasing amount of municipal solid waste (MSW) that is generated and disposed of is clearly a concern for local officials. Nearly 200 billion beverage containers are sold in the United States each year, two-thirds of which are land-filled, are incinerated, or end up as roadside litter. Beverage-container recycling, however, is decreasing, from 53.5 percent in 1992 to 33.5 percent in 2004. More important, sales of plastic bottles of water have eclipsed sales of other noncarbonated beverages, increasing more than 115 percent, from 13 billion in 2002 to 27.9 billion in 2005, according to a 2007 study by the Container Recycling Institute. Bottled water commanded only 2 percent of the market share of beverages in 1997, but by 2005, that share had increased to 14 percent.[2]

Although eleven states currently have container-deposit laws, more commonly known as *bottle bills*, most do not cover plastic water bottles. Oregon, which passed the first statewide bottle bill in 1973, expanded its legislation in June 2007 to cover bottled-water containers effective in January 2009. Chicago is the first city to implement a tax on plastic water bottles.

While waste and recycling are at the forefront of many local governments' motivation for reducing bottled-water consumption, there are three other policy drivers: energy efficiency, economics, and a backlash against the sale of water as a commodity, especially in poorer areas. The environmental impact of plastic bottled water is related not only to waste, but also to the fact that bottled water must be transported miles from the source, requiring the burning of fossil fuels and increased emissions into the atmosphere. In addition, an estimated 17 million barrels of crude oil per year are needed to manufacture the 29 billion plastic bottles used for water in the United States each year.[3]

Money is a second major factor driving municipal officials' decisions on bottled water. Chicago's bottled water tax was initially estimated to generate $10.5 million in annual revenues by adding about 30 percent to the overall cost of a case of bottled water; cases make up about 90 percent of all bottled water sold in that city. San Francisco, which prohibited city funds from being used to purchase single-serving bottled water in 2007, had been spending $500,000 yearly on bottled water in plastic containers.

The Conference of Mayors' 2007 resolution also focuses on the availability of high-quality, safe drinking water, a $43-billion-per-year investment for local government. One-quarter of the bottled water sold each year comes from the same source as tap water, which means consumers are paying 1,000 to 10,000 times more for bottled water than the water they can get from their own home faucets. California governor Arnold Schwarzenegger signed a bill increasing annual water vending-machine license fees from $10 to $40 in an October 2007 measure to discourage the growth of the vending machines, which frequently show up outside grocery stores.

Groups like Corporate Accountability International (CAI) have identified a third reason for banning plastic bottles of water through what they term a "challenge to the corporate control of water." They cite a growing use of resources by water-intensive industries and the privatization of public water systems as the way private corporations are "reducing a shared common resource into simply another opportunity to profit." Their Think Outside the Bottle campaign urges consumers to rely on refillable containers, and to protect public water systems both in the United States and abroad. CAI points to companies like Coca-Cola, Pepsi, and Nestle that they say are taking advantage of World Bank policies and loans for water privatization.[4]

While cities are certainly feeling the bottled-water backlash, the food and beverage industries are not simply giving in to the bans and boycotts. Representatives of the Illinois Retail Merchants Association, for instance, argue that the Chicago tax will cause customers to migrate to other cities, jeopardizing 4,500 jobs and $270 million in wages earned by local bottled-water industry workers. Retail officials also believe the tax is regressive, since wealthier consumers will be able to buy their cases of water outside the city to avoid paying the tax. An alliance of trade associations has promised to sue the city over the levy, claiming that existing state laws prohibit the city from singling out a single product like water. They wonder what's next. They ask, "What is to preclude the City Council from deciding to tax salad dressing or lawn mowers?"[5]

The bottled-water initiatives are actually part of a bigger issue question, though. Which level of government is best suited to deal with the public's increasing demands to do something about environmental problems? A December 2006 Government Accountability Office report faulted the EPA for failing to establish performance measures or to collect comprehensive data on municipal recycling, so city officials have taken action on their own. In 2007, San Francisco became the first U.S. city to ban biodegradable bags in supermarkets and large chain pharmacies, and similar bans are being considered in dozens of other cities. Still, the United States is behind many other cities and countries that have already taken such steps, and the pace of international campaigns is speeding up more rapidly than many U.S. officials realize. Bottled-water bans may be the first step in a larger campaign to reduce consumer packaging, starting at the tap.

CARBON CAPTURE AND SEQUESTRATION

The U.S. Department of Energy (DOE) estimates that the United States has a 250-year supply of coal, constituting 95 percent of the country's fossil energy reserves. Because coal is both abundant and low-cost, it remains at the heart of energy production, accounting for more than half of the energy generated in the United States. Roughly one-third of the United States' carbon emissions come from power plants and other large sources. With current attention being focused on carbon dioxide (CO_2) and global warming, scientists and policymakers are looking at various technological solutions to deal with emissions produced by fossil-fueled power plants, biomass energy facilities, natural-gas processing, synthetic-fuel plants, and hydrogen-production plants. Among the many ideas that have been developed is the largely theoretical concept of carbon capture and sequestration (CCS), also referred to as *carbon capture and storage*. The basic process involves capturing CO_2 emissions at the source, such as a large fossil-fueled power plant, before the emissions are released into the atmosphere.

Once captured, the emissions would be compressed for injection or transported, and then stored in a geological formation, such as oil and gas reservoirs, unmineable coal seams, deep saline reservoirs, and geologic formations such as basalt. The CCS process might also include pumping CO_2 gas into a reservoir to push out oil or natural gas—enhanced oil and gas recovery. The revenues from recovered oil and gas products can then be used to offset the cost of sequestering the carbon or coal-bed methane.

Another form of CCS is terrestrial sequestration, a process where natural ecosystems, such as forests or wetlands, are maintained or manipulated to increase their ability to store carbon. Techniques include massive forestation and deforestation abatement, estimated to sequester as much as 2 billion metric tons of carbon per year. Another potential technique is ocean sequestration, such as directly injecting CO_2 into ocean masses at depths of 1,000 meters or more. Currently, however, there is an incomplete understanding of the ecological effects of ocean sequestration, including how to ameliorate costs, potential changes in ocean ecosystems and the impact on marine organisms, and the effects of CO_2 on the acidity of ocean water.

Although theoretically feasible on a large scale, there are numerous problems associated with these processes, most of which have never gone past the research phase. For instance, even though the technology is available, currently available CCS commercial technology would add about 75 percent to the cost of electricity for a new pulverized-coal plant, and 35 percent to the cost of a new advanced gasification-based plant, according to the DOE.[6] In addition to adding to the cost of electricity, once captured, the CO_2 would have to be transported, most likely through a dedicated pipeline system, although it might be possible to transport it on ships. Although there is evidence that CO_2 could potentially be stored for millions of years, there is also a question of leakage from geological storage sites. One method of dealing with potential leakage would be to establish a system of measurement, monitoring, and verification to ensure safe permanent storage.

From a policy perspective, there have been a variety of public and private efforts to advance research and development into carbon capture and sequestration. At the federal level, the DOE established a Carbon Sequestration Program within the Office of Fossil Energy in 1997, followed by a basic research program two years later. The goal is to cover the entire "life cycle" of capture and separation, sequestration, transportation, and storage or reuse. Similar programs are being considered for two other greenhouse gases: methane and nitrous oxides. In December 2009, the department announced it was awarding grants totaling nearly $1 billion to speed up the development of commercial-scale projects at three coal-fired plants in New Haven, West Virginia; Mobile, Alabama; and Odessa, Texas.

At the private level, the U.S. Climate Action Partnership issued *A Call for Action* in January 2007 seeking congressional legislation to reduce levels of greenhouse-gas emissions, and a recommendation that Congress require the Environmental Protection Agency (EPA) to issue regulations on geological sequestration of CO_2 along with funding for at least three to five large-scale sequestration demonstration projects, their operation, and a fund for postclosure facility management.[7]

Research is being conducted by several consortiums and institutions. One example, CSiTE (Carbon Sequestration in Terrestrial Ecosystems), is comprised of the Argonne, Oak Ridge, and Pacific Northwest National Laboratories, as well as several universities. The consortium was established in 1999 and is sponsored by the Climate Change Research Division of the Office of Biological and Environmental Research within the DOE. In addition to addressing questions related to the physical, biological, and chemical processes of soil carbon inputs and storage, CSiTE seeks to develop sustainable technologies to enhance carbon sequestration and its potential for mitigating climate change. In November 2008, Montana State University received a $67 million grant to demonstrate the feasibility of using underground geologic formations for storage, with a plan to inject up to 1 million tons of CO_2 into a sandstone repository in southwestern Wyoming.

Despite the fact that the United States is one of the top emitters of CO_2, carbon sequestration is more than just a domestic issue. Worldwide, there were an estimated 273 projects underway in 2009, 64 of them at a commercial scale. Of those, seven are operational end-to-end, although none as yet generate electricity and none have been adapted for use in clusters of power stations. An alternative carbon-capture technique, called Oxyfuel technology, is being tried in Germany, and China plans to open a $1 billion clean-coal plant in 2010.[8] There is also an international Carbon Sequestration Leadership Forum (CSLF), a voluntary climate initiative of developed and developing nations that are responsible for more than three-quarters of all human-caused carbon-dioxide emissions and about 60 percent of the world's population. The group, composed of twenty-four countries and formed in 2003, shares technology and holds informational conferences on near-term strategies for carbon capture and storage. In 2009, for instance, at its meeting in London, the CSLF recognized ten new CCS projects, endorsed CCS as a key component of international plans to combat climate change, and created a capacity-building program to assist member nations.[9] Still, CCS is, for the most part, at an experimental stage, with the concept accepted among the science and policy communities but still largely untested.

ENVIRONMENTAL REFUGEES

The projections vary from as few as 50 million to as many as 500 million, but the problem is clear: Millions of people around the world will be displaced because of rising sea levels, desertification, drought, weather-related flooding, and other environmental changes. Environmental problems are already facing tens of millions of people who do not have access to government grants, subsidies, and programs that provide food, shelter, medical care, or other services because they are not recognized in the same way as political refugees. Their numbers are growing so rapidly that researchers with the Red Cross now estimate that there are more people displaced by environmental disasters than by war.[10]

There is some debate over the proper term for such people, with some arguing that the United Nations' term, "environmentally induced migrants" fails to distinguish those who are in the category of migrants due to climate change. The term was first used in the 1980s to define "people who have been forced to leave their traditional habitat, temporarily or permanently, because of a marked environmental disruption (natural and/or triggered by people) that jeopardized their existence and/or seriously affected the quality of their life." Subsequent scholars have used the terms "climigrant" and "climate exile" to refer to those who specifically move because of changes in climate.[11]

What is disturbing to many policymakers is the fact that the problem is not new but, as two leading scholars point out, the issue "has all but dropped from sight as other consequences of climate change have taken center stage." Norman Myers and Jennifer Kent, who wrote about the emerging crisis of environmental refugees in 1995,[12] have continued to sound the alarm, predicting that several hundred million people could be driven to involuntary migration for environmental reasons during the twenty-first century. The impacts of climate change, they say, are just beginning, and will "steadily multiply and intensify. Present-day environmental crises such as drought, water scarcity, soil erosion, and desertification will aggravate land-use conflicts and trigger further environmentally induced migration."[13]

International organizations have also identified the problem. The Intergovernmental Panel on Climate Change stated in 1990 that "one of the gravest effects of climate change may be those of human migration. The United Nations Population Fund (UNPF) has also documented the problem, noting that both the nature and scale of environmentally induced population movements have begun to change. The organization predicts that there is a high probability that changes in sea levels, climate, and other environmental conditions will cause major increases in movement in the coming decades. "Societies would do well to consider now how to address environmentally induced movements of people."[14]

It is the latter point that is of primary concern to policymakers. Since many of the cases of environmental refugees involve internal problems, with a smaller proportion of movement between neighboring countries and even smaller numbers of persons migrating long distances, many of the solutions will involve national governments, many of which are unprepared for the onslaught of migrants within their own borders. New types of changes, such as sea-level rise, may require resettlement of affected populations. Marginalized populations, such as the poor, elderly, women, and children, tend to bear the brunt of environmental change, and may be most in need of services. The UNPF notes that it is essential to mainstream considerations of gender, age, and diversity into climate-change consequences and to "focus policy responses on these groups."[15]

There are already examples where the problem of environmental refugees has begun to overwhelm government agencies. In Yemen's capital, Sana'a, the population has doubled on average every six years since 1972, now standing at 900,000. The city depends on an aquifer that is falling by six meters a year, and may be exhausted by 2010, according to the World Bank. The low-lying island state of Tuvalu has struck an agreement with New Zealand to accept its nearly 12,000 citizens in the event rising sea levels swamp the country.[16] Myers sees "hot spots" for refugee areas in the coastal zones of South, Southeast, and East Asia, and in deltas such as those of the Nile and the Niger River, along with regions prone to prolonged drought in the drier sections of Sub-Saharan Africa and China.[17]

Despite the scientific uncertainty of the impact of climate change and other environmental factors, Myers and Kent argue that "absence of evidence of a problem does not constitute evidence of absence. As in other situations beset with uncertainty, it will be better for us to find we have been roughly right than precisely (and belatedly) wrong. The time for concerted action is now if we are to get on top of the problem before it gets on top of us."[18]

GREEN-COLLAR JOBS

For generations, a person's work could be described by the types of clothing the wearer put on to go to work: blue-collar shirts for manufacturing and industrial sector positions, blouses with pink collars for secretarial and low-level administrative jobs, and white collars for higher-level administrative, technical, and government workers. More recently, a new item of apparel has been added to the list: the green collar. The term is used to describe career-track positions that pay wages sufficient to support a family, and that contribute directly to preserving or enhancing environmental quality. The U.S. Conference of Mayors estimated that over 750,000 workers were directly employed in the green economy in 2006, with many of those jobs related to clean energy. According to the Apollo Alliance, a coalition of groups that is working toward the creation of more green-collar jobs, a $500 billion investment in clean energy over ten years will create 5 million direct and indirect jobs.[19]

Jobs in the green economy can be divided into six sectors, with a variety of positions represented in each one, the Alliance predicts. Most of the job descriptions already exist (see the list below); the change would be the application of those positions to changing business sectors.

- *Building Retrofitting*: electricians, heating and air-conditioning installers, carpenters, construction-equipment operators, roofers, insulation workers, carpenter helpers, industrial truck drivers, construction managers, building inspectors

- *Mass Transit/Freight Rail*: civil engineers, rail track layers, electricians, welders, metal fabricators, engine assemblers, bus drivers, dispatchers, locomotive engineers, railroad conductors

- *Smart Grid*: computer software engineers, electrical engineers, electrical-equipment assemblers and technicians, machinists, team assemblers, construction laborers, operating engineers, electrical power-line installers and repairers

- *Wind Power*: Environmental engineers, iron and steel workers, millwrights, sheet-metal workers, machinists, electrical-equipment assemblers, construction-equipment operators, industrial truck drivers, industrial production managers, first-line production supervisors

- *Solar Power*: electrical engineers, electricians, industrial machinery mechanics, welders, metal fabricators, electrical-equipment assemblers, construction-equipment operators, installation helpers, laborers, construction managers
- *Advanced Biofuels*: chemical engineers, chemists, chemical-equipment operators, chemical technicians, mixing- and blending-machine operators, agricultural workers, industrial truck drivers, farm-product purchasers, agricultural and forestry supervisors, agricultural inspectors[20]

Response to the idea of creating green jobs has come from the national, state, and local levels. Congress enacted the Green Jobs Act as part of the Energy Independence and Security Act of 2007. It amended previous workforce legislation, authorizing $125 million for the creation of an Energy Efficiency and Renewable Energy Worker Training Program. Administered by the Department of Labor and the DOE, grants are made available for a variety of purposes, from researching labor-market data to tracking workforce trends and job training. The legislation is aimed at multistakeholder partnerships, including five existing programs in Oakland, Los Angeles, New York, Richmond, and Chicago.

The actual implementation of the Green Jobs program will involve a variety of stakeholders. Grants will be given to labor-management training programs, and also distributed to states for the purpose of labor research and to administer state energy-efficient workforce development programs. The legislation also requires the Secretary of Labor to track market data on workforce trends through the Bureau of Labor Statistics. The Department of Labor will also work with the Pathways Out of Poverty Program for labor-training partnerships that serve low-income demographics.

LOCAVORES

The locavores are coming! The locavores are coming!

Perhaps you're not aware that the locavores are on their way, and they hope to affect the way we buy our food and eat.

Never heard of a "locavore"? The term was the *New Oxford American Dictionary's* 2007 Word of the Year (with runners-up like *upcycling* and *cloudware*) and the topic has been featured in articles in *Fortune*, *Time*, and the *New York Times*. Locavores are people who try to eat only "locally grown" food. The term was coined in 2005 by four San Franciscan women who encourage residents to buy, cook, and eat from within a 100-mile radius of their foodshed. It is, advocates believe, the best way to support the environment, and an important way to promote sustainability. Buying locally also helps reduce the number of "food miles" that items like imported produce travel between the fields where they are picked to the supermarkets where they are sold. The Natural Resources Defense Council (NRDC) relies on estimates that most produce grown in the United States travels an average of 1,500 to 2,500 miles before it is sold.[21]

The locavore movement has challenged consumers' choices on an individual basis, but supporters are also targeting schools, prisons, and other institutions that purchase food. In the Litchfield, Arizona, Elementary School District, for

Another View, Another Voice: Jerome Ringo

Jerome Ringo is used to being called "the first," and although the designation applies in many ways, the label as a "conservationist" is perhaps more important. In 2006, he was named one of *Ebony* magazine's most influential African Americans, and he notes that his role model is Dr. Martin Luther King Jr. and "young children who ask the right questions—who will sit down and share their concerns."

Born in 1955 in the bayou area of southern Louisiana, Ringo was one of six children; his mother was a nurse and his father, a postal worker, sought to integrate the racially segregated schools in his community. He became involved in the Boy Scouts, and was the first black ranger at the world's largest scout ranch in New Mexico, teaching scouts about survival. Although he attended Louisiana Technical University and McNeese State University, planning to major in education, he did not finish his degree, choosing instead to take a lucrative job in the petrochemical industry. He served as a union leader, becoming active in environmental justice issues near the plant where he worked until he accepted early retirement at age thirty-nine. At that point, he decided to become a full-time activist.

One factor that made his conservation efforts somewhat different from those of other leaders is that he continued to work at the petrochemical plant while organizing local communities against the chemical discharges from that plant. He adds that although he was not sure how comfortable the company was with his activism, they were not going to fire him because they at least wanted to project themselves as being friends of the environment.

In 2005 he joined the Apollo Alliance, named in honor of President John F. Kennedy's Apollo program, which put a man on the moon in 1969. He serves as president of the Alliance, a coalition of labor organizations, civil rights and environmental groups, and business leaders representing more than 17 million people. The Alliance's goals include making the United States independent of foreign oil sources, developing green jobs, and rebuilding the nation's cities and ensuring good stewardship of natural resources.

Among the firsts on his résumé is that in 2005, he was named the chairman of the board of the National Wildlife Federation, becoming the first African American to chair a major environmental organization. In 2007, he was invited to serve on the National Parks and Conservation Association board of directors, and he also serves on *Newsweek* magazine's advisory panel on climate change. He was the only black delegate to the global-warming treaty negotiations in Kyoto, Japan, in 1998, and he represented the National Wildlife Federation at the UN conference on sustainable development in 1999. On his webpage, he lists his involvement with Al Gore's climate advisory panel, as a participant in the Sundance Channel's "The Green," and as an associate research scholar at Yale University.

SOURCES:
Apollo Alliance. "Staff." http://www.apolloalliance.org/about/staff. Accessed June 15, 2009.
Erik Kancler. "The Pioneer: An Interview with Jerome Ringo." *Mother Jones*. April 25, 2005. http://motherjones.com/environment/2005/04/pioneer-interview-jerome-ringo. Accessed June 15, 2009.
"Power Shift 2009 Is Reactivating Activism, Says Jerome Ringo." http://www.itsgettinghotinhere.org/2009/02/28. Accessed June 15, 2009.

instance, the schools' food director, who is also a registered dietician, is buying locally grown food whenever possible. There once were farms across the street from the schools in what was a predominantly rural, agricultural area outside Phoenix. Those farms are gone now, replaced by new suburban housing developments. But the district is feeding nearly 8,000 students produce that comes straight from the field, having some delivered and picking up some of the food.

Locavores are also promoting the "Eat Local Challenge" in much the same way mayors and other officials have been asked to support global climate-change pledges. The locavore pledge:

If not locally produced, then organic.

If not organic, then family farm.

If not family farm, then local business.

If not a local business, then fair trade.

The approach is also called "relationship marketing" in a book by Joel Salatin called *Holy Cows and Hog Heaven: The Food Buyer's Guide to Farm Friendly Food*.[22] Salatin urges consumers to take the extra step of getting to know the farmers in their area, and to purchase products from those they know as a way of guaranteeing food integrity. He runs a small farm in Swoope, Virginia, where he sells eggs and meat from chickens and livestock he raises. The farm does not ship its products long-distance, or wholesale its food. Customers drive to the farm to pick up their orders.

Several authors have also reported on their efforts to take the Eat Local pledge or to eat only foods grown within a 100-mile radius of their homes. Ecologist Gary Nabham and novelist Barbara Kingsolver are among those who have written about the dearth of knowledge Americans have about where their food comes from and the role corporate production plays in the growing, processing, transporting, marketing, and sale of the food they eat.

The locavore movement also discourages people from eating food that is listed as endangered, out of season, or produced using practices that are not sustainable. Monkfish, for instance, is an endangered species, and many restaurants have taken it off their menus. Produce such as raspberries imported from New Zealand may even be organic, but critics note that the berries travel thousands of miles to get to the supermarket. Reducing the amount of meat, dairy products, fruits, and vegetables bought outside the foodshed reduces the amount of fossil fuels used to transport them. The NRDC notes that each year, more than 270 million pounds of grapes are sent in cargo ships from Chile to California, and then are trucked to market. The 5,900-mile journey releases 7,000 tons of global-warming emissions each year. For government entities trying to reduce their carbon footprints, buying local agriculture supports the local economy and reduces carbon emissions at the same time.

The Eat Local Challenge may seem a challenge in itself, especially for those trying to find local foods in an urban area or far from farms. Advocates note that state departments of agriculture are now developing lists of resources and developing websites for those seeking to find local sources. They also recommend that consumers look to foods that they might not otherwise consider as locally produced, such as flour, wine, spices, or sausage. Produce managers are often a valuable source of information on where products come from, and store managers might be convinced to buy items in bulk if customers are willing to commit to purchasing them regularly.

There are, however, challengers of the locavore movement, including critics like James McWilliams, whose 2009 book questioned the local-food concept and argued for a broad pattern of regionally integrated, technologically advanced, middle-sized farms and an increased reliance on aquaponics.[23] He notes that transportation and food miles account for only about 10 percent of overall energy that goes into producing food, and that 14 percent of total food purchases are tossed in the trash, with produce accounting for 27 percent of that waste.

McWilliams, who became a vegetarian after writing his book, also says that there is a danger that the locavore movement will become a victim of its own success. "When I listen to locavores, I'm just not hearing enough about this looming global food crisis I think we're facing."[24]

Still, the founders of the locavore movement continue to tout the benefits of eating within a 100-mile radius. "Recognition of one's residence within a foodshed can confer a sense of connection and responsibility to a particular locality. The foodshed can provide a place for us to ground ourselves in the biological and social realities of living on the land and from the land in a place that we can call home, a place to which we are or can become native."[25]

RECLAIMED WATER

The reuse of treated water, also known as *recycled* or *reclaimed water*, is not a recent phenomenon; it is a growing strategy to try to stretch existing water sources, especially in areas such as the Southwest that suffer from severe drought. And at the global level, the use of reclaimed water is considered a valuable idea, with tremendous potential as a water resource as technology has expanded to make the process both more cost-effective and safer for further use.

There is evidence of the use of wastewater for irrigation among ancient civilizations, ranging from the city of Jerusalem to the Chinese and Japanese. As cities grew during the Industrial Revolution, the science of wastewater management grew almost as quickly as the population, and by 1900, reuse systems were in place in England, France, Mexico, and Australia. Augusta, Maine, installed the first system in the United States in 1872, and by the 1900s, reclaimed water was being widely used in Texas and California. The National Park Service began using reclaimed water at the Grand Canyon to flush toilets, irrigate the landscape, and for dust control beginning in 1926, and Los Angeles County's sanitation districts have used reclaimed water for irrigation in parks and golf courses since 1929.[26]

One of the most controversial issues related to reclaimed water is what types of uses it is suitable for. The Clean Water Act of 1972 ended the practice of dumping raw sewage, but the EPA does not regulate reclaimed water; states have jurisdiction over what standards and classifications are used through the issuance of permits. In Arizona, for instance, reclaimed water is regulated by the state's Department of Environmental Quality, requiring extensive testing to determine the concentrations of various substances such as nitrogen. The highest grade possible is A+; the higher the grade of water, the more uses it can serve. The A and A+ water can be used for irrigation of food crops, residential landscape irrigation, school-ground landscape irrigation, urinal and toilet flushing, fire-protection systems, spray irrigation of an orchard or vineyard, commercial closed-loop air-conditioning systems, vehicle and equipment washing, and snowmaking. But even this level of water cannot be used in any situation where ingestion or body contact is possible, ruling out the use of reclaimed water for swimming pools, misting systems, evaporative coolers, and most uses inside the home.[27] Water rated as B or B+ can be used for surface irrigation of an orchard or vineyard; golf-course irrigation, dust control, soil compaction and other construction activities; pasture for milking animals; dairy-animal watering; concrete and cement mixing; materials washing and sieving; and street cleaning. Finally, grade C water can only be used for livestock watering of nondairy animals; irrigation of sod farms; irrigation of fiber, seed, forage, and similar crops; and silviculture.

Within wastewater management, there are multiple concerns about the quality of reclaimed water and the potential public health effects of its use.[28] Treated wastewater, also known as *effluent*, may contain pathogens and high levels of parasites such as Giardia that could be transferred to humans through contact or inhalation. There may also be environmental and health impacts from substances known as *endocrine-disrupting chemicals*, compounds often found in reclaimed water. Current methods of treatment, some believe, are insufficient, and more advanced forms of treatment including the use of reverse osmosis and ozonation may be required to make wastewater safe for most uses. To further protect the public, states require those using effluent to place a sign warning the public not to drink from irrigation systems.

Reclaimed water can be sold like any commodity, and in some areas, it has the potential to serve as a substitute for potable water. Orange County, California, for instance, uses a Groundwater Replenishment System that takes wastewater from one treatment plant and sends it to spreading basins, where it percolates into the aquifer below. Nearby wells pump water out of the aquifer for municipal use. Many cities have effluent-dependent wetlands constructed in conjunction with wastewater treatment plants, some of which double as riparian habitats. Projects such as these expand the capacity of municipal governments by increasing the amount of water that can recharge the local aquifer, and in some instances, the artificial wetlands have become sites for birding and watching wildlife that gather to drink.

There are two regulated uses that have met with considerable controversy. One involves the use of reclaimed water for cooking and drinking. Thus far, advocates have been unable to convince consumers that effluent, even when treated to standards beyond those required for drinking water, is "pure" enough for these purposes. There is a common belief that this water is tainted by its original source. Consumers are wary of using reclaimed water and have shown reluctance to allow policymakers to approve its use in the same way they approve using reclaimed water to irrigate golf courses.

The second controversy, which is so acrimonious that it reached the level of the U.S. Supreme Court, has been the use of reclaimed water for snowmaking. The U.S. Forest Service granted a permit to a company in northern Arizona to make snow using reclaimed water from the communities below the San Francisco Peaks, where a ski resort is located. If the permit was not granted, the company said, it did not have a dependable source of snow and its economic future was uncertain. But Native-American tribes argued that the Peaks were sacred to their cultural beliefs, and that using reclaimed water dishonored those beliefs, analogous to allowing someone to use a church as a toilet.[29]

Environmental groups presented a different argument, saying that there were unknown public-health risks from using reclaimed water. After years of court battles, the Supreme Court agreed with the Forest Service in 2009, finally giving the ski resort the approval it needed to make artificial snow. The tribes vowed they would not give up the fight, in a debate that split the community's leaders and citizens in a bitter dispute. They appealed the court decision in federal court, arguing that the Forest Service failed to consider the human health risks of ingesting artificial snow.[30] For reasons that are still unclear, the Forest Service stalled on granting the resort owners the permit to begin snowmaking operations, telling the parties that there was a need for further negotiations. The lack of a clarification of the agency's position further postponed the debate over the use of reclaimed water, and further economic uncertainty for the affected communities.[31]

FURTHER READING

David B. Brooks, Oliver M. Brandes, and Stephen Gurman, eds. *Making the Most of the Water We Have: The Soft Path Approach to Water Management.* London: Earthscan Publications, 2009.

Tony Clarke. *Inside the Bottle: An Exposé of the Bottled Water Industry.* Ottawa, Canada: Canadian Centre for Policy Alternatives, 2008.

Amy Cotler. *The Locavore Way: Discovering the Delicious Pleasures of Eating Fresh, Locally Grown Food.* North Adams, MA: Storey Publishing, 2010.

Scott M. Deitche. *Green Collar Jobs: Environmental Careers for the 21st Century.* Westport, CT: Praeger, 2010.

Marco Grasso. *Justice in Funding Adaptation under the International Climate Change Regime.* New York: Springer, 2010.

A. Bronwyn Llewellyn. *Green Jobs: A Guide to Eco-Friendly Employment.* Cincinnati, OH: Adams Media, 2008.

Klaus Lorenz and Rattan Lal. *Carbon Sequestration in Forest Ecosystems.* New York: Springer, 2010.

James Meadowcroft, ed. *Caching the Carbon: The Politics and Policy of Carbon Capture and Storage.* Northampton, MA: Edward Elgar Publishing, 2010.

Elizabeth Royte. *Bottlemania: How Water Went on Sale and Why We Bought It.* New York: Bloomsbury USA, 2008.

Appendix A

Major U.S. Environmental Legislation, 1947–2010

Year	President	Legislation
1947	Truman	Federal Insecticide, Fungicide, and Rodenticide Act
1956	Eisenhower	Water Pollution Control Act
1963	Kennedy	Clean Air Act
1964	Johnson	Land and Water Conservation Fund Act
1965	Johnson	Water Quality Act
		Highway Beautification Act
1966	Johnson	Endangered Species Preservation Act
1967	Johnson	Air Quality Act
1968	Johnson	National Wild and Scenic Rivers Act
		National Trails System Act
1969	Nixon	National Environmental Policy Act
		Endangered Species Act Amendments
1970	Nixon	Clean Air Act Amendments
		Water Quality Improvement Act
		Resource Recovery Act
		Environment Education Act
1971	Nixon	Alaska Native Claims Settlement Act
1972	Nixon	Federal Water Pollution Control Act
		Federal Environmental Pesticides Control Act
		Coastal Zone Management Act
		Marine Protection Research and Sanctuaries Act
		Noise Control Act

(continued)

Year	President	Legislation
1973	Nixon	Endangered Species Act
1974	Nixon	Safe Drinking Water Act
1976	Ford	Toxic Substances Control Act
		Resource Conservation and Recovery Act
		Federal Land Policy and Management Act
		National Forest Management Act
1977	Carter	Clean Air Act Amendments
		Clean Water Act Amendments
		Surface Mining Control and Reclamation Act
		Soil and Water Conservation Act
1978	Carter	Public Utility Regulatory Policies Act
		National Energy Act
1980	Carter	Comprehensive Environmental Response, Compensation, and Liability Act
		Alaska National Interest Conservation Act
		Fish and Wildlife Conservation Act
1982	Reagan	Nuclear Waste Policy Act
1984	Reagan	Resource Conservation and Recovery Act Amendments
1985	Reagan	Food Security Act
1986	Reagan	Safe Drinking Water Act
		Superfund Amendments and Reauthorization Act
1987	Reagan	Clean Water Act Amendments
		Nuclear Waste Policy Act Amendments
		Global Climate Protection Act
1988	Reagan	Federal Insecticide, Fungicide, and Rodenticide Act Amendments
		Ocean Dumping Act
1990	Bush	Clean Air Act Amendments
1992	Bush	Energy Policy Act
1994	Clinton	California Desert Protection Act
1996	Clinton	Safe Drinking Water Act Amendments
		Food Quality Protection Act
2002	G.W. Bush	Small Business Liability Relief and Brownfields Revitalization Act
2003	G.W. Bush	Healthy Forests Restoration Act
2005	G.W. Bush	Energy Policy Act
2009	Obama	Omnibus Public Lands Management Act

Appendix B

Major International Environmental Agreements, 1900–2009[*]

Year	Environmental Agreement
1906	Convention Concerning the Equitable Distribution of the Waters of the Rio Grande for Irrigation
1916	Convention for the Protection of Migratory Birds
1933	Convention on the Preservation of Fauna and Flora in Their Natural State
1946	International Convention for the Regulation of Whaling
1947	General Agreement on Tariffs and Trade
1951	International Plant Protection Convention
1954	International Convention for the Protection of the Seas by Oil
1958	Convention on the Continental Shelf
1958	Convention on the Territorial Sea and Contiguous Zone
1958	Convention on the High Seas
1958	Geneva Convention on Fishing and Conservation of the Living Resources of the High Seas
1959	Antarctic Treaty
1960	Paris Convention on Third Party Liability in the Field of Nuclear Energy
1963	Berne Convention on the International Commission for the Protection of the Rhine against Pollution

(continued)

[*]These agreements are in various stages of implementation, based upon the status and participation of the parties involved. Stages include adoption, ratification, acceptance or approval, acts of formal confirmation, entry into force, and accession.

Year	Environmental Agreement
1963	Vienna Convention on Civil Liability for Nuclear Damage
1964	International Convention for the Conservation of Atlantic Tunas
1968	African Convention on the Conservation of Nature and Natural Resources
1970	Declaration of Principles Governing the Seabed and the Ocean Floor, and the Subsoil Thereof, Beyond the Limits of National Jurisdiction
1971	Ramsar Convention on Wetlands of International Importance Especially as Waterfowl Habitat
1972	Convention for the Protection of the World Cultural and Natural Heritage
1972	Convention on the Prevention of Marine Pollution by Dumping of Wastes and Other Matter
1973	Stockholm Declaration of the United Nations Conference on the Human Environment
1973	International Convention for the Prevention of Pollution by Ships
1979	International Convention on Long-Range Transboundary Air Pollution
1980	Convention on the Conservation of Antarctic Marine Living Resources
1982	United Nations Convention on the Law of the Sea
1982	World Charter on Nature
1983	Cartagena Agreement
1985	Vienna Convention for the Protection of the Ozone Layer
1985	International Tropical Timber Agreement
1987	Montreal Protocol on Substances that Deplete the Ozone Layer
1989	Basel Convention on the Control of Transboundary Movements of Hazardous Wastes and Their Disposal
1990	Wellington Convention for the Prohibition of Fishing with Long Driftnets in the South Pacific
1991	Bamako Convention on the Ban of Import into Africa and the Control of Transboundary Movement and Management of Hazardous Wastes within Africa
1991	Protocol on Environmental Protection to the Antarctic Treaty
1991	Declaration on the Protection of the Arctic Environment
1992	Framework Convention on Climate Change
1992	Convention on Biological Diversity
1992	North American Free Trade Agreement
1992	Rio Declaration on Environment and Development
1994	Convention to Combat Desertification in Those Countries Experiencing Serious Drought and/or Desertification, Particularly in Africa
1994	Vienna Adjustments to the Montreal Protocol
1994	Convention on Nuclear Safety
1995	Global Program of Action for the Protection of the Marine Environment from Land-Based Activities

Year	Environmental Agreement
1995	Washington Declaration on Protection of Marine Resources from Land-Based Activities
1995	Straddling Stocks Convention
1996	Protocol to the Convention on the Prevention of Marine Pollution by Dumping of Wastes and Other Matter
1997	Kyoto Protocol to the Framework Convention on Climate Change
1997	Montreal Amendments and Adjustments to the Montreal Protocol
1997	Convention on the Law of the Non-Navigational Uses of International Watercourses
1997	Protocol to Amend the 1963 Vienna Convention on Civil Liability for Nuclear Damage
1997	Convention on Supplementary Compensation for Nuclear Damage
1998	Convention on Access to Information, Public Participation in Decision Making and Access to Justice in Environmental Matters
1998	Rotterdam Convention on Prior Informed Consent Procedure for Certain Hazardous Chemicals and Pesticides in International Trade
1998	Protocol on Persistent Organic Pollutants
1998	Protocol on Heavy Metals
1999	Protocol to the Cartagena Agreement
1999	Protocol to Abate Acidification, Eutrophication, and Ground-Level Ozone
1999	Protocol on Liability
1999	Beijing Amendments and Adjustments to the Montreal Protocol
2000	Cartegena Protocol on Biosafety to the Convention on Biological Diversity
2001	Stockholm Convention on Persistent Organic Pollutants
2001	International Treaty on Plant Genetic Resources for Food and Agriculture
2002	Delhi Ministerial Declaration
2002	Convention for Cooperation in the Protection and Sustainable Marine and Coastal Environment of the Northeast Pacific (Antigua Convention)
2003	Protocol on Pollutant Release and Transfer Registers
2005	Treaty on the Conservation and Sustainable Development of the Forest Ecosystems of Central Africa
2005	Framework Convention on the Value of Cultural Heritage for Society
2006	International Tropical Timber Agreement
2006	Southern Indian Ocean Fisheries Agreement
2007	International Convention on the Removal of Wrecks
2007	Agreement on the Conservation of Gorillas and Their Habitats
2008	Protocol on Integrated Coastal Zone Management in the Mediterranean
2009	Statute of the International Renewable Energy Agency

Notes

Chapter 1

1. Executive Summary, *Environmental Performance Index 2008*, http://www.yale.edu/epi/files/2008EPI_Text.pdf accessed December 17, 2009.

2. Felicity Barringer, "U.S. Given Poor Marks on the Environment," *New York Times*, January 23, 2008, http://www.nytimes.com, accessed December 17, 2009.

3. Ibid.

4. Executive Summary, *Environmental Performance Index*, http://www.yale.edu/epi/files/2008EPI_Text.pdf accessed December 17, 2009.

5. "Emerging Economy Front Runner in Climate Policy for the First Time," news release, Climate Action Network Europe and Germanwatch, December 14, 2009, http://www.germanwatch.org/presse/2009-12-14e, accessed December 17, 2009.

6. Ibid.

7. John W. Kingdon, *Agendas, Alternatives, and Public Policies*, 2nd ed. (New York: Longman, 2003), 96.

8. For more on the development of environmental awareness, see Roderick Nash in *American Environmentalism*, 3rd ed. (New York: McGraw-Hill, 1990); *The American Conservation Movement* (St. Charles, MO: Forum, 1974); *Wilderness and the American Mind*, 4th ed. (New Haven, CT: Yale University Press, 2001); and *The Rights of Nature:*

A History of Environmental Ethics (Madison: University of Wisconsin Press, 1988).

9. Roderick Nash, *Wilderness and the American Mind*, 4th ed. (New Haven, CT: Yale University Press, 2001).

10. Roderick Nash, *American Environmentalism*, 3rd ed. (New York: McGraw-Hill, 1990), xi.

11. David Cushan Coyle, *Conservation* (New Brunswick, NJ: Rutgers University Press, 1957), 8–9, 21.

12. Donald Worster, *American Environmentalism: The Formative Period, 1860–1915* (New York: Wiley, 1973), 3.

13. Among the historians who have researched the sportsmen's movement is John E. Reiger; see *American Sportsmen and the Origins of Conservation* (Norman: University of Oklahoma Press, 1986).

14. Ibid., 53.

15. The biographical materials on these early pioneers provide an excellent background on the formation of the early conservation movement. See, for example, George T. Morgan Jr.; *William B. Greeley, A Practical Forester* (St. Paul, MN: Forest History Society, 1961); and Wallace Stegner, *Beyond the Hundredth Meridian: John Wesley Powell and the Second Coming of the West* (Boston: Houghton Mifflin, 1954).

16. Another major contributor to the field of American environmental history is Joseph Petulla; see *Environmental Protection in the United*

States (San Francisco: San Francisco Study Center, 1987).

17. Suellen Hoy, "Municipal Housekeeping: The Role of Women in Improving Urban Sanitation Practices," in *Pollution and Reform in American Cities 1870–1930*, ed. Martin Melosi (Austin: University of Texas Press, 1980), 173–198.

18. See Harold McCracken, *George Catlin and the Old Frontier* (New York: Dial, 1959), for a biographical perspective on one of the frontier environmentalists.

19. There are two ways to gauge Thoreau's impact on the development of the environmental movement, especially his sojourn at Walden Pond. One is to read his own words, such as *The Annotated Walden* (New York: Potter, 1970) and *Consciousness in Concord* (Boston: Houghton Mifflin, 1958). Many biographers have attempted to characterize this complex individual; see Milton Meltzer and Walter Harding, *A Thoreau Profile* (New York: Crowell, 1962); Sherman Paul, *The Shores of America: Thoreau's Inward Exploration* (Urbana: University of Illinois Press, 1959); and Robert Richardson, *Henry Thoreau: A Life of the Mind* (Berkeley: University of California Press, 1986).

20. The urban sanitation issue became one of the cornerstones of urban environmentalism. See George Rosen, *A History of Public Health* (New York: MD Publications, 1958).

21. See Suellen Hoy, *Chasing Dirt: The American Pursuit of Cleanliness* (New York: Oxford University Press, 1995), 117–120.

22. Few comprehensive studies of the early organizations exist, except for those produced by the groups themselves. See, for example, Michael Cohen, *The History of the Sierra Club 1892–1970* (San Francisco: Sierra Club, 1988).

23. For more information on this early period, see Henry Clepper, *Origins of American Conservation* (New York: Ronald Press, 1966); and Peter Wild, *Pioneer Conservationists of Western America* (Missoula, MT: Mountain Press, 1979).

24. Samuel P. Hays, *Conservation and the Gospel of Efficiency* (Cambridge, MA: Harvard University Press, 1959), 5.

25. To see how Pinchot's view contrasted with Muir's, see Muir's books, *Our National Parks* (Boston: Houghton Mifflin, 1901) and *The Yosemite* (New York: Century, 1912). One of the most widely researched environmental pioneers, Muir has been the subject of dozens of biographers, including Michael P. Cohen, *The Pathless Way: John Muir and the American Wilderness* (Madison: University of Wisconsin Press, 1984); Stephen Fox, *John Muir and His Legacy* (Boston: Little, Brown, 1981); Frederick Turner, *Rediscovering America: John Muir in His Time and Ours* (New York: Viking, 1985); and Linnie M. Wolfe, *Son of the Wilderness: The Life of John Muir* (New York: Knopf, 1945).

26. Samuel P. Hays, *Conservation and the Gospel of Efficiency* (Cambridge, MA: Harvard University Press, 1959), 132.

27. The activities of the Conservation Congresses are outlined by Grant McConnell in "The Conservation Movement—Past and Present," *Western Political Quarterly*, 7, no. 3 (September 1954): 463–478.

28. Samuel P. Hays, *Conservation and the Gospel of Efficiency* (Cambridge, MA: Harvard University Press, 1959), 69.

29. Many historians and analysts of the Progressive period have downgraded its importance to contemporary environmentalism. See Geoffrey Wandesforde-Smith, "Moral Outrage and the Progress of Environmental Policy: What Do We Tell the Next Generation about How to Care for the Earth?" in *Environmental Policy in the 1990s*, ed. Norman J. Vig and Michael E. Kraft (Washington, DC: Congressional Quarterly Press, 1990), 334–335.

30. For a discussion of the evolution of public health and environmental protection, see Robert Gottlieb, *Forcing the Spring: The Transformation of the American Environmental Movement* (Washington, DC: Island Press, 2005).

31. For a summary of the development of the parks and wilderness areas, see Dyan Zaslowsky and the Wilderness Society, *These American Lands* (New York: Henry Holt, 1986).

32. There is a wealth of historical information on the National Park Service and its programs, including the following books: William C. Everhart, *The National Park Service* (New York: Praeger, 1972); Ronald A. Foresta, *America's National Parks and*

Their Keepers (Washington, DC: Resources for the Future, 1984); Alfred Runte, *National Parks: The American Experience* (Lincoln: University of Nebraska Press, 1982); David J. Simon, ed., *Our Common Lands* (Washington, DC: Island Press, 1988); and National Parks Conservation Association, *Investing in Park Futures: A Blueprint for Tomorrow* (Washington, DC: Author, 1988).

33. Rachel Carson, *Silent Spring* (Greenwich, CT: Fawcett, 1962). For biographical material on the woman who is largely credited with reviving the contemporary environmental movement, see Paul Brooks, *The House of Life: Rachel Carson at Work* (Boston: Houghton Mifflin, 1972); Carol Gartner, *Rachel Carson* (New York: Ungar, 1983); H. Patricia Hynes, *The Recurring Silent Spring* (New York: Pergamon Press, 1989); and Philip Sterling, *Sea and Earth: The Life of Rachel Carson* (New York: Crowell, 1970).

34. Paul Ehrlich, *The Population Bomb* (New York: Ballantine, 1968).

35. For an account of this event, see Carol Steinhart and John Steinhart, *Blowout: A Case Study of the Santa Barbara Oil Spill* (Belmont, CA: Wadsworth, 1972). An extensive bibliography on the spill was compiled by Kay Walstead, *Oil Pollution in the Santa Barbara Channel* (Santa Barbara: University of California, Santa Barbara Library, 1972).

36. Dyan Zaslowsky and the Wilderness Society, *These American Lands* (New York: Henry Holt, 1986), 37.

37. See Lewis L. Gould, *Lady Bird Johnson and the Environment* (Lawrence: University of Kansas Press, 1988). See also Cormac O'Brien, *The Secret Lives of the First Ladies* (Austin, TX: Eakin Press, 2005).

38. John C. Esposito, *Vanishing Air* (New York: Grossman, 1970), 292.

39. Samuel P. Hays, "From Conservation to Environment," *Environmental Review*, 6 (Fall 1982): 37.

40. Jack Lewis, "The Spirit of the First Earth Day," *EPA Journal*, 16, no. 1 (January–February 1990): 9–10.

41. See John C. Whitaker, *Striking a Balance: Environment and Natural Resources Policy in the Nixon-Ford Years* (Washington, DC: American Enterprise Institute, 1976), 6.

42. Samuel P. Hays, *Beauty, Health and Permanence: Environmental Politics in the U.S., 1955–1985* (Cambridge: Cambridge University Press, 1987), 61.

43. See Lois Gibbs, *Love Canal* (Albany: State University of New York Press, 1983); and Adeline Gordon Levine, *Love Canal: Science, Politics and People* (Lexington, MA: Heath, 1982).

44. Robert Cameron Mitchell, "The Public Speaks Again: A New Environmental Survey," *Resources*, 60 (September–October 1978): 2.

45. David Rapp, "Special Report," *Congressional Quarterly*, January 20, 1990, 138.

46. "Household Waste Threatening Environment; Recycling Helps Ease Disposal Problem," *Gallup Report* 280, January 1990, 30–34.

47. See Riley E. Dunlap, "Public Opinion in the 1980s: Clear Consensus, Ambiguous Commitment," *Environment*, 33, no. 8 (October 1991): 9–15, 32–37.

48. George Gallup Jr., and Frank Newport, "Americans Strongly in Tune with the Purpose of Earth Day 1990," *Gallup Poll Monthly*, April 1990, 6.

49. The increasingly global nature of perceptions about the nature of environmental problems is illustrated by a series of public opinion polls conducted in 1992. See the press release "Environment Given Priority over Economic Growth in Both Rich and Poor Nations" (Washington, DC: George H. Gallup International Institute, May 4, 1992). See also Riley E. Dunlap, George H. Gallup Jr., and Alec M. Gallup, *The Health of the Planet Survey* (Washington, DC: George H. Gallup International Institute, May 1992).

50. Albert Gore, *Earth in the Balance* (Boston: Houghton Mifflin, 1992).

51. Margaret Kriz, "Quick Draw," *National Journal*, November 13, 1993, 2711–2716, quote on 2713.

52. Keith Schneider, "New View Calls Environmental Policy Misguided," *New York Times*, March 21, 1993, 1.

53. See Ed Gillespie and Rob Shellhas, eds., *Contract with America* (New York: Times Books, 1994), 125–141. For a discussion of the history and

evolution of the Contract with America, see Elizabeth Drew, *Showdown: The Struggle between the Gingrich Congress and the Clinton White House* (New York: Simon and Schuster, 1996), 28–34.

54. Quoted in Cindy Skryzycki, "Hill Republicans Promise a Regulatory Revolution," *Washington Post*, January 4, 1995, A1.

55. Craig E. Richardson and Geoff C. Ziebart, *Red Tape in America: Stories from the Front Lines* (Washington, DC: Heritage Foundation, 1995), v.

56. B. J. Bergman, "Standing Up for the Planet," *Sierra* (March–April 1995): 79–80.

57. Tom Kenworthy, "In Smooth Water Now," *Washington Post National Weekly Edition*, December 11–17, 1995.

58. "Harris Poll: Americans Want Conservation Laws," *Columbia University Record*, 21, no. 13 (January 19, 1996): 29.

59. Humphrey Taylor, "Nation's 'Feel Good Index' Rises Sharply," *The Harris Poll #26*, June 3, 1998.

60. White House news release, "President Clinton: Saving America's Natural Treasures," April 22, 1998.

61. White House, "Protecting the Environment: President Clinton and Vice President Gore," http://www.whitehouse.gov/CEQ, accessed March 18, 2000.

62. *American Trucking Association v. U.S. Environmental Protection Agency*, 175 F3d 1027 (D.C. Cir., 1999).

63. Traci Watson, "Study: 4 of 10 Factories Violated Clean Air Act," *USA Today*, May 20, 1999, 3A.

64. "Toxic Chemical Release Rises," *Arizona Republic*, May 23, 1999, A28.

65. White House, "Protecting the Environment: President Clinton and Vice President Gore," http://www.whitehouse.gov/CEQ, accessed March 18, 2000.

66. Joseph Carroll, "Environment Not Highest-Priority Issue This Election Year," *Gallup Poll Monthly*, no. 420 (September 2000): 15–16.

67. Riley E. Dunlap and Lydia Saad, "Only One in Four Americans Are Anxious About the Environment," *Gallup Poll Monthly*, no. 427 (April 2001): 6.

68. Ibid.

69. Frank Newport and Lydia Saad, "Americans Consider Global Warming Real, but Not Alarming," *Gallup Poll Monthly*, no. 427 (April 2001): 2–3.

70. Matthew Daly, "Bush Administration Takes Up Review of Landmark Environmental Law," *San Francisco Chronicle*, August 29, 2002, http://www.sfgate.com, accessed August 30, 2002.

71. Memorandum, Council on Environmental Quality, "NEPA Task Force," April 10, 2002, http://ceq.eh.doe.gov, accessed September 1, 2002.

72. See "Internal Forest Service Memo Suggests Changes to Northwest Forest Plan," *The Forestry Source*, 7, no. 8 (August 2002): 1; Tom Detzel, "Bush Team Looks at Forest Plan Facelift," *The Oregonian*, August 26, 2002, http://www.oregonlive.com/environment/oregonian, accessed September 1, 2002; Matthew Koehler, "Mark Rey Wants to Take Our Forests Away," *Forest Advocate*, Summer 2002, 1.

73. American Enterprise Institute, "Polls on the Environment," http://www.aei.org/docLib 11, accessed May 16, 2005.

74. Ibid.

75. "As Interior Turns," *High Country News*, January 5, 2009, 8–9.

76. "Problems and Priorities," PollingReport.com, http://www.pollingreport.com/priority, accessed October 2, 2009.

77. "NRDC Applauds Obama's Environmental Record Ahead of Climate Summit," Environmental News Service, December 15, 2009, http://www.ens-newswire.com, accessed December 17, 2009.

78. Ibid.

Chapter 2

1. McKenzie Funk, "Firestarter," *Outside*, September 2007, 116.

2. Ibid., 105.

3. For various perspectives on the Vail incident and ELF, see Daniel Glick, *Powder Burn: Arson, Money, and Mystery on Vail Mountain* (New York: Public Affairs, 2001); Alex Markels, "Backfire," *Mother Jones*, March–April 1999, 60–64, 78–79; and Michelle Nijhuis, "ELF Strikes Again," *High Country News*, February 1, 1999, 3.

4. McKenzie Funk, "Firestarter," *Outside*, September 2007, 115.

5. Ibid., 116.

6. William McCall, "11 Indicted by U.S. in Ecoterrorism," *Arizona Republic*, January 21, 2006, A12.

7. William McCall, "Radical Environmentalism on the Wane," *USA Today*, July 22, 2007, http://www.usatoday.com/news/nation/environment/2007-07-22-radical-environmentalism_N.htm, accessed July 8, 2009.

8. Ibid.

9. Statement of John Lewis, U.S. Senate Committee on Environment and Public Works, May 18, 2005, http://epw.senate.gov/hearing_statements.cfm?id=237817, accessed May 23, 2005.

10. See Robert Hunter, *Warriors of the Rainbow: A Chronicle of the Greenpeace Movement* (New York: Holt, Rinehart and Winston, 1979); Paul Watson, *Sea Shepherd* (New York: Norton, 1982); Rick Scarce, *Eco-Warriors: Understanding the Radical Environmental Movement* (Chicago: Noble Press, 1990); and Dave Foreman, *Confessions of an Eco-Warrior* (New York: Harmony Books, 1991).

11. Scott Sunde and Paul Shukovsky, "Elusive Radicals Escalate Attacks in Nature's Name," *Seattle Post-Intelligencer*, June 18, 2001, http://www.seattlepi.com/local/27871_ecoterror18.shtml?dpfrom=thread, accessed August 7, 2001.

12. Harold D. Lasswell, *Politics: Who Gets What, When, How* (New York: P. Smith, 1936).

13. For the classical tenets of group theory, see David Truman, *The Governmental Process* (New York: Knopf, 1951), and Earl Latham, *The Group Basis of Politics* (New York: Octagon Books, 1965).

14. Riley E. Dunlap and Angela G. Mertig, "The Evolution of the U.S. Environmental Movement from 1970 to 1990: An Overview," in *American Environmentalism: The U.S. Environmental Movement, 1970–1990*, ed. Riley E. Dunlap and Angela G. Mertig (Washington, DC: Taylor & Francis, 1992), 4.

15. See Michael S. Greve, "Private Enforcement, Private Rewards: How Environmental Suits Became an Entitlement Program," in *Environmental Politics: Public Costs, Private Rewards*, ed. Michael S. Greve and Fred L. Smith Jr. (New York: Praeger, 1992), 105–109.

16. Greenpeace, "About Us," http://www.greenpeace.org/international/about, accessed August 30, 2009.

17. Norman Miller, *Environmental Politics: Stakeholders, Interests, and Policymaking*, 2nd ed. (New York: Routledge, 2009).

18. "About the Blue Green Alliance," http://www.bluegreenalliance.org/about_us, accessed June 17, 2009.

19. "Myers Withdraws His Judicial Nomination," *Earthjustice: In Brief* (Spring 2007): 6–7.

20. Robert D. Bullard, *Dumping in Dixie: Race, Class, and Environmental Quality*, 3rd ed. (Boulder, CO: Westview, 2000), 10.

21. See, for example, Allan Schnaiberg, *The Environment: From Surplus to Scarcity* (New York: Oxford University Press, 1980); Bunyan Bryant and Paul Mohai, eds., *Race and Incidence of Environmental Hazards* (Boulder, CO: Westview Press, 1992); Richard Hofrichter, ed., *Toxic Struggles: The Theory and Practice of Environmental Justice* (Philadelphia: New Society, 1993); Bunyan Bryant, ed., *Environmental Justice: Issues, Policies, and Solutions* (Covelo, CA: Island Press, 1995); and David E. Camacho, ed., *Environmental Injustices, Political Struggles: Race, Class, and the Environment* (Durham, NC: Duke University Press, 1998).

22. United Church of Christ Commission for Racial Justice, *Proceedings: The First National People of Color Environmental Leadership Summit* (New York: United Church of Christ Commission for Racial Justice, 1993), xiii–xiv.

23. Robert D. Bullard, ed., *Confronting Environmental Racism: Voices from the Grassroots* (Boston: South End Press, 1993), 17.

24. Robert D. Bullard, "The Environmental Justice Movement Comes of Age," *Amicus Journal*, 16, no. 1 (Spring 1994): 32–37.

25. U.S. Environmental Protection Agency, "National Environmental Justice Advisory Council Overview," http://www.epa.gov/environmentaljustice/nejac/index.html, accessed May 23, 2005; and U.S. Environmental Protection Agency, "Environmental Justice: Frequently Asked Questions," http://www.epa.

gov/compliance/resources/faqs, accessed May 23, 2005.

26. Christopher H. Foreman Jr., *The Promise and Peril of Environmental Justice* (Washington, DC: Brookings Institution, 1998), 3, 133.

27. United Church of Christ Justice & Witness Ministries, *Toxic Wastes and Race at Twenty 1987–2007*, http://www.ucc.org/justice, accessed May 9, 2007.

28. Segun Gbadegesin, "Multinational Corporations, Developed Nations, and Environmental Racism: Toxic Waste, Exploration, and Eco-Catastrophe," in *Faces of Environmental Racism: Confronting Issues of Global Justice*, ed. Laura Westra and Bill E. Lawson (Lanham, MD: Rowman & Littlefield, 2001).

29. Samuel P. Hays, *Beauty, Health and Permanence: Environmental Politics in the United States 1955–1985* (Cambridge: Cambridge University Press, 1987), 295.

30. Ibid., 308.

31. Sheldon Kamieniecki, *Corporate America and Environmental Policy: How Often Does Business Get Its Way?* (Stanford, CA: Stanford University Press, 2006).

32. Perspectives on the role of industry in environmental policymaking vary widely. See, for example, Neil Gunningham, Robert A. Kagan, and Dorothy Thornton, *Shades of Green: Business, Regulation, and Environment* (Stanford: Stanford University Press, 2003); Hugh S. Gorman, *Redefining Efficiency: Pollution Concerns, Regulatory Mechanisms, and Technological Change in the U.S.* (Akron, OH: University of Akron Press, 2001); and Jack Doyle, *Taken for a Ride: Detroit's Big Three and the Politics of Pollution* (New York: Four Walls Eight Windows, 2000).

33. For different views of the grassroots movements, see Alan M. Gottlieb, ed., *The Wise Use Agenda* (Bellevue, WA: Free Enterprise Press, 1989); Ron Arnold, *Ecology Wars: Environmentalism As If People Mattered* (Bellevue, WA: Free Enterprise Press, 1987); David Helvarg, *The War against the Greens: The "Wise Use" Movement, the New Right, and Anti-Environmental Violence* (San Francisco: Sierra Club Books, 1994); John Echeverria and Raymond Booth Eby, eds., *Let the People Judge: Wise Use and the Private Property Rights Movement* (Washington, DC: Island Press, 1995); Philip D. Brick and R. McGreggor Cawley, eds., *A Wolf in the Garden: The Lands Rights Movement and the New Environmental Debate* (Lanham, MD: Rowman & Littlefield, 1996); and Paul R. Ehrlich and Anne H. Ehrlich, *The Betrayal of Science and Reason* (Washington, DC: Island Press, 1996).

34. Keith Schneider, "A County's Bid for U.S. Land Draws Lawsuit," *New York Times*, March 9, 1995, A1.

35. Laurel Hagen, "Report from the Paria River," Wildlands CPR, May 13, 2009, http://www.wildlandscpr.org/blog/report-paria-river-protests, accessed June 2, 2009.

36. Patty Henetz, "Feds Reviewing BLM Evidence from ATV Protest Ride," *Salt Lake Tribune*, May 12, 2009, http://www.sltrib.com/ci_12347329, accessed June 2, 2009; "Counties Attack Grand Staircase-Escalante National Monument Resource Protections," http://www.highway-robbery.org/lands/utah13.htm, accessed June 2, 2009.

37. Patty Henetz, "Feds Reviewing BLM Evidence from ATV Protest Ride," *Salt Lake Tribune*, May 12, 2009, http://www.sltrib.com/ci_12347329, accessed June 2, 2009.

38. Roger W. Cobb and Charles D. Elder, *Participation in American Politics: The Dynamics of Agenda-Building*, 2nd ed. (Baltimore: Johns Hopkins University Press, 1983).

39. James Anderson, *Public Policymaking*, 4th ed. (Boston: Houghton Mifflin, 2000), 100.

40. Peter Bachrach and Morton Baratz, *Power and Poverty* (New York: Oxford University Press, 1970), 44.

41. Gregg Easterbrook, *A Moment on the Earth: The Coming Age of Environmental Optimism* (New York: Viking, 1995), 493.

42. Jake Coyle, "Is Twitter Becoming the News Outlet for the 21st Century?" *Arizona Republic*, July 9, 2009, E2.

43. On the role of the media, see, for example, J. Robert Cox, ed., *Environmental Communication and the Public Sphere*, 2nd ed. (Thousand Oaks, CA: Sage, 2010); Doris A. Graber, *Mass Media and American Politics* (Washington, DC: CQ Press, 2010); and Anders Hansen, *Environment, Media and Communication* (New York: Routledge, 2010).

44. J. P. Rodriguez et al., "Globalization of Conservation: A View from the South," *Science* 317 (August 10, 2007): 755–756.

45. See Chen Gang, *Politics of China's Environmental Protection: Problems and Progress* (Hackensack, NJ: World Scientific Publishing, 2010); Tim Swanson and Tun Lin, *Environmental Growth and Environmental Regulation: China's Path to a Brighter Future* (New York: Routledge, 2010); and Bryan Tilt, *Struggling for Sustainability in Rural China: Environmental Values and Civil Society* (New York: Columbia University Press, 2010).

46. See Benjamin Seel, Matthew Paterson, and Brian Doherty, eds., *Direct Action in British Environmentalism* (London: Routledge, 2000); Derek Wall, *Earth First! and the Origin of the Anti-Roads Movement* (London: Routledge, 1999); and Russell J. Dalton, *The Green Rainbow: Environmental Groups in Western Europe* (New Haven, CT: Yale University Press, 1994).

47. "Twentieth Anniversary of the American Green Movement," http://www.greenparty.org/intro.php, accessed November 10, 2004.

48. Jonathan Finer and Spencer S. Hua, "Repeat Role as Spoiler Is Unlikely," *Washington Post*, November 3, 2004, http://www.washingtonpost.com/wp-dyn/articles/A19764-2004Nov2.html, accessed November 10, 2004; Green Party USA. "Green Party Election Highlights," at http://www.gp.org/2004election, accessed November 10, 2004.

49. "November 2008 Green Party Election Results," http://www.gp.org/2008-elections/November-2008ElectionResults.htm, accessed June 16, 2009.

50. Anna Bramwell, *The Fading of the Greens: The Decline of Environmental Politics in the West* (New Haven, CT: Yale University Press, 1994).

51. John Rensenbrink, "A Brief History of the Global Green Network," http://www.globalgreens.info/ggn_ggnbriefhistory.html, accessed November 10, 2004.

52. Marvin S. Soroos, "Global Institutions and the Environment: An Evolutionary Perspective," in *The Global Environment*, ed. Norman J. Vig and Regina S. Axelrod (Washington, DC: Congressional Quarterly Press, 1999), 27–51.

53. United Nations, *Agenda 21: Report of the United Nations: Conference on Environment and Development* (New York: United Nations, 1992).

Chapter 3

1. "Obama Signs the Omnibus Public Lands Management Act of 2009," *New York Times*, March 30, 2009, http://www.nytimes.com/2009/03/30/us/politics/30lands-text.html, accessed March 31, 2009.

2. Ibid.

3. Juliet Eilperin, "Obama Signs Major Land Conservation Law," *Washington Post*, March 30, 2009, http://www.voices.washingtonpost.com/44/2009/03/30/obama_signs_major_land_conserv.html, accessed March 31, 2009.

4. "A Ghost of the 1970s," *High Country News*, April 13, 2009, 5.

5. Norman Miller, *Environmental Politics: Stakeholders, Interests, and Policymaking*, 2nd ed. (New York: Routledge, 2009), 20.

6. "Key Legislation in Omnibus Public Land Management Act of 2009," The Wilderness Society, http://www.wilderness.org, accessed July 17, 2009.

7. Norman Miller, *Environmental Politics: Stakeholders, Interests, and Policymaking*, 2nd ed. (New York: Routledge, 2009), 23.

8. For an overview of the presidential role, see Dennis L. Soden, ed., *The Environmental Presidency* (Albany: State University of New York Press, 1999).

9. Alfred A. Marcus, *Promise and Performance: Choosing and Implementing an Environmental Policy* (Westport, CT: Greenwood Press, 1980), 87.

10. Ibid., 85.

11. John Quarles, *Cleaning Up America: An Insider's View of the EPA* (Boston: Houghton Mifflin, 1976), 34.

12. Steven A. Cohen, "EPA: A Qualified Success," in Sheldon Kamieniecki et al., *Controversies in Environmental Policy* (Albany: State University of New York Press, 1986).

13. John Quarles, *Cleaning Up America: An Insider's View of the EPA* (Boston: Houghton Mifflin, 1976), 17–19.

14. John McCormick, *Reclaiming Paradise: The Global Environmental Movement* (Bloomington: Indiana University Press, 1989), 110. See also Karen M. Hult and Charles E. Walcott, *Empowering the White House: Governance under Nixon, Ford, and Carter* (Lawrence: University Press of Kansas, 2003).

15. Marc K. Landy, Marc C. Roberts, and Stephen R. Thomas, *The Environmental Protection Agency: Asking the Wrong Questions*, expanded ed. (New York: Oxford University Press, 1994), 41.

16. Lou Cannon, *President Reagan: The Role of a Lifetime* (New York: Simon and Schuster, 1991), 530–531.

17. C. Brant Short, *Ronald Reagan and the Public Lands* (College Station: Texas A&M University Press, 1989), 57.

18. Lou Cannon, *President Reagan: The Role of a Lifetime* (New York: Simon and Schuster, 1991), 531.

19. Jonathan Lash, Katherine Gillman, and David Sheridan, *A Season of Spoils: The Reagan Administration's Attack on the Environment* (New York: Pantheon Books, 1984), 231.

20. Ron Arnold, *At the Eye of the Storm: James Watt and the Environmentalists* (Chicago: Regency Gateway, 1982), 94.

21. Ibid., 93.

22. Lou Cannon, *President Reagan: The Role of a Lifetime* (New York: Simon and Schuster, 1991), 532.

23. Jonathan Lash, Katherine Gillman, and David Sheridan, *A Season of Spoils: The Reagan Administration's Attack on the Environment* (New York: Pantheon Books, 1984), 287–297.

24. Needless to say, Burford's account of the personnel loss and her subsequent fall from grace is somewhat different. She attributes the changes to natural attrition within the agency. See Anne Burford with John Greenya, *Are You Tough Enough?* (New York: McGraw-Hill, 1986).

25. See Richard E. Cohen, "The Gorsuch Affair," *National Journal*, January 8, 1983, 80.

26. Haynes Johnson, *Sleepwalking through History: America in the Reagan Years* (New York: Norton, 1991), 170.

27. *Public Papers of the President of the United States: Ronald Reagan*, 1983 (Washington, DC: U.S. Government Printing Office, 1984), 388–389.

28. Haynes Johnson, *Sleepwalking through History: America in the Reagan Years* (New York: Norton, 1991), 171.

29. Marc K. Landy, Marc C. Roberts, and Stephen R. Thomas, *The Environmental Protection Agency: Asking the Wrong Questions*, expanded ed. (New York: Oxford University Press, 1994), 252.

30. Ibid., 256.

31. Tom Turner, "Changing the Guards," *Mother Earth News*, May–June 1989, 56.

32. William K. Reilly, "Pollution Prevention: An Environmental Goal for the '90s" *EPA Journal*, 16, no. 1 (January–February 1990): 5.

33. "A Vision for EPA's Future," *EPA Journal*, 16, no. 6 (September–October 1990): 5.

34. "William Reilly's Green Precision Weapons," *The Economist*, March 30, 1991, 28.

35. Executive Office of the President, Council on Environmental Quality, *The 21st Annual Report of the Council on Environmental Quality* (Washington, DC: U.S. Government Printing Office, 1991).

36. "Quailing over Clean Air," *Environment*, 33, no. 6 (July–August 1991): 24.

37. Allan Freedman, "After Interior's Smooth Ride, Some Issues Left Behind," *Congressional Quarterly Weekly Report*, October 5, 1996, 2858.

38. Gary Lee, "Agency Takes a Hit from One of Its Own," *Washington Post*, June 27, 1997, A27.

39. Robert L. Paarlberg, "A Domestic Dispute: Clinton, Congress, and Environmental Policy," *Environment*, October 1996, 16–28.

40. See Colin Campbell and Bert A. Rockman, eds., *The Clinton Presidency: First Appraisals* (Chatham, NJ: Chatham House Publishers, 1996).

41. One notable exception was the administration's acceptance of the Safe Harbor program, initiated by the Environmental Defense Fund and the National Cattlemen's Beef Association. Under a safe harbor agreement, a landowner commits to restoring or enhancing habitats for endangered species and the government pledges not to "punish" the landowner by placing any new restrictions on the land if their actions result in the natural introduction of endangered species.

42. Martin Nie, "It's the Environment, Stupid! Clinton and the Environment," *Presidential Studies Quarterly*, 27, no. 1 (Winter 1997): 39–51.

43. Maurie J. Cohen, "George W. Bush and the Environmental Protection Agency: A Midterm Appraisal," *Society and Natural Resources*, 17 (2004): 69–88.

44. Ibid., 72.

45. "Dozens of Doozies: Keeping Tabs on George W. Bush," *Sierra*, 86, no. 4 (July–August 2001): 21.

46. Natural Resources Defense Council, *Rewriting the Rules: The Bush Administration's First Term Environmental Record*, Executive Summary at http://www.nrdc.org/legislation/rollbacks/execsum.asp, accessed February 20, 2005.

47. "Ins and Outs: Bush Cabinet Shuffle," *CBS News*, December 3, 2004, http://www.cbsnews.com.com/stories/2004/12/03/politics/main659055.shtml, accessed December 31, 2004.

48. Michael Doyle, "Veneman Ends Role as First Female USDA Chief," November 15, 2004, http://www.knoxstudio.com, accessed December 13, 2004; Dan Looker, "Bush Announces Veneman Resignation as Ag Secretary," November 15, 2004, at http://www.agriculture.com, accessed December 13, 2004; and "Remarks by the President and Secretary of Agriculture Nominee Governor Mike Johanns," at http://www.lincolnjournalstar.com, accessed December 13, 2004.

49. Jacqueline Vaughn and Hanna J. Cortner, *George W. Bush's Healthy Forests: Reframing the Environmental Debate* (Boulder: University Press of Colorado, 2005), 23.

50. Jonathan H. Adler, "Post-Whitman EPA," *National Review*, June 2, 2003, at http://www.nationalreview.com, accessed November 28, 2003.

51. See Christie Todd Whitman, *It's My Party Too: The Battle for the Heart of the GOP and the Future of America* (New York: Penguin Press, 2005).

52. "A Get-Along Voice at the EPA," *New York Times*, August 13, 2003, http://www.nytimes.com, accessed August 13, 2003.

53. Environmental News Service, "Northwestern Hawaiian Islands Proclaimed a National Monument," June 15, 2006, http://www.ens-newswire.com/ens/jun2006/2006-06-15-03.asp accessed February 20, 2007.

54. Juliet Eilperin, "Hawaiian Marine Reserve to Be the World's Largest," *The Washington Post*, June 15, 2006, http://www.washingtonpost.com, accessed February 20, 2007.

55. David A. Rochefort and Roger Cobb, *The Politics of Problem Definition: Shaping the Policy Agenda* (Lawrence: University Press of Kansas, 1994).

56. OpenSecrets.org, "Lobbying Database," http://www.opensecrets.org/lobby/index.php, accessed June 11, 2009.

57. James Anderson, *Public Policymaking*, 4th ed. (Boston: Houghton Mifflin, 2000), 152–155.

58. Bureau of Land Management, "Factsheet on Challenges Facing the BLM in its Management of Wild Horses and Burros," http://www.blm.gov/wo/st/en/prog/wild_horse_and_burro/wh_b_information_center/blm_statements/new_factsheet.html, accessed August 2, 2009.

59. Jean-Pierre Ruiz, "US House Passes Legislation to Protect Burros and Wild Horses," *Seattle Examiner*, August 2, 2009, http://www.examiner.com/x-9726-Seattle-Pet-Laws-Examiner~y2009m8d2-US-House-passes-legislation-to-protect-burros-and-wild-horses, accessed August 3, 2009.

60. "7 Preserves Envisioned to Manage Wild Horses," *New York Times*, October 7, 2009, http://www.nytimes.com/2009/10/08/us/08horses.html, accessed October 9, 2009.

61. Ibid.

62. Erin Kelly, "House OKs Plan to Avert Slaughter of Wild Horses," *Arizona Republic*, July 18, 2007, A1, A7.

63. Michael E. Kraft, "Environmental Gridlock: Searching for Consensus in Congress," in *Environmental Policy in the 1990s*, ed. Norman J. Vig and Michael E. Kraft (Washington, DC: Congressional Quarterly Press, 1990), 103–124.

64. Walter A. Rosenbaum, *Environmental Politics and Policy*, 2nd ed. (Washington, DC: Congressional Quarterly Press, 1991), 83.

65. USDA Forest Service, "About Us," at http://www.fs.fed.us/aboutus, accessed April 4, 2005.

66. 5 U.S.C. 551 (4).

67. See Cornelius M. Kerwin, *Rulemaking: How Government Agencies Write Law and Make Policy*, 2nd ed. (Washington, DC: CQ Press, 1999).

68. For more on the role of the courts, see Rosemary O'Leary, "Environmental Policy in the Courts,"

in Norman J. Vig and Michael E. Kraft, *Environmental Policy: New Directions for the Twenty-First Century* (Washington, DC: CQ Press, 2010): 125–146.

69. Frederick R. Anderson, *NEPA and the Courts* (Baltimore, MD: Johns Hopkins University Press, 1973), 17. For more on NEPA, see Matt Lindstrom and Zachary Smith, *The National Environmental Policy Act: Judicial Misconstruction, Legislative Indifference, and Executive Neglect* (College Station: Texas A&M University Press, 2001.

70. The case that is generally regarded as opening the door to environmental group litigation is *Scenic Hudson Preservation Conference v. Federal Power Commission*, 453 F. 2d 463 (2nd Cir. 1971). The local conservation group challenged the application of New York Edison Company to build a power plant on Storm King Mountain in the Hudson River Valley and was granted standing by the Second Circuit Court under the Federal Power Act, which directs the Federal Power Commission to consider the impact of proposed projects.

71. See Robert V. Percival, "Environmental Law in the Courts: Highlights From the Marshall Papers," *Environmental Law Reporter*, 23, no. 10 (October 1993): 10606; and Richard E. Levy and Robert L. Glicksman, "Judicial Activism and Restraint in the Supreme Court's Environmental Law Decisions," *Vanderbilt Law Review*, 42 (March 1989): 343–431.

72. 121 S.Ct. 2448 (2001).

73. *Tahoe-Sierra Preservation Council, Inc. v. Tahoe Regional Planning Agency* 122 S.Ct. 1465 (2002). For commentary on the two cases, see John R. Nolan, "When Environmental Regulations Go 'Too Far,'" *New York Law Journal*, 227 (June 19, 2002): 5; and Peter R. Paden and Laurence A. Horvath, "Takings in 'Tahoe': U.S. Supreme Court Veers to the Center," *New York Law Journal*, 227 (July 1, 2002): 9.

74. See Defenders of Wildlife, "Weakening the National Environmental Policy Act: How the Bush Administration Uses the Judicial System to Weaken Environmental Protections"; "Undercutting National Forests Protections: How the Bush Administration Uses the Judicial System to Weaken Environmental Laws"; and

"Sabotaging the Endangered Species Act: How the Bush Administration Uses the Judicial System to Undermine Wildlife Protections"; http://www.defenders.org/publications/index.php, accessed April 8, 2005.

75. *Save the Manatee Club v. Ballard*, Unpubl'd, July 9, 2002. (D. DC No. 00-76).

76. See *Whitman v. American Trucking Associations, Inc.* 121 S.Ct. 903 (2001).

77. 213 F.3d 663 (DC. Cir. 2000). For a commentary on the ruling, see Nathan J. Brodeur, "Michigan v. U.S. Environmental Protection Agency," *Ecology Law Quarterly*, 28, no. 2 (2001): 275–296.

78. See, for example, Robert D. Behn, *Rethinking Democratic Accountability* (Washington, DC: Brookings Institution Press, 2001); Nancy C. Roberts, "Keeping Public Officials Accountable through Dialogue: Resolving the Accountability Paradox," *Public Administration Review*, 62, no. 6 (2002): 658–669; and Nancy Manring, "From Postdecisional Appeals to Predecisional Objections: Democratic Accountability in National Forest Planning," *Journal of Forestry*, 102, no. 2 (2004): 43–47.

79. J. Clarence Davies, *The Politics of Pollution* (New York: Pegasus, 1970).

80. See Samuel P. Hays, *Beauty, Health, and Permanence: Environmental Politics in the United States, 1955–1985* (Cambridge: Cambridge University Press, 1987), 441.

81. Barry G. Rabe, *Fragmentation and Integration in State Environmental Management* (Washington, DC: The Conservation Foundation), 31.

82. Samuel P. Hays, *Beauty, Health, and Permanence: Environmental Politics in the United States, 1955–1985* (Cambridge: Cambridge University Press, 1987), 433.

83. For an explanation of the new role of the states, see Barry G. Rabe, "Racing to the Top, the Bottom, or the Middle of the Pack," in *Environmental Policy: New Directions for the Twenty-First Century*, 6th ed., ed. Norman J. Vig and Michael E. Kraft (Washington, DC: Congressional Quarterly Press, 2010), 27–50.

84. Susan J. Buck and Edward M. Hathaway, "Designating State Natural Resource Trustees under the Superfund Amendments," in *Regulatory Federalism, Natural Resources, and*

Environmental Management, ed. Michael S. Hamilton (Washington, DC: American Society for Public Administration, 1990), 83–94.

85. James P. Lester, "A New Federalism?" in *Environmental Policy in the 1990s*, ed. Norman J. Vig and Michael E. Kraft (Washington, DC: Congressional Quarterly Press, 1990), 59–79.

86. "Governor Schwarzenegger Calls for One Million Solar Energy Systems in California Homes," news release, August 20, 2004, http://www.governor.ca.gov/state, accessed April 10, 2005.

87. Denise Scheberle, *Federalism and Environmental Policy: Trust and the Politics of Implementation* (Washington, DC: Georgetown University Press, 1997), 12–16.

88. David Roberts, "School of Rocky: An Interview with Salt Lake City Mayor and Green Innovator Rocky Anderson," *Grist*, February 6, 2007 at http://www.grist.org/article/anderson1/, accessed February 13, 2007.

89. Barry G. Rabe, "Racing to the Top, the Bottom, or the Middle of the Pack," in *Environmental Policy: New Directions for the Twenty-First Century*, 6th ed., ed. Norman J. Vig and Michael E. Kraft (Washington, DC: Congressional Quarterly Press, 2010).

90. Christopher McGrory Klyza and David J. Sousa, *American Environmental Policy 1990–2006*, Cambridge, MA: MIT Press, 2008).

Chapter 4

1. Peter Graff, "'Poetry for the Soul' in First Afghan National Park," Reuters News Service, June 18, 2009, http://www.reuters.com/article/idUS TRE55H5GK20090618, accessed June 18, 2009.

2. "Afghans Get First National Park," BBC News, April 22, 2009, http://neww.bbc.co.uk/go/pr/fr/-/2/hi/south_asia/8013017.stm, accessed June 18, 2009.

3. Peter Graff, "'Poetry for the Soul' in First Afghan National Park," Reuters News Service, June 18, 2009, http:// http://www.reuters.com/article/idUSTRE55H5GK20090618, accessed June 18, 2009.

4. Roderick Frasier Nash, *Wilderness and the American Mind*, 4th ed. (New Haven, CT: Yale University Press, 2001), 109–110.

5. Michael P. Dombeck, Christopher A. Wood, and Jack E. Williams, *From Conquest to Conservation: Our Public Lands Legacy* (Washington, DC: Island Press, 2003), 9–13.

6. The Sonoran Institute, "Western 'Crown Jewel' Public Lands Threatened," news release, July 8, 2009, http://www.sonoraninstitute.org, accessed August 24, 2009.

7. Dennis Wagner, "Groups, Feds Join to Push Law Aimed at Saving Lands in West," *Arizona Republic*, March 3, 2008, A1.

8. Denzel Ferguson and Nancy Ferguson, *Sacred Cows at the Public Trough* (Bend, OR: Maverick Publications, 1983), 171–172.

9. Richard West Sellars, *Preserving Nature in the National Parks: A History* (New Haven, CT: Yale University Press, 1997), 9–10.

10. Gregory M. Lamb, "U.S. National Parks Endangered by Climate Change," *Christian Science Monitor*, October 2, 2009, http://www.csmonitor.com/Environment/Bright-Green/2009/1002/us-national-parks-endangered-by-climate-change, accessed October 9, 2009.

11. The Yosemite Fund, http://www.yosemitefund.org, accessed June 16, 2005.

12. The California Desert Protection Act of 1994, P.L. 103-433.

13. For a general overview of U.S. forest policy, see Frederick W. Cubbage, Jay O'Laughlin, and Charles S. Bullock III, *Forest Resource Policy* (New York: Wiley, 1993); Christopher McGrory Klyza, *Who Controls Public Lands? Mining, Forestry, and Grazing Policies, 1970–1990* (Chapel Hill: University of North Carolina Press, 1996), 67–107; Elizabeth May, *At The Cutting Edge* (San Francisco: Sierra Club Books, 1998).

14. See Marion Clawson, *The Federal Lands since 1956: Recent Trends in Use and Management* (Baltimore: Johns Hopkins University Press, 1967); and Paul Culhane, *Public Lands Policies* (Baltimore: Johns Hopkins University Press, 1981).

15. George Hoberg, "The Emerging Triumph of Ecosystem Management: The Transformation of Federal Forest Policy," in *Western Public Land and Environmental Politics*, 2nd ed., ed. Charles Davis (Boulder, CO: Westview Press, 2001), 55–85.

16. For perspectives on the U.S. Forest Service and its employees, see the classic work by Herbert Kaufman, *The Forest Ranger: A Study in Administrative Behavior* (Baltimore: Johns Hopkins University Press, 1960); Harold K. Steen, *The U.S. Forest Service: A History* (Seattle: University of Washington Press, 1976); Robert D. Baker, Robert S. Maxwell, Victor H. Treat, and Henry C. Dethloff, *Timeless Heritage: A History of the Forest Service in the Southwest* (College Station, TX: Intaglio Press, 1988); David A. Clary, *Timber and the Forest Service* (Lawrence: University Press of Kansas, 1986). Some recent commentaries can be found in Roger A. Sedjo, ed., *A Vision for the U.S. Forest Service: Goals for Its Next Century* (Washington, DC: Resources for Future Press, 2000); William Dietrich, *The Final Forest: The Battle for the Last Great Trees of the Pacific Northwest* (New York: Penguin Books, 1992): 161–168.

17. See William Dietrich, *The Final Forest: The Battle for the Last Great Trees of the Pacific Northwest* (New York: Penguin Books, 1992): 161–168.

18. Ibid.

19. Chris Carrel, "A Patchwork Peace Unravels," *High Country News*, November 23, 1998, 1.

20. The foremost authority on the role of fire is Stephen J. Pyne, whose research explores the role of fire in culture, details about specific fires such as the one in 1910, and the history of wildland fire. See, for example, Stephen J. Pyne, *Fire in America: A Cultural History of Wildland and Rural Fire* (Seattle: University of Washington Press, 1982); Pyne, *Fire: A Brief History* (Seattle: University of Washington Press, 2001; Pyne, *Tending Fire: Coping with America's Wildland Fires* (Washington, DC: Island Press, 2004). See also Stephen F. Arno, *Flames in Our Forest: Disaster or Renewal?* (Washington, DC: Island Press, 2002).

21. William R. Jordan III, "Restoration, Community, and Wilderness," in *Restoring Nature: Perspective from the Social Sciences and Humanities*, ed. Paul H. Gobster and R. Bruce Hull (Washington, DC: Island Press, 2000), 23–36. See also Eric Katz, *Nature As Subject: Human Obligation and Natural Community* (Lanham, MD: Rowman & Littlefield, 1997); Eric Katz, "The Problem of Ecological Restoration," *Environmental Ethics*, 18 (1994): 222–224; Eric Katz, "The Call of the Wild: The Struggle Against Domination and the Technological Fix of Nature," *Environmental Ethics*, 14 (1992): 265–273; Andrew Light and Eric Higgs, "The Politics of Ecological Restoration," *Environmental Ethics*, 18 (1996): 227–247; Andrew Light and Eric Katz, *Environmental Pragmatism* (New York: Routledge, 1996).

22. Thomas G. Alexander, "Struggle in an Endangered Empire: The Search for Total Ecosystem Management in the Forests of Southern Utah, 1976–1999," in *Forests Under Fire*, ed. Christopher J. Huggard and Arthur R. Gomez (Tucson: University of Arizona Press, 2001), 234. For more on the controversy, see Tom Kenworthy, "Burn Now or Burn Later," *Washington Post National Weekly Edition*, September 9–15, 1996, A22.

23. "U.S. Forest Service. Federal Wildland Fire Management: Policy and Program Review. (Darby, PA: Diane Publishing Company, 1995).

24. "Bush Sparks Protest with Planned National Forest Logging for Fire Prevention," August 24, 2002, at http://www.cbc.ca, accessed August 24, 2002.

25. "President Announces Healthy Forests Initiative," Remarks by the President on Forest Health and Preservation, August 22, 2002, Central Point, Oregon, http://georgewbush-whitehouse.archives.gov/news/releases/2002/08/20020822-3.html, accessed August 23, 2002.

26. Natural Resources Defense Council, "Bush's Forest Proposal a 'Smokescreen,' Says NRDC," news release, August 22, 2002, http://www.nrdc.org/media/pressreleases/020822.asp, accessed August 24, 2002.

27. The Wilderness Society, "Analysis: Bush Administration's 'Healthy Forests Initiative,'" fact sheet, August 22, 2002, http://www.wildernesssociety.org/newsroom, accessed August 23, 2002.

28. Jeff Barnard, "Forest Plan Faces Obstacles," *The Missoulian*, August 26, 2002, http://www.missoulian.com, accessed August 26, 2002.

29. National Association of State Foresters, "NASF Commends Presidential Forest Health Initiative," news release, August 23, 2002, http://www.stateforesters.org/news, accessed August 26, 2002.

30. Office of the Governor of the State of Idaho, "Kempthorne: President's Fire Plan Just What

Idaho and the West Needs," news release, August 22, 2002, http://www.state.id.us/gov, accessed August 24, 2002.

31. Jennifer McKee, "Martz: Ban Logging Appeals," *Billings Gazette*, August 22, 2002, http://www.billingsgazette.com, accessed August 26, 2002.

32. "USDA and DOI Deliver Legislation to Implement President's Healthy Forests Initiative," news release, September 5, 2002, http://www.doi.gov/news, accessed September 7, 2002.

33. The parallel strategy of introducing the Healthy Forests proposals in Congress and the bureaucracy are outlined in Jacqueline Vaughn and Hanna J. Cortner, *George W. Bush's Healthy Forests: Reframing the Environmental Debate* (Boulder: University Press of Colorado, 2005).

34. Andy Stahl, "Ashes to Ashes, Dust to Dust," *Forest Magazine*, Spring 2005, 5.

35. USDA Forest Service, "Forest Service Publishes Planning Rules for Better Management of National Forests and Grasslands," news release, December 22, 2004, http://www.fs.fed.us/news/ 2004/releases, accessed December 23, 2004.

36. Andy Stahl, "Ashes to Ashes, Dust to Dust," *Forest Magazine*, Spring 2005, 5.

37. Jacqueline Vaughn and Hanna J. Cortner, *George W. Bush's Healthy Forests: Reframing the Environmental Debate* (Boulder: University Press of Colorado, 2005), 223.

38. Tania Schoennagel et al., "Implementation of National Fire Plan Treatments Near the Wildland-Urban Interface in the Western United States," *Proceedings of the National Academy of Sciences* (June 2009), www.pnas.org/content/106/26/10706.full?sid=8fb36fe6-452b-4bcd-a08b-54be84b88493, accessed September 9, 2009.

39. Ibid.

40. George Ochenski, "Feeling Burned: Study Cuts Down the Healthy Forests Restoration Act," *Missoula News*, June 11, 2009, http://www.missoulanews.bigskypress.com/Missoula/ochenski, accessed September 9, 2009.

41. Char Miller, *Gifford Pinchot and the Making of Modern Environmentalism* (Washington, DC: Island Press, 2001), 5.

42. U.S. Department of Agriculture, "Roadless Area Conservation: Background Paper," http://www.roadless.fs.fed.us/xdocuments.shtml, accessed May 6, 2005.

43. Mike Anderson, "A Decade of National Forest Roadless Area Conservation: Background Paper," http://wilderness.org/files/Roadless-Background%20.pdf, accessed August 5, 2009.

44. Bettina Boxall, "Court Restores Restrictions on Road-Building in National Forests," *Los Angeles Times*, August 6, 2009, http://articles.latimes.com/2009/aug/06/nation/na-court-roads6, accessed August 6, 2009.

45. Jeff T. Green, "Clinton-Era Rule Protecting Forests Upheld," *New York Times*, http://green-inc.blogs.nytimes.com/2009/08/05/court-up-holds-clinton-era-roadless-rule/, accessed August 5, 2009.

46. Michael P. Dombeck, Christopher A. Wood, and Jack E. Williams, *From Conquest to Conservation: Our Public Lands Legacy* (Washington, DC: Island Press, 2003), 17. For a comprehensive history of grazing policies, see George A. Gonzalez, "Ideas and State Capacity, or Business Dominance? A Historical Analysis of Grazing on the Public Grasslands," *Studies in American Political Development*, 15, no. 2 (Fall 2001): 234–244. See also Wesley Calef, *Private Grazing and Public Lands* (Chicago: University of Chicago Press, 1960); Phillip O. Foss, *Politics and Grass* (Seattle: University of Washington Press, 1960); Gary D. Libecap, *Locking Up the Range* (Cambridge, MA: Ballinger, 1981).

47. Colorado Cattlemen's Association, "Ending All Grazing on Public Lands Can Hurt Everyone," news release, November 12, 2003, at http://cca.beef.org, accessed June 17, 2005.

48. National Public Lands Grazing Campaign, "Conservationists Mail Letter to 22,000 Federal Grazing Permittees," at http://www.publiclandsranching.org, accessed June 17, 2005.

49. USDA Forest Service, "BLM and Forest Service Announce 2009 Grazing Fee," news release, January 30, 2009, http://www.blm.gov/wo/st/en/info/newsroom/2009/january/NR_01_30_2009.html, accessed October 9, 2009.

50. See William E. Riebsame, "Ending the Range Wars?" *Environment*, 38, no. 4 (May 1996): 4–9,

27–29; J. M. Feller, "What Is Wrong with the BLM's Management of Livestock Grazing on the Public Lands?" *Idaho Law Review*, 30, no. 3 (1993–1994): 555–602.

51. William L. Graf, *Wilderness Protection and the Sagebrush Rebellions* (Savage, MD: Rowman & Littlefield, 1990), 229.

52. 104th Congress, H.R. 643.

53. Bureau of Land Management, "Questions and Answers Regarding the BLM's New Grazing Regulations," at http://www.blm.gov, accessed June 17, 2005.

54. Center for Biological Diversity, "U.S. Bureau of Land Management's New Regulations Undercut Public Participation and Threaten Wildlife and Water With Hand-Outs to the Livestock Industry," news release, June 16, 2005, at http://www.biologicaldiversity.org/news/press_releases/grazing6-16-05.html, accessed June 17, 2005.

55. Ibid.

56. Julie Cart, "U.S. Altered Study, Scientists Say," *Arizona Republic*, June 19, 2005, A10.

57. Ibid.

58. Bureau of Land Management, "Questions and Answers Regarding the BLM's New Grazing Regulations," at http://www.blm.gov, accessed June 17, 2005.

59. Christopher McGrory Klyza, *Who Controls Public Lands? Mining, Forestry, and Grazing Policies, 1970–1990* (Chapel Hill: University of North Carolina Press, 1996), 28–29.

60. In 1970, Congress enacted the Mining and Minerals Policy Act (consisting of three short paragraphs); but rather than reform practices, it simply provided that the Secretary of the Interior prepare a report on the domestic mining industry. The statute provided explicit support for domestic mineral production and has been termed "little more than a rhetorical device intended to placate the mining industry." See R. McGreggor Cawley, *Federal Land, Western Anger: The Sagebrush Rebellion and Environmental Politics* (Lawrence: University Press of Kansas, 1993); John D. Leshy, *The Mining Law: A Study in Perpetual Motion* (Washington, DC: Resources for the Future Press, 1987).

61. Wilderness Society, *Bush Strikes Out on the Environment: A State of the Environment Report* (Washington, DC: Author, January 24, 2002), 7–8.

62. See Joshua Footer and J. T. VonLunen, "A Legacy of Conflict: Mining and Wilderness," in *Contested Landscape: The Politics of Wilderness in Utah and the West*, ed. Doug Goodman and Daniel McCool (Salt Lake City: University of Utah Press, 1999), 117–136.

63. *Village of Euclid v. Ambler Realty Co.*, 272 U.S. 365 (1926).

64. Randy Stapilus, "Ballot Box Hangover," *High Country News*, September 18, 2006, http://www.hcn.org/issues/330/16544, accessed February 20, 2007.

65. *Pennsylvania Coal Co. v. Mahon*, 260 U.S. 393 (1922).

66. Richard Epstein, *Takings: Private Property and the Power of Eminent Domain* (Cambridge, MA: Harvard University Press, 1985).

67. For a discussion of the strategies used by property-rights groups, see Bruce Yandle, ed., *Land Rights: The 1990s' Property Rights Rebellion* (Lanham, MD: Rowman & Littlefield, 1995); John D. Echeverria and Raymond Booth Eby, eds., *Let the People Judge: Wise Use and the Private Property Rights Movement* (Washington, DC: Island Press, 1995); David Helvarg, *The War against the Greens: The "Wise Use" Movement, the New Right, and Anti-Environmental Violence* (San Francisco: Sierra Club Books, 1994); and Jacqueline Vaughn Switzer, *Green Backlash: The History and Politics of Environmental Opposition in the U.S.* (Boulder, CO: Lynne Rienner, 1997.

68. See Karol J. Ceplo, "Land Rights Conflicts in the Regulation of Wetlands," in *Land Rights: The 1990s Property Rights Rebellion*, ed. Bruce Yandle (Lanham, MD: Rowman & Littlefield, 1995), 106.

69. Heidi J. Albers, Amy W. Ando, and Daniel Kaffine, "Land Trusts in the United States: Analyzing Abundance," *Resources*, Spring 2004, 9–13; Richard Brewer, *Conservancy: The Land Trust Movement in America* (Dartmouth, NH: University Press of New England, 2003); Sally K. Fairfax and Darla Guenzler, *Conservation Trusts* (Lawrence: University Press of Kansas, 2001).

Chapter 5

1. Shaila Dewan, "Tennessee Ash Flood Larger than Initial Estimate," *New York Times*, December 27, 2008, http://www.nytimes.com/2008/12/27/us/27sludge.html, accessed October 21, 2009.

2. Ibid.

3. U.S. Environmental Protection Agency, "Summary of Past and Current EPA Response Activities Regarding the TVA Kingston Coal Ash Spill," http://www.epa.gov/region4/kingston/summary.html, accessed October 21, 2009.

4. Shaila Dewan, "Tennessee Ash Flood Larger than Initial Estimate," *New York Times*, December 27, 2008, http://www.nytimes.com/2008/12/27/us/27sludge.html, accessed October 21, 2009.

5. Shaila Dewan, "Clash in Alabama over Tennessee Coal Ash," *New York Times*, August 30, 2009, http://www.nytimes.com/2009/08/30/us/30ash.html, accessed October 21, 2009.

6. Ibid.

7. Martin V. Melosi, *Garbage in the Cities: Refuse, Reform and the Environment, 1880–1980* (College Station: Texas A&M University Press, 1981), 3. For a contemporary view, see Martin V. Melosi, *Effluent America: Cities, Industry, Energy, and the Environment* (Pittsburgh, PA: University of Pittsburgh Press, 2001).

8. Ibid., 189–192. In fairness to industry, however, it should be noted that the development of packaging has many beneficial consequences. Packaging has extended the shelf life of many goods (especially produce and dairy products) that otherwise might rot or spoil. Packaging also allows products to be stored and shipped in bulk and often results in lower consumer prices.

9. U.S. Environmental Protection Agency, "Municipal Solid Waste Generation, Recycling, and Disposal in the United States: Facts and Figures for 2007," http://www.epa.gov/waste/nonhaz/municipal/pubs/msw07-fs.pdf, accessed August 26, 2009.

10. Ibid.

11. Ibid.

12. Ibid.

13. Ibid.

14. Ibid.

15. Ibid.

16. Ibid.

17. Sarah Gauch, "Egypt Dumps 'Garbage People,'" *Christian Science Monitor*, January 6, 2003, http://www.csmonitor.com/2003/0106/p07s02-woaf.html, accessed April 13, 2007; Janice E. Perlman, "Innovative Solutions Create Urban Sustainability," *Global Issues Electronic Journal*, http://usinfo.org/wf-archive/2000/000424/epf107.htm, accessed April 13, 2007.

18. "Final Report: Evaluation of EPA Efforts to Integrate Pollution Prevention Policy Throughout EPA and at Other Federal Agencies," http://www.epa.gov/p2/pubs/docs/p2integration.pdf, accessed March 10, 2010.

19. "China Bans Free Plastic Bags," *Environment News Service*, January 10, 2008, http://www.ens-newswire.com/ens/jan2008/2008-01-10-03.asp, accessed January 13, 2008.

20. Louis Blumberg and Robert Gottlieb, *War on Waste: Can America Win Its Battle With Garbage?* (Washington, DC: Island Press, 1989), 63.

21. See William L. Kovacs and John F. Klusik, "The New Federal Role in Solid Waste Management: The Resource Recovery and Conservation Act of 1976," *Columbia Journal of Environmental Law*, 3 (March 1977): 205.

22. *City of Philadelphia* v. *New Jersey*, 437 U.S. 617 (1978).

23. See Rosemary O'Leary, "Trash Talk: The Supreme Court and the Interstate Transportation of Waste," *Public Administration Review*, 57, no. 4 (July–August 1997): 281–284.

24. See "Recent Developments, Federal Regulation of Solid Waste Reduction and Recycling," *Harvard Journal on Legislation*, 29 (1992): 251–254. For a more comprehensive analysis of the policy process as it relates to both the RCRA and Superfund, see Charles E. Davis, *The Politics of Hazardous Waste* (Englewood Cliffs, NJ: Prentice-Hall, 1993).

25. For an estimate of Superfund costs and issues, see Katherine N. Probst and David M. Konisky, *Superfund's Future: What Will It Cost?* (Washington, DC: Resources for the Future Press, 2001).

26. U.S. Environmental Protection Agency, "Superfund National Accomplishments Summary Fiscal

Year 2004," http://www.epa.gov/superfund/
accomp/numbers08.htm, accessed October 26,
2009.

27. Ibid.

28. U.S. Environmental Protection Agency, "New
Report Projects Number, Cost, and Nature of
Contaminated Site Cleanups in the U.S. over
Next 30 Years," news release, http://www.epa.
gov/superfund/accomp/news/30years.htm,
accessed December 6, 2004.

29. John Heilprin, "EPA Sees Toxic Waste Sites,
Costs Growing," *Newsday*, December 3, 2004,
http://www.newsday.com/news/politics/wire,
accessed December 6, 2004.

30. Bob Anez, "W. R. Grace Accused of Hiding
Cancer Risk," http:www.chej.org/WRDis_
Grace.htm, accessed February 10, 2005.

31. Carrie Johnson and Dina ElBoghdady,
"Prosperity Turned to Poison in Mining
Town," *Washington Post*, February 8, 2005,
http://www.washingtonpost.com/wp-dyn/
articles/A6243-2005Feb7.html, accessed
February 10, 2005.

32. Carrie Johnson and Dina ElBoghdady, "Md.
Firm Accused of Asbestos Coverup," *Washington
Post*, February 8, 2005, http://www.washing-
tonpost.com/wp-dyn/articles/A5493-2005Feb7.
html, accessed February 10, 2005.

33. Bob Anez, "W. R. Grace Accused of Hiding
Cancer Risk," http://www.chej.org/WRDis_
Grace.htm accessed February 10, 2005.

34. "$800M Lawsuit Against W.R. Grace Barred by
Judge," http://www.asbestos.com/news/2009/
04/15/800m-lawsuit-against-wr-grace-barred-
by-judge/, accessed August 26, 2009.

35. U.S. Environmental Protection Agency, "About
Brownfields," http://www.epa.gov/brown-
fields/about.htm, accessed August 18, 2009.

36. National Oceanic and Atmospheric Administration, "Revitalizing Ports to Benefit Economic
Activity and Healthy Ecosystems," http://
coastalmanagement.noaa.gov/portfields.html,
accessed August 18, 2009; U.S. Environmental
Protection Agency, "Portfields – The Wave of
the Future," http://www.epa.gov/brownfields/
success/portfields.pdf, accessed August 18, 2009.

37. Ibid.

38. Matthew J. Wald, "Study Aids Opponents of
Nevada Burial," *Arizona Republic*, April 7, 2005,
A3.

39. Spencer Abraham, "One Safe Site Is Best,"
Washington Post, March 26, 2002, A-19.

40. Shelley Berkley, "Yucca Mountain: A History of
Nuclear Politics," March 13, 2002, http://www
.house.gov/Berkley/2002/edit_2002_0313.html
accessed April 18, 2002. Berkley is a member of
the U.S. House of Representatives from Nevada.

41. See Tony Davis, "Nuclear Waste Dump Opens,"
High Country News, April 12, 1999, 5; and James
Brooke, "Deep Desert Grave Awaits First Load
of Nuclear Waste," *New York Times*, March 26,
1999, A-17.

42. Kenny C. Guinn, "Statement of Reasons
Supporting the Governor of Nevada's Notice of
Disapproval of the Proposed Yucca Mountain
Project," April 8, 2002, http://www.state.nv.us/
nucwaste/news2002/nn11650.pdf, accessed
March 1, 2010.

43. "Senate Approves Yucca Mountain Nuclear
Waste Site," July 10, 2002, http://www.cnn.
com/2002/ALLPOLITICS/07/09/yuccamoun-
tain.ap/index.html, accessed July 21, 2002.

44. Doug Abrahams, "Bush Approves Yucca Site for
Nation's Nuclear Waste," *Arizona Republic*, July
24, 2002, A-6.

45. "Nevada Panel Optimistic Yucca Mountain
Project Can Be Killed," *Las Vegas Sun*, February
5, 2005, http://www.lasvegassun.com, accessed
February 7, 2005.

46. Barack Obama, "Letter to the Editor," *Las Vegas
Review Journal*, May 20, 2007, http://www.lvrj
.com/opinion/7598337.html, accessed
September 9, 2009.

47. "Mountain of Trouble," *Washington Post*, March
8, 2009, http://www.washingtonpost.com/
wp-dyn/content/article/2009/03/07/AR20090
30701666.html, accessed September 9, 2009.

48. Timothy Noah, "Good Riddance, Yucca
Mountain," *Slate*, March 3, 2009, http://www
.slate.com/id/2212792, accessed September 9,
2009.

49. Lisa Mascaro, "Despite Obama's Opposition,
Congress Tangles over Yucca," *Las Vegas Sun*,
July 19, 2009, http://www.lasvegassun.com/

news/2009/jul/19/despite-obamas-opposition-congress-tangles-over-yu/, accessed September 9, 2009.

50. See Michael Renner, "Military Mop-Up," *WorldWatch*, 7, no. 5 (September–October 1994): 23–29; and Seth Shulman, *The Threat at Home: Confronting the Toxic Legacy of the U.S. Military* (Boston: Beacon, 1992).

51. Katherine N. Probst, "Long Term Stewardship and the Nuclear Weapons Complex," *Resources*, Spring 1998, 14–16.

52. Michael Cabanatuan, "Settlement to Ease Public Monitoring of Nuclear Weapons Cleanup Sites," *San Francisco Chronicle*, December 15, 1998, A-22.

53. Joanisabel Gonzalez-Velazquez, "Navy in Advanced Stage to Begin Vieques Cleanup," *Puerto Rico Herald*, August 13, 2003, http://www.puerto-herald.org/issues/2003/vol7n34/Navy AdvancedVQ-en-shtml accessed May 27, 2005.

54. U.S. Fish and Wildlife Service, "Vieques and Culebra Proposed Superfund Listing," http://www.fws.gov/southeast/vieques, accessed May 27, 2005.

55. "Protest in Vieques: The Navy Is 'Bombing' Again," *San Francisco Bay View*, May 18, 2005 http://www.sfbayview.com/051805/bombinga gain051805/shtml accessed May 27, 2005.

56. Rep. Jose E. Serrano, "Serrano Secures $1 Million for Vieques Cleanup," news release, December 3, 2004, http://www.house.gov/list/press/ny16_serrano/041203Vieques.html, accessed May 27, 2005.

57. This terminology is derived from both the U.S. Environmental Protection Agency language and that of the OECD.

58. Kate O'Neill, *Waste Trading among Rich Nations: Building a New Theory of Environmental Regulation* (Cambridge, MA: MIT Press, 2000), 35.

59. See Ed Bellinger et al., eds., *Environmental Assessment in Countries in Transition* (New York: CEU Press, 2000).

60. Kate O'Neill, *Waste Trading among Rich Nations: Building a New Theory of Environmental Regulation* (Cambridge, MA: MIT Press, 2000), 37–41.

61. See Jennifer Clapp, *Toxic Exports: The Transfer of Hazardous Wastes from Rich to Poor Countries*

62. Ibid., 82–83.

63. Kate O'Neill, *Waste Trading among Rich Nations: Building a New Theory of Environmental Regulation* (Cambridge, MA: MIT Press, 2000), 209–210.

64. "The Ship Breakers of Bangladesh," CBS News, *60 Minutes*, August 29, 2007, http://www.cbsnews.com/stories/2006/11/03/60minutes/main2149023.shtml, accessed August 30, 2009.

65. "Ship Breaking Ordered Shut," http://www.ban.org/ban_news/2009/090318_shipbreaking_ordered_shut.html, accessed August 30, 2009.

66. Greenpeace, "Ship Breaking," http://www.greenpeace.org/india/campaigns/toxics-free-future/ship-breaking, accessed August 30, 2009.

Chapter 6

1. Kenneth C. Clarke and Jeffrey J. Hemphill, *The Santa Barbara Oil Spill: A Retrospective* (Honolulu: University of Hawaii Press, 2002), 157–162.

2. Ibid.

3. Steve Gorman, "California County Retreats on Offshore Drilling," April 7, 2009, http://www.reuters.com/article/idUSTRE5370G020090408, accessed October 2, 2009.

4. U.S. Department of the Interior, "Unprecedented Public Outreach for Comprehensive Offshore Energy Plan Generates More than 450,000 Comments," news release, September 22, 2009, http://www.interior.gov/news/09_News_Releases/092209.html, accessed October 2, 2009.

5. William A. Pizer, "Setting Energy Policy in the Modern Era," *Resources*, 156 (Winter 2005): 9.

6. H. Joseph Herbert, "Poll: High Gas Prices Alter Americans' Energy Views," *Arizona Republic*, July 2, 2009, A6.

7. Ian W. H. Parry and J.W. Anderson, "Petroleum: Energy Independence Is Unrealistic," *Resources*, 156 (Winter 2005): 12.

8. Ibid.

9. Edward Teller, *Energy from Heaven and Earth* (San Francisco: Freeman, 1979), 2.

10. There are numerous accounts of the development of American energy resources. See, for

example, Robert J. Kalter and William A. Vogely, eds., *Energy Supply and Government Policy* (Ithaca, NY: Cornell University Press, 1976); Daniel Yergin, *The Prize: The Epic Quest for Oil, Money, and Power* (New York: Simon and Schuster, 1991); Richard Rudolph and Scott Ridley, *Power Struggle: The Hundred-Year War over Electricity* (New York: Harper and Row, 1986); and Walter Rosenbaum, *Energy Politics and Public Policy*, 2nd ed. (Washington, DC: Congressional Quarterly Press, 1987).

11. Laura Paskus, "The Winds of Change," *High Country News*, 37, no. 8 (May 2, 2005):

12. Robert L. Bamberger, *Energy Policy: Setting the Stage for the Current Debate* (Washington, DC: Congressional Research Service, May 7, 2002), 3–4.

13. Richard G. Newall, "The Hydrogen Economy," *Resources*, 156 (Winter 2005): 23.

14. Nick Timiraos, "Inside Bush's Energy Proposals," *Wall Street Journal*, January 27–28, 2007, A7.

15. Jad Mouawad, "Obama Tries to Draw Up an Inclusive Energy Plan," *New York Times,* March 17, 2009, http://www.nytimes.com/2009/03/18/business/energy-environment/18offshore.html, accessed September 9, 2009.

16. Ryan Wiser et al., "Renewables Portfolio Standards: A Factual Introduction to Experience from the United States," Lawrence Berkeley National Laboratory, Report No. 62569 (April 2007).

17. Louis Sahagun, "Environmental Concerns Delay Solar Projects in California Desert," *Los Angeles Times*, October 18, 2009, http://articles.latimes.com/2009/oct/19/local/me-solar19, accessed October 19, 2009.

18. Jim Motavalli, "Catching the Wind: The World's Fastest-Growing Renewable Energy Source Is Coming of Age," *E Magazine*, January–February 2005, http://www.emagazine.com/view/?2176, accessed January 16, 2005.

19. Ibid.

20. Doug Abrahms, "Wind Power Set to Soar," *Arizona Republic*, January 5, 2005, D-1.

21. "Project at a Glance," http://www.capewind.org/modules.php?op=modload&name=Sections&file=index&req=viewarticle&artid=24&page=1, accessed October 19, 2009.

22. For perspectives on what happened at WPPSS and Shoreham, see Howard Gleckman, *WPSS: From Dream to Default* (New York: The Bond Buyer, 1983); and Karl Grossman, *Power Crazy* (New York: Grove Press, 1986).

23. Taylor Moore and John Carey, "License Renewal Revitalizes the Nuclear Industry," *EPRI Journal*, 25, no. 3 (Fall 2000): 8.

24. U.S. Department of Energy, "Building New Nuclear Plants," http://www.ne.doe.gov/pdfFiles/factSheets/BuildingNewNuclearPlants.pdf, accessed August 11, 2009.

25. Energy Information Administration, "Status of Potential New Commercial Nuclear Reactors in the United States," http://www.eia.doe.gov/cneaf/nuclear/page/nuc_reactors/reactorcom.html, accessed September 9, 2009.

26. Ibid.

27. Paul R. Portnoy, "Penny-Wise and Pound Fuelish? New Car Mileage Standards in the United States," *Resources*, 147 (Spring 2002): 11.

28. U.S. Department of Transportation, "Secretary Peters Proposes 25 Percent Increase in Fuel Economy Standards Over 5 Years for Passenger Vehicles, Light Trucks," news release, April 22, 2008, http://www.dot.gov/affairs/dot5608, accessed October 14, 2009.

29. Paul R. Portnoy, "Penny-Wise and Pound Fuelish? New Car Mileage Standards in the United States," *Resources*, 147 (Spring 2002): 15.

30. James Everett Katz, *Congress and National Energy Policy* (New Brunswick, NJ: Transaction Books, 1984), 5–7.

31. See John C. Whitaker, *Striking a Balance: Environmental and Natural Resources Policy in the Nixon-Ford Years* (Washington, DC: American Enterprise Institute, 1976), 66–68.

32. Eric R. A. N. Smith, *Energy, The Environment, and Public Opinion* (Lanham, MD: Rowman & Littlefield, 2002), 87–90.

33. See Claude E. Barfield, *Science Policy from Ford to Reagan: Change and Continuity* (Washington, DC: American Enterprise Institute, 1982); and Don E. Kash and Robert W. Rycroft, *U.S. Energy Policy: Crisis and Complacency* (Norman: University of Oklahoma Press, 1984).

34. Holly Idelson, "National Energy Strategy Provisions," *Congressional Quarterly*, November 28, 1992, 3722–3730.

35. Susan Dentzer, "RIP for the BTU Tax," *U.S. News and World Report*, June 21, 1993, 95.

36. Howard Gleckman, "Gas Pump Politics," *BusinessWeek*, May 13, 1996, 40–41.

37. Marc Sandalow, "Boxer Calls for Total Ban on New Offshore Oil Drilling," *San Francisco Chronicle*, August 1, 1998, A-1.

38. "Offshore Oil Rigs: More in California's Future?" *San Francisco Chronicle*, August 9, 1998, A-1.

39. Mike Soraghan, "Battles Over Drilling Shifting to Rockies," *Denver Post*, http://www.denverpost.com/cda, accessed April 23, 2002.

40. Dan Morgan and Ellen Nakashima, "Search for Oil Targets Rockies," *Washington Post*, April 18, 2002, A-1. See also Ray Ring, "Local Governments Tackle an In-Your-Face Rush on Coalbed Methane," *High Country News*, September 2, 2002, 1.

41. Robert F. Kennedy Jr., "Dick Cheney's Energy Crisis," *Sierra* (October–November 2004).

42. Lydia Saad, "Americans Mostly 'Green' in the Energy vs. Environment Debate," *Gallup Poll Monthly*, no. 426 (March 2001): 33–34.

43. White House, "Securing Our Nation's Energy Future," fact sheet, March 9, 2005, http://fire.pppl.gov/us_energy_bush_030905.pdf, accessed March 11, 2005.

44. U.S. Department of Energy, Energy Information Administration, "International Energy Outlook 2009," May 27, 2009, http://www.eia.doe.gov/oiaf/ieo/highlights.html, accessed October 28, 2009.

45. Ibid.

46. Karl Gawell and Griffin Greenberg, "2007 Interim Report Update on World Geothermal Development," May 1, 2007, http://www.geo-energy.org/publications/reports/GEA%20World%20Update%202007.pdf, accessed October 19, 2009.

47. Mycle Schneider, "2008 World Nuclear Status Report: Global Nuclear Power," *Bulletin of the Atomic Scientists*, September 16, 2008, http://www.thebulletin.org/web-edition/reports/2008-world-nuclear-industry-status-report/2008-world-nuclear-industry-status-rep, accessed August 11, 2009.

48. See Judith Thornton and Charles E. Ziegler, eds., *Russia's Far East: A Region at Risk* (Seattle: University of Washington Press, 2002); Paul R. Josephson, *Red Atom: Russia's Nuclear Power Program from Stalin to Today* (New York: Freeman, 2000).

49. Mycle Schneider, "2008 World Nuclear Status Report: Global Nuclear Power," *Bulletin of the Atomic Scientists*, September 16, 2008, http://www.thebulletin.org/web-edition/reports/2008-world-nuclear-industry-status-report/2008-world-nuclear-industry-status-rep, accessed August 11, 2009.

50. U.S. Department of Energy, Energy Information Administration, "International Energy Outlook 2009," May 27, 2009, http://www.eia.doe.gov/oiaf/ieo/highlights.html, accessed October 28, 2009.

51. Ian Phillips, "World's Dams Damaging Environment, Report Says," *Arizona Republic*, November 17, 2000, A-4; "The Great Dam of China," *Mother Jones*, May–June 2002, 74.

52. U.S. Department of Energy, Energy Information Administration, "International Energy Outlook 2009," May 27, 2009, http://www.eia.doe.gov/oiaf/ieo/highlights.html, accessed October 28, 2009.

Chapter 7

1. Elizabeth Grossman, "A Canoe in Singing Waters," *Yes Magazine*, Winter 2004, http://www.yesmagazine.org/issues/whose-water/a-canoe-in-singing-waters, accessed February 20, 2007.

2. Ibid.

3. Ibid.

4. Matt Jenkins, "Columbia River Dams Revived," *High Country News*, April 3, 2006, http://www.hcn.org/issues/319/16210, accessed February 20, 2007.

5. Nancy L. Barber, "Summary of Estimated Water Use in the United States in 2005," U.S. Geological Survey, Fact Sheet 2009-3098, http://pubs.usgs.gov/fs/2009/3098/pdf/2009-3098.pdf, accessed November 28, 2009.

6. Ibid.

7. Ibid.

8. Jacques Leslie, "Running Dry: What Happens When the World No Longer Has Enough Freshwater?" *Harper's*, 301, no. 1802 (July 2000): 37–52.

9. See George Wharton James, *Reclaiming the Arid West: The Story of the United States Reclamation Service* (New York: Dodd, Mead, 1917).

10. Robert Gottlieb, *A Life of Its Own: The Politics and Power of Water* (New York: Harcourt Brace Jovanovich, 1988), 48.

11. See Wallace Stegner, *This Is Dinosaur* (New York: Knopf, 1955). At that time, the Bureau of Reclamation also had the proposed Glen Canyon Dam near the Arizona–Utah border on the drawing boards; the project was eventually built after the Echo Park controversy. Even though the Glen Canyon project provides hydroelectric power to 400,000 people in seven states, its original purpose was to store water in Lake Powell, which holds 26.7 million acre-feet of water when full. Environmentalists are now seeking to see Lake Powell drained to restore Glen Canyon to its original beauty.

12. See Constance Elizabeth Hunt, *Down by the River* (Washington, DC: Island Press, 1988), 11–14.

13. See Tom Harris, *Death in the Marsh* (Washington, DC: Island Press, 1991).

14. Robert Gottlieb, *A Life of Its Own: The Politics and Power of Water* (New York: Harcourt Brace Jovanovich, 1988), 270–271.

15. Shaun McKinnon, "State's Draw of River Water Declines," *Arizona Republic*, June 24, 2005, B1.

16. The issues were discussed as part of a series of border roundtable discussions in 2000 and 2001 in preparation of the Draft Border XXI Plan.

17. See Benedykt Dziegielewski and Duane D. Baumann, "Tapping Alternatives: The Benefits of Managing Urban Water Demands," *Environment*, 34, no. 9 (November 1992): 6–11.

18. Lewis M. Cowardin, Virginia Carter, Francis C. Golet, and Edward T. LaRoe, *Classification of Wetlands and Deepwater Habitats of the United States* (Washington, DC: U.S. Fish and Wildlife Service, December 1979), http://www.npwrc. usgs.gov/resource/wetlands/classwet/index.htm, accessed June 25, 2005.

19. 40 CFR 230.3(t).

20. Jon Kusler, "Common Questions: Wetland Definition, Delineation, and Mapping," http://www.aswm.org/propub/14_mapping_6_26_06.pdf, accessed July 27, 2009.

21. T. E. Dahl, *Status and Trends of Wetlands in the Conterminous U.S. 1998–2004* (Washington, DC: U.S. Department of the Interior; Fish and Wildlife Service, 2006), http://www.fws.gov/wetlands/_documents/gSandT/National Reports/StatusTrendsWetlandsConterminous US1998to2004.pdf, accessed July 27, 2009.

22. U.S. Environmental Protection Agency, "Fact Sheet: National Wetland Condition Assessment," http://www.fws.gov/wetlands/_documents/gSandT/OtherInformation/EPANationalWetlandConditionAssessmentFS.pdf, accessed July 27, 2009.

23. See Frank Graham Jr., "Of Broccoli and Marshes," *Audubon*, 7, (July 1990): 102.

24. William K. Stevens, "Panel Urges Big Wetlands Restoration Project," *New York Times*, December 12, 1991, A16.

25. U.S. Environmental Protection Agency, "River Corridor and Wetland Restoration," http://www.epa.gov/owow/wetlands/restore/defs.html, accessed July 27, 2009.

26. Coastal America, "1992 Memorandum of Understanding," http://www.coastalamerica.gov, accessed June 25, 2005.

27. 33 CFR Section 328.3 (a) (3).

28. White House, "President Announces Wetlands Initiative on Earth Day," news release, April 22, 2004, http://georgewbush-whitehouse.archives.gov/news/releases/2004/04/20040422-4.html, accessed June 25, 2005.

29. Coastal America, "President Bush's Wetlands Initiative on Track."

30. "Obama Administration Seeks Wetlands Clarity," July 1, 2009, http://www.rockproducts.com/green/rock_obama_administration_seeks/, accessed November 28, 2009.

31. Marjory Stoneman Douglas, *The Everglades: River of Grass* (Sarasota, FL: Pineapple Press, 1997). Douglas writes about the Everglades in another

genre in *A River in Flood, and Other Florida Stories* (Gainesville: University Press of Florida, 1998).

32. See Steven M. Davis and John C. Ogden, eds., *Everglades: The Ecosystem and Its Restoration* (Delray Beach, FL: St. Lucie Press, 1994); Thomas E. Lodge, *The Everglades Handbook: Understanding the Ecosystem* (Delray Beach, FL: St. Lucie Press, 1994); David McCally, *The Everglades: An Environmental History* (Gainesville: University Press of Florida, 1999); Ted Levin, *Liquid Land: A Journey Through the Florida Everglades* (Athens: University of Georgia Press, 2003).

33. Comprehensive Everglades Restoration Plan, "About Everglades Restoration," http://www.evergladesplan.org/about/landing_about.aspx, accessed June 11, 2005.

34. Ibid.

35. Florida Department of Environmental Protection, "Everglades Forever Act," http://www.dep.state.fl.us/evergladesforever, accessed June 11, 2005.

36. Pamela Smith Hayford, "Everglades Restoration to Top $600 Million," *News-Press*, June 9, 2005, http://www.news-press.com, accessed June 11, 2005.

37. "Comprehensive Everglades Restoration Plan 2007–2008 Update," http://www.evergladesplan.org/pm/pm_docs/cerp_2008_rpt_to_public.pdf, accessed July 27, 2009.

38. "Remarks at the Signing of the Water Quality Act of 1965, October 2, 1965," *Public Papers of the President: Lyndon B. Johnson* (Washington, DC: U.S. Government Printing Office, 1966), 1035.

39. Robert Gottlieb, *A Life of Its Own: The Politics and Power of Water* (New York: Harcourt Brace Jovanovich, 1988), 163.

40. The Court's interpretation is outlined in *United States v. Republic Steel Corporation*, 362 U.S. 482 (1960); *United States v. Standard Oil Company*, 384 U.S. 224 (1966).

41. James Ridgeway, *The Politics of Ecology* (New York: Dutton, 1970), 51.

42. David Hosansky, "Drinking Water Bill Clears, Clinton Expected to Sign," *Congressional Quarterly Weekly Report*, August 3, 1996, 2179.

43. Jonathan H. Adler, "Wrong Way On Water," *National Review Online*, November 13, 2001, http://www.nationalreview.com, accessed July 27, 2002.

44. Ibid.

45. Pete Yost, "Money, Politics and Pollution: How Policy Is Changed," *Detroit News*, February 16, 2004, http://www.detnews.com/2004, accessed January 1, 2005.

46. California Department of Health Services, "MTBE Regulations," http://www.cdph.ca.gov/certlic/drinkingwater/Pages/MTBE.aspx, accessed January 1, 2005.

47. Environmental Protection Agency, "Achieving Clean Air and Clean Water: The Report of the Blue Ribbon Panel on Oxygenates in Gasoline (EPA420-R-99-021)," September 15, 1999, http://www.epa.gov/air/caaac/mtbe/r99021.pdf, accessed January 1, 2005.

48. Pete Yost, "Money, Politics and Pollution: How Policy Is Changed," *Detroit News*, February 16, 2004, http://www.detnews.com/2004, accessed January 1, 2005.

49. Ibid.

50. Charles Duhigg, "Millions in U.S. Drink Dirty Water, Records Show," *New York Times*, December 8, 2008, http://www.nytimes.com/2009/12/08/business/energy-environment/08water.html?_r=1, accessed December 8, 2009.

51. Philip P. Pan, "The Wetlands Are Running Dry," *Washington Post National Weekly Edition*, July 9–15, 2001, 17.

52. Baruch Boxer, "Global Water Management Dilemmas," *Resources*, Winter 2001, 5–9.

53. Robin Clarke, *Water: The International Crisis* (Cambridge, MA: MIT Press, 1993), 91–92.

54. David Hunter, James Salzman, and Durwood Zaelke, *International Environmental Law and Policy*, 2nd ed. (New York: Foundation Press, 2002), 794–796.

55. Christopher J. Bosso, *Environment, Inc.: From Grassroots to Beltway* (Lawrence: University Press of Kansas, 2005), 64.

56. Murray Feshbach, Ecological Disaster: Cleaning Up the Hidden Legacy of the Soviet Regime (New York: Twentieth Century Press, 1995), 106.

Chapter 8

1. Robin Lloyd, "Beijing Olympics' Air Pollution: Worse than L.A.," *Live Science*, June 22, 2009, http://www.livescience.com/environment/etc/090622-beijing-olympics-air-pollution-worse.html, accessed October 15, 2009.

2. David G. Streets et al., "Air Quality during the 2008 Beijing Olympic Games," *Atmospheric Environment*, 41 (2007): 480–492.

3. Tini Tran, "Study: Beijing's Air Worse than at Past Olympics," Associated Press wire report, http://www.usnews.com/science/articles/2009/06/21/study-beijings-air-worse-than-at-past-olympics.html, accessed June 21, 2009.

4. Ed Ainsworth, "Fight to Banish Smog, Bring Sun Back to City Pressed," *Los Angeles Times*, October 13, 1946, 7.

5. For a chronology of the early air-pollution efforts, see James E. Krier and Edmund Ursin, *Pollution and Policy* (Berkeley: University of California Press, 1977), 46–47. The history of discovery of atmospheric chemicals, urban air pollution, and impacts are covered in Mark Z. Jacobson, *Atmospheric Pollution: History, Science, and Regulation* (Cambridge, UK: Cambridge University Press, 2002).

6. For information on criteria air pollutants, see http://www.epa.gov/air/urbanair/

7. W. James Gauderman et al., "The Effect of Air Pollution on Lung Development from 10 to 18 Years of Age," *New England Journal of Medicine*, 315, no. 11 (September 9, 2004): 1057–1067.

8. James E. Krier and Edmund Ursin, *Pollution and Policy* (Berkeley: University of California Press, 1977), 47.

9. For a description of the London episode, see Peter Brimblecombe, *The Big Smoke* (London: Methuren, 1987) and Fred Pearce, "Back to the Days of Deadly Smogs," *New Scientist*, December 5, 1992, 25–28.

10. John C. Esposito, *Vanishing Air: The Ralph Nader Study Group Report on Air Pollution* (New York: Grossman, 1970), vii.

11. John C. Whitaker, Striking a Balance: Environment and Natural Resources Policy in the Nixon-Ford Years (Washington, DC: American Enterprise Institute, 1976), 94.

12. See Marc K. Landy, Marc J. Roberts, and Stephen R. Thomas, *The EPA: Asking the Wrong Questions: From Nixon to Clinton*, expanded ed. (New York: Oxford University Press, 1994).

13. See Alfred Marcus, "EPA," in *The Politics of Regulation*, ed. James Q. Wilson (New York: Basic Books, 1980), 267–303.

14. *International Harvester* v. *Ruckelshaus*, District of Columbia Court of Appeals, 155 U.S. App. DC 411 (February 10, 1973).

15. John C. Whitaker, *Striking a Balance: Environment and Natural Resources Policy in the Nixon-Ford Years* (Washington, DC: American Enterprise Institute, 1976), 104.

16. Alfred A. Marcus, *Promise and Performance: Choosing and Implementing an Environmental Policy* (Westport, CT: Greenwood Press, 1980), 123.

17. John C. Whitaker, *Striking a Balance: Environment and Natural Resources Policy in the Nixon-Ford Years* (Washington, DC: American Enterprise Institute, 1976), 104.

18. *Sierra Club* v. *Ruckelshaus*, 344 F.Supp. 256 (1972). For an analysis of the case, see Thomas M. Disselhorst, "*Sierra Club v. Ruckelshaus*: On a Clear Day . . ." *Ecology Law Quarterly*, 4 (1975): 739–780.

19. See Arnold W. Reitze Jr., "A Century of Air Pollution Law: What's Worked, What's Failed, What Might Work," *Environmental Law*, 21, no. 4:2 (1991): 1549–1646.

20. For a detailed chronology of these events, see Richard E. Cohen, *Washington at Work: Back Rooms and Clean Air* (New York: Macmillan, 1992).

21. See Norman W. Fichthorn, "Command and Control vs. the Market: The Potential Effects of Other Clean Air Act Requirements on Acid Rain Compliance," *International Law*, 21, no. 4:2 (1991): 2069–2084; and Alyson Pytte, "A Decade's Acrimony Lifted in the Glow of Clean Air," *Congressional Quarterly Weekly Report*, October 27, 1990, 3587–3592.

22. Michael Weisskopf, "Writing Laws Is One Thing—Writing Rules Is Something Else," *Washington Post National Weekly Edition*, September 30–October 6, 1991, 31; see also Henry Waxman, "An Overview of the Clean Air Act Amendments of 1990," *Environmental Law*, 21, no. 4:2 (1991): 1721–1816.

23. Henry V. Nickel, "Now, the Rush to Regulate," *Environmental Forum*, 8, no. 1 (January–February 1991): 19.

24. Mark Mardon, "Last Gasp Next 185,000 Miles?" *Sierra*, 76, no. 5 (September–October 1991): 38–42.

25. See U.S. Senate Committee on Environment and Public Works, "Three Years Later: Report Card on the 1990 Clean Air Act Amendments," November 1993.

26. U.S. Environmental Protection Agency, "New EPA Data Shows Dramatic Air Quality Improvements from Clear Skies Initiative," news release, July 1, 2002, http://yosemite.epa.gov/opa/adm-press.nsf/b1ab9f485b098972852562e7004dc686/3feaba8793ea23c885256be9005c5e75?Open Document, accessed July 21, 2002.

27. Max Barman, "Bush's Utility Rule Proposal Fuels Debate Over Dirty Air," *Arizona Republic*, June 14, 2002, A1.

28. U.S. Environmental Protection Agency, "Clean Air Interstate Rule," http://www.epa.gov/CAIR/, accessed March 11, 2005.

29. U.S. Environmental Protection Agency, "Basic Information," http://www.epa.gov/CAIR/basic.html, accessed March 11, 2005.

30. Americans for Balanced Energy Choices, "EPA Issues New Air Quality Rules," news release, March 10, 2005, http://www.highbeam.com/doc/1P2-13194742.html, accessed March 11, 2005.

31. Environmental Defense, "Big Win for Clean Air," http://www.edf.org/article.cfm?ContentID=4358, accessed March 11, 2005.

32. Environmental Protection Agency, *Air Quality Criteria for Ozone and Related Photochemical Oxidants* (Washington, DC: EPA), July 1996.

33. Earthjustice, "The Campaign to Protect Public Health From Ground Level Ozone: A Third of a Century and Counting," May 30, 2002, http://www.earthjustice.org/library/policy_factsheets/ozone_control_chronology.pdf, accessed September 15, 2005.

34. *American Trucking Association* v. *US EPA*, 175 F.3d 1027 (D.C. Cir. 1999).

35. H. Josef Hebert, "EPA Threatened with Ozone Suit," *Arizona Republic*, May 31, 2002, A6.

36. U.S. Environmental Protection Agency, "8-Hour Ozone Area Summary," April 11, 2005, http://www.epa.gov/air/oaqps/greenbk/gnsum.html, accessed May 11, 2005.

37. Darren Samuelsohn, "EPA Agrees to Reassess Ozone Cleanup for Rural Areas," Greenwire, January 21, 2005, http://www.eenews.net/Greenwire, accessed May 11, 2005.

38. "Appeals Court Denies EPA Attempt to Weaken Air Quality," Earthjustice, news release, June 8, 2007, http://www.earthjustice.org/news/press/007/appeals-court-denies-epa-attempt-to-weaken-air-quality.html, accessed September 30, 2007.

39. See *Breath-Taking: Premature Mortality Due to Particulate Air Pollution in 239 American Cities* (New York: Natural Resources Defense Council, May 1996). See also Douglas W. Docker et al., "An Association between Air Pollution and Mortality in Six U.S. Cities," *New England Journal of Medicine*, 329, no. 24 (December 9, 1993): 1753–1759; and C. Arden Pope III et al., "Particulate Air Pollution as a Predictor of Mortality in a Prospective Study of U.S. Adults," *American Journal of Respiratory Care Medicine*, 151 (1995): 669–674.

40. Environmental Protection Agency, "EPA Announces Final Designations for First Fine Particle Standard," news release, December 17, 2004, http://yosemite.epa.gov/opa/admpress.nsf/e1fffb2c795ec9b2852570210055ba60/bc63cfdda235542585256f6d005e6738!OpenDocument, accessed January 2, 2005.

41. Juliet Eilperin, "New Emissions Curbs for Diesel Trains, Ships," *The Washington Post*, March 3, 2007, http://www.washingtonpost.com/wp-dyn/content/article/2007/03/02/AR2007030201348.html, accessed March 6, 2007.

42. Ibid.

43. Terence Chea, "Pollution Rules Get OK," *The Arizona Republic*, December 10, 2005, A32.

44. Environmental Protection Agency, "EPA Proposes to Slash Harmful Ship Emissions along the Nation's Coastlines to Save Lives," news release, March 30, 2009, http://yosemite.epa.gov/OPA/ADMPRESS.NSF/d0cf6618525a9efb85257359003fb69d/b7129c28691a2b8685257589005ba9af!OpenDocument, accessed June 22, 2009.

45. Earthjustice, "EPA Proposes to Slash Harmful Ship Emissions, Leaves Out Arctic Protections," news release, March 30, 2009, http://www.earthjustice.org/news/press/2009/us-epa-proposes-to-slash-harmful-ship-emissions-leaves-out-arctic-protections.html, accessed March 9, 2010.

46. U.S. Environmental Protection Agency, Technology Transfer Network, National Air Toxics Assessment, "Frequently Asked Questions," http://www.epa.gov/ttn/atw/nata/natsafaq.html, accessed May 15, 2005.

47. Blake Morrison and Brad Heath, "Health Risks Stack Up for Students Near Industrial Plants," *USA Today*, December 10, 2008, http://www.usatoday.com/news/nation/environment/school-air1.htm, accessed June 22, 2009.

48. "EPA to Test Air Around 62 Schools in 22 States," ABC News, March 31, 2009. http://ww.abcnews.go.com/Politics/wireStory?id=7217569, accessed March 26, 2010.

49. David Hunter, James Salzman, and Durwood Zaelke, *International Environmental Law and Policy*, 2nd ed. (New York: Foundation Press, 2002), 516.

50. The Trail Smelter case can be found as *United States* v. *Canada*, Arbitral Tribunal, 1941, 3 UN Rep.Int'l. Arb. Awards. It later became the genesis for Principle 21 of the Stockholm Declaration.

51. Tex. Govt. Code Section 481.0075(a) (1995).

52. Tini Tran and John Heilpin, "'Brown Clouds' Threaten Health and Crops, UN Says," *Arizona Republic*, November 14, 2008, A20.

53. Randolph E. Schmid, "Asian Pollution Affects Pacific Storms," Associated Press, March 7, 2007, http://earthhopenetwork.net/Asian_Pollution_Affects_Pacific_Storms.htm, accessed March 3, 2006.

54. For more on the European response to the transboundary convention, see *United Nations Economic Commission for Europe, Strategy for EMEP 2000–2009* (Geneva: United Nations, 2001).

Chapter 9

1. International Union for the Conservation of Nature, "Wildlife Crisis Worse than Economic Crisis," http://www.iucn.org/?3460/Wildlife-crisis-worse-than-economic-crisis–IUCN, accessed July 2, 2009.

2. International Union for the Conservation of Nature, "The IUCN Red List of Threatened Species: A Key Conservation Tool," http://cmsdata.iucn.org/downloads/the_iucn_red_list_a_key_conservation_tool_factsheet_en.pdf, accessed July 29, 2009.

3. International Union for the Conservation of Nature, "Wildlife Crisis Worse than Economic Crisis," http://www.iucn.org/?3460/Wildlife-crisis-worse-than-economic-crisis–IUCN, accessed July 2, 2009.

4. International Union for the Conservation of Nature, "Extinction Crisis Continues Apace," http://www.iucn.org/?4143/Extinction-crisis-continues-apace, accessed November 4, 2009.

5. Dan Shapley, "Brother, Can You Spare $4.7 Trillion?" *San Francisco Chronicle*, July 29, 2009, http://articles.sfgate.com/2009-07-29/living/17118726_1_climate-change-ecosystem-warming, accessed July 29, 2009.

6. Integrated Taxonomic Information System, "What's New," http://www.itis.gov/whatsnew.html, accessed August 2, 2009.

7. Jerome A. Jackson, "Ivory Billed Woodpecker," *Birds of North America*, http://bna.birds.cornell.edu/bna/species/711/articles/introduction, accessed July 30, 2009.

8. Juha V. Siikamaki, "Biodiversity," *Resources*, Spring 2008, 13–17.

9. U.S. Executive Office of the President, U.S. Council on Environmental Quality, *The Evolution of National Wildlife Law* (Washington, DC: Government Printing Office, 1977).

10. U.S. Fish and Wildlife Service, "Listing a Species as Threatened or Endangered," http://www.fws.gov/endangered/factsheets/listing.pdf, accessed August 9, 2009.

11. See Brian Czech and Paul R. Krausman, *The Endangered Species Act: History, Conservation Biology, and Public Policy* (Baltimore: Johns Hopkins University Press, 2001).

12. U.S. Fish and Wildlife Service, *Endangered Species Bulletin* 34, no. 1 (Spring 2009), http://www.fws.gov/endangered/bulletin/2009/bulletin_spring2009-all.pdf, accessed August 7, 2009.

13. U.S. Fish and Wildlife Service, "Invasive Species: Laws and Regulations," http://www.fws.gov/invasives/laws.html, accessed July 29, 2009.

14. Shaun McKinnon, "Mussels Invading Arizona Waterways," *Arizona Republic*, January 23, 2007, A1, A10.

15. Bob Benenson, "Conferees' Interior Initiatives May Get Clinton's Veto," *Congressional Quarterly Weekly Report*, September 23, 1995, 2883–2884.

16. The White House, "President Clinton: Saving America's Natural Treasures," news release, April 22, 1998, http://clinton6.nara.gov/1998/04/1998-04-22-president-clinton-on-saving-american-natural-treasures.html, accessed April 23, 1998.

17. U.S. Fish and Wildlife Service, "Delisted Species Report," June 8, 2005, http://ecos.fws.gov/tess_public/DelistingReport/do, accessed June 8, 2005.

18. U.S. Fish and Wildlife Service, "Number of U.S. Listed Species per Calendar Year," http://www.ecos.fws.gov, accessed June 8, 2005; Juliet Eilperin, "Endangered Species Act's Protections Are Trimmed," *Washington Post*, July 4, 2004, http://www.washingtonpost.com/wp-dyn/articles/A26242-2004Jul3.html, accessed April 9, 2005.

19. James A. Tober, *Wildlife and the Public Interest: Nonprofit Organizations and Federal Wildlife Policy* (New York: Praeger, 1989), 59–83; Mark Crawford, "The Last Days of the Wild Condor?" *Science*, 229 (August 30, 1985): 845; David Phillips and Hugh Nash, *The Condor Question: Captive or Forever Free?* (San Francisco: Friends of the Earth, 1981); William W. Johnson, "California Condor: Embroiled in a Flap Not of Its Own Making," *Smithsonian*, December 1985, 73–80; "Condor Chick Deaths Alarm Biologists," CNN.com, October 24, 2002, "Condor Death Frustrates Biologists," Associated Press, October 23, 2002, http://www.highbeam.com/doc/1P1-68934324.html, accessed October 25, 2002.

20. National Geographic, "California Condor," http://animals.nationalgeographic.com/animals/birds/california-condor.html, accessed July 29, 2009.

21. Center for Biological Diversity, "Suit Filed to Overturn Bush-Era Removal of Protections for Preble's Meadow Jumping Mouse in Wyoming," news release, June 23, 2009, http://www.biologicaldiversity.org/news/press_releases/2009/prebles-meadow-jumping-mouse-06-23-2009.html, accessed August 7, 2009; John Heilprin, "Builders Hear Roar of Tiny At-Risk Mouse," *Arizona Republic*, January 26, 2006, A8.

22. Greater Yellowstone Coalition, "Wildlife: Buffalo in Greater Yellowstone," Greater Yellowstone Coalition," Wildlife: Bison: Give Them A Home Outside Yellowstone." http://www.greateryellowstoneog/issues/wildlife/Feature.php?id=64, accessed January 9, 2005.

23. Greater Yellowstone Coalition, "National Park Service Slaughtering Yellowstone Buffalo," news release, March 5, 2003, http://www.greateryellowstone.org, accessed January 9, 2005.

24. "Panel OKs Resumption of Buffalo Hunt in Montana," *Billings Gazette*, December 17, 2004, http://www.billingsgazette.com/news/state-and-regional/montana/article_4c811397-0723-5888-8e3e-c5ff7c097fe5.html, accessed January 9, 2005.

25. "Montana Should Not Call Bison Slaughter a Hunt," *Idaho State Journal*, January 7, 2005, http://www.journalnet.com, accessed January 9, 2005.

26. "Montana Wildlife Commission May Cancel Bison Hunt," *Arizona Daily Sun*, January 7, 2005, A4.

27. Montana Fish, Wildlife, and Parks Commission, "FWP Commission Agrees to Hold Drawing for 10 Bison Hunting Licenses," news release, January 11, 2005, http://fwpiis.mt.gov/news/article_3291.aspx, accessed January 14, 2005.

28. 115 S. Ct. 2407 1995.

29. See John H. Cushman Jr., "Environmentalists Win Victory, But Action by Congress May Interrupt the Celebration," *New York Times*, June 30, 1995; and "Regulating Habitat Modification," *Congressional Digest*, March 1996, 72.

30. "*Sweet Home* v. *Babbitt*," update (Stewards of the Range, Boise, ID, August 1995), 3.

31. Defenders of Wildlife, "Sabotaging the Endangered Species Act: How the Bush Administration Uses the Judicial System to Undermine Wildlife Protections," Executive Summary, I, http://www.defenders.org, accessed April 8, 2005.

32. Ibid.

33. Ibid.

34. Pam Easton, "Peregrines Make a Comeback," August 25, 1998, http://www.abcnews.com, accessed August 25, 1998.

35. James A. Tober, *Wildlife and the Public Interest: Nonprofit Organizations and Federal Wildlife Policy* (New York: Praeger, 1989), 24.

36. Center for Biological Diversity, "Conservationists Will Sue for Protection of 55 Endangered Species, 8.7 Million Acres of Habitat," news release, August 27, 2009 http://www.enn.com/press_releases/2127, accessed October 15, 2007.

37. John Heilprin, "Ex-Official's Decisions on Wildlife Scrutinized," *Arizona Republic*, July 21, 2007, A18.

38. Charlie Savage, "Report Finds Meddling in Interior Dept. Actions," *New York Times*, December 16, 2008, http://www.nytimes.com/2008/12/16/washington/16interior.html, accessed August 7, 2009.

39. Juliet Eilperin, "Fewer Species Make Endangered List," *Arizona Republic*, March 23, 2008, A10.

40. Krista West, "Lion versus Lamb: In New Mexico, a Battle Brews between Two Rare Species," *Scientific American*, 286, no. 5 (May 2002): 20–21.

41. United States Fish and Wildlife Service, "Rare White Mountains Plant Recovers: Endangered Species Success Story," news release, August 28, 2002, http://www.fws.gov/news/newsreleases/r5/C3314775-90A8-4608-9A5159013020D017.html, accessed October 11, 2002.

42. World Wildlife Fund, "CITES, Elephant Ivory Deadlock Broken," June 14, 2007, http://www.panda.org/who_we_are/wwf_offices/south_africa/news/?106780/CITES-Elephant-ivory-deadlock-broken, accessed November 4, 2009.

43. John Frederick Walker, "Selling Ivory to Save the Elephants," *Washington Post*, October 17, 2009, http://www.washingtonpost.com/wp-dyn/content/article/2009/10/16/AR2009101602729.html, accessed November 4, 2009.

44. David Hunter, James Salzman, and Durwood Zaelke, *International Environmental Law and Policy*, 2nd ed. (New York: Foundation Press, 2002).

45. "61st Annual and Associated Meetings, International Whaling Commission," news release, June 22, 2009, http://www.iwcoffice.org/meetings/meeting2009.htm, accessed September 9, 2009.

46. International Whaling Commission, "Final Press Release," http://www.iwcoffice.org/meetings/specmeeting2002.htm, accessed October 23, 2002.

47. "Australia to Lead Protest Against Japan's Whaling," Reuters, June 2, 2005, http://www.reuters.com, accessed June 8, 2005.

48. Ibid.

49. Emma Tom, "A Modest Proposal: Let's Eat Japanese Scientists," *Courier-Mail*, June 8, 2005, http://www.couriermail.com.au, accessed June 8, 2005.

50. David E. Pitt, "A Biological Treaty to Save Species Becomes Law," *New York Times*, January 2, 1994, 1–4; Kal Raustiala and David G. Victor, "The Future of the Convention on Biological Diversity," *Environment*, 38, no. 4 (May 1996): 17–20, 37–45.

51. "World Heritage Committee Inscribes 9 New Sites on the World Heritage List," http://whc.unesco.org/en/news/156, accessed October 11, 2002.

52. Convention on Biological Diversity, "Background," http://www.cbd.int/2010-target, accessed November 6, 2009.

53. World Resources Institute, "Temperate and Boreal Forests," http://www.wri.org/wri/biodiv/temperate, accessed October 11, 2002.

54. See Chris Tollefson, ed., *The Wealth of Forests: Markets, Regulation and Sustainable Forestry* (Vancouver: University of British Columbia Press, 1999).

55. Anjali Acharya, "Plundering the Boreal Forests," *WorldWatch* (May–June 1995): 21–29.

56. Ibid.

57. Western Canada Wilderness Committee, "How to Save Jobs in the B.C. Woods," *Educational Report*, 12, no. 8 (Winter 1993–1994).

58. See B. Willems-Braun, "Buried Epistemologies: The Politics of Nature in (Post) Colonial British Columbia," *Annals of the Association of American Geographers*, 87 (1997): 3–31; Government of British Columbia, *British Columbia's Forest Renewal Plan* (Victoria: Queen's Printer, 1994): 1–5.

59. For a general background on the Clayoquot Sound dispute, see Ronald MacIssac, Anne Champagne, and Ron MacIssac, eds., *Clayoquot Mass Trials: Defending the Rainforest* (Philadelphia, PA, and Gabriola Island, BC: New Society Publishers, 1994); Tzeporah Berman, *Clayoquot and Dissent* (Vancouver: Ronsdale Press, 1994). The evolution of British Columbia's forest-management policies is outlined by Sheldon Kamieniecki in "Testing Alternative Theories of Agenda Setting: Forest Policy Change in British Columbia, Canada," paper presented at the annual meeting of the American Political Science Association, Boston, 1998.

60. Solon L. Barraclough and Krishna B. Ghimire, Agricultural Expansion and Tropical Deforestation: Poverty, International Trade and Land Use (London: Earthscan, 2000).

61. See Kari Keipi, ed., *Forest Resource Policy in Latin America* (Baltimore: Johns Hopkins University Press, 1999). Greenpeace reports on the mahogany trade in "Lust for 'Green Gold' Drives Amazon Destruction," October 17, 2002, http://www.atlanticinlandenvironmental.com/news/12040015.html, accessed October 25, 2002.

62. Tim Johnson, "China Protects Its Timber But Imports Rare Woods," *Arizona Republic*, March 6, 2005, A28.

63. "More Negotiations in June," ITTO Tropical Forest Update, http://www.itto.int/direct/topics/topics_pdf_download/topics_id=9340000&no=1, accessed June 9, 2005.

64. John Heilprin, "Brazilian Wood Held at US Ports," *Arizona Republic*, May 5, 2002, A10.

Chapter 10

1. Paul Dragos Aligica, "Rethinking Institutional Analysis: Interviews with Vincent and Elinor Ostrom," Interview, Mercatus Center at George Mason University, 2003, http://www.mercatus.org/publication/rethinking-institutional-analysis-interviews-vincent-and-elinor-ostrom, accessed October 15, 2009.

2. Catherine Rampell, "Elinor Ostrom and Oliver E. Williamson Win Nobel in Economic Science," *New York Times*, October 12, 2009, http://economix.blogs.nytimes.com/2009/10/

elinor-ostrom-and-oliver-e-williamson-win-nobel-in-economic-science/, accessed October 15, 2009.

3. Garrett Hardin, "The Tragedy of the Commons," *Science*, 162 (December 13, 1968): 1243–1248.

4. See Lynda M. Warren, "Protecting the Global Commons," *Forum for Applied Research and Public Policy*, 16, no. 3 (Fall 2001): 6–13; John A. Baden and Douglas S. Noonan, *Managing the Commons*, 2nd ed. (Bloomington: Indiana University Press, 1998); and Susan J. Buck, *The Global Commons: An Introduction* (Covelo, CA: Island Press, 1998).

5. See, for example, J. D. Hays, John Imbrie, and N. J. Shackleton, "Variations in the Earth's Orbit: Pacemakers of the Ice Ages," *Science*, 194 (December 10, 1976): 1121–1131. The authors conclude, "A model of future climate change based on the observed orbital-climate relationships, but ignoring anthropogenic effects, predicts that the long-term trend over the next several thousand years is towards extensive Northern Hemisphere glaciation" (p. 1131).

6. See James E. Lovelock, *Gaia* (Oxford, UK: Oxford University Press, 1979).

7. World Commission on Environment and Development, *Our Common Future* (Oxford, UK: Oxford University Press, 1987).

8. Bettina Boxall, "Wildfires Linked to Global Warming," *Arizona Republic*, November 7, 2004, A12.

9. See Clark A. Miller, "Challenges in the Application of Science to Global Affairs: Contingency, Trust, and Moral Order," in *Changing the Atmosphere: Expert Knowledge and Environmental Governance*, ed. Clark A. Miller and Paul N. Edwards (Cambridge, MA: MIT Press, 2001): 247–285.

10. Dian J. Gaffen, "Falling Satellites, Rising Temperatures?" *Nature*, 394 (August 13, 1998): 615–616.

11. American Geophysical Union, Statement, January 29, 1999, http://www.agu.org/sci_soc, accessed February 1, 1999.

12. H. Josef Hebert, "Global Warming Costs Analyzed by White House," *San Francisco Chronicle*, August 1, 1998, A8.

13. Alec Gallup and Lydia Sand, "Public Concerned, Not Alarmed about Global Warming," Gallup

Poll, December 2, 1997, http://www.gallup.com, accessed January 5, 1998.

14. John A. Krosnick, Penny S. Visser, and Allyson L. Holbrook, "American Opinion on Global Warming," *Resources*, 133 (Fall 1998): 5–9.

15. See Daniel Bodansky, "The History of the Global Climate Change Regime," in *International Relations and Global Climate Change*, ed. Urs Luterbacher and Detlef F. Sprinz (Cambridge, MA: MIT Press, 2001), 23–40.

16. "Vice President Gore Announces New Data Showing Warmest June on Record," News release, July 14, 1998, http://www.whitehouse.gov/ceq, accessed July 15, 1998.

17. Allan Freedman, "Clinton's Global Warming Plans Take Heat from Congress," *Congressional Quarterly Weekly Report*, October 25, 1997, 2598. Other criticisms came from American business interests. See "Big U.S. Industries Launch Attack on Warming Treaty," *Wall Street Journal*, December 12, 1997, A3.

18. See David G. Victor, *The Collapse of the Kyoto Protocol and the Struggle to Slow Global Warming* (Princeton, NJ: Princeton University Press, 2001).

19. Quirin Schiermeier, "Accord in Morocco Breathes Fresh Life into Kyoto Protocol," *Nature*, 414, no. 6861 (November 15, 2001): 238.

20. "Environment Ministers to Bush: Kyoto Still Alive," April 22, 2001, http://www.enn.com, accessed July 31, 2002.

21. "Bush Offers Alternative Environment Plan," June 11, 2001, http://archives.cnn.com/2001/ALLPOLITICS/06/11/bush.global.warming/index.html, accessed July 31, 2002; Andrew C. Revkin, "Dispute Arises Over a Push to Change Climate Change Panel," *New York Times*, April 2, 2002, http://www.nytimes.com/2002/04/02/science/02CLIM.html?pagewanted=1, accessed April 2, 2002. See also Bette Hileman, "Bush's Plan to Cut CO2 Emissions," *Chemical and Engineering News*, 80, no. 7 (February 18, 2002): 10.

22. "Introduction and Overview," *U.S. Climate Action Report 2002*, http://www.grio.org/CAR 2002?car2002ch1.pdf accessed March 28, 2010.

23. Seth Borenstein, "Global-Warming Treaty Is Approved by Russians," *Arizona Republic*, October 1, 2004, A22.

24. "Kyoto Ratification," *Washington Post*, November 6, 2004, http://www.washingtonpost.com/wp-dyn/articles/A29459-2004Nov5.html, accessed November 6, 2004; Steven Lee Myers, "Putin Ratifies Kyoto Protocol on Emissions," *New York Times*, November 6, 2004, http://www.nytimes.com/2004/11/06/international/europe/06kyoto.html, accessed November 6, 2004.

25. Pew Research Center for People and the Press, "Fewer Americans See Solid Evidence of Global Warming," http://www.people-press.org/report/556/global-warming, accessed October 23, 2009.

26. Ibid.

27. Nicole Winfield, "Climate Talks Put Nations At Odds," *Arizona Republic*, July 10, 2009, A5.

28. Urs Luterbacher and Detlef F. Sprinz, "Conclusions," in *International Relations and Global Climate Change*, ed. Urs Luterbacher and Detlef F. Sprinz (Cambridge, MA: MIT Press, 2001), 297–307.

29. Arthur Max, "US Aid Offer Boosts Deal at UN Climate Talks," Associated Press, December 17, 2009, http://abcnews.go.com/Technology/wireStory?id=9359273, accessed December 17, 2009.

30. Michael Casey and Jennifer Loven, "Diplomatic Frenzy at Final Day of UN Climate Talks," Associated Press, December 18, 2009, http://www.physorg.com/news180364123.html, accessed December 18, 2009.

31. Charles J. Hanley, "Little to Show for U.N. Climate Talks, but Small Steps Are a Positive Sign," *Arizona Republic*, December 20, 2009, A6.

32. Michael Casey and Jennifer Loven, "Diplomatic Frenzy at Final Day of UN Climate Talks," Associated Press, December 18, 2009, http://www.physorg.com/news180364123.html, accessed December 18, 2009.

33. *Massachusetts* v. *EPA*, 549 U.S. 497 (2007).

34. U.S. Environmental Protection Agency, "California Greenhouse Gas Waiver Request," http://www.epa.gov/oms/climate/ca-waiver.htm, accessed October 19, 2009.

35. Robin Bravender, "EPA Air Chief Offers 'No Apologies' for Greenhouse-Gas Permitting Rule," *New York Times*, October 7, 2009 http://www.nytimes.com/gwire/2009/10/07/

07greenwire-epa-air-chief-offers-no-apologies-for-greenhou-73773.html, accessed October 7, 2009.

36. Anne Underwood, "Mayors Take the Lead," *Newsweek*, April 16, 2007, 68.

37. Mayors Climate Protection Center, *Survey on Mayoral Leadership on Climate Protection*, U.S. Conference of Mayors (Summer 2007).

38. For a narrative description of the rise of the ozone-depletion issue to the top of the environmental-protection agenda, see John J. Nance, *What Goes Up: The Global Assault on Our Atmosphere* (New York: Morrow, 1991).

39. See Susan Solomon et al., "On Depletion of Antarctic Ozone," *Nature*, 321 (June 19, 1986): 755–758.

40. Martha M. Hamilton, "The Challenge to Make Industry Ozone-Friendly," *Washington Post National Weekly Edition*, October 7–13, 1991, 21.

41. Steven J. Shimburg, "Stratospheric Ozone and Climate Protection: Domestic Legislation and the International Process," *Environmental Law*, 21, no. 2175 (1991): 2188.

42. Peter M. Morrisette, "The Montreal Protocol: Lessons for Formulating Policies for Global Warming," *Policy Studies Journal*, 19, no. 2 (Spring 1991): 152–161. Many researchers believe it is essential that joint implementation be used as a strategy to gain compliance with international environmental agreements. See, for example, Farhana Yamin, "The Use of Joint Implementation to Increase Compliance with the Climate Change Convention," in *Improving Compliance with International Environmental Law*, ed. James Cameron, Jacob Werksman, and Peter Roderick (London: Earthscan, 1996), 229–242; and Axel Michaelowa, "Joint Implementation—The Baseline Issue," *Global Environmental Change*, 18, no. 1 (April 1998): 81–92.

43. Information about both books and the film is available at http://www.climatecrisis.net.

44. Richard E. Benedick, *Ozone Diplomacy: New Directions in Safeguarding the Planet*, enlarged ed. (Cambridge, MA: Harvard University Press, 1998), 331–332.

45. The Stratton Commission, *Our Nation and the Sea* (Washington, DC: United States Government Printing Office, 1969), http://www.lib.noaa.

gov/noaainfo/heritage/stratton/title.html, accessed June 5, 2005.

46. P.L. 89-454.

47. Ibid.

48. National Oceanic and Atmospheric Agency, "A History of NOAA," http://www.history.noaa.gov, accessed June 5, 2005.

49. P.L. 106-256.

50. Pew Charitable Trust, Pew Oceans Commission, "America's Living Oceans: Charting a Course for Sea Change," May 2003, vii, http://www.pewtrusts.org/our_work_report_detail.aspx?id=30009, accessed September 18, 2005.

51. Ibid., viii.

52. Ibid., x.

53. Adrienne Froelich, "Washington Watch: A Sea Change for U.S. Ocean Policy?" American Institute of Biological Sciences, http://www.aibs.org/washington-watch/washington_watch_2002_03.html, accessed June 5, 2005.

54. U.S. Department of State, Bureau of Oceans and International Environmental and Scientific Affairs, "Oceans, Fisheries, and Marine Conservation," http://www.state.gov/g/oes/ocns/, accessed June 5, 2005.

55. Ibid.

56. Natural Resources Defense Council, "Testing the Waters 2009," http://www.nrdc.org/water/oceans/ttw/titinx.asp, accessed August 6, 2009.

57. Ibid.

58. "Sweeping Restrictions Put on Fishing Along the Coast," *Arizona Republic*, August 6, 2009, A2.

59. Merry Camhi, "Overfishing Threatens Sea's Bounty," *Forum for Applied Research and Public Policy*, Summer 1996.

60. Government of Canada, Overfishing and International Fisheries Governance, "State of Global Fishery," http://www.dfo-mpo.gc.ca/overfishing-surpeche/isu-state-eng.htm, accessed June 6, 2005.

61. Brian J. Rothchild, "How Beautiful Are Ocean Fisheries?" *Consequences*, 2 (1996): 15.

62. Gary Lee, "Tuna Fishing Bill Divides Environmental Activists," *Washington Post*, July 8, 1996, A7; Tim Eichenberg, "End Sea Mammal Massacre," *Los Angeles Times*, August 19, 2002,

http://articles/latimes/com/2002/aug/19/opinion/oe-eichen19.

63. David Hunter, James Salzman, and Durwood Zaelke, *International Environmental Law and Policy*, 2nd ed. (New York: Foundation Press, 2002), 710.

64. Ibid., 731.

65. United Nations, Division for Ocean Affairs and Law of the Sea, "A Historical Perspective," http://www.un.org/Depts/los/convention_agreements/convention_historical_perspective.htm, accessed June 5, 2005.

66. "Sea Law Convention Enters into Force," *UN Chronicle*, 32 (March 1995): 8–12.

67. Steven Greenhouse, "U.S., Having Won Changes, Is Set to Sign the Law of the Sea," *New York Times*, July 1, 1994, A1.

68. Robert O. Keohane, Peter M. Haas, and Marc A. Levy, "The Effectiveness of International Environmental Institutions," in *Institutions for the Earth: Sources of Effective International Environmental Protection*, ed. Peter M. Haas, Robert O. Keohane, and Marc A. Levy (Cambridge: MIT Press, 1993), 3–24.

Chapter 11

1. Angelina Martyn, "Working to End Acid Attacks in Bangladesh by 2015," http://www.unfpa.org/public/News/pid/3917, accessed October 7, 2009.

2. Ibid.

3. United Nations Population Fund, "Looking Back, Moving Forward: Commemorating 15 Years of Progress and Lessons Learned," http://www.unfpa.org/icpd/15/index.cfm, accessed October 7, 2009.

4. Office of Population Affairs, "Office of Family Planning," http://www.hhs.gov/opa/familyplanning/index.html, accessed October 19, 2004.

5. U.S. Department of State, "Bureau of Population, Refugees, and Migration," http://www.state.gov/g/prm/, accessed January 1, 2005.

6. Phillip Davis, "The Big O: Zero Population Growth," *Buzzworm*, November–December 1992, 54.

7. Peter J. Donaldson and Amy Ong Tsui, "International Family Planning Movement," *Population Bulletin*, 45, no. 3 (November 1990): 14.

8. P.L. 104-208.

9. The president's actions are outlined in his January 10, 2002, statement, "President Signs Foreign Operations Appropriations Act," http://georgewbush-whitehouse.archives.gov/news/releases/2002/01/20020110-14.html, accessed October 6, 2002, and in Presidential Determination No. 2002-32, http://edocket.access.gpo.gov/cfr_2003/3CFRSept30.htm, accessed October 6, 2002.

10. Liz Sidoti and Matthew Lee, "Obama Reverses Bush Abortion-Funds Policy," January 23, 2009, Associated Press, http://www.msnbc.msn.com/id/28812519/, accessed January 23, 2009.

11. Ibid.

12. "Population Beyond the Numbers," *WorldWatch Magazine*, September–October 2004, http://www.worldwatch.org/node/1795, accessed June 6, 2005.

13. Alan B. Durning, *Poverty and the Environment: Reversing the Downward Spiral*, WorldWatch Paper 92 (Washington, DC: WorldWatch Institute, 1989), 40–41.

14. For further discussion of these issues, see World Commission on Environment and Development, *Our Common Future* (New York: Oxford University Press, 1987); Robert Repetto, "Agenda for Action," in *The Global Possible: Resources, Development, and the New Century*, ed. Robert Repetto (New Haven, CT: Yale University Press, 1985), 496–519.

15. Donella H. Meadows et al., *The Limits to Growth* (New York: Universe Books, 1972).

16. Gregg Easterbrook, *A Moment on the Earth: The Coming Age of Environmental Optimism* (New York: Viking Penguin, 1995), xvi.

17. Julian Simon, "Pre-Debate Statement," in *Scarcity or Abundance? A Debate on the Environment,* ed. Norman Myer and Julian L. Simon (New York: Norton, 1994), 5–22.

18. Tom Tietenberg, *Environmental and Natural Resource Economics*, 3rd ed. (New York: HarperCollins, 1992), 356–357.

19. Thomas F. Homer-Dixon, quoted in William K. Stevens, "Feeding a Booming Population

without Destroying the Planet," *New York Times*, April 5, 1994.

20. See Philip Appleman, ed., *Thomas Robert Malthus: An Essay on the Principle of Population* (New York: Norton, 1976). For biographical material on Malthus and his theories, see Jane S. Nickerson, *Homage to Malthus* (Port Washington, NY: Kennikat Press, 1975); David V. Glass, *Introduction to Malthus* (New York: Wiley, 1953); William Petersen, *Malthus* (Cambridge, MA: Harvard University Press, 1979); Donald Winch, *Malthus* (New York: Oxford University Press, 1987).

21. For a historical perspective on demographic transition theory, see the work of Kingsley Davis, "The World Demographic Transition," *Annals of the American Academy of Political and Social Science*, 237 (January 1945): 1–11; George Stolntiz, "The Demographic Transition: From High to Low Birth Rates and Death Rates," in *Population: The Vital Revolution*, ed. Ronald Freedman (Garden City, NY: Anchor Books, 1964).

22. See, for example, Ansley Coale, "The History of the Human Population," *Scientific American*, 231 (1974): 40–51; Kingsley Davis, "The Theory of Change and Response in Modern Demographic History," *Population Index*, 29, no. 4 (1963): 345–366.

23. "Population Beyond the Numbers," *WorldWatch Magazine*, September–October 2004, http:// www.worldwatch.org/node/1795, accessed June 6, 2005.

24. United Nations Population Fund, "State of the World Population 2004," http://www.unfpa. org/swp/2004/pdf/en_swp04.pdf, accessed June 6, 2005.

25. "Population Beyond the Numbers," *WorldWatch Magazine*, September–October 2004, http:// www.worldwatch.org/node/1795, accessed June 6, 2005.

26. See Michael Grubb et al., *The Earth Summit Agreements: A Guide and Assessment* (London: Earthscan, 1993), 106–108.

27. Emily MacFarquhar, "Unfinished Business," *U.S. News and World Report*, September 19, 1994, 57.

28. United Nations Conference on Population, "Programme of Action," September 1994, Paragraph 8.25, http://www.iisd.ca/Cairo/program/ p00000.html, accessed September 20, 2005.

29. Alan Cowell, "Does This Mean Abortion?; Vatican and U.S. Battle Over Document for Population Talks." *New York Times*, August 11, 1994, http://www.nytimes.com/1994/08/11/world/ does-this-mean-abortion-vatican-and-us-battle-over-document-for-population-talks.html? scp=38sq=Alan+Cowell+Is+This+Abortion% 3F8st=nyt, accessed March 28, 2010.

30. Barbara Crossette, "U.N. Meeting Facing Angry Debate on Population," *New York Times*, http:// www.nytimes.com/1994/09/04/world/un-is-facing-angry-debate-on-population.html?scp= 18sq=U.N.+Meeting+Facing+Angry+Debate+ On+Population, accessed March 25, 2010.

31. United Nations Population Fund, "State of the World Population 2004," http://www.unfpa.org/ swp/2004/pdf/en_swp04.pdf, accessed June 6, 2005.

32. Ibid.

33. See Julie Fisher, "Third World NGOs: A Missing Piece in the Population Puzzle," *Environment*, 36, no. 7 (September 1994): 6–11.

34. "China Region Allows More 2-Kid Clans," *Arizona Republic*, August 25, 2002, A24.

35. Universal Declaration of Human Rights, Article 16 (1948).

36. Garrett Hardin, "Sheer Numbers," *E Magazine*, 1, no. 6 (November–December 1990): 40–47.

37. United Nations Population Fund, "State of the World Population 2004," http://www.unfpa. org/swp/2004/pdf/en_swp04.pdf, accessed June 6, 2005.

38. David R. Francis, "Can Obama's Family-Planning Policies Help the Economy?" *Christian Science Monitor*, January 26, 2009, http://www. csmonitor.com/Money/2009/0126/p16s01-wmgn.html, accessed December 15, 2009.

Chapter 12

1. U.S. Conference of Mayors, http://usmayors. org/resolutions/76th_conference/environ-ment_07.asp, accessed March 30, 2010.

2. Jennifer Gitlitz and Pat Franklin, *Water, Water Everywhere: The Growth of Non-Carbonated Beverages in the United States* (Washington, DC: Container Recycling Institute, February 2007),

http://www.container-recycling.org, accessed April 14, 2007.

3. Janet Larsen, "Bottled Water Boycotts: Back-to-the-Tap Movement Gains Momentum," Earth Policy Institute, December 7, 2007, http://www.earth-policy.org/index.php?/plan_b_updates/2007/update68, accessed March 9, 2010.

4. Corporate Accountability International, "Water," http://www.stopcorporateabuse.org/water-campaign, accessed December 29, 2007.

5. Karoun Demirjian, "Food and Beverage Retailer Alliance Plans to Sue Chicago Over Bottled-Water Tax," *Chicago Tribune*, December 27, 2007, http://archives.chicagotribune.com/2007/dec/27/business/chi-watertax_27dec27, accessed December 29, 2007.

6. U.S. Department of Energy, "Carbon Capture and Storage R & D Overview," http://www.fossil.energy.gov/sequestration/overview.html, accessed November 27, 2009.

7. U.S. Climate Action Partnership, "Principles for Legislation: Geologic Carbon Storage," June 8, 2007, http://www.us-cap.org/policystatements/USCAPGeologic%20CarbonStorageRecommendations070608.pdf, accessed November 27, 2009.

8. Andrew Charlesworth, "Talking Energy: Carbon Capture and Storage," *The Telegraph* http://www.telegraph.co.uk/sponsored/lifestyle/talkingenergy/6672153/Talking-Energy-carbon-capture-and-storage.html, accessed November 27, 2009.

9. U.S. Department of Energy, "Carbon Sequestration Leadership Forum," http://www.fossil.energy.gov/sequestration/cslf/index.html, accessed November 27, 2009.

10. Larry West, "Scholars Predict 50 Million 'Environmental Refugees' by 2010," http://www.environment.about.com/od/globalwarming/a/envirorefugees.htm, accessed December 8, 2009.

11. Sujatha Byravan and Sudhir Chella Rajan, "The Climate Exile Alarm," http://www.thehindu.com/2009/07/15/stories/2009071553330800.htm, accessed December 8, 2009.

12. *Environmental Exodus: An Emergent Crisis in the Global Arena* (Washington, DC: Climate Institute). See also Norman Myers, "Environmental Refugees in a Globally Warmed World," *Bioscience*, 42, no. 11 (December 1993): 752–761.

13. Norman Myers and Jennifer Kent, "Special Report: Preparing for 500 Million Environmental Refugees," December 1, 2009, http://www.peopleandplanet.net/doc.php?id=3673, accessed December 8, 2009.

14. United Nations Population Fund, "On the Move," http://www.unfpa.org/swp/2009/en/ch3.shtml, accessed November 29, 2009.

15. Ibid.

16. Larry West, "Scholars Predict 50 Million 'Environmental Refugees' by 2010," http://www.environment.about.com/od/globalwarming/a/envirorefugees.htm, accessed December 8, 2009.

17. Norman Myers and Jennifer Kent, "Special Report: Preparing for 500 Million Environmental Refugees," December 1, 2009, http://www.peopleandplanet.net/doc.php?id=3673, accessed December 8, 2009.

18. Ibid.

19. Apollo Alliance, "Workforce Development and the New Apollo Program," http://www.apolloalliance.org/wp-content/uploads/2009/04/memo-nap-and-workforce-development-final-011709.pdf, accessed June 15, 2009.

20. Ibid.

21. Wendy Gordon, "Food Essentials: Shop Wisely, Cook Simply, Eat Well," http://www.simple-steps.org/food/eating-well/food-essentials-shop-wisely-cook-simply-eat-well, accessed November 9, 2009.

22. Joel Salatin, *Holy Cows and Hog Heaven: The Food Buyer's Guide to Farm Friendly Food* (Swoope, VA: Polyface Publishing, 2005).

23. James E. McWilliams, *Just Food: Where Locavores Get It Wrong and How We Can Truly Eat Responsibly* (Boston: Little Brown, 2009).

24. Christine Gillham, "Swallowing Eco-Hype," *Newsweek*, September 23, 2009, http://www.newsweek.com/id/216034, accessed November 9, 2009.

25. locavore.com, accessed November 9, 2009.

26. Susanna Eden, Joe Gelt, and Claire Landowski, "Once Shunned, Wastewater Now Viewed as a Valuable Resource," *Arroyo*, May 19, 2009, Water Resources Research Center, University of Arizona.

27. Ibid.

28. David B. Brooks, Oliver M. Brandes, and Stephen Gurman, eds., *Making the Most of the Water We Have: The Soft Path Approach to Water Management* (London: Earthscan Publications, 2010).

29. For an analysis of the discourse of the dispute, see Ophir Sefiha and Pat Lauderdale, "Sacred Mountains and Profane Dollars: Discourses about Snowmaking on the San Francisco Peaks," *Social and Legal Studies*, 17, no. 4 (2008): 491–511, http://sls.sagepub.com/cgi/content/abstract/17/4/491, accessed November 29, 2009.

30. For the perspective of one group that has protested against the use of reclaimed water, see Save the Peaks, "*What's in the Wastewater?*" http://www.savethepeaks.org/index.php?option=com_content&view=article&id=5&Itemid=8, accessed November 29, 2009.

31. Felicia Fonseca, "Feds Acknowledge Withholding Permits for Snowbowl," *Arizona Republic*, November 25, 2009, http://www.azcentral.com/news/articles/2009/11/25/20091125ski-flap25-ON.html, accessed November 29, 2009.

Index